Management Information Systems for the

Information Age, Second Edition

Stephen Haag
Daniels College of Business
University of Denver

Maeve Cummings
Pittsburg State University

James Dawkins
Deltek Systems, Inc.

Irwin
McGraw-Hill

Boston   Burr Ridge, IL   Dubuque, IA   Madison, WI   New York   San Francisco   St. Louis
Bangkok   Bogotá   Carácas   Lisbon   London   Madrid
Mexico City   Milan   New Delhi   Seoul   Singapore   Sydney   Taipei   Toronto

Irwin/McGraw-Hill

A Division of *The McGraw·Hill Companies*

Management Information Systems for the Information Age

This book is printed on acid-free paper.

domestic   1 2 3 4 5 6 7 8 9 0 VNH VNH 9 4 3 2 1 0 9
international   1 2 3 4 5 6 7 8 9 0 VNH VNH 9 4 3 2 1 0 9

ISBN 0-07-231535-0

Vice President/Editor-in-chief: Michael W. Junior
Senior sponsoring editor: Rick Williamson
Developmental editor: Christine Wright
Senior marketing manager: Jodi McPherson
Senior project manager: Mary Conzachi
Senior production supervisor: Madelyn S. Underwood
Freelance design coordinator: Mary Christianson
Freelance cover designer: Jamie O'Neal
Cover illustration: © Don Baker
Senior photo research coordinator: Keri Johnson
Supplement coordinator: Marc Mattson
Compositor: Cecelia G. Morales
Typeface: 11/13 Bulmer MT
Printer: Von Hoffmann Press, Inc.

Library of Congress Cataloging-in-Publication Data

Haag, Stephen.
    Management information systems for the information age / Stephen
Haag, Maeve Cummings, James Dawkins. -- 2nd ed.
       p.   cm.
    ISBN 0-07-231535-0
    1. Management information systems. 2. Information technology.
I. Cummings, Maeve. II. Dawkins, James. III. Title.
T58.6.H18   1999
658.4'038--dc21   98-53861

http://www.mhhe.com

DEDICATIONS

For Pam, Indy, and Bo. I truly cannot imagine life without you.

- Stephen Haag

To my parents Dolores and Steve Lyons, whose love is the bedrock upon which my life is built.

- Maeve Cummings

To Patti: my wife, my love, and my inspiration.

- James Dawkins

FEATURES

ON YOUR OWN PROJECTS

TEAM WORK PROJECTS

ELECTRONIC COMMERCE

GROUP PROJECTS

vi

Brief
CONTENTS

CONTENTS

CHAPTER 5

DECISION SUPPORT AND ARTIFICIAL INTELLIGENCE 172
Brainpower for Your Business
A Decision Support System to Save Lives

CHAPTER 8

PLANNING FOR IT SYSTEMS 318
Knowing Where You're Going
Chaos in California

CHAPTER 9

DEVELOPING IT SYSTEMS   360
Bringing IT Systems to Life
Programmers Get One Slice of Pizza for Every Nine Lines of Code

CHAPTER 10

MANAGING IT SYSTEMS   410
Staying on Track

To Whom Do Doctors Go For Help?

CHAPTER 11

PREPARING FOR THE FUTURE   452
It's Your World

The Business of the Future—The Cyber Corporation

PHOTO CREDITS

It is the information age, truly a time when knowledge is power. More so than ever before, businesses all over the world are focusing on information as a key resource. And those businesses will enter the 21st century with an even greater focus on information. That's why you constantly see such terms as *competitive intelligence*, *knowledge worker*, *competitive scanning*, *business geography*, and the *learning organization* in the popular business trade press. The information age, with its focus on information as a key business resource, has changed the way we view the role of information technology (IT) and management information systems (MIS) in an organization.

In previous years, people approached IT primarily as a tool to increase efficiency, either by cutting costs, time, and/or energy spent. In the information age, however, the role of IT is much different—IT is an essential enabler of innovation and a tool for getting the right information into the hands of the right people at the right time. That's why you also see such terms as *business geography*, *data warehouse*, *data mart*, *knowledge database*, *individualized electronic advertising*, *data mining*, and *electronic commerce* in the popular business trade press.

The role of MIS has changed as well. No longer is MIS left solely to IT specialists; today, knowledge workers (who work with and produce information as a product) actively participate in the MIS function by developing their own systems, by using query tools to build their own reports, and by taking advantage of telecommunications technologies to usher in a whole new generation of telecommuters. MIS is no longer buried deep in the organizational chart. Indeed, most organizations now have chief information or technology officers who report directly to strategic management.

We've written the second edition of this text—*Management Information Systems for the Information Age*—specifically to address the changing role of information technology and management information systems in organizations today. It truly is the information age; IT and MIS have surfaced as key competitive tools for all organizations. After all, the word "information" is the most important part of the terms *information* technology and management *information* systems.

In this second edition, we focused a great deal of our efforts in updating what is perhaps the most exciting and innovative feature of the text—the *Real HOT Electronic Commerce* projects. Those projects will take you and your students through a deep exploration of Internet-based electronic commerce functions such as

ordering products, making travel arrangements, finding investment opportunities, and building a Web page. To support the electronic commerce projects, we've included over 1,000 great links on our Web site at http://www.mhhe.com/business/mis/haag. You should have no trouble in motivating your students to take advantage of this great repository of Internet sites that demonstrate the true capabilities of electronic commerce.

The Organization of This Text

To help you present the ever-changing role of IT and MIS to your students, we've grouped the material in this text into five major sections.

- **Chapters 1 through 3**—These chapters lay the foundation for the information age, the role of IT and MIS, and the use of technology to gain a strategic and competitive business advantage. In these chapters, you'll introduce your students to such concepts as data vs. information, ethics, the information age, transaction processing systems, artificial intelligence, interorganizational systems, total quality management, information partnerships, virtual organizations, learning organizations, and business process reengineering.

- **Chapters 4 through 7**—In these chapters, you'll help your students explore the specific technologies that enable an organization to succeed. These technologies include: databases and data warehouses (Chapter 4); decision support systems, geographic information systems, neural networks, and genetic algorithms (Chapter 5); telecommunications technologies, client/server, and the role of networks in achieving electronic commerce (Chapter 6); emerging technologies such as virtual reality, electronic or digital cash, multimedia, global positioning systems, and intelligent home appliances (Chapter 7).

- **Chapters 8 through 10**—In these chapters, you'll provide your students with a view of the organizational and people issues associated with the planning for, development, management, and use of information technology in an organization. These issues include: aligning organizational goals and IT, value chains, information architectures, cost-benefit analysis, and contingency planning (Chapter 8); the systems development process, prototyping, the knowledge worker development of systems, and outsourcing (Chapter 9); the role of information as both raw material and capital, ergonomics, disaster recovery, telecommuting, and cross-cultural diversity (Chapter 10).

■ **Real HOT Group Projects**—these projects will enable your students to come to understand the true productivity benefit of the use of technology as they solve nontrivial business problems. These projects focus on the use of spreadsheet, database, and presentation graphic software. In the following section, we address these projects in more detail.

■ **Appendices A through C**—Using these appendices, you'll have the opportunity to cover other topics in greater detail. Appendix A, for example, provides an overview of basic technology tools such as input and output devices and the CPU and internal memory; Appendix B introduces your students to the fundamental workings of the Internet and includes some great scavenger hunts that require learning how to take advantage of various Internet search tools to find information; Appendix C allows you to explore in more detail with your students the concept of object-oriented technologies and their increasing role in the use of technology.

According to your needs, you can easily incorporate the coverage of the Real HOT group projects and the appendices into your coverage of the chapter material. In the Instructor's Manual that accompanies this text, we've provided many suggestions concerning how to do this.

The Key Pedagogical Components of This Text

Regardless of the topic or body of material, the most effective learning tool is always an interactive environment in which both students and teachers actively participate. In MIS, we expand that interactive environment even further to include technology itself as an important role

player. To help you create the most successful and dynamic learning environment, we've provided several pedagogical components to foster the interactivity between (1) you as the instructor and your students and (2) your students and technology.

Real HOT Electronic Commerce Projects

To help create the best interactive learning environment between your students and technology, we've developed two hands-on components; both of these require your students to literally "roll up their sleeves" and use technology or technology-related tools to solve a problem or take advantage of an opportunity. We've entitled these two components "Real **HOT**" which stands for "Real **H**ands **O**n **T**echnology." The first of these components is entitled "**Real HOT Electronic Commerce— Business and You on the Interne**t."

This component (which appears at the end of each chapter) focuses on how individuals and businesses can and do use the Internet for electronic commerce. As your students work through these projects, they will be "electronic commerce consumers." However, many of the questions they must answer encourage them to consider aspects of being an "electronic commerce provider." Specifically, we focus on the following electronic commerce concepts (presented in order by chapter):

■ Using the Internet as a Tool to Find a Job

■ Ordering Products on the Internet

■ Finding Investment Opportunities Using the Internet

■ Searching Online Databases and Information Repositories

■ Starting Your Own Business

■ Getting Health Care Information on the Internet

■ Finding News, Weather, and Sports Information

■ Finding Freeware and Shareware on the Internet

■ Building the Perfect Web Page

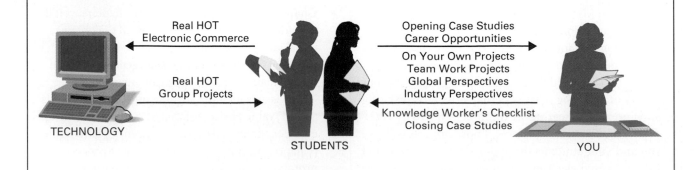

TECHNOLOGY   Real HOT Electronic Commerce   Real HOT Group Projects   STUDENTS   Opening Case Studies   Career Opportunities   On Your Own Projects   Team Work Projects   Global Perspectives   Industry Perspectives   Knowledge Worker's Checklist   Closing Case Studies   YOU

- Making Travel Arrangements on the Internet
- Continuing Your Education Through the Internet

These projects include hundreds of great Web sites to visit and exercises that require your students to do work on the Internet. In some instances, these exercises require your students to find information or information resources, while others require your students to gather material concerning how to perform electronic commerce on the Internet and issues relating to electronic commerce on the Internet. Because we realize that some of your students may have had limited previous exposure to the Internet and its basic operational aspects, we've developed Appendix B which is an introduction to the Internet.

Real HOT Group Projects

The second component that fosters an interactive and hands-on environment for your students is that of **Real HOT group projects**. These projects require your students to use personal productivity software and other technology-related tools to solve a problem or take advantage of an opportunity. We've included 14 Real HOT group projects at the end of the text (after Chapter 11 and before Appendix A). In the Instructor's Manual, we've provided some recommendations concerning which Real HOT projects go with which chapters and grading criteria for evaluating the work of your students.

We should make a note here about the Real HOT group projects. These are by no means simple projects that can be completed in a short period of time. For example, we have two group projects that deal with assessing the value of information and using spreadsheet software to analyze information and make a decision. The first of these projects deals with evaluating 819 carrier transactions over the last 27 months for a home electronics manufacturer and determining the best carrier(s) for future distribution needs. The second of these projects deals with evaluating 600 real estate transactions and determining the best housing projects in which to direct future sales efforts.

Both of these projects, which in scope are representative of all the Real HOT group projects, require significantly more effort than projects found in other MIS texts. As most of the Real HOT group projects require your students to use existing electronic files, we provide those files in a variety of ways including: (1) on the instructor's CD-ROM so you can place them on a network and (2) on the Web site that supports this text so your students can download them.

Opening Case Studies

Each chapter begins with a case study that covers many of the topics introduced in the chapter. These opening case studies provide you with a mechanism for addressing the practical and business use of the chapter material.

Industry Perspectives

Each chapter includes 9 different Industry Perspectives components. These components address the business use of certain technologies as they are applied to various industry settings. These industries include entertainment & publishing, financial services, food, hospitality & leisure, health care, IT & telecommunications, manufacturing, retail, and transportation. These are particularly helpful for your students, especially for those who have already determined a specific industry in which they hope to find employment.

Career Opportunities

Within the chapter text, we take the time to break away from traditional textbook prose and really speak to your students about their career opportunities and why the covered material is so important. These Career Opportunities will definitely help you answer this question for your students—"Why am I reading this material?"

On Your Own and Team Work Projects

Throughout each chapter, you'll find several projects to be completed by individual students (On Your Own projects) and by groups of students (Team Work projects). Many of these projects can be completed in class and make great break-out exercises, while others require some outside work. We have placed these projects within the text so you can easily integrate them into your presentation and so your students can more easily identify the chapter material that relates to each project.

Global Perspectives

A constant theme you'll find throughout this text is that business is now global—competitors, distributors, suppliers, and customers for any business now exist all over the world. To reinforce this, we've included Global Perspectives features in each chapter that discuss specific concepts within the context of a global business environment.

Knowledge Worker's Checklist

At the close of each chapter, we address the learning objectives list to summarize the material for your students. This is consistent with the teaching adage of "Tell them what you're going to tell them, tell them, and then tell them what you told them."

Closing Case Studies

Each chapter includes 2 closing case studies which will help your students apply what they just learned. These case studies profile an actual business and then require your students to use the chapter material to answer a variety of questions.

The Web Site and Online Learning Center (http://www.mhhe.com/business/mis/haag)

To help keep our text as up-to-date as possible and create interactivity among you, your students, and technology, we've created a Web site that both you and your students will find invaluable. In it, you'll find the following sections:

■ **AND THE DEBATE RAGES ON**—a great forum for your students to express their opinions concerning controversial issues surrounding technology. For example – "Should you have a satellite-detectable microchip on your body?"

■ **GROUPWARE**—a review of some of the latest and best groupware tools such as suites and work flow automation software.

■ **ABOUT THIS TEXT**—an overview of this text, including the projects, industry and global perspectives, and the chapters.

■ **THE WEIRD, WILD, AND WACKY**—some of the wildest and most unusual uses of technology. Definitely good for a laugh.

■ **ELECTRONIC COMMERCE SUPPORT**—coverage of some of the best Web development tools, online databases, electronic commerce resources, and much more.

■ **FROM & ABOUT THE AUTHORS**—read about us and our thoughts concerning information technology and management information systems.

■ **NEW!! IN THE NEWS**—a review of some of the new uses of technology in business today.

■ **CULTURE**—odd and interesting differences of people all over the world.

■ **CAREER LINE**—career pointers from us, online graduate schools, job databases, and much more.

■ **EMERGING TECHNOLOGIES**—coverage of new and existing emerging technologies such as ASR systems and data warehouses.

■ **MULTIMEDIA**—a review of multimedia authoring tools and other multimedia-related developments and products.

■ **SYSTEMS DEVELOPMENT**—discussion of systems development tools such as CASE tools and enterprise software suites.

■ **OBJECT-ORIENTED TECHNOLOGIES**—including object-oriented databases and object-oriented programming languages.

■ **ELECTRONIC COMMERCE PROJECTS**—links to over 1,000 Web sites for your students to use as they complete the Real HOT electronic commerce projects.

■ **REAL HOT GROUP PROJECT FILES**—all the files your students need in downloadable form to complete the Real HOT group projects.

These sections may very well change over time as we endeavor to frequently add new material and expand our coverage of the newest and hottest topics in IT and MIS.

The Support Package

As both authors and teachers, we realize that no textbook is complete without a well-rounded teaching support package. To facilitate your efforts in the classroom, we've provided five components in the support package for this text. In creating these, it was our sincere goal to support your unique efforts and teaching style. The support package for this textbook includes an Instructor's Resource Guide, Instructor's Manual, a test bank, a PowerPoint slide presentation, and our Web site.

■ **Instructor's Resource Guide**
  ◆ A wealth of material to help instructors prepare to teach the MIS course
  ◆ Sample syllabi for 5 week, 10 week, and 15 week terms
  ◆ Recommended uses of the various pedagogical features
  ◆ Recommended uses of the various support package features such as the PowerPoint slides
  ◆ Sample testing mechanisms for (1) two exams and a final exam and (2) a midterm exam and a final exam

■ **Instructor's Manual**
  ◆ Teaching tips and suggestions for presenting each chapter
  ◆ How to use the various pedagogical features, such as the opening and closing case studies
  ◆ Pop quizzes for each chapter

- ◆ Solutions to the Real HOT group and electronic commerce projects
- ◆ Guidelines for implementing the On Your Own and Team Work projects
- ■ **Test Bank**
  - ◆ Completely automated
  - ◆ Over 1500 true/false, fill-in-the-blank, multiple-choice, and short-answer questions
  - ◆ Facilities for generating exams and adding your own questions
- ■ PowerPoint Slide Presentation
  - ◆ Approximately 40 slides per chapter
  - ◆ Supplemental in-text art work files for you to choose from
- ■ **Web Site**
  - ◆ At http://www.mhhe.com/business/mis/haag
  - ◆ An invaluable resource for both you and your students
  - ◆ Coverage of the latest uses of technology
  - ◆ Coverage of new technology advancements
  - ◆ Over 1,000 great links for completing the Real HOT electronic commerce projects
  - ◆ All the files your students need to complete the Real HOT group projects

We would like to further address our newest feature of the support package—the **Instructor's Resource Guide**. We realize the tremendous faculty constraint that teaching an MIS course places on a department; daily, more and more students are enrolling in an MIS course and departments are attempting to meet those increased needs with the same or fewer faculty. In many instances, the MIS course is taught by new faculty with limited previous classroom exposure.

The Instructor's Resource Guide is particularly valuable to new faculty teaching in the MIS area. We've developed such support as sample syllabi for a variety of term formats and suggested testing mechanisms as well. Where the Instructor's Manual focuses on the use and presentation of the actual text material, the Instructor's Resource Guide focuses on helping you develop a strategy for the overall presentation of the MIS course. And, if you've previously used another MIS text, the Instructor's Resource Guide will aid you in making the transition to *Management Information Systems for the Information Age*.

Acknowledgments

It has been our privilege this past year to work with a host of talented individuals, all of whom wanted this book to be as successful as possible. Unfortunately, we haven't the space to name everyone; in reality, we probably don't know the names of absolutely everyone involved. To those behind the scenes and whose names we never heard—our deepest and most heartfelt regards.

We would like specifically to mention a few people. They include: Cecelia G. Morales, the book's compositor; Francis Owens, our art director; Christine Wright, our developmental editor; Mary Conzachi, our project manager; and Rick Williamson, our editor who brought the book to life. Without the encouragement and support of each of these people, our efforts would not be nearly as successful.

Our gratitude is also extended to helpful reviewers of the manuscript. They took on a thankless job that paid only a portion of its true worth. We had the best. They include:

Noushin Ashrafi, *University of Massachusetts–Boston*
Jack D. Becker, *University of North Texas*
Alice Jacobs, *University of Phoenix*
Teresita S. Leyell, *Washburn University*
Stephen L. Loy, *Eastern Kentucky University*
Ross A. Malaga, *University of Maryland–Baltimore County*
B. Dawn Medlin, *Appalachian State University*
John Melrose, *University of Wisconsin–Eau Claire*
Harold Palmer, *Ferris State University*
Michael D. Reimann, *University of Texas–Arlington*
Stephanie Robbins, *University of North Carolina–Charlotte*
Roberta M. Roth, *University of Northern Iowa*
William David Salisbury, *Mississippi State University*
Jayne Stasser, *Miami University*
Mani R. Subramani, *University of Minnesota*
Connie E. Wells, *Nicholls State University*

From Stephen Haag . . .

Over the past 15 years, I've been proud to be a part of the creation of 11 books. My co-authors and everyone else associated with these books have made each experience truly one that is unforgettable and exhilarating. I would not trade those experiences for anything in the world. To all of you—everyone at Irwin/McGraw-Hill and our reviewers—I thank you all.

On a more personal note, I'm extremely grateful for the opportunity to work again with Maeve and Jim. I also had the encouragement of many friends and family during this project. I'll not name them all—they know who they are. My wife Pam supported me with unending patience and love. She did so even when my countless hours of work and boring stories did nothing to excite her, much less keep her awake. Finally, to Indy and Bo—simply because you are two of my dearest friends.

From Jim Dawkins . . .

I am so grateful to the many people who contributed to this work. I will always be grateful to Tom Devane of Premier Integration who gave me my start in management consulting and taught me so much. And to Don McCubbrey at the University of Denver who introduced me to the joy of teaching. I am grateful to Stephen Haag who opened my eyes to the extraordinary experience of creating a manuscript. And to Rick Williamson and all those at Irwin/McGraw-Hill, I express my sincere gratitude.

Of course I could not have pursued any of these professional challenges without the unending support of my loving wife, Patti. For her love and the joy she brings me, I cannot thank her enough. And finally to our children—Devin and Kristin—who never let me forget what is truly important in life.

From Maeve Cummings . . .

I am very fortunate to have had continuous support, both practical and moral, from so very many people. I want to mention a few of these individuals in recognition of their outstanding contributions. Dr. Felix Dreher, chair of our department, was enormously helpful in providing me with resources and assistance. Kevin Bracker, Barbara Clutter, Jane and Henry Crouch, Vicki Dennett, John Gephardt, Kathryn Richard, Malcolm Turner, and Don Viney gave freely of their time and expertise, and their assistance was invaluable. The wonderful folks at Irwin/McGraw-Hill helped at every step of the journey.

I will always be thankful to Stephen Haag for inviting me into this project. Working with Steve, who is tireless in his quest for excellence, is an extraordinary experience. My husband's unwavering support has seen me through many difficult times, and without his love and help I would not have been able to meet the many challenges along the way.

ABOUT THE AUTHORS

Stephen Haag is a professor of Information Technology and Electronic Commerce in the University of Denver's Daniels College of Business. Stephen holds a B.B.A. and M.B.A. from West Texas State University and a Ph.D. from the University of Texas at Arlington. Stephen has published numerous articles appearing in such journals as *Communications of the ACM*, *The International Journal of Systems Science*, *Applied Economics*, *Managerial and Decision Economics,* and *Socio-Economic Planning Sciences*.

Stephen is also the author of 10 other books including *Interactions: Teaching English as a Second Language* (with his mother and father), *Case Studies in Information Technology* (with Maeve and Jim), *Information Technology: Tomorrow's Advantage Today* (with Peter Keen), and *Exceling in Finance* (with Ed Boyer). Stephen lives with his wife, Pam, and their two sons, Indiana and Bosephus, in Highlands Ranch, Colorado.

Maeve Cummings is a professor of Information Systems at Pittsburg State University. She holds a B.S. in Computer Science, an M.A. in Mathematics, and an M.B.A. from Pittsburg State University; and a Ph.D. in Information Systems from the University of Texas at Arlington. She has published in various journals including the *Journal of Global Information Management* and the *Journal of Computer Information Systems*. She is on the editorial board of several journals including the *Journal of Global Information Technology Management* and the *Midwest Quarterly*. She is the co-author of *Case Studies in Information Technology*. She lives in Pittsburg, Kansas with her husband, Slim.

James P. Dawkins is a sales consultant with Deltek Systems, Inc., in Englewood, Colorado, specializing in the Allegro Resource Management System. Jim previously served as a system consultant for Deltek. Jim provided systems and management consulting with Fortune 500 firms independently for five years prior to joining Deltek. Previous to that Jim spent eight years as a practicing engineer.

Jim holds a B.S. in Mechanical Engineering from Texas A&M University and an M.B.A. from the University of Denver. He is a co-author of *Case Studies in Information Technology*. Jim, along with his wife Patti, and their two children, Devin and Kristin, live in Aurora, Colorado.

Management Information Systems for the **Information Age,** Second Edition

CASE STUDY

Would You Paint Your House with Yogurt?

Well, perhaps you can't actually paint your house with yogurt, but you could base the color of the paint on your favorite flavor of yogurt. That's exactly what one woman did. She so loved Stonyfield Farm's apricot-mango yogurt that she had her bedroom painted an apricot-mango color.

Gary Hirshberg, CEO and president of Stonyfield Farm Inc., based in Londonderry, New Hampshire, loves listening to stories like that, as well as any other comments customers want to make. In fact, when you call Stonyfield with a comment, suggestion, or complaint, you actually have a personal conversation with one of the many people who make yogurt instead of an operator who reads questions to you from a script. Gary believes this creates more personalized service and focused marketing.

IN THE NEWS

4 Knowledge workers in the United States outnumber all other workers by a four-to-one margin.

7 Customer moment of value means providing service when, where, and how the customer wants it.

12 Top 50 world industrial leaders by country from 1975 to 1995 (Figure 1.4).

13 Would you pay $500 for a birthday cake for your pet? Some people do.

14 Over 15 million people in the United States telecommute, and that figure is expected to grow by 20 percent over the next several years.

15 Electronic commerce addresses the use of information technology as an essential enabler of business.

18 The five categories of information-processing tasks include capturing, conveying, creating, cradling, and communicating information (Table 1.1).

19 A typical CD-ROM can hold the equivalent of 325,000 pages of printed text.

24 An East Coast retail store manager stocks diapers and beer on the same aisle to increase sales.

25 Are you a professional, expert, or innovator?

27 Have you ever been flamed?

29 It's estimated that one of every two copies of software in use in the world today is a pirated copy (Figure 1.9).

CHAPTER 1

The Information Age in Which You Live

Changing the Face of Business

So, when he received a note from Christine Ahearn, the consumer-relations coordinator, that a customer had called with a request for chocolate yogurt, he immediately wanted to know if there had been any other requests for chocolate yogurt, how often chocolate yogurt requests came in, and the regions of the country in which the chocolate requests originated. To his dismay, there was no way of sorting through the massive paper-flows of customer suggestions to answer such questions.

That's when Gary realized that, although his toll-free number was a great way to create customer loyalty, the company had no way of capitalizing on a great source for new product ideas. Gary quickly enlisted the services of Cocci Computers Inc. to create a system for tracking customer calls. Cocci proposed a $10,000 system that included all the necessary hardware, software (Microsoft Access), and about $8,000 worth of programming and development to create the necessary files, data entry screens, and report formats.

Today, all customer information is kept in a database. Using Microsoft Access, Stonyfield's employees can quickly and easily retrieve information in any order they want—by flavor, by type of complaint or suggestion, by region, and even by stores that do and do not carry certain flavors. This gives Stonyfield the flexibility to follow up within seconds any comments that a customer may make.

FEATURES

IN THE INFORMATION AGE, KNOWLEDGE WORKERS UNDERSTAND...

1. *The Management Information Systems Challenge* and management information systems

2. Important factors shaping the new business

3. The role of information technology in the new business

4. Information as a key business resource and its dimensions

5. Their role as information-literate knowledge workers

Incidentally, Gary used the database to determine that 11 customers had requested chocolate yogurt in 1 week alone. A few months later, Stonyfield Farm chocolate yogurt hit the shelves in grocery stores around the country.

Now, you might not think that yogurt making is an information-intensive task, but just like all businesses today, information is a driving force defining the success of creating products and services that people want. And information is what we focus on in this chapter—how it's the basis for today's economy, how businesses are exploiting such concepts as databases, important dimensions of information that define a business's success, and how you can be an information-literate knowledge worker in today's exciting, fast-paced, and ever-changing business world.[1,2] ❖

Introduction

Throughout the history of the world people have characterized its existence by time periods or ages. Long ago we had the Ice Age and the Neolithic time period; in more modern times we've had the Renaissance period, the agricultural age, the age of enlightenment, and the industrial age. Today we have moved into another age that is different from any other. What is it? It is the *information age*—a time when knowledge is power. Today, more than ever, businesses are using information to gain a competitive advantage. You'll never find a successfull business whose slogan is "What you don't know can't hurt you." Businesses understand that what they **don't know** can become an Achilles heel and a source of advantage for their competitors.

Sound like some pretty bold statements? Not actually; it's simply the reality of today's business world. Businesses that have realized the true value of information are succeeding today; businesses that haven't, unfortunately, cannot expect to survive much less succeed. What does all of this mean for you? Think about your major. Whether it's marketing, finance, accounting, productions and operations management, human resource management, or any of the many other specializations in a business program, you're preparing to enter the business world as a *knowledge worker*. Simply put, a *knowledge worker* works with and produces information as a product. According to *U.S. News & World Report*, knowledge workers in the United States outnumber all other workers by a four-to-one margin.[3]

Sure, you may work with your hands to write notes or use a mouse and keyboard to produce a spreadsheet, but what you've really done is use your mind to work with, massage, and produce more information. If you're an accountant, you generate profit and loss statements, cash flow statements, statements of retained earnings, and so on. Those are information-based products; they may physically appear on paper, but your task was not to create a piece of paper, rather, it was to produce information on the paper. To say that an accountant produces paper is like saying Michelangelo painted ceilings.

Still not sure of the importance of information to today's businesses? Consider the examples in Photo Essay 1-1 on pages 6–7. Dreyer's, GE Plastics, Lands' End, and Cigna are just a few of the many thousands of businesses using information to gain a competitive advantage. We could easily fill hundreds of pages with examples of other businesses doing the same; in fact, you'll read about the success of several hundred businesses throughout this text. Now, is information important to today's businesses?

Let's review the Dreyer's discussion. Consider the sentence, "... Dreyer's reps enter a grocery store armed with handheld computers and track inventory levels and immediately send that information back to headquarters where it's carefully poured over and analyzed by product line specialists." Think about that sentence for a moment and try to identify the key components or resources that define the success of Dreyer's ability to know the consumer market. In essence, there are three key resources working together for Dreyer's—information (inventory levels), information technology (handheld computers), and people (reps and product line specialists). And how to plan for, develop, manage, and use those three key resources are what this text is about. In fact, the title of this text names those three key resources indirectly—that is, management information systems.

Take a careful look at the phrase *management information systems*. What does it mean? We define it as follows:

Management information systems (MIS) deals with the planning for, development, management, and use of information technology tools to help people perform all tasks related to information processing and management.

In that definition, you can find the three key resources—information, information technology, and people. You'll also find various functions that you as a knowledge worker must undertake to ensure that your organization maximizes its advantage. It doesn't matter if you're preparing to work in the area of finance, human resource management, logistics, marketing, or even information technology, you'll still have responsibilities that include planning for, developing, managing, and using the MIS function within your area of expertise.

Let's take a closer look at the challenge facing today's information-based business and at you as tomorrow's knowledge worker who will use the three key resources of information, information technology, and people.

The Management Information Systems Challenge

Many people believe that information technology is the key resource in MIS. Indeed, information technology is a critically important set of tools for working with information and supporting the information and information-processing needs of your organization. But information technology (which we'll simply abbreviate to IT) is not a panacea. You have to realize that the success of IT as a set of tools in your organization depends on the careful planning for, development, management, and use of IT with the two other key business resources—people and information. And that's what MIS is all about—planning for, developing, managing, and using IT tools to help people work with information.

To help you better understand the role of IT and MIS in an information-based organization, we have created *The Management Information Systems Challenge (The MIS Challenge)* that *all* businesses must strive to meet (see Figure 1.1). Notice that we emphasize the word *all* and

stress that all businesses—whether service- or product-oriented, whether large or small—must address the challenge of MIS to be successful. Let's take a closer look at *The MIS Challenge* and see what it involves.

There are three aspects of *The MIS Challenge*, including

1. What businesses do
2. Customer moment of value
3. The role of information technology

Let's look at these three aspects in more detail.

What Businesses Do

In a nutshell, businesses service their customers. And it really doesn't matter whether you own a business that makes dog treats or are employed by an organization that provides telecommunications services around the world or sells auto parts in a small community, the goal of the business (and the only reason it will continue to stay

Business is in the business of servicing its customers. Whether it's building cars, mowing lawns, or providing telecommunications around the world, a business will only survive if it provides perfect service to its customers.

Perfect service occurs at the customer's moment of value. That is, perfect service occurs when the customer wants it (time), where the customer wants it (location), how the customer wants it (form), and in a manner that is guaranteed to the customer. We call the guarantee to the customer "perfect delivery."

Today perfect service is only possible if a business has the right information in the hands of the right people at the right time; this occurs through the appropriate use of information technology. Therefore the challenge facing any business is to plan for, develop, manage, and use its three most important resources—information, information technology, and people—to provide perfect service at the customer's moment of value. The planning for, development, management, and use of these three fall within the function of management information systems, or MIS.

FIGURE 1.1

The Management Information Systems Challenge

Information Is Big Business

Dreyer's

According to Rick Cronk, cofounder of Dreyer's Grand Ice Cream Inc., "Ice cream is fragmented to the nth degree, and there is the opportunity." What Rick simply means is that the ice cream market is defined by an almost countless number of flavors and styles to meet the sometimes whimsical desires of the consumer market. And the opportunity lies in having information about the whimsical desires of the consumer market. Dreyer's reps enter a grocery

store armed with handheld computers and track inventory levels and immediately send that information back to headquarters where it's carefully poured over and analyzed by product line specialists. For instance, Dreyer's found that markets dominated by older people prefer more sugar-free varieties, whereas most urban consumers prefer coffee flavors. Dreyer's has now embarked on a bold 5-year initiative to become the nation's largest provider of packaged ice cream. This will mean doubling

sales by the year 2000. Rick and Gary Rogers (the other cofounder) believe they can do this because they'll have the right information at the right time to make the right decisions.[5]

GE Plastics

GE Plastics recently went live with information relating to technical and support information concerning its various product lines. The goal: to help customers improve their productivity (while cutting costs) through faster access to information. Now any of GE's customers, including internal customers such as scientists, designers, and engineers, can simply use the Internet to gain access to information they need. The Web site for GE includes Hotlists where customers can save the addresses for the sources of information they frequently use. It also contains five special newsgroup buttons that quickly take customers to topics relating to automotive, building and construction, computers, designs, and plastics. Information in these

GE Plastics

newsgroup sites is updated on a weekly basis. For GE Plastics, this method of providing information means improving customer loyalty.[6]

in business) is to service its customer base. Consider Case Corp., a manufacturer of construction and farm equipment located in Racine, Wisconsin.[4] During 1991 and 1992, operating losses for Case soared to almost $900 million. Why? Because Case had made ignoring the customer into a virtual art. Then things changed. According to Jean-Pierre Rosso, the CEO, "We need to be asking what the farmer and contractor really need." And that's just what Case did.

For example, Case asked longtime customer Larry Willingham to fly in and test a new backhoe model. For three 11-hour days, the engineers at Case had Larry loading and leveling dirt and digging ditches. In the end,

Larry still wasn't satisfied—the new backhoe weighed too much, and he would need a bigger truck if he bought one. A year later, when the new model was revealed, Larry was quite surprised. The engineers at Case had listened—the new model had all the bells and whistles Larry wanted, *and* it weighed only 12,900 pounds (the model Larry originally tested weighed almost 16,000 pounds). As a result of such customer-oriented projects, net income for Case skyrocketed to $165 million on $4.3 billion in sales in 1994. From this, Case learned that servicing its customers was its primary mission, and the only way to do that was to listen to what the customers had to say.

Lands' End

Lands' End, located in the small town of Dodgeville, Wisconsin, is big in the business of retail merchandising and catalog mail ordering. Every time one of Lands' End's 20 million customers places an order or requests a catalog, that information is added to a data warehouse. The data warehouse contains other vital information as well, including shipping dates and orders for merchandise not currently in stock. Lands' End developed its data warehouse for two reasons: first, to create a single source of all information and, second, to support the many decision support functions that the ever-changing retail industry faces each day. Because of the way the information is arranged in the data warehouse, Dan Rourke, vice president of information services, says, "[it] . . . allows me to give my merchants not only what I sold, but also what my customers wanted to buy." This advantage is huge, and Lands' End knows it. Today Lands' End is well-regarded as one of the key leaders in the retail industry, and its leadership position is partly defined by its ability to access and use information located in its database.[7]

Cigna

In 1993, Cigna Corp.'s portfolio of U.S. P&C business lost $251 million. Twelve months later that loss became an $87 million profit because of its new knowledge base built around the concept of structural intellectual capital. Says consultant Harry Lasker, "We found significant latent know-how in the organization. There were experts, but not a good means of extracting and publishing that know-how." Now, managers build and maintain a knowledge base that underwriters use to process applications. For example, if a nursing home in California wants insurance, the knowledge base can provide information about the proximity of earthquake fault lines, extent of staff training, quality of the sprinkler systems, and so on. The cost of this system? Harry responds, "Very little. They were collecting all the information anyway, but it just went into files." Now that information goes into a knowledge base that is instantly accessible by anyone.[8]

Customer Moment of Value

Servicing the needs of customers extends beyond just providing products and services—it includes providing perfect service to the customer, which occurs at the customer's moment of value. *Customer moment of value* is defined as providing service

1. When the customer wants it (time)
2. Where the customer wants it (location)
3. How the customer wants it (form)
4. In a manner guaranteed to satisfy the customer (perfect delivery)

The first three characteristics of customer moment of value—time, location, and form—are the basis by which many organizations today are succeeding in retaining their current customer base and attracting new customers. Consider these examples.

Continental Says, "Just Get Them There on Time" In 1995, for the first time since 1986, Continental expected to turn a profit.[9] Why? Consider this: In 1994 Continental ranked dead last among the major airlines in on-time performance. But in March and April of 1995, Continental was ranked number one for the first time ever. And that's Continental's focus. It wants to attract business flyers who sometimes pay premium ticket prices to fly somewhere the next day for an important business meeting. For Continental, the most important characteristic of a customer's moment of value is time or, more specifically, getting somewhere on time.

CAREER OPPORTUNITY

Many businesses, unfortunately, have forgotten about the customer, just as Case Corp. had done. Some have failed to regain their customer perspective and are now out of business. In your career, take every opportunity to make your customers number one—**they** are the reason you're in business.

Ford Says, "Location, Location, Location" In the United States it may still be the big 3—Ford, Chrysler, and General Motors—but in Asia it's "Oh what a Toyota."[10] As late as the end of 1995, Toyota sold 1 of every 4 cars traveling down the roads of Asia, whereas Ford sold only 1 of every 40. So, Ford has decided that the best way to sell cars in Asia is to actually make them there. In 1994 and 1995, Ford invested $240 million in plants in China, $102 million in Vietnam, $500 million in Thailand, and $50 million in India. W. Wayne Booker, Ford's vice president for international automotive operations, predicts that the investments will pay off within 5 years. And a 5-year return on investment means big bucks in the automobile industry.

Car Dealers Say, "Terrific Bargains Come in Different Forms" Today's average price for a new automobile is right around $20,000, up some 18 percent from 1990.[11] And that has a lot of car dealers worried—what if customers simply cannot afford to pay one-fifth of what most of them paid for an entire home? For many car dealers (and automobile manufacturers), the solution is to offer customers two incentives to buy a new car no matter what the price. The first of these is cash-back rebates. Among the United States' big 3, the average cash-back rebate is now over $800, and Infiniti even offered a rebate as high as $7,000 to boost the sale of its luxury sedan line. The second incentive is a lease option. In fact, 32 percent of all U.S. auto sales happen to be leases, and car dealers don't think that figure will go anywhere but up. In a time when prices of automobiles seem to be skyrocketing, car dealers are carefully crafting the form and method of payments to keep consumers happy.

The final characteristic of a customer's moment of value deals with providing the first three—time, location, and form—in a manner guaranteed to satisfy the customer (what we call *perfect delivery*). In business, perfect delivery amounts to saying, "We know our customers' moment of value according to time, location, and form, and we're

Defining Customers and Their Moment of Value

In reality, businesses have many different sets of customers. Consider a plastics manufacturing firm. It has customers who consume or use its products, the community from which it draws employees, stockholders and financial institutions who have invested money, and various government agencies that regulate certain business aspects.

Your school is no different. It too has many sets of customers to whom it must provide perfect service at the appropriate moment of value.

1. Define each set of customers for your school.
2. For each customer set, define the products and services your school provides.
3. For each customer set, define the moment of value in terms of time, location, form, and perfect delivery.

As a student, how does your school use technology to provide you with products and services at your moment of value? How else can your school use technology to better provide you with products and services according to your moment of value? ❖

Getting the Right Airline Information When You Want It

On the Internet, you can find almost any information you want, from the current temperature in Tokyo, to stock quotes, to the latest Nielson ratings. You can also check on the status of airline flights by connecting to any of the many Web sites that airlines provide. But if you connect to an airline Web site, do you really get the right information? According to Antoine Toffa, the answer is no. As he explains, "Airlines have an agenda—it [the Web] is a selling point for them to claim on-time status. But their flight data is often bogus. They don't tell you until the last minute that a flight is late."

So, Antoine set out to provide the correct flight information by connecting his new Web-based service to the Federal Aviation Administration (FAA). By connecting to http://www.thetrip.com, you can search for detailed information about the exact arrival time and location of any flight at any time. You don't even have to know the flight number; instead, you can use the airline name, tail number, or departure and city destination. While you are at Antoine's site, you can also book flights, make hotel and rental car reservations, and even plan a route to an unfamiliar city by using an interactive, graphic mapping system.

The Internet is definitely going to have an impact on customer moment of value. You will not only have instantaneous access to information when you want it (time moment of value), but also some assurance that the information you're getting is correct (perfect delivery).[12] ❖

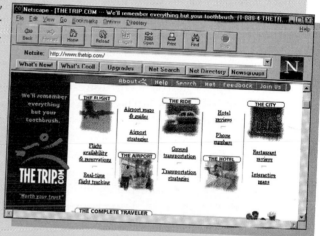

willing to guarantee that we can meet those characteristics." This guarantee of perfect delivery comes in many forms. For example, if an auto parts store doesn't have a part you need, it may be willing to call around town to help you find the part. That same store may even have someone deliver it to you so you don't have to drive across town (location perfect delivery). Pizza delivery businesses may also guarantee perfect service by giving you a free pizza if delivery does not occur within a given amount of time (time perfect delivery).

The Role of Information Technology

An organization's ability to provide perfect service at customer moment of value depends on three things:

❶ Knowing the time at which the customer's moment of value occurs

❷ Knowing the location where the customer's moment of value occurs

❸ Knowing the form in which the customer's moment of value occurs

All these can be summed up easily—it's having **knowledge**, and **knowledge comes from having information**. Gaining knowledge through information is the role of IT in today's information-based business. IT is a set of tools that can help provide the right people with the right information at the right time. This will help those people make the best decisions possible about the time, location, and form of the customer's moment of value.

From that you might say, "Okay, let's provide an IT structure that will allow people to share and use information. Then we'll be successful." Unfortunately, that's only part of the solution, and a small one at that. The real solution lies in fundamentally changing the way an organization works and the processes it undertakes so that people will share and use information (through IT) as a natural part of their respective jobs. Says Daniel Shubert of Electronic Data Systems Corp., "The problem is not with the technology, but with the corporate processes. Companies must fundamentally change the way they do business, and that's hard."[13] The article in which that statement appears goes on to say, "You can't assume people will share information, just because the network allows

them to...." Indeed, it's far easier to develop a complex IT system for supporting information sharing than it is to get people to change the way they think about business processes and share information as naturally as they would expect a paycheck at the end of each month.

The MIS Challenge, and specifically planning for, developing, managing, and using the coordinated efforts of an organization's three most important resources (information, IT, and people) comprise the intellectual and structural framework for this text (see Figure 1.2). In Chapters 1 through 3, we focus on the information resource in an organization. In Chapters 4 through 7, we focus on four important facets of IT that can help your organization provide perfect service at the customer's moment of value. These aspects of IT include databases and data warehouses (Chapter 4), decision support systems and artificial intelligence (Chapter 5), networks (Chapter 6), and emerging technologies (Chapter 7). Finally, we devote Chapters 8 through 10 to the people resource. In those chapters, you'll learn about your role as a knowledge worker while planning for, developing, and managing IT in your organization.

INDUSTRY PERSPECTIVE   **Manufacturing**

Using Information Technology to Share 100 Million Pages of Information

For you as a knowledge worker, knowledge (from information) is power, and sharing that knowledge with your fellow colleagues can result in unbelievable power for your organization. Unfortunately, most organizations store their information on paper. As you might well guess, that makes it hard to share information—if you have it, someone else doesn't.

At Westinghouse Savannah River Co., a manufacturer of nuclear weapons components, the problem of information sharing cannot be overcome without technology. Over 12,000 Westinghouse employees share 100 million pages of information daily. What's even worse is that those same employees generate another 20 million pages of information annually. To create better information sharing, Westinghouse turned to document management software. Now, each paper document is scanned into an enterprisewide system and then tagged by key words such as product ID, supplier number, and date. Employees can

then enter the document management system and find whatever information they need, whenever they need it, regardless of who else is working with it.

But the transition to the new system hasn't been easy. Westinghouse's previous document system deployed information at the department level, often prohibiting some departments from gathering information maintained by other departments. So, Westinghouse is radically changing the way it performs workflows and business processes. This has required that everyone rethink how the business should work.[14] ❖

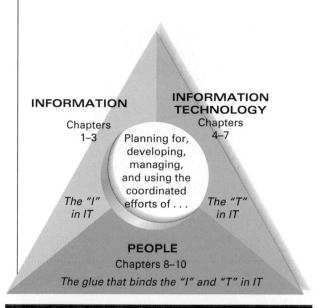

FIGURE 1.2

Your Resource Focus: Information, Information Technology, and People

Characteristics of Today's New Business

In preparing to enter today's fast-paced, ever-changing, and exciting business environment, you need to understand the new thinking in business. To do that, let's examine some of the most important factors shaping today's business and the many changes that have come about as a result of those factors. Figure 1.3 lists six such factors including globalization, competition, information as a key resource, the virtual workplace and telecommuting, electronic commerce, and knowledge worker computing. These and other factors have created dramatic changes in the workplace. Some of these factors are external forces that have provided outside pressure and have forced organizations to change within. Others are simply internal results of external pressure.

Why is it important for you as a knowledge worker to understand these factors? Simply put, they translate into a substantial opportunity for you, if you understand them and prepare through your education to take advantage of them.

Globalization

Look around your room. How many products do you think are wholly domestic? It might surprise you to learn that many of them are "foreign." For example, if you're taking notes with a pencil it may have come from Japan, and the paper on which this text is printed may very well have come from Canada. Business today is global business. Even if you own a small business and have suppliers and customers who are wholly domestic, you probably have some sort of foreign competition.

Consider the graph in Figure 1.4. It charts the world's industrial leaders from 1975 to 1995. Notice the gradual and consistent increase in the number of companies outside the United States. But don't let the numbers scare you. Although it's true that there are many foreign companies competing for consumer dollars in the U.S. market, U.S.-based companies enjoy marketing their products and services throughout most of the world. So, while foreign companies are competing for dollars in the United States from some 260,000,000 consumers, U.S. companies are selling products and services to a market of more than 5,642,000,000 (that's over 5 billion) consumers worldwide.[15]

Globalization, a factor shaping today's business, is a result of many factors, including privatization, deregulation, improved worldwide transportation and telecommunications, the emergence of transnational firms, and trade blocs. Think about trade blocs for a moment. The three that dominate the world today are the World Trade Organization (formally known as the General Agreement on Trades and Tariffs, or GATT), the European Union (EU), and the North American Free Trade Agreement

FIGURE 1.3

Factors Changing the Landscape of Business Today

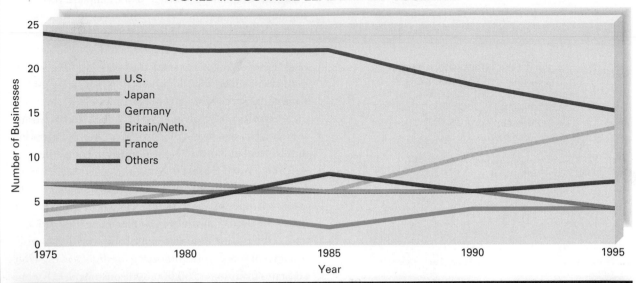

FIGURE 1.4

Where the Big Companies Are[16]

(NAFTA). NAFTA, alone, has opened a market of 134,000,000 people in Chile, Canada, and Mexico to U.S. businesses. For you, globalization represents a substantial career opportunity. In fact, you may have taken courses in international finance, international marketing, global logistics, or international business. Even if you haven't, you should realize that most large businesses operate as *transnational firms*—firms that produce and sell products and services in countries all over the world. Think of how much better your resume would look if you could speak a foreign language or had knowledge in subjects relating to all aspects of international commerce.

Competition

Competition is everywhere. It doesn't matter what business you're in, there are countless other businesses all over the world competing against you. Why? Many reasons actually. Obviously, globalization has increased competition. In the automobile industry, for example, the big 3—Ford, Chrysler, and General Motors—used to

dominate. Today, it's more like the big 26. In 1995, 26 of the world's largest 500 companies were automobile manufacturers (or parts manufacturers), and 22 of those had home offices outside the United States, including Turkey.[17] It's interesting to note that the old big 3 were still ranked one, two, and six (in the automotive and parts industry) in spite of fierce global competition.

Information technology is another reason competition is heating up. Daniel Schulman, AT&T's marketing vice president for small business, explains, "Technology is going to be a tremendous equalizer. Size will no longer be as important in determining market strength. Creativity and innovation are the main factors."[18] Technology tools, such as the Internet, fax machines, and toll-free numbers are helping seemingly small businesses compete with larger ones. Consider Intercontinental Florist Inc. William Marquez purchased Intercontinental Florist in 1993 (it accumulated $144,000 in sales that year). At the end of 1995, sales skyrocketed to an amazing $11 million.[19] Using a fax service with automated dialing and callback features, William can reach 25,000 businesses in a single night. With his detailed logs of toll-free calls, he can quickly redirect advertising efforts to areas with the highest demand. And his $15,000 investment in advertising on the Internet has already paid for itself many times over. William happily predicts that his high-tech florist business could blossom into a $100 million plus business.

For consumers competition is good. It means lower prices and better service. It will also allow tomorrow's

CAREER OPPORTUNITY

Remember, the optimist sees the donut, whereas the pessimist sees the hole. Today's optimistic knowledge worker sees globalization as an opportunity to expand internationally; the pessimistic knowledge worker sees globalization as a threat to the "home front." Which are you?

knowledge workers, like you, to adopt creative and innovative means of reaching customers and providing those customers with what they want when they want it.

Information as a Key Resource

In the introduction to this chapter, we alluded to the importance of information in today's business environment. This truly is a time when knowledge is power, and knowing your competition as well as your customers will define the success of your organization. Everyday, you can pick up any business magazine such as *Forbes, Business Week,* or *Fortune* and read about the many information-based success stories of businesses in all industries. But why is information so important—why must businesses have information to be successful?

Again, there are many reasons; one such reason is the fact that we now operate in a wants-driven economy. Some 30 years ago that wasn't true—people mainly purchased only what they needed. Not so today, when wants often exceed needs and consumers are more than willing to spend their money on products and services they want rather than spend their money on just what they need. Consider a seemingly trivial example: tennis shoes in which the heels light up with the pressure of each footstep. Now, how many people do you think really **need** tennis shoes with rear lights? Very few, if any, but if that's what they want, that's what they'll buy.

Consider another example: dog bakeries, some of which even offer dog birthday cakes that range in price from $150 to $500. Now, if you ask a dog, it would probably say (that is, if it could speak) that dog treats (mail carrier cookies that taste like beef, fire hydrant cookies that taste like chicken, and so on) are very necessary. But in reality, neither people nor dogs need dog treats—some dog owners simply want to indulge their pets. By the way, the owners of the Three Dog Bakery in Kansas City expect to do over $1 million in gross revenues this year.[20]

For business, this requires a dramatic shift in thinking, marketing, and product research and development. Businesses can no longer base product decisions on what people need. Businesses must do their research and find out what people want, or figure out how to make people want a product they're producing. This need to capture and record information about what people want has led to the many IT-based databases and data warehouses of which businesses are now boasting. These databases and data warehouses contain valuable information detailing customers' wants and desires.

The Virtual Workplace and Telecommuting

Today, many organizations are restructuring in a variety of ways—rightsizing, horizontal flattening, eliminating departmental barriers based on function and the creation of teams defined by product or product lines, outsourcing,

I Want It!

Tennis shoes with lighted heels are just one of the many wants-based products that have recently surfaced. Take a walk around a mall, see how many wants-based products you can find, and then fill in the table below. Critically think about what information a business must know about its customers to identify potential buyers. Also, stay away from foods—we need very few actual food products, but our taste buds deserve variety.

Now that you've identified a few wants-based products, consider how technology could help you capture and process information relating to people who buy those products. Where would that information come from? Could you use technology to capture that information? Once you have the information, what technologies could you use to process that information? ❖

Product	Price	Why People Want It	What Kind of People Buy It

Pizza Hut, Kentucky Fried Chicken, and Taco Bell in One Database

A database is an important repository of information for an organization. It contains everything from who made the last purchase to the expected delivery date of the next raw materials shipment. PepsiCo maintains many databases, and it has one large one for all the financial information con-

cerning its three most popular fast-food chains—Pizza Hut, Kentucky Fried Chicken, and Taco Bell. In that database, PepsiCo planners have access to information on more than 3,000 stores in 29 countries.

Using the database, restaurant site planners can evaluate the ever-changing wants and purchases of the consumer market. But PepsiCo's planners don't just evaluate Taco Bell information when considering where to open a new Taco Bell restaurant. They also sift through the information for Pizza Hut and Kentucky Fried Chicken

sites in the same area as the proposed Taco Bell. What planners hope to do is understand the buying trends in that area and determine if the area can support another restaurant.

In a wants-driven economy in which consumers spend billions of dollars annually on fast foods, PepsiCo has more information on its plate than most of the competition. And that information equates to making better decisions in providing consumers with what they want.[22] ❖

and workplace virtualization and telecommuting. And, no matter which of these approaches a business adopts, it must fundamentally rethink the way it does business and how it performs processes. That, in a nutshell, is your advantage. You are not bogged down in the previous thinking and philosophy of business. You have the ability to think in new ways and redefine the way an organization works. Let's look at the virtual workplace and telecommuting and what they mean to an organization and to you as you prepare to enter the workforce.

CAREER OPPORTUNITY

Telecommuting and the virtual workplace represent a substantial career opportunity for you. Think about it for a moment—would an organization ask you to work from home if you didn't know how to use e-mail? Videoconferencing software? Other communications technology, such as fax machines and modems? The answer, unfortunately, is no. Tomorrow's telecommuters who will thrive in a virtual workplace are learning to use IT today. You should too.

The virtual workplace and telecommuting go hand in hand. Consider these definitions:

Virtual workplace—a technology-enabled workplace. No walls. No boundaries. Work anytime, anyplace, linked to other people and information you need, wherever they are.[21]

Telecommuting—the use of communications technology to work in a place other than a central location.

Telecommuter —someone who works for an organization either at home or a satellite work location at least part of the time while connected to the main office through some form of communications technology.[23]

Notice that the definitions of the virtual workplace and telecommuting are almost identical. Basically, the concepts of the virtual workplace and telecommuting focus on using communications technology (for example, fax, voice mail, and videoconferencing software) to allow people to work together or individually to perform work-related tasks while in another location.

Today, it's estimated that over 15 million people in the United States telecommute, and that figure is expected to grow by 20 percent over the next several years.[24] Wouldn't it be a great surprise if you went to a job interview and were asked if you would mind working from home instead of slogging through traffic 5 days a week to get to and from work? If you don't really believe it could happen, take a look at the graph in Figure 1.5 and see how many businesses are planning to increase their number of telecommuting employees.

Electronic Commerce

The success of the virtual workplace and telecommuting depends, in part, on your organization's ability to do business electronically. Today, the popular term for doing

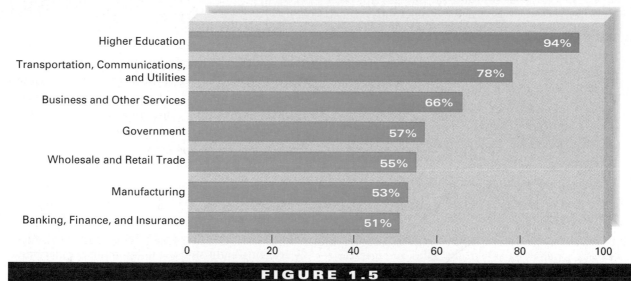

% OF SITES THAT PLAN TO ADD TELECOMMUTERS

- Higher Education — 94%
- Transportation, Communications, and Utilities — 78%
- Business and Other Services — 66%
- Government — 57%
- Wholesale and Retail Trade — 55%
- Manufacturing — 53%
- Banking, Finance, and Insurance — 51%

FIGURE 1.5

Attention Knowledge Workers! Work from Home[25]

business electronically is electronic commerce. Consider the following definition:

> **Electronic commerce** is a modern methodology that addresses the use of information technology as an essential enabler of business. Electronic commerce supports both internal and external business functions. That is, *external electronic commerce* addresses the use of information technology to support how a business interacts with the marketplace, and *internal electronic commerce* addresses the use of information technology to support internal processes, functions, and operations.

This definition encompasses two themes: (1) information technology in support of how a business interacts with the marketplace and (2) information technology in

Bloomberg Mobilizes Its Customers

Bloomberg Financial Markets is a global multimedia-based distributor of financial information services. It provides 140,000 financial professionals in 52 countries with portable computers that can access Bloomberg's mainframe computer 24 hours a day 365 days a year. These 140,000 financial professionals aren't Bloomberg employees; rather, they are people who work for other businesses but subscribe to the financial services that Bloomberg provides.

So why provide customers with mobile technologies? It's simple. Most of the customers of Bloomberg are telecommuters and need to do their jobs and access Bloomberg's financial information services from anywhere in the world. If they couldn't do this, some of them might not use

THE GLOBAL PERSPECTIVE

the services Bloomberg provides. So, Bloomberg outfitted a Texas Instruments TravelMate portable computer for its customers to use, specifically hoping they would continue to utilize Bloomberg's financial information services. And they do—from a hotel or their own home, or even on an airplane, customers use the TravelMate equipped with a modem, customized keyboard, Quicken, and Microsoft Works to do their work anywhere, anytime.

It's a win-win situation for everyone. For the customers it's a way to telecommute and access the valuable services Bloomberg provides. For Bloomberg it simply means happy telecommuting customers who will continue to use its services, perhaps more often than ever before.[26, 27] ❖

support of internal processes, functions, and operations. For businesses, electronic commerce includes

- Performing transactions with customers over the Internet for purposes such as home shopping, home banking, and electronic cash use

- Performing transactions with other organizations through the use of electronic data interchange (EDI)—the direct computer-to-computer transfer of transaction information contained in standard business documents, such as invoices and orders

- Gathering information relating to consumer market research and competitors (called *competitive scanning*)

- Distributing information to prospective customers through interactive advertising, sales, and marketing efforts

Electronic commerce is a great new business horizon, and we have yet to realize its full potential. Says Don McCubbrey, director of the Center for the Study of Electronic Commerce, "In electronic commerce, there will be serious winners and losers. Electronic commerce is more than ever before a strategic business issue. The future success of businesses will depend on their ability to (1) use EDI to reengineer interorganizational business processes, (2) perform functions in the electronic marketplace such as finding customers and suppliers, and (3) internalize EDI to support the virtual workplace."

For you, electronic commerce is obviously a great career opportunity. No longer do you have to use paper documents to distribute information contained in sales invoices, purchase orders, advertising flyers, and the like. By realizing and using the full potential of electronic commerce, you'll be able to create strategic outsourcing

INDUSTRY PERSPECTIVE

Entertainment & Publishing

KRFX FM 103.5 The Fox Radio Station Gets Sly on the Internet

Thousands of businesses are taking advantage of the Internet everyday to perform electronic commerce. But, for some of these businesses, it almost seems odd that you would find them on the Internet. Radio stations are one such group. That's right—radio stations are setting up Web sites. Why? For a variety of reasons. If you check out some of their sites, you'll find the ability to interactively chat with DJs, request music to be played on the radio, hear clips of new music, and see photos of radio personalities whose voices you've only heard up to now.

"We may be a radio station, but you won't just find us on the radio," says production manager Mark Coulter at The Fox Radio Station in Denver, Colorado. "We constantly court all types of media to advertise our radio station—television, newspapers, billboards, and now the Internet. We see the Internet as the next big advertising tool. Currently, we average about 1,400 accesses per day to our Web page. That figure was as high as 17,000 on the day the O. J. Simpson verdict was announced."

In May 1995 Mark viewed the Internet as an interesting tool for advertising. Today he sees it as the future for electronic commerce. The Fox is even planning to go live with its programming on the Internet some time soon. "We want to market the radio station to an extreme, and the Internet is an excellent tool," explains Mark. For Mark and The Fox, the Internet is not only different from other advertising tools such as billboards, but also better because it's interactive.

The Fox is also using its Web site to build a valuable database. To achieve this, The Fox regularly has giveaways on the Internet. You can, for example, get a Fox bumper sticker by clicking on the bumper sticker icon and providing your name and address. You'll receive a bumper sticker through regular mail, but your name and address goes into a database that The Fox uses for its various advertising campaigns.

At FM 103.5 The Fox innovation means excellence and market share. And The Fox truly is one of the leading radio station innovators at exploiting the Internet. One final thought from Mark: "If you're going to advertise on the Internet, then notify as many information lists and newsgroups as possible of your Web address. To put up a Web page and not let people know of its existence is like opening a donut shop and not telling the police." ❖

alliances, form electronic partnerships with other organizations, and reach literally millions of potential customers on the Internet with a few clicks on a mouse.

At the end of each chapter, you'll find a section entitled "*Real HOT—Electronic Commerce*." In these sections, you'll learn how businesses are performing (and how you can perform) electronic commerce functions such as accepting orders over the Internet, competitive scanning, finding business opportunities, and finding investors. In the "*Real HOT*" section at the end of this chapter, you'll learn how to perform an electronic commerce function vitally important to you—that of finding a job on the Internet.

Knowledge Worker Computing

In every organization today, you'll find people sitting at powerful workstations and PCs doing their own information processing. Some of these people may be performing simple tasks, such as writing letters and generating graphs, but others are developing sophisticated order-entry systems that run on a network or three-dimensional drawings to demonstrate certain product features. All these are examples of knowledge worker computing. *Knowledge worker computing* places technology, technology power, software, information, and technology knowledge in the hands of those who need it—knowledge workers. So, knowledge worker computing involves you in more than just developing a budget using spreadsheet software, creating a presentation using presentation graphics software, or using a system that someone else developed. It requires you to take an active role in developing systems that support your specific needs or the needs of a team. Knowledge worker computing might involve

- Giving you telecommuting tools so that you can work wherever and whenever needed
- Letting you develop personal database applications so you can maintain information for your own processing needs
- Setting up networks that allow departments to develop and maintain their own applications
- Setting up Web sites so customers can order products and services
- Giving access to information to those people who need it so they can make the right decisions at the right time

The list of possibilities is endless. But the most important thing to know about knowledge worker computing is that it places *technology knowledge* in your hands. As a knowledge worker, your responsibilities may very well

include using telecommuting tools, setting up a personal database, evaluating hardware technologies to determine the best one for a given situation, and so on.

Throughout this text, we specifically address many of the aspects of knowledge worker computing. For example, in Chapter 2, we introduce you to groupware technologies that can help your team develop high-quality applications quickly; in Chapter 4, we show you how to develop a personal database; in Chapter 5, we discuss how you can develop a decision support system to facilitate problem solving; and in Chapter 6, we discuss the many technology-related issues of developing an organizationwide IT structure that will support your information-processing efforts. Knowledge worker computing is here to stay, and your success in business will depend, in part, on your abilities to use knowledge worker computing concepts successfully.

Information Technology
Its Role in the New Business

Information technology, as both an industry and business resource, is still in its infancy. In the 1950s, businesses embarked on the first widespread use of computers primarily as tools for recording and processing accounting transactions. Thus IT has only really been a part of business for about the last 40 years. Nonetheless, IT is one of the most important resources in today's business environment, and successful businesses are investing heavily in IT. But what exactly is information technology, or IT, and how are businesses using information technology?

Formally defined, *information technology (IT)* is any computer-based tool that people use to work with information and support the information and information-processing needs of an organization. IT includes keyboards, mice, screens, printers, modems, payroll software, word processing software, and operating system software, just to name a few. And how are businesses using IT? They use IT in three ways: (1) to support information-processing tasks, (2) as an enabler of innovation, and (3) as a collapser of time and space.

Supporting the Information-Processing Tasks in an Organization

First and foremost, businesses are using IT to support information-processing tasks. These tasks range from computing and printing payroll checks, to creating presentations, to setting up Web sites from which customers can order products. Because IT is a set of tools for working with information, you can easily categorize various IT tools according to what information-processing task you need to perform. In Table 1.1, you can see that the five categories of information-processing tasks include capturing, conveying, creating, cradling, and communicating information.

You can consider each of these information-processing tasks individually, but eventually you have to combine them to create a system that handles all the tasks. This is true because any particular business function—whether finance, marketing, human resource management, or distribution—always involves these five information-processing tasks. If this is your first introduction to IT or you need a quick refresher of the various IT tools within each category, we encourage you to read Appendix A (*The Technology Tree*), which discusses

not only these categories of IT tools in detail but also the real "brains" of an IT system—the processing engine (CPU and internal memory).

Information Technology as an Enabler of Innovation

IT tools not only support the information-processing tasks of an organization, they also enable innovation. Consider FedEx—the first package freight company to offer package delivery software that its customers could use to electronically request package pickup and check the status of packages during delivery. All the other major package delivery services—UPS and RPS, just to name two—were forced to quickly develop similar software or risk losing their customer base to a company that provided

TABLE 1.1	**Categories of Information-Processing Tasks and IT Tools**	
Information-Processing Task	**Description**	**IT Tools**
CAPTURING information	Obtaining information at its point of origin	Input technologies *Examples:* • Mouse • Keyboard • Bar code reader
CONVEYING information	Presenting information in its most useful form	Output technologies *Examples:* • Screen • Printer • Speakers
CREATING information	Processing information to obtain new information	Software technologies *Examples:* • Word processing • Payroll • Expert system
CRADLING information	Storing information for use at a later time	Storage technologies *Examples:* • Hard disk • CD-ROM • Tape
COMMUNICATING information	Sending information to other people or to another location	Telecommunications technologies *Examples:* • Modem • Satellite • Digital pager

Ski Aspen!

Aspen Skiing Co. wants your business, and it's using IT in innovative ways to make certain you ski Aspen when you're in Colorado. For people already on the slopes Aspen has set up four multimedia touch-sensitive kiosks that can show you views from the tops of local mountains and give you up-to-the-minute weather reports.

And if you're trying to decide where to ski, try connecting to Aspen's Web site at http://www.aspenonline.com.

Once there, you can check current ski conditions, area shopping, dining places, cultural festivities, or directions to Aspen, local banks, and ATMs. You can even view skiing video clips.

While you're online with Aspen, you can also reserve a room at the lodge. Aspen even plans to add photos to show you exactly what your room looks like and the

view you'll have from your balcony. Now that's an innovative use of IT. ❖

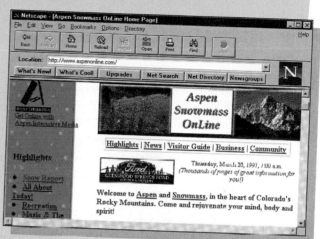

a more innovative and efficient way to handle the information-processing tasks related to delivering packages.

Information Technology as a Collapser of Time and Space

If you want to take a more pragmatic view of the role of IT in business today, you can say IT is essentially a collapser of space and time. Consider space: A typical CD-ROM can hold 650 megabytes (MB) of information, or roughly 650 million characters of printed text. If you assume that a page of double-spaced printed text holds about 2,000 characters, then a CD-ROM can hold the equivalent of about 325,000 pages of text. That's approximately 650 five hundred-sheet reams of paper! So, IT allows organizations to store huge amounts of information in one small, convenient space.

An organization can then use various IT tools to collapse the time it takes to process and massage that information. As a collapser of time, we're talking about IT speed. For example, a typical home computer today can execute about 450 million instructions per second. You should probably stop for a moment and really think about that number—450 million instructions processed in a single second.

To help you gain some perspective, think about this. Suppose you had an automatic paint roller that could

ON YOUR OWN

Redefining Business Operations Through IT Innovation

FedEx and its customer-oriented package delivery software is just one of hundreds of examples of IT innovation that you'll find in business every day and in your personal life. Below, we've listed several different business environments that have used IT for innovation to change the way you live your life. For each, define its innovation through IT.

1. Airlines
2. Banks
3. Grocery stores
4. Phone companies
5. Hotels
6. Fuel stations
7. Utility companies
8. Cable TV providers

Can you think of any other types of businesses that have found innovation through IT and changed the way you live your life? ❖

continuously apply an endless amount of paint and could paint 1 square foot per second. In the time it would take to paint that 1 square foot, a "pseudo" IT painting system (with the ability to paint 450 million square feet in a second) could paint almost 17 square miles! Now, of course, there are no such IT painting systems, but the example does give you some idea of the sheer speed with which an IT system can perform processing functions.

As a collapser of time and space, IT represents a tremendous advantage for businesses. Businesses can use IT to store huge amounts of information in a single location and process, massage, and query that information at unbelievable speeds. Because of this, many organizations are beginning to reengineer their daily processes, work, and information flows around the use of IT. In Chapter 3, when we look at the strategic and competitive opportunities of IT, you'll read more about the successful reengineering efforts of many organizations.

Information

A New Key Business Resource

Information is one of the three key business resources in *The MIS Challenge*, and it is the basis by which many organizations operate in today's business environment, which brings us to an interesting question. What is information? You can't really put your hands on it, which means that it's intangible and its value is extremely difficult to measure. But today's businesses are banking on their information, so it must be important.

To understand the nature of information and exactly what it is, you must understand another term—data. *Data* are any raw facts or observations that describe a particular phenomenon. For example, the current temperature, the cost of a part, and your age are all data. *Information*, then, is simply data that has a particular meaning within a specific context. For example, if you're trying to decide what to wear, the current temperature is information because it's pertinent to your decision at hand (what to wear)—the cost of a part, however, is not. Information may be data that have been processed in some way or presented in a more meaningful fashion. In business, for instance, the cost of a part may be information to a sales clerk, but it may represent only data to an accountant who is responsible for determining the value of current inventory levels. For the accountant, the cost of the part and current quantity on hand represent data that he or she uses to calculate the current value of inventory for that part. The current value of inventory for that part is the information the accountant derives from the two pieces of data.

Dimensions of Information

Defining Information Value

In our simple part cost example, you can see that information to one person is not necessarily information to another. If you receive information that is not pertinent to what you're doing, it really has no value. If you receive information today that you needed yesterday, that

Charging Your Information

Richard Fairbank has figured out that issuing credit cards isn't banking, but an information business. Says Richard, "It's all about collecting information on 150 million prospective customers, and on the basis of data alone, making credit and marketing decisions."

That's what he told the Signet Corp., and Signet's credit card business, known as Capital One Financial Corp., grew from less than $1 billion in receivables to $8.9 billion in mid-1995. Why? Because Signet now tracks information on potential credit card holders. What the analysts at Signet are looking for are good credit risks who don't pay off their balances each month. Many of these people carry balances near $5,000 and pay interest at annual rates ranging from 13 to 17 percent.

Signet even goes further customizing a credit card offering to a potential holder. After careful analysis of the available information, Signet may offer a particular customer a card with 5.9 percent interest and a $20 initiation fee, 6.9 percent interest and no initiation fee, or a card that offers features such as transferring other credit card balances.

If you own a Signet credit card, you can even call Signet and request better rates and features. The analysts at Signet can quickly review information concerning your payment history and help you get a better deal. Credit cards, interest rates, initiation fees, and information—they all go hand in hand.[30, 31] ❖

information has no value to you because it's now old and outdated. And if you receive information that's been incorrectly calculated, it certainly has no value. As a knowledge worker this issue of information value is an important one. Because you work with and produce information as a product, information is one of your most valuable resources.

So, how do you determine the value of information? What makes certain information highly valuable, and other information completely worthless? Unfortunately, it's impossible to put an exact dollar figure on the value of information. But what you can do is define your needs according to the three *dimensions of information*—time, content, and form (see Figure 1.6). Using these three dimensions, you can define the characteristics of information that has value to you. Let's look at these dimensions and the characteristics within each.

The Time Dimension of Information

Whether you're providing your customers with information about products and services or using information to make a decision, the time dimension of information is critical. The time dimension of information deals with the "when" aspect of information. Time characteristics of information include

Timeliness: Information when you need it

Currency: Information that is up to date

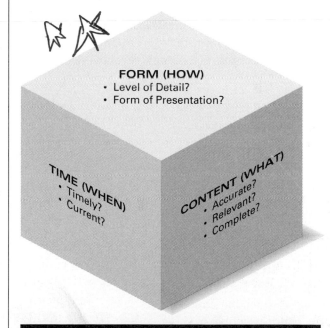

Dimensions of Information—What Defines the Value of Your Information?[32]

Timeliness means having information when you need it. If you don't have the right information at the right time, it's almost impossible to make the right decision. *Currency* means having the most recent or up-to-date information. In today's fast-paced business environment, yesterday's information is often obsolete and of no use to a knowledge worker.

The Content Dimension of Information

Content is often considered the most critical dimension of information. It deals with the "what" aspect of information, and its characteristics include

Accuracy:	Information free of errors
Relevance:	Information useful to what you're trying to do
Completeness:	Information that completely details what you want to know

The *accuracy* characteristic of information specifies that the information you receive is information that has been processed correctly. It may do you no good to know yesterday's sales totals if those totals were added incorrectly. The *relevance* and *completeness* characteristics of information go hand in hand. That is, you should receive only information that is relevant to your task (relevance), and you should receive all the information you need (completeness). In many instances, our IT-based environment has made it too easy to ignore relevance and overload people with more information than they can assimilate or with information that they don't need.

When you receive information that is complete, you're receiving all the information you need to perform a task or make a decision. For example, if you receive a report that details last month's utility expenses, is that information complete? Well, it depends on what you're trying to do. If you're trying to develop a budget, you might also want to know how those expenses compare to the same month last year.

The Form Dimension of Information

The last dimension of information is form, which deals with the "how" aspect of information. Form characteristics of information include

Detail:	Information detailed to the appropriate level
Presentation:	Information that is provided in the most appropriate form—narrative, graphics, color, print, video, sound, and so on

The *detail* characteristic of information deals with receiving information that either summarizes or details information at the appropriate level. For example, if you're a floor supervisor in a department store, you'll want sales figures for each of your salespeople. On the other hand, if you're a sales analyst in the corporate office, you'll want sales figures broken down by store but not by salesperson. This issue of detail is called *information granularity*.

The Language of the Internet

On the Internet today, you can connect to millions of Web sites all over the world. But if you stop and think about it, doesn't that mean that there are literally hundreds of languages used on the Internet? The answer is definitely yes. For English-speaking countries that's not a problem, because almost 80 percent of the host computers on the Internet are located in English-speaking countries.

But for people in other language-specific countries, cruising the Internet and taking advantage of its vast information resources is not so simple. In Europe, for example, "the Internet has been a bit slow to develop because the perception is that there's too much content in English," explains James Lewis, president of Globalink Inc., a translation program company. And according to Tony Laszlo, a lecturer at Tokyo's Wako University, "Japan is fighting the concept of English [language dominance]," on the Internet.

But that problem certainly hasn't slowed down the explosive growth of the Internet all over the world. In fact, it's opened up a whole business segment—software that translates e-mail and Web sites from one language to another. For example, Globalink is now marketing a Netscape add-on that translates between English, Japanese, German, French, and Spanish.

English is already the language of international business and science. Right now, it's also the language of the Internet. But, soon, the language in which a Web site is developed won't matter; anyone anywhere in the world will be able to read it.[33] ❖

THE GLOBAL PERSPECTIVE

Information with a fine granularity details information to a great extent, whereas information with a coarse granularity summarizes information to a great extent.

The *presentation* characteristic of information deals with the form in which you receive information—perhaps graphically, narratively, or even in video form. Information presentation wins (and loses) many business deals today. Indeed, some business deals are won based purely on the fact that information was presented graphically, which is easier to understand. Presentation also includes the technology used to provide you with information. For example, you can receive information in printed form; displayed on a screen with or without motion, video, and animation; in an audio form; and even physically (as with virtual reality systems).

Using the appropriate dimensions of information will, in part, define your success. It's crucial to have the right information (content) when you want it (time) and how you want it (form). Now the question becomes, "How do you determine what information you need, when you will need it, and how you want it?" The answer to that question—and a few others—will make you an information-literate knowledge worker.

Knowledge Workers
Information and Technology Users

To this point, we've looked at *The MIS Challenge*, characteristics of today's new business, information technology, and information as a new business resource. We have done so to give you a broad overview of the nature of business and the role of IT and information. Let's

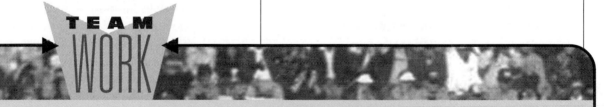

Would You Like Some Information with Your Coffee?

Just like big businesses, small businesses are turning to information to decide where to open their doors. Suppose you and several of your friends wanted to open a coffee house in your town. As a group, find two possible locations for your coffee house and decide on the best location. As you evaluate the two different locations, complete the tables below for the information you did and did not use.

The first table is to be completed regarding information that you found to be useful in your decision-making process. The second table is to be completed for information that you came across but did not find useful in your decision-making process. ❖

IMPORTANT INFORMATION YOU CONSIDERED		
Description	**Dimension and Characteristic**	**Why Was This Information Important?**

INFORMATION YOU DID NOT CONSIDER	
Description	**Why Was This Information Not Important?**

now turn our attention to the most important resource in business—you as a knowledge worker. Recall that, as a knowledge worker, you work with and produce information as a product. And it really doesn't matter if you use a high-powered workstation or a calculator, you're still a knowledge worker, responsible for processing information that your business needs to survive.

To succeed as a knowledge worker in today's information-based business environment, you need to understand the true nature of information, what it means to be an information-literate knowledge worker, and the ethical responsibilities of working with information. We've already discussed the nature of information (information dimensions in the previous section); let's now focus on the remaining two and why they're important to you as a knowledge worker.

Being an Information-Literate Knowledge Worker

In the Information Age

Knowing the appropriate time, content, and form dimensions of your information needs is a major step toward becoming an information-literate knowledge worker in the information age. But it doesn't stop there—knowing what you need is only part of the information equation. You also need to know such things as how and where to obtain that information and what the information means once you receive it. Let's consider the following definition for an information-literate knowledge worker:

An *information-literate knowledge worker* can define what information is needed, knows how and where to obtain that information, understands the meaning of the information once received, and can act appropriately, based on the information, to help the organization achieve the greatest advantage. In all instances, an information-literate knowledge worker always uses information according to ethical and legal constructs.

It may seem like a mouthful of a definition, but if you look at it closely it's actually composed of five distinct charges to you. These include

Charge 1—You must define what information you need.

Charge 2—You must know how and where to obtain information.

Charge 3—You must understand the meaning of the information.

Charge 4—You must act appropriately based on the information.

Charge 5—You must use information adhering to both legal and ethical constructs.

In the next section, we'll address the fifth charge (ethical and legal considerations regarding the use of information); right now let's focus on the first four.

Consider a unique, real-life example of an information-literate knowledge worker. Several years ago, a manager of a retail store on the East Coast received some interesting information—diaper sales on Friday evening accounted for a large percentage of total diaper sales for the week. Most people in this situation would immediately jump to charge 4 and decide to make sure that diapers are always well stocked on Friday or run a special on diapers during that time to increase sales, but not our information-literate knowledge worker. She first looked at the information and decided it was not complete. That is, she needed more information before she could act.

She decided the information she needed was why a rash of diaper sales occurred during that time and who was buying them (charge 1—define the information you need). That information was not stored within the system, so she stationed an employee in the diaper aisle on Friday evening who recorded any information pertinent to the situation (charge 2—know how and where to obtain information). The store manager learned that young businessmen purchased the most diapers on Friday evening. Apparently, they had been instructed to buy the weekend supply of diapers on their way home from work (charge 3—understand what the information means). Her response, which is charge 4, was to stock premium domestic and imported beer near the diapers. Since then, Friday evening is not only a big sale time for diapers but also for premium domestic and imported beer.

These four charges of becoming an information-literate knowledge worker in the information age are actually all about problem solving. That is, understanding the problem (or in the diaper case, opportunity) and determining what information you need to solve the problem or take advantage of the opportunity; knowing where and how to get the information you need to make a decision; evaluating the information once it's received and formulating several alternatives to address the problem or opportunity; and finally, acting appropriately based on the information.

IT tools are great for helping you through this problem-solving or advantage-realizing process. In fact, many IT-based systems are designed specifically to help you solve a problem or take advantage of an opportunity. We call these decision support systems and artificial intelligence, and you'll learn more about them in Chapters 2 and 5, including group decision support systems, expert systems, neural networks, and genetic algorithms.

Chasing the Latest Fashions at J. C. Penney

If there ever was a fast-paced, extremely volatile market, it's definitely women's clothing. Trendy and hip fashions seem to change as often as the weather. And awareness of these changes and willingness (and sometimes enough bravery) to market new lines of clothing in hopes of keeping up with trends defines Marilee Cumming, J. C. Penney's chief of women's apparel, as a true information-literate knowledge worker.

In the early 1990s, J. C. Penney enjoyed huge profits based on its well-made, conservative private-label brands, such as its Original Arizona denim line, with sales in excess of $1 billion a year. It didn't matter that Penney's lines weren't cutting edge; they were at least reliable and that's all that mattered.

The consumer market, however, soon began to move away from "reliable" clothing in search of the more trendy and cutting-edge apparel. And, unfortunately, J. C. Penney didn't see it coming, or chose not to react to it. During the last 6 months of 1994, the company's profits dropped by 13.6 percent. And 1995 was even worse, with profits plunging nearly 21 percent.

That's when Marilee stepped into her new role as chief of women's apparel and began making sweeping changes. The new women's apparel lines are still "reliable," but they also include lambskin leather vests and silk leopard-print blouses. "Quite honestly, this is not what you'd expect from Penney. But this is definitely the direction we're going in," explains Marilee. She has even started a 1-hour show broadcast every other Monday to its 1,238 store managers. The show gives the managers a look at new apparel that has sold well at other stores, so they can order them while they're still in fashion.[34] ❖

Charges 1 and 2 are usually related to the task you're trying to perform. For example, if you're trying to decide where to build a new store, it's up to you to decide what information you need as well as where that information might be located and in what way you need to go about getting it. Charges 3 and 4 are related not only to the task you're trying to perform, but also to your ability to see what's "not there" or "around the corner" and be innovative and creative in choosing the right alternative. Your abilities to do this will measure what we refer to as your *level of information literacy*. Levels of information literacy include being a professional, an expert, or an innovator (see Figure 1.7). In the previous diaper example, these three levels might look like this:

Professional—"I'm aware that diaper sales increase on Friday evenings, so

let's make sure that diapers are well stocked during that time."

Expert—"I understand that diaper sales increase on Friday evenings and that we could capitalize on that by keeping diapers well stocked and running a sale during that time to increase revenue."

Innovator—"The majority of diaper sales can be attributed to businessmen coming home from work. Let's make sure diapers are always well stocked but, more important, let's place premium beer near the diapers to entice the businessmen to purchase a product with a high gross margin."

Notice also from Figure 1.7 that as a professional and expert you deal mainly with "what to think," and that's what your curriculum is designed to do. In this textbook for example,

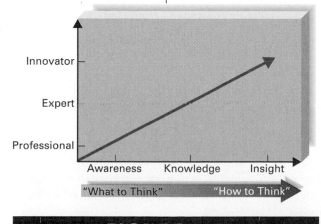

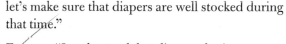

FIGURE 1.7

Levels of Information Literacy

you'll learn about the various issues involved in MIS (awareness) and the potential ramifications of those issues and how you deal with them (knowledge). What neither we nor any other text or instructor can teach you is how to gain insight from your knowledge. We can teach you "what to think" but not "how to think." Your ability to learn how to think will define you as a true innovator.

Being a Socially Responsible Knowledge Worker

In the Information Age

The first four charges in becoming an information-literate knowledge worker challenge you to learn how to use information to benefit your organization. But you must also realize that you have certain social responsibilities as well. A college athletic coach, for instance, is charged with creating a winning team for the school. At the same time, however, he or she is also charged with making certain the athletes succeed in their studies and do not take any drugs (such as steroids) that might improve their performance, but harm them.

As a knowledge worker, your charge is similar. You're charged with using information in the best possible way, but you're also charged with using that information in a socially responsible way. The last charge—use information adhering to both legal and ethical constructs—falls into the general category of ethics. *Ethics* are sets of principles or standards that help guide behavior, actions, and choices.

Open Wide and Let Everyone See Your Information

According to a 1993 Harris poll, 85 percent of the physicians surveyed said that protecting the confidentiality of patient medical records was very essential and high on their priority lists. Is 85 percent good or bad? Look at it this way: If there are 35 students in your class and each uses a different doctor, 5 of you have doctors who don't care about protecting the confidentiality of your medical records. Some doctors even make their computerized records available to drug companies in return for equipment discounts.

Long before IT became widespread as a use for computerizing patient medical records, patient confidentiality was suspect. For instance, your doctor's handwritten medical records could be subpoenaed by a court without your knowledge or consent. This happened to a woman in California whose records were subpoenaed after a car accident. Her records revealed that she had given up a child for adoption 30 years earlier.

The computerized medical record is here to stay and, when used appropriately or ethically, is of great benefit to you. *Telemedicine*—which can electronically transfer your records to any doctor in the country at any time—is a great concept if you live in Montana and get injured while on vacation in Florida. But, beware—perhaps your most sensitive information is now traveling throughout a vast network of computer users.

If you're concerned about the confidentiality of your medical records, take action. These suggestions provide a starting point.

1. Never disclose anything to your doctor that is not health-related. It may be recorded in your file, which could be transferred to another organization, such as an insurance provider.

2. Ask your doctor if any of your records can be accessed by individuals or organizations outside his or her office. If they can, ask for what purpose.

3. Always ask to review your medical records for accuracy and content.

4. Ask your doctor to notify you in writing if your records are ever subpoenaed. Also, state that only information relevant to the case be disclosed.

There is a great need to share information in the medical field for medical studies and the like. That doesn't mean, however, that you have to give up your right to privacy. This is a key issue that will dominate the health care industry as it pushes further to provide you with the best possible medical treatment through the use of IT.[35, 36] ❖

Ethical conduct is a key concern in business today, especially in the use of information and IT. As a knowledge worker, you need to understand that ethics are different from laws. Laws require or prohibit some action on your part, whereas ethics are more a matter of personal interpretation. Consider the following examples:

❶ Copying software you purchased or making copies for your friends and charging them for the copies

❷ Making an extra backup of your software just in case both the copy you are using and the primary backup fail for some reason

❸ Giving out the phone numbers and names of your friends and family to MCI for its Friends & Family calling plan, without asking them for permission

Each of these is either ethically or legally incorrect. In the second example, you may have been ethically correct in making an extra backup copy (because you did not share it with anyone), but according to most software licenses you're prohibited by law from making more than one backup copy.

To help you better understand the relationship between ethical and legal acts (or the opposite), consider the table in Figure 1.8. The table is composed of four quadrants, and you always want to remain in quadrant I. If all your actions fall in that quadrant, you'll always be acting legally and ethically, and thus in a socially responsible way.

In business, the question of ethics is an overriding concern because of the widespread use of IT to capture information. For example, if a business invests money to capture information about you as you make a purchase, does that information then belong to the business that captured the information or do you still have privacy rights regarding its distribution? Here are a few more examples to ponder:

■ If you find a coin in a pay telephone, does it belong to you, should you turn it over to the phone company, or should you try to find the person who last used the phone?

■ Does a business have the right to read your e-mail if it explicitly reserved that right in the employment contract you signed? Is the business then

financially and legally responsible for any flaming e-mail you distribute? ***Flaming*** is the distribution of an online communication that offends someone because of the use of obscene, derogatory, or inappropriate language.

■ Do organizations have the right to generate mailing lists of their customers and sell those lists to other businesses?

■ If you see a physician for lower back pain that turns out to be nothing more than a result of bad sitting posture and then later apply for health insurance, does the physician have the right to notify the insurance carrier of your previous problem?

■ If you find a money clip in the parking lot of a mall, are you required to take it to the lost and found and turn it in? What if it contains $2? $100? $1,000?

■ If you receive an unsolicited product in the mail along with a bill, can you keep the product without paying for it? Should you send it back? Was the company acting ethically or legally in sending you an unsolicited product and then asking you to pay for it?

Throughout this textbook, you'll read about becoming a socially responsible knowledge worker with respect to the use of IT and information. Many of our discussions will focus on various IT crimes such as viruses, hacking, and violating the privacy rights of individuals. The ethical and legal aspects of using information and IT are not only important for business, but also expensive—whether violating ethical standards (as with Chevron) and laws or taking measures to avoid unethical and illegal acts.

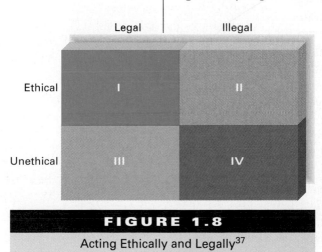

FIGURE 1.8

Acting Ethically and Legally[37]

For example, it's estimated that one of every two copies of software in use in the world today is a pirated copy (see Figure 1.9). Imagine how much money software manufacturers are losing to pirated software. Their sales and net revenues would easily double if pirated software were nonexistent.

We've written this text specifically for you as you prepare to become a knowledge worker in today's information age and to introduce you to management information systems within a business environment. It doesn't matter if you plan to be a financial analyst, a tax accountant, a marketing specialist, a compensation director, or a computer programmer, this text will help you understand that the use of technology in any organization will be successful only if **you** help plan for, develop, manage, and use the three most important business resources in *The MIS Challenge*. Those three resources are information, information technology, and people. Without all three working together in a coordinated and meaningful fashion, IT will not be successful, the right information will not be made available to the right people at the right time, and the organization will ultimately suffer.

ON YOUR OWN

E-Mail: Electronic Mail or Expensive Mail?

In February 1995, an employee at Chevron came across what he thought was an interesting and funny list—"25 Reasons Why Beer Is Better Than Women." He quickly logged into his e-mail and distributed the list to many people. The only problem was that one of the people who received the e-mail was a woman, and she was offended by it. What followed was a lot of legal mumbo jumbo and an eventual out-of-court settlement worth $2 million that Chevron had to pay to the offended employee—definitely an example of when e-mail becomes expensive mail.

Most people agree that the original sender should not have distributed the list. It was mail that was potentially embarrassing and offensive to some people and, therefore, should not have been distributed as a matter of ethics. What people don't agree on, however, is whether or not the company was at fault for not monitoring and stopping the potentially offensive mail. What are your thoughts? Before you decide, follow the accompanying diagram and consider the consequences of your answers.[38] ❖

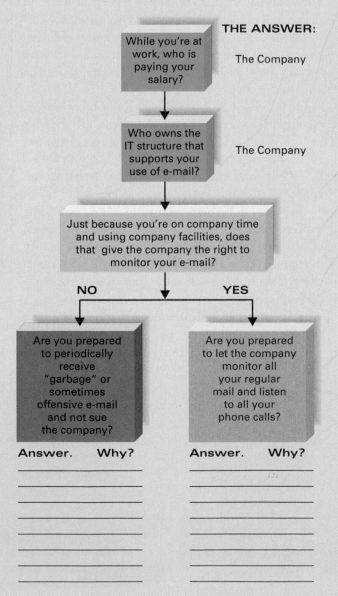

THE ANSWER:

While you're at work, who is paying your salary? — The Company

Who owns the IT structure that supports your use of e-mail? — The Company

Just because you're on company time and using company facilities, does that give the company the right to monitor your e-mail?

NO — Are you prepared to periodically receive "garbage" or sometimes offensive e-mail and not sue the company?

Answer. Why?
_____
_____
_____
_____
_____
_____
_____

YES — Are you prepared to let the company monitor all your regular mail and listen to all your phone calls?

Answer. Why?
_____
_____
_____
_____
_____
_____
_____

| PIRATED SOFTWARE LOSERS AND USERS | | | |
| TOP LOSERS | | TOP USERS | |
Revenues Lost by Software Publishers (in billions)		Percentage of Illegally Acquired Software	
Japan	$1.31	China	98
United States	$1.05	Russia	95
France	$0.48	Thailand	92
Italy	$0.26	India & Pakistan	87
United Kingdom & Ireland	$0.24	Czech & Slovak Republics	84
WORLD TOTAL	$8.08	WORLD AVERAGE	49

FIGURE 1.9

Pirates on the Prowl[39]

Your career opportunity lies in making these three resources work together effectively. To do that, you need to learn about information, information technology, people, and the issues involved in bringing these together.

CLOSING CASE STUDY: CASE 1

Information Sells Disney Resorts

Time-share vacations are big business in the hospitality and leisure industry. Basically, a time-share vacation gives you (as the purchaser) the right to use a vacation facility for a given number of weeks each year. While you're not using the vacation facility, the company can and does sell time shares to other people. Some time-share agreements even give you the right to trade your time-share vacation at one location for another time-share vacation spot, which can be anywhere in the world. In fact, according to the American Resort Development Association, in 1996 Europe surpassed the United States in terms of growth of new time-share owners. Finding good candidates for this type of vacation plan amounts to gathering information about people who like to travel frequently, go to fascinating and sometimes expensive vacation spots, and don't mind paying as much as $10,000 up front and yearly maintenance fees of $1,500 to always have a guaranteed vacation spot two weeks every year.

In 1991, Walt Disney Corp. decided to enter this lucrative market and sell time-share vacations at Disney resorts. These resorts, incidentally, are located within Walt Disney theme parks, which means time-share vacationers will probably be spending as much money at the theme parks as they pay for their vacation time. The first obstacle to overcome in developing the Disney time-share strategy was to build a warehouse of information that completely described potential time-share vacationers. After only 15 months and about $500,000, Disney had its warehouse (called a database) built and ready for information. Disney loaded the database with users of Disney credit cards, Walt Disney Corp. shareholders, and lists of customers who had stayed at other Disney hotels.

Now, Disney has 15,000 customers in its time-share database and 300,000 great prospects. Disney regularly sends a direct-marketing letter to each prospect. It includes personalized stories about the fun Disney resort customers are having and general information about time-share vacation possibilities. Disney also contacts its current time-share customers for referrals. For each referral that eventually buys a time-share vacation, Disney awards free stays and gifts to the members who made the referral. To date, the referral process has yielded over 3,000 leads.

Disney expects time-share sales to increase dramatically over the next several years. These time-share vacation purchases are important to Disney because they account for about 6 percent of the company's total revenue.[40,41] ❖

◀ Questions ▶

1. Disney Vacation Development is the division of Walt Disney Corp. that markets time-share vacations. Within *The Management Information Systems Challenge*, address the following questions:

KNOWLEDGE WORKER'S ✓-LIST

The Management Information Systems Challenge and **Management Information Systems.** *The Management Information Systems Challenge* addresses three aspects:

1. *What businesses do:* Service their customers.
2. *Customer moment of value:* Providing service when the customer wants it (time), where the customer wants it (location), how the customer wants it (form), and in a manner guaranteed to the customer (perfect delivery).
3. *The role of information technology:* To supply a set of tools that provide the right people with the right information at the right time.

   Management information systems (MIS) deals with the planning for, development, management, and use of information technology tools to help people perform all tasks related to information processing and management. No matter what career path you choose, you will be responsible for some portion of the MIS function.

Important Factors Shaping the New Business. There are many factors shaping today's new business environment. They represent a significant career opportunity for you if you understand them and are prepared to take advantage of them in the workplace. Some of the factors include

1. *Globalization:* The opportunity to expand internationally and reach a market of over 5 billion consumers.
2. *Competition:* A new environment in which creativity and innovation will help you provide customers with what they want when they want it.
3. *Information as a key resource:* Knowledge is power, and knowledge comes from having information.
4. *The virtual workplace and telecommuting:* The ability to work anywhere—without regard to time or location—because of your knowledge of the various IT tools that support the virtual workplace and telecommuting.
5. *Electronic commerce:* The performance of all functions related to business in an electronic fashion.
6. *Knowledge worker computing:* The placement of technology, technology power, software, information, and technology knowledge in the hands of those who need it—knowledge workers.

The Role of Information Technology in the New Business. Information technology (IT) is one of the three key resources in *The MIS Challenge*. Formally defined, **information technology (IT)** is any computer-based tool that people use to work with information and support

---

A. What business does Disney Vacation Development engage in?
B. What is its customer moment of value in time, location, and form?
C. What is the role of IT?

2. Do some research and find other companies that are competing with Disney in the market of time-share vacations. What features do some of these companies offer to compete with the location of Disney time-share vacations near Disney theme parks?

3. How are time-share vacations a part of a wants-driven economy? To effectively market Disney time-share vacations, what information do you think Disney provides to potential vacationers?

4. Target marketing is a primary concern for Disney. If you were a marketing specialist for Disney, what would be the ideal customer profile for a potential time-share vacationer or family?

5. What are the ethical issues relating to how Disney gathers information? Do you think Disney is acting ethically in gathering information from referrals, lists of Walt Disney shareholders, lists of Disney credit card users, and lists of people who stay at other Disney hotels?

CLOSING CASE STUDY: CASE 2

Does Acxiom Corp. Know Your Height and Weight?

It may seem like an odd question considering most people have never even heard of Acxiom Corp., but the

the information and information-processing needs of an organization. For you, the role of IT is

1. *To support the information-processing tasks of an organization*—using IT tools to capture, convey, create, cradle, and communicate information
2. *As an enabler of innovation*—learning the basics of IT and then determining how IT can significantly alter what your business does to achieve the greatest advantage
3. *As a collapser of time and space*—bringing vast amounts of information together in one small place and using IT tools to sift quickly through that information

Information as a Key Business Resource and Its Dimensions. Information is one of the three key business resources in *The MIS Challenge*, and it is the basis by which many organizations operate in today's business environment. *Information* is data that have a particular meaning within a specific context, and *data* are any raw facts or observations that describe a particular phenomenon.

The dimensions of information include

1. *Time*—information that is timely and current
2. *Content*—information that is accurate, relevant, and complete

3. *Form*—information at the appropriate level of detail and provided in the most appropriate form (for example, graphically)

Their Role as Information-Literate Knowledge Workers. Knowledge workers outnumber all other types of workers by a four-to-one margin. This simply means that businesses rely on information and, more important, on knowledge workers who understand the nature of information and how to use it. Knowledge workers who can do this are called information-literate knowledge workers. As an information-literate knowledge worker, you understand

1. *The dimensions of information*—according to time, content, and form.
2. *Your charges*—(1) defining what information you need, (2) knowing how and where to obtain information, (3) understanding the meaning of information, and (4) acting appropriately based on information. Meeting these four charges will define your ability to be a true innovator.
3. *Your charge as an ethical user of information*—being socially responsible as you manage and use information. ❖

answer may surprise you. Acxiom specializes in providing information to organizations that want to market product and services. Since the mid-1980s, Acxiom has been gathering information and building a special file called InfoBase. InfoBase now contains some or all of the following facts on 195 million Americans: home ownership, age, estimated income, cars owned, occupation, buying habits, types of credit cards used, children, and even height and weight. In 1995 alone, Acxiom sifted through the InfoBase file and created prospect lists totaling 3.7 billion people. Consider what Acxiom has done for the two organizations below.

Marriott Vacation Club International Just like Disney Resorts in the first case, Marriott Vacation Club International is exploiting all types of information in hopes of selling vacation time

shares. Initially, Marriott provides Acxiom with a list of names, mostly hotel guests. Then Acxiom sifts through motor vehicle records, property records, warranty cards, and lists of people who have made purchases through the mail in search of Marriott's hotel guests. When a match is found, Acxiom provides additional information such as children's ages, what cars they drive, and even if they play golf.

Allstate Corp. For Allstate, Acxiom retrieves an insurance applicant's credit reports, driving records, claims history, and family relationships (just in case you have a relative who likes to speed). Acxiom then electronically passes that information to Allstate's automated underwriting system. Because of the speed with which Acxiom can provide the information, Allstate can confirm a price on a new policy in 1 to 5 days, down from 35 days in 1989.[42] ❖

◄ Questions ►

1. What is the role of information technology at Acxiom? Could it still maintain and provide such a wealth of information without using IT? Acxiom's InfoBase file holds 350 terabytes of information on consumers. How much information is that? How many double-spaced pages would it take to hold all that information?

2. Within *The MIS Challenge*, what business does Acxiom engage in? What is its customer moment of value in terms of time, location, and form?

3. What are the ethical and legal issues relating to the fact that Acxiom may know your height and weight and is certainly willing to sell that information if the price is right? Can Acxiom legally own that information and sell it to any and every organization? How does it make you feel to know that your personal information is available for the right price?

4. Within each dimension of information—time, content, and form—what characteristics are most important to Allstate when receiving information from Acxiom? What about Marriott—which characteristics are most important when receiving information from Acxiom?

5. Do some research and find other companies that specialize in providing marketing information. What companies did you find? Do they provide information on people all over the country or just in your town or state? Did any of these companies state that they could provide the height and weight of individuals?

REAL [H·O·T]
Electronic Commerce
Business and You on the Internet

Using the Internet as a Tool to Find a Job

Electronic commerce is a great new business horizon. And it's not "just around the corner." Electronic commerce is already here and businesses all over the world are taking advantage of it. By using telecommunications technologies, such as the Internet, businesses can electronically perform a number of tasks, including selling products and services, providing service and support, advertising, and researching customers and competitors in the marketplace. But electronic commerce is not limited to the business environment. As an individual, you can use the Internet to perform a vitally important task—that of finding a job.

Today, information technology can help you land a job in two ways. First, most employers are looking for candidates with IT skills. If you doubt this, just ask several graduating seniors what information they've included on their resumes. You'll find that they all include information about their education, work experience, extracurricular activities, and awards and honors. You'll also find that they include a section that details such IT skills as the application software, hardware, and operating systems with which they're familiar.

Second, you can use your knowledge of IT and IT itself to help you find potential employers, place your resume in their hands, locate summer internships, and learn the art of selling yourself during the interview and negotiation process. How? By simply cruising the Internet and using online job database and service providers as well as accessing information about how to prepare for an interview (among other things).

Although no one knows the exact numbers, it's estimated that over 4 million people daily cruise the Net in search of job opportunities and employers at hundreds of different Web sites. Those same people are also building and posting e-resumes (electronic resumes) and accessing sites that provide tips for interviewing and negotiating that first big raise. So, the question we ask you is, are you one of those people taking advantage of the Internet to find a job? If you're not, we'd like to help by introducing you to just a few of the thousands of Web sites that can help you find a job.

In this section, we've included a number of Web sites related to finding a job through the Internet. On the Web site that supports this text (http://www.mhhe.com/business/mis/haag, select "Electronic Commerce Projects"), we've provided direct links to all these Web sites as well as many, many more. These are a great starting point for completing this Real HOT section. We would also encourage you to search the Internet for others.

Job Database and Service Providers

When most people think of using the Internet to find a job, they think of the hundreds of online job database and service providers such as Career Mosaic, JobTrak, and Online Career Center. These job database and service providers offer you a wealth of information and services that range from hundreds of thousands of job postings, to powerful search engines for searching through those postings, to tips and helpful hints for building an electronic resume. Let's first explore searching these job databases, and then we'll look toward building an electronic resume.

Searching Job Databases

There are—quite literally—thousands of sites that provide you with databases of job postings. Some are better than others; some focus on specific industries; and still others offer only postings for executive managers. For the best review of job Web sites, connect to two different places. The first is Web21's 100 Hot Jobs and Careers at http://www.100hot.com/jobs. This site ranks the most popular job Web sites according to traffic (number of hits). The second is the Career Resources Homepage at http://www.rpi.edu/dept/cdc/homepage.html. This site provides the most comprehensive list of the available job Web sites. There, you'll find a list of over 1,000 job Web sites.

So, let's explore some of these databases—hopefully, you'll find the perfect job. Think for a moment about the job you want. What would be its title? In which industry do you want to work? In what part of the country do you want to live? What special skills do you possess (e.g., if you're looking for an accounting job, you may be specializing in auditing)? Is there a specific organization for which you would like to work?

Now that you've thought about your job, connect to five different job database sites. In the table on page 36, we've provided a list of the more popular job databases and where you can find them on the Internet. And on the Web site that supports this text, you'll find a list of many others. As you connect to five different databases and search for your job, answer the following questions for each database.

A. What is the date of last update?

B. Are career opportunities abroad listed as a separate category or are they integrated with domestic jobs?

C. Can you search for a specific organization?

D. Can you search by geographic location? If so, how? By state? By city? By zip code?

E. Does the site provide direct links to Web sites or provide some other profile information for those organizations posting jobs?

F. Does the site provide direct links to e-mail addresses for those organizations posting jobs?

G. Can you apply for a position online? If so, how do you send your resume?

H. Can you search by a specific industry?

I. Can you specify your desired position as entry level, advanced, managerial, and so forth?

Hopefully, your search of five different databases led you to some potential job opportunities. If not, search through a few more of the databases. There are jobs out there for you.

Creating and Posting an Electronic Resume

Most, if not all, the job databases you just explored focus on two groups—employers and employees. As a potential

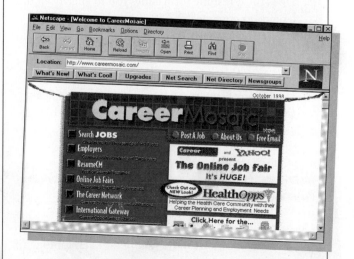

employee, you search to find jobs that meet your qualifications and desires. Likewise, employers need to search job databases that contain resumes so they can find people (like you) who meet their qualifications and desires. In this instance, you need to build an electronic resume (e-resume) and leave it at the various job database sites as you perform your searches. That way, organizations can perform similar searches, in the hope of finding you.

What you need to understand first is that building an e-resume is quite different from creating a paper resume. It really is! An e-resume (and the search for an e-resume) is built on key words. For example, if you put "tele-marketing experience" in your e-resume and a potential employer searches for "telemarketing experience," your e-resume may not appear as a match. Likewise, if a potential employer is looking for someone who can start work during the first of the summer and you enter your first available date as June 15, is that a match? So, building an e-resume is an important process and one that you should not take lightly.

Almost all the job database sites we've listed give you the ability to create and post an electronic resume. Visit two new job database sites (different from those you visited to find a job). In each, go through the process of creating an e-resume, posting it, and making some sort of modification to it. As you do, answer the following questions for each of the sites.

A. Do you have to register as a user to build an e-resume?

B. Once a potential employer performs a search that matches your e-resume, how can that employer contact you?

C. What valuable tips for building a good e-resume are available?

D. Once you build your e-resume, can you use it to perform a job search?

E. Does the e-resume form allow you to specify all the languages you speak?

F. When you modify your e-resume, can you update your existing e-resume or must you delete the old one and create a new one?

G. How many key terms concerning your qualifications can you include in your e-resume?

H. For what time frame does your e-resume stay active?

Searching Newspapers the New-Fashioned Way

One of today's most popular ways to find a job is to search the classified sections of newspapers. Each Sunday (if

your library is open) and Monday you can visit your local library and find a gathering of people searching through the classified sections of the *Los Angeles Times*, *Boston Herald*, and *Dallas Morning News* in the hope of finding a job. Most of these people are attempting to find a job in a specific geographic location. For example, a person looking in the *Dallas Morning News* is probably most interested in finding a job in the Dallas/Fort Worth area.

And as you might well guess, newspapers are not to be left off the Internet bandwagon. Today, you can find hundreds of online editions of daily newspapers. And the majority of these provide their classified sections in some sort of searchable electronic format. In the table on page 36, we've provided a list of newspapers and where you can find them on the Internet. Don't forget that the Web site that supports this text contains direct links to all these plus many others. Pick five newspapers, perform an online search for a job that interests you at each newspaper, and answer the following questions. You may want to include your local newspaper in your list of five. To obtain a comprehensive list of online newspapers all over the world, connect to http://www.newspapers.com. There, you'll find a map of the United States—simply point at and click on your state.

A. Can you search by location/city?

B. Can you search back issues or only the most recent issue?

C. Does the newspaper provide direct links to Web sites or provide some other profile information for those organizations posting jobs?

D. Does the newspaper provide direct links to e-mail addresses for those organizations posting jobs?

E. Is the newspaper affiliated with any of the major job database providers? If so, which one?

F. Does the newspaper provide direct links to a major job database provider so you can post your resume?

G. Can you use your electronic resume to perform a job search? If so, was your search successful?

H. Does the newspaper provide a true, searchable database of job opportunities or simply its classified ad section in an electronic form?

Locating That All-Important Internship

Have you ever noticed that a large number of jobs require experience. That being the case, how does someone gain experience through a job when experience is required to get the job? As it turns out, that's a perplexing dilemma

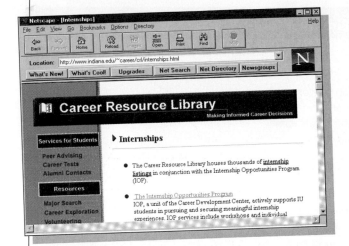

for many college students. And one way to avoid it is by obtaining an internship. Internships provide you with valuable knowledge about your field, pay you for your work, and offer you that valuable "experience" you need to move up in your career.

In the table on page 36, we've listed Web sites that describe internship programs and job opportunities, and we've provided many more on the Web site that supports this text. Connect to a total of four of these sites. Did you find any internships in line with your career? What about pay—did you find both paying and nonpaying internships? Compared to the more traditional job database sites you looked at earlier, how do these internship sites compare? Why do you think this is true?

Interviewing and Negotiating

The Internet is a vast repository of information—possibly more information than you'll ever need in your entire life. During the job search process, however, the Internet can offer you very valuable information. In the area of interviewing and negotiating, for example, the Internet contains over 1,500 sites devoted to interviewing skills, negotiating tips, and the like.

Interviewing and negotiating are just as important as searching for a job. Once you land that first important interview, you can still lose the job if you're not properly prepared. And, if you do receive a job offer, you may be surprised to find that you can negotiate such things as moving expenses, signing bonuses, and allowances for technology in your home.

In the table on page 36, we've provided Web sites that address the interviewing and negotiating skills you need in today's marketplace. And on the Web site that supports this text, you'll find a list of additional sites devoted to these two important skill sets. Review some of these sites (and any others that you may find). Then,

develop a list of dos and donts for the interview process. Finally, develop a list of tips that will increase your effectiveness during the negotiation process. Once you've developed these two lists, prepare a short class presentation concerning your findings.

Going Right to the Source— The Organization You Want

Today, many organizations are posting positions they have open on their own Web sites. The thought process is simple. If you like an organization enough to visit its Web site, you might just want to work there. For example, if you connect to the Gap at http://www.gap.com and buy clothes online, you might consider working there if the opportunity were right.

In the table on page 36, we've listed a few organizations and where you can find them on the Internet (there are many others on the Web site that supports this text). Choose five of these and then choose five other organizations not listed. For each organization, connect to its Web site, look for job opportunities, and answer the following questions.

A. Are you able to find job opportunities?

B. How difficult is it to find the job opportunities?

C. Are positions grouped or categorized by type?

D. Is a discussion of career paths included?

E. How do you obtain an application form?

F. Are there international opportunities available?

G. Do the job descriptions include a list of qualifications?

H. Are there direct links to e-mail addresses for further questions?

I. Are fax numbers listed? Can you fax your resume to those numbers?

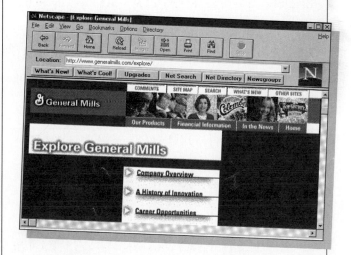

Web Sites for Finding a Job

Service	Address
America's Job Bank	http://www.ajb.dni.us
NationJob Online Jobs Database	http://www.nation.job.com
Online Career Center	http://www.occ.com
Career Mosaic	http://www.careermosaic.com
Interactive Employment Network	http://www.espan.com

Newspapers	Address
LA Times	http://www.latimes.com
Minneapolis Star Tribune	http://www.startribune.com
Dallas Morning News	http://www.dallasnews.com
Denver Post	http://www.denverpost.com
Atlanta Journal-Constitution	http://www.accessatlanta.com

Internship Sites

http://www.indiana.edu/~career/crl/internships.html
http://www.wm.edu/csrv/career/stualum/jintern.html
http://sailor.lib.md.us/topics/emp_cat/vol.html
http://www.hanover.edu/career_center/intern.html
http://www.westga.edu/~coop/internships.html

Interviewing and Negotiating Sites

http://www.pipelinepress.com/data/rlr/interview.html
http://www.academic.marist.edu/career/informative-1.htm
http://www.olemiss.edu/depts/career_services/int_view.htm
http://www.careermag.com/newsarts/interviewing/1003.html
http://www.bsu.edu/careers/intrview.html

Organization	Address
IBM	http://www.ibm.com
Ford	http://www.ford.com/us
General Mills	http://www.generalmills.com
United Airlines	http://www.ual.com
Hertz	http://www.hertz.com

Go to the Web site that supports this text: **http://www.mhhe.com/business/mis/haag** and select "Electronic Commerce Projects."

We've included links to over 100 Web sites for using the Internet as a tool to find a job as well as Employment With the Government.

KEY TERMS AND CONCEPTS

Competition
Customer Moment of Value
Data
Dimensions of Information
Electronic Commerce
Ethics
Flaming
Globalization
Information
Information Age
Information-Literate Knowledge Worker

Information Technology (IT)
Knowledge Worker
Knowledge Worker Computing
Levels of Information Literacy
Management Information Systems (MIS)
Management Information Systems Challenge
Perfect Delivery
Telecommuter
Telecommuting
Transnational Firm
Virtual Workplace

SHORT-ANSWER QUESTIONS

1. What is a knowledge worker?
2. What is management information systems (MIS)? What are the three key resources of MIS?
3. What are the three aspects of *The Management Information Systems Challenge*?
4. What are important factors shaping today's business?
5. How is IT a collapser of time and space?
6. What is the difference between data and information? What are the dimensions of information?
7. What are the five charges of being an information-literate knowledge worker?
8. What are ethics?
9. What are the four characteristics of customer moment of value?
10. How is a wants-driven economy related to information as a key resource in the new business?
11. What is knowledge worker computing? Why is it important to you?

DISCUSSION QUESTIONS

1. Knowledge workers dominate today's business environment. However, many industries still need workers who do not fall into the category of knowledge workers. What industries still need skilled workers who are not knowledge workers? Can you see a time when these jobs will be replaced by knowledge workers?
2. Put yourself in the shoes of a bank CEO and focus specifically on customers with checking and savings accounts. What is their moment of value in terms of time, location, form, and perfect delivery? How have banks already used IT to deliver perfect service at the customer's moment of value? In what ways could banks further exploit IT to achieve greater customer satisfaction?
3. The three key resources in *The Management Information Systems Challenge* are information, information technology, and people. Which of these three resources is the most important? Why? The least important? Why?
4. We identified six important factors that are changing business today. What other factors are

also causing changes? Has IT had some sort of involvement in their presence?
5. Telecommuting is like all things—it has a good side and it has a bad side. What are some of the disadvantages or pitfalls of telecommuting? How can these be avoided?
6. As an information-literate knowledge worker for a local distributor of imported foods and spices, you've been asked to prepare a customer mailing list that will be sold to international cuisine restaurants in your area. If you do, would you be acting ethically? If you don't consider the proposal ethical, what if your boss threatened to fire you if you didn't prepare the list? Do you believe you would have any legal recourse if you didn't prepare the list and were subsequently fired?
7. How is your school helping you prepare to take advantage of knowledge worker computing? What courses have you taken that included teaching you how to use technology? What software packages were taught?

CASE STUDY

Levi Strauss Is Losing Its Pants to Vanity Fair

Along with its line of women's undergarments, Vanity Fair (VF) is also the producer of Lee and Wrangler jeans, and its sales of Lee and Wrangler jeans are beating the pants off of its $6-billion-a-year rival, Levi Strauss & Co. Since 1991 VF has boasted a compound annual growth rate of almost 20 percent, something very few big companies can match. What's behind the success of VF? It's a computerized "market-response system" that cuts inventory replenishment times for large retailers like Wal-Mart and J. C. Penney to as little as 3 days.

Take Wal-Mart as an example. VF has connected its computers to those of Wal-Mart. When a customer buys a pair of Wrangler jeans on Wednesday, that information is sent by computer to VF that evening. If VF has a replacement pair in stock, it's immediately sent out on Thursday and

IN THE NEWS

43 X-Treme Rocky Accessories is creating a new organizational structure based on information and the use of various IT systems to achieve the greatest advantage.

44 At Bank of America, phone representatives receive over 100,000 calls a day from credit card customers.

46 US West's *Global Village* is an intranet, a special type of internal Internet.

51 Customer integrated systems place technology in the hands of an organization's customers and allow them to process their own transactions. ATMs are a great example.

59 Videoconferencing systems for your home computer cost less than $1,500.

64 Work flow automation software helped IBM Credit increase the rate of throughput one hundredfold (not 100 percent, but one hundred times).

66 Genetic algorithms mimic evolutionary, survival-of-the-fittest processes to help people generate increasingly better solutions to problems.

70 R. J. Reynolds cut purchase order costs from $75 to just 93 cents by using electronic data interchange.

Information Technology Systems

arrives at Wal-Mart on Saturday. Three days for inventory replenishment is an astounding feat, especially when you consider that it can take up to 1 month for Wal-Mart to receive Levi's.

But speed isn't VF's only advantage. The market-response system also takes the guess-work out of reordering and provides retailers with only the best-selling styles and lines. Explains Robert Wildrick, merchandising chief of Belk Stores Services, "We get more sales out of the same amount of inventory, because we now have in stock more of the sizes the customer wants."

And VF CEO Lawrence Pugh still isn't satisfied. He has even embarked on creating an extension of the market-response system that will analyze the sales databases of retailers and determine groups of goods—for instance, matching jeans, shirts, and jackets—to help retailers forecast ideal supply levels.

Vanity Fair is like many businesses today that are striving to create IT based systems that will help them manage information more efficiently and effectively. VF's market-response system is actually three IT systems rolled into one. First, the system that allows retailers to electronically transfer sales information to VF is called an *interorganizational system*. Second, the system that processes the sales information and updates VF's database is called a *transaction processing system*. Finally, the system that determines which styles and sizes to send to retailers and which groups of goods might sell best is a type of *decision support system* (or perhaps even *artificial intelligence*).[1,2] ❖

FEATURES

IN THE INFORMATION AGE, KNOWLEDGE WORKERS UNDERSTAND...

1. How organizations can be structured, both horizontally and vertically

2. The nature of decentralized computing and shared information

3. How information flows in an organization and what information can describe

4. The information-processing tasks that take place in an organization and IT systems that support those tasks

CHAPTER 2

Introduction

Vanity Fair not only provides an excellent example of some of the different types of IT systems you can find in an organization, but also illustrates how one organization has achieved a competitive advantage through using IT to perform a variety of information-processing tasks. And that's the focus of this chapter—information technology systems in an organization, how your organization can use IT systems to perform information-processing tasks, and how your organization can use those systems to achieve a competitive advantage.

The phrase "information technology systems in an organization" is composed of three distinct parts: (1) an organization, (2) information in an organization, and (3) information technology systems in an organization (see Figure 2.1). So, let's review an organization and information in an organization, and then we'll explore the seven different information technology systems (IT systems) used by organizations.

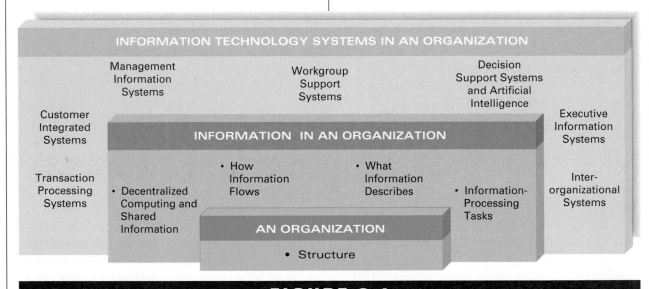

FIGURE 2.1

Your Focus in This Chapter

Who Is X-Treme Rocky Accessories?

X-Treme Rocky Accessories (XRA) is a manufacturer of mountain bicycle parts and accessories located in Denver, Colorado. The recent boom in outdoor recreational activities, especially mountain biking, prompted XRA to find innovative ways to structure its organization, develop new parts and accessories, and market its products.

"When mountain biking was a little-known recreational activity, we were a fairly stable organization. Now, competition is fierce—if we can't be innovative every single day, we'll go out of business. Not only that, our customers want some of the most unusual products. For ex-

ample, one customer wanted to know if we made plastic water bottles that glowed in the dark. Why anyone would want to mountain bike in the dark is beyond me. Anyway, we started making glow-in-the-dark water bottles, and today we sell about 50,000 per year."

—R. F. "Spike" Havel, CEO of XRA

Today, XRA employs 148 people and generates annual revenues in excess of $45 million. As we proceed through this chapter, we will explore XRA's organizational structure, information flows, IT structure, and the IT systems that give XRA a significant advantage in the marketplace. ❖

As we proceed through this chapter, we'll also introduce you to X-Treme Rocky Accessories, a parts and accessories manufacturer of mountain bikes. Like most other organizations, X-Treme Rocky Accessories is creating a new organizational structure based on information and the use of various IT systems to achieve the greatest advantage.

An Organization

Most people view a traditional organization as a four-level triangle (see Figure 2.2). At the top is *strategic management*, which provides an organization with overall direction and guidance. The second level is often called *tactical management*, which develops the goals and strategies outlined by strategic management. The third level is *operational management*, which manages and directs the day-to-day operations and implementation of the goals and strategies. Finally, the fourth level of the organization comprises nonmanagement employees, those people who actually perform daily activities, such as order processing, developing and producing goods and services, and servicing customers.

This traditional triangular view of an organization really describes only two dimensions of an organization—length and width. In reality, all organizations have a third dimension—depth. That is, an organization is multifaceted or has many sides. In Figure 2.3, you can see General Motors' organizational structure. Notice that GM is

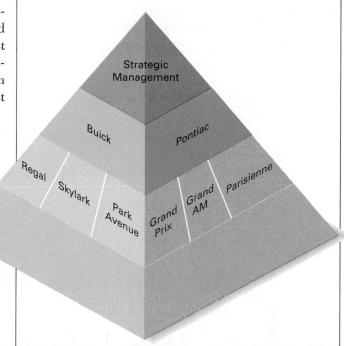

Vertical and Horizontal Structuring at General Motors

structured vertically by product lines (Buick, Pontiac, and so on) and horizontally by specific automobiles within each product line. In this instance, GM has chosen an organizational structure based on specific products rather than traditional business functions, such as production, finance, and so on.

Structuring an organization according to its products or services, instead of general business functions, makes sense but also creates problems. For example, does this type of structure at GM mean that there is a group of people in the Pontiac division designing car seats for just Pontiacs, another group in the Buick division designing car seats for just Buicks, and yet another group in the Chevrolet division designing car seats for just Chevrolets? The answer, unfortunately, is both yes and no.

To a certain extent, each of these groups must be concerned only with the design of the seats for their respective automobiles. But there are also many overlapping concerns. For example, no matter which GM car or truck you buy, you choose a fabric from a common group—cloth, vinyl, leather, and so on. Therefore these seemingly diverse workgroups need to work together and independently. Later in this chapter, we'll explore IT systems (called workgroup support systems) and specific IT products that can help these groups or teams work effectively; and in Chapter 3, you'll read about the many team strategies and competitive opportunities in an organization.

A Traditional View of an Organization

Organizational Structure

XRA is like many organizations today—it has found that structuring specifically according to traditional business functions has its merits, but also some drawbacks. Therefore, XRA's organizational structure includes five basic business functions (called divisions)—Finance & Accounting, Production & Development, Marketing & Sales, Human Resource Management, and Information Technology (IT). But, within some of these divisions, department structures are built around specific product sets and customer sets.

For example, Production & Development includes three departments: (1) Tires & Foot Pedals; (2) Seats & Handle Bar Grips; and (3) Plastic Water Bottles, Helmets, & Elbow and Knee Pads. And

Marketing & Sales includes two departments: (1) Retail Center Accounts and (2) Manufacturer Accounts. Why structure the organization in this fashion?

"Well, we market and sell to two major customer sets—retail centers and actual bike manufacturers. Retail centers buy products and accessories from all three Production & Development departments. Bike manufacturers only buy products and accessories from two Production & Development departments. Bike manufacturers don't buy our products that include plastic water bottles, helmets, and elbow and knee pads."

—Jennifer Gance, director of Marketing & Sales ❖

Strategic Management

Production & Development

Marketing & Sales

Plastic Water Bottles, Helmets, & Elbow and Knee Pads

Seats & Handle Bar Grips

Tires & Foot Pedals

Manufacturer Accounts

Retail Center Accounts

Information in an Organization

In Chapter 1, we looked at the various dimensions of information—time, content, and form. Those dimensions define information in terms of when you need it (time), what information you need (content), and how you want the information (form). As you might well guess, knowledge workers at different levels need and work with different kinds of information and different dimensions of information. For example, knowledge workers in upper levels of an organization are more concerned with information that exhibits a coarse granularity (sales by year), whereas those in the lower levels are more concerned with information that exhibits a fine granularity (sales by day or week).

Besides the dimensions of information, you also need to consider

❶ The concept of shared information through decentralized computing

❷ The directional flow of information

❸ What information specifically describes

❹ The information-processing tasks your organization undertakes

Shared Information Through Decentralized Computing

At Bass Brewery—one of England's largest beer manufacturers—variety is the spice of life that guarantees a high level of sales in a market that demands widely varying products and batch sizes.[3] Bass produces more than 50 types of beer in more than 150 different packages. These include beer for domestic consumption, beer for international exporting, cask-conditioned beers, and beer in pint packages. To support this vast variety of beer production, Bass uses an automated, state-of-the-art networked computer system that manages two facilities—the brew house and the packaging hall. The brew house is where the beer is manufactured, and the packaging hall is where the beer is placed in the appropriate containers with various labels attached. With this networked computer system, Bass has reduced product transition time from hours to just a few minutes.

With the touch of a computer screen, the production manager can switch all the production facilities from one type of beer to another. This includes starting cleaning fluid throughout the brew house and electronically sending recipes to the brew house vats and information about bottling sizes and labels to the packaging hall. Throughout the process, production information from both the automated brew house vats and the packaging hall is relayed to the production manager. Bass's computer-integrated manufacturing system is an excellent example of the state-of-the-art use of technology for managing information and coordinating work processes in an organization. The key for Bass is twofold—***decentralized computing*** and ***shared information***. To understand these concepts, let's take an interesting historical perspective of technology and information in an organization.

As recently as the late 1970s and early 1980s, most organizations exhibited centralized computing and isolated information (see Figure 2.4a). Centralized computing is characterized by the use of large mainframe computers

to manage an organization's information and handle all information-processing tasks. In a centralized computing environment, people typically access the mainframe through a terminal, which has a combination of a keyboard and screen but no storage or processing capabilities. In spite of the central proximity of information (all of it contained within the mainframe), it is still largely isolated. That is, as computing applications are developed, separate files of information are set up for each. This simply means that most applications do not and cannot share information unless that information is duplicated.

As computing technologies became less expensive, more powerful, and smaller, organizations began to decentralize their computing structures. This flood of ever more powerful systems included minicomputers and microcomputers or workstations. The decentralization of computing allowed organizations to split computing power and locate it in functional business areas (see Figure 2.4b). These systems, however, still maintained their own information, which meant that isolated information was still a problem. This type of environment could be characterized as decentralized computing with isolated information.

 **Divisions and Departments Must Work Together**

"Creating departments like this allows our employees to create cross-functional teams that work together during the development of a new product or accessory. For example, last year we set out to develop a new line of helmets for children. Our people in retail center Marketing & Sales and helmet Production & Development joined together to create a simply fantastic line of children's helmets. We even go so far as to require people to periodically work in different departments. Sometimes, our design engineers go on sales calls with people from Marketing & Sales. And all Marketing & Sales employees must spend at least two weeks per year on the manufacturing floor. That way, everyone can do a better job because they understand what happens all over the organization."

—Bill Polland, director of Production & Development

"Where does Finance & Accounting, Human Resource Management, and IT fit in? In a nutshell, they fit in everywhere. These functions are fundamental to our entire organization. Everyone works with everyone. For example, we have IT people who

are permanently assigned to certain departments. Those IT people constantly train employees concerning new IT products, and the IT people also relay to me what departments need. Traditional organizational structures simply don't support this cross-functional approach."

—Jarod Green, director of IT ❖

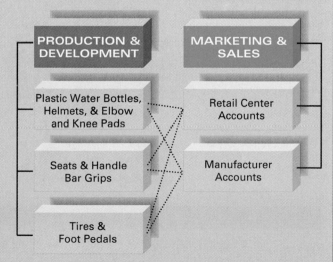

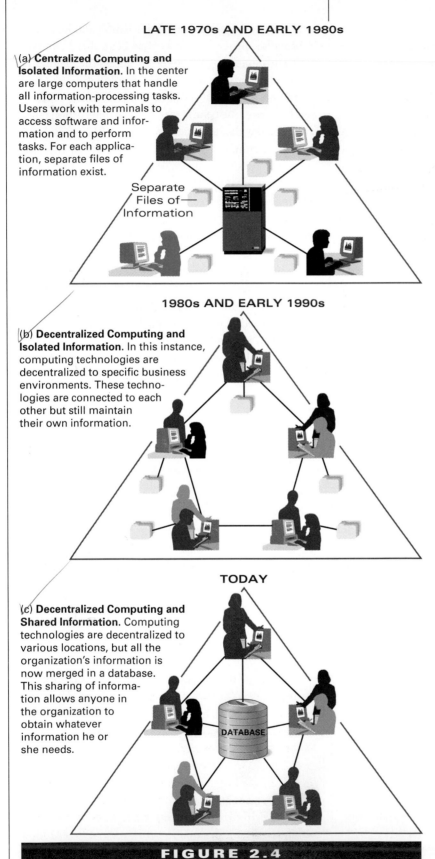

LATE 1970s AND EARLY 1980s

(a) **Centralized Computing and Isolated Information.** In the center are large computers that handle all information-processing tasks. Users work with terminals to access software and information and to perform tasks. For each application, separate files of information exist.

Separate Files of Information

1980s AND EARLY 1990s

(b) **Decentralized Computing and Isolated Information.** In this instance, computing technologies are decentralized to specific business environments. These technologies are connected to each other but still maintain their own information.

TODAY

(c) **Decentralized Computing and Shared Information.** Computing technologies are decentralized to various locations, but all the organization's information is now merged in a database. This sharing of information allows anyone in the organization to obtain whatever information he or she needs.

DATABASE

FIGURE 2.4

The Movement Toward Decentralized Computing and Shared Information

Today, many organizations are like Bass—they have maintained their decentralized computing structures while bringing together the entire spectrum of the organization's information in an orderly fashion so that it can be accessed and used by anyone who needs it. This structure of ordered information is called a *database*, which is designed to directly support the concept of shared information (see Figure 2.4c). Throughout the organization, people now use software to provide specific updates to databases and have access to powerful software that lets them drill down through the database to find any information they need. This drill down concept has led to the popular terms of "information mining" and "data mining" to describe the process of sifting through or massaging a database to find information.

At Bank of America, phone representatives receive over 100,000 calls a day from credit card customers. Instead of simply responding to customer requests, the phone reps mine through a database in hopes of selling customers another product while they have them on the phone. For example, a phone rep may discover that a certain customer has bounced a couple of checks, so he or she might try to sell the customer overdraft protection. Drilling down through a customer's information is what gives Bank of America the ability to sell more-tailored products. Having this kind of insight into a customer's behavior is so advantageous that Luke Helms, vice chairman in charge of retail banking at Bank of America, says ". . . it's almost like you're cheating."[4]

Decentralized computing and shared information make the most business sense. Decentralized computing provides groups of people (for instance teams, departments, and business units) with the flexibility to handle their own specific information-processing tasks. Information sharing,

Information Technology

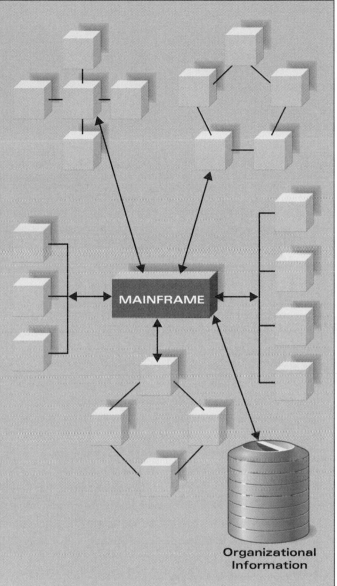

Organizational
Information

"**O**ur IT structure is definitely decentralized. We currently have a mainframe computer on which we run all of our basic business functions—payroll gathering, order processing, collections, and so on. But within each division or department, we have small networks connected to the mainframe. That way, everyone has access to the mainframe but is also free to do information processing unique to them. For example, Production & Development can always look up what new orders have come in, but they also have a CAD/CAM (computer-automated design/computer-automated manufacturing) system that only that division uses. Still, because we're all connected, Production & Development can easily send me a product design for review."

—Sevilla Williamson, Manufacturer
Accounts representative

"Information sharing is a must. Anyone in any division or department can always access information stored on the mainframe. However, we do restrict who can do what with that information. For example, if someone in Human Resource Management wants to access the daily production schedule, they are completely free to do so. But, they can't alter the production schedule in any way. Only people in Production & Development can do that. Information sharing may be critical, but so is developing the appropriate security that controls who can do what to the information."

—Julie Ko, IT operations manager ❖

on the other hand, guarantees everyone in the organization—regardless of location—access and use of any needed information.

How Information Flows in an Organization

Because of the nature of shared information and decentralized computing, information in an organization flows in three directions—up, down, and horizontally (see Figure 2.5). Information that flows upward, or the *upward flow of information*, describes the current state of the organization based on its daily transactions. When a sale occurs, for example, that information originates at the lowest level of the organization and then is passed up through various levels of management. And don't forget, as information of this nature flows upward, it becomes increasingly more concise. IT plays a vital role in the upward flow of information. Information gathered as part of everyday operations is consolidated by IT and passed upward to decision makers who monitor and respond to problems and opportunities.

The *downward flow of information* consists of the strategies, goals, and directives that originate at one level and are passed to lower levels. For example, in 1991 Honda's strategic management responded to lagging sales (information that was passed up through the organization) by terminating its CRX automobile and

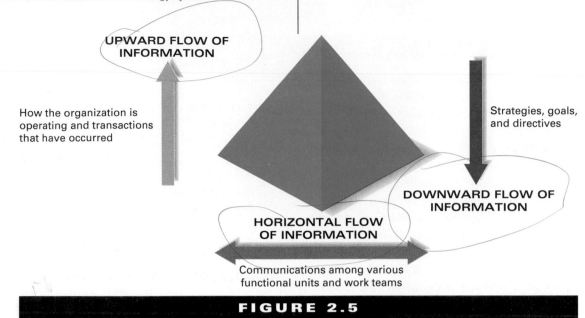

FIGURE 2.5

The Flow of Information in an Organization

developing the new Del Sol. This strategic management decision was passed downward to tactical management, which determined how to rid the company of its CRX inventory. Those decisions were passed to car dealers, who determined how to advertise the CRX closeout sale and what incentives to offer. Dealer decisions, in turn, were passed downward to the salespeople who were responsible for making the sales.

Information that flows horizontally, or the *horizontal flow of information,* is between functional business units and work teams. In our earlier example of GM and the car seat teams within the product line groups, horizontal flows of information would include new product designs, changes to proposed product designs, and completed product designs (see Figure 2.6). Communications here are essential to consolidate ideas and create car seats that can be used in most, if not all, GM automobiles.

At US West, some 15,000 employees in 14 states use an internal Internet to create upward, downward, and horizontal information flows.[5] This type of internal Internet is called an **intranet**, and, like US West, many companies are creating their own internal Internet to support information flows. US West's intranet is called the *Global Village.* Employees can connect to the *Global Village* and meet in online chat rooms, exchange documents, and discuss ongoing projects, even with employees located in remote geographic areas. US West eventually plans to allow service

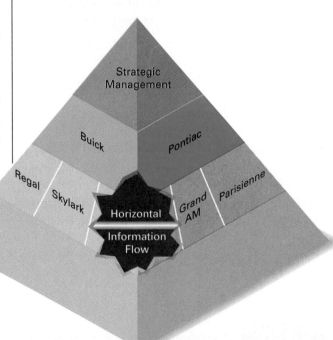

FIGURE 2.6

The Horizontal Flow of Information in an Organization

representatives to access the *Global Village* to fill orders for customers while they wait on the phone. You could, for example, call US West and request call waiting. The service representative would simply use the *Global Village* to enter your request, which would then be routed immediately to the appropriate phone-switching network, where your call waiting would be activated—in a matter of seconds.

What Information Describes

Different jobs need different information, so different people in an organization need different types of information. Information may be internal, external, objective, subjective, or some combination of the four. *Internal information* describes specific operational aspects of the organization, whereas *external information* describes the environment surrounding the organization. *Objective information* quantifiably describes something that is known; *subjective information* attempts to describe something that is currently unknown. For example, you know today's prime interest rate, so it's objective information; however, you don't know what the prime interest rate will be 6 months from now, so your projection of it represents subjective information.

Every business—no matter how small or large—works with internal, external, objective, and subjective information every day. Consider a small convenience store that sells gas. To determine the best price per gallon, the store must consider competitors' prices (external and objective information), the cost of gas to the store (internal and objective information), projected movements in the price of crude oil (external and subjective information), as well as a host of other types of information.

Information-Processing Tasks in Your Organization

When most people think of information processing, they usually think in terms of arithmetically manipulating information. For example, determining the accrued interest on your credit card balance is an arithmetic information-processing task as is determining your tuition

bill based on the classes for which you enroll. But information processing extends well beyond arithmetic. In Chapter 1, we introduced you to the five categories of information-processing tasks—capturing, conveying, creating, cradling, and communicating information. Let's review these.

Capturing information means obtaining information at its point of origin. The key to capturing information is in obtaining information at its **point of origin**. Organizations today must strive to capture information only once at its point of origin and not require people to reenter information as they need it. *Conveying information* is the exact opposite of capturing information. That is, *conveying information* involves presenting information in its most useful form to people who need it. The key to conveying information is in presenting it in its **most useful form**. That is, do you need information in a graphic form, printed on paper in numeric form, or perhaps presented to you in audio form? The information-processing task of conveying information is closely related to the form dimension of information.

XRA   Horizontal Flow of Information

"**W**e couldn't achieve our cross-functional team approach without IT that supports the horizontal flow of information. For example, when Marketing & Sales wants to develop a different kind of bicycle seat, they can formulate the requirements, create simple drawings, and interactively share and discuss that information with Production & Development. Even when sales reps are on the road, they can use their laptops to electronically communicate this information. I've even seen our Production & Development people approve a product modification while the sales rep sat in the office of a bicycle manufacturer. It's amazing—we can actually design products here while our sales reps work with manufacturers anywhere in the country."

—Jimmy Surlan, design engineer ❖

Determining Savings Rates at Banks and Savings and Loans

If you think all banks and S&Ls offer the same rates on such instruments as deposit accounts and CDs, think again. Below is a list of the nation's best rates for 5-year CDs during the fall of 1998.

Institution	Rate
Capital One, Glen Allen, VA	6.20%
Central State Bank, Calera, AL	6.00%
Abbotsford St., Abbotsford, WI	6.00%
Advanta Nat. Bank, Wilmington, DE	6.00%
Eastern Savings, Hunt Valley, MD	6.00%

What this means is that banks and S&Ls have some flexibility in setting their own rates. If you were in charge of setting rates, what information would go into your decision-making process? Enter each piece of information in the table below and identify whether it's internal, external, objective, subjective, or a combination of the four. We've completed one such piece of information to help you get started.

It may help to interview a bank or S&L officer in order to better understand how this type of decision is made.

For each specific piece of information you identify, also determine how that information flows in an organization. Does it flow upward, downward, horizontally, or perhaps some combination of the three? ❖

Information	Internal	External	Objective	Subjective
Prime Rate Today		X	X	

Creating information is the most commonly understood information-processing task. It involves processing information to obtain new information. Our previous example of determining the interest on your credit card balance involves creating information. That is, the interest on your credit card balance is created by determining your average daily balance and multiplying that amount by the monthly interest rate. Creating information takes on two forms—transaction processing and analytical processing. *Transaction processing* is exactly what its name implies—the processing of transactions that occur within an organization. For example, determining your tuition bill, computing payroll for employees, and calculating applicable tax for products you purchase are all examples of creating information through transaction processing.

Analytical processing, on the other hand, is creating information to support your decision-making tasks. For example, if you use regression analysis to determine the extent to which advertising has an effect on sales, you're

creating information through analytical processing. Likewise, creating information through analytical processing would involve your using spreadsheet software to help you determine how to allocate your investments in various financial markets.

From a technology point of view as well as yours, transaction and analytical processing are quite different. If you're using technology for transaction processing, the technology itself can handle all the information processing. For example, grocery stores use IT to calculate the amount you owe for your purchase. No one takes the register receipt and then verifies that the computations were correct—everyone assumes, and rightfully so, that the technology added the numbers correctly. With analytical processing, however, some of the information processing still rests with you as a decision maker. If you consider our earlier example of using spreadsheet software to allocate your investments, the spreadsheet software will quickly and easily compute any combination of investments in various markets. But it's still up to you to decide what action to take.

The fourth information-processing category is that of cradling information. *Cradling information* involves storing information for use at a later time. Today information cradling or retention is critical in all organizations. Remember, we are in the information age, and cradling information for use at a later time is invaluable. Finally, the last information-processing category is that of *communicating information*. It involves sending information to other people or to another location. Communicating information is achieved through telecommunications technologies, such as modems, digital pagers, satellites, and microwaves. Forces shaping today's new business, such as globalization and electronic commerce, have made communicating information a must for all organizations.

For you as a knowledge worker, understanding the nature of information-processing tasks in your organization is key. For example, if your responsibilities include

capturing information, then you'll know that you need to use input technologies. And if your responsibilities include creating information through analytical processing, you'll be better able to determine which type of software is most appropriate. Perhaps the most important reason you need to understand the nature of information-processing tasks in your organization is because it will help you determine which type of information technology system (IT system) is best. In the remaining sections, we discuss the seven types of IT systems in use today. Some support creating information through transaction processing; some support creating information through analytical processing; and still others are designed primarily to support the communication of information between people and organizations.

To determine which of the seven is best for a given situation, you must understand first what information-processing tasks you want to perform. By defining your information-processing tasks first, you'll then be able to define what technology support you need. The order

INDUSTRY PERSPECTIVE

Transportation

Analytical Processing Keeps Union Pacific on Track

Union Pacific has always been a leader among railroad organizations in developing high-quality systems that process transaction information, but not necessarily in developing systems that support analytical processing. For example, if someone needed a report on the status of fleet maintenance to make a decision, they received an overwhelming stack of paper. And it wasn't just a single report—it was numerous reports, making it extremely time-consuming and tedious to reconcile the information.

That's when Union Pacific decided to create a central

data warehouse. A *data warehouse* is a logical collection of information gathered from all over the organization that supports business analysis activities and decision-making tasks. Thus data warehouses are a special way to organize information to support analytical processing as opposed to transaction processing. Now marketing specialists can analyze rate and pricing information to quote the most competitive price; logistics analysts use some of the same information to determine the most cost-effective route; and financial analysts use much of the same information to review profitability.

Has its data warehouse that supports analytical processing paid off? You bet. Consider these numbers:

■ An accounts payable project that saved $500,000 in the

first year, with a projected savings of over $2 million over the next 4 years

■ A tax-exempt purchase identification project that saved over $1 million

■ An accounts receivable project that saves $1.5 million a year by cutting receivable cycles by just 1 day

■ A logistics project that saves $2 million a year by alerting knowledge workers to where competitors' cars are located

When organizations, such as Union Pacific, can share information among knowledge workers to support analytical processing, the benefits are unbelievable.[6] ❖

here is key. Never let technology define what information-processing tasks you can perform. Rather, ensure that your information-processing tasks always drive your decision of what technology and IT system to use.

Transaction Processing and Customer Integrated Systems
The Heart of Every Organization

Fundamental to the success of an organization are IT systems whose primary responsibilities are to capture information at its point of origin, create new information based on the captured transaction information, and cradle both the captured and created information in an operational database. For these systems, the creation of information involves transaction processing. For example, the system you use at school to register for classes is primarily responsible for capturing your registration requests, creating new information based on your requests (your tuition bill, class schedule, and so on), and cradling that information in your school's database. That same registration system may also display or print your class schedule for you (convey information) and electronically send that information to various state agencies (communicate information). However, its primary responsibilities are capturing, creating, and cradling information.

These vitally important capturing, creating, and cradling systems include transaction processing systems and customer integrated systems. Before we look at each, let's step back and consider capturing, creating, and cradling systems in general. These systems may seem boring and mundane to the casual viewer, because many people downplay the significance of systems that do nothing more than capture, create, and cradle information. It's important to remember, however, that capturing, creating, and cradling information are the most important information-processing tasks in an organization.

Consider this—what if you called an airline to purchase a ticket but couldn't because the reservation agent said the system is "down"? What would you do? More than likely you'd call another airline. In this instance, the first airline lost money because its transaction processing system wasn't working. Consider another example: As an inventory manager for L. L. Bean, you expect a report every day that details purchases and returns. One day you receive that report but its numbers seem dramatically low. What you eventually learn is that not all of the transactions were entered because the system failed for some reason. Can you still effectively manage the inventory?

These examples illustrate the two reasons transaction processing and customer integrated systems are the most important systems in an organization. First, these systems are an organization's primary interface to its customers. Because the system was down for the airline, you took your business elsewhere. For customers, when these systems don't work the whole organization has failed. Second, these systems capture, create, and cradle information that is eventually used throughout the organization. If these systems fail or malfunction in any way whatsoever, the whole organization suffers because the right information is not available at the right time for the right people.

Transaction Processing Systems

A *transaction processing system (TPS)* is exactly what its name implies—a system that processes transactions that occur within the organization. Therefore, TPSs are mainly responsible for capturing transactions, creating new information, and cradling (storing) these transactions and information in a database. TPSs also have a secondary responsibility that includes conveying information to users. When XRA receives orders from retail centers, for example, the order-entry TPS performs the following functions (see Figure 2.7):

1. *Captures* information concerning the order
2. *Creates* new information such as the total purchase and applicable tax
3. *Conveys* that information to the order-entry specialist
4. *Cradles* or stores the order information

XRA   **Importance of a TPS**

"**W**e have transaction processing systems all over the place. Without our TPSs, I dare say our organization would come to a grinding halt. In fact, that happened about two years ago when the mainframe went down unexpectedly because of a power shortage. Today, we have battery backups that can keep our systems running for two hours even if we completely lose electrical power."

—Spike, CEO ❖

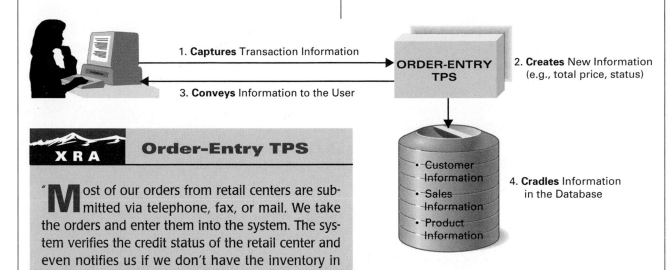

1. **Captures** Transaction Information

2. **Creates** New Information (e.g., total price, status)

3. **Conveys** Information to the User

4. **Cradles** Information in the Database

ORDER-ENTRY TPS

- Customer Information
- Sales Information
- Product Information

XRA Order-Entry TPS

"**M**ost of our orders from retail centers are submitted via telephone, fax, or mail. We take the orders and enter them into the system. The system verifies the credit status of the retail center and even notifies us if we don't have the inventory in stock. That way we can tell the retail center the date they can expect a shipment."

—*Jonathan Haggard, order-entry specialist* ❖

FIGURE 2.7
Order-Entry TPS

A few years ago, Avon Products realized the full potential of a good TPS.[7] Originally, a large number of Avon's 12 million yearly orders came handwritten to the home office. An order-entry clerk had the painstakingly slow task of deciphering the handwriting and then entering the order. Many of the orders were full of errors, and other errors were created simply because the order-entry clerk could not decipher the handwriting correctly. These errors resulted in orders that were filled incorrectly and delivery delays. To reduce order-entry and processing errors, Avon implemented a document-imaging system to scan the incoming orders and allow a computer to decipher the writing, which was then automatically fed into Avon's order-entry TPS. A year later, Avon reported that the new system had improved accuracy by 76 percent, improved productivity by 75 percent, and cut order-processing times by an amazing 67 percent. All these improvements led to a decrease in order-entry costs of over 65 percent.

TPSs are found in all functions of an organization. Large automobile manufacturers like Ford, General Motors, and Chrysler each have different TPSs for processing transactions related to payroll, inventory management, customer billing, administrative overhead, shipments to dealerships, warranty claims, and a host of other activities. For manufacturers alone, losses because of system downtime during 1992 were estimated at almost $2.5 billion, and many of those "systems" were in fact

TPSs.[8] In yet another study, Dr. Stephen Lunce found that most businesses estimated they would lose 50 percent of their respective revenues if their IT systems failed for only 15 days.[9]

CAREER OPPORTUNITY

Customer integrated systems promise to change the relationship between an organization and its customers forever. Your career opportunity lies in looking at an organization's interface with its customers through "fresh eyes" and trying to find ways to put technology in the customers' hands. It's a win-win-win situation for everyone. The organization wins, the customers win, and, most important, you as an employee win.

Customer Integrated Systems

A *customer integrated system (CIS)* is an extension of a TPS that places technology in the hands of an organization's customers and allows them to process their own transactions. Automated teller machines (ATMs) are perhaps the most common example of a CIS. ATMs provide you with the ability to do your own banking anywhere at any time. What's really interesting is that ATMs actually

Will the London Stock Exchange Come Falling Down?

The London Stock Exchange is among the oldest and most highly regarded financial institutions in the world. But the London Stock Exchange is in serious jeopardy of losing its worldwide status. And the problem is seemingly a simple one—it has an old and outdated transaction processing system that posts buy and sell quotes on an electronic bulletin board.

Competitors are acutely aware of this problem and have taken advantage of it. For example, the stock exchanges in Amsterdam, Paris, Milan, and Frankfurt recently installed electronic posting TPSs. These new systems are not only improving their information flow and cutting transaction costs, but also luring away many big traders from the London Stock Exchange. Even private stock exchanges, such as Tradepoint Investment Exchange in London, are offering their customers faster buy and sell posting times.

Financial markets are among the fastest moving and most volatile industries of any in the world. At the heart of the success of financial institutions playing in these markets are TPSs that process transaction information. Who would have thought the London Stock Exchange would be in jeopardy from not having such a seemingly simple system?[10] ❖

THE GLOBAL **PERSPECTIVE**

do nothing "new," but they give you greater flexibility in accessing and using your money. For financial institutions, ATMs represent a whole new way of doing business at a substantial savings. When you use an ATM, you essentially become your own bank teller, which means that banks no longer have to employ as many people. This alone has saved banks millions of dollars each year in human resource costs. Some banks are even encouraging their customers to use ATMs by charging a fee if they go into the bank and use a real teller.

CISs further decentralize computing power in an organization by placing that power in the hands of customers (see Figure 2.8). For that reason, CISs are also responsible for communicating information. Consider our ATM example again. Banking by ATM, you can check your account balance, transfer money from one account to another, and even withdraw money from virtually anywhere in the world. You can perform these tasks because the worldwide ATM network structure handles all the communication between you and your financial institution.

Banks aren't the only organizations that are taking advantage of CISs. Colleges and universities across the country are using CISs to allow students to register for classes by touch-tone telephone. Convenience stores use

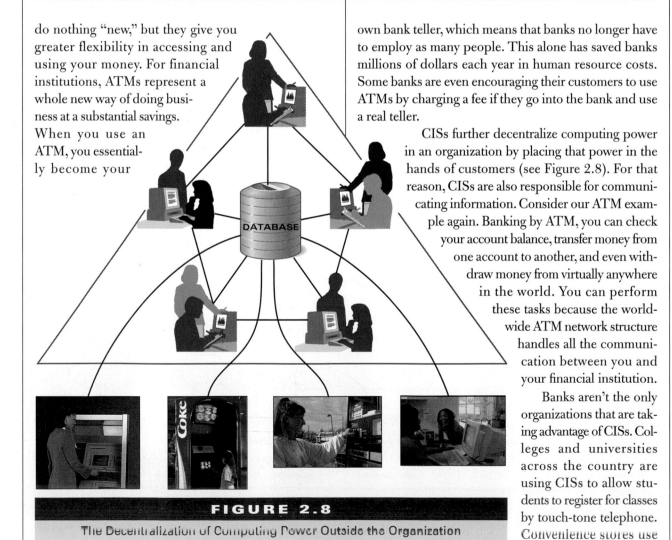

FIGURE 2.8
The Decentralization of Computing Power Outside the Organization

ON YOUR OWN

Going Customer-Oriented at Your School

Develop a plan for a complete customer integrated system at your college or university. This CIS should provide students with the ability to perform all their own transaction processing from initially applying to receiving grades each semester or quarter.

As you develop the plans for this system, write down each individual function that students should be able to perform (paying tuition, for example). For each function, write down which technology tools would be most important according to which information-processing tasks will be performed.

Has your school already implemented any of these functions as a customer integrated system? If your school were to completely implement your plan, could you live anywhere in the country and still attend classes at your school? Receive counseling for class selections? Get a diploma? ❖

---

them to allow customers to pay for gas at the pump instead of inside. You may even be able to pay your utility and telephone bills electronically from your home computer.

Bergen Brunswig, an $8 billion distributor of drugs and supplies to pharmacies, created a CIS by accident.[11] In 1992, Bergen Brunswig decided to equip its sales representatives with portable computers that included a multimedia product encyclopedia and customers' account information. As the sales reps began their pitch with their new systems, a curious thing happened. Many of the pharmacists asked if the reps would leave the portable so that they could view it at their leisure over the next several days. That's when Jim McLaughlin, head of technology and R&D at Bergen Brunswig, had an idea—why

---

Customer Integrated Systems, the Internet, Concerts, and Movies

If you need a good example of a customer integrated system, just cruise the Internet for a while. There, you'll find the ability to order almost any product imaginable, from automobiles to sweaters for your pet. You'll also find numerous ticket-selling agencies. For example, Ticketmaster is at http://www.ticketmaster.com, Playbill is at http://playbill.com, and MovieFone is at http://movielink.com. According to Bob Perkins, vice president of online services at Ticketmaster, "We feel like the Internet is where [electronic] commerce is going."

What's really great about setting up a CIS on the Internet for ticket-selling agencies is that they don't necessarily have to spend a lot of money distributing technology to you as a customer. After all, if you order concert or movie tickets over the Internet, you're using your computer and you're paying for time to an online service.

Now the ticket-selling agencies need only to develop the necessary software. Incidentally, there's a high degree of correlation between being an Internet user and being a concert goer. Can you figure out why?[12] ❖

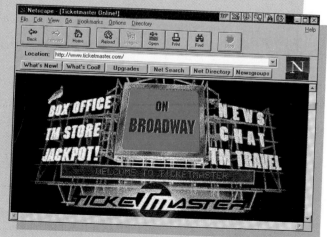

not modify the system so that it included order-entry software and simply provide it to every pharmacist free of charge? That's just what Bergen Brunswig did. Today, pharmacists receive regular updates through CD-ROM about twice a month.

Management Information Systems
Providing Predetermined Views of Information

Once TPSs and CISs capture information, process it, and cradle or store it in a database, people all over the organization need to access that information in some form or fashion. Among the different types of systems that help people access that information are management information systems. A ***management information system (MIS)*** is a system that provides periodic and predetermined reports that summarize information within a database (see Figure 2.9).

So, MISs are systems that have information-processing responsibilities that include creating information through analytical processing and conveying information to whoever needs it. MISs are often called *management alerting systems* because they "alert" people (usually management) to the existence (or potential existence) of problems or opportunities. This is an important distinction between an MIS and other systems that support management efforts. MISs are designed primarily to summarize what has occurred and point people toward the existence of problems or opportunities. Reports generated by MISs rarely tell someone why a problem or opportunity exists or offer solutions.

In some instances, however, MIS reports can help people determine where and when to take action. For example, if you were in charge of product inventory and received a daily report that showed which product inventories had fallen below reorder points, you would take action to order more to assure that a stockout didn't occur. From your report, you wouldn't necessarily know why inventory levels had fallen, but you would know what action to take. Usually, these types of problems are structured. That is, the action you take to solve the problem has structure and does not require a lot of analysis. Problems (or opportunities) that are not as structured as inventory reordering require more analysis and comprise systems in the category of decision support and artificial intelligence—which we'll discuss in an upcoming section.

Like many organizations, Hechinger Stores was originally a mainframe-based operation with all applications and information located within a centralized IT structure. In a move to decentralize its IT structure—while creating an information-sharing environment—Hechinger created a new decision support and management analysis system called PRISM (profitability of inventory and sales management).[13] This new system is capable of supporting decision-making functions (discussed later in this chapter), as well as preparing periodic and predetermined reports that summarize information (an MIS or management information system). Says Russ Gazaille, director of applications systems development, "In marketing, for example, it could take three weeks to build a single report under the old system. With PRISM, it takes less than a day. Similarly, in merchandising, the new system has reduced what used to be a daylong activity of collating reports into 20 minutes of data analysis." These various reports in marketing, merchandising, and other areas all serve to alert management personnel to the existence of potential problems or opportunities.

MISs provide reports in many different forms. From our definition, you can easily see that an MIS produces

MANAGEMENT INFORMATION SYSTEMS . . .

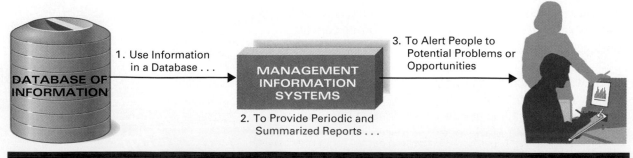

1. Use Information in a Database . . .

2. To Provide Periodic and Summarized Reports . . .

3. To Alert People to Potential Problems or Opportunities

FIGURE 2.9

Management Information Systems at Work

Standard MIS Reports

"From a traditional point of view, we have a pretty standard MIS. Each week, managers receive various reports that help them make fairly straightforward decisions. Many times, they don't even have to make decisions—it's just nice to know the status of how things are working. For example, I receive a weekly report of overtime hours. If we're extremely busy, I don't pay much attention to the report because I know we're working a lot of overtime. But, if we're not real busy and overtime hours seem high, it does alert me to a potential problem."

—Todd McGlaughlin, assistant production floor supervisor ❖

reports that are periodic and summarized. ***Periodic reports*** are reports that are produced at a predetermined time interval—daily, weekly, monthly, yearly, and so on. ***Summarized reports*** are simply those reports that aggregate information in some way. For example, sales by salespeople, defective returns by product line, and the number of students by class enrollment are all MIS reports. MISs can also generate exception and comparative reports. ***Exception reports*** show only a subset of available information based on some selection criteria. As you might guess, ***comparative reports*** show two or more sets of similar information in an attempt to illustrate a relationship.

In Figure 2.10, you can see an example of an MIS report that is summarized, periodic, exception, and comparative in nature. In accounting, this type of report is often called an "aging schedule." It is a summary report because it shows total credit sales by customer. It is a periodic report because it's generated at the end of the month (notice the subtitle). It is an exception report because it lists when payments were made (the selection criteria). It's also a comparative report because it provides footnotes that compare percentage of total sales receipts within specific periods. Again, this MIS report only points you toward the existence of problems and opportunities.

MAXIMUM OFFICE PRODUCTS
For Period Ending January 31, 1997

Customer	0–10 Days*	11–30 Days	31–60 Days	61–90 Days	91–120 Days	Past 120 Days
ACME Hardware		$2,400				
Bellows Meats		700	$300			
Darin Publicity						$2,000
Federal Inc.	$1,400					
Jake's Fidelity	7,000					
Malloy Realty		1,600				
P. J.'s Floral				$600	$200	
Shann Landscape						
Whitt Federal						1,500
Yellow Truck	9,500					
Zeno Fishery		6,000				
Totals	$17,900	$10,700	$300	$600	$200	$3,500
Total sales:	$33,200					
% of total	53.9%	32.2%	0.9%	1.8%	0.6%	10.5%

*Terms are given 2/10, net 30. $358 total discounted for payments within 10 days.

FIGURE 2.10

An Aging Schedule MIS Report

It does not tell you why they exist. For example, nonpayment by Darin Publicity and Whitt Federal is a problem, but from the report you can't tell why the problem exists.

You may have noticed that these types of systems have the same name as this particular field of study—management information systems. Don't confuse the field of study and the system, however—one offers a very specific view of a system that provides periodic reports and the other presents a very broad view of a field of study that deals with the planning for, development, management, and use of information technology tools to help people perform all tasks related to information processing and management. If you find yourself struggling to differentiate the two, think of the term "medicine." The field of medicine deals with the study of preventing, alleviating, and curing diseases, whereas types of medicines—such as cough drops or nasal decongestants—relieve specific symptoms of physical ailments.

Workgroup Support Systems

Communicating Information Among Team Members

In Chapter 1, we discussed many of the forces that are changing the shape of today's business environment, including globalization, competition, and the virtual workplace and telecommuting. Another change that you'll see is a restructuring of an organization through the use of workgroups or teams. These workgroups or teams are often called *cross-functional teams* because they are composed of people working in a variety of departments throughout the organization regardless of job title or department.

Supporting Financial Decisions

"It seems like our business changes every day. Every time I turn around, it seems like we're facing a new problem or a new opportunity. A couple of months ago we had a chance to restructure our debt position by selling stock. I put together a team of financial analysts to determine our best overall debt strategy. That team used a package called Collabra, which is groupware. It supported their ability to simultaneously review alternatives, make recommendations, and eventually come up with the best alternative. By the way, the best alternative was to do nothing at all—we were right where we needed to be."

—*Cory Tillman, chief accountant* ❖

Teams are developed for one of two reasons. First, many organizations are building *project teams* to solve a specific problem or take advantage of a specific opportunity. For example, a team of accountants and financial analysts may be created to define a new debt structure that will take advantage of declining interest rates. This type of team literally has a one-time goal. When it's met, the team disbands to move on to other projects. Second, organizations are simply creating *permanent teams* that sometimes include people from all departments of the organization to perform a flow of work more effectively and efficiently. These types of teams are more permanent and require consistent and continuous support. For either of these types of teams to collaborate effectively, they need first-rate workgroup support systems that primarily support the sharing, dissemination, and flow of information.

A *workgroup support system (WSS)* is a system that is designed specifically to improve the performance of teams by supporting the sharing and flow of information. For a project team—such as the accountants and financial analysts in our example—a WSS helps them effectively communicate, share information, and exchange ideas as they solve a problem or take advantage of an opportunity. For permanent teams, a WSS not only supports the flow of information but also the underlying business process that's being automated.

The foundation of any WSS is *groupware*—the popular term for the software component that supports the collaborative efforts of a team. Groupware is one of the newest

INDUSTRY PERSPECTIVE

Health Care

Practicing Medicine with Groupware and the Internet

Eleven weeks into her pregnancy, Cathie St. Laurent discovered she had bone marrow cancer and desperately needed to see a specialist. The only problem was that she lived 7 hours away from the nearest bone marrow specialist, and the thought of driving that long on dangerous mountain roads did not excite her. So her family physician arranged for a two-way video link between Cathie and the specialist. An hour later, the specialist and Cathie decided to delay the surgery until after her child was born. Cathie's story is not uncommon from the point of view of using technology to practice *telemedicine*. Every day, doctors transfer medical records all over the country through the Internet and meet with patients on two-way video hookups.

The National Jewish Center (NJC) is even allowing its patients to use the Internet to gain access to its workgroup support system. Its WSS supports a team that includes nurses and doctors within NJC, doctors in other organizations, and patients. For example, by an agreement with Denver-based University Hospital, NJC patients are often referred to University Hospital for lab work. Using the Internet, the patient lab results are then passed back to NJC, where they are stored in a group document database. Patients then can access the WSS, review their lab results and other medical information, and leave any questions to which they need answers.[15, 16] ❖

IT-based tools that you'll find in an organization. Although groupware can be difficult to use, it can help your organization achieve the greatest advantage. In Chapter 3, we'll explore many of the rich advantages and uses of groupware; and in Chapter 6, we'll explore the hardware necessary to support a WSS. Right now, let's simply focus on groupware as the software component of a WSS.

Groupware

The most critical component of a WSS is the underlying software, or groupware. Unfortunately, no matter what literature you read or which conference you attend, everyone has a different view of what's included in groupware. Lotus, for example, the maker of Lotus Notes, will tell you that groupware contains three components. Other vendors will tell you differently. In the popular trade press, you can read that groupware contains anywhere from four to nine primary components. To introduce you to this no-standards, no-definition, no-agreement, and no-boundary confusing field, let's consider that groupware contains software components for supporting the following three functions (see Figure 2.11):

❶ Team dynamics

❷ Document management

❸ Applications development

TEAM DYNAMICS

• E–mail, Electronic Bulletin Boards, Intranets
• Electronic Meeting Support:
  • Group Scheduling Software
  • Electronic Meeting Software
  • Videoconferencing Software
  • Whiteboard Software

DOCUMENT MANAGEMENT

A group document database that acts as a powerful storage facility for organizing and managing all documents related to specific teams

APPLICATIONS DEVELOPMENT

• Prewritten Applications
• Programming Tools for Creating Customized Applications
• Work Flow Automation Software

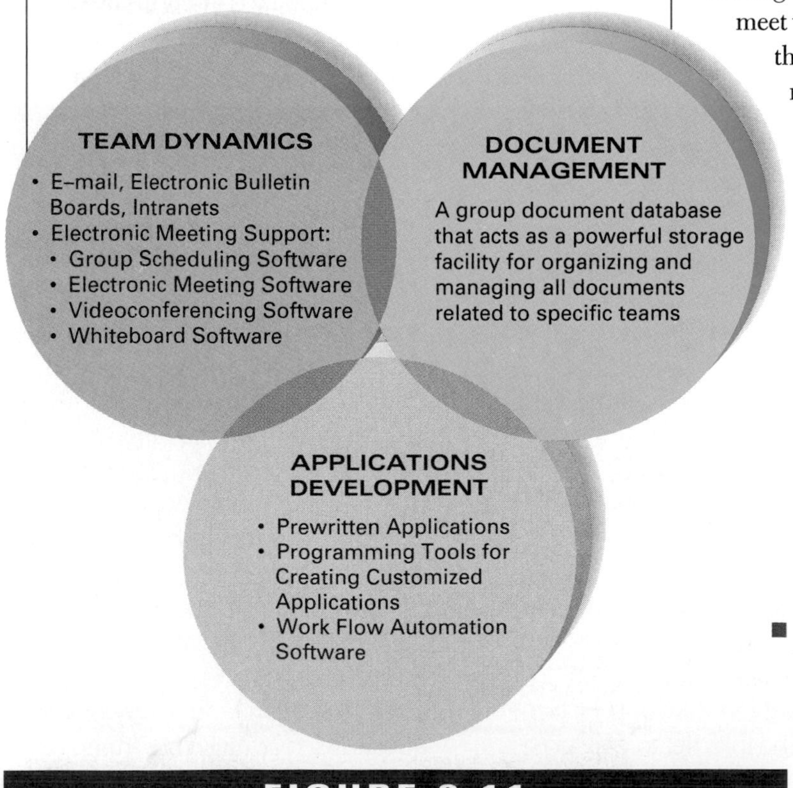

FIGURE 2.11

The Groupware Environment

Team Dynamics

Team dynamics is the most basic and fundamental support provided by groupware. Team dynamics includes the facilitation and execution of meetings and any communications between team members as they solve a problem, take advantage of an opportunity, or perform a flow of work more efficiently and effectively. Among the important groupware components that support team dynamics are electronic messaging and electronic meeting support.

If you review our definition of a workgroup support system, you'll see that communicating information is the primary information-processing responsibility. That is, the primary responsibility is supporting the flow of information from one location to another and between people. *Electronic messaging* is the software component of groupware that helps team members communicate. The electronic messaging component of groupware may include simple e-mail; electronic bulletin boards, where notes can be posted and read; and vendor-provided internal messaging systems. Each of these helps team members communicate with each other through IT. Both project and permanent teams use electronic messaging extensively.

Intranets—internal company Internets—are another important component of electronic messaging. Earlier we discussed US West's *Global Village,* which US West employees use to participate in online chat rooms, exchange documents and discuss ongoing projects, and meet with staff located in remote geographic areas. As the use of WSSs increases in the business environment, you can expect to see more businesses develop intranets.

As you might well guess, team members must meet. And it's often no small task to get everyone together at a convenient time and in a convenient location. Indeed, if you've ever worked in a group for a class project, you understand how difficult this can be. *Electronic meeting support* is the component of groupware that helps you schedule meetings and carry out those meetings. You'll find that both project teams and permanent teams make extensive use of the electronic meeting support component of groupware. Components of electronic meeting support include

■ For the scheduling of meetings:

◆ *Group scheduling software*—provides facilities for maintaining the day-to-day electronic calendars of team members and evaluating those calendars to schedule optimal meeting times. Some group scheduling software will even

Supporting Product Design

"Our workgroup support system is permanent. All we basically do every day is review and modify current designs and develop designs for new products. Our WSS completely stores all our designs and suggested changes in a huge database. As many as 15 design engineers can simultaneously review the same design, make modifications, see how those changes will affect the production process, and perform feasibility studies. Without it, we'd be forced to all meet in the same room at the same time and make drawings on the board. We used to do that, and it took weeks to get a finalized design. We can now do that in less than two days thanks to our WSS."

—Melanie Burleson, quality control analyst ❖

help you reserve a certain room and any equipment (for example, an overhead projector) that you may need.

■ For the actual execution of meetings:

◆ *Electronic meeting software*—lets a team have a "virtual" meeting through IT. For example, electronic meeting software helps you create an agenda and electronically send it to everyone. Each member can then read and respond to each agenda item. Their responses would be "tagged" according to agenda item, date, time, and name of the person who provided the response. Each response would be sent to each member so that others can also respond. This type of software is great for discussing agenda items that do not require a quick response or solution. In many instances, these types of virtual meetings may take place over a period of several weeks.

◆ *Videoconferencing software*—allows a team to have a "face-to-face" meeting when members are geographically dispersed. You've probably seen ads on television showing people in one location meeting with others who appear on a large screen or monitor. Today you can purchase a videoconferencing system (complete with a microphone and camera) for your home computer for less than $1,500. These types of systems are called "desktop videoconferencing systems."

◆ *Whiteboard software*—lets team members meet and interactively edit and share documents. For example, you could develop a spreadsheet on your screen and have your work automatically displayed on the screen of someone in a remote location. That person could also makes changes to the spreadsheet, which would automatically be displayed on your screen.

Document Management

Perhaps the most critical software component of any groupware product is document management, which is achieved through a group document database. A *group document database* is a powerful storage facility for organizing and managing all documents related to specific teams. The complete group document database will contain documents from many different teams (see Figure 2.12). Because of this, group document databases support many levels of security to control access to database documents, authenticate the identity of the people creating new documents or making changes to existing documents, and guard against wrongful use.

A team can store, access, track, and organize a wealth of information inside a group document database. This information can be in many forms—traditional database tables, text files, sound, and even video. As you create

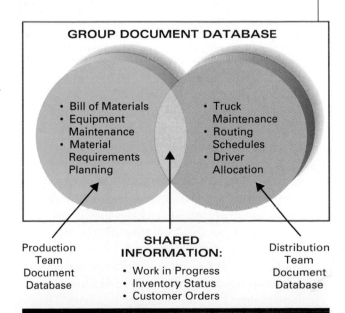

GROUP DOCUMENT DATABASE

- Bill of Materials
- Equipment Maintenance
- Material Requirements Planning

- Truck Maintenance
- Routing Schedules
- Driver Allocation

Production Team Document Database

SHARED INFORMATION:
- Work in Progress
- Inventory Status
- Customer Orders

Distribution Team Document Database

FIGURE 2.12

Multiple Teams in a Group Document Database

Maximizing Team Efforts and Groupware

You have more in common with businesses than you might imagine. Every day in business, meetings are held. You probably have team meetings almost daily at school as well.

Phase 1

Consider the challenges you've faced in your own team projects. Gather together and discuss problems you've experienced as a team in trying to achieve a common goal. List the problems you've experienced in the first column below. In the second column, identify which components of groupware (electronic messaging, group scheduling software,

electronic meeting software, videoconferencing software, or whiteboard software) would help you overcome these problems. How effective do you think these groupware tools would really be?

Phase 2

Just like most types of packaged application software, different products and manufacturers abound for electronic meeting support software in the marketplace. Connect to the Web site for this text to obtain a list of several such products.

As a team, choose one category of software and do some research. For the packages you choose, determine their price, capabilities, and limitations. If you had to make a recommendation, which would you choose? Why? Also, did you find any new packages during your research? ❖

Team Problem	Solved By

different views or reports of the information in a group document database, you can even attach spreadsheets, graphs, or text from other applications, such as word processing and presentation graphics.

Within the group document database area for your specific team, you can perform full text searches that will completely analyze all the information, regardless of form. Finally, group document databases provide sophisticated tracking mechanisms to identify who has updated which version of each document. For example, if a person on your team made modifications to a document, the group document database would notify you that those changes had been made and by whom. The group document database will also let you easily maintain previous versions of a document that are stamped with the date and time of the last modification.

Group document databases are central to the success of effective team environments. No matter what the specific function or goal, any team needs to (or rather, *must*) create, organize, and track a wealth of documents that differ in form (for example, table versus graph versus text), are created by different people, and constantly change over time.

Applications Development

The final software component of a groupware environment is that of applications development (or applications development facilities). In groupware, ***applications development facilities*** constitute a wealth of basic building blocks that you can use to create applications quickly, so teams can literally "get to work." These basic building blocks include prewritten applications and programming tools that developers can use to create customized applications.

Prewritten applications include those functions that most businesses commonly perform. For example, most businesses need customer service applications for tracking customer inquiries, managing customer relations, and routing information concerning customers to people throughout the organization. Prewritten applications are also commonly used in human resource management and accounting departments. Groupware environments also support a number of programming tools that can be used to create applications unique to your organization or a specific team within your organization. Many of these tools can also be used to modify prewritten applications for greater suitability to your specific task.

One specific applications development facility that has received much attention recently is work flow automation software. *Work flow automation software* is software designed to automate the flow of business documents in a specific work process or procedure. By using work flow automation software, companies have significantly increased the productivity of permanent teams, while also increasing intangible benefits such as customer satisfaction. Consider the case of the IBM Credit Corporation, a wholly owned subsidiary of IBM, which provides

financing for computers, software, and services that IBM sells.[17] Without work flow automation software, the work process included the following steps:

> **Step #1** A salesperson called in a request for financing, which was recorded on paper by 1 of 14 people.
>
> **Step #2** Someone physically walked the paper request to the credit department, where a credit specialist entered the request into a computer and checked the credit status of the customer. From there, the paper-based credit report was delivered to the business practices department.
>
> **Step #3** The business practices department modified a standard loan agreement according to any special requests by the customer. The special terms arrangement document was attached to the original request (still on paper) and delivered to a pricer.
>
> **Step #4** The pricer keyed all the information into a spreadsheet and determined the appropriate interest rate. This figure was written onto the other forms and delivered to the clerical group.
>
> **Step #5** The clerical group converted all paper documents into a quote letter and delivered it back to the salesperson through FedEx.

continued on page 64

Work Flow Automation Software and the Paperless Office

Here's an interesting figure to consider—companies that gross more than $1 billion in annual revenue process more than 88 million pages of information each year, according to Priscilla Emery, senior vice president at the Association for Information and Image Management. 88 million pages stacked on top of each other is almost 4 miles high. That has certainly led many financial service firms to adopt work flow automation software in hopes of tearing down the mountain of paper and creating a paperless office.

Two such firms are Texas Commerce Bank and the Virginia Retirement System. At Texas Commerce Bank, the stack of trust fund files alone was 6 miles high, which equates to over 130 million pages of information. According to Anita Ward, vice president and manager of the reengineering program at Texas Commerce, the bank is now running work flow automation software in 13 different areas. Those applications have reduced the amount of paper, and Anita boasts that access to information is now more readily available.

For Jane Pugh, manager of IT at the Virginia Retirement System, the primary goal was not really to eliminate all the paper, but just to be able to process it all. As Jane explains, "We had tremendous amounts of paper coming in and few people to process it." Thanks to work flow automation software, Jane radically changed business processes at Virginia Retirement. Her efforts brought about smoother work flows, faster processing of the incoming information, and even a reduction in the reams of paper that flowed through the processes.[18] ❖

PHOTO ESSAY 2-1 Lotus Notes . . . The Leader in Groupware

Overview

Lotus Notes is the leader in groupware today. Designed specifically to work on a client/server platform, Lotus Notes includes a document database, an applications development environment, and a sophisticated messaging system.

The ability to quickly create applications that are customized to your particular business needs is a welcome feature. And Notes gives you this capability. These applications are centered around a powerful document database where you can store traditional database tables, spreadsheet applications, graphic images, electronic mail, faxes, and a host of other business-related documents. With the internal messaging system, you can then route all this information to provide the most efficient distribution throughout your organization.

Notes works well with most major network operating systems and can run on a variety of hardware platforms. It also supports an open interface that allows you to access the document database through other applications.

If you want to learn more about this promising product, visit Lotus's Web site at http://www.lotus.com.

Document Database

As you build your applications, the document database becomes a repository of your information needs. Inside the document database, you can store all information relating to specific workgroup needs. This information can be in many forms—text, graphics, sound, and even video. You can even import information from spreadsheet, presentation graphics, and word processing applications, as well as a host of other applications.

You can also perform a full text search feature that allows you to quickly find the information you need. With the full text feature, you can search all or part of the database for words, phrases, numbers, and even dates. What's more, you'll be able to find that information no matter how it's stored—tables, word processing documents, video, or sound.

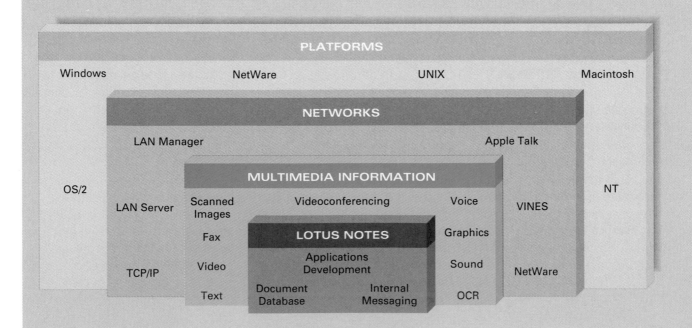

PLATFORMS

Windows · NetWare · UNIX · Macintosh

NETWORKS

LAN Manager · Apple Talk

OS/2 · NT

MULTIMEDIA INFORMATION

LAN Server · Scanned Images · Videoconferencing · Voice · VINES

Fax · LOTUS NOTES · Graphics

Video · Applications Development · Sound · NetWare

TCP/IP

Text · Document Database · Internal Messaging · OCR

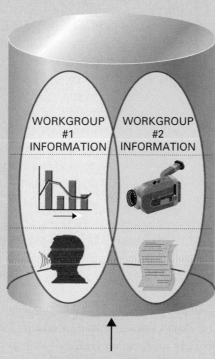

LEVEL #3
SECURITY
Open to
Department
Heads

LEVEL #2
SECURITY
Open to
Project Leaders

LEVEL #1
SECURITY
Open to
All Team
Members

WORKGROUP #1 INFORMATION

WORKGROUP #2 INFORMATION

FULL TEXT SEARCHES

Lotus Notes also provides multiple levels of security to ensure a well-protected environment. You can easily control access to all or part of the database by workgroup and by individuals. For the users, these security levels are completely transparent.

Applications Development

Lotus Notes supports three forms of applications development. First, it includes 25 templates that allow you to quickly create workgroup applications. These built-in applications include customer service, project management, and product research and development.

Second, as a user you can customize the built-in applications or develop your own applications using forms, views, and macros. Forms allow you to create a document and capture information. Views give

you the ability to index, sort, and view information contained in the document database. And macros give you the ability to automate business functions that need to be performed repetitively.

Finally, Lotus Notes supports a large number of programming tools that advanced developers can use to create more complicated business processes. These programming tools include Notes Applications Programming Interface, Lotus Notes ViP (the visual programming environment for Notes), and many third-party tools.

Internal Messaging

The internal messaging component is designed to (1) help people in a workgroup communicate and (2) automate the flow of business documents throughout an organization. You can even access Lotus Notes through the Internet or company-supported mail systems.

When automating the flow of business documents, you can quickly specify the routing of information and develop macros that will execute at designated time intervals. This helps assure that people throughout the organization always have the most up-to-date information. ❖

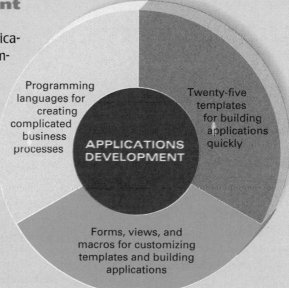

Programming languages for creating complicated business processes

Twenty-five templates for building applications quickly

APPLICATIONS DEVELOPMENT

Forms, views, and macros for customizing templates and building applications

The entire process took 6 days on the average and sometimes as long as 2 weeks. As you can imagine, this slow and lengthy process did nothing to help a salesperson close a sale quickly. In fact, many potential sales were lost because customers simply couldn't or didn't want to wait that long.

To fully understand the problem, two senior managers decided to personally walk a credit request through the process. At each step, they asked the appropriate people to set aside whatever they were doing and handle the one specific request immediately. The senior managers found that the actual work took only 90 minutes, with the rest of the time (literally days) consumed by just moving the information from one place to the next.

This example may seem almost unbelievable, especially for a large company like IBM Credit, but it's actually true. Eventually, IBM Credit adopted a technique called business process reengineering (which is discussed at length in Chapter 3) and work flow automation software to completely redesign the flow of work. The new system led to a 90 percent reduction in cycle time while increasing the rate of throughput one hundredfold (not 100 percent, but one hundred times). The new system also dramatically increased customer satisfaction by providing financing in 4 hours on the average, instead of 6 days.

Decision Support Systems and Artificial Intelligence

Creating New Information to Support Decision Making

In your personal life, you face decision-making tasks every day—what to wear, what groceries to buy, which way to drive to school, and so on. The same is true in business, but many business decision-making tasks tend to be very complex and time-consuming. For example, if you're considering different locations for a new distribution center, your decision will be affected by the quality of the workforce, projected fluctuations in interest rates, tax incentives offered by each location, proximity to other warehouses and distribution centers, proximity to major transportation outlets, and so on.

These types of business decision-making tasks are not simple, and the decision you make will affect the success of your organization. All businesses need IT systems that can help them make the best decision—we call these systems decision support systems and artificial intelligence.

Decision support systems and artificial intelligence are any IT tools that create information through analytical processing to facilitate decision-making tasks that require significant effort and analysis. Therefore, decision support systems and artificial intelligence are primarily responsible for the information-processing task of creating information. A secondary information-processing task is that of conveying the created information to the user. As you can see in Figure 2.13, decision support systems and artificial intelligence use information already contained in a database, often combined with information in a data warehouse and new information the user enters.

IT systems in this category include

- Decision support systems
- Group decision support systems ⎤
- Geographic information systems ⎦ Special types of decision support systems
- Neural networks ⎤
- Genetic algorithms ⎥
- Expert systems ⎥ Artificial intelligence
- Intelligent agents ⎦

Chapter 5 is devoted to the decision support systems and artificial intelligence used by all types of organizations today. Our discussions in that chapter focus on specific aspects of each, numerous business examples, how they are developed, and the ethics of using technology to support the decision-making process. Here, we'll simply introduce you to a few examples.

Decision Support Systems

A *decision support system (DSS)* is a highly flexible and interactive IT system that is designed to support decision

DECISION SUPPORT SYSTEMS AND ARTIFICIAL INTELLIGENCE . . .

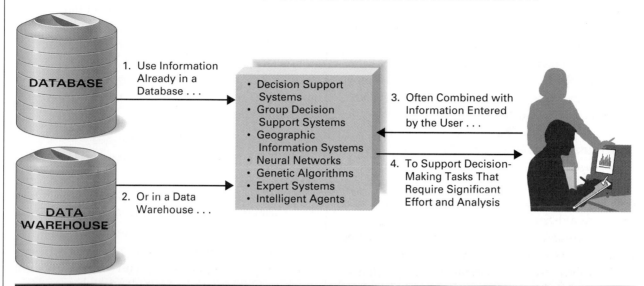

FIGURE 2.13

Decision Support Systems and Artificial Intelligence at Work

making when the problem is not structured. Spreadsheet software is the most common example of a DSS. With spreadsheet software, you can perform a variety of decision-making tasks—budget your monthly expenses and income, project your overall GPA based on your estimated semester or quarterly GPA, and estimate how much money you'll need for your next vacation.

Typically, DSSs are very interactive. This gives you the ability to (1) perform a series of "what-if" analyses to see how certain inputs will affect the outputs and (2) use

Predicting Room Rates a Year in Advance

For many hotels, yield management—maximizing rates and occupancies—is the only way to stay in business. Yield management is no simple process. You must gather past sales and occupancy information, perform a series of complicated mathematical models, and then adjust room rates. Along the way, you also have to factor in the weather, any special civic events, airline ticket prices, and a host of other information. Because of the complicated and time-consuming nature of yield management, most hotels are turning to special decision-support software.

One such hotel is Hilton International. Using 2 years of performance history, Hilton's system forecasts future arrivals, optimizes the information based on any special conditions (for example, holidays), and then recommends room rates for every day up to a year in advance. According to Kathleen Sullivan, Hilton's director of revenue management systems, the system works great—Hilton has experienced an 8 percent increase in market share.

Hilton's system not only generates more business through higher occupancy rates and better pricing structures, but also provides information that goes into marketing strategies. Using system-generated reports concerning projected future occupancies, Hilton can determine the best times of the year to implement marketing strategies, such as advertising campaigns on television.

IT systems, such as decision support systems and artificial intelligence, are an integral part of many organizations. For the hotel industry, they are a necessary part of survival.[19] ❖

different modeling tools (for example, regression, goal seeking, and analysis of variance) to analyze information. This is an important distinction between MISs and DSSs. MISs typically provide predetermined reports that may alert you to potential problems or opportunities. DSSs, on the other hand, allow you to enter new levels of inputs and determine their effect on outputs and use different modeling tools to analyze information.

Geographic Information Systems

A *geographic information system (GIS)* is a decision support system designed specifically to work with spatial information. A GIS stores and manipulates information as a digital map, with each digital map (and components of it) referenced by a specific geographic location. GISs are beneficial in decision-making tasks in which you must consider the geographic distribution of people and other resources.

Dallas Area Rapid Transit (DART) makes extensive use of a GIS as it works with, makes changes to, and plans for future additions to the many bus, van, and light-rail public transportation modes in the Dallas area. Using a GIS, DART employees can analyze the impact of proposed bus, van, and light-rail routes, determine optimal

locations for new stops (there are over 13,500 right now), and even obtain exact street addresses of those stops. Before using a GIS, DART employees were forced to create new service maps manually and pour over several maps at once to respond to some 5,000 daily customer inquiries. With the new system, a few simple clicks on a mouse can provide the exact information needed—and in graphic form.

Artificial Intelligence

Artificial intelligence (AI) is the science of making machines imitate human thinking and behavior. When viewing the field of AI, always remember the key word is "artificial" and not "intelligence." Although it's true that many AI systems can mimic human intuition and thought processes, you or someone else must still program them to do so. Computers are incapable of thinking and reasoning on their own, so their intelligence really is *artificial*.

Genetic Algorithms

A *genetic algorithm* is an artificial intelligence system that mimics the evolutionary, survival-of-the-fittest process

---

INDUSTRY PERSPECTIVE

IT & Telecommunications

Curing Computer Viruses

No one is immune to computer viruses, those pesky pieces of software that cause your system to malfunction in some way. The malfunction may be as simple as having GOTCHA! appear on the screen each time you hit the Enter key or as catastrophic as having your hard disk reformat itself. Whatever the case, most people now have antivirus software that can check for, detect, and remove any known virus.

But what about new and unknown viruses? They crop up every day. In fact, some people estimate that approximately a dozen new viruses are created each day. That's over 4,000 new viruses a year. How can antivirus software that you bought last year recognize a new virus that was created only yesterday? Unfortunately, most antivirus software can't, and that creates a real problem, especially for people who frequently download information from the Internet.

But don't despair. IBM is hard at work on a new type of antivirus software that can detect a virus that it's never seen. IBM's new software is based on a neural network technology. A *neural net-*work is an artificial intelligence that is literally capable of learning from its own past experiences. To do so, a neural network develops a recognition pattern based on numerous previous inputs. Over time, the neural network can match new patterns to old ones to determine what they are. Applied to antivirus software, a neural network will be able to recognize a new virus based on what previous viruses have looked like. Won't that be great—buy one piece of antivirus software and it's good for the rest of your life (or your computer's life)?[20] ❖

Production Scheduling Expert System

"**W**hen we were small, I used to be completely in charge of developing our two-week production schedule. It was no big deal, and I could complete it in about a day. Not anymore—we have so many products and so many requests that there's no way I could do it in less than a month. We purchased a special expert system that now handles our production scheduling. It uses a set of rules to evaluate our product demand, current inventory levels, material levels, priority statuses, and so on to create the optimal production schedule. I simply review the proposed schedule to make sure it's correct. No matter what anyone ever tells you, computers will never be as smart as people. You still have to carefully review the recommendations made by a system—even if it's called an 'expert' system."

—Lawrence Middleton,
production scheduling supervisor ❖

to generate increasingly better solutions to a problem. These evolutionary processes include crossover, mutation, and selection. As a genetic algorithm attempts to solve a problem, it may use *crossover* to combine two or more steps in an attempt to create a step that yields a better result. *Mutation* involves randomly ordering or combining different steps and evaluating the outcome. Finally, with *selection* only those steps (or set of steps) that produce better outcomes are retained—the poorer steps are literally removed from the genetic algorithm to make room for better ones.

If you've ever flown on a Boeing 777, you were propelled through the air by an engine that was developed using a genetic algorithm. General Electric, the producer of the Boeing 777 engine, successfully used a genetic algorithm to create an engine that was 1 percent more efficient than previous versions. One percent may not sound like much—but it's pure profit for the company.[21]

Expert Systems

An *expert system* is an artificial intelligence system that applies reasoning capabilities to reach a conclusion. Rules are gathered from experts and stored in a knowledge base and have associated actions that will be executed based on the user's input. For example, General Motors has developed an expert system called Expert System Scheduling (ESS) to automate the scheduling process in its production facilities.[22] The ESS contains rules, supplied by an experienced human factory scheduler about all scheduling decisions. Using the ESS, General Motors is able to respond more efficiently to changes in production requirements and plant floor conditions.

Again, we've devoted all of Chapter 5 to decision support systems and artificial intelligence, so we've just briefly introduced you to a few of them here.

Executive Information Systems
Supporting the Information Needs of Strategic Management

In previous sections, we've looked at management information systems and various decision support systems and artificial intelligence. These two system categories (1) point toward the existence of potential problems or opportunities, (2) help knowledge workers understand why those problems or opportunities exist, and (3) help determine strategies for solving problems or taking advantage of opportunities. We now want to look at a system that combines both and adds even more reporting and data analysis flexibility—an executive information system (see Figure 2.14).

An *executive information system (EIS)* is a highly interactive MIS combined with decision support systems and artificial intelligence for helping managers identify and address problems and opportunities. Similar to an MIS, an EIS allows managers to view information from different angles. Additionally, it provides managers with the flexibility to easily create more views to better understand the problem or opportunity. And, similar to DSSs and AI, an EIS provides tools for further analyzing information and for creating strategies for solving a problem or taking advantage of an opportunity. These tools can include personal productivity software such as spreadsheet software, and more sophisticated DSS and AI tools such as expert and geographic information systems. Thus an EIS is responsible for the information-processing tasks of creating information through analytical processing and conveying that information to the user.

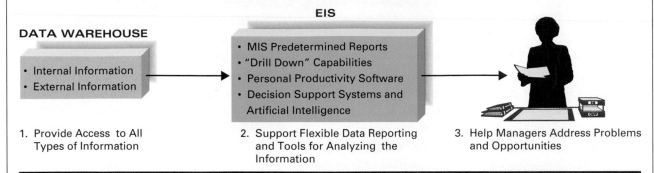

EXECUTIVE INFORMATION SYSTEMS . . .

EIS

DATA WAREHOUSE

• Internal Information
• External Information

• MIS Predetermined Reports
• "Drill Down" Capabilities
• Personal Productivity Software
• Decision Support Systems and Artificial Intelligence

1. Provide Access to All Types of Information

2. Support Flexible Data Reporting and Tools for Analyzing the Information

3. Help Managers Address Problems and Opportunities

FIGURE 2.14

Executive Information Systems at Work

Key Features of an Executive Information System

The following are key features of an EIS at work.

■ **Use of a Data Warehouse.** In Figure 2.14 you can see that EISs provide access to information in a data warehouse—a collection of information used in a decision-making task. In organizations today, data warehouses can consist of information from

operational databases such as inventory, and from external sources such as demographics. We cover data warehouses at length in Chapter 4, so, for now, let's just say that a data warehouse is a collection of information that a decision maker needs.

■ **Drill Down Capabilities.** From a reporting perspective, an EIS contains highly summarized information and allows a manager to drill down through the information to obtain more revealing

---

INDUSTRY PERSPECTIVE **Retail**

Calgary Co-op Beats the Larger Chains with an Executive Information System

Competing in today's retail environment means going up against big competition. Large retail chains such as REI, Cub Foods, and Sam's Club all enjoy the benefits of economies of scale and can cut the already narrow margins to pennies and still survive. Thanks to technology, however, Calgary Co-op is not losing any ground to its larger competitors.

Calgary's technology is an executive information system that includes an easy-to-use graphic interface, predetermined and flexible reporting features, forecasting capabilities, and drill down capabilities. Specifically, Calgary's EIS provides

■ A "quick-look monitor board" that highlights the best, worst, and acceptable product performers

■ Sales performance forecasting capabilities that reveal business trends over time

■ Drilling down to the lowest level of detail to provide answers concerning highlighted

products on the monitor board

■ The assurance that decision making is consistent by using the appropriate set of criteria for the decision at hand

According to Ken Doherty, Calgary's vice president of information services, store managers are able to better monitor product movement and sales, as well as personnel and administrative costs. Information that previously required over 2 weeks to analyze can now be quickly and easily evaluated with the EIS.[23] ❖

and precise information. Initially, an EIS presents a manager with a series of reports. After choosing a particular report, the manager would then be able to point to icons or specific points in the report to receive information in greater detail.

■ **Flexible Data Presentation.** As you can see, an EIS provides much greater reporting flexibility than an MIS. Where MISs provide predetermined views of information, an EIS starts with predetermined views and then allows a manager to select from a variety of other report formats (the concept of drilling down) that provide more revealing and in-depth information. This reporting flexibility distinguishes MISs and EISs. Although both provide predetermined views of information, an EIS goes even further to provide easy-to-use mechanisms for displaying information from different points of view, even to the point where you could request that numeric information be presented in graphic form.

■ **Identification of Information Responsibility.** Most EIS packages identify the person responsible for certain information. For example, if a manager had drilled down as far as the EIS allowed and still needed more information, the EIS would identify the person in the organization who could provide more.

■ **Use of DSS and AI Tools.** From a data analysis perspective, an EIS gives a manager the ability to quickly view information from different angles (flexible reporting), which can often be used as a method of data analysis. An EIS also supports many DSS and AI tools that help managers understand why a problem or opportunity exists so they can develop strategies. For example, a complete EIS environment would include spreadsheet software into which a manager could import information to perform a "what-if" analysis and perhaps a fuzzy system that could handle imprecise information.

■ **Access to Varieties of Information.** Finally, EISs provide managers with access to all types of information. This information includes not only internally generated information, but also external information that describes the environment surrounding the organization.

Have Executive Information Systems Been Misnamed?

Executive information systems sound really great; they give executives and managers the flexibility to view information from many angles and provide various tools for supporting data analysis. But consider this: Are there other people besides executives in organizations who need the same capabilities? The answer is definitely yes. People throughout any organization—regardless of status or title—need flexible data access, drill down capabilities, and tools for supporting decision making. And there are many good EIS prewritten software packages available on the market at an affordable price.

> ## CAREER OPPORTUNITY
>
> In the business world, don't think of EISs as executive information systems. Think of EISs as *employee information systems*—systems that support **any** employee's efforts to flexibly view information and make decisions.

 **Employee Information Systems**

"Executive information systems are somewhat of a misnomer at XRA. In reality, we have *employee information systems* that anyone can use to "drill down" through information to get at whatever they need. For example, a while back we apparently produced several thousand plastic water bottles that didn't solidify well in the casting process. We started with bottles that went into that batch and drilled down to machines and people. Once we had determined that almost all the production employees had used different casting machines to produce the bad bottles, we were able to eliminate employees and machines as the problem. As we drilled even further, we eventually determined that the bad bottles were all made from the same plastic raw material batch. So, there was our problem. We don't limit this type of "drilling down" to our executives—we encourage all our employees to do this to find a problem or figure out how to do something better."

—Bill Polland, Production & Development director ❖

Interorganizational Systems

Communicating Information Among Organizations

In Chapter 1 we discussed electronic commerce as an important force shaping the landscape of business today. Electronic commerce supports a "virtual market" in which product manufacturers, service suppliers, distributors and wholesalers, retailers, and customers gather to do business. To do this effectively, businesses must provide first-rate technologies that support the flow of information among all parties involved—we call these technologies interorganizational systems. An ***interorganizational system (IOS)*** automates the flow of information between organizations to support the planning, design, development, production, and delivery of products and services (see Figure 2.15). Therefore, IOSs are responsible for the information-processing task of communicating information.

In fact, we've already looked at a special form of an IOS—a customer integrated system. These systems allow an organization to electronically communicate with you as a customer while you order a product or service. So, CISs are essentially a type of IOS that supports the flow of information between an organization and its customers for the purpose of directly supporting the delivery of products and services.

Just as organization-to-customer IOSs can provide an organization with significant competitive advantage, so can organization-to-organization IOSs. Organization-to-organization IOSs not only support the delivery of products and services, they can also support the timely exchange of information throughout the entire product cycle—from planning to delivery. Let's consider three IOS examples—R. J. Reynolds; the World Insurance Network; and the alliance of IBM, Apple, and Motorola.

CAREER OPPORTUNITY

Interorganizational systems—regardless of their level—are not tomorrow's business advantage. Rather, they are today's required way of doing business. Large organizations, such as Sears and General Motors, will no longer do business with suppliers that are not linked to them through EDI. The federal government has even announced that all contractors wanting government contracts must be linked to the government by the year 2000. And, according to a 1995 *Computerworld* survey, 92 percent of the companies said they had EDI capabilities with their customers, and 81 percent said they had the same links with their suppliers.[24] If your business can't do EDI, it may not remain in business.

R. J. Reynolds will no longer do business with suppliers or distributors that do not have an IOS to support electronic data interchange.[25] ***Electronic data interchange (EDI)*** is the direct computer-to-computer transfer of transaction information contained in standard business documents, such as invoices and purchase orders, in a standard format. So, when distributors need to order products from R. J. Reynolds, they do so by electronically communicating (via EDI) their order information. Literally no paper is moved to and from R. J. Reynolds as its distributors order products. Likewise, when R. J. Reynolds orders materials from its suppliers, it does so electronically through EDI. Before using an IOS and EDI, a paper-based purchase order cost R. J. Reynolds $75 to process. Now, the electronic-based purchase order costs only 93 cents to process. This alone has saved R. J. Reynolds almost $1 million annually.

Today less than 1 percent of all global insurance transactions are moved between organizations through IOSs. That's why the world's six largest insurance brokers have pooled their resources to create the World Insurance Network.[26] When complete, insurance companies worldwide will be able to handle all insurance transactions electronically and gain instant access to policy

FIGURE 2.15

Interorganizational Systems at Work

Communicating with Customers Through EDI

"**W**e require that all bike manufacturers be connected to us through EDI. That way they can electronically send their order requests to us. Once our system receives an order request, it passes that information to the production system which processes it and sends back a projected delivery date. We electronically send the projected delivery date back to the bike manufacturer as confirmation that we received the order. And when I say 'we,' I really mean the system. We don't do anything."

—Yolanda Feruz, Bike Manufacturer accounts manager ❖

information and prices of all major insurance providers. This will allow small insurance agencies to find the best competitive pricing for prospective customers. Notice that this type of IOS takes advantage of economies of scale in technologies and provides all participating organizations with access to product and service pricing information. Without this type of IOS, the individual participating organizations could not develop a system with these vast capabilities.

In the early 1990s, IBM, Apple, and Motorola formed a strategic alliance in hopes of breaking Intel's dominance in the CPU market. Using an IOS to communicate information, these three organizations shared product development expertise and other forms of vitally important competitive information. The result of this alliance was the PowerPC chip, which Apple now uses almost exclusively in its line of workstation and portable computers. With this type of IOS and information sharing, the alliance of the partnering organizations often becomes transparent to the customers. Indeed, many Apple users are unaware that Apple teamed with its arch rival IBM to bring the PowerPC chip to the market.

IOSs definitely offer significant advantages to all participating organizations. For R. J. Reynolds, its distributors, and its suppliers, EDI translates into moving transaction information more quickly and inexpensively than doing so with paper documents. The participants in the World Insurance Network will be able to use their IOS to obtain product and service pricing information as well as information about insurance customers. And IBM, Apple, and Motorola have used their IOS to join forces in creating a completely new product, the PowerPC chip.

INDUSTRY PERSPECTIVE — Food

Quaker Oats Hopes to Move Snapple Electronically

Over the past several years, Quaker Oats has been on a beverage buying spree, buying both Gatorade and Snapple. Today, Quaker is the third-largest beverage company after Coke and Pepsi, and it's the largest vendor of noncarbonated beverages.

But being the biggest today doesn't mean that you'll always be that way. So, Quaker hopes to sell even more Snapple through technology. Quaker plans to create an interorganizational system that will connect it to the top 50 distributors of Snapple. Then Quaker will tap into the distributors' databases, monitor their inventory levels, and replenish Snapple supplies at a moment's notice.

This sort of IOS that supports information sharing between organizations is not that uncommon. Quaker already does it for its Gatorade distributors. And it must be working—Gatorade commands 80 percent of the sports drink market. Snapple's current market share is 15 percent in teas and 24 percent in fruit drinks. Imagine the revenues if those figures skyrocket to 80 percent or better.[27] ❖

Caterpillar Moves Fast Around the World

THE GLOBAL PERSPECTIVE

With an interorganizational system that links Caterpillar's factories, distribution centers, dealers, and large customers in some 1,000 locations across 23 time zones in 160 countries, Caterpillar moves around the world with ease. Consider this scenario. A sensor on a part on a Caterpillar machine in Uruguay detects a malfunction and relays that information to a remote monitoring center. A technician at the monitoring center pushes a few buttons on a computer, which causes an alert to be routed to the nearest field technician's portable computer. The alert contains information concerning the nature of the malfunction, which the portable computer uses to perform a diagnostic, recommend needed repairs, and even prepare an electronic order form for the necessary parts.

Next, the field technician notifies the customer of the exact cost of the repairs and a time frame within which the repair can be made. When the customer approves the cost of the repair, the field technician uses the portable computer to submit the electronic order for the parts. Upon arrival in Uruguay a few days later, the field technician finds the parts waiting.

If that sounds too good to be true, think again. Caterpillar has such a system, it is worldwide, and it links hundreds of organizations together through technology. The benefits are obviously enormous. According to James Baldwin, vice president of the Parts and Service Support Division, "The amount of time that will be saved is probably in the range of 20 percent to 30 percent. When you consider that field service workers are billed out at $20 to $50 an hour, that's a significant savings."[28] ❖

Some Final Thoughts About IT Systems in Organizations

In this chapter, we've looked at various ways to create organizational structures, information as it moves through an organization, the five categories of information-processing tasks, and seven IT systems that help your organization work with information and perform tasks related to information processing. As you consider the seven IT systems in an organization, keep the following points in mind:

- *Functional systems are combinations of the seven IT systems.* Consider Vanity Fair's market-response system in the opening case study. It supports the flow of information between organizations (an example of an IOS), it processes incoming information and updates Vanity Fair's database (an example of a TPS), and it removes much of the guesswork from product reordering (an example of a DSS).

- *All systems perform all five information-processing tasks.* As we discussed each system, we identified its primary (and sometimes secondary) information-processing responsibilities. That can often be

a matter of interpretation and different in many instances. Voice mail, for example, is primarily responsible for communicating information—sending messages between people. But it also captures information when you speak, conveys information when you listen to a message, and stores information when you save a message.

CAREER OPPORTUNITY

The real business world rarely operates as ideally as it appears in textbooks. For example, you can't look at a specific system and just call it a TPS or say that it only captures information. Your opportunity lies in understanding that systems in organizations perform many tasks and support the varying information needs of many different people.

- *Your information-processing needs should drive all your technology decisions.* We cannot stress this enough. You should never let technology dictate what you can or cannot do with respect to information processing. As a knowledge worker, it's up to you to define your information-processing needs first, and then determine the best IT system.

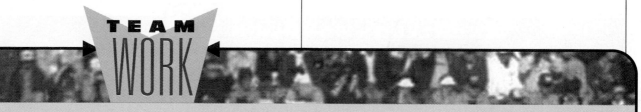

TEAM WORK

Creating Interorganizational Systems with the Internet

A growing number of companies are using the Internet to create interorganizational systems and check out the competition. For creating interorganizational systems, most organizations are simply using the Internet to create customer integrated systems and perform electronic data interchange with suppliers and customers. Others have begun to take advantage of the Internet to form electronic information partnerships for sharing information.

For checking out the competition, many organizations are hiring "Net Cruisers" whose sole responsibility is to cruise the Internet all day, check out competitors' Web sites, and find any new products or services that the competition is planning to offer.

Task 1

Explore the Internet and find Web sites that are examples of customer integrated systems and electronic data interchange. Find at least five Web sites. Can you foresee a time when all organizations—grocery stores, utility companies, video rental stores, colleges and universities, and others—will use the Internet for these purposes? What is currently the most significant drawback to using the Internet for these purposes?

Task 2

Suppose you had been hired as a Net Cruiser. Develop a list of competitor Web sites that you would want to check frequently. Also, develop a list of key feature, product, and service offerings that you would want to monitor carefully. You can choose from the organizations listed below as your employer or come up with your own.

IBM	MGM Studios
General Motors	General Electric
American Airlines	Coca-Cola
Apple	Merrill Lynch
Microsoft	General Mills ❖

ON YOUR OWN

Information-Processing Responsibilities

B elow is a table of the seven IT systems we introduced in this chapter. For each, identify the primary and secondary information-processing tasks. To do this place a "P" (for Primary) and an "S" (for Secondary) in the appropriate columns. Be prepared to justify your decisions. ❖

	Capture	Convey	Create	Cradle	Communicate
Transaction processing system					
Customer integrated system					
Management information system					
Workgroup support system					
Decision support system and artificial intelligence					
Executive information system					
Interorganizational system					

KNOWLEDGE WORKER'S -LIST

How Organizations Can Be Structured, Both Horizontally and Vertically. Typically, an organization is viewed in a triangular or pyramid form with four levels. These four levels include *strategic management, tactical management, operational management,* and *nonmanagement employees.*

Organizations can also be structured horizontally and vertically according to *business function* (for example, production, finance, and human resource management) or according to *specific products and services.* Whatever the case, businesses today are making extensive use of workgroups or teams.

The Nature of Decentralized Computing and Shared Information

Decentralized computing—the placement of technology within groups of people (for instance teams, departments, and business units) to give them the flexibility to handle their own specific information-processing tasks

Shared information—the placing of all the organization's information in a database and giving people software to (1) provide specific updates to the database and (2) drill down through the database to find any information they need

How Information Flows in an Organization and What Information Can Describe. How information flows:

Upward—typically describing the state of the organization in terms of how it's operating and the transactions that have occurred

Downward—consisting of the strategies, goals, and directives that originate at one level and then are passed to lower levels

Horizontal—defining the communications that exist among various functional business units and work teams

What information can describe:

Internal—specific operational aspects of the organization

External—the environment surrounding the organization

Objective—something that is quantifiably known

Subjective—something that is currently unknown

CLOSING CASE STUDY: CASE 1

Marriott Takes Information Technology Around the World

Marriott hotels boast an amazing 80 percent occupancy rate at a time when the industry average is around 65 percent. Marriott has achieved this by implementing an integrated approach that includes (1) identifying customers, (2) reaching them effectively, (3) developing programs to keep them loyal, and (4) delivering a quality program. Marriott's technology-based global distribution system (GDS) stands behind this integrated approach.

Marriott's GDS is the most powerful hotel GDS in the industry, and owners worldwide have found it to be a powerful selling tool. In 1994 alone, Marriott's 2,000 sales professionals handled over 21 million phone calls and generated $4 billion in sales. Marriott's GDS also has the highest connectivity rate to airline reservation systems in the industry. Many travel agents have even decided to use Marriott's GDS as their primary interface for booking hotels and airline flights around the world. By the end of 1995, Marriott projected that travel agents (using Marriott's GDS) will have booked nearly 6 million room nights and generated $600 million in sales for Marriott's owners.

But Marriott's use of technology doesn't stop with its interorganizational GDS. Says Bruce Wolff, vice president of distribution systems, "Each property uses Marriott's revenue management and demand forecasting systems to set its goals for occupancy and rate. Our reservations staff has access to that information when making bookings and can work with the strategy the property has set up. We measure our reservations staff on how well they follow and execute the properties' revenue management strategies. By working in tandem with the properties, we were able

The Information-Processing Tasks That Take Place in an Organization and IT Systems That Support Those Tasks. Information-processing tasks:

Capturing—obtaining information at its point of origin

Conveying—presenting information in its most useful form

Creating—processing information to obtain new information

Cradling—storing information for use at a later time

Communicating—sending information to other people or locations

IT systems:

Transaction processing system (TPS)—processes transactions that occur within an organization. Primary information-processing tasks include capturing, creating, and cradling. Secondary information-processing tasks include conveying.

Customer integrated system (CIS)—extension of a TPS that places technology in the hands of an organization's customers and allows them to process their own transactions. Primary information-processing tasks include capturing, creating, cradling, and communicating. Secondary information-processing tasks include conveying.

Management information system (MIS)—provides periodic and predetermined reports that summarize information within a database. Primary information-processing tasks include creating and conveying.

Workgroup support system (WSS)—designed specifically to improve the performance of workgroups by supporting the sharing and flow of information. Primary information-processing tasks include communicating.

Decision support system and artificial intelligence (DSS/AI)—facilitates the processing of information to support decision-making tasks in environments that require significant analysis. Primary information-processing tasks include creating.

Executive information system (EIS)—highly interactive MIS combined with various decision support systems and artificial intelligence to help people identify and address problems and opportunities. Primary information-processing tasks include creating and conveying.

Interorganizational system (IOS)—automates the flow of information between organizations and customers for the purpose of supporting the planning, design, development, production, and delivery of products and services. Primary information-processing tasks include communicating. ❖

to generate $2 million in incremental business in 1994, while defending both rate and occupancy." Bruce firmly believes that this team-oriented philosophy has encouraged the reservations staff to always find a sale.

For example, the reservations staff can mine through the data warehouse to optimize cross-selling. "If one hotel is full, our agents can suggest another Marriott hotel in the area. One out of every ten rooms sold is processed this way. This creates satisfied customers and keeps more people loyal to our brands," comments Bruce. Reservation staff members even share their ideas on which accounts they're looking for and what works best through national meetings and important conference calls. Almost 500 members of the staff participate on these national teams, creating a vital synergy that boosts the visibility of and market for each property.

In a time when the hospitality and leisure industry seems flat, Marriott is using technology to create customer loyalty and increase brand preference.[29,30] ❖

◄ Questions ►

1. How would you characterize the organizational structure for Marriott? Does it follow typical business functions, products and services offered, or some other? How has Marriott integrated its use of teams to compete more effectively?

2. Marriott's global distribution system is an example of an interorganizational system. How has Marriott been able to attract travel agents to use its GDS? Can you think of other features that Marriott might add to encourage even more use by travel agents?

3. Within Marriott's organizational structure, there are many flows of information, traveling up, down, and horizontally, that describe different aspects of the business. Identify specific information flows, describe their direction, and identify whether they are internal, external, objective, or subjective information flows.

4. How has Marriott taken advantage of the concepts of a data warehouse and "data mining" to increase revenue? In what other ways could data mining further increase revenue and marketability?

AlliedSignal Serves Up Its Very Own Groupware

Groupware is undoubtedly one of the hottest topics in business today—not only in computer circles but in any circumstance in which a group of people want to improve the performance of a team. And, while many organizations are choosing to purchase popular groupware products such as Lotus Notes and Collabra, AlliedSignal Technical Services decided to create its own.

Called TQSoft, AlliedSignal's proprietary groupware product services its 87,000 employees grouped into over 3,000 teams spread throughout 30 countries. AlliedSignal's primary reason for developing and using TQSoft was to avoid "reinventing the wheel" every time a project team tackled the reengineering of a business process. That problem was actually quite common before AlliedSignal developed TQSoft. Many project teams were devoted to just reengineering existing business processes to make them more efficient and streamlined. One group in New Jersey, for example, duplicated the efforts of other groups who had tackled the same business process in another part of the country or world.

With TQSoft, AlliedSignal is now able to consolidate all business process information into a single repository that everyone can access. The sharing of this information alone is expected to eliminate redundant work by as much as 90 percent. But TQSoft supports more than just the consolidation of information. Employees can also share tips, messages, and notes through an e-mail component of TQSoft. And anyone can literally "drill down" through the information repository to discover new ways of solving problems or determine a list of other employees who had worked on similar problems. TQSoft also supports the storing of information in a variety of formats such as videos, graphs, spreadsheets, and PowerPoint slides. Employees can then easily link these types of information to any other stored information to create logical relationships within and among business processes.[31] ❖

◄ Questions ►

1. Which of the three functions mentioned in this chapter—team dynamics, document management, and applications development—does TQSoft

5. Of the seven IT systems discussed in this chapter, which are identified in this case? What are their primary information-processing responsibilities? What levels do they support?

support? In what ways? If you find that TQSoft didn't support a particular function, do you think AlliedSignal omitted such a function by design or because of some limitation? Justify your answer.

2. How is TQSoft similar to an executive information system? How is TQSoft different from an executive information system? How would you characterize TQSoft—as an "executive" information system or an "employee" information system?

3. For AlliedSignal, TQSoft doesn't support business process reengineering with work flow automation software but it still supports the reengineering of business processes. How? In what other ways could a groupware product support the reengineering of business processes?

4. What sort of security issues do you think AlliedSignal faces by letting everyone have access to the single repository of business process information? What types of information might be stored in that repository that could be potentially damaging to an individual or department? Does AlliedSignal have any ethical or legal responsibility to protect sensitive departmental or personal information?

5. How would you characterize the information stored in the repository according to how information flows—upward, downward, or horizontally—and according to what information describes—internal, external, objective, or subjective information? In general, would you say that most workgroup support systems are designed to support the upward, downward, or horizontal flow of information? Why?

6. Creating information takes on two forms—transaction processing and analytical processing. Which does TQSoft support? How? Would your answer differ if TQSoft were designed to support permanent teams instead of project teams? Does the type of team matter? Why or why not?

Electronic Commerce
Business and You on the Internet

Ordering Products on the Internet

For most people, electronic commerce is all about business-to-customer. That is, most of us think of electronic commerce as an essential enabler for allowing businesses to interact with their individual customers (you and me). Think about ATMs—they enable your financial institution to interact with you electronically, giving you instant access to your money without having to go to the traditional brick-and-mortar place of business.

That business-to-customer aspect of electronic commerce certainly dominates the Internet right now. On the Internet, you (as an individual customer) can purchase groceries, clothes, computers, automobiles, music, antiques, books, and much more. In fact, if you want to buy it, there's probably an Internet site selling it. Even more so, there are probably hundreds of Internet sites selling what you want, giving you the opportunity to shop for the best buy.

In this section, we've included a number of Web sites related to ordering products on the Internet. On the Web site that supports this text (http://www.mhhe.com/business/mis/haag, select "Electronic Commerce Projects"), we've provided direct links to all these Web sites as well as many, many more. These are a great starting point for completing this Real HOT section. We would also encourage you to search the Internet for others.

We would offer a couple of words of caution before you begin this project. Those words are *caveat emptor* or "let the buyer beware." You can indeed find almost anything to buy on the Internet. However, you should carefully consider the person or organization from whom you're making the purchase. This is especially true if you have to provide a credit card number to make the purchase.

So, let's explore just the tip of the iceberg concerning products you can buy on the Internet. And remember—this is just the beginning. If you want it, it's probably for sale somewhere on the Internet.

Books and Music

Books and music make up one category of products you can readily find on the Internet to purchase. In fact, one of the most widely known and acclaimed Internet sites performing electronic commerce is Amazon.com at http://www.amazon.com. Amazon boasts over 3 million book and music titles for sale. Amazon and many other book and music sites even carry a wide selection of textbooks for you to order.

Of course, as with all products you buy on the Internet, you need to consider price and the amount you'll save on the Internet compared to purchasing books and music from local stores. Sometimes, prices are higher on the Internet, and you can certainly expect to pay some sort of shipping and handling charges. So don't blindly purchase any product on the Internet without first checking local stores.

In the table on page 80, we've listed some sites on the Internet where you can purchase books and music (we've also included many more on the Web site that supports this text).

Make a list of five books or music albums (CDs, cassettes, or whatever) that you're interested in purchasing. For each of these, find their price at a local store. Next,

visit five books and music Web sites and answer the following questions.

A. What are the five books or music albums you're interested in?

B. What are their prices at a local store? ~ \$50

C. Can you find them at each Internet site? yes

D. How does each site categorize its books and music?

E. Are the local prices higher or lower than the Internet prices?

F. How do you order and pay for your products?

G. How long is the shipping delay? ~ 2-3

H. What is the shipping charge?

I. Overall, how would you rate your Internet shopping experience compared to your local store shopping experience?

Clothing and Accessories

It might seem odd, but many people purchase all types of clothing on the Internet—from shoes to pants to all kinds of accessories, including perfume. The disadvantage in shopping for clothes on the Internet is that you can't actually try them on and stand in front of the mirror. But, if you know exactly what you want (by size and color), you can probably find and buy it on the Internet.

In the table on page 80, we've provided a list of five clothing shops and where you can find them on the Internet. Connect to several of these sites (as well as any of the others we've listed on the Web site that supports this text) and experience cyber-clothing shopping. As you do, consider the following. How do you order and pay for merchandise? What sort of description is provided about the clothing—text, photos, perhaps 3D views? What is the return policy for merchandise that you don't like or doesn't fit? Can clothing retail stores expect to see a decline in sales as more people shop on the Internet? Finally, is shopping for clothes on the Internet as much fun as going to the mall? Why or why not?

Computers and Accessories

It only makes sense that the Internet (a computing-based environment) is full of online stores where you can purchase anything computing-related. And what's really great is that most of these sites provide product reviews, the ability to customize your own system, and technical

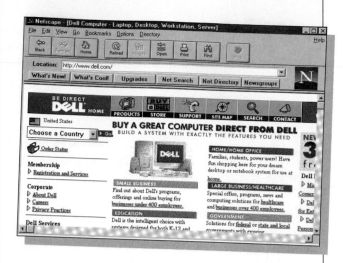

support once you make your purchase. To see how purchasing a computer on the Internet works, think about the system you'd like to have—CPU speed, internal memory size, storage peripherals, and monitor characteristics.

In the table on page 80, we've provided just a few of the hundreds of sites where you can order computing technology. On the Web site that supports this text, you'll find many more. Connect to at least three sites (definitely consider connecting to Dell, Gateway, Hewlett-Packard, or Computers.com) and evaluate their effectiveness in allowing you to shop for a computer system. As you do, answer the following questions for each site.

A. What is the cost of your dream system?

B. How do you specify the characteristics of your system?

C. How do you order your system?

D. What packaged software, if any, comes with your system?

E. Does the site offer any financing?

F. Does the site offer any "special" already-built systems?

G. What sort of technical support is provided once you purchase your system?

H. How long does it take for your system to be shipped to you?

Many of the sites you visited may as well offer product reviews and recommendations concerning how to configure the best system. What they probably don't do is provide a list of pricing alternatives as compared to other Web sites. And before you buy a computer online, you should definitely do some competitive pricing. Fortunately, there are some sites devoted to providing you with that information. At Price Scan (http://www.prices-can.com), for example, you can obtain a great review of competitive pricing on almost any technology-related product. If you search around the Internet (using search terms such as "computer" and "buyers guide"), you'll undoubtedly find a great number of sites that provide similar information.

Internet Auction Houses

As you search for products on the Internet, you'll find a lot of individuals and traditional organizations such as the Gap selling their wares. You'll also come across a variety of Internet auction houses. These auction houses act as clearing stations on which you can sell your products or purchase products from other people in an auction format. And auction houses represent some serious electronic commerce on the Internet. Ebay, one of the more popular auction houses, boasts an amazing 140 million hits per week.

It works quite simply. First, you register as a user at a particular auction house. Once you do, you'll have a special user ID (perhaps your e-mail address or a special name you give yourself) and password that allow you to post products for sale or bid on other products. When the auction is complete for a particular product (auction houses set time limits that last typically from one to seven days), the auction house will notify the seller and the winning bidder of the final price. Then, it's up to you and the other person to exchange money and merchandise.

In the table on page 80, we've listed a few of the more popular auction houses on the Internet (many more are included on the Web site that supports this text). Now, think of a product you'd like to buy or sell—perhaps a rare coin, a computer, a hard-to-find Beanie Baby, a bottle of wine, or a car. Connect to at least five Internet auction houses and answer the following questions for each.

A. What is the registration process to become a user?

B. Do you have to pay a fee to become a user?

C. Is your product of interest listed?

D. How does the auction house categorize products?

E. How do you bid on a product?

F. What does the auction house charge you to sell a product?

G. What is the duration of a typical auction?

H. Can you set a minimum acceptable bid for a product you want to sell?

I. How does the auction house help you evaluate the credibility of other people buying and selling products?

Shipping Information

When you order something through the Internet—much as you would over the phone or through traditional mail order—you'll probably incur shipping and handling charges and perhaps the cost of insuring the package. Of course, most companies have already preset these charges and pass them along to you. But have you ever wondered just how much shipping and insurance actually costs?

As well as buying, you can sell your merchandise through several Internet shops and malls (especially Internet auction houses). In that case, you certainly want to know the proper shipping and insurance charges. Well, it's easy enough to find out   all you need to know is the zip code from where you're shipping, the zip code you're shipping to, the weight of the package, and any special characteristics (e.g., speed of delivery, oversize boxes, and insurance requirements).

In the table on page 80, we've listed the Internet sites for the U.S. Postal Service, UPS, and FedEx. Connect to those three sites and complete the table at the top of the next page by entering your zip code and the rates charged by each organization.

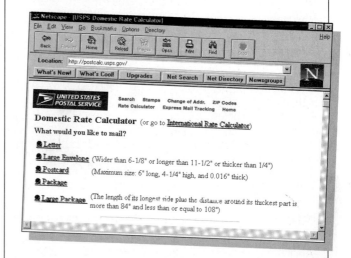

Your Zip	Destination	Weight	Speed	Rates		
	55812	4.5 lbs.	Next day	USPS: _____	UPS: _____	FedEx: _____
	80126	1.2 lbs.	2-3 days	USPS: _____	UPS: _____	FedEx: _____
	79007	10 lbs.	Slowest	USPS: _____	UPS: _____	FedEx: _____
	01890	6 ozs.	Next day	USPS: _____	UPS: _____	FedEx: _____
	24412	3 lbs.	2–3 days	USPS: _____	UPS: _____	FedEx: _____

Web Sites for Ordering Products

Book and Music Stores	Address
Amazon	http://www.amazon.com
Barnes and Noble	http://www.barnesandnoble.com
Borders	http://www.borders.com
Blockbuster Books	http://www.blockbuster.com/books
Book Zone	http://www.bookzone.com

Clothing and Accessory Stores	Address
Fashionmall.com	http://www.fashionmall.com
L.L. Bean	http://www.llbean.com
Birkenstock Express	http://www.footwise.com
Bugle Boy	http://www.bugleboy.com/virtualstore
Eddie Bauer	http://www.eddiebauer.com/home/home.asp

Computer Stores	Address
CDW	http://www.cdw.com
Cyberian Outpost	http://www.outpost.com
Hewlett-Packard	http://www.hp.com
Dell	http://www.dell.com
Gateway	http://www.gateway.com

Auction Houses	Address
Ebay	http://www.ebay.com
Napa Valley Wine	http://www.nvwa.org/nvwa/lots/149.html
Web Auction Center	http://www.webauctioncenter.com
Rotman Collectibles	http://www2.wwcd.com/rotman
New York Computer Exchange	http://www.nyceonline.com/html/auction.htm

Shipping Services	Address
The U.S. Postal Service	http://postcalc.usps.gov
UPS	http://www.ups.com/using/services/rave/rate.html
FedEx	http://www1.fedex.com/us/rates

Go to the Web site that supports this text: **http://www.mhhe.com/business/mis/haag** and select "Electronic Commerce Projects."

We've included links to over 100 Web sites for ordering products on the Internet, including automobiles.

KEY TERMS AND CONCEPTS

Analytical Processing
Applications Development Facility
Artificial Intelligence (AI)
Comparative Report
Customer Integrated System (CIS)
Data Warehouse
Decentralized Computing
Decision Support System (DSS)
Electronic Data Interchange (EDI)
Electronic Meeting Software
Electronic Meeting Support
Electronic Messaging
Exception Report
Executive Information System (EIS)

Expert System
External Information
Genetic Algorithm
Geographic Information System (GIS)
Group Document Database
Group Scheduling Software
Groupware
Internal Information
Interorganizational System (IOS)
Intranet
Management Information System (MIS)
Objective Information

Operational Management
Periodic Report
Shared Information
Strategic Management
Subjective Information
Summarized Report
Tactical Management
Transaction Processing
Transaction Processing System (TPS)
Videoconferencing Software
Whiteboard Software
Work Flow Automation Software
Workgroup Support System (WSS)

SHORT-ANSWER QUESTIONS

1. How do organizations differ structurally both horizontally and vertically?
2. What are the four types of information in an organization?
3. Why is decentralized computing coupled with shared information the best structure in an organization?
4. Why are transaction processing and customer integrated systems the most important systems in an organization?
5. How do executive information systems differ from management information systems?
6. What three functions do workgroup support systems support?
7. What are the five categories of information-processing tasks? Which IT systems support each?

DISCUSSION QUESTIONS

1. Worldwide interorganizational systems always create new problems—quality of electrical service, impact of environmental factors, cultural barriers, and so on. Which do you think is the greatest barrier for organizations to overcome—technological, time, geographic, or cultural barriers? Which do you think is the least daunting barrier for an organization to overcome?
2. Management information systems (as a specific IT system) are quickly becoming an everyday part of executive information systems. As more people in an organization use executive information systems, do you think management information systems will become a system of the past? Why or why not?
3. Of the seven IT systems discussed in this chapter, which do you think must have the easiest to use interface for the user? Why? Which system is concerned the least with the user interface? Why?
4. As mentioned in the text, many firms are moving technology into the hands of their customers through the use of customer integrated systems. Why do you think this is the case today and was not the case 15 years ago? What has changed? Is it the technology or something else? Do you think this is a growing trend? Why or why not?
5. The use of such advanced artificial intelligence techniques as expert systems is growing. Using such systems a firm may target you as a new customer by analyzing your credit card purchasing trends. Is this an invasion of your privacy?

CASE STUDY

Creating Vision for a New Way to Do Business

When you're winning—is it still important to improve? That's the question faced by Andersen Corp., the world's largest wood-window manufacturer. It is unusual for a successful firm to ask the question. But to take that next step and answer yes gives Andersen an enormous competitive advantage. For Andersen, "yes" is *business process reengineering*—a radical redesign to achieve dramatic improvements. This 3-year, seven-phase reengineering project will add more than $10 million in profits per year to the firm when it is completed. Still, can you imagine your firm investing $5 million to reinvent the way it does business when it outsells its top three competitors? Why not wait until there's a problem?

IN THE NEWS

Strategic and Competitive Opportunities

Using IT to Generate Organizational Horsepower

However, this is Andersen, where the company motto is "different and better." As a result, competitive advantage is everywhere. Not long ago Andersen developed and produced a line of easy-to-clean Tilt-Wash windows in less than half the time required for a typical major product development—21 months compared to 4 years. Soon after, information technology enabled Andersen to reduce those 21 months to 14 months. To accomplish this, Andersen needed *electronic data interchange (EDI)* to link to suppliers. This EDI foundation will pave the way for future information partnerships. With its suppliers online, Andersen turned to other opportunities.

Next, Andersen completely reorganized its manufacturing operations. Taking *just-in-time* concepts, Andersen reduced work stoppages and delays using *cross-functional teams.* By bringing together employees from all disciplines and allowing them to work together in teams, Andersen was able to discover new and innovative solutions to old manufacturing problems. Finally, Andersen looked to the future to address a challenge created by a changing market—more and more homeowners are demanding unique windows for their homes. Offering more styles has caused Andersen's catalogs to grow, and price quotes as long as 15 pages began taking hours to calculate; getting all these increasingly complex

FEATURES

IN THE INFORMATION AGE, KNOWLEDGE WORKERS UNDERSTAND...

1. The important role information technology plays in enabling perfect service

2. The way in which organizations develop organizational horsepower and how this affects their competitiveness

3. How quality forms the foundation of organizational competitiveness

4. The role of various organizational horsepower strategies in creating a competitive organization

5. When to adopt an organizational horsepower strategy using a radical improvement process

orders right was growing harder. By 1991, 20 percent of Andersen's truckloads contained at least one order discrepancy, double the number in 1985. So Andersen implemented a *paperless* product ordering system using a product database that calculates price quotes right in retail stores and then transmits the order directly to Andersen. Each window is then tracked with bar codes through the assembly line to the warehouse. As a result, in 1995 Andersen offered a whopping 188,000 different products, yet fewer than 1 in 200 truckloads contained an order discrepancy. Certainly, "different and better."[2, 3] ❖

Introduction

As you can see, Andersen is truly an innovative company. The people at Andersen have learned to think about their business in an entirely new way. Andersen employed such concepts as business process reengineering, EDI, a just-in-time approach, cross-functional teams, and the paperless office. We'll examine these ideas and many others as ways to increase the power of your organization in this chapter.

Gaining a competitive advantage through effective business strategies is what this chapter is all about. And you'll gain an understanding of how to get there from here. That is—you'll examine a road map for creating power in your organization. You'll discover that no single strategy fits all situations, and so you'll look at how to pick the strategy or strategies that are right for your situation.

As we mentioned in Chapter 1, there are many forces shaping today's business, and one of them is competition. Alert companies sense heightened competition and use information technology to level the playing field. Examples abound—take County Fair Food Stores, for instance.[1] Do you think a big retailer like Kmart has anything on this two-store grocery chain in South Dakota? Well, maybe not. Kmart has a satellite communications system to play commercials and broadcast discount information over its speakers—so does County Fair. Kmart uses a special printing firm to crank out signs for specials on products—but not County Fair. It goes one step further and does it all in-house with a special printing system. Employees at County Fair simply scan a product bar code, punch in the sale price, enter the date the sale starts, and press a button. In just a few minutes out comes a store-ready sale sign. You see, County Fair is aware of its competitive environment and uses technology to help reduce any advantage a competitor like Kmart might have.

Let's take a look at a competitive environment a bit nearer to home. Have you ever satisfied that last-minute hunger attack with a call to your favorite Chinese food restaurant? Or maybe that call was to Domino's or Pizza Hut for pizza? Ever wondered why your Chinese restaurant didn't use the same telephone database technology as Pizza Hut? You know the one—the technology that allows you to call Pizza Hut and give an operator your phone number, which loads up your name, address, last order, and even the nearest delivery location. Often you never know which store delivered the pizza! Well, if you live in Mountain View, California, you know a Chinese restaurant that *does* use that technology.[4] Of course the owner, Roger Kao, isn't looking to offer the *same* service as Pizza Hut or Domino's. Roger says, "I admire Domino's approach. But I saw that I could do some things even better." Roger understands both his customers' expectations and his own business. He also knows firsthand how IT can enable a competitive advantage.

Gaining a Competitive Advantage

You know that businesses are in the business of servicing their customers—even daring to provide *perfect service* to customers. Many fall short of this goal. But that hasn't stopped customers from expecting it or businesses from striving to achieve it. It is this struggle that forms the basis of competition. So, for a company to gain a ***competitive advantage***, it must provide the best perceived perfect service at the customer's moment of value. And it's only customers who evaluate this competitive advantage. You see, a customer's perception of perfect service is what makes a sale. If you want Chinese food *fast* and you live in Mountain View, California, you call Roger Kao's restaurant. Roger's business has a competitive advantage.

The trouble with a competitive advantage is it doesn't last very long. You may recall from Chapter 1 that FedEx was the first freight company to offer package delivery software to its customers. Within months, however, UPS also provided similar software to its customers. Even more recently, UPS beat FedEx to the Internet with a Web site where you can schedule package pickup, check delivery routes, and calculate rates.[5] In turn, FedEx responded to this competitive challenge by doing the same.

So, sustaining a competitive advantage may not be possible. In fact, the only true sustainable competitive advantage is the one that's constantly renewed. Successful firms nurture innovation to provide this renewal. Take 3M, for example, the firm that created Post-it Notes.[6] For the people at 3M, nurturing innovation means allowing the creative process to run its course. As William Coyne, research and development chief at 3M, explains, "We're managing in chaos, and that's the right way to do it." 3M knows that innovation requires supportive strategies and tools, but you never know what idea may provide you advantage. Some consider the creation of Post-it Notes almost serendipitous, others consider it innovative. Nevertheless, most would agree creating an organization that fosters such new ideas is invaluable. Leon Royer, the leader of the tape division that invented Post-it Notes, adds, "An environment to free up your imagination—that's the whole idea." And, so, this chapter is all about helping you find new strategies to help your organization compete.

Organizational Horsepower

Force and Speed Combined

Organizations create their competitive advantages differently. How your organization creates an advantage depends on two factors: (1) knowledge of your competitive environment and (2) knowledge of your own business. In Chapter 8, we will cover how you can better understand your competitive environment by gathering competitive intelligence. For now, let's take a closer look at knowing your business and how you can improve its ability to compete.

No doubt you have seen a great deal in the business press about different strategies to improve an organization. This has been and will continue to be a source of much research. You see, the forces that act upon a company change over time, and the responding strategy will change as well. You'll remember from Chapter 1 that seven important forces shape today's business environment. Responding to, or taking advantage of, these seven forces is how your business competes. And that takes organizational horsepower.

What Exactly Is Organizational Horsepower?

What do you think of when you hear the term horsepower? Do you envision race cars with massive engines? Well, it's an appropriate image, but let's take it a bit further. Horsepower is not only about force, but also about force delivered with speed. One without the other is far less powerful than both combined. Imagine a large,

powerful boxer who can deliver a punch so quickly you can barely see it. Now that's horsepower.

We can apply these concepts of force and speed to an organization. ***Organizational horsepower (OHP)*** is a measure of organizational competitiveness generated through organizational force and speed. But what do we mean by organizational force and speed? ***Organizational force*** is meeting as many customer expectations as possible. An organization hopes to meet more expectations than its competitors and thus gain a competitive advantage. ***Organizational speed*** is meeting customer expectations quickly. Again, an organization hopes to meet these expectations before its competition does in order to gain a competitive advantage. Organizational force and organizational speed are both components of OHP and, together, they provide a framework for evaluating how various strategies can empower your organization (see Figure 3.1).

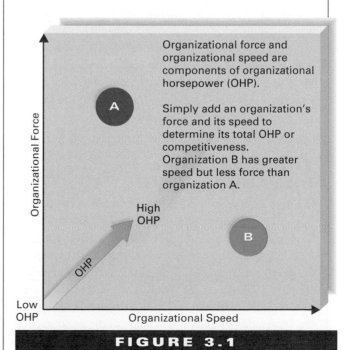

FIGURE 3.1
What Creates Organizational Horsepower?

As you can see in Figure 3.1, two organizations are charted, A and B, based on their organizational force and speed capabilities. In the figure, B generates greater organizational speed than does A, but less organizational force. And if you look at the components of force and speed together for each organization, you get OHP—a measure of competitiveness. In our example, organization A's force and speed together provide more horsepower than organization B. As you can see, both organizational force and speed give organizations competitiveness. The trouble is, few organizations have the resources to pursue both speed and force at the same time. So you must choose how you wish to compete based on what you can accomplish in your own organization. Fortunately, there are organizational strategies to fit all organizations. For example, you might wish to increase organizational force by expanding your hours of operation; with longer hours you can serve more customers and create a competitive advantage, if you can afford the personnel.

Whether your organization pursues organizational force or speed or both, it's IT that creates the opportunities. You may decide, for example, to broaden your organization's customer base by operating internationally. Such a move could generate organizational force, but only if IT systems link the international operations. Otherwise, all the operations pursue independent goals and no single operation benefits. And remember Daniel Shulman of AT&T from Chapter 1, "Size will no longer be important in determining market strength." IT can crank up your organizational force by making your product available everywhere—locationless operations. Or, IT can crank up your organizational speed by helping you respond quickly to customers with products—the just-in-time approach. IT enables these powerful strategies and more, as discussed in this chapter. Let's take a look at a summary of the various OHP strategies available to your firm.

The Strategies for Increasing OHP

In this chapter we will examine seven strategies to increase organizational competitiveness using IT. Each strategy is depicted on the OHP graphic framework in Figure 3.2. The framework depicts organizational force and speed for each strategy, as well as the OHP magnitude for each strategy. To illustrate, let's look at one strategy. The just-in-time approach generates mostly organizational speed (as depicted by the dark shading near the organizational speed axis). The just-in-time approach does not, however, generate much organizational force (as depicted by no shading near the organizational force axis). Finally,

the just-in-time approach generates the lowest total OHP of all the strategies. Now let's look at each strategy individually.

Just-in-Time Approach

The *just-in-time (JIT)* approach is producing or delivering a product or service *when* the customer wants it. Customers don't like to wait for their products, and the JIT approach seeks to deliver products and services to internal as well as external customers as the products are required. The JIT approach generates strong organizational speed through quick customer response enabled by IT telecommunications and scheduling systems. JIT generates very little organizational force. Comparatively, JIT generates the least OHP of all the strategies we'll discuss.

Teams in an Organization

A *team* is a group of people with a shared goal and task interdependence. Teams are used to bring diverse perspectives to an organizational problem. Teams, enabled by groupware, generate strong organizational force by helping the organization reach more customers. Teams generate very little organizational speed. Teams generate more OHP than the JIT approach but less than other strategies.

Information Partnerships

An *information partnership* is an agreement between organizations for the sharing of information to strengthen each partner organization. Information partnerships can pursue organizational speed using EDI, or organizational force using other IOSs. By sharing strategic information, information partnerships can generate both organizational force and speed. These OHP components of force and speed permit information partnerships to generate greater OHP than teams and the JIT approach, but less than the remaining strategies.

Timeless and Locationless Operations

Timeless operations operate without regard to time. *Locationless operations* operate without regard to location. With timeless operations, organizations operate 24 hours a day, if necessary, using IT systems that never sleep. These timeless operations generate organizational speed through quick, timely customer response. With locationless operations, customers are always near a location, often using IT systems like "virtual stores" on the Internet. These locationless operations generate organizational force by allowing the organization to reach

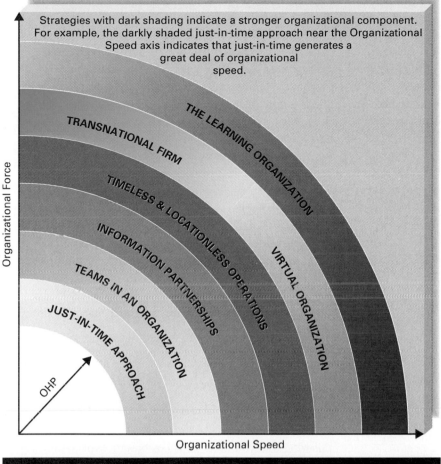

Strategies with dark shading indicate a stronger organizational component. For example, the darkly shaded just-in-time approach near the Organizational Speed axis indicates that just-in-time generates a great deal of organizational speed.

THE LEARNING ORGANIZATION

TRANSNATIONAL FIRM

TIMELESS & LOCATIONLESS OPERATIONS

INFORMATION PARTNERSHIPS

VIRTUAL ORGANIZATION

TEAMS IN AN ORGANIZATION

JUST-IN-TIME APPROACH

OHP

Organizational Force

Organizational Speed

FIGURE 3.2

How Strategies Generate Organizational Force, Speed, and Organizational Horsepower

forming a fully functional firm, generates a great deal of organizational speed. The magnitude of this speed is matched only by the magnitude of the organizational force generated by the transnational firm. All this speed gives the virtual organization OHP at least as great as that of the transnational firm, even though both get their OHP from completely different OHP components—one through force, one through speed.

The Learning Organization

A *learning organization* is an organization whose people are continually discovering how to learn together while, at the same time, altering their organization as a result of what they learn. By learning from your mistakes your organization can serve your customers better and faster—generating organizational speed. This strategy provides the most potential organizational speed because a learning organization is self-perpetuating. That is, a learning organization invents new strategies for serving its customers internally, based on its own knowledge of its customers. To generate such tremendous OHP, information must be shared throughout the organization at all levels, enabled by groupware, artificial intelligence systems, and networks.

more customers. Together, timeless and locationless operations generate *both* organizational force and speed. The total magnitude of the resulting OHP is greater than that of information partnerships.

The Transnational Firm

A *transnational firm* produces and sells products and services in countries all over the world in coordinated cooperation. All operations share information and resources, using IT networks, making the notion of a "headquarters" irrelevant. This firm's extensive international market exposure generates tremendous organizational force and OHP.

The Virtual Organization

A *virtual organization* is a network of independent organizations linked together by IT to exploit market opportunities by sharing skills, costs, and market access. The ability of independent organizations to respond to customer needs by coming together quickly and, in effect,

Achieving Competitive Advantage Using OHP

Now that you have some understanding of each strategy, examine the OHP graphic framework and the OHP strategies depicted in Figure 3.2. The framework graphically communicates how each individual strategy affects your organization as well as how one strategy compares to another. You can use this framework to choose an appropriate strategy or combination of strategies for your organization. This requires, however, a more complete understanding of each strategy so that you can evaluate the knowledge and resources required to implement each strategy. Shortly, we'll take a detailed look at each of the OHP strategies. However, we are still missing one piece essential to competitiveness. And that piece is *quality*.

Organizational speed is all about customer responsiveness, whereas organizational force is all about reaching lots of customers. Both OHP components assume that the customer wants what you have to offer. Ensuring that you produce products and services valuable to the customer is the foundation of all OHP strategies. We call that OHP foundation quality. Before we examine each of the OHP strategies, let's look closely at the foundation for all strategies—quality.

CAREER OPPORTUNITY

OHP is "organizational" horsepower, which simply means that it's not confined to how you use information technology. It addresses all business resources including people, distribution and logistics, product development, capital funding, and so on. Consider an organization that can quickly develop new products but doesn't possess good distribution channels to reach wide markets. That organization possesses speed (in product development) but not force (limited market reach). When you think about OHP, consider all organizational resources in addition to technology.

Quality

Your Competitive Foundation

When asked what two attributes are most important to a company's performance, 11,000 executives said, "quality of management" and "quality of products or services."[7] Consumers find quality important as well, placing it as the second most important criterion in a purchase decision behind "experience with a brand."[8] Very few terms in business are more misunderstood than "quality." What exactly is quality? Is a $40,000 luxury car of a higher quality than a $16,000 compact car? If so, does that mean that the compact car manufacturer isn't appealing to consumers and the 11,000 executives mentioned above?

Quality is not goodness, prettiness, or luxury. Products cannot have relative worth described by "good quality" and "bad quality." Precisely defined, *quality* is meeting customer expectations. So, your customers define quality. But what do we mean by *customer expectations*? Remember in Chapter 1, we examined the concept of providing perfect service to your customers. Perfect service is what customers expect. They expect you to provide service to them when, where, and how they want it. So, if luxury car customers expect a car with a leather interior and a smooth ride, delivered to

their home, then providing that product/service package is providing a quality product. If a compact car customer expects an economical, affordable car purchased with no hassles, then providing that product/service package is providing a quality product. To suggest simply that the luxury car is quality and the compact car is not, is simply wrong. This misperception persists, however. Different customers have different expectations, none of them wrong.

Meeting your customer expectations is all about knowing what those expectations are. To produce a quality product or service, your firm must constantly gather customer expectation information directly from your customers. You gather and analyze this information through your organizational IT systems at the point of customer contact, using CISs for example. Still, once you gather customer expectation information, how do you ensure that you can meet those expectations? That's a good question—let's examine a method of managing the quality foundation.

Total Quality Management

Keeping the Quality Foundation Strong

Ensuring that you meet your customer's expectations, that is, produce a quality product or service, requires a consistent quality implementation. For that, you can employ a process called total quality management—one of the many quality improvement processes you can implement in your organization. ***Total quality management (TQM)*** is meeting customer expectations through continuous improvement and organizationwide quality ownership. TQM includes three important ingredients. These ingredients are

1. Meeting customer expectations
2. Continuous improvement
3. Organizationwide quality ownership

Let's examine each of these closely.

Meeting Customer Expectations

The goal of TQM is quality, or meeting customer expectations. This goal is the very reason TQM is at the foundation of an organization's horsepower. If you don't meet your customer's expectations, it really doesn't matter what else you do—you will fail. So what do your customers expect? The most recent customer satisfaction survey reveals three key expectations—defect-free products, excellent service, and a competitive price.[9] In each industry the order of importance may be different, but all three exist. Take your telephone long-distance carrier for example. Clearly this is an area where competition is fierce. Television commercials air nightly with each carrier claiming to have the lowest rates. Interestingly enough, what long-distance customers want most is a superior connection and good customer service—both ahead of rates.

The challenge is in discovering exactly what your customers want along with when, where, and how they want it. And this is an important role for information technology—enabling quality. That's certainly what the Royal Bank of Canada discovered.[10] Recently it made a comprehensive customer database available online to all of its branches and offices to facilitate loan processing. In doing so, however, it discovered that its customers were purchasing only 3 financial services from the Royal Bank for every 14 they purchased elsewhere. Bank executives immediately reduced their efforts to market to new customers and refocused on existing customers whose expectations hadn't been met. The Royal Bank gathered customer information at the point of customer contact using CISs. Once gathered, the bank used data mining, which we discuss in Chapter 4, to determine customer expectations. You could also use decision support systems, discussed in Chapter 5, to detect new trends in customer expectations.

Once you've defined what your customers expect, you have to put systems in place to ensure that you meet those expectations day in and day out. The best way to do this is to measure all that you do and compare these measurements against your customer's expectations definition. ***Statistical process control (SPC)*** is a method of gathering and analyzing these measurements to identify and solve quality problems. We use two key SPC tools to analyze quality measurements. The principal SPC tool is the control chart. A ***control chart*** is a graphic means of identifying causes to problems that are controllable. Another helpful tool is a histogram. A ***histogram*** is a graphic representation of frequency distributions, or counts of how often different things occur. You then examine how the frequencies are distributed to see if

INDUSTRY PERSPECTIVE   **Transportation**

Meeting Customer Expectations Through a Quality Standard

Can you predict the future? Today's customers often want you to. If you give them a product exactly like the one they want they then ask for proof that you can provide that very same product again in the future. That's certainly what the big 3 automakers in North America have asked of their suppliers. General Motors, Chrysler, and Ford not only tell their suppliers what they'd like them to provide, but also demand certain standards compliance. So if you had a company that produced auto parts and you wanted to sell the parts to one of these big 3 automakers, you'd need to provide the exact product the manufacturer requested and also prove that you can produce that product reliably by becoming QS-9000 certified.

QS-9000 is a quality certification built on the more widely accepted ISO 9000 standard. The QS-9000 standard, however, is an expanded version with requirements tailored to the automotive industry. Becoming QS-9000 certified tells auto manufacturers that you have a well-organized system to satisfy their product needs. Such quality standards are less and less an option. William Petty, CEO of J. B. Tool & Machine in Wapakoneta, Ohio, says that comprehensive quality control systems keep increasingly demanding satisfied customers. The results? J. B. Tool was a $10 million company 6 years ago. Today, it's a $50 million plus company. And the next time a customer tells J. B. Tool to "prove it" it can easily respond with its QS-9000 certification.

Many organizations find it helpful to compare their quality success against a standard. For some, this means competing for awards such as the *Malcolm Baldrige National Quality Award* or the *Deming Award*. For others, the standard is ISO 9000 certification. Competing for one of the quality awards and seeking ISO 9000 certification are huge organizational efforts in which you'll likely participate. To learn more about the Baldrige Award, the Deming Award, and ISO 9000 and QS-9000 certification, look for them on the Web site that accompanies this book.[11] ❖

meeting customer expectations is even possible. For example, if most of the coffee you sell at your coffee shop is weaker than customers expect, then your brewing process may need some work. Both SPC tools are supported by IT systems. In large organizations, the control information is gathered and monitored by automated quality control systems. In smaller organizations, the control information is gathered manually and input into desktop computing systems to compute the SPC tools' variables. Because of the large amount of information gathered, IT systems enable much more extensive monitoring and enforce a rigor to the SPC tool process.

Continuous Improvement

You'd think that once you understood your customer's expectations and learned to meet them you'd be done. But those expectations change and so must you. And don't forget about your competition. They're always trying to beat you on product, service, and price. Consider Toronto-based Cadet Uniform Services Ltd., a uniform cleaning company that never takes its customers for granted.[12] "You have to improve the quality of your product to survive," says Cadet founder Quentin Wahl. For Quentin, continually improving has paid off. The company has lower per unit costs than most of its competitors, and that allows it to stay price competitive. And it boasts a customer retention rate of 99 percent, the highest in the industry. Those customers stick with Cadet because it never stops trying to improve. In the uniform cleaning industry, where thousands of similar-looking garments are cleaned and sorted, mistakes are common. But at Cadet, Quentin developed a fabric label that, when scanned, identifies the garment's owner and company. Now, Quentin says, only 3 to 6 garments a week out of 400,000 end up missing.

Of course, to improve you must identify the areas that provide the most opportunity for improvement. Three tools can help in this search. The fishbone diagram, or the cause and effect diagram, can facilitate this identification. A *fishbone diagram* is simply a line diagram that begins with a problem (the effect) and branches out into problem causes. Once completed, the diagram resembles the bones of a fish. The benefit of using a fishbone diagram is that you can separate root problem causes from causes that are simply the result of other causes. The pareto analysis is a tool related to the histogram. In a *pareto chart*, you gather frequencies of various problem causes, sort them, and calculate percentages for each. This analysis is used to target improvement efforts, because a small percentage of causes determine a large percentage of quality problems.

A scatter diagram is another tool. You create a *scatter diagram* by simply plotting paired data on a two-

axis graph. For example, for each worker we might plot the number of customer complaints against the hours of customer service training each has received. The scatter diagram will graphically depict any patterns in the data plotted. The customer complaint diagram then could reveal that training reduces the number of complaints a worker receives. Desktop computing resources support both the pareto analysis and the scatter diagram in organizations. The fishbone diagram is a tool used in group brainstorming environments and is best supported by networks and groupware systems.

> ## CAREER OPPORTUNITY
>
> Many other quality improvement tools are available to you. You can use these to facilitate brainstorming sessions in virtually any meeting. In fact, most of these tools exist in software form. Seek out these packages and incorporate them into your management tool kit.

Organizationwide Quality Ownership

TQM requires a commitment from every individual in the organization—quality is everyone's job. Along with this commitment everyone must have the power to ensure quality, which requires executive support and clear customer focus. When you combine individual commitment and power, employees develop a sense of ownership for their contributions to quality. And they communicate that sense of ownership to customers through better customer service. Quality ownership is practiced throughout Rod Stasik's The Lube Stop, a quick-oil-change company with 30 stores in the Cleveland area.[13] "Straightening out misunderstandings with customers is the job of everyone in the company," says Rod. "We're selling convenience and customer service. That's what customers expect," he explains. And quality ownership means employees do all they can to meet those customer expectations. Haven't you ever felt frustrated when a customer representative with whom you're dealing can't fix your problem? Have you ever wondered why you even bothered to talk to this person? Have you ever wished they would "own-up" to their responsibilities as a representative for that company? For every customer, the point-of-contact person *is* the company to the customer. And if that representative can't help that person, then from his or her perspective, the company just doesn't care. So, it doesn't matter if you work in accounting or engineering, everyone throughout the organization must own the job of quality.

TEAM WORK

Getting to the Bottom of a New Customer Problem

Suppose you work for a small bottled water company that has been advertising actively for new customers. The advertisements mention a new low introductory monthly price for a home bottled water dispenser. In some respects, the advertising campaign seems to be working. That is, customers are calling to request a dispenser and bottled water service. The problem is that they always seem to change their minds once the delivery person arrives. Why are they doing this?

Construct a fishbone diagram to diagnose the root cause or causes of this customer problem. Remember, many obvious causes of problems are actually the result of other causes. The goal is to find the root causes that we can target for improvement.

Below is an example fishbone diagram to get you started. The "head" of the fish is the problem statement. Each "bone" of the fish is a cause of the problem. Some of these causes have causes themselves that are listed on smaller "bone branches" (subcauses). For each root cause, brainstorm a solution. ❖

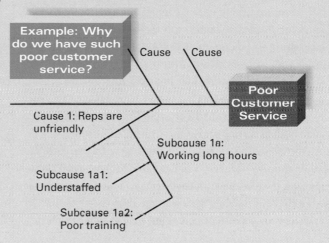

The Just-in-Time Approach

No Product Before Its Time

It's Saturday night and you're hunting for something good to watch on television. Just your luck, nothing's on. But wait, you have that satellite television hookup. You push a few buttons and the latest action thriller pops up on your screen. Just the movie you want, just when you want it. Instant gratification? Well, in business we call that just-in-time. The image of a surgeon sticking out a hand while barking scalpel, and a nurse instantly slapping one in the surgeon's hand, may not make us think of instant gratification. We think of great precision and teamwork. But it's also just-in-time.

The Just-in-Time Approach

What is the just-in-time approach?	■ The just-in-time approach is producing or delivering a product or service *when* the customer wants it.
What does just-in-time do?	■ It increases flexibility.
	■ It reduces inventory levels.
	■ It increases quality.
How does just-in-time affect OHP?	■ It increases organizational speed by decreasing the time to respond to a customer.
	■ The increased speed increases OHP.
How is just-in-time IT-enabled?	■ The just-in-time approach is built on IT telecommunications and scheduling capabilities. ❖

The approach of just-in-time is all of the above and more. Once confined to the manufacturing floor, just-in-time now applies to retail stores, the medical field, the entertainment and publishing industries, and to many others as well. Strictly defined, the *just-in-time (JIT)* approach is producing or delivering a product or service when the customer wants it. The JIT approach may be viewed from two perspectives—*internal* and *external* to your organization. From the external perspective, you would look at the firm as a customer or supplier. So, when a customer walks into your auto-repair shop and wants his or her car repaired today, you could use the JIT approach.

Traditionally, that could mean extra capacity, that is, extra mechanics, to handle any walk-in clients. But those mechanics could end up just sitting around. Using the JIT approach, you could form a partnership with other repair shops supported by an interorganizational system. Then, when a customer walks in when you're booked up, you would just check your IT system to find extra capacity at an affiliated shop and communicate your request. The customer would leave his or her car with you and the other shop would deliver a mechanic to fix the car, allowing you to deliver same day service. The customers get what they want, when they want it. Your shop responded instantly to customer need. That's an excellent example of organizational speed. And you used the JIT approach as seen from an external perspective.

From an internal perspective, JIT means supplying internal products and services just as they are needed. If shipping requires different products daily, the production department must be flexible; otherwise delays are certain to occur. For the manufacturing floor, this means producing one product one day and another the next. Compaq, a computer manufacturer, uses a method called cell manufacturing to implement just-in-time.[14] Manufacturing in small "cells" or workstations instead of on assembly lines means Compaq must first receive an order, and *then* it produces the computer. So, on cell manufactured products, Compaq doesn't produce products in the hope that a customer will buy them. This kind of flexibility generates organizational speed, which allows Compaq to respond at the moment customer want is identified. Employing JIT is both efficient and powerful.

But Why Just-in-Time?

Producing products and services precisely when they are required is a powerful strategy to meet emerging customer wants and needs. This also means that you won't be producing what customers don't want. Responding quickly to demand prevents overproducing. Maybe this

INDUSTRY PERSPECTIVE **Health Care**

Just-in-Time Surgery

Don't tell Joe, but some 200 items for his coronary bypass surgery didn't arrive at the hospital until just as Joe was being rolled into the operating room. Joe, and many other patients like him, are experiencing, firsthand, the just-in-time delivery system called ValueLink, employed by Baxter International of Deerfield, Illinois. As a supplier of medical products, Baxter relieves hospitals from the cost of carrying inventory. With the costs of health care rising fast, Baxter customers,

like Dr. Bruce Capehart at Duke University Medical Center, find the just-in-time system appealing. He says, "We're not simply slowing the rate of increase in the cost of health care. We've achieved a real decrease."

Still, Baxter has extended the concept of just-in-time delivery by entering into risk-sharing agreements. Each year, Baxter and its risk-sharing partners split any cost savings they achieve—or jointly cough up for overruns. So far, the agreements have generated savings for Baxter's customers by standardizing the items required for surgical procedures. For example, in the case of arthroscopic

knee surgery, Baxter persuaded eight Duke physicians to eliminate excessive variety and use more of the same items. That move reduced the cost per operation by 25 percent. Before the agreement, Duke's supply costs had risen 31 percent from 1991 to 1994. Using this approach, both Duke and Baxter benefit. Duke's medical supply costs drop because of reduced variety and reduced inventory. Baxter achieves a higher level of customer satisfaction while the reduced product variety eases the task of just-in-time delivery.[15] ❖

is an obvious point, but the benefits are not always obvious. Overproducing creates several problems, including

- *Unsold inventories* that must be stored in costly warehouses
- *New-product delays* until existing inventories are sold
- *Quality lapses* when defects aren't caught until quality control catches up with inventory

The JIT approach prevents such problems from occurring by focusing on production timing and quantity, all driven by customer demands. So JIT allows your firm to reduce the costs associated with overproduction and gain the benefits of meeting customer needs. And along the way, JIT will increase your organization's speed by reducing delays associated with inventories. All of these factors create significant competitive advantages.

Just-in-Time Supported by Sophisticated Technology

Implementation of the JIT approach from the external perspective requires interorganizational systems to streamline the customer-to-supplier communication. EDI, discussed in Chapter 2, supports fast product and service delivery by providing quick informational delivery in support of this commerce.

Internal implementation of the JIT approach requires the proactive support of several IT systems. These systems don't wait until the customer places an order; rather they help you anticipate the demand. Without these systems, customers have to either hope the product is in stock or wait for the entire product to be manufactured. Let's look at these supporting IT systems. First, you must be able to predict accurately your production processes. ***Production scheduling*** systems provide detailed plans for producing all components of a final product. These systems use sales forecasts and existing customer orders to predict how much product must be produced. As customer wants change frequently, organizations need the accuracy and speed of IT systems in calculating required production from sales numbers. Many manufactured products have so many raw materials and components that the production calculation becomes much more complicated.

Material requirements planning (MRP) systems take the production schedule and determine which raw materials and components are required and when. Each component used to create a product has a *bill of material* that lists materials required for construction. MRP systems take the bill of material information and dissect it to discover the required raw materials. Most raw materials

ordered from suppliers have some lead time between the time ordered and the time received. In addition, it takes time to construct components from these raw materials. All of these material requirements and their necessary lead times create a complicated matrix of needs that the MRP system works through each time the input production schedule changes. This means an organization using the JIT approach can quickly and accurately determine which raw materials to order and when, often as frequently as customers change their minds.

Extending the MRP concept beyond manufacturing resulted in a new system name, ***manufacturing resource planning II (MRP II)***. MRP II systems tie material requirements from MRP systems into other organizational systems to integrate financial, human resource, and marketing needs into the scheduling. Changes in customer wants affect more than the raw materials the manufacturing department needs. These customer changes also affect resource requirements in a number of departments, including finance, human resources, purchasing, accounting, and marketing. For example, if customer demand increases, the finance department may need to process more credit applications. Likewise, the accounting department must process more accounts receivables from those customers and more accounts payables to suppliers. Most departments can benefit from the resource planning capabilities of MRP II. Extending resource planning with IT beyond the manufacturing function permits extension of the JIT strategy beyond the manufacturing function as well. Thus departments from accounting to sales can deliver services internally just-in-time to the internal customer of those services. For example, if the accounting department can plan accounts receivable work, then the accounting department can more easily deliver these accounts to the credit department as needed. MRP II helps allocate resources stretched thin by the JIT strategy.

Teams in an Organization

More Than Just Departments

The use of teams in organizations seems such a simple concept, deceivingly simple actually. But they can be so powerful in an organization. Teams built the Boeing Co.'s newest airliner, the 777.[16] Eight thousand employees from 200 disciplines had to figure out how to create an airplane that has 2 million parts while designing it completely on a computer. That, alone, would be a challenge for any organization. But Boeing also wanted to reduce

What are teams in an organization?	▪ A team is a group of people with a shared goal and task interdependence.
What do teams in an organization do?	▪ They provide diverse perspectives for a collaborative effort.
How do teams in an organization affect OHP?	▪ Team productivity greatly increases organizational force and thus OHP.
How are teams in an organization IT-enabled?	▪ Groupware supports working in teams. ❖

design changes and rework by 50 percent. Not satisfied with 50 percent, Boeing's 777 teams achieved reductions of 60 to 90 percent. The ultimate success, though, is in the competitive advantage Boeing gained. Thanks to the 777 project, Boeing gained a 68 percent market share and over 100 orders for the 777.

Strictly defined, a *team* is a group of people with a shared goal and task interdependence. That definition really contains three parts—a group of people, a shared goal, and task interdependence. Teams contain groups of people that gather from all corners of the organization, called *cross-functional teams.* For the team to have a focus, all team members must share a common goal. Last, team members must work together on tasks that depend upon one another, that is, *task interdependence.*

There are two main types of teams in an organization—project teams and permanent teams. The team effort at Boeing is an example of a project team. **Project teams** are designed to accomplish specific one-time goals and disband once the project is complete. These teams are similar to the temporary workgroups mentioned in Chapter 2. **Permanent teams** are designed to support permanent processes and are not intended to be disbanded. These teams are similar to the permanent workgroups in Chapter 2. They might be continuous improvement teams in a TQM program, or they could be business process teams that manage a process.

Permanent teams may augment or replace a more traditional departmental structure. At Medtronic Inc., the Minneapolis-based maker of heart pacemakers, permanent teams are the new organizational structure.[17] Since 1991, the company has been reorganizing into two permanent teams, designers and manufacturers. The culture in the two processes is so different, two teams seemed a natural approach. You see, designers at Medtronic are quite free-spirited and experimental. And that culture clashes with the highly disciplined manufacturers. Has it helped? From 1991 to 1996, Medtronic's sales have increased 70 percent, with earnings up even

higher at 120 percent. For Medtronic, at least, permanent teams are creating tremendous OHP.

Permanent teams as a new organizational structure have many benefits over a departmental structure. Because teams unite employees from different functional areas the members' diverse backgrounds promote new idea generation. Many organizations using permanent teams as part of their structure evaluate the team as a group and even base team members' compensation on the team's performance. Even without linking group performance with pay, it's important to reinforce team responsibility with team power. This extends to team spirit as well. Teams within your organization should work cooperatively, otherwise they fall into the trap of competitive spirit. Although competitiveness can be helpful, it often means employees pursue very different goals, sometimes in conflict with other teams or perhaps even the overall strategic direction of the organization.

All teams, whether project or permanent, create OHP by generating organizational force. They allow an organization to reach new markets with ideas that are new to the firm. Teams also create a synergy of ideas that firms often don't even realize they have. For them, it's new-found strength. However, because such idea generation between cross-functional team members is so hard to predict, teams often reduce an organization's speed. Clearly, organizations must recognize this OHP trade-off and strive to gain more OHP through force than they might lose in speed.

Information Technology Enables Teams

ITT Hartford Insurance Group needed help.[18] Everyone from underwriters to customer support personnel seemed to be working against each other. An analysis revealed that the average time to process a new customer's application was 19 days, when the total time spent actually working on the application was only 3 hours. "The

INDUSTRY PERSPECTIVE

Food

Learning to Collaborate at Nabisco

Teams can powerfully affect an organization's ability to innovate. That is, of course, if the organization's various functional areas know how to work together. Sometimes this is quite a struggle. At Nabisco Corp. in Parsippany, New Jersey, exchanging ideas across functional lines required some help at first.

Nabisco found its solution in groupware; by using it to support the public exchange of ideas, Nabisco "introduced collaboration to users," recalls Erik Iversen, director of application development services. The electronic interface helped break down organizational barriers and allowed accountants to become accustomed to discussing ideas with engineers, for example. This first step facilitated the use of teams within Nabisco. Today, more than 3,500 people participate in discussion groups at Nabisco.

Using groupware to promote collaborative efforts within cross-functional teams is an excellent way to overcome cultural barriers. The groupware interface is really faceless; you are evaluated only on the merit of your ideas. But in addition to overcoming cultural barriers, groupware breaks time and location barriers as well. Maybe you have manufacturing engineers who work on a graveyard shift. Losing their input because of inconvenient team meeting schedules can now be avoided.[19] ❖

---

assembly line way of doing things was seriously impeding our ability to get quotes out of the door and win business," explained Jack Crawford, senior vice president for ITT Hartford.

So ITT Hartford organized its branch offices into cross-functional teams with common goals and a common base of information. The team structure gave local employees more power and responsibility. The tools they needed were information connectivity and work flow automation software. ITT Hartford linked together the team members within each office, as well as in the branch offices. Links were established using a local area network and telecommunications, which we'll discuss in more detail in Chapter 6. Work flow automation software provided another key to team productivity. As applications or other transactions require attention, the work flow automation software routes the necessary documents automatically from person to person at the appropriate time. Team members also make extensive use of e-mail to facilitate communication.

Have teams and the supporting IT helped ITT Hartford? Remember those pesky policy quotes that took so long to process? Well, team members now process those business account quotes within a day. And information-empowered team members can now answer most customer questions in a single phone call instead of several calls. ITT Hartford uses groupware technology to support its teams. But that support extends beyond e-mail and work flow automation software to include

- Group scheduling software ⎤
- Electronic meeting software |
- Videoconferencing software | Team Dynamics Support
- Whiteboard software ⎦

This software supports the team dynamic. Transaction processing systems and management information systems also support teams as an organizational structure, just as they support a departmental structure.

The Information Partnership

Learning to Share

In Chapter 2 we discussed interorganizational systems (IOSs) that automate the flow of information between organizations. We examined EDI as the fundamental IOS required for all sharing of information between organizations. IOSs support an OHP strategy called information partnerships. An ***information partnership*** is an agreement between organizations for the sharing of information to strengthen each partner organization. Information partners gain increased organizational force by reaching a greater market. Information partners also gain organizational speed by automating the information flow between partner organizations. When partners share strategic information, they gain both organizational

The Information Partnership

What is an information partnership?	■ An information partnership is an agreement between organizations for the sharing of information to strengthen each partner organization.
What does an information partnership do?	■ It creates organizational synergy from complementary resources at participating organizations.
How does an information partnership affect OHP?	■ It increases organizational force by reaching new customers or discovering new cost-reduction techniques. ■ It increases organizational speed by streamlining the purchasing and receiving process.
How is an information partnership IT-enabled?	■ EDI forms the bedrock of the information partnership. ❖

force and speed by reaching markets they've never considered before and by bringing products to market more quickly through a combined design effort. So we have three different information partnership strategies, each characterized by the type and magnitude of OHP they generate, as you can see in Figure 3.3.

All three information partnership strategies generate OHP by leveraging information sharing. The purpose or the focus may differ but all information partnerships involve organizations that share information. And this sharing is supported by IOSs, although their application differs depending on the partnership

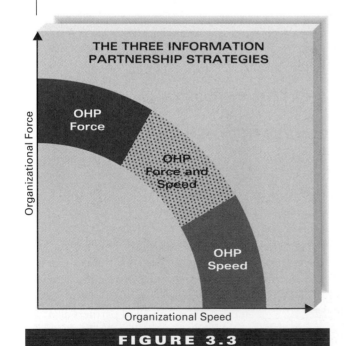

THE THREE INFORMATION PARTNERSHIP STRATEGIES

OHP Force

OHP Force and Speed

OHP Speed

Organizational Force

Organizational Speed

FIGURE 3.3

Three Information Partnership Strategies

focus. Let's examine each variation on the information partnership strategy, noting the purpose of each variation as well as how an IOS might support the strategy.

An Information Partnership for OHP Speed

The simplest information partnership strategy generates organizational speed by automating the information flow between partner organizations. The partners usually assume the role of customer and supplier and share information necessary to complete business transactions, like product sales, for example. Because the information flow is automated, business transactions can proceed much more quickly. Business volume in general increases for both organizations and, because the transaction information is in a standard form, transaction errors are greatly reduced. Partners do not modify their product offerings or their target markets. Simply put, the partners do what they've always done, just faster. An IOS using EDI supports this information partnership strategy.

Westinghouse implemented EDI to streamline the procurement process for many of its larger customers. One such customer is Portland General Electric (PGE). Because PGE now uses EDI with Westinghouse, time from order to delivery has been cut from 15 days to ½ day, and processing costs have been slashed from $90 to $10.

An Information Partnership for OHP Force

Another information partnership strategy is the pursuit of OHP force generated by sharing information to reach a larger market. For example, many grocery chains issue preferred customer cards that give customers discount coupons when they make purchases. The grocery chain shares the purchase information with supplier organizations. However, few customers know that this sharing takes place. Suppliers can now target coupon mailings directly to customers who use their products. In so doing, they expand their market reach and OHP force. This information partnership strategy owes its significance to two trends. First, organizations today regularly capture customer information while conducting business. Information in electronic form can be used, manipulated, and sold. The advent of efficient TPSs has facilitated this development. Second, organizations have learned to gather the information in a meaningful way. For example, an organization will not only capture a customer's name and address, but relate that information to average income information for the customer's neighborhood. In this way, the information becomes more meaningful and thus more valuable. With such value attributed to the information, other organizations now view the sharing of information as worthwhile.

The information sharing is not always about customers, however. The consulting firm, Price Waterhouse, recently established an organizational best-practices partnership.[20] This partnership allows all participating organizations to share quantitative measures of performance, like how long it takes a firm to design a new product. This information partnership strategy, however, joins organizations through information only. No organizational joining or breaking of organizational barriers occurs. So, EDI and IOSs using networking technology support this strategy.

An Information Partnership for OHP Force and Speed

Some organizations take the concept of an information partnership much further. These organizations share information that is strategic in nature and affects their fundamental business strategy. A bakery firm might share information about its decision to expand into other food products, for example. A potential information partner might wish to be in the bakery business and decide to share that information with the bakery. The information

---

INDUSTRY PERSPECTIVE　　　　**Retail**

Retailers Who Avoid Safety

Do you *avoid* safety? Some retailers do. You see, to ensure that they have what you want, most retailers stock slightly more than they've forecasted you'll buy. They call this extra inventory safety stock and it's expensive to store. Today, experts value industry safety stock inventories at over $700 billion. To reduce that inventory cost the nation's largest retailer, Wal-Mart Stores, Inc., in Bentonville, Arkansas, and one of its suppliers, Warner-Lambert Co. in Morris Plains, New Jersey, have entered into an information partnership for organizational speed. What's unique about this partnership for speed is how far beyond EDI the partnership goes.

Most information partnerships for speed center around the use of electronic data interchange (EDI) for sending and receiving purchase orders and confirmations in a standard format. The partnership between Wal-Mart and Warner-Lambert uses the Internet to allow partners to communicate interactively about sales forecasts. The partners use this interorganizational system (IOS) to share information about virtually everything that might impact sales—from planned changes in store layouts to precise meteorological data about pollen counts and when flu season will hit a certain region. The partners then jointly create sales forecasts. The IOS requires communication standards that are much broader than those for EDI so that partners can share a much wider range of information. For

Wal-Mart and Warner-Lambert, they have taken a full 2 ½ weeks off the time a product spends in the supply chain. That is, how long from the time a product is manufactured to the day it's bought. And that 2 ½ weeks translates into millions saved in reduced inventory. So, with benefits like that, retailers and their suppliers are reconsidering the highly confidential way in which they now create sales forecasts. If you or your organization is interested in creating sales forecasts through an information partnership, visit the Web site for the Collaborative Forecasting and Replenishment Initiative (CFAR) (http://www. benchmarking.com) for communication specifications.[21] ❖

sharing is synergistic in that both partners benefit by innovating new business strategies. Each respective partner reaches these innovations faster than he or she would alone and therefore gains OHP speed. Partners also reach more customers than before and therefore gain OHP force. The information sharing required for both OHP force and speed involves breaking down organizational barriers, and customers often see a new product or service that has no visible relationship to the founding partners. This differs quite a bit from either the partnership for force or the partnership for speed.

An excellent example of an information partnership for OHP force and speed is that between JM Mold of Piqua, Ohio, and Futura Plastics of Louisville, Kentucky.[22] Recently, when Hydro Systems of Cincinnati, Ohio, contacted Futura about a project, Futura did some preliminary work and then suggested JM Mold participate in some sales calls. Before long, the partners won the contract, with Futura handling manufacturing and JM Mold handling the tooling. The key is the way they structured this relationship. Both organizations worked interactively on design changes. Neither organization could have handled the entire project alone, and could not have overcome the budget and time constraints by outsourcing part of the work. Only through working together, sharing real-time information, were both organizations able to win the business and profit.

Surprisingly, technology was not the largest hurdle to overcome for this partnership strategy. IOSs easily support the interactive design and production work. The toughest part for the organizations was in reconsidering their respective places in the market. Ed Kinsella, a JM Mold manager, put it nicely, "Don't think of your company as a small pool of resources surrounded by fierce competitors. Think of yourself in the middle of a very large resource pool controlled by competitors who can be your partners. That way you can take on just about any job."

Information partnerships for force and speed create many benefits for the partner organizations. These benefits include

- Sharing of resources, informational as well as fixed assets, expertise, and funds

- Gaining access to new customers of the member organizations

- Taking advantage of new opportunities such as products or services not previously provided or capable of being produced

All of the above benefits require more trust, more communication, and more IOSs than does a partnership for either force or speed alone. Still, these benefits generate great OHP force and speed to support a growing business.

Timeless and Locationless Operations

Anywhere, 24 Hours a Day

Quite a few years ago, Sears & Roebuck devised a way to take the store to the customer—Sears called it mail order. As a result, customers could have the product *where* they wanted it—at home. But even ordering through the mail left room for improvement, so mail-order firms installed toll-free numbers to handle the customer's orders.

Timeless and Locationless Operations

What are timeless operations?	■ Timeless operations are operations that use IT to operate without regard to time.
What are locationless operations?	■ Locationless operations are operations that use IT to operate without regard to location.
What do timeless and locationless operations do?	■ They put an organization to work 24 hours a day. ■ They create a presence for the organization everywhere.
How do timeless and locationless operations affect OHP?	■ They increase organizational force by reaching more customers at the customer's location. ■ They increase organizational speed through simultaneous, independent work and by serving customers whenever they want.
How are timeless and locationless operations IT-enabled?	■ Timeless and locationless operations require IT to tie the operations together. ❖

Virtually any time a customer called, an operator was waiting to take the order. This meant that customers could order *whenever* they wanted. IT now allows such firms to install automated phone-order systems to take orders 24 hours a day. Finding a way to deliver when and where a customer wants with IT gives your firm a competitive advantage.

You can apply a timeless and locationless strategy to almost any operation within a business. Precisely what do we mean by timeless and locationless? Well, simply put, *timeless operations* operate without regard to time. For example, e-mail allows a worker in Hong Kong to communicate with a colleague in New York long after the worker in New York has gone to sleep. *Locationless operations* operate without regard to location. Using electronic commerce, for example, businesses can create virtual stores that exist wherever the customer is. There is only one time and place that truly matters for a business, and that is the time and the place the customer wants service. Using a timeless operational strategy, organizational speed increases by allowing customers to order 24 hours a day from "virtual stores." Those same virtual stores generate organizational force by placing them everywhere the customer wants them. Even maximizing the internal operations located around the globe with telecommunications means your organization develops products and services faster. IT systems never sleep and can provide a time bridge enabling consecutive operation. Locationless operations allow your firm to establish operations at geographically suitable sites. This might mean cost-effective manufacturing in Mexico, marketing expertise in Canada, or just an engineer working from home.

But What Operation?

Timeless and locationless strategies apply to many organizational operations. And the list grows every day, as IT systems that enable them become more available. The best approach to selecting target operations within your firm is to examine how other firms apply this strategy. Take a look at Table 3.1 for a summary of targeted operations. Then we'll review the firms that have met with success in targeting these operations.

Locationless Retail Sales

Perry and Monica Lopez's Hot Hot Hot store in Pasadena, California, occupies only 300 square feet.[23] Certainly that tiny store couldn't possibly serve as many customers as a large Wal-Mart store. But that doesn't mean there isn't a strategy to allow them to do so. Perry and Monica established a virtual store on the Internet, and now more than 1,500 people drop by every day (http://www.hothothot.com). To match that exposure in their Pasadena store, Perry and Monica would have to see more than three new customers every minute. This implementation is not solely timeless or locationless. The Lopez's virtual store is open 24 hours a day. Certainly not something Perry and Monica want for their Pasadena store. But from the customer's perspective, Hot Hot Hot is *where* the customer wants it (on their home computer) *and* available *when* they want it (24 hours a day).

Timeless Meter Reading

If you've ever lived in a house where the electric meter is hard to access (maybe in a locked backyard), you know how annoying it is to miss the meter reader. Most utility

---

TABLE 3.1   Successful Timeless and Locationless Operations

Which Operation?	Timeless or Locationless?	What Benefit?	What Firm?
Retail sales	Locationless	Can see more customers than could fit in the store	Hot Hot Hot
Meter reading	Timeless	Never fail to capture customer consumption	Kansas City Power & Light
Customer service	Timeless	Customers service themselves whenever they want	Cisco Systems
Manufacturing	Locationless	The small fixed-asset investment reduces risk	Dell Computers
Knowledge worker	Locationless	Can work anywhere	Paul, Hastings, Janofsky & Walker

companies make a guess at your electrical consumption and wait until an actual meter reading can take place, sometimes months later. If the utility company's guess was low, you get a bill for the difference. And that can be something of a shock. These problems are history for customers of Kansas City Power & Light Company.[24] The utility installed radio transmitters in homes throughout Kansas City to communicate customer consumption of electricity, and even water and gas. The power company's customers want to do business regularly every month. Now time is no longer an ugly barrier between the utility company and its customers. The communication capability the utility company installed results in timeless customer transactions and improved customer service.

Timeless Customer Service

For companies in the technology business, customer service is a critical organizational operation. The sophisticated nature of the products requires extensive after-the-sale service. This is a taxing operation that drains OHP. Customers want that after-the-sale service whenever they need it and have little tolerance for delays. Cisco Systems, a computer-networking company, has found a solution in online customer service.[25] Cisco has grown rapidly over the last few years, and so have its

customer service inquires. Because customer service engineers cost Cisco as much as $100,000 a year, you can see why the company sought to reduce that cost. With online customer service on the Internet, customers can read manuals, ask specific questions, get automated responses, and even get personal alerts about problems with their software. All of this occurs on demand, day or night. This keeps customers happy and saves Cisco over $45 million a year.

Locationless Manufacturing

Have you ever bought a Dell Computer? Maybe you know someone who has. Where was it manufactured? Do you even care? That was at least a part of the reasoning behind Dell Computers' locationless manufacturing strategy. You see, Dell doesn't manufacture anything. Dell buys components, designed specifically for it, and simply puts them all together in its own warehouse. The strategy works for Dell for two reasons. First, the manufacturing location is unimportant to the customer. Customers receive their computers through the mail. Second, component manufacturing is not Dell's strength. Dell excels in marketing computers and has little desire to dilute its OHP with poor operations. So, financially, Dell can boast almost $50 in sales for every dollar invested in plant and equip-

INDUSTRY PERSPECTIVE — IT & Telecommunications

Who Are You Calling?

When you call a toll-free number from an Apple Computer advertisement, are you really calling Apple? If you call AT&T WorldNet to sign up for Internet access, are you really calling AT&T? From the other end of a telephone line it's a bit hard to tell, but the answer to both questions is, of course, no. Either phone call will connect you to TeleTech Holdings Inc., in Denver, Colorado. The reasoning behind TeleTech's business is clear—companies can't handle all their customer service calls. In the past, companies competed primarily in their own domestic market, which limited their customer base. Today, companies compete in the global marketplace and find supporting all those customer calls is more than they can handle. And today's IT systems place all of a company's customer and product information in databases at the tip of a customer service rep's fingers, regardless of where that rep is located or for whom he or she works. Therein lies the opportunity for firms like TeleTech.

IT systems are the key to *locationless* customer service operations. Most people would guess that if you called with questions about a new service offered by United Parcel Service (UPS), for example, the rep might need to reference volumes of manuals. TeleTech, however, which handles some UPS calls, maintains a *paperless office*. Reference materials are all read on computer screens and even notes are handled electronically, all of which provides TeleTech's customers with cost-effective customer support. And with such knowledgeable reps, callers never feel as if they got a wrong number.[26] ❖

ment versus $3.50 for a real computer manufacturer like IBM. Dell's locationless manufacturing means customers receive their computers *where* they want them (on their doorsteps) and Dell profits.

Locationless Knowledge Workers

Imagine driving through Atlanta, Georgia, during the 1996 Summer Olympic Games. You might have spent more time in traffic jams than actually driving. Certainly, businesses in Atlanta worried about workers being able to get to work during the Olympic Games. One local law firm armed 75 attorneys and law clerks with computers and sent them home.[27] These workers from the law firm of Paul, Hastings, Janofsky & Walker avoided the traffic snarls and conducted "business as usual" from home. In fact, few clients were even aware that their respective attorneys weren't at the office. It's likely that this strategy will increase. "One thing to come out of the Olympics is an increased demand for telecommuting after the Games as employees say, 'This is neat—I can do my job from home,'" added Steve Saussy, supervisor of MIS for the Atlanta law firm. And this Atlanta law firm is not alone in promoting telecommuting. In fact, this type of locationless strategy is so prevalent it deserves a closer look.

In Support of the Telecommuter

Lawyers represent but one group of telecommuting professionals. You can telecommute, or work away from the main office, in many types of jobs. And businesses with telecommuting workers have begun to value the locationless business—one that is less dependent upon geographic space. Some barely have a location at all. At EDS, a Plano, Texas, consulting firm, over 2,000 of its 3,000 consultants work outside the Plano office.[28] With so many people working outside the "base" office, the geographic location of the home office could be a matter of opinion. And just maybe, it's irrelevant. Still, all these people are full-time EDS employees and EDS must manage and motivate them in the same way it motivates its traditional employees.

Making Telecommuting Work

Telecommuters and their employers must create their own work space—a virtual workplace. From the employer's perspective, the virtual workplace has requirements over and above those of the "real" workplace. Figure 3.4 lists five components of the virtual workplace. Let's discuss them.

First, you'll need *communication technology* to transfer assignments and work, both in progress and completed.

This technology includes phone lines, modems, and e-mail software. Second, it's important to maintain *constant communication* with all telecommuters. There is a real tendency to procrastinate necessary dialogue just because employees are off-site. E-mail is an excellent tool for everyday communication because of its timeless nature. If you're going to use e-mail, though, your employees must use it diligently as well. Third, create a program for *goal setting and monitoring*. Telecommuting isn't for everyone, and you must track performance to determine which employees are best suited for telecommuting. Laurie Coots, chief operating officer for the advertising agency Chiat/Day in Los Angeles, puts it bluntly, "It's goal-oriented: Did you do what you said you'd do? We're not interested in chair warmers."[29]

The fourth requirement is scheduling *physical meetings*. Bringing off-site employees to the main office cultivates teamwork and loyalty. Remember, these telecommuters are your employees and must understand the vision of your firm. Fifth, you must provide your telecommuters with *information access*—they must have access to the firm's collective knowledge. On-site employees can step into the file room, stroll down the hall to a coworker's office, or even ask another department manager for details about a project. Off-site employees lack these conveniences, so you must help them stay connected to organizational information, perhaps through databases or data warehouses.

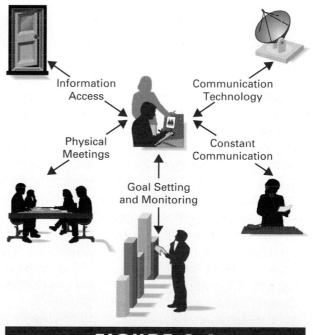

FIGURE 3.4
Key Components of Your Virtual Workplace

Key Timeless and Locationless Ingredients

All timeless and locationless operations share certain key ingredients. Information technology is an absolutely essential key ingredient to creating timeless and locationless operations. Your business must understand electronic commerce and support its operation. Telecommunication networks are also a key ingredient. Networks are discussed in Chapter 6. Establishing locationless operations also requires a working relationship with other businesses that sell complementary products and services. And, of course, your firm must have customers who expect round-the-clock access to you. Even if your customers do not yet have that expectation, you should anticipate it.

The Transnational Firm

Everywhere You Want to Be

The transnational firm extends the locationless operations strategy around the globe. So much so that it's difficult to know which country is the firm's home country. That's certainly true with automobile manufacturers like Honda, an auto manufacturer headquartered in Japan that is now manufacturing more cars outside than inside Japan.[30] Honda also sells globally. Amazingly, it exports more cars from the United States than does General Motors, Ford, or Chrysler. Operating extensively outside the country of origin is a hallmark of the transnational firm. But why should your organization go international with its operations? That's a good question—let's find some answers.

Operating internationally benefits a firm because it gains access to more customer markets around the globe. Using IT to link these geographically dispersed operations, organizational force is magnified more than any other OHP strategy. Having a presence in every major market in the world commands a powerful competitive position. Your firm also can generate organizational force through the economies of scale that accrue through massive global production. And a firm operating internationally with IT accumulates diverse intellectual resources

INDUSTRY PERSPECTIVE

Entertainment & Publishing

Where the Left and Right Sides of the Brain Meet

If you could imagine a place that brought the worlds of art and science together, where would that place be? Strangely enough, that spot may be the Internet, where time and location have no meaning. Although precisely how the Internet will be used in the future is a matter for debate, there is little argument over the need for Web sites that are both technically sophisticated and aesthetically pleasing.

Consider SonicNet's attempts to meet Internet needs. SonicNet provides information about alternative music through the Internet (http://www.sonicnet.com). Nicholas Butterworth, SonicNet's creative director, finds operating on the Internet requires skills from many worlds. "How do you get someone from a technical background to work with someone from a film background? An illustrator may know nothing about quality assurance, and a programmer may not understand why a copy editor takes so long worrying over one sentence. The hard part is developing a common language, and that's what we're trying to do." Developing a common language is key, although the timeless, locationless nature of the Internet reduces other barriers to communication that surface in face-to-face meetings. So it may be that the Internet is not only the ultimate timeless and locationless medium, but also the ultimate bridge between art and science.[31] ❖

The Transnational Firm

What is the transnational firm?	■ A transnational firm is one that produces and sells products and services in countries all over the world in coordinated cooperation.
What does the transnational firm do?	■ It expands the scope and breadth of a firm's operations.
How does the transnational firm affect OHP?	■ It geographically disperses operations to strengthen a firm's organizational force.
	■ It may positively or negatively affect organizational speed, depending on implementation.
How is the transnational firm IT-enabled?	■ Extensive use of IT networks facilitates coordination and synergy for the transnational firm. ❖

not available to domestic firms. This IT enabled resource synergizes a firm's market competitiveness.

International operations also diversify a company's market risk. Often windows of opportunity in one market offset the lack of opportunity in another. And some opportunities might be invisible without benefit of a firm's operations in another country. For example, a transnational firm operating in both the United States and Mexico would see that the labor cost in Mexico is 15 percent that of the United States.[32] A firm operating in the United States alone might not be aware of that opportunity.

Clearly, operating internationally is a forceful strategy for your firm. Implementing this international strategy begins with three different configurations—global, multinational, and transnational (see Photo Essay 3-1). In a **global configuration**, all international operations depend on headquarters for resources and direction. Therefore information directives travel one way from headquarters to operations. In a **multinational configuration**, international operations operate independently, reporting only financial information to headquarters. Or a firm may construct a **transnational configuration**, becoming a **transnational firm** that produces and sells products and services in countries all over the world in coordinated cooperation. All operations share information and resources, so the notion of a "headquarters" becomes irrelevant.

Transnational Firm Critical Success Factors

Two critical factors determine the success of transnational operations. First, to adopt a transnational firm strategy your organization must carefully balance local uniqueness with global uniformity. Customers around the world want your firm to cater to their unique cultural and national needs. Your firm's international operations must reflect that uniqueness in marketing, sales, human resources, and legal conformance. At the same time, your firm must operate with a global standard of excellence. Whether a customer walks into a McDonald's restaurant or a Citibank bank, he or she wants that comforting feeling of familiarity. Customers want you to reinforce their selection of your specific firm. For example, Citibank operates 1,200 branch offices in 41 countries, each with the same blue awning and Citibank feel.[33] From any branch you can access your Citibank account whether it was opened next door or on the other side of the world.

Second, adopting a transnational firm strategy means your organization must create a global IT *infrastructure* that supports the first critical success factor. That is, hardware, software, and telecommunications networks must support both a global brand and local independence. You are far more likely to travel internationally than your ancestors were. And that means you're far more likely to do business with a transnational firm's international operations. You might need access to your checking account back home, for example. In the past, such an international transaction was very unlikely, so consumers' expectations did not include real-time international transactions. Today, however, you would expect a bank to readily cash your international check in one visit to the bank. You expect to use your Visa card in almost any shop in the world, instantly. These customer expectations require you to establish international transaction processing systems (TPSs) and customer integrated systems (CISs).

Three Configurations for Operating Internationally

THE GLOBAL CONFIGURATION

Headquarters directs all international operations, and the operations are dependent on headquarters for most resources.

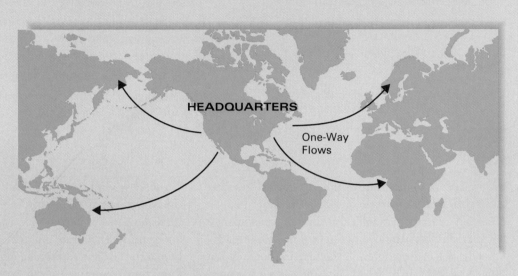

THE MULTINATIONAL CONFIGURATION

International operations report to headquarters while operating mostly independently.

THE TRANSNATIONAL CONFIGURATION

All operations share information and other resources with each other.

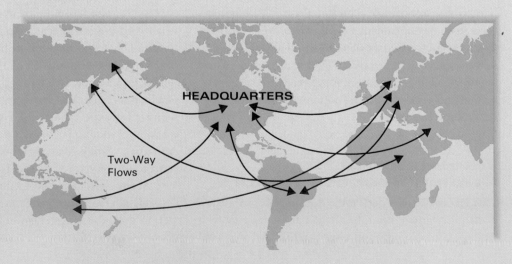

Transnational firms need more than just TPSs and CISs; they must access their global knowledge resources. Geographically dispersed experts need to work together in deciding the firm's direction. That means establishing global decision support systems (DSSs), management information systems (MISs), and workgroup support systems (WSSs).

Transnational Firm Challenges

With resources spread across the globe, the transnational firm must ensure that resource duplication does not occur among locations. Multinational firms maintain independent operations and often duplicate resources because they lack interoperational communication. To benefit from transnational integration, international operations must communicate with each other to eliminate this redundancy. Communicating in this way also reduces the isolation of international operations. Often language or cultural barriers create isolation. The multitude of translation tools available today can break those barriers. For example, you can purchase Internet communication software, like Netscape Navigator, that translates between 18 different languages and dialects. Other software allows you to translate even more languages.

In addition to integrating operations, transnational firms must learn to integrate strategies as well. If a transnational firm decides to incorporate a team organizational strategy, then multifunctional teams will be *multinational* teams as well. Common processes, such as purchasing, will probably occur in locations all over the globe, so redesigning these processes to take advantage of teams requires input from each of those operations.

Although transnational firms operate in an almost borderless fashion, real political borders still exist and create hurdles. For example, sending financial information to a colleague in Taiwan could be problematic. Information crossing borders, called ***transborder data flows***, is subject to customs regulations just like any other product.

To create a transnational information infrastructure, the telecommunications standards in various countries must be considered. For example, if telephone service is unavailable or unreliable, you would consider using cellular or satellite services. Will you use existing telecommunications media or build your own? Will the country's government allow such an investment?

Operating internationally can create some surprising ethical challenges. Taking advantage of a competitive opportunity in one country may be viewed as exploitation in another. For example, inexpensive labor costs in one country may be the result of what another country considers unethical labor practices. Avoiding such dilemmas requires coordination on a global basis. It is important to understand cultural standards as well as communication practices across the transnational firm.

Listening All Over the World

THE GLOBAL **PERSPECTIVE**

Countless times every day, up to 420 passengers travel in the same airplane, at the same time, and go to the same place. That's the role of the world's largest passenger aircraft, the Boeing 747. It seems hard to imagine the need for an aircraft any larger, doesn't it? And that might have been the thinking at Boeing Co. of Seattle, Washington; but listening to the customers, wherever they may be, is a prime tenet of any truly *transnational* firm.

In Asia, airlines must move passengers in and out of highly congested airports. Therefore, increasing aircraft capacity has become important for Asian airlines, like Hong Kong-based Cathay Pacific Airways Ltd. So it's critical to the success of Boeing to communicate this information back to the decision makers. Rod Eddingtion, Cathay Pacific managing director, knows Boeing's communication channels are open all the way to the CEO of Boeing, Phil Condit. "Phil Condit has done a terrific job of involving the customer at every stage of development," Rod confirms. As a result, Boeing has announced plans for two new high-capacity jumbo jets—the 747-500 (a 460-passenger jet) and the 747-600 (a 550-passenger jet). Operating a transnational firm requires this type of two-way, open communication to provide perfect service all over the globe.[34] ❖

The Virtual Organization

Becoming Bigger Than You Are

If you think of a transnational firm as located everywhere, think of the virtual organization as located nowhere. The virtual organization is the distributed firm of the future—and the present. Take the Cole Group of, well, everywhere.[35] Founded by David Cole, this newspaper technology consulting and publishing firm generates revenues in excess of $250,000 per year. David does some consulting and writes the *Cole Papers* newsletter from San Francisco, California, while a group in Illinois prints and mails the newsletter. Correspondents in several states contribute to the *Cole Papers*, while consultants in Honolulu and Boca Raton assist in the consulting business. The distant members of the Cole Group communicate through e-mail and a Web site (http://www.colegroup.com).

The organization created by David is an example of a virtual organization. A ***virtual organization*** is a network of independent organizations linked together by IT to exploit market opportunities by sharing skills, costs, and market access. Many virtual organizations operate on a project-only, temporary basis. These organizations are created solely to meet newly identified customer needs faster than building an organization from scratch. All member organizations share in this type of organizational speed. Project-only virtual organizations also permit member organizations to reach new customers beyond their current capabilities and thus share an organizational force. Tying the member organizations together with IT enables the organizations to operate as one and create organizational forces unattainable by any single member.

Some virtual organizations, on the other hand, operate as permanent companies. Member organizations join in a flexible network, establishing permanent relationships to produce certain products and services. Even though the virtual organization is permanent, member organizations remain independent and free to do business outside the virtual organization. In a permanent arrangement, the simultaneous production at member organizations creates shared organizational speed. Member organizations share the organizational force only if each of them actively contacts customers to extend the market reach. Katie La Chance and Maureen Robinson operate a tiny firm, Legal Services Institute Inc., that typifies the permanent virtual organization.[36] You see, Katie lives in Clearwater, Florida, and Maureen lives in south Philadelphia, Pennsylvania. They've met only twice—and not before they joined forces, which confirms the power of telecommunications technology to create new business forms. Katie and Maureen are scopists—they create a polished transcript from a court reporter's notes. Individually, they generated about $30,000 per year. Together, they have generated more than six figures annually. Legal Services Institute germinated as a modest idea and rapidly blossomed to hit the market with great speed. Both Katie and Maureen contact customers and both benefit from a market reach much larger than either could attain individually.

Whatever characteristics virtual organizations have, they all differ from locationless operations and outsourcing. Outsourcing was mentioned briefly in Chapter 1. Table 3.2 will help us differentiate characteristics

The Virtual Organization

What is the virtual organization?	■ A virtual organization is a network of independent organizations linked by IT to exploit market opportunities by sharing skills, costs, and market access.
What does the virtual organization do?	■ It extends the concept of locationless operations beyond the organization's boundaries.
How does the virtual organization affect OHP?	■ It facilitates the greatest organizational speed of any OHP strategy except for the learning organization.
	■ With a virtual organization, however, synergy is lacking and organizational force suffers.
How is the virtual organization IT-enabled?	■ Organizations participating in the virtual organization are linked through telecommunications, as in telecommuters. ❖

TABLE 3.2	Defining a Virtual Organization	
Locationless Operations	**Virtual Organization**	**Outsourcing**
Unlimited life	Unlimited life	Specified lifetime
Employee run	Partnership run	Contractual operation
Share assignments and tasks to complete assignments	Share market knowledge and resources	Share only that which is required

for each topic. For example, when you outsource operations, you do so for a contractually specified time period. However, that's not the case for either a virtual or locationless operation. In addition, employees run locationless operations, whereas partners run virtual operations. At times these partners may be working part-time for another firm. Contract provisions dictate all outsourced operations. There is little room for synergy. The type of information that is shared among operations provides another distinction. Organizations with locationless operations share assignments and completed tasks with distant employees. By comparison, virtual organizations share almost everything about markets, prices, and customers among operations. And again, when outsourcing, contracts specify what information the outsourcer requires to complete its tasks.

Special Information Technology Considerations for the Virtual Organization

Because the virtual organization joins independent businesses, creating links with IT can present special challenges, including

- Linking incompatible hardware and software
- Fostering creativity without human contact
- Effectively communicating concepts online

Independent organizations have their own telecommunications hardware and software, and linking them is the first hurdle a virtual organization must overcome. Another hurdle faces virtual organizations that provide creative

Paperless Payments

Many organizations today ask the same, nagging question: When will we get paid? For some who do business with governments slow to pay, the question can loom quite large. Pharmacists working with the British Columbia Ministry of Health used to wait as long as 60 days to get word of when they would get paid. Today, however, pharmacists receive the same decision within 20 seconds–online. In the old prescription claim system, claims were paper-based and all were processed manually. The new online system eliminates the need for paper claims and saves the ministry the equivalent of 30 full-time jobs. Communicating information electronically has other benefits as well. In addition to filing claims online, pharmacists can check prescription histories for 2.8 million people within seconds. This allows the pharmacist to ensure new prescriptions won't create adverse side effects with existing prescriptions. Providing benefits to the pharmacist users of the system encourages system use. The pharmacists benefit and the ministry benefits by encouraging pharmacists to avoid paper claims. All told, this paperless system will pay for itself in just 6 months. So, now, the ministry isn't the only one who knows when pharmacists get paid.[37] ❖

THE GLOBAL PERSPECTIVE

Is a Virtual Organization Right for You?

Virtual organizations sell products and service customers. Some have been more successful than others. Examine the different types of firms in the list below, and check the strategy that you think is most appropriate. For each, try to imagine how a day of business or a customer transaction is processed to aid in your decision.

What characteristic of each business caused you to decide one way or the other? For each firm, try to remain open to new ways of doing business. ❖

	Traditional Firm	Virtual Organization
A mail-order firm		
A pharmaceuticals manufacturer		
A software company		
A management consulting firm		
A moving company		
A dress boutique		

services for clients, for example, marketing and advertising services. Cultivating a creative environment electronically for these organizations, in itself, requires creativity. You should consider the use of videoconferencing, as well as workgroup support software (see Chapters 2 and 5). A final IT hurdle results from the fact that virtual organizations share much more than just what *to do,* as is the case for both locationless and outsourced operations. They share a vision of where the organization wants *to be,* which means that all partners help decide what should and shouldn't be done. Communicating this type of information requires constant contact, either electronically or in face-to-face meetings. In many respects, this level of information sharing resembles an information partnership. You can see, though, that the virtual organization has a much more distributive network of partners. Most information partnerships include only two partners, and they often create a single unifying location from which to operate the business.

The Learning Organization

The Organization That Never Stops Learning

Can organizations learn? If they make mistakes, will they repeat them? Creating an environment within a company to foster learning is an important strategy for increasing OHP. And it may well be *the* critical strategy for the company of the future. That's because it's really much more than a strategy. When you create a company that learns, you've developed an environment that develops its own new strategies and makes existing strategies more effective. Take total quality management, our foundation for all strategies, for example. Imagine the power of an organization that not only monitors its continuous improvement efforts, but also learns how to improve them.

If you've strolled into a Boston Market restaurant for a bite recently, you've sampled one organization's attempt to create this learning environment.[38,39] From 1992 to 1997, Boston Chicken Inc., the company that operates the Boston Market restaurant, opened over 1,150 stores. Yet in June of 1998 it laid off more than a quarter of its corporate workforce and saw its stock price drop over 90 percent. What did Boston Chicken learn from this bumpy ride? Early on Boston Chicken created a structure that supported easy information flows from store to store and back to headquarters. Customers with complaints could call a toll-free number and, within a few hours, the firm's telecommunications system relayed the complaint to headquarters and to the local store. But simply listening to customers wasn't enough; the organization needed to learn how to learn as well. What does that mean? It means that not assuming current successes provide the knowledge to avoid future failure. You see, Boston Chicken expanded so fast it lost sight of what made it successful in the first place—providing quality homestyle dinners. Perhaps

The Learning Organization

What is the learning organization?	■ A learning organization is an organization whose people are continually discovering how to learn together while, at the same time, altering their organization as a result of what they learn.
What does the learning organization do?	■ It provides an organizational structure that can change as rapidly as customers' needs.
How does the learning organization affect OHP?	■ It provides more potential than any other strategy by creating new strategies. ■ It increases organizational speed by learning from past experience the true cause of problems and eliminating them.
How is the learning organization IT-enabled?	■ Organizational learning only occurs when IT systems acquire and disseminate information among all employees. ❖

Scott Beck, co-founder and CEO, put it best, "We got too far off strategy. We are going back to our roots." Scott epitomizes the continuous learning credo, even in the face of tough setbacks, by recalling a Winston Churchill quote, "Success is never final. Failure is never fatal."

Boston Market is striving to create a company called a learning organization. A *learning organization* is an organization whose people are continually discovering how to learn together while, at the same time, altering their organization as a result of what they learn. By modifying your organization through organizational learning you can serve your customers better and faster. Your organization develops more organizational speed by finding the root causes of production slowdowns and eliminating them.

How Information Technology Can Help Your Organization Overcome Learning Barriers

Companies don't learn for three reasons. Some companies still manage by commanding and controlling all employees and their actions. Others seem to place more importance on blame than problem solving. Still others make it difficult to see beyond individual functions and make it impossible for those individuals to experience the outcome of their actions. Let's examine these three learning barriers, along with the opportunities that information technology provides in overcoming them.

Command It to Control It

Has a boss ever given you a job that seemed completely unnecessary? Your difficulty in executing that job arose from your exclusion from the decision-making process

that assigned the job. By the time the job reached you, it was too late to alter the decision. In a *command and control* structure, the people who perform the jobs are rarely part of the decision-making process. The command and control organizational structure achieves efficient, consistent execution of tasks. But this is possible only if the market changes infrequently. The structure is inflexible and often incapable of learning. Its inflexibility is due to rigorous job definitions that are designed to maintain control and increase efficiency. All decisions to change a job come from the top of the organization. And information flows only from top to bottom. So, if customers communicate a need for change to a customer representative, the information does not reach the decision makers and no change occurs.

IT systems can make that bottom-to-top information flow possible. When you call Boston Market's toll-free number, the information you provide the representative flows up to the local manager and even up to corporate management. Along the way, many different people within the organization have the information they need to make a change. Allowing information to flow in both directions supports a learning organization's need for information diversity. Getting the information to the people who need it is a good first step in organizational learning.

It Shouldn't Be a Blame Game

One morning while you are driving to work one of your tires goes flat, making you late for the morning staff meeting. Was it your fault that you were late? Your boss probably thought so. Of course, you might blame the bad tire. In any case, how will assigning blame prevent the result from happening again? Probably not much. Nevertheless,

Seeing Beyond What You Do

Seeing beyond your job classification to your role in the organization as a whole is a difficult task. Job titles tend to pigeonhole employees and make them forget their impact. All of us work within organizationwide processes. And these processes have suppliers (supplying us with raw materials or raw information) and customers (to whom you deliver the result of your work). However, you may have difficulty identifying the ultimate supplier and ultimate customer for your process because of their time and location distance from you. Still, how can you learn how to better serve your customer if you don't know the ultimate customer of your labors? How can you communicate to your supplier what you need to serve this customer if you don't know your ultimate supplier? To accomplish both tasks, you must develop a *big picture*—or see the process as a whole.

For each job title below, consider the particular task that person performs and identify the supplier and customer of the entire organizational process. While you do so, ask yourself if an IT system could effectively shrink the logical distance from supplier to customer. For example, a customer database for a process enlightens the process workers as to the identity and needs of individual customers. ❖

Job Title	Task	Process	Supplier	Customer
Accountant	Paying vendors			
Buyer	Negotiating purchases			
Engineer	Designing a new product			
Salesperson	Making a sale			
Parts assembler	Putting parts together			
Systems analyst	Creating design specs for new systems			
Researcher	Researching a new product material			

assigning blame is a common organizational practice. So why do we assign blame? For most of us, it's simply a misguided attempt to find a cause for events. The reason the attempt is misguided is that when we assign blame, we make an assumption that it wasn't *our* fault. For organizations, this assumption can be devastating. You see, when your organization looks to you for the cause of a problem, that means it's no longer your organization's problem. And now you're on your own to learn why something happened and you must try to fix it. Suppose, in your personal learning process, you discovered the problem was greater than just you? Well, that's too bad, because it's no longer the organization's problem.

Assigning blame promotes individual learning, which is not at all the same as organizational learning. In learning together we stand a better chance of finding true causes to problems as well as maintaining our unified customer focus. In large organizations, steering clear of assigning blame is facilitated by IT. Whiteboard software, for example, allows many individuals to work electronically to solve problems. When one individual makes a change, all the other individuals can see the impact simultaneously. Each will formulate his or her own cause and effect, tested by all the participants. "Virtual" meetings, where individuals gather together through teleconferencing, allow many members of the organization to hear problem descriptions and possible solutions and offer their input. Now everyone in the meeting can apply this newly learned problem solving to other problems and the organization as a whole has learned.

Learning from Your Experiences

If your organization assigns blame to individuals, its challenge is greater than just finding *a* single individual to blame. Often there is a whole series of actions, or causes and effects, that can be traced back to the root cause. To trace the causes, everyone must be able to see the "big picture." That is, to discover both the final effect and the root cause you must see the entire organizational system of causes and effects at the same time. Unfortunately, these causes and effects are often separated by both time and location. Imagine turning on the water to a long hose where the end is out of sight. The distance between the cause and effect makes it virtually impossible for you to control the effect. It certainly would be helpful if you had someone positioned at the end of the hose to yell out how much water is flowing through the hose. Without feedback, your actions are a guess at best, and you have no way of learning from your experience of turning on the water.

How can you eliminate these barriers? You can use IT systems to bring the root cause and final effect together in time and location. A simple example would be to put a water flowmeter at the end of your long hose, so when you turn on the faucet (the cause) you gauge the water pressure or emission (the effect). That way, a single individual now has enough information to connect cause and effect and, as a result, the organization learns. When you operate the faucet to the hose, you can pass on to the organization which water faucet settings are optimal. By collapsing time and location, the information technology allows you to see the organizational big picture.

In addition, you can utilize *artificial intelligence*, discussed in Chapter 5, to learn from your experiences. Artificial intelligence systems like *neural networks* are patterned after the human brain and can look at a situation and identify patterns that suggest a solution. Then

---

For Sale: One Million Dollar CAVEs

Well, not caves as we know them. Cave Automatic Virtual Environments (CAVEs) are three-dimensional virtual reality chambers for testing product designs. Although computers' ability to create and display environments in a "virtually realistic" manner has existed for several years, this technology has only recently been applied to collaborative learning.

The lifeblood of a manufacturing firm is its ability to produce innovative products that meet customers' needs. Product design, however, is most often a collaborative effort, whereas testing is done by individuals. As a result, design engineers don't get the necessary feedback. To attempt to correct this inadequacy, Caterpillar of Peoria, Illinois, created a *permanent team* to work with the University of Illinois at Urbana-Champaign, where the first industrial CAVE was built in 1993. The team is creating a network of CAVEs, a collaborative virtual environment, if you will, to test new earthmoving vehicle designs with many engineers participating. If you're thinking this is all just for show, hear what Kem Ahlers, the executive in charge of the program, says: "We normally don't spend money on flash. We and other companies are solving real-life problems in the CAVEs. We can improve products and meet customer needs more quickly." Could a better case be made for this collaborative learning environment? Clearly Caterpillar does not think so.[40] ❖

neural networks apply this pattern identification to new problems. If the organization must solve a problem with potentially thousands of solutions, a *genetic algorithm* might be applied. This type of artificial intelligence system mimics an evolutionary process to generate increasingly better solutions. Because complex cause and effect relationships prevail in large organizations, genetic algorithms can speed up the learning process by evaluating thousands of scenarios for an optimal solution.

Selecting and Adopting Organizational Horsepower Strategies

How Information Technology Enables the Organizational Transformation

You've examined seven organizational horsepower strategies to increase your organization's competitiveness. Each strategy offers your firm opportunity for improvement, but in different ways. With so many different strategies, how do you go about selecting a strategy for your organization? Let's examine a process to select your OHP strategy.

Selecting an Organizational Horsepower Strategy

Selecting an appropriate OHP strategy is a four-step process. Each step contains questions, the answers to which will help you define your organizational need. The strategy you select is based on this need. The four steps are listed below.

❶ How do your customers define perfect service? When, where, and how do your customers expect delivery of your product or service?

❷ Does your organization have a strategic plan? If so, how do your strategic goals translate into organizational force and speed? How do your organizational goals for IT development translate into organizational force and speed?

❸ Based on your customers' definition of perfect service and your strategic plan, which organizational strategy, or combination of strategies, best fits your organization's needs?

❹ Does your organization have the resources to adopt the strategy you've selected? Do your organization's goals for IT systems fit with the IT systems required for your chosen strategy?

The four-step OHP strategy selection process ensures that the OHP strategy your organization selects fits within the goals of your organization. In these four steps, you consider three major organizational goals—perfect service goals, organizational strategic goals, and organizational IT systems goals. Considering all three, with the customer paramount, ensures that your OHP strategy promotes existing organizational goals and doesn't take your organization in an unintended direction.

You may select more than one OHP strategy. Many of the strategies we have discussed complement one another. For example, establishing a just-in-time EDI link between your organization and your customers promotes the creation of an information partnership between your firm and your customer. Likewise, if you select a virtual organization strategy, you'll make use of telecommunications technology that can be used in a transnational firm strategy. You only have to ensure that selecting more than one strategy promotes your organizational goals, and that your organization has sufficient resources to adopt the strategies. Once you select your strategy or strategies, your organization must now adopt that strategy.

Adopting an Organizational Horsepower Strategy

Adopting an OHP strategy begins with designing its application. Each strategy may be applied in many different ways, as illustrated by the numerous business examples in this chapter. In addition to *how* the selected strategy will be applied, your organization must decide *by what process* it will be applied. Three issues must be considered in adopting the selected strategy. First, determine which aspects of the selected strategy will be applied. Each strategy may be applied comprehensively or partially. For example, adopting a transnational firm strategy may involve 2 or 20 nations. Adopting a team strategy may involve a few project teams or a permanent restructuring with work teams. The extent to which the strategy will be adopted will also be determined by the number of resources your organization can devote to this effort.

Second, determine which technology the selected strategy requires. Are the resources available to implement this supporting technology? And, possibly more important, does your organization have the IT knowledge to implement this technology? Many of these IT systems issues, such as when to hire outside help, are covered in Chapter 9. Third, determine the most appropriate process by which to adopt the selected strategy. Your organization will select from two processes to adopt your OHP strategy. One possibility is a continuous improvement process. Continuous improvement was covered in our discussion of total quality management. This process is appropriate for adopting strategies in stages or incrementally. For example, if you wish to adopt a transnational firm strategy, you might do so in one or two countries at a time. The change to the organization is less radical and more in keeping with this process. If, however, you wish to adopt a strategy at once, your organization will require a more radical improvement process called *business process reengineering*. This process is used extensively in business to facilitate radical organizational improvement. Let's take a close look at this process and how it might compare to the continuous improvement process.

What Is the Business Process Reengineering Improvement Process?

Business process reengineering is an essential tool in an organization's improvement. Just imagine getting approval for a home loan in minutes over the phone instead of waiting the usual 2 to 4 weeks. Of course, you don't really have to imagine it—just call the Bank of Montreal today and experience it yourself.[41] In fact, a recent survey of 100 large, publicly held firms revealed that 83 percent have adopted business process reengineering in their improvement efforts.[42] Of those firms, 70 percent became more productive, 61 percent achieved greater cost efficiencies, and 42 percent improved profits. It's apparent from these numbers, however, that the goal of business process reengineering varies from company to company.

If you searched issues of business magazines for just the last few years alone, you would find several hundred references to "reengineering." Some articles use the phrase

Adopting a Transnational Strategy, Radically

Radically going global is risky for any firm, but it's even riskier if you're in the financial services Industry. Emerging financial markets in the Third World can quickly plummet in value and take your investments there with them. Still, firms like the Morgan Stanley Group of New York, New York, are leading the way. Morgan Stanley's office in India is an example of how to reduce the risk associated with strategy adoption. The office is located on the fourth floor of a 90-year-old building with a broken elevator and questionable phone service. But on that fourth floor you'll find a modern office with its own power and telecommunications lines isolating Morgan Stanley from outside risks.

Power and telecommunications, however, don't shield the company from or eliminate all risks. In April 1994, Morgan Stanley became the first foreign company to launch a domestic mutual fund for retail customers in India. The leap began wonderfully with over 1.5 million investors pouring $310 million into the fund in just 2½ days. From that start, however, the fund has declined 16.5 percent, mostly as a result of inadequate advertising planning. "People thought they were buying a Morgan Stanley share, not an emerging-market fund," says K. N. Vaidyanathan of Morgan Stanley. Moving quickly with a radical strategy adoption is a risky endeavor, but one that is possible with adequate planning.[43] ❖

business process reengineering, some business reengineering, and others just reengineering. What do these terms mean? Well, unfortunately, these terms are often misused and misunderstood. So, let's clarify things a bit.

Business process reengineering (BPR) is the reinventing of processes within a business. Many OHP strategies require a reinvention of processes. You reengineer in organizational units called *processes*. **Business processes** are sequences of activities that take raw materials from a supplier and serve outcomes to a customer. For example, a mortgage loan process takes loan information (raw materials) from applicants (suppliers) and delivers a decision (outcome) to the new clients (customers). These processes cut across and connect departments like accounting and sales. A representative sales order process is illustrated with a process map in Figure 3.5.

What does it mean to *reinvent* a process? In Chapter 2, IBM Credit reinvented its credit review process using work flow automation software. But was this really reinventing a process or just incrementally improving it? From what we know of TQM, how does continuously improving a process compare to BPR? If it is similar, does that mean BPR is really just another type of TQM? The answer is a resounding no! Let's take a look at Figure 3.6 to clarify.

BPR is a radical undertaking that requires innovative strategies to create dramatic improvements in serving your customers. TQM focuses on continuous improvement. The very nature of a continuous improvement process conflicts with radical improvement. IBM Credit took a credit review process of 6 days and slashed it to just 4 hours—drastic reinventing. The distinction is important in approaching the process of implementing an OHP strategy. For example, the bank that redesigns deposit slips to speed a teller's work through an improvement program is practicing TQM. The bank that put in the first ATM to replace teller visits, however, was practicing BPR. Both may require IT systems to implement them, but one incrementally improves a process (redesigning deposit slips) and the other creates a whole new process (installing an ATM).

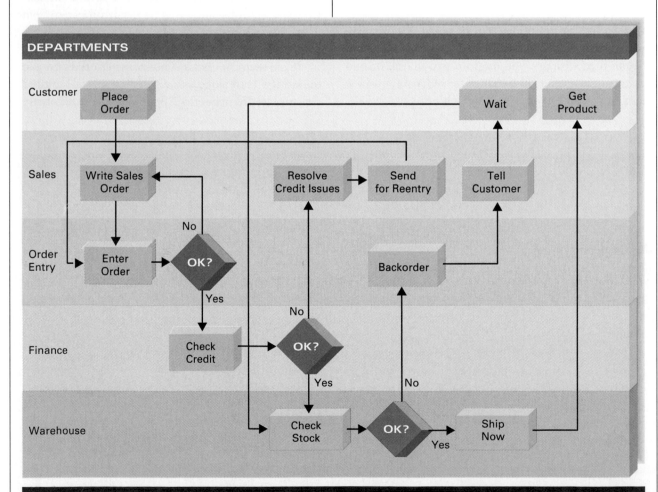

FIGURE 3.5

The Sales Order "As-Is" Process Map at Brothers Copiers

MYTHS

BUSINESS PROCESS REENGINEERING *IS NOT*
• Just Eliminating Jobs
• Incremental Improvement
• Redesigning IT Alone
• Continuous Improvement
• Efficiency-Focused

REALITY

BUSINESS PROCESS REENGINEERING *IS*
• Radical and Innovative
• For Dramatic Improvement
• Redesign Enabled by IT
• A Targeted Project
• Effectiveness-Focused

FIGURE 3.6

Business Process Reengineering Myths and Reality

Possibly the best way to think about these two improvement processes is this. TQM says, "There *might* be a *better* way to do this. If there is, let's find it and improve it." BPR says, "It's broken, we *must* build a new process. We must dramatically change the way we serve our customers." With TQM, your company must commit itself to continual improvement, which is an essential process and the foundation of OHP. However with BPR, your company must carve the company to improve it. BPR is much riskier, much more painful, and is not always appropriate. Ultimately BPR means changing more than you keep. TQM means keeping more than you change.

Performing Business Process Reengineering

Using BPR in your organization is a straightforward six-step process. The six steps include

❶ Defining the OHP strategy you wish to adopt
❷ Identifying the affected processes that need to be reengineered
❸ Identifying the goal for each process
❹ Identifying process participants and a facilitator for each process
❺ Mapping the "as-is" process
❻ Designing the "to-be" process

Let's take a look at each of these six steps. Step 1 ties the BPR effort to the organizational goals by first identifying where you wish your organization to go using your OHP strategy. Otherwise, unfocused BPR efforts can take your organization far from its intended strategic direction. Step 2 identifies the business processes that will be affected by the OHP strategy. For example, establishing a locationless "virtual" store on the Internet will affect not only how you take orders, but also your entire sales order process. Step 3 identifies the goal of each process. Over time, processes within your business can stray from their intended purpose. A credit approval process, for example, may begin to gather competitive company information based on the credit clerk's ability to analyze company financials. Although competitive information gathering is a worthy task, it does nothing to speed your customers' credit approval—your process goal. Identifying each process goal will refocus old processes and clarify your process redesign effort.

ON YOUR OWN

Creating a New Process at Brothers Copiers

Suppose you were redesigning the sales order process at the fictitious copier sales company in Figure 3.5. Using the general format of the process map, depicting departments horizontally and processes as boxes, create a new reinvented process map. Be certain to consider the following concerns.

1. Is there a need for the order entry department? Who else could perform that task?

2. When should credit checks be done? Will moving *when* the credit checks are done change the number of process boxes?

3. Who should be doing backorders? And when should stock be checked?

Always ask *why* you are doing something as well as *who* is the best choice to do it. In general, try moving all valuable processes up as close to the first step as possible. Imagine what OHP strategy will best fit your new way of serving the customer. ❖

Don't Forget Quality

When selecting an appropriate OHP strategy, never forget the foundation of all organizational horsepower—quality. Even in rugged manufacturing environments, IT systems can support your quality foundation. At OMC-Milwaukee, a unit of Waukegan, Illinois-based Outboard Marine Corp., a challenging factory floor didn't stop OMC from finding an IT system solution. OMC recognized the need to promote organization-wide quality ownership by providing production line personnel with a simple means of gathering quality data. In addition, OMC wanted to link all data gathering together so everyone could benefit from what was happening on the manufacturing floor.

OMC's solution was a wireless local area network (LAN). Essentially, personal computers were used to gather quality data at workstations around the factory. But, because of safety concerns, wires to connect these workstations could not be at ground level, and running conduit to house the wires was deemed too expensive. So OMC decided on wireless transmitters for each workstation to communicate the data instantly through receiver modules placed at various points in the ceiling. With this solution, the IT system was built within budget while promoting organizationwide quality ownership.[44] ❖

TEAM WORK

Finding the Best Organizational Horsepower Strategy for Your Industry

Regardless of the improvement process that you select to adopt your organization's OHP strategy, ensuring that the OHP matches your organizational goals is critical. To simplify the selection process even further, you might consider which OHP strategies work best with the various industries profiled in the Industry Perspectives boxes in each chapter of this book. Match the OHP strategies on the left with the most appropriate industry across the top. Each strategy can match more than one industry. For each match, write at least one reason why this match is appropriate. ❖

OHP Strategies	Hospitality & Leisure	Financial Services	Health Care	Retail	IT & Telecommunications	Transportation	Food	Entertainment & Publishing	Manufacturing
Just-in-time approach									
Teams in an organization									
Information partnerships									
Timeless & locationless operations									
Transnational firm									
Virtual organization									
The learning organization									

Industries

Step 4 identifies all those individuals within your organization who participate in each process. When redesigning processes, each participant's input is essential to both understanding the process and including all participants' needs. You'll also identify a BPR facilitator who is trained in conducting process redesign sessions. Facilitators ensure that the redesign sessions stay focused on the problem and that everyone participates. In Step 5 process participants map the current, or "as-is," process graphically to facilitate an understanding of the process by all participants (a technique often applied to the learning organization). Many participants have seen only their own small pieces of the process. With an understanding of the entire process, they can consider all process needs better. An example process map is shown in Figure 3.5. Last, Step 6 asks all participants to redesign a new, or "to-be," process in support of your new OHP strategy. The participants consider the previously defined process goal, what the process must accomplish based on the old as-is process, and what the process must accomplish based on your new OHP strategy.

Business Process Reengineering Ethical Considerations

Using a BPR improvement process can trigger ethical concerns. For example, is it ethical to ask employees to participate in BPR that results in elimination of their jobs? You can certainly understand why many employees hesitate to join in such processes. But is it even right to ask them to do so? And is it ethical for a firm to look at opportunities to save money through job elimination without also looking at opportunities for revenue growth through job retraining? Firms that use BPR to take advantage of a competitive opportunity are more likely to consider new jobs than eliminate old jobs. Unfortunately, most firms take on BPR to increase productivity or decrease costs. Less than one-half the firms practicing BPR have done so to increase profits. And eliminating jobs always appears at the top of the "reduce costs" list.

CLOSING CASE STUDY: CASE 1

GE Transforms Itself

The most valuable company in the world, General Electric Co. (GE), has decided it needs a new strategy. Not satisfied to maintain current revenues, GE is looking to the future and searching for ways to transform this manufacturing giant into a more profitable firm. Although strong industrial sales have propelled GE to

where it is today, its CEO, Jack Welch, hopes for more from the firm. Espousing the concept of perfect service, Jack says, "Our job is to sell more than just the box." So GE is moving on all fronts to do just that.

On the medical products front, GE has entered into a partnership with Columbia/HCA to share product and cost information, with Columbia saving tens of millions of dollars while GE gains a greater lock on one of its biggest customers. How close is the partnership? "They've become part of our team," enthuses Columbia chief financial officer Sam Greco. To encourage such partnerships with other medical customers, GE produces educational programming, transmitted by way of a satellite system, to train hospitals in how best to use their equipment.

On the aircraft engine front, GE now services the engines it sells and offers to assist customers in pursuing organizational horsepower strategies of their own. With British Airways PLC (BA), GE performs 85 percent of BA's engine maintenance while moving the firm to a just-in-time inventory system and instituting project teams. On the power generation front, GE has extended its global reach through a joint venture with the Milan-based power company Societa Nordelettrica to offer utility maintenance services throughout Europe. In total, GE is reinventing all that it does to provide better service to its present customers and to the new customers it has yet to reach.[45] ❖

◄ Questions ►

1. Does GE's OHP strategy fit our definition of BPR? Why or why not? Compare the BPR myths and realities from this chapter to the GE effort. How does this support or detract from our BPR concept?

2. What information partnership strategy is GE pursuing? Which component of organizational horsepower is most likely to be greater: organizational force, organizational speed, or both? Why?

3. How has GE pursued timeless or locationless operations? What technology has it used to enable this strategy? How might GE benefit from this strategy?

4. On what OHP strategies has GE provided consulting? How would it have obtained this knowledge? How might this help GE other than in consulting revenues?

5. What international operating configuration is GE pursuing? Why do you think GE has selected this configuration? How has this strategy fit into the overall company strategy?

KNOWLEDGE WORKER'S ✓-LIST

The Important Role Information Technology Plays in Enabling Perfect Service. Information technology enables your organization to provide customers products and services *when* they want them, *where* they want them, and *how* they want them. IT enables the when, where, and how of customer service. With IT, you can gain a **competitive advantage** by providing the best perceived perfect service at the customer's moment of value.

The Way in Which Organizations Develop Organizational Horsepower and How This Affects Their Competitiveness. **Organizational horsepower (OHP)** is a measure of an organization's ability to exert force in the market with speed. Organizational horsepower is made up of two components—organizational force and organizational speed. **Organizational force** is meeting as many customers' expectations as possible. **Organizational speed** is meeting customers' expectations quickly. Both components combine to create an organization's competitiveness, or OHP.

How Quality Forms the Foundation of Organizational Competitiveness. **Quality** is meeting customer expectations. IT systems gather customer information and help define customer expectations. **Total quality management (TQM)** is meeting customer expectations through continuous improvement and organizationwide quality ownership. TQM ensures that a firm continuously pursues quality in all that it does.

The Role of Various Organizational Horsepower Strategies in Creating a Competitive Organization. OHP strategies can generate both organizational force and speed. But each OHP strategy generates different magnitudes of force and speed, if any at all, that affect an organization's competitiveness differently. The seven OHP strategies are outlined in the table on page 119.

When to Adopt an Organizational Horsepower Strategy Using a Radical Improvement Process. Continuous improvement is improving what you have by using TQM. Radical improvement, like **business process reengineering (BPR)**, is the reinventing of processes within a business. A **business process**, a sequence of activities that takes raw materials from a supplier and serves an outcome to a customer, is the unit of improvement. BPR is an appropriate OHP strategy adoption process when processes require radical redesign.

CLOSING CASE STUDY: CASE 2

3M Fights Back

Lately, the Minnesota Mining & Manufacturing Co. (3M) hasn't been the company it once was. In 1995, for the first time in years, 3M didn't achieve its financial goals. In 1996, 3M announced the biggest restructuring in its 93-year history. You could blame these woes on many causes, but one seems to sum it all up nicely. Competitive advantages are fleeting and 3M needs a new competitive advantage. Innovations like Post-it Notes lead the market for only a while and must be replaced by new ones constantly.

One source of irritation at 3M is the lack of a clear strategy. The closest 3M comes to a strategy is this statement from its CEO, "Desi" DeSimone: "We're going to do two principal things: be very innovative, and satisfy our customers in all aspects." Sounds a little like perfect service. And innovation in business is all about guessing what customers will want tomorrow. More than anything, 3M needs to know when to let go of those innovations. 3M stayed in the magnetic-storage business (diskettes, videotape, etc.) for 10 years after problems were evident. It did the same in electronic components packaging.

One challenge for 3M is finding a strategy to help it manage its 33 technology platforms. Each technology platform is an area of research that seems promising and could support multiple products. In fact, managers at 3M view 3M as having 500 to 1,000 different businesses derived from those technology platforms. Some of this is due to 3M's application of project teams. If you have an idea, you form an ad-hoc group of maybe two to four people. You're given a small percentage of your time to see if your idea produces anything. If not, you return to your regular job full-time. If the idea works, you get funding for

	OHP Component		
OHP Strategy	**Force**	**Speed**	**IT Support**
The **just-in-time (JIT)** approach is producing or delivering a product or service *when* the customer wants it.		✓	Communication systems and production scheduling software
A **team** is a group of people with a shared common goal and task interdependence.	✓		Groupware
An **information partnership** is an agreement between organizations for the sharing of information to strengthen each partner organization.	✓	✓	EDI, electronic information partnerships, and electronic strategic alliances
A **timeless operation** means operating without regard to time; and a **locationless operation** means operating without regard to location.	✓	✓	Electronic commerce and telecommunication networks
A **transnational firm** produces and sells products and services in countries all over the world in coordinated cooperation.	✓		Global IT infrastructure including IT systems of all kinds implemented internationally
The **virtual organization** is a network of independent organizations linked together by IT to exploit market opportunities by sharing skills, costs, and market access.		✓	Linked telecommunication networks and workgroup support software
The **learning organization** is an organization whose people are continually discovering how to learn together while, at the same time, altering their organization as a result of what they learn.		✓	(1) Transaction processing systems and management information systems that support vertical information flows; (2) workgroup support software ❖

it to fully test it. At any one time, 3M has hundreds of project teams working on hundreds of diverse ideas. Some would argue that this promotes innovation. Others might argue that it's a waste of time and resources.

3M does make use of a partnership with customers to mine them for new product ideas. 3M uses "major customer" teams that include reps from every department from R&D to sales. These teams meet with significant customers to discover their current and future needs. By using these teams, much guesswork is eliminated.[46] ❖

◄ Questions ►

1. What type of information partnership does 3M have with its customers—a partnership for force, a partnership for speed, or a partnership for both force and speed? What characteristics convince you of this?

2. 3M uses project teams for several purposes. Is this an appropriate use of project teams or should permanent teams be considered? Why or why not?

3. 3M openly admits that it lacks a clear strategy. Is this a good approach? What is 3M's argument for such an approach? Can you think of any strategy discussed in this chapter that might help 3M's business?

4. 3M is undergoing some internal change. Is this change total quality management or business process reengineering? What characteristics about the change support your choice?

5. What strategy is 3M using to support a goal of perfect service? How does this strategy do this? Are there IT systems that can facilitate this strategy?

Electronic Commerce
Business and You on the Internet

Finding Investment Opportunities Using the Internet

When you buy stock in a company, you're betting on the success of that firm. Sometimes that bet is a good one, and other times it's not. Finding a company that's a good bet involves a great deal of research. And to further complicate matters, some people prefer investing in large, safe companies, whereas others prefer the potential higher return of a small, more risky firm. So how do you make sense of all the options? Well, now you have access to financial information that professional investors use to evaluate stocks. And the access is instant on the Internet. The Internet brings together information-hungry investors with companies that are anxious to reach out to investors. In fact, over 900 companies now offer investment information on the Internet, and the number is increasing rapidly.

Before you begin your investment research, though, be sure you consider the reliability of the information you may find on the Internet. Start by considering your source; that is, look at the Web site sponsor and ask yourself if you've heard of them before and if they might have any incentive to slant their information offerings. As you know, investments traded on public markets like the New York Stock Exchange can move up or down in price quickly on the basis of new information about the company. An individual or an organization posting information about a company on the Internet may be just that, reliable information, or it might be false information posted simply to affect the price of an investment to favor the sponsor of the information. So, be cautious. And be especially leery of Web sites sponsored by individuals or organizations not known to you. Remember, no one guarantees the results of your investments. Investing involves risk, and the point of the research is to reduce that risk. Don't increase it by believing everything you read. Do your best to verify the source of any information.

In this section, we've included a number of Web sites related to finding investment opportunities using the

Internet. On the Web site that supports this text (http://www.mhhe.com/business/mis/haag, select "Electronic Commerce Projects"). We've provided direct links to all these sites as well as many, many more. These are a great starting point for completing this Real HOT section. We would also encourage you to search the Internet for others.

Learning about Investing

Investing can be as simple as finding a company that performs well financially and buying some of its stock. Or, if you want to spread your investment over a number of stocks and don't want to personally select each stock, you can invest in a mutual fund. A mutual fund buys many different stocks for you. This way you leave the research of individual stocks to the mutual fund. Of course, there are thousands of mutual funds with all types of investment objectives. So, any way you go, you must pick your investment wisely. And to help you get up to speed quickly, you'll find many helpful Web sites on the Internet.

For starters, you might explore sites aimed at first-time investors like http://onlineinvestors.com. There you'll find ratings for online brokerages as well as general investing advice. Another source of investment information is the National Association of Securities Dealers (NASD) at http://www.nasdr.com. NASD will brief you on the risks involved in online investing. Then, once you understand the risks involved, you might want to retrieve more general information from the online versions of traditional print media like *The Wall Street Journal* or *Money* magazine.

Now that you've thought about your knowledge of investing, connect to five different investment reference sites. In the table on page 123, we've provided a list of investment reference sites that will help bring you up to speed concerning online investing and where you can find them on the Internet. And on the Web site that supports this text, you'll find a list of many others. As you connect to five different investment reference sites, answer the following questions.

A. Is the site designed for first-time investors or those who are more experienced?

B. Can you search for a specific topic?

C. Are specific stocks or mutual funds reviewed or evaluated?

D. Does the site provide direct links to brokerage or stock quoting sites?

E. Is a forum for submitting questions available? If so, are frequently asked questions (FAQs) posted?

F. Who sponsors the site? Does it seem as if the sponsor is using the site to advertise its own products or services?

G. Can you download reference documents to read later?

Researching the Company Behind the Stock

One excellent way to pick a stock investment is to research the company behind that stock. Focusing on items such as sales revenues and profits to pick a stock is called *fundamental research*. So you might choose to invest in Boeing stock because you've discovered sales revenues for Boeing have been climbing steadily for the last three years. Or you might initially consider buying some Disney stock but change your mind when you find that EuroDisney revenues have been below expectations.

Now that you're ready to research a stock investment, connect to four different stock investment sites using the table on page 123. The Web site that supports this text includes a list of many other stock investment sites. As you connect to four different stock investment sites, look up each company's financials, and answer the questions that follow. You'll probably want to include at least two companies with which you are familiar and two

that are new to you. In addition to reviewing company financials, look around each company site and see to what degree it is investor-oriented.

A. Do all the company sites offer financial information?

B. Is the information targeted at investors? How can you tell?

C. Can you download financial information to your computer and use it in a spreadsheet?

D. Can you download the company's annual report? Is it a full-color version?

E. Does the site provide direct links to e-mail addresses for requesting additional information?

F. Do the companies provide comparisons to others in their industry?

G. Does the site provide stock quotes as well as financials?

H. Can you search the site for related information like press releases?

I. Is there a charge for retrieving the financial information?

Finding Other Sources of Company Financials

Searching for a company's financials may be a bit more difficult than you first imagined. First, you must determine the Internet address for the company either by guessing the address and typing it in or using one of the many search engines available. Both of these methods are fraught with error. For example, if you guessed that http://www.amex.com was the address for American Express you'd be wrong. And even if you find the company's site, you may still not find its financials. Take Adidas, for example, at http://www.adidas.com. No financials are available at this site.

The reason many companies don't provide financials on their Web sites is that they view the primary purpose of their sites as reaching consumers, not investors. So, many companies elect to post their financials on a financial provider site or simply to let investors view the company's submissions to the Securities and Exchange Commission at the SEC's Web site.

In the table on page 123, we've provided a list of five Web sites that list or distribute financial information on companies. And on the Web site that supports this text, you'll find a list of many others. Pick three providers of financial information, access their Web sites, and answer the following questions.

A. Is there a charge for retrieving the information?

B. Do you have a choice for the information's format?

C. Are companies listed alphabetically?

D. Does the site offer more than just annual reports?

E. Are there direct links from the site to the desired company's site?

F. Can you find more companies at the site than by searching the Web for individual company Web sites?

G. How many companies are available on each Web site?

H. Are the represented companies mostly large and established or small and relatively unknown?

Making Trades Online

If you want to invest in stocks or mutual funds, you'd probably do what everyone else does—go to a stockbroker. A stockbroker has the licensing and connections to make a trade in securities traded on markets all over the world. So it makes sense to call or visit a stockbroker. However, many of the same services offered by stockbrokers are available on the Internet.

Virtually all of the stockbrokers with offices you can visit near you have Web sites that support online investing and more. These services include providing research reports, financial planning, and online investing services. Before we go online to look at some of these stockbrokers, you should be sure you understand the difference between a full-service brokerage house and a discount brokerage house. As the names imply, the full-service brokerage offers many more services than the discount brokerage. And it's important to understand that the costs for many of these services are built into the fees to buy and sell stocks and mutual funds. So you pay for having these services available even if you don't use them at a full-service brokerage. So, let's venture online and see what the various brokerages have to offer. In the table on page 123 you'll find a list of brokerages and where you can find them on the Internet. And on the Web site that supports this text, you'll find a list of many others.

Pick five of the brokerages, examine what it takes to conduct an online investment transaction, and answer the following questions.

A. Must you already have an investment account with the brokerage to purchase stocks or mutual funds?

B. Which sites are full-service brokerages and which are discount brokerages? How can you tell?

C. Is online research available? Is it free?

D. Can you retrieve stock price quotes for free?

E. If you already have an account with the brokerage, does it offer special services for its customers? What kind of services are offered?

F. Is the site aimed at experienced investors or new investors?

G. If you're investing for the first time, would you feel comfortable using online investing? If so, why? If not, why not?

Retrieving Stock Quotes

Once you find the right stock to buy, you'll then be asking yourself, How much will this stock cost me? Stocks and mutual funds are both offered by the share, so you can easily buy as much or as little of the stock or mutual fund as you like. Still, some individual shares are priced in the hundreds of dollars and that alone might make the purchase undesirable to you.

In addition to pricing individual shares to assess the affordability of an investment, you'll probably want to see how the price has varied over time. Even though most financial advisers will tell you that historical price variations provide no indication of future performance, most everyone uses price history to get a feel for whether the investment is trading at all-time highs or lows. So finding a chart of a stock price online might be helpful when making your purchase.

And even after you've made your purchase, you'll probably want to follow how your investment is doing. The thrill of realizing a paper profit is enough to keep many investors checking their investments daily. Of course, realizing a paper loss can be equally disappointing. And even if daily tracking isn't for you, you'll certainly want to check on your investments regularly, and doing so online can be quick and painless. In the table below, you'll find a list of online stock and mutual fund quoting services and where you can find them on the Internet. And on the Web site that supports this text, you'll find a list of many others.

Pick five of the stock quoting services, examine what it takes to retrieve a stock or mutual fund quote, and answer the following questions.

A. Are the quotes provided free of charge or for a fee?

B. Does the site require a ticker symbol (the abbreviation used by experienced investors), or can you type in a company name?

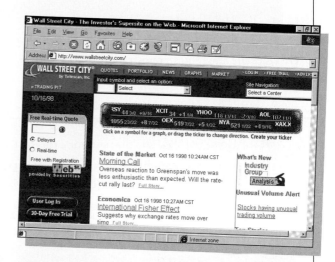

Web Sites for Finding Investment Opportunities

Investment References	**Address**
The Basics of Investing	http://www.investor.nasd.com/ni_module_menu.html
Microsoft Money Insider	http://moneyinsider.msn.com/home.asp
Investing Basics	http://www.aaii.com/invbas
CBS MarketWatch Investor's Primer	http://cbs.marketwatch.com/news/primer
The Syndicate	http://www.moneypages.com/syndicate/index.html

Companies	**Address**
Disney	http://www.disney.com/investors
Coca-Cola	http://www.coca-cola.com/co
Century 21 Real Estate	http://www.century21.com
Boeing	http://www.boeng.com/company offices/financial
Hughes	http://www.hughes.com/Invest.html

Providers	**Address**
Investors Relations Information Network (IRIN)	http://www.irin/com
Securities and Exchange Commission (SEC)	http://www.sec.gov/edgarhp.htm
Barron's Annual Report Service	http://www.icbinc.com/cgi-bin/barrons.pl
Hoover's Online	http://www.hoovers.com
Tana Interactive Annual Reports List	http://www.tanagraphics.com/ti/ar_list

Brokerages	**Address**
Merrill Lynch	http://www.ml.com
Charles Schwab	http://www.schwab.com
American Express Financial Advisors	http://www.americanexpress.com/financial
Smith Barney	http://www.smithbarney.com
E*Trade	http://www.etrade.com

Quoting Services	**Address**
Yahoo Finance	http://quote.yahoo.com
PC Quote Online	http://www.pcquote.com
CNN Financial News Stock Quotes	http://cnnfn.com/markets/quotes.html
Microsoft Investor	http://investor.msn.com
Wall Street City	http://www.wallstreetcity.com

C. Are the quotes real-time or are they delayed (15–20 minutes old)?

D. Does the site require registration?

E. Are historical prices available?

F. Are price charts available? Can you customize the chart display?

G. Can you create and save a personal portfolio of stocks and track the overall value?

 Go to the Web site that supports this text:
http://www.mhhe.com/business/mis/haag
and select "Electronic Commerce Projects."

We've included links to over 100 Web sites for finding investment opportunities using the Internet as well as getting the latest market news.

KEY TERMS AND CONCEPTS

Business Process
Business Process Reengineering (BPR)
Competitive Advantage
Control Chart
Fishbone Diagram
Global Configuration
Histogram
Information Partnership
Just-in-Time (JIT)
Learning Organization
Locationless Operation

Material Requirements Planning (MRP)
Manufacturing Resource Planning II (MRP II)
Multinational Configuration
Organizational Force
Organizational Horsepower (OHP)
Organizational Speed
Paperless Office
Pareto Chart
Permanent Team

Production Scheduling
Project Team
Quality
Scatter Diagram
Statistical Process Control (SPC)
Team
Timeless Operation
Total Quality Management (TQM)
Transborder Data Flow
Transnational Configuration
Transnational Firm
Virtual Organization

SHORT-ANSWER QUESTIONS

1. What is OHP and what are its components?
2. What are the seven OHP strategies? Which strategies provide OHP speed, which provide OHP force, and which provide both?
3. What is quality? What is TQM?
4. What are the three TQM ingredients and the purpose of each?
5. What is the just-in-time approach?
6. What is a learning organization?
7. What three reasons prevent an organization from learning?
8. What is the virtual organization?

9. What is a project team? What is a permanent team? What is the difference between the two?
10. What is an information partnership? What IT systems support an information partnership?
11. What are timeless and locationless operations? Give an example for each.
12. What is a transnational firm? What international configuration does it pursue? What are other international configurations?
13. What is business process reengineering? How is it different from total quality management?

DISCUSSION QUESTIONS

1. How does OHP affect an organization's ability to compete? How do each of the two OHP components affect how an organization competes?

2. What is quality, and does it mean something different to different people? To different organizations? How can you create a quality product or service if quality means different things?

3. How would you apply just-in-time to a service organization? To a product organization? Why are they different? Which has more value, if any? Why or why not?

4. How could teams replace departments as an organizational structure? What areas must be excluded, and what areas might be included? Why or why not?

5. Explain what is meant by organizational learning. List and explain three reasons why organizations don't learn.

6. What is the difference between a virtual organization, locationless operations, and outsourcing? When might you use each of these strategies?

7. Information partnerships require a great deal of trust. Under what circumstances would a firm enter into one with a competitor? Justify your answer with a business example.

8. How might the transnational firm seem like a virtual organization? Is the difference simply geographic? And how is either of these different from a locationless operation?

9. Why would a firm be willing to undergo business process reengineering? Is it a process to pursue regularly?

10. Of all the OHP strategies, which is the best strategy? Which is the worst? How did you reach these conclusions? Or did you?

CASE STUDY

Using Databases and Data Warehouses Instead of Shopping Carts

If you go into a retail store, you grab a shopping cart and start shopping. Would you believe that store employees also use those same shopping carts to haul around information? It's true. "Mervyn's had people who spent hours pouring over shopping carts full of paper reports," explains Sid Banjeree. Product line planners and buyers literally worked their way through shopping carts full of reports to make a decision.

Mary McCormick, Mervyn's director of planning and technology, decided something had to change. In the fast-paced, cutthroat retail industry, decision makers at Mervyn's needed a powerful repository of information that was easy to use and easy to get to. They also needed powerful

IN THE NEWS

Databases and Data Warehouses

A Gold Mine of Information

software that would work quickly through the information.

Mervyn's solution was to build a data warehouse—a collection of information just for supporting decision-making activities. To access the data warehouse, Mervyn's purchased data mining tools—special software that allows decision makers to slice and dice their way through the information. According to Sue Little, Mervyn's manager of merchandise planning and logistics systems, "We're finally comparing apples to apples, and now we're spending only 10 percent of our time gathering data and 90 percent acting upon it, rather than the other way around."

Using the data warehouse and data mining tools, buyers and inventory managers can now look online and see product information by units,

by dollars, by a single store, by season, by region, and even by ad zone, all within a few seconds. This helps them quickly decide in which ad zones to increase or reduce inventory. They can now perform these tasks in less than a minute, compared to over an hour using the shopping carts full of reports.

Mervyn's is a subdivision of Dayton Hudson Corp. And Dayton Hudson completely supports the data warehouse concept. Dayton Hudson is the fifth-largest retailer in the world, behind only Wal-Mart, Sears, Kmart, and Kroger in annual sales. Being—and staying—among the top five retailers in the world is a strategic goal for Dayton. It will only be able to do so through concepts such as data warehouses that support decision-making activities.[1, 2] ❖

FEATURES

IN THE INFORMATION AGE, KNOWLEDGE WORKERS UNDERSTAND...

1. The importance of separating the logical from the physical concerning the organization of information

2. The role of databases and database management systems in an organization

3. How to develop a knowledge worker database application

4. The role of data warehouses and data mining tools in an organization

5. Key issues in managing the information resource

Introduction

Imagine that you're the inventory manager for a multi-million dollar firm and that you can accurately predict selling trends by the week, territory, salesperson, and product line. Imagine that you own an accounting firm and can accurately predict which and how many of your clients will file for tax extensions. Imagine that you're an accounts manager and can accurately determine credit-worthy risks. Sound impossible? Not really—it's quite possible that you could make these predictions with a 95 percent accuracy rate, or even higher. How? Obviously your education has something to do with it. But so does access to and the ability to work with a resource that every organization owns today—information. *Access to* information implies that it's organized in such a way that you can easily and quickly get to it. *Working with* information implies that you have the right information-processing tools. That's what this chapter is all about—organizing information and having the right tools to work with that information.

Most people believe that working with information—especially while making a decision—is much more difficult than organizing it. And who knows, perhaps it is. But unless you organize your information in a way that is easily accessed with your tools, those tools are useless. To organize information today, most organizations rely on databases and data warehouses. To work with that information, all organizations use software—the technology tools for creating information. As applied to databases and data warehouses, the software tools are called database management systems and data mining tools, respectively.

Throughout this chapter, we will focus on (1) databases and data warehouses—the most popular methods for organizing and managing information and (2) database management systems and data mining tools—the software you use to work with information in databases and data warehouses. We have also included a vitally important section to help you learn how to develop your own personal database application. Knowing how to develop a personal database application is an important part of the concept of knowledge worker computing and a substantial career opportunity for you.

Information in an Organization Revisited

Throughout the first three chapters, we've viewed various perspectives of information, including dimensions, flows, what information describes, and isolated versus shared information. In Chapter 2, specifically, we addressed the issue of creating information by looking at transaction and analytical processing. Keeping those concepts in mind, let's now address this question: "What do organizations do with information as an important resource?" Basically, organizations do three things with information: (1) process information in the form of transactions, (2) use information to make decisions, and (3) manage information while using it.

Processing Information in the Form of Transactions

First, organizations process information in the form of transactions, as we discussed in Chapter 2. Consider your school's registration system. It processes information by capturing your registration requests and processing those requests to create your class schedule and tuition bill and update the various classes for which you've registered. In capturing and processing that information, your school's registration system is supporting the concept of online transaction processing. *Online transaction processing (OLTP)* involves gathering input information, processing that information, and updating existing information to reflect the gathered and processed information. Most organizations today use databases and database management systems to support OLTP. Databases that support OLTP are most often referred to as *operational databases*.

Using Information to Make a Decision

Once your organization captures and processes information, many people need to analyze that information to perform various decision-making tasks. In your registration system, for example, an administrator may wish to know, "How many senior-level marketing majors have not taken statistics?" This is a form of online analytical processing. *Online analytical processing (OLAP)* is the manipulation of information to support decision making. OLAP is essentially an IT-based extension of creating information through analytical processing, which we also discussed in Chapter 2.

At H-E-B Grocery Co., the largest privately held grocer in the United States with annual sales exceeding $4 billion per year, OLAP is a must.[3] All employees—category managers, buyers, accountants, sales analysts, and merchandisers—tap into a powerful data warehouse and perform queries (OLAP) to make important decisions. But that wasn't the way it used to be. Originally, recalls Greg Friedrichs, H-E-B's manager of decision support systems, "All the data resided in flat files. We could do some ad hoc queries every now and then, but there were only three people in our IS department capable of doing them." With the new system—built on the concept of a data warehouse—any user can easily perform a query from his or her desktop personal computer.

A data warehouse is, in fact, a special form of a database that contains information specifically for supporting decision-making tasks. Data warehouses differ from most other types of databases, because they are designed chiefly to support OLAP and not OLTP. Figure 4.1 provides examples that distinguish between OLTP and OLAP.

Managing Information While It Is Used

Your organization must manage its information at the same time its knowledge workers are using it. Managing information is no small task. Indeed, for most organizations it's quite a challenge. Many large organizations today track hundreds of thousands of pieces of information that must be organized and stored in a way that allows immediate access by each knowledge worker whenever he or she requires it. Let's look at Bank of America for example.[4] In 1986, its data warehouse

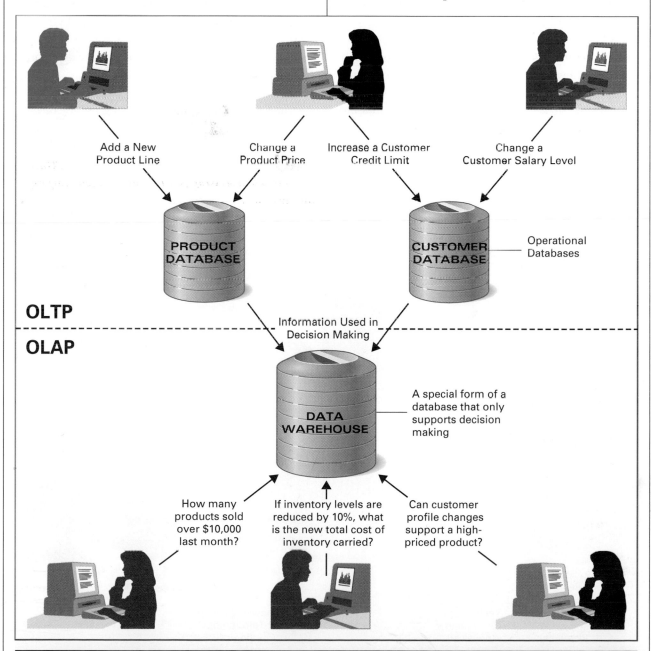

FIGURE 4.1

Online Transaction and Analytical Processing

consisted of 15 gigabytes of information and was accessed only five times a day, but each of those five queries cost Bank of America $2,430. Today, Bank of America's data warehouse has grown to 800 gigabytes, and roughly 2,000 inquiries are submitted daily at a cost of $24 each. When Robert Menicucci, senior vice president, goes to work, he can easily ask such questions as, "How many Silicon Valley residents own Acura Legends and golf club memberships?" Queries of this sort give Bank of America a competitive advantage, because it can better define its customers' lifestyles, which allows Bank of America to tailor its services and products to customer needs and wants.

Managing information includes a variety of tasks such as determining who can view or use what information, specifying how to back up information, determining how long to retain information, and identifying what storage technologies to use. Most important, managing information includes choosing the appropriate technology to organize information so that knowledge workers can *logically* use it without having to know anything about its physical

organization. The difference between logical and physical is key. In managing information, *physical* deals with the structure of information as it resides on various storage media, whereas *logical* deals with how knowledge workers view their information needs. In the optimal information-based environment, knowledge workers need to know nothing about the physical characteristics of information storage. They simply need to know the logical characteristics of their information needs. In Figure 4.2, you can see the difference between logical and physical information organization. On the physical side, technology manages information according to where it resides on various storage media and includes such terms as bits, bytes, and words. On the logical side, knowledge workers view information as logical collections of characters, fields, records, files, databases, and data warehouses.

For a knowledge worker, the smallest logical unit of information is a *character*. A logical grouping of characters is called a *field* (a person's name, a product number, price, and so on). A logical grouping of fields is a *record*. For example, all fields associated with a particular

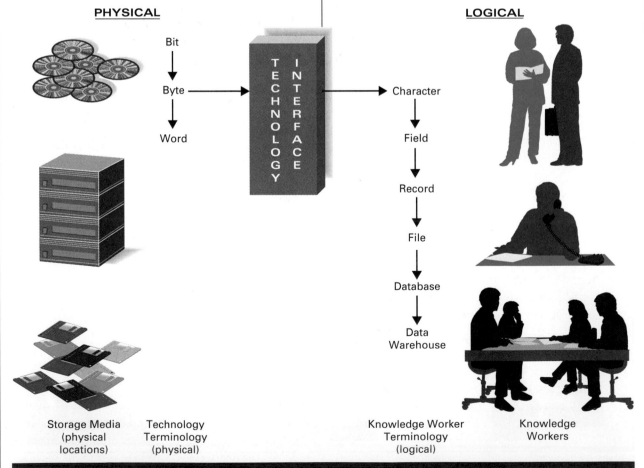

PHYSICAL

Bit → Byte → Word

TECHNOLOGY INTERFACE

Character → Field → Record → File → Database → Data Warehouse

LOGICAL

Storage Media (physical locations)   Technology Terminology (physical)

Knowledge Worker Terminology (logical)   Knowledge Workers

FIGURE 4.2

The Difference Between Logical and Physical Information Organization

Be in My Database and I'll Take You on a Cruise

Almost all business application software today uses the database concept to effectively organize and manage information. But big businesses aren't the only ones reaping the rewards of database technologies. Small businesses are also reaping benefits.

Peg Otsby, the owner of Creative Cruises, uses a sales automation package called Gold-Mine to focus her efforts on gaining new customers and retaining existing customers. For example, Peg used GoldMine to generate and then maintain a huge volume of group-sales business in the beauty salon industry.

First, Peg sent press releases to various salon trade magazines. She then used GoldMine to compile a list of 9,000 current and potential salon clients who had responded in some way to her press releases. GoldMine, which organizes and manages information in a database, allows her to easily send follow-up letters and brochures to those clients "the same day, not once or twice a week, like when everything was done manually," Peg explains. Peg can even track her salon-based clients by cruise purchase, number of cruise purchases per client, and favorite cruise destinations of each.[5, 6] ❖

product are the product record. All logically associated records comprise a *file*. For example, all product records constitute the product file. When you bring together logically associated files, you create a *database*. A product database, for example, would include a product file, an order file, and a distributor file, among others.

CAREER OPPORTUNITY

We cannot stress enough the importance of separating logical from physical when talking about information management. If you have to spend time trying to find the location of information, you have in fact **wasted** time. As a knowledge worker, you should spend all your time dealing with information logically, not physically. Need a simple example? How about a phone book. It's logically organized (alphabetically). When looking up a phone number, people don't care about page numbers—they care only about spelling.

The most recent addition to this logical view of information is a data warehouse. Data warehouses are composed of information from several databases and are central to today's logical view of information. Data warehouses bring together a wide spectrum of information from various databases to support the decision-making information needs of knowledge workers and decision makers in the form of OLAP.

Again, the key is to separate the logical from the physical. Knowledge workers should only have to know the logical characteristics of the information they need. The technology interface should then take over and convert logical information requests into their physical equivalent. If your organization does this correctly, knowledge workers can spend more time dealing with information logically as opposed to physically. To create this separation between logical and physical, tools such as databases, database management systems, data warehouses, and data mining tools provide the technology interface that allows knowledge workers to logically work with information without having to know its physical details. This technology interface is vitally important.

The Database and Database Management System Environment

In most organizations, databases and database management systems provide the foundation for organizing, managing, and working with information. In a database and database management system environment, the database contains the information, and the database management system is the collection of software tools that supports management of a database and performance of

OLTP and OLAP functions (see Figure 4.3). Employees throughout your organization—whether knowledge workers or IT specialists, such as database programmers—interact with a database by using database management system software tools.

What Is a Database?

The term "database" is perhaps one of the most overused and misunderstood terms in today's business environment. Many of the people who will tell you they have a database, in fact, have only files. Others simply refer to a gathering of information as a file. In reality, many of these files are probably databases. Consider these definitions of a database:

- Collection of data organized to serve many applications
- Collection of related files
- Integrated collection of computer data
- Collection of files
- Superset of related files

You can see why it's easy to misunderstand the database concept. Each definition refers to a database as a "collection," but describes the collection differently. Let's adopt the following definition of a database:

A **database** is a collection of information that you organize and access according to the logical structure of that information.

So you can see that a database is actually composed of two distinct parts: (1) the information itself and (2) the logical structure of that information. Let's look at a portion of an inventory database to further explore the characteristics of a database.

Important Characteristics of a Database

A Collection of Information In Figure 4.4 we've created a view of a portion of an *Inventory* database. Notice that the *Inventory* database contains two files: *Part* and *Facility*. (In reality, it would contain many more files including *Orders*, *Distributors*, and so on.) A facility is simply a storage place for parts (similar to a warehouse). Most often, a database contains two or more files with related information (although some databases may contain only one file). The *Part* and *Facility* files are logically related for two reasons. First, parts are stored in various facilities, so each file contains a common field—*Facility Number*. Second, you would use both files to manage your inventory, a common function in almost any business.

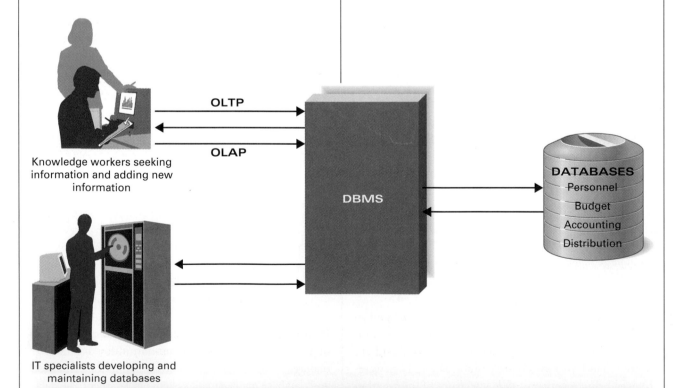

OLTP

OLAP

Knowledge workers seeking
information and adding new
information

DBMS

DATABASES
Personnel
Budget
Accounting
Distribution

IT specialists developing and
maintaining databases

FIGURE 4.3

Databases and Database Management Systems

INVENTORY DATABASE

. . . is composed of

PART FILE

Part Number	Part Name	Cost	Percentage Markup	Facility Number	Bin Number
1003	50' Tape Measure	$11.90	40.00%	291	2988
1005	25' Tape Measure	$9.95	40.00%	291	3101
1083	10 Amp Fuse	$0.07	50.00%	378	3984
1109	15 Amp Fuse	$0.07	50.00%	378	3983
2487	25 Amp Fuse	$0.08	50.00%	378	3982
2897	U.S. Socket Set	$29.75	25.00%	411	8723
3789	Crimping Tool	$14.50	30.00%	411	3298
3982	Claw Hammer	$9.90	30.00%	291	2987
4101	Metric Socket Set	$23.75	25.00%	411	4123
5908	6" Pliers	$7.45	25.00%	411	4567
6743	8" Pliers	$7.90	25.00%	411	4385

FACILITY FILE

Facility Number	Facility Name	Phone Number	Street Location	Manager Name
291	Pegasus	378-4921	3578 W. 12th St.	Greg Nelson
378	Medusa	379-2981	4314 48th Ave.	Sara Wood
411	Orion	298-8763	198 Red Ln.	James Riley

FIGURE 4.4

A Portion of an Inventory Database

A Logical Structure Using a database, you organize and access information according to its logical structure, not its physical position. A *data dictionary* contains the logical structure of information in a database. When you create a database, you first create the data dictionary. The data dictionary contains important information or logical properties about your information. The screen in Figure 4.5 shows how you can build the data dictionary for the *Part* file using Microsoft Access (a popular personal database package). Notice that the data dictionary identifies all field names, type (Currency for *Cost*, for example), size, format, default values, and so on.

This is quite different from other ways of organizing information. For example, if you want to access the information in a certain cell in most spreadsheet applications, you must know its physical position—row number and column character. With a database, however, you need only know the field name of the column of information (for example, *Percentage Markup*) and its logical row, not its physical row. As a result, in our *Inventory* database example, you could easily change the percentage markup for part number 1003, without knowing where that information is physically stored (by row or column).

Logical Ties Among the Information In a database environment, you create ties or relationships among the information that show how files relate to each other.

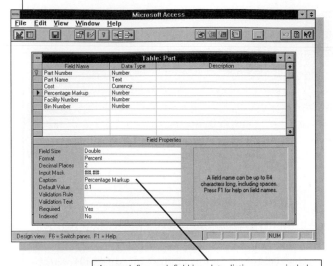

As you define each field in a data dictionary, you include certain properties that define its logical structure. The properties given here are for the field *Percentage Markup*.

FIGURE 4.5

Defining the Logical Structure of a Database

Before you can create these relationships among files, you must first specify the primary key for each file. A *primary key* is a field in a database file that uniquely describes each record. In our Inventory database, *Part Number* is the primary key for the *Part* file and *Facility Number* is the primary key for the *Facility* file.

From Figure 4.4, you can also see that *Facility Number* also appears in the *Part* file. This creates the logical relationship between the two files and is an example of

a foreign key. A *foreign key* is a primary key of one file that also appears in another file.

Built-in Integrity Constraints By defining the logical structure of information in a database, you're also developing *integrity constraints*—rules that help ensure the quality of the information. For example, by stating that *Facility Number* is the primary key of the *Facility* file and a foreign key in the *Part* file, you're saying that a part (in the *Part* file) cannot be assigned to a facility number that does not exist in the *Facility* file. Also, because you've identified *Part Number* as the primary key of the *Part* file, you're saying that no two parts can have identical part numbers.

In 1994, *Consumer Reports* rated the Ritz-Carlton first among luxury hotels.[7] Why? It's simple—Ritz-Carlton has created a powerful guest preference database to provide customized, personal, and high-level service to guests at any of its hotels. For example, if you leave a message at a Ritz-Carlton front desk that you want the bed turned down at 9 P.M., prefer no chocolate mints on your pillow, and want to participate in the 7 A.M. aerobics class, that information is passed along to the floor maid and also stored in the guest preference database. The next time you stay in a Ritz-Carlton hotel, in Palm Beach for example, your information travels with you and the hotel staff immediately knows of your desires.

For the management at Ritz-Carlton, achieving customer loyalty starts first with knowing each customer individually. That includes your exercise habits, what you most commonly consume from the snack bar in your room, how many towels you use daily, and whether you

Standardizing Information Means Ensuring Quality in Australia

The New South Wales Department of Health often found itself wrestling with differing information needs among areas and strategic management. This led to real problems—if several areas organized their information differently, there was no way they could share in the use of that information, or have strategic management consolidate information from all areas.

The only way to solve the problem was to create a standardized, organizationwide database structure. Within that structure, the Department of Health will specify integrity constraints that dictate the form of the information as well as the logical relationships that tie the information together. That standardized structure serves two purposes. First, it ensures that transaction processing (OLTP) will be uniform among all the departments. Second, it will support a variety of strategic analytical processing (OLAP) needs. As Peter Williams explains, "You can formulate queries on the fly—you can get a lot more adaptable and tap into that resource. From a strategic point of view, that was the driver."[8] ❖

THE GLOBAL PERSPECTIVE

like a chocolate on your pillow. The guest preference database contains all this information, and employees use it to fill your every need (or whim).

What Is a Database Management System?

When you use word processing software, you develop and work with a document. When you use spreadsheet software, you develop and work with a template or spreadsheet. When you use personal information management software, you develop and work with a phone book or appointment calendar. The same is true in a database environment—you use software to develop and work with a database. A *database management system (DBMS)* is the software you use to specify the logical organization for a database and access it. A DBMS contains five important software components (see Figure 4.6):

1. DBMS engine
2. Data definition subsystem
3. Data manipulation subsystem
4. Application generation subsystem
5. Data administration subsystem

DBMS Engine
Providing the Logical-to-Physical Bridge

The DBMS engine is perhaps the most important—yet seldom recognized—component of a DBMS. The *DBMS engine* accepts logical requests from the various other DBMS subsystems, converts them to their physical equivalent, and actually accesses the database and data dictionary as they exist on a storage device. Therefore, the DBMS engine allows you to work with database information from a logical point of view, without having to worry about physical and technical details. Again, the distinction between *logical* and *physical* is important in a database environment. The *physical view* of information deals with how information is physically arranged, stored, and accessed on some type of secondary storage device, such as a magnetic hard disk or CD-ROM. The *logical view* of information, on the other hand, focuses on how you as a knowledge worker need to arrange and access information to meet your particular business needs.

Databases and DBMSs provide two really great advantages in separating the logical from the physical view of information. First, the DBMS handles all physical tasks. So you, as a database user, can concentrate

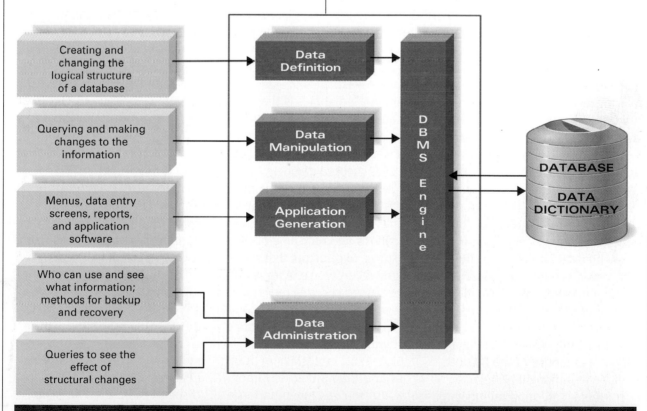

FIGURE 4.6
Software Subsystems of a Database Management System

solely on your logical information needs. Second, although there is only one physical view of information, there may be numerous knowledge workers who have different logical views of the information in a database. That is, according to what business tasks they need to perform, different knowledge workers logically view information in different ways. The DBMS engine can process virtually any logical information view or request into its physical equivalent.

Data Definition Subsystem
Defining the Logical Structure of a Database

The *data definition subsystem* of a DBMS helps you create and maintain the data dictionary and define the structure of the files in a database. Recall that a data dictionary contains the logical structure of information in a database. The data definition subsystem of a DBMS is often called the "data definition language" or DDL. Figure 4.5 on page 134 contains a DDL screen for the *Part* file.

The most important function of the data definition subsystem is that it supports your ability to define the logical structure or properties of the information when you first create a database. Once again, as you do this the DBMS engine, not you, is responsible for developing the physical structure of the information as it will appear on a storage device. Logical structures of information include the following:

Logical Structures (Properties)	Example
Name	*Part Number, Bin Number*
Type	Alphabetic, numeric, date, time, etc.
Form	Is an area code required for a phone number?
Default value	If no percentage markup is entered, the default is 10%.

Saving Lives with Information

Kaiser Permanente is the largest and oldest HMO in the United States. It has remained the largest HMO for many years by providing the best possible health care at an affordable price. Recently, Kaiser took a bold step toward a new method of improving and prolonging the lives of diabetics. No, it's not a new medical procedure or drug. It's called a data warehouse—a large collection of information designed specifically to help people make decisions.

In 1994, Kaiser set up a data warehouse of the 84,000 diabetics among its 2.4 million northern California members. The data warehouse includes information from billing, ad-missions, various lab departments, doctor's records, and surveys. What Kaiser found was alarming, to say the least.

Although diabetes is the leading cause of blindness, Kaiser discovered that only 15 to 20 percent of its diabetic patients were getting their eyes checked routinely. Kaiser also discovered that medical practitioners in routine office visits were not making strong enough recommendations for combating obesity and stress, two factors that make diabetes even worse. As a result, Kaiser is now enforcing more rigorous eye-screening programs and setting up patient support groups for obesity and stress.

Blue Plus, an HMO of Blue Cross and Blue Shield of Minnesota, also realizes the importance of information-based preventive programs. It has developed a mammography program called *A Decision for Life.* The database that supports the program now contains information on over 30,000 women aged 50 to 75. Using various data manipulation tools, Blue Plus sends reminders to those women, urging them to have a mammogram. Those reminders are paying off—the number of Blue Plus patients aged 50 and older coming in for mammograms increased from 68 to 84 percent in 2 years.

The key to the success of the Kaiser and Blue Plus programs is IT tools such as databases and DBMSs that support the concepts of data warehousing and mining. The health care industry as a whole is expected to spend more than $6 billion in 1996 on information technology.[9,10] ❖

Validation rule	Can percentage markups exceed 100%?
Is an entry required?	Must you enter a *Facility Number* for a part or can it be blank?
Can there be duplicates?	Primary keys cannot be duplicates, but what about percentage markups?

Once you've created a database, the data definition subsystem also allows you to define new fields, delete fields, or change field properties. For example, you could easily add a new field—*Price*—to the *Part* file and define it as *Cost* * (1 + *Percentage Markup*).

Data Manipulation Subsystem
Mining and Changing
Information in a Database

The ***data manipulation subsystem*** of a DBMS helps you add, change, and delete information in a database and mine it for valuable information. Software tools within the data manipulation subsystem are most often the primary interface between you as a user and the information contained in a database. In most DBMSs, you'll find a variety of data manipulation tools, including views, report generators, query-by-example tools, and structured query language.

Views Views are perhaps the simplest tools to use when you want to mine information from a database or change information contained in a database. A *view* allows you to see the content of a database file, make whatever changes you want, perform simple sorting, and query to find the location of specific information. The screen in Figure 4.7 shows a view in Microsoft Access for the *Part* file of our *Inventory* database. At this point, you could click on any specific field and change its content. You could also point to an entire record and click on the cut icon (the scissors) to remove a record. If you want to add a record, simply click the *Part Number* field of the first blank record and begin typing. Notice, we've sorted the file in ascending order by *Part Number*. You can easily achieve this by clicking on the A → Z sort button in the view window. If you want to sort in descending order by *Percentage Markup*, simply point to any *Percentage Markup* field and click the Z → A sort button. You can also perform searches within views. For example, if you want to find all parts that have the term "pliers" in the *Part Name* field, simply point anywhere in that

column, click on the "find text" button (the binoculars) and enter "pliers." Access will respond by highlighting each *Part Name* field where the word "pliers" appears.

Report Generators *Report generators* help you quickly define formats of reports and what information you want to see in a report. Once you define a report, you can simply view it on the screen or print it. Figure 4.8 shows an intermediate screen in Microsoft Access that allows you to specify which fields of information are to appear in a report. We have chosen to include all fields in the report except *Part Name* and *Bin Number*. Following a simple and easy-to-use set of screens, we went on to specify that sorting should take place by *Facility Number* and that the name of the report should be "Parts by Facility Location." The completed report is shown in Figure 4.9. Notice that it only displays those fields we requested, that it's sorted by *Facility Number*, and that the title is "Parts by Facility Location."

Query-by-Example Tools *Query-by-example (QBE) tools* help you graphically design the answer to a question. In our *Inventory* database, for example, "What are the names and phone numbers of the facility managers who are in charge of parts that have a cost greater than $10?" The question may seem simple considering that we have only 3 facilities and 11 parts in our database. However, can you imagine trying to answer that question if 100 facilities and 70,000 parts were involved? It would not be fun.

Fortunately, data manipulation tools such as QBE can help you answer questions or perform queries in a matter of seconds. In Figure 4.10, you can see a QBE screen that

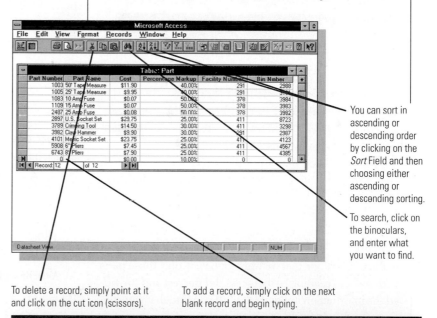

To delete a record, simply point at it and click on the cut icon (scissors).

To add a record, simply click on the next blank record and begin typing.

You can sort in ascending or descending order by clicking on the *Sort* Field and then choosing either ascending or descending sorting.

To search, click on the binoculars, and enter what you want to find.

FIGURE 4.7
A View in Microsoft Access

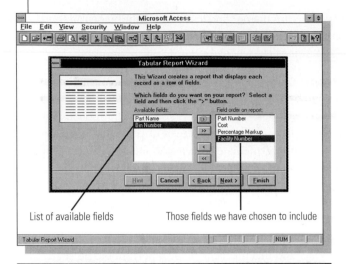

FIGURE 4.8

Specifying Fields for a Report

Parts by Facility Location			
09-Jun-96			
Part Number	Cost	Percentage Markup	Facility Number
1005	$9.95	40.00%	291
1003	$11.90	40.00%	291
3982	$9.90	30.00%	291
1083	$0.07	50.00%	378
1109	$0.07	50.00%	378
2487	$0.08	50.00%	378
2897	$29.75	25.00%	411
3789	$14.50	30.00%	411
4101	$23.75	25.00%	411
5908	$7.45	25.00%	411
6743	$7.90	25.00%	411

FIGURE 4.9

The Completed Report

answers our question. When you perform a QBE, you (1) identify the files in which the information is located, (2) drag any necessary fields from the identified fields to the QBE grid, and (3) specify selection criteria.

For names and phone numbers of facility managers in charge of parts with costs over $10, we first identified two files—*Part* and *Facility*. Second, we dragged *Part Number*, *Facility Number*, and *Cost* from the *Part* file to the QBE grid and dragged *Manager Name* and *Phone Number* from the *Facility* file to the QBE grid. Finally, we specified in the Criteria box that we wanted to view only those parts with costs exceeding $10. Access did the rest and provided the information in Figure 4.11. If you find that you consistently use a certain query such as the one above, you can save it. When needed later, you would simply specify the name of the query, and it would automatically be performed.

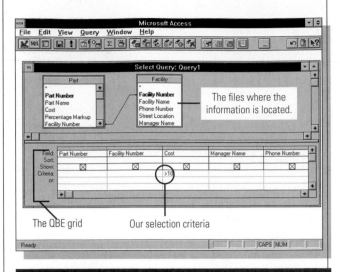

FIGURE 4.10

Specifying Information for a Query-by-Example

Structured Query Language *Structured query language (SQL)* is a standardized fourth generation query language found in most database environments. By standardized, we mean that a committee has developed a set of guidelines stating how SQL should work, no matter which hardware or DBMS software you use. Standardized languages, such as SQL, are of great benefit to you because once you learn them for a particular system you don't have to relearn how they work for other systems. This is not true for views, QBE, and report generators which operate differently for different DBMSs.

SQL performs the same function as QBE, except that you perform the query by creating a statement instead of pointing, clicking, and dragging. In other words, SQL is sentenced-based rather than graphics-based. The basic form of an SQL statement is

SELECT ... FROM ... WHERE ...

After the SELECT, you list the fields of information you want; after the FROM, you specify in what files those fields are located; and after the WHERE, you specify any selection criteria. If we consider the query performed above using QBE, the SQL statement would be:

SELECT   DISTINCTROW Part.[Part Number], Part.[Facility Number], Part.Cost, Facility.[Manager Name], Facility.[Phone Number]

FROM   Part INNER JOIN Facility ON Part.[Facility Number] = Facility.[Facility Number]

WHERE   ((Part.Cost>10));

This SQL statement is identical to the previous QBE example and provides the same results. Consider the SELECT clause. It requests *Part Number, Facility Number,* and *Cost* from the *Part* file (the file name is

Part Number	Facility Number	Cost	Manager Name	Phone Number
4101	411	$23.75	James Riley	298-8763
3789	411	$14.50	James Riley	298-8763
1003	291	$11.90	Greg Nelson	378-4921
2897	411	$29.75	James Riley	298-8763

FIGURE 4.11

The Results of Our Query-by-Example

given before each field name followed by a period). It also requests *Manager Name* and *Phone Number* from the *Facility* file. The FROM clause creates a join between the fields listed for the two files and matches the joining information when *Facility Number* is a match. Finally, the WHERE clause states that the only desired information is when *Cost* exceeds $10.

As you can tell, QBE is much simpler and easier to use than SQL for answering simple questions or performing simple queries. However, QBE becomes limited when you want to gather information from more than two files. SQL, on the other hand, will allow you to build a query that may include information from as many as 10 different files.

Application Generation Subsystem
Developing Database Applications

The ***application generation subsystem*** of a DBMS contains facilities to help you develop transaction-intensive applications. These types of applications usually require that you perform a detailed series of tasks to process a transaction. Application generation subsystem facilities include tools for creating data entry screens, programming languages specific to a particular DBMS, and interfaces to commonly used programming languages that are independent of any DBMS. In Figure 4.12, you can see a sample data entry screen for entering new parts into our *Inventory* database. This data entry screen is much more visually appealing and easier to use than a view. We could also add other helpful features to this data entry screen, including a pull-down list in the *Facility Number* field that would let the user choose from a list of available facilities in which to store the new part.

Each DBMS also comes with its own programming language that you can use to write transaction-intensive applications. In the personal database environment, for example, Microsoft Access has its own programming language as do other popular DBMS packages like Paradox, FoxPro, and dBASE. DBMS packages for larger

systems such as DB/2 also provide their own programming languages.

Because databases are such an integral part of today's business environment, most DBMS packages support an interface to today's more popular general-purpose

CAREER OPPORTUNITY

Knowledge workers always ask the same question about data manipulation subsystem tools: "Which are best?" Unfortunately, the answer is, "It depends on what you're trying to do." If you're working with only a few files that contain only a few records, views and QBE are great. If you want to just generate reports and not change any information, report generators are the way to go. If, on the other hand, you're trying to perform complex queries using numerous files with large amounts of information, SQL is probably best. What does all this mean for you? Learn how to use all the data manipulation tools available to you.

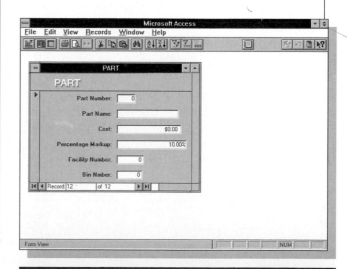

FIGURE 4.12

A Sample Data Entry Screen

programming languages. In COBOL for example—the most widely used programming language for business applications—SQL statements can be embedded to quickly and rapidly access database-stored information. Other languages such as C++ and Smalltalk also support embedded SQL statements.

Data Administration Subsystem
Managing the Database

The *data administration subsystem* of a DBMS helps you manage the overall database environment by providing facilities for backup and recovery, security management, query optimization, reorganization, concurrency control, and change management. The data administration subsystem is most often used by a data administrator or database administrator—people responsible for assuring that the database environment meets the entire information needs of the organization.

Backup and recovery facilities provide a way for you to (1) periodically back up information contained in a database and (2) restart or recover a database and its information in case of a failure. These are important functions you cannot ignore in today's information-based business environment. Organizations that understand the importance of their information in a database take precautions

TEAM WORK

Defining Information Privileges During University Registration

uppose your school supports complete online paperless registration of classes—from class scheduling by the faculty, to class selection approval by advisers, to actual registration by you. In this type of environment, people need different types of information access privileges. As a student, for example, you need "view" privileges of available classes but not the privilege of adding a new class.

Consider further that the registration environment is restricted to four groups of information—Student, Course, Class, and Courses Taken (similar to your transcript). In this instance, we define a class as a scheduled course. For example, a course may be Introduction to Financial Markets, while scheduled instances of that course (called classes) would be section I at 9:00 on MWF and section II at 8:00 on TTH.

1. For each of these four groups of information, identify specific pieces of information that would need to be stored. For example, Student information would include Student I.D., Name, Major, and so on.

2. After you've identified specific pieces of information for each group, determine the access privileges for the following people. For each of the people, identify whether they should have "view," "add," "change," or "delete" privileges.

Students	Instructional Faculty
Deans	Department Chairs
Director of Registration	Director of Housing
Director of Financial Aid	President/Provost

If you want, you can build a grid. To do so, list the people above in the columns and the pieces of information in the rows. Then, in the appropriate cells, place a "V" for view privileges, an "A" for add privileges, a "C" for change privileges, and/or a "D" for delete privileges.

What would be the potential impact if these access privileges were not properly controlled by the DBMS administration subsystem? ❖

ON YOUR OWN

DBMS Support for OLTP, OLAP, and Information Management

In the table below, we've listed the various DBMS subsystems or tools. For each of these, identify whether it supports online transaction processing, online analytical processing, both online transaction and analytical processing, or the management of a database. ❖

DBMS Tool	OLTP	OLAP	Both	Management
DBMS engine				
View				
Report generator				
QBE				
SQL				
Data entry screen				
DBMS programming language				
Common programming language				
Data administration subsystem				

to preserve it by running backup databases, a DBMS, and storage facilities parallel to the primary database environment. These backup systems can immediately take over if the primary system fails, often without interrupting service to the users and application software.

Security management facilities allow you to control who has access to what information and what type of access those people have. In many database environments, for example, some people may need only "view" access to database information, but not "change" privileges. Still others may need the ability to add, change, and/or delete information in a database. Through a system of user-specification and password levels, the data administration subsystem allows you to define which users can perform which tasks and what information they can see. At car dealership JM Family Enterprises (JMFE), security management facilities are an absolute must because its technology environment is highly decentralized and includes many users of mobile technologies.[11] JMFE's system supports encryption and passwords to protect databases, files, and many hardware resources. The system even supports automatic log-offs after a certain amount of time if users accidentally leave their system running.

Query optimization facilities often take queries from users (in the form of SQL statements or QBEs) and restructure them to minimize response times. In SQL,

for example, you can build a query statement that might involve working with as many as 10 files. Fortunately, you don't have to worry about structuring the SQL statement in the most optimized fashion. The query optimization facilities will do that for you and provide you with the information you need in the fastest possible way.

CAREER OPPORTUNITY

Which DBMS software component or subsystem is most important? The answer is that they all are equally important. No matter what you're trying to do, the DBMS engine, data definition, data manipulation, application generation, and data administration subsystems are vital. To create a successful database in your organization, you must exploit each of these subsystems fully. Your career opportunity lies in understanding the major tasks each subsystem performs. Although you may never personally be involved in backing up a database, having information backed up may become crucial to you if your primary database fails.

Reorganization facilities continually maintain statistics concerning how the DBMS engine physically accesses information. In maintaining those statistics, reorganization facilities can optimize the physical structure of a

Finance Firms Put On the Technology Gloves for a Real Fight

According to Dudley Nigg, executive vice president for direct distribution at Wells Fargo Bank, "If we're going to stay competitive, we'll have to stay competitive technologically." If there ever was a statement in support of using technology to stay in business and gain a competitive advantage, that may very well be it. Banks alone were estimated to have spent over $19 billion on technology in 1996.

Financial service firms seeking a competitive advantage are using technology in a variety of ways. Fidelity Investments, for example, has implemented customer-oriented voice recognition technology. And Charles Schwab & Co. leads the way in electronic account management on the Internet, with 24 percent of its transactions occurring on PCs all over the world.

But technology alone isn't enough; these firms also need information about current and potential customers. Therefore, many of them are building databases and data warehouses that contain internally generated information and information purchased from external database providers about their customers. Using this information, financial service firms are determining customers' (current and potential) exact tastes and predicting their future buying decisions. With that information, these firms are then able to get customers to buy more financial products through sophisticated mail and telephone solicitations.

Information technology is a vitally important tool. But don't ever forget what you use technology for—to work with information.[12] ❖

database to further increase speed and performance. For example, if you frequently access a certain file by specific order, the reorganization facilities may maintain the file in that presorted order or create an index that maintains the sorted order of the file.

Concurrency control facilities ensure the validity of database updates when multiple users attempt to access and change the same information. This is crucial in today's networked business environment. In an airline reservation system, for example, if two reservation agents attempt to simultaneously reserve the same seat on a flight for two different passengers, who gets the seat? What happens to the person who did not get his or her requested seat? These are important questions that must be answered and, once answered, defined in the database environment using concurrency control facilities.

Change management facilities allow you to assess the impact of proposed structural changes to a database environment. For example, if you decide to add a character identifier to a numeric part number, you can use the change management facilities to see how many files will be affected. Recall that *Part Number* would be the primary key for a *Part* file and that it would also be a foreign key in many other files. Sometimes, structural changes may not have much effect on the database (adding a four-digit zip code extension), but others can cause widespread

changes that you must assess carefully before implementing.

The Relational Database Model

When your organization decides to create a database environment, one of the most important questions to answer is which database model to adopt. There are actually four database models in use today—the hierarchical, network, relational, and object-oriented database models. The hierarchical and network database models are the oldest of the four and the least used. In this section, we concentrate on the most widely used model—the relational database model; in the next section we'll look at the object-oriented database model—the newest of the four.

The relational database model is the most widely used model for modeling information in a database, for both personal and business environments (see Figure 4.13). The **relational database model** uses a series of two-dimensional tables or files to store information. The term **relation** describes each two-dimensional table in the relational model (hence its name *relational database model*).

Our previous example of the *Inventory* database is in fact a relational database. It maintains part information

1993 Use for "Most Important" Databases

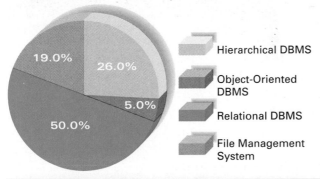

Hierarchical DBMS

Object-Oriented DBMS

Relational DBMS

File Management System

1995 Use for "Most Important" Databases

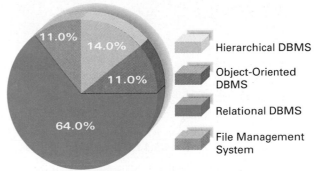

Hierarchical DBMS

Object-Oriented DBMS

Relational DBMS

File Management System

FIGURE 4.13

Database Models and Their Use in 1993 and 1995

in a two-dimensional table and maintains facility information in another two-dimensional table. Each table or relation in a relational database model stores information pertaining to a particular entity class. An *entity class* is a concept—typically people, places, or things—about which you wish to store information and that you can identify with a unique key (called the primary key).

Entity classes are easy to find. At your college or university, for example, entity classes would include students, classes, courses, rooms, faculty, departments, and so on. You are an *instance* of the "student" entity class. That is, an *instance* is an occurrence of an entity class that can be uniquely described (for you, it would be with your student I.D. number or social security number).

Let's consider another example—a video rental store—and look more closely at the relational model. In Figure 4.14, you can see the relational database model for a small video rental store. Notice that there are four relations that contain information pertaining to four different entity classes—*Customer, Video, Video Rental,* and *Distributor.* The information in each of these four relations is logically related to other relations by the presence of foreign keys—primary keys of one relation that exist in another relation.

For example, *Dist Num* is the primary key of the *Distributor* relation that uniquely identifies each distributor from which the video rental store buys videos. *Dist Num* also appears as a foreign key in the *Video* relation—this allows you to define which videos were purchased from which distributor. If you look closely at the *Video Rental* relation, you'll notice that two fields make up the primary key—*Cust ID* and *Video Num.* In this particular instance, the primary key of the *Video Rental* relation is a *composite primary key*—a primary key that uses more than one field to create a unique description (a primary key that uses only one field is an *atomic primary key*).

The composite key is necessary because a customer can rent many videos, and a video can be rented by many different customers (at different times). So the composite primary key for the *Video Rental* relation is composed of two foreign keys—the primary key *Cust ID* in the *Customer* relation and the primary key *Video Num* in the *Video* relation.

The greatest advantage of the relational database model is that it's built on the relatively simple concept of representing information in two-dimensional tables (relations). Most people can easily identify entity classes and then create and work with simple two-dimensional tables that contain information describing those entity classes. Julie Cox, at Lucile Salter Packard Children's Hospital in Palo Alto, hopes that a relational database will bring the hospital into 1990s technology and make it more information-accurate.[13] She explains, "There is a huge amount of duplication in using traditional paper and processes and the new system [a relational database] provides much more accuracy and timeliness." At the 160-bed facility, there are about 1,400 terminals and personal computers from which doctors, nurses, and other professionals will be able to access information in the relational database. Doctors will even be able to access the information by dialing into the system while they are away from the hospital.

The Object-Oriented Database Model

Technology—its abilities, how you use it, and how you perceive its use in business—is changing every day. The same is certainly true for database technologies. In past years, the network and hierarchical database models were the most widely used; today it's the relational model.

Customer Relation

Cust ID	Name	Phone	Address
47857	Jake Stevens	237-6871	2352 8th Ave.
47952	Abigail Green	237-2310	124 Northland
67098	C. J. Smerud	239-7101	P.O. Box 124a
97832	Devin Cash	446-7987	1372 Ivanhoe

Primary key   Foreign key   Primary keys

Video Rental Relation

Cust ID	Video Num	Date Rented	Date Returned
97832	1111-2	3-11-97	3-13-97
47952	4371-1	4-14-97	4-17-97
47952	4781-2	4-14-97	

Foreign key

Video Relation

Video Num	Name	Type	Dist Num	Days	Rental Price
1111-1	Tides Gone Bad	Drama	457	2	$3.00
1111-2	Tides Gone Bad	Drama	457	2	$3.00
2356-1	Horror Night	Horror	235	2	$1.50
4371-1	The Alien	Sci Fi	381	2	$3.00
4781-1	Phobia	Horror	457	1	$3.00
4781-2	Phobia	Horror	457	1	$3.00

Primary key

Because *Dist Num* is the primary key of the *Distributor* relation and also appears in the *Video* relation, it's a foreign key in the *Video* relation.

Primary key

Distributor Relation

Dist Num	Name	Phone
235	Hughes Films	(800) 234-8000
986	ABC Enterprises	(212) 543-9822
457	North Film Works	(800) 320-2000
381	NBC Capitol	(800) 632-9721

FIGURE 4.14

A Relational Database Model for a Video Rental Store

Using a Database to Dominate Niche Marketing

Some retailers believe that households with annual incomes of less than $25,000 are bad credit risks. Fingerhut thinks otherwise. Located in Minnetonka, Minnesota, Fingerhut is the fourth-largest mail-order company in the United States, focusing on households whose annual incomes are less than $25,000. And it's paying off. Fingerhut currently has over 13 million "good credit" customers and has a 14 percent annual growth rate, even during the recession.

Fingerhut's strategy is to dominate a market niche through sophisticated customer information analysis. In 1992, for example, Fingerhut had over 150 specialty catalog mailings and major promotional campaigns. Each of these was based on statistically determined predictions about consumer behavior. What makes these predictions possible is a huge database of customer information.

For each existing and potential customer, Fingerhut tracks over 1,400 pieces of information. This includes demographic information, such as income level, home ownership status, appliance ownership, and purchasing histories from various categories of products. For each household, Fingerhut also tracks the name, age, sex, and birth date of each child. When a child has a birthday, the parents receive a personalized mailing that often says, "Here's wishing Dominique a happy birthday in May. We've enclosed a catalog of some great gifts for her. And when you order any of these, we'll send her a free surprise birthday gift."

Because of its extensive use of technology, specifically the development of predictive models based on a consumer database, Fingerhut's marketing strategy differs dramatically from other retailers and mail-order companies. Indeed, Fingerhut is succeeding where others have failed, thanks in part to its use of a consumer database.[14, 15] ❖

A new database model, however, has emerged that very well may define how the majority of tomorrow's databases will look and work. That new database model is the object-oriented database model.

The object-oriented database model cannot be properly defined without some understanding of its underlying foundation—an object. An **object** is a software module containing information that describes an entity class along with a list of procedures that can act on the information describing the entity class. In this instance, an entity class is the same as for the relational database model. So an object includes (or encapsulates) both information about a specific entity class and the software instructions (procedures) to work with that information.

In Figure 4.15, you can see the four object representations for the video rental store (the relational representation for the video rental store is in Figure 4.14). Notice that each object contains both information and procedures. For example, the VIDEO RENTAL object contains *Date Rented* and *Date Returned* as well as the procedures for updating those two fields—*Create New Video Rental* (which would specify today's date as *Date Rented*) and *Change Date Returned*. Notice also that the VIDEO RENTAL object contains two other objects— CUSTOMER and VIDEO. This is necessary because the transaction is called a video rental when a customer rents a video.

Now that you understand something about objects, let's return to object-oriented databases. An **object-oriented database** (**O-O database** or **OODB**) is a database model that brings together, stores, and allows you to work with both information and procedures that act on the information. An **object-oriented database management system** (**O-O DBMS** or **OODBMS**) is the DBMS software that allows you to develop and work with an object-oriented database. Unlike the relational database model, which stores information in a two-dimensional table separate from the procedures that act on that information, an O-O database combines both.

In Appendix C, we cover object-oriented technologies in more detail. But from our example here, you can see several key features that have led many people to believe that object-oriented technologies will become the foundation for how organizations will store and work

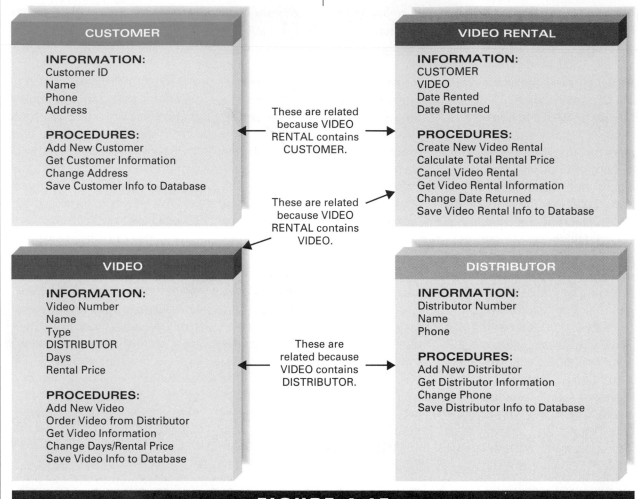

FIGURE 4.15

An Object Representation for a Video Rental Store

with information in the future. First, combining information and procedures more closely models how an organization works as opposed to the relational database model. When you consider the inventory function in a typical business for example, you don't think only about information (quantity on hand, reorder points, cost, price, and so on), and you don't think only of procedures (back ordering, processing invoices, and so on). Instead, you actually consider information and procedures together as a series of business processes. Again, other database models, such as the relational model, actually require you to consider and model information separately from procedures.

The second key feature of object-oriented technologies is that of reuse. *Reuse* simply means that, once you define a set of procedures for a given object, those procedures can also be used by other objects. For example, in Figure 4.15 you can see that the VIDEO RENTAL object contains the CUSTOMER object. So, while a clerk is in the process of checking out a video to a customer

(using the VIDEO RENTAL object), the customer could request that his or her address be changed. Because the VIDEO RENTAL object contains the CUSTOMER object (which would include all information and procedures), the clerk can easily make the address change without having to stop the video rental process, go to another part of the system, change the customer's address, and return to the video rental process.

Knowledge Worker Computing and Developing Your Own Database

Databases and DBMSs are everywhere—in small businesses (for example, the video rental store above), in medium-sized businesses, and in large businesses. Using a DBMS, you can mine these databases for valuable information to help identify problems or opportunities, which can help your organization be more competitive in the marketplace. But what about your personal information needs? Can building a personal database help you do a better job? In many instances, the answer is most definitely yes. But using a personal database amounts to more than using the various DBMS tools. You must also know how to actually build a database. "Knowing how" falls within the concept of knowledge worker computing, because knowledge worker computing includes placing technology knowledge in your hands.

So let's take a look at how you would go about building a database that meets your personal information needs. The four steps include:

❶ Defining entity classes and primary keys

❷ Defining relationships among entity classes

❸ Defining information (fields) for each relation

❹ Using a data definition language to create the database

Let's assume that you own a small business and are interested in tracking employees by the department in which they work, job assignment, and number of hours assigned to each job. You have no IT specialists working for you, so it's up to you to build the database. Each of your employees can be assigned to only one department, but a department may have many employees (a department, however, may not have any employees assigned to it). Further, each employee can be assigned to any number of jobs and a job can have many employees assigned to it, but it's not necessary that any employees be assigned to a certain job. Figure 4.16 contains a sample employee report that you could generate.

Step 1: Defining Entity Classes and Primary Keys

The first and most important step in developing a relational database is to define the various entity classes and the primary keys that uniquely identify each instance within each entity class. For your database, you can easily

INDUSTRY PERSPECTIVE

Transportation

Reengineering Through Objects

To reengineer or not to reengineer was never the question. For Skyway Freight Systems, a California-based transportation systems company, it was simply *how* to reengineer. Skyway chose to reengineer using an object-oriented approach, and it has never looked back or regretted its decision.

Before going to objects, Skyway employed five people in its claims processing department. Now, because of the use of objects, the claims processing department has shrunk to three people. But their productivity has risen by 400 percent, while reducing the time to process a claim from 10 days to 5 days and reducing data entry from 30 minutes to a mere 5 minutes.

The programmers at Skyway program with objects in unique ways. Says David Moore, "Object-oriented programming takes the grunge work out of programming." When methods such as object-oriented programming and object-oriented databases increase process productivity and programmer satisfaction, they become important business tools.

If you're interested in learning more about object-oriented programming and databases, check out these Web sites:

http://www.cs.usask.ca/grads/wlml125cmpt856/linkobj.html— Object-oriented links page

http://src.doc.ic.ac.uk/bySubject/Computing/Languages.html— Links to programming languages

http://src.doc.ic.ac.uk/bySubject/Computing/Languages.html— Index or object-oriented resources from SIGS Publications, Inc.

http://volta.polito.it/marco/oosites.html—Index of object-oriented sites

You can also connect to the Web site for this text at http://www.mhhe.com/business/mis/haag. There, you'll find a list of the most popular object-oriented database technologies, including vendor names and phone numbers.[16] ❖

Emp ID	Name	Dept	Dept Sup	# Emp	Job	Job Name	Hours	Job	Job Name	Hours
1234	Jones	43	Halston	3	14	Acct	4	23	Sales	4
2345	Smith	15	Dallas	1	14	Acct	8			
6548	Joslin	43	Halston	3	23	Sales	6	46	Admin	2
9087	Mills	43	Halston	3	23	Sales	5	14	Acct	3
8797	Jones	69	Irving	1	39	Maint	8			

FIGURE 4.16
A Sample Report in Your Personal Database Environment

identify the entity classes as *Employee*, *Department*, and *Job*. Now you have to identify their primary keys.

For most entity classes, you cannot use names as primary keys because duplicate names may exist. For example, you have two employees with the last name of Jones. From the sample employee report, however, you can see that each employee, department, and job has a number, and the number assigned to each is unique. Therefore, the primary key for *Employee* is *Emp ID*, the primary key for *Department* is *Dept*, and the primary key for *Job* is *Job*.

Step 2: Defining Relationships Among Entity Classes

The next step in developing a relational database model is to define the relationships among the identified entity classes. To help you do this, we'll use an entity-relationship diagram. An ***entity-relationship diagram (E-R***

diagram) is a graphic method of representing entity classes and their relationships. An E-R diagram includes seven basic symbols:

1. A rectangle to denote an entity class
2. A diamond to denote a relationship between two entity classes
3. A line to connect symbols
4. A "1" to denote a single occurrence
5. An "M" to denote multiple occurrences
6. A "|" to denote a required relationship
7. An "o" to denote an optional relationship

In Figure 4.17, you can see the E-R diagram for your database using these symbols. Let's take some time to explore how to create and read an E-R diagram.

Consider the portion of the E-R diagram shown at the top of the next page. To help you read the symbols, we've added dashed lines and arrows.

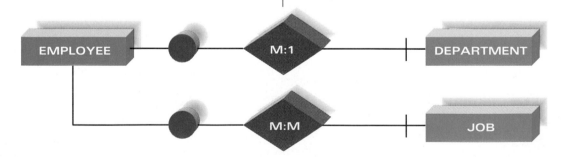

ENTITY-RELATIONSHIP DIAGRAM SYMBOLS

	A rectangle denotes an entity class.	——— A line connects symbols.	**M** An M denotes multiple occurrences.	● A circle denotes an optional relationship.
	A diamond denotes a relationship between two entity classes.	**1** A 1 denotes a single occurrence.		A dash denotes a required relationship.	

FIGURE 4.17
An Entity-Relationship Diagram

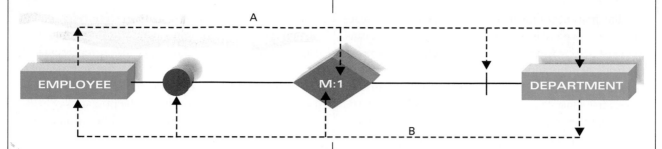

Following the arrows marked "A," you would read the E-R diagram as, "An *Employee* is assigned to one and must be assigned to one *Department*." So, that part of the E-R diagram states that the relationship between *Employee* and *Department* is that an *Employee* must be assigned to one *Department* and that no *Employee* can be assigned to more than one *Department*. Following the arrows marked "B," you would read the E-R diagram as, "A *Department* may have many *Employees* assigned to it but is not required to have any *Employees* assigned to it." So, that part of the E-R diagram states the relationship between *Department* and *Employee*. It's important that you understand that E-R diagrams are read in both directions between two entity classes. Our portion of the E-R diagram includes the relationship between *Employee* and *Department* and between *Department* and *Employee*.

Building the initial E-R diagram is a relatively simple process. All you have to do is draw the entity class rectangles on a sheet of paper and decide whether relationships exist between two entity classes. If they do, draw the diamond between the two entity classes and determine whether a "1" or an "M" (many) is appropriate. Finally, you have to determine whether the relationship between two entity classes is required or optional.

After developing the initial E-R diagram, it's time to begin the process of normalization. ***Normalization*** is a process of ensuring that a relational database structure can be implemented as a series of two-dimensional tables. The complete normalization process is quite extensive and outside the scope of this text. For our purposes, we will focus on the following three rules of normalization:

❶ Eliminate repeating groups or M:M relationships

❷ Assure that each field in a relation depends only on the primary key of that relation

❸ Remove all derived fields from the relations

ON YOUR OWN

Finding One-to-One Relationships in the Real World

In the real world, one-to-many (1:M), many-to-one (M:1), and many-to-many (M:M) relationships between entity classes are easy to find. What's really difficult to find are one-to-one (1:1) relationships. Consider the E-R diagram below for a blood bank. It states that there is a one-to-one relationship between a unit of blood and a unit of plasma. That is, a unit of blood can be converted to one unit of plasma, at most, and that one unit of plasma comes from one unit of blood.

When most people think of one-to-one relationships, they come up with husband to wife, but in many countries that's not true. Other people may say there is a one-to-one relationship between a mother and a child. But a mother can have many children.

How many examples of one-to-one relationships can you think of? Because there is a relationship, the primary key of one entity class must appear in the other entity class. Where would you put the foreign key? Does it matter? What about for our unit of blood and unit of plasma relationship? ❖

BLOOD — 1:1 — PLASMA

The first rule of normalization states that no repeating groups can exist in an entity class (or that an M:M cannot exist between two entity classes). Repeating groups are fields of information that appear more than once in an entity class. You can find repeating groups in two ways. First, look at your Employee report in Figure 4.16. Note that three fields—*Job*, *Job Name*, and *Hours*—appear twice as columns of information. Second, the presence of a many-to-many (M:M) relationship in an E-R diagram also identifies a repeating group. You can look at the E-R diagram in Figure 4.17 and see that there is a many-to-many (M:M) relationship between *Employee* and *Job*. To develop the best relational database model, you cannot have repeating groups or many-to-many relationships between entity classes. Let's look at how to eliminate the repeating group in your E-R diagram.

In Figure 4.18, we have developed the appropriate relationship between *Employee* and *Job* by removing the repeating groups. Notice that we started with the original portion of the E-R diagram and created a relationship in between *Employee* and *Job* called *Employee-Job*, which

is an intersection relation. An ***intersection relation*** is a relation you create to eliminate a repeating group. It is called an intersection relation because it represents an intersection of primary keys between the first two relations. That is, an intersection relation will have a composite primary key that consists of the primary key fields from the two intersecting relations. The primary key fields from the original two relations now become foreign keys in the intersection relation. When combined, these two foreign keys make up the composite primary key for the intersection relation.

For your database, the intersection relation *Employee-Job* represents which employees are assigned to each job. If you read the relationship between *Employee* and *Employee-Job*, it states that an employee can have many jobs and that an employee must have at least one job. The relationship in reverse (between *Employee-Job* and *Employee*) states that an employee found in the *Employee-Job* relation must be found and can be found only one time in the *Employee* relation. Figure 4.19 shows the E-R diagram after you remove the many-to-many relationship.

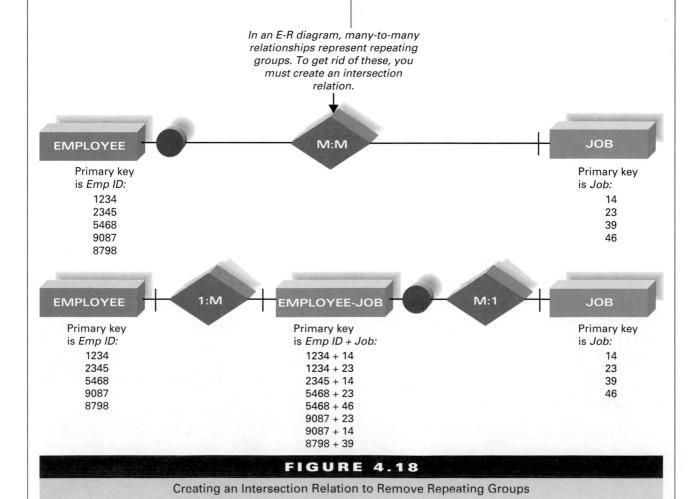

In an E-R diagram, many-to-many relationships represent repeating groups. To get rid of these, you must create an intersection relation.

FIGURE 4.18

Creating an Intersection Relation to Remove Repeating Groups

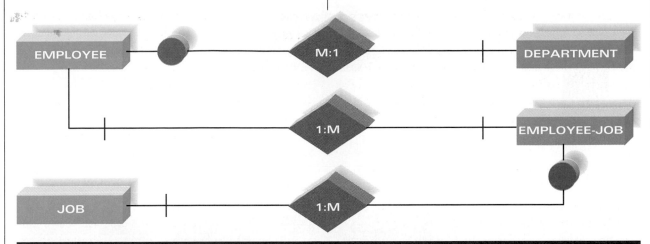

FIGURE 4.19

The Completed E-R Diagram for Your Database

Step 3: Defining Information (Fields) for Each Relation

Once you've completed steps 1 and 2, you must define the various pieces of information that each relation will contain. Your goal in this step is to make sure that the information in each relation is indeed in the correct relation and that the information cannot be derived from other information—the second and third rules of normalization.

In Figure 4.20 (on page 152), we've developed a view of the relations based on the new E-R diagram with the intersection relation. To make sure that each piece of information is in the correct relation, look at each piece of information and ask, "Does this piece of information depend only on the primary key for this relation?" If the answer is yes, the information is in the correct relation. If the answer is no, the information is in the wrong relation.

Let's consider the *Employee* relation. The primary key is *Emp ID*, so each piece of information must depend only on *Emp ID*. Does *Name* depend on *Emp ID*? Yes—so that information is in the correct relation. Does *Dept* depend on *Emp ID*? Yes, because each employee's department designation depends on the particular employee you're describing. Does *Dept Sup* depend only on *Emp ID*? The answer here is no. The supervisor for a particular department doesn't depend on which employee is in that department.

So the question becomes, "In which relation should *Dept Sup* appear?" The answer is in the *Department* relation, because *Dept Sup* depends on the primary key that uniquely describes each department. Therefore, *Dept Sup* should not appear in the *Employee* relation but, rather, in the *Department* relation. Take a look at the intersection relation *Employee-Job*. Notice that it includes the field called *Hours*. *Hours* is located in this

TEAM WORK

Building an E-R Diagram for the Video Rental Store

If you return to the video rental store example in Figure 4.14 on page 144, you'll notice that there are four relations—*Customer*, *Video Rental*, *Video*, and *Distributor*. What would the E-R diagram look like for the video rental store? For each relationship you identify (between two entity classes), develop a set of statements that describes the 1s and Ms and whether the relationship is required or optional.

Your completed E-R diagram will include an intersection relation. Which one is it? Which foreign keys from other relations make up the primary key for the intersection relation? ❖

EMPLOYEE RELATION

Emp ID	Name	Dept	Dept Sup
1234	Jones	43	Halston
2345	Smith	15	Dallas
5468	Joslin	43	Halston
9087	Mills	43	Halston
8798	Jones	69	Irving

JOB RELATION

Job	Job Name
14	Acct
23	Sales
39	Maint
46	Admin

DEPARTMENT RELATION

Dept	Dept Sup	# Emp
15	Dallas	1
43	Halston	3
69	Irving	1

EMPLOYEE-JOB RELATION

Emp ID	Job	Hours
1234	14	4
1234	23	4
2345	14	8
5468	23	6
5468	46	2
9087	23	5
9087	14	3
8798	39	8

Hours belongs in this relation because it depends on a combination of who *(Emp ID)* is assigned to which job *(Job)*.

FIGURE 4.20

A First Look at the Relations in Your Database

relation because it depends on two things—the employee you are describing and the job to which he or she is assigned.

CAREER OPPORTUNITY

Learning how to develop your own database represents a significant career opportunity for you. Businesses today allow knowledge workers to develop many of their own applications—including database applications that support an individual or a workgroup. Your opportunity lies in learning how to identify your information needs, developing the best logical information model, implementing that logical model in the form of a database, and then taking advantage of data manipulation tools to add, change, and delete information and mine the database for valuable information.

If you follow this line of questioning for each relation, you'll find that all other fields are in their correct relation. Now you have to look at each field to see whether you can derive it from other information. If you can, the derived information should not be stored in the database. When we speak of "derived" in this instance, we are referring to information that you can mathematically derive—counts, totals, averages, and the like. Currently, you are storing the number of employees (*# Emp*) in the *Department* relation. Can you derive that information from other information? The answer is yes—all you have to do is count the number of occurrences of each department number in the *Employee* relation. So you should not store *# Emp* in your *Employee* database.

Once you've completed step 3, you have completely and correctly defined the structure of your database and identified the information each relation should contain.

Figure 4.21 shows your database and the information in each relation. Notice that we have removed *Dept Sup* from the *Employee* relation (following the second rule of normalization) and that we have removed *# Emp* from the *Department* relation (following the third rule of normalization).

Step 4: Using a Data Definition Language to Create the Database

The final step in developing a relational database is to take the structure you created in steps 1 to 3 and use a data definition language to actually create the relations. In this step, you'll develop a data dictionary, which is the logical structure of the information and files in the database. This step also includes such specific functions as defining the various relations, primary keys, properties of each

of the fields, and how relations are logically related (foreign keys).

Once you've done this, you're ready to use any of the many data manipulation subsystem tools to enter information, create reports, make queries, and make changes to the information content of the database.

Data Warehousing and Data Mining
Prospecting for Gold in Information

As a manager at Victoria's Secrets, suppose you wanted to know the total revenues generated from the sale of shoes last month. That's a simple query, which you could

EMPLOYEE RELATION

Emp ID	Name	Dept
1234	Jones	43
2345	Smith	15
5468	Joslin	43
9087	Mills	43
8798	Jones	69

JOB RELATION

Job	Job Name
14	Acct
23	Sales
39	Maint
46	Admin

DEPARTMENT RELATION

Dept	Dept Sup
15	Dallas
43	Halston
69	Irving

EMPLOYEE-JOB RELATION

Emp ID	Job	Hours
1234	14	4
1234	23	4
2345	14	8
5468	23	6
5468	46	2
9087	23	5
9087	14	3
8798	39	8

FIGURE 4.21

The Correct Structure of Your Database

easily implement using either SQL or a QBE tool. But what if you wanted to know, "By actual versus budgeted, how many size 8 shoes in black did we sell last month in the southeast and southwest regions, compared with the same month over the last 5 years?" That task seems almost impossible, even with technology. And, if you were actually able to build an SQL query for it, you would probably bring the organization's operational database environment to its knees.

People today need to know answers to that type of question and many others that may be even more complex. For your organization to succeed (and survive), users must have (1) a way to easily develop the logical structure of such questions and (2) the needed information presented to them quickly without sacrificing the speed of various operational systems and databases. To support such intriguing, necessary, and complex queries, many organizations are building data warehouses and providing data mining tools. A data warehouse is simply the next step (beyond databases) in the progression of representing an organization's information logically, and data mining tools are the tools you use to mine a data warehouse for valuable information. Let's consider each in turn.

What Is a Data Warehouse?

Data warehouse is one of the newest and hottest buzz words and concepts in the IT field and the business environment. A ***data warehouse*** is a logical collection of information—gathered from many different operational databases—that supports business analysis activities and decision-making tasks. Sounds simple enough on the surface, but data warehouses represent a fundamentally

---

Getting People Involved Can Be More Difficult Than Building a Database

When you're developing a personal database application, it's relatively easy to get the user involved. You are in fact the user you're developing the application for. But when you develop organizational database applications, getting the users involved is sometimes not so easy. Consider Dennis Gaukel's task at Pioneer Hi-Bred.

Pioneer Hi-Bred International Inc., based in Iowa, is one of the nation's largest producers of seed corn. In the midwest, Pioneer employs some 4,000 sales representatives. In the south and west, the company distributes seed corn through over 3,000 independent dealers. When Dennis Gaukel was hired as the marketing manager at Pioneer, he had one directive—to build a database to strengthen customer relationships.

All Dennis had to do was gather the necessary information from the 4,000 sales reps and 3,000 independent dealers, build the database, and let people start using it. It sounds relatively simple, but it was not. Dennis faced two major obstacles—convincing people to turn over their valuable information and mine the new database for whatever information they needed.

The first obstacle was definitely a problem because many of the sales reps believed they would be replaced by technology once their information was in a database and not in their heads. So Dennis spent the first year just meeting with sales reps to convince them that their jobs were not in jeopardy and that the new database would help them do a better job. Slowly but surely, the sales reps came around and warmed to the idea.

To help the sales reps mine the new database, Dennis hired six technical information specialists. These specialists are available 24 hours a day and regularly conduct training courses in the field on how sales reps can best use the new database.

Today the database contains information on over 600,000 farm operators. Pioneer regularly uses the database to mail customized fliers to each farm operator. The database is a big success. But building it wasn't the difficult part. The most difficult part was convincing the end users to provide information and use the information once it was stored in the database.

Building a technology environment is often far easier than getting people to use it. This is a substantial career opportunity for you. Your skills at motivating the active participation of end users are a definite plus in business.[17, 18] ❖

Entertainment & Publishing

Data Warehouses Help Sega Sell Video Games

The sale of video games accounts for a huge portion of the revenues generated in the entertainment and publishing industry. And it's definitely a fiercely competitive and cut-throat market. To stay on top, Sega of America, the $1.5 billion electronic games company, uses a data warehouse to more effectively distribute its $40 million a year advertising budget.

Sega regularly gathers sales information from the operational databases of such retailers as Toys'R'Us, Wal-Mart, and Sears to create its data warehouse. Sega's product line specialists and marketing strategists then use the information in the data warehouse to "drill" into trends of each retail chain. Their goal is to find buying trends that will help them better determine which advertising strategies are working best and how to reallocate advertising resources by media and territory.

Video games are a part of our wants-driven economy. To sell

these products, video game manufacturers must know the desires of their customers. Sega is learning those facts by tapping into the operational databases of retail stores all over the country.

Incidentally, Sega is planning to add Internet-access capabilities to its new games. When it does so, Sega game players will be able to cruise the Internet. More important, those players will be able to connect to Sega's Web site, review new games, and even purchase and download those new games.[19, 20] ❖

---

different way of thinking about organizing and managing information in an organization. Consider these key features.

Data Warehouses Combine Information from Different Databases Data warehouses combine information—by summarizing and aggregating—from different operational databases in your organization. As you extract information from various operational databases to create a data warehouse, you gather only required information for decision making (see Figure 4.22). This "required information" is defined by users according to their logical

decision-making information needs. So a data warehouse contains only information relevant to user needs for decision making.

Data Warehouses Are Multidimensional In the relational database model, information is represented in a series of two-dimensional tables. Not so in data warehouses—most data warehouses are multidimensional, meaning that they contain layers of columns and rows. For this reason, most data warehouses are really *multidimensional databases*. The layers in a data warehouse

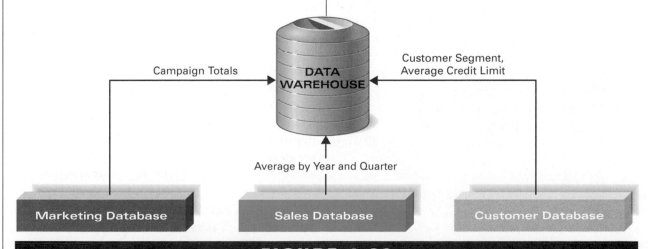

FIGURE 4.22

Building a Data Warehouse from Operational Databases

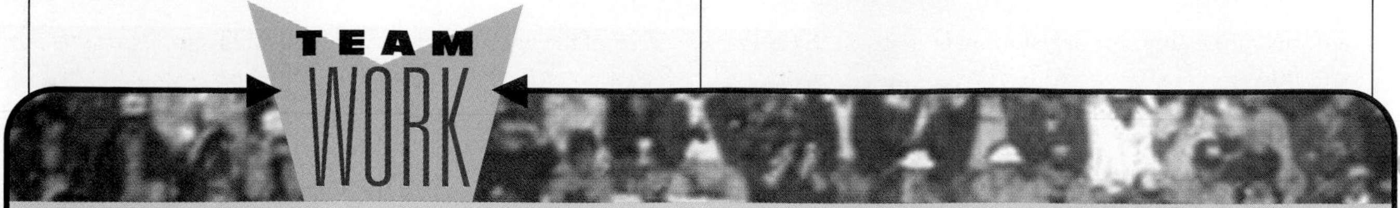

Politically Correct Data Mining

Suppose your group is in charge of a political campaign for a candidate running for mayor in your town. Your job includes two primary tasks: (1) developing marketing material and (2) advising the candidate concerning which groups of people feel strongly for or against certain issues. Suppose also that you wanted to build a voter data warehouse to support your information needs. Address the following issues and perform the following tasks:

1. What information would you include by what dimension?

2. Design a hypercube that would incorporate the various dimensions you indicated.

3. Graphically, what would it look like?

4. For each piece of information, specify where you would obtain this information. ❖

---

represent information according to different dimensions. This multidimensional representation of information is referred to as a *hypercube.*

In Figure 4.23, you can see a hypercube that represents product information by product line and region (columns and rows), by year (the first layer), by customer segment (the second layer), and by credit sales (the third layer). Using this hypercube, you can easily ask, "According to customer segment A, what percentage of total sales for product line 1 in the southwest territory were credit sales?" You should also notice that the information in Figure 4.23 is a summary of information located in one or more operational databases.

Data warehouses are a special form of databases. Recall that a database is a collection of information that you organize and access according to the logical structure of the information. The same is true for a data warehouse. Users of a data warehouse express their information needs logically and are not concerned about row, column, or layer. Data warehouses also have a data dictionary. Data warehouse data dictionaries maintain the logical structure of the information and include two additional important characteristics—origin and method. That is, a data warehouse data dictionary always tracks from which operational databases information originated and by which method (total, count, average, standard deviation, and so on).

Data Warehouses Support Decision Making, Not Transaction Processing In an organization, most databases are transaction-oriented. That is, most databases support online transaction processing (OLTP) and, therefore, are operational databases. Data warehouses are not transaction-oriented—they exist to support various decision-making tasks in your organization. Therefore data warehouses support online analytical processing (OLAP).

What Are Data Mining Tools?

Data mining tools are the software tools you use to query information in a data warehouse. These data mining tools support the concept of OLAP—the manipulation of

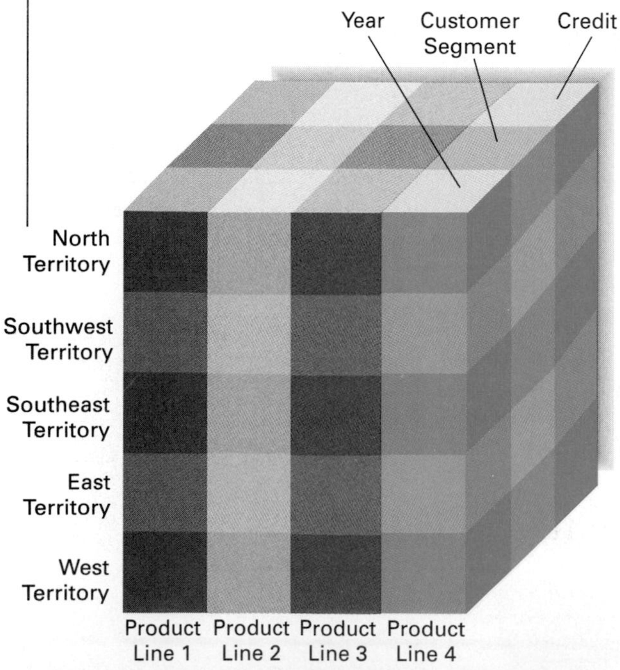

FIGURE 4.23

The Multidimensional Aspect of Data Warehouses

information to support decision-making tasks. Data mining tools include query-and-reporting tools, intelligent agents, and multidimensional analysis tools (see Figure 4.24). Essentially, data mining tools are to data warehouse users what data manipulation subsystem tools are to database users.

Query-and-Reporting Tools *Query-and-reporting tools* are similar to QBE tools, SQL, and report generators in the typical database environment. In fact, most data warehousing environments support simple and easy-to-use data manipulation subsystem tools such as QBE, SQL, and report generators. Most often, data warehouse users use these types of tools to generate simple queries and reports.

Intelligent Agents *Intelligent agents* utilize various artificial intelligence tools such as neural networks and fuzzy logic to form the basis for "information discovery" in OLAP. For example, Wall Street analyst Murray Riggiero uses OLAP software called Data/Logic, which incorporates neural networks to generate rules for his highly successful stock and bond trading system.[21] Other OLAP tools, such as Data Engine, incorporate fuzzy logic to analyze real-time technical processes.

Intelligent agents represent the growing convergence of various IT tools for working with information. Previously, intelligent agents were considered only within the context of artificial intelligence and were seldom thought to be a part of the data organizing and managing functions in an organization. In Chapter 5, we'll explore artificial intelligence techniques such as intelligent agents.

Multidimensional Analysis Tools *Multidimensional analysis (MDA) tools* are *slice-and-dice techniques* that allow you to view multidimensional information from different perspectives. For example, if you completed

either of the two recommended Real HOT group projects for Chapter 1, you were using spreadsheet software to literally slice and dice the provided information.

North Memorial Medical Center uses an MDA tool called Forest & Trees to help managers slice and dice their way through information for 10,000 daily patient records.[22] Managers hope to learn how well the hospital (which has several locations) is serving the needs of its patients in billing, admissions, testing and lab work, radiology, pharmaceuticals, and outpatient counseling. MDA tools (such as Forest & Trees) help these managers view information according to hospital location and according to specific business area.

Important Considerations in Using a Data Warehouse

Do You Need a Data Warehouse?

If you ask most people in the business world if they need a data warehouse, they'll immediately say yes. But they may be wrong. Although data warehouses are a great way to bring together information from many different databases and data mining tools are a great way to manipulate that information, they're not necessarily the best technologies for all businesses.

Why? Three reasons. First, there's the expense associated with a data warehouse. Building a data warehouse takes considerable time, and time is money. Data mining software is also not exactly inexpensive. You must also be prepared to spend money in training potential data warehouse users.

Second, and perhaps most important, some organizations simply don't need data warehouses and data mining tools. For these organizations, users can easily extract

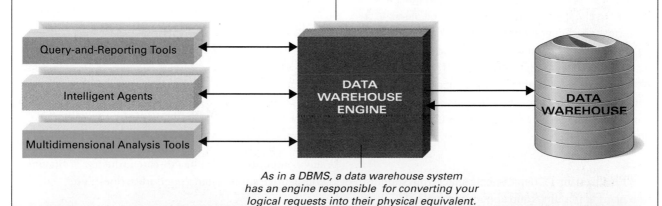

As in a DBMS, a data warehouse system
has an engine responsible for converting your
logical requests into their physical equivalent.

FIGURE 4.24

The Data Miner's Tool Set

How Up-to-Date Should Data Warehouse Information Be?

Information timeliness is a must in a data warehouse—old and obsolete information leads to poor decision making. Below is a list of decision-making processes that people go through for different business environments. For each, specify whether the information in the data warehouse should be updated monthly, weekly, daily, or by the minute. Be prepared to justify your decision.

1. To adjust class sizes in a university registration environment

2. To alert people to changes in weather conditions

3. To predict scores for professional football games

4. To adjust radio advertisements in light of demographic changes

5. To monitor the success of a new product line in the clothing retail industry

6. To adjust production levels of foods in a cafeteria

7. To switch jobs to various printers in a network

8. To adjust CD rates in a bank

9. To adjust forecasted demands of tires in an auto parts store ❖

needed information from operational databases without sacrificing performance. To support the multidimensional analysis of information as it resides in a relational database, organizations can choose from a variety of data mining tools called *relational OLAP technologies.* Relational OLAP technologies allow you to view and query relational database information from many dimensions. Relational OLAP technologies include Axsys by Information Advantage, Beacon by Prodea Software, and Metacube by Stanford Technology.

CAREER OPPORTUNITY

The choice of implementing a data warehouse in your organization is an important one. In a nutshell, you have to ask yourself two questions. First, does the current use of queries for decision making slow the performance of operational databases? Second, do people within your organization need to slice and dice their way through multiple dimensions of information? If the answer is yes to either of these questions, then you should seriously consider building a data warehouse and using data mining tools to find valuable information.

Finally, many IT departments suffer from supporting too many applications and application tools. If your organization chooses the data warehouse route, it must be prepared to provide support. Says David Tanaka, a DSS manager at Hospital Health Plan Management Corp., "Right now, we are support-strapped. If we introduce

something like OLAP, we will have to give it a lot of support."[23] Every organization must carefully ask itself if there truly is an information need for such technologies and if it can devote time toward developing and supporting those technologies. If the answer is no, then a data warehouse is inappropriate.

Do You Already Have a Data Warehouse?

Many organizations already have data warehouses in place and provide users with data mining tools. Where? Most commonly, EISs use a form of data warehouse and data mining tools. Recall from Chapter 2 that an EIS makes use of a special database that contains information from other databases. This EIS database, in fact, may be a data warehouse. If this is the case, then you should consider expanding the EIS so other users can have access to it.

In some instances, an organization may choose to abandon its EIS and develop a completely new data warehouse that can be used throughout the organization. That's what Blue Cross/Blue Shield of Maryland decided to do. Says Mark Max, director of financial systems, "Adopting OLAP allowed Blue Cross/Blue Shield of Maryland to better examine its volume of data and stay competitive in the health-care industry."[24] Staying competitive sounds like a good idea, doesn't it?

Who Will the Users Be?

To build the best data warehouse, you must understand the information requirements. To determine those information requirements, you have to know who the users will be. Only data warehouse users can define the logical information requirements. As with all types of technology, data warehouses will serve no meaningful purpose unless you ask users what they need.

Sometimes knowing your users is extremely difficult. Think about MasterCard International and its data warehouse, MasterCard On-Line.[25] What makes this data warehouse unique—besides the fact that it will be the world's largest data warehouse when in full production—is that MasterCard plans to let its 22,000 banks, retailers, restaurants, and other partners mine it for valuable information. If you were working for a restaurant and wanted to give away airline tickets as part of a promotional campaign, MasterCard would allow you to build OLAP queries such as, "What are the preferred flight destinations of people who frequent our restaurant at least twice a month?"

These types of data warehouses—those that people outside the providing organization can use—fall into the category of interorganizational systems (IOSs from Chapter 2). That is, they allow many organizations to share vitally important market and customer information. By the way, MasterCard's data warehouse will contain one terabyte (trillion) of information concerning 8.5 million daily credit and debit card transactions.

How Up-to-Date Must the Information Be?

Data warehouses contain information from other databases. From an operational perspective, it's important to consider how often you should extract information

from those databases and update the data warehouse. Instantaneously is usually not feasible in most organizations because of communication costs and performance considerations. So some organizations take "snapshots" of databases every 30 minutes and update the data warehouse, whereas other organizations perform updates nightly.

At DowElanco, for example, a joint venture of The Dow Chemical Company and Eli Lilly and Co., every needed transaction in any Dow Chemical company as well as DowElanco is passed nightly to DowElanco's data warehouse. As that information is passed, it is summarized into monthly views to help sales analysts determine which products customers really need.[26] This issue goes back to knowing the information requirements of users. Some users, because of the time sensitivity of their decision-making tasks, may need almost continuously updated information. Others may not. Whatever the case, updating is an issue to be taken seriously.

What Data Mining Tools Do You Need?

User needs determine which data mining tools are necessary—query-and-reporting tools, multidimensional analysis tools, intelligent agents, or some combination of the three. This is where training comes in. It's important for your organization to make users aware of the potential of all data mining tools, so they can best describe the software they'll need to mine the data warehouse for valuable information.

INDUSTRY PERSPECTIVE · **Manufacturing**

Tracking Historical Sales with Data Warehouses

Data warehouses and data mining tools offer many benefits. First, data warehouses gather information from several different operational databases. Second, you can specify how up-to-date that gathered information should be—daily, monthly, and so on. Third, you

can then use a variety of data mining tools to slice and dice your way through that information.

At Subaru, marketing specialists enjoy all those benefits, while taking the guesswork out of determining which auto makes and models are selling the best. Subaru's data warehouse contains enormous quantities of information, ranging from dealer codes and vehicle identification numbers, to regional identifiers for each sale. And just as important,

that information is updated on a daily basis.

Using SQL and report generator data mining tools, the Subaru marketing specialists sift through all the information daily. Their ability to do so helps the company maximize sales. And if they can't perform these tasks, Subaru stands to have hundreds of new but unsold "clunkers" on dealer lots.[27] ❖

Managing the Information Resource in an Organization

As you prepare to enter today's fast-paced, exciting, and information-based business world, you must be prepared to help your organization manage and organize its information. After all, you will be a knowledge worker—a person who works primarily with information. Your organization will be successful, in part, because of your ability to organize and manage information in the way that best moves the organization toward its goals. Below is a list of questions that you should keep in mind. The answers to some are definitely moving targets. As business and technology changes, your answers may have to change as well.

How Will Changes in Technology Affect Organizing and Managing Information?

If there ever has been a moving target that businesses are trying to hit, it's most probably information technology. It seems every day that businesses are faced with new technologies that are faster, better, and provide more capabilities than the technologies of yesterday. Chasing technology in a business environment can be very expensive.

For example, converting a relational database application to an object-oriented approach can cost your organization millions of dollars, not to mention many years.

What you have to remember is that technology is simply a set of tools for helping you work with information, including organizing and managing it. As new technologies become available, you should ask yourself whether those technologies will help you organize and manage your information **better**. You can't simply say, "A new technology is available that will allow us to organize and manage our information in a different way, so we should use it." The real question is whether that different way of organizing and managing information is better than what you're currently doing. If the answer is yes, you should seriously consider the new technology in light of the strategic goals of the organization. If the answer is no, stay with what you've got until a tool comes along that allows you to do a **better** job.

One of the greatest technological changes that will occur over the coming years is a convergence of different tools that will help you better organize and manage information. Environment Canada's Ice Services, for example, is providing a combination of a data warehouse and Internet-based information resources that seafarers can use.[28] This new system gathers ice charts stored in the Internet and logically organizes them in the form of a data warehouse. Using this new system, seafarers can obtain updated maps and charts that reflect changing ice conditions every 4 hours instead of every 12 hours. Who knows—

Types of Databases Found in Organizations

- **Centralized databases**—databases that maintain all database information in one location.

- **Distributed databases**—databases in which information is distributed to various locations. The two main forms of a distributed database are partitioned and replicated. A **partitioned database** maintains certain files of information in different locations—usually where that information is most often used. A **replicated database** maintains multiple copies of information in different locations.

- **External** or **online databases**—databases that exist outside an organization. Examples of external or online databases include Dow Jones QuickSearch (current stock quotes), CENDATA (U.S. census statistical data), and MEDIS (medical journal reference).

- **Knowledge worker databases**—databases designed and maintained by knowledge workers to support their personal information needs.

- **Operational databases**—databases designed specifically to support online transaction processing (OLTP). Examples include an inventory database, an accounts receivable database, and a personnel database.

- **Data warehouses**—a logical collection of information gathered from many different operational databases that supports business analysis activities and decision-making tasks. Data warehouses therefore support online analytical processing (OLAP) and not online transaction processing. ❖

Databases and Data Warehouses Are Just What the Doctor Ordered

Most organizations have found that today they need many types of databases, including data warehouses. We are certainly in the information age, and that has made it necessary to have access to all types of information that may be contained in a variety of databases.

For GlaxoWellcome, a pharmaceutical maker in London, developing an operational database and a data warehouse became a priority in the summer of 1996. That summer, GlaxoWellcome announced a combination of two of its drugs that was effective in treating AIDS. GlaxoWellcome's distributors all over the world quickly scrambled to order as much of the drugs as they could. With its high-powered operational

THE GLOBAL PERSPECTIVE

database, GlaxoWellcome was able to process all the incoming orders and even streamline distribution processes. Once the information was processed in the operational database, it was passed to a data warehouse. Using the information there, market analysts were able to track the size and sources of demand in just a few hours. Their efforts translated into constant availability of the combination of drugs.

GlaxoWellcome's effective organization and management of information has certainly added to its bottom-line profits. But, more important, GlaxoWellcome's ability to efficiently work with that information probably saved the lives of many people all over the world.[29] ❖

the *Titanic* might still be here today if this system had been available in 1912!

What Types of Database Models and Databases Are Most Appropriate?

Successful use of database and database applications depends on many factors, including type of database model and type of database. Today most organizations use the relational and object-oriented database models, but the choice between the two is not clear. Functional requirements play an important part in determining which database model is best.

The same is true for type of database. In the box on the previous page, you can read about different types of databases, including centralized, distributed (partitioned and replicated), external or online, operational, data warehouses (analytical databases), and knowledge worker. Here again, the choice depends on the application. If you need applications that use information gathered outside the organization, an external or online database may be best. If you need to support transaction-intensive basic business functions, an operational database is probably best.

This may not be a major consideration in the future of business. Today's data warehouses—designed to bring together the full spectrum of information in an

organization—may eliminate several types of databases. But, then again, they may not.

Who Should Oversee the Organization's Information?

In organizations today, you can find chief executive officers (CEO), chief operating officers (COO), and chief financial officers (CFO). You can also find another title—chief information officer. The *chief information officer (CIO)* is responsible for overseeing an organization's information resource. A CIO's responsibilities may range from approving new knowledge worker project development to monitoring the quality and use of an organizational data warehouse.

Two important functions associated with overseeing an organization's information resource are data and database administration. *Data administration* is the function in an organization that plans for, oversees the development of, and monitors the information resource. It must be completely in tune with the strategic direction of the organization to assure that all information requirements can be met.

Database administration is the function in an organization that is responsible for the more technical and operational aspects of managing the information contained in organizational databases. Database administration functions include defining and organizing database structures and contents, developing security procedures, developing database and DBMS documentation, maintaining DBMS software, and approving and monitoring the development of databases and database applications.

In organizations of any great size, both functions are usually handled by a steering committee rather than a single individual. These steering committees are responsible for their respective functions and reporting to the CIO. It's definitely a team effort to manage most organizational resources—information is no different. In Chapter 8, we'll further discuss the role of a CIO and the data and database administration functions.

Is Information Ownership a Consideration?

Information sharing in your organization means that anyone—regardless of title or department—can access and use whatever information he or she needs. But information sharing brings to light an important question—does anyone in your organization own any information? In other words—if everyone shares information, who is ultimately responsible for providing that information and assuring the quality of the information? Information ownership is a key consideration in today's information-based business environment. Someone must accept full responsibility for providing specific pieces of information and ensuring the quality of that information. If you find that the wrong information is stored in the organization's data warehouse, you must be able to determine the source of the problem and whose responsibility it is.

This issue of information ownership is similar to other management functions. If you manage a department, you're responsible for the work in the department as well as expenses and people. The same is true for information. If information originates in your department, you essentially own that information because you're providing it to those who need it and ensuring its quality.

What Are the Ethics Involved in Organizing and Managing Information?

Throughout this text, we address many ethical issues associated with information and information technology.

INDUSTRY PERSPECTIVE   **IT & Telecommunications**

Is Database Information Free on the Internet?

The answer to that question is both yes and no. Many online databases, such as those provided by the federal government, are free. Others, however—such as Nexis, a popular but pay-as-you-go database of published information in magazines and the like—are not. That creates a real problem for cyber cruisers and organizations offering access to database information for a fee. For cyber cruisers, it raises the issue of whether or not you want to put your credit card number on the Internet for a $6 fee to access a database. For organizations offering those pay-access databases, it means having to handle hundreds or even thousands of small credit card transactions.

Fortunately, IBM may have a solution to make everyone happy. IBM offers an electronic-content clearinghouse called InfoMarket that acts as an intermediary between you as a cyber cruiser and organizations offering information. When you subscribe to IBM's service, you provide your credit card, and you only have to do it once. Then you can use InfoMarket's powerful search engines to locate information you need. If that information is in a fee-charge database, you can still access it. When you do, IBM automatically charges your credit card and forwards that amount to the database provider.

IBM's InfoMarket takes much of the hassle out of obtaining information on the Internet. As a customer, you're not saddled with always providing your credit card information. For information providers, they no longer have to process thousands of small transactions each month.[30] ❖

Many of our discussions focus on your organization's societal obligations with respect to customers. Within the organization, those same issues are a concern. By bringing together vast amounts of information into a single place (a database or data warehouse) and providing software (a DBMS or data mining tools) that anyone can use to access that information, ethics and privacy become important concerns.

For example, as a manager of marketing research, should you be able to access the salaries of people in distribution and logistics? Should you be able to access medical profiles of those in accounting? Should you be able to access counseling records of those in manufacturing? The answer to some of these questions is obviously no. But how does an organization safeguard against the unethical use of information within the organization?

While most DBMS packages provide good security facilities, it's far easier for someone within your organization to obtain information than it is for someone outside the organization. So what's the key? Unfortunately we don't know the answer and neither does anyone else. But it all starts with each person always acting in the most ethical way with respect to information. Ethics, security, and privacy will always be great concerns. You can do your part by always acting ethically. Remember, this is another step toward becoming an information-literate knowledge worker.

How Should Databases and Database Applications Be Developed and Maintained?

There are many ways your organization can go about developing and maintaining databases and database applications. Which to choose is always a function of what you're trying to do. For example, if a workgroup responsible for building a new distribution center needs a database, then you should consider a workgroup support system such as Lotus Notes. It contains a group document database structure and built-in templates that will help you develop applications quickly.

If, on the other hand, you're interested in developing transaction-intensive applications such as payroll, you may decide to follow an organizational development process and choose the DBMS environment most suited to your organization as a whole. Many organizations are even choosing to outsource these functions for non-critical databases and applications. Whatever the case, the choice of *how* to develop and maintain databases and database applications is an important one for any organization.

Zeneca Pharmaceuticals Cures Its Problems with a Data Warehouse

Zeneca's data warehousing system, called Zeneca Integrated Contracting System (ZICS), has certainly cured many information organization and management problems. Using ZICS, for example, Zeneca determined that its prostate cancer drug, Zolodex, wasn't selling as well as TAP Pharmaceuticals' (a major competitor of Zeneca) Lupron drug. That was disturbing, but what made it even worse was that Lupron was far more expensive than Zolodex and offered no additional medicinal benefits over Zolodex. Armed with information, Steve Crane, a Zeneca business manager, persuaded several customers to switch from Lupron to Zolodex. The customers themselves saved tens of thousands of dollars, and Zeneca watched its bottom line grow.

But determining information of that nature and acting on it wasn't always so easy at Zeneca. In the early 1990s, Zeneca's business managers had no OLAP capabilities. Instead, each month they received a 6-inch-high stack of reports that contained some 6 million records. As Keith Megay explains, "It could take as long as 2 days for a manager to find the pertinent data." But not anymore. Thanks to the data warehouse organization of information, managers can slice and dice their way through information concerning account types, customers, product classes, contract terms, prescription drug pricing, and sales and contract histories.

As they do, ZICS provides a graphic and very easy-to-use interface. For example, if a manager wants to see how much of a given prescription drug an HMO has ordered over the last year, the process amounts to clicking on the HMO's name, the name of the drug, and then the appropriate time frame button. This flexible interface allows managers to view information from many dimensions. "With OLAP, you analyze data online and interactively, without preconceived ideas about the relationships. You can make indirect connections and find new correlations," explains David McGoveran. That certainly doesn't hold true for other database technologies such as the relational model, which requires that you define relationships among information when creating a database with the data definition subsystem.[31] ❖

◄ Questions ►

1. How was Zeneca able to determine the sales figures for Lupron, a drug of its arch rival TAP Pharmaceuticals? From where might that information have come?

2. Behind Zeneca's data warehousing are important operational databases that provide information. A sales database is one such database. In it, products and customers would be entity classes, and there is a many-to-many relationship between them. That is, a customer can order many products, and a product can be ordered by many customers. How would you eliminate this many-to-many relationship? What did you call the intersection relation?

3. How up-to-date do you believe Zeneca's data warehouse information must be? Does it differ for different types of information? For example, prices probably need to be very current, but what about inventory levels? Does the currency of the information depend on what decision-making task you're trying to perform? Why or why not?

4. How many dimensions of information can you find in this case study that would be important to consider when constructing Zeneca's multidimensional data warehouse? What information dimensions not mentioned in the case might also be important?

5. The ZICS system cost Zeneca a total of $230,000 for software acquisition and the actual construction of the data warehouse. That figure doesn't include training or ongoing maintenance. Does that figure seem unreasonable? How can you cost-justify systems that support analytical processing?

KNOWLEDGE WORKER'S -LIST

The Importance of Separating the Logical from the Physical Concerning the Organization of Information. The *physical view* of information organization deals with how information is physically arranged, stored, and accessed on some type of secondary storage device. The *logical view* of information organization, on the other hand, focuses on how knowledge workers need to arrange and access information to meet a particular business need. Separating the logical from the physical is key in information management. The less time knowledge workers have to be concerned with the physical aspects of information organization, the more time they can spend determining their logical information needs.

The Role of Databases and Database Management Systems in an Organization. A *database* is a collection of information that you organize and access according to the logical structure of the information. Databases today represent the most popular way of organizing information. Databases contain two distinct parts—the information itself and the logical structure of the information, which is called a *data dictionary*.

A *database management system (DBMS)* is the software you use to specify the logical organization for a database and access it. A DBMS contains software components for providing the logical to physical bridge (*DBMS engine*), defining the logical structure of a database (*data definition subsystem*), mining and changing information in a database (*data manipulation subsystem*), developing transaction-intensive applications (*application generation subsystem*), and managing the database environment (*data administration subsystem*).

Although databases and DBMSs support online analytical processing through views, QBE tools, report generators, and SQL, they are mostly designed to support online transaction processing.

How to Develop a Knowledge Worker Database Application. Database application development can be achieved in numerous ways, including through knowledge worker development and from an organizational point of view. For knowledge worker development, the steps include:

1. Defining entity classes and primary keys
2. Defining relationships among the entity classes
3. Defining information (fields) for each relation
4. Using a data definition language to create the database

When developing a database application, you make use of two techniques—an entity-relationship diagram and normalization. An *entity-relationship (E-R) diagram* is a graphic method of representing entity classes and their relationships. *Normalization* is a process of assuring that a relational database structure can be implemented as a series of two-dimensional tables.

The Role of Data Warehouses and Data Mining Tools in an Organization. A *data warehouse* is a logical collection of information gathered from many different operational databases that is used to support business

What Happens When Your Data Warehouse Is Too Big, Too Good, and Too Hard to Use?

Lands' End is big, with $1 billion in annual revenues. So why shouldn't Lands' End have an equally big data warehouse? That's what Dan Rourke, vice president of information systems, thought. With that in mind, Dan coordinated the development of an enterprisewide data warehouse for Lands' End that included all marketing, financial, and merchandising information. Unfortunately, Dan discovered that there's truth to the old adage "too much of a good thing."

Instead of diving headlong into the vast information resources of the data warehouse, many knowledge workers still requested very simple reports from the MIS department. For example, some knowledge workers requested reports for describing the performance of a particular swim suit or how many people had responded to the latest catalog. All that information (and a lot more) was in the data warehouse. Why weren't people using it? "We realized a lot of our business users were too intimidated to fully exploit the systems," explains Dan. Indeed, the data warehouse system contained so many features and so much information that most users didn't even know where to begin.

---

analysis activities and decision-making tasks. Therefore data warehouses are designed to support online analytical processing and not online transaction processing. Data warehouses are multidimensional, meaning that they represent many dimensions of information in the form of a hypercube.

Data mining tools are the software tools you use to query information in a data warehouse. Data mining tools include **query-and-reporting tools** such as QBE and SQL, **intelligent agents** or certain forms of artificial intelligence such as neural networks that support "information discovery," and **multidimensional analysis (MDA) tools** that let you slice and dice information to view it from different perspectives.

Key Issues in Managing the Information Resource.
How will changes in technology affect organizing and managing information? Changes in technology occur every day. The key is to decide whether those changes provide better ways of organizing and managing information. If they do, seriously consider them. If they don't, wait for one that will.

What types of database models and databases are most appropriate? The two popular database models include the relational database model and the object-oriented database model. By type, databases include **centralized databases** that maintain information in one location, **distributed databases** that allocate information to different places, **external** or **online databases** that rest outside the organization, **knowledge worker databases** that support personal information needs, **operational**

databases that support online transaction processing, and **data warehouses** that support online analytical processing. The choice is important.

Who should oversee the organization's information? Today, the responsibility of an organization's information rests with the **chief information officer (CIO)**, who is responsible for **data administration** (planning, overseeing the development of, and monitoring the information resource) and **database administration** (the technical and operational aspects of managing information contained in organizational databases).

Is information ownership a consideration? Information ownership deals with who is responsible for providing specific information and assuring the quality of that information. Ultimately, information ownership must rest with someone.

What are the ethics involved in organizing and managing information? Internally, organizations must still protect the privacy and information rights of their employees. It's far easier for someone inside the organization to gain access to information than for someone outside the organization. We must all do our part to act ethically regarding the use of information.

How should databases and database applications be developed and maintained? Database and database applications can be developed and maintained in a variety of ways including knowledge worker development, development and maintenance from an organizational point of view, and outsourcing. The choice is a key one. ❖

Dan's solution to the problem was to create several smaller, more-specialized data warehouses called data marts. A *data mart* is a subset of a data warehouse, in which a highly summarized or focused portion of the data warehouse is kept. For example, Dan created a data mart just for the merchandising department. That data mart contains only merchandising-specific summaries of information and not any information that would be unique to the finance department. Because of the smaller, more manageable data marts, knowledge workers at Lands' End are now performing their own queries.

Data marts—along with enterprisewide data warehouses—are some of the hottest buzz words in business today; not only because they support online analytical processing, but also because they're easily paying for themselves. Consider these numbers. According to a recent International Data Corp. study, the returns on investment for data warehouses and data marts are a whopping 321 percent and 532 percent, respectively. Additionally, the payback period for a data warehouse is 2.73 years and an even better 1.57 years for a data mart.[32] ❖

◄ Questions ►

1. Data marts are of tremendous benefit to the knowledge workers in whose departments they reside. But consider data marts from an organizational perspective. Don't data marts essentially represent "isolated" information? If you're in marketing, for example, and need information contained in the data mart of the production department, you can't get to it. By creating data marts, have organizations really recreated one of the problems they were trying to avoid—isolated information?

2. Data marts are subsets of a larger data warehouse. Does that then make them really just databases? After all, a database is also a subset of a data warehouse, because a data warehouse contains information from many databases.

3. What steps could Lands' End have taken to help users overcome being intimidated by the enterprise-wide data warehouse? If these efforts had been successful, do you think they would still have needed the smaller data marts? Why or why not?

4. The International Data Corp. study states that data marts demonstrate a higher ROI and shorter payback period than enterprisewide data warehouses. Why do you think this is true?

5. One of the reasons that many organizations are turning to data marts instead of data warehouses is because of the lack of agreement on basic definitions of terms such as "customer," "sales," and "profit." Consider your school as an example. What terms might have different meanings to people in different departments or divisions? For example, is there a difference between "course" and "class" or can they be used interchangeably?

6. One alternative to creating data marts is to have knowledge workers use existing database technologies to perform their queries and analyze information. What would be some of the problems associated with using databases instead of data marts or data warehouses for OLAP?

Electronic Commerce
Business and You on the Internet

Searching Online Databases and Information Repositories

In short, the Internet is a valuable information resource— you can find just about everything you'd ever want to know on the Internet. As you've already seen in the Real HOT Electronic Commerce sections of Chapters 1 and

3, you can find a variety of information on the Internet relating to finding a job and investing. And in the remaining sections throughout this text, you'll work through exercises for finding information relating to starting a new business (Chapter 5), medicine and health (Chapter 6), news, weather, and sports (Chapter 7), freeware and shareware (Chapter 8), building a Web page (Chapter

9), business travel (Chapter 10), and continuing your education (Chapter 11).

As you find sites on the Internet that provide information, many of them will do so in the form of a database—a searchable grouping of information that allows you to find specific information by entering key words and phrases. These words and phrases are in fact some sort of key (similar to primary and foreign keys we discussed in this chapter) that are used as matching criteria in a field of the database.

You'll also come across sites that provide information but not in the form of a database as we strictly defined it in this chapter. These sites are more like information repositories, with textual descriptions and perhaps links to other related sites. Whatever the case, the Internet is a great place to find information.

In this section, you'll explore a variety of information topics that you can find on the Internet either in the form of a database or a simple information repository. To help you, we've included a number of Web sites related to searching online databases and information repositories. On the Web site that supports this text (http://www.mhhe.com/business/mis/haag, select "Electronic Commerce Projects"), we've provided direct links to all these Web sites as well as many, many more. These are a great starting point for completing this Real HOT section. We would also encourage you to search the Internet for others. As you review these sites, think critically about their nature as a true database. Some will be, and some won't.

Financial Aid Resources

As we explore online databases and information repositories on the Internet, let's first look toward an area that may be of great interest to many of you—finding financial aid. You are all aware of the rising cost of education (of course, the cost of ignorance is much greater), including text books, tuition and fees, and living expenses in general. Besides requiring a four-year commitment from you, getting an education also costs money.

In pre-Internet days, students turned to the financial aid office of their institution to seek assistance. Now, you can turn to the Internet to quickly, easily, and inexpensively (free in most instances) find financial aid. In the table on page 169, we've provided a list of financial resources on the Internet and where you can find them, and we've included a list of several others on the Web site that supports this text.

Connect to at least four of these sites and review what they have to offer. As you do, answer the following questions for each.

A. Do you have to register as a user to access information?

B. Do you have to pay a fee to access information?

C. Can you build a profile of yourself and use it as your search?

D. Does the site support only financial aid for specific groups of students or all students in general?

E. Who is the provider of the site?

F. What type of key words and phrases can you use to search for financial assistance?

G. Can you find financial assistance that meets your criteria?

Libraries

Throughout your educational career, you'll face the task of writing term papers for various classes. Writing those papers involves research, namely library research to find relevant books and articles. You've undoubtedly already undertaken that task, and you've probably found it to be a sometimes frustrating experience. Well, the Internet may offer easier ways.

As a distribution channel for information, the Internet has become a tremendous repository of books, articles, and manuscripts. Many libraries now offer a great selection of materials online. Just by knowing the author, the title, or even a keyword or phrase, you can search for information at library resources on the Internet. In the table on page 169, we've provided a list of library sites on the Internet and where you can find them (don't forget to connect to the Web site that supports this text for direct links to these as well as many others).

Think for a moment about a term paper you're currently writing or may have to write soon. What is the major topic? What are the related subtopics? What would you hope to find at a library? Now connect to several of the library sites on the Internet and try to find some of that information. As you do, answer the following questions for each site.

A. What organization supports the site?

B. Do you have to pay a subscription fee to access the information provided?

C. Does the site offer true searching capabilities for information?

D. How can you obtain printed versions of information you find?

E. If you are able to search periodicals, how up to date are the issues?

F. Is finding information in libraries on the Internet easier or more difficult than finding information in a traditional "brick-and-mortar" library?

As you search various sites and answer the questions above, you should definitely connect to your school's library and do the same. Does your school's library offer search mechanisms over the Internet or must you use a computer in the library itself? And, with respect to Internet searches in general, how does performing an online library search compare to using the standard Internet search engines such as Yahoo!, WebCrawler, and AltaVista?

Consumer Information

The business world is not always safe. Almost daily, you can read about business scams that bilked investors for millions of dollars. And on a more personal level, you've probably had a bad buying experience or felt you were not completely informed concerning a product or service you purchased. Well, think about how much more easily that can happen on the Internet. In cyberspace, illegitimate business happens by the second.

And whether you're doing business on the Internet or face-to-face, you need to protect yourself as a consumer. For that reason, consumer protection advocates such as Ralph Nader founded organizations to protect your rights as a consumer in a business transaction. The government also plays an important role here, establishing all sorts of functions related to credit reporting, fair trade practices, consumer information, and fraud alerts.

These consumer organizations have found that the Internet is a great resource for distributing consumer information. And you benefit from that. With a few simple clicks on the mouse, you can check your credit report, read government reports concerning fraudulent business dealings, and obtain buyers' guides for almost any product. In the table on page 169, we've listed sites on the Internet where you can find consumer information. We've also provided several other great consumer information sites on the Web site that supports this text.

Connect to several of these sites and review the information they offer. As a consumer, did you find any of the information to be helpful? Did you find any of the information to be opinion only, completely factual, or a combination of the two? Will you use some of that information for a future purchase? How important will this type of consumer information become as electronic commerce becomes more widespread on the Internet?

Demographics

If you recall from Chapter 1, you can characterize our economy today as wants-driven. That is, a large portion of purchases are made based on what people want and not necessarily what they need. This presents a real marketing and product development challenge. It's relatively easy to determine what people need—basic necessities such as food and shelter. The real challenge lies in determining what people want (e.g., children's shoes with rear lights).

For organizations focusing on meeting those wants or desires, the demographic makeup of the target audience is key. It's simple—the more you know about your target audience, the better equipped you are to develop and market products based on wants. So, most organizations today expend a great deal of time and effort in just learning about their target audience—their income levels, number of household members, age distribution, and so on.

In the table on page 169, we've provided a list of sites on the Internet that offer demographic information and many others are listed on the Web site that supports this text. Of course, the government is a large provider of demographic information. If you're interested in quickly accessing many of the government's sites, we recommend you connect to http://www.fedworld.gov. As well, the Real HOT Electronic Commerce section in Chapter 5 (Starting Your Own Business), lists numerous great sites that provide customer-specific information, including demographics.

Connect to five demographics-related Internet sites and see what they have to offer. As you do, answer the following questions for each.

A. What is the target audience of the site?

B. Who is the provider of the site?

C. Is the provider a private (for-profit) organization or a not-for-profit organization?

D. How often is the demographic information updated at the site?

E. Does the site require that you pay a subscription fee to access its demographic information?

F. For accessing the information, can you perform your search online, obtain printed reports, or download electronic files?

G. How helpful would the information be if you wanted to start a new business and sell various products (e.g., children's clothing, expensive watches, real estate/homes, and so forth)?

Web Sites Containing Online Databases and Information Repositories

Financial Aid	Address
FastWeb	http://www.fastweb.com
Financial Aid Information Page	http://www.finaid.org
CollegeNET	http://www.collegenet.com
FundFinder from the College Board	http://www.collegeboard.org/fund/finder/bin/fundflnd01.p1
Scholarship Resource Network	http://www.rams.com/srn

Library	Address
Annual Reports Library	http://www.zpub.com/sf/arl
Bodleian Library (Oxford University)	http://rsl.ox.ac.uk
BUBL Information Service Web Server	http://www.bubl.bath.ac.uk/BUBL/home.html
Cline Library—Special Collections and Archives	http://www.nau.edu/~cline/speccoll/imagedb.html
Interlibrary Loan and Document Delivery	http://www.nlc-bnc.ca/ifla/II/ill.htm

Consumer Information	Address
Consumer World	http://www.consumerworld.org
Consumer Information Center Catalog	http://www.pueblo.gsa.gov
Consumer Fraud Alert Network	http://www.world-wide.com/Homebiz/Fraud.htm
Better Business Bureau	http://www.bbb.org
Consumer Law Page	http://consumerlawpage.com

Demographic Information	Address
Acxiom Case-in-Point	http://www.acxiom.com/cip-00.htm
U.S. Census Bureau	http://www.census.gov
Mediamark Research	http://www.mediamark.com
Claritas Solutionseries	http://www.demographics.com/adlinks/claritas/solution.htm
Maritz Marketing Research	http://www.maritz.com/mmri

Real Estate	Address
Real Estate News	http://realtimes.com/consumer.htm?opendocument
Recent Sales	http://products.dataquick.com/consumer/input.asp?product_code=411_HSRCOUNT
Realtor Search	http://www.REALTOR.com/nbyp.htm?gate=webcrawler
Timeshare Sales	http://www.classifieds2000.com/cgi-cls/display.exe?wc-whr+Rental+Timeshare+Search
Realtor.Com	http://webcrawler.com/home_and_real_estate/sell

In the coming years, you can expect our economy and society to become even more wants-driven than it currently is. That simply means that demographic information will increase in importance. We definitely recommend that you frequently revisit the site that supports this text and see what new demographics-related sites are available.

Real Estate

Everyone on the Internet seems to be buying or selling something, from automobiles to children's clothing to pets. And people have also found that the Internet is a great place for the real estate business (homes, commercial properties, rentals, timeshares, and land). Especially when you consider that people are changing jobs and moving all over the country more than ever before, the Internet is indeed a great place to find real estate in your own neighborhood or in a city in another state.

In addition to the buying and selling of real estate, you'll also find a variety of related information. For example, there are sites that take you through a step-by-step process for buying your first home, provide mortgage and interest rate calculators, and even offer crime reports by neighborhood.

In the table on page 169, we've provided a list of real estate–related sites and where you can find them on the Internet. You should also check the Web site that supports this text to find a list of many others. If you're really interested in searching for a home via the Internet, we recommend you connect to http://homescout.homeshark.com, one of the largest collections of links to homes for sale on the Internet, with over 300,000 homes on over 120 real estate Web sites.

Connect to five real estate sites on the Internet and review their offerings. As you do, answer the following questions for each.

A. What is the focus of the site (homes, commercial real estate, real estate–related information, and so forth)?

B. Does the site require that you register as a user to access its services?

C. Does the site require you to a pay a subscription fee to access its services?

D. How can you search for information (by state, by zip code, by price range)?

E. How often is information on the site updated?

F. Does the site offer real estate–related information and services such as a mortgage calculator and interest rates?

G. Does the site offer links to other sites that provide real estate financing?

Go to the Web site that supports this text: **http://www.mhhe.com/business/mis/haag** and select "Electronic Commerce Projects."

We've included links to over 100 Web sites concerning online databases and information repositories, including a review of general Internet search tools such as Yahoo! and WebCrawler.

KEY TERMS AND CONCEPTS

Application Generation Subsystem
Atomic Primary Key
Centralized Database
Character
Chief Information Officer (CIO)
Composite Primary Key

Data Administration
Data Administration Subsystem
Data Definition Subsystem
Data Dictionary
Data Manipulation Subsystem
Data Mart

Data Mining Tool
Data Warehouse
Database
Database Administration
Database Management System (DBMS)

Database Management System
  Engine (DBMS Engine)
Distributed Database
Entity Class
Entity-Relationship (E-R) Diagram
External Database
Field
File
Foreign Key
Instance
Integrity Constraint
Intelligent Agent
Intersection Relation
Knowledge Worker Database

Logical View
Multidimensional Analysis (MDA)
  Tool
Normalization
Object
Object-Oriented Database
  (O-O Database or OODB)
Object-Oriented Database
  Management System (O-O
  DBMS or OODBMS)
Online Analytical Processing (OLAP)
Online Database
Online Transaction Processing
  (OLTP)

Operational Database
Partitioned Database
Physical View
Primary Key
Query-and-Reporting Tool
Query-by-Example (QBE) Tool
Record
Relation
Relational Database Model
Replicated Database
Report Generator
Structured Query Language (SQL)
View

SHORT-ANSWER QUESTIONS

1. What is the difference between online transaction processing (OLTP) and online analytical processing (OLAP)?
2. Why is separating logical from physical important in information organization?
3. What is a database? What are the two distinct parts of a database?
4. What are the five subsystems of a database management system? For what are they responsible?
5. What tools can you use to query a database?
6. What are the primary differences between the relational and object-oriented database models?
7. What are the four steps in developing a knowledge worker computing relational database application?
8. What are the various types of databases that can be found in an organization?
9. What is a data warehouse? How does it differ from traditional, operational databases?
10. What are the tools used to mine a data warehouse?

DISCUSSION QUESTIONS

1. Of the seven IT systems we discussed in Chapter 2, which primarily support the concept of online transaction processing (OLTP)? Which primarily support the concept of online analytical processing (OLAP)? Are there some IT systems that really support neither? Which are they and why?
2. Object-oriented technologies are used widely in organizations to reengineer processes. Why do you think this is true? If object-oriented technologies are indeed the best way to model business processes, why are organizations still using relational database technologies?
3. Some people believe that data warehouses will eventually replace most other types of databases, including operational ones. If this is to occur, how must data warehouses and data mining tools change? What do you see as the greatest drawback(s) to data warehouses replacing operational databases?
4. In Chapter 3, we discussed the virtual organization and the paperless office. Which types of databases

and database models best support these two concepts? As businesses move further toward the virtual organization and the paperless office, will the role of databases and data warehouses increase, decrease, or remain about the same? Be prepared to justify your answer.
5. Of the online databases you explored in the electronic commerce section of this chapter, which databases do you think were relational and which were object-oriented? Were any of those databases really data warehouses in disguise?
6. Knowledge worker computing databases are created on desktops every day in business around the globe mostly because of the readily availab[...] DBMSs on the market. Many [...] workers have not been expose[...] techniques like those describe[...] What do you think are the most [...] or omissions made by these peop[...]

CASE STUDY

A Decision Support System to Save Lives

You cannot see, hear, or smell nuclear radiation, but it's deadly all the same. In 1986 about 3.5 million people in Belarus, Russia, and Ukraine were exposed to it when there were two explosions in Unit 4 of the Chernobyl Nuclear Power plant. Some of the effects are only now emerging, like the high incidence of thyroid cancer in children. Experts agree that many health problems would have been avoided if an evacuation plan had been in place.

To avoid such a human tragedy in Virginia, power plant administrators commissioned the development of TEDSS to assist in creating an evacuation plan in case of a nuclear power plant disaster there. TEDSS is a special type of IT system called a *decision support system*. If a

IN THE NEWS

Decision Support
and Artificial
Intelligence

Brainpower for Your Business

CHAPTER 5

nuclear disaster were to occur, planners can use TEDSS to quickly determine the best evacuation routes and how best to notify the public of those routes.

For TEDSS to help determine the best evacuation strategies, it uses information that includes

- The behavior of radioactive gasses, such as dispersion rates
- Highway system characteristics, such as number of lanes
- Population distributions, such as densities and the location of people with disabilities
- Current weather conditions, such as wind direction

If this information were static, administrators would have no need for a decision support system because the evacuation route would be developed once and the job would be done. However, the information fluctuates constantly depending on the time of day, time of year, and meteorological and economic conditions. Population densities also change, as does the highway system. The task, then, is to analyze all the information given the specific conditions of the moment, find the best solution, and find it quickly.

Some of the information that TEDSS needs resides within the power plant organization, such as the layout of the power plant, information on deadly gasses, and the escalation rate of the

FEATURES

IN THE INFORMATION AGE, KNOWLEDGE WORKERS UNDERSTAND...

1. Categories of decisions and the process of decision making

2. The various types of decision support systems and their respective roles in effective decision making

3. The different types of artificial intelligence systems and how they contribute to better decision making

4. How to choose an IT system to suit your decision

accident. Other information is supplied by state agencies and other external sources.

By processing this information in its simulation models, TEDSS provides output—some of it in graphic form—on the following factors:

- Evacuation routes and paths from any origin to assigned shelters
- Projected volumes of traffic on the highway system

- Highways that may become severely blocked by radiation
- The time that will have elapsed before the last vehicle clears the area

With these outputs produced by TEDSS, planners can evaluate traffic management strategies, such as one-way operation of highways, shoulder use, and flashing signals to reduce traffic congestion and to improve evacuation time.[4, 5] ❖

Introduction

In the opening case study, power plant disaster planners use IT to make informed evacuation plans in the event of a nuclear disaster. The role of IT is crucial for several reasons. First, the planners must consider an enormous amount of information, both internal and external. Second, they must analyze and consolidate all this information to create new information. Finally, they must do it quickly—time is of the essence. With their decision support system, planners are able to more effectively and efficiently make decisions about how to direct the evacuation operation.

People in business regularly make decisions as complex as those that face power plant disaster planners, though not necessarily as grave in a life-and-death sense. Clearly, IT can help in decision-making processes, regardless of whether the decisions contribute to human or organizational survival. In a nutshell, IT can provide brainpower.

The big winners in tomorrow's business race will be those organizations, according to *Management Review,* that are "big of brain and small of mass."[1] For example, with only 35 people, the Adtrack company is able to track 10 million records (in a data warehouse) of information pertaining to newspaper and magazine ads. These 35 people perform complex tasks to provide newspapers and ad agencies with information on their relative position against competitors.[2, 3]

For many years, computers have been crunching numbers faster and more accurately than people can. A computer can unerringly calculate a payroll for 1,000 people in the time it takes a pencil to fall from your desk to the floor. Because of IT, knowledge workers have been freed of much of the drudgery of manually handling day-to-day transactions. And now IT power is augmenting brainpower and thought processes in ways previously seen only in science fiction. In some cases, IT power is actually **replacing** human brainpower.

Businesses, like individuals, use brainpower to make decisions, some big, some small, some relatively simple, and some very complex. As an effective knowledge worker, you'll have to make decisions on issues such as whether to expand the workforce, extend business hours, use different raw materials, or start a new product line. IT can help you in most, if not all, of these decisions. The extended brainpower that IT offers you as a decision maker comes in the form of decision support systems and artificial intelligence.

Whether to use a decision support system (there are several variations) or some form of artificial intelligence depends on the type of decision you have to make and how you plan to go about making that decision. So let's first look at different types of decisions and the process you go through to make a decision. Then we'll discuss decision support systems and artificial intelligence—IT brainpower (see Figure 5.1).

Decisions, Decisions, Decisions

Decision making is one of the most significant and important activities in business. Organizations devote vast resources of time and money to the process. In this section, we'll consider different decision types and the phases of decision making to help you better understand how IT can benefit that process.

Types of Decisions You Face

Some decisions are easier to make than others. Consider, for example, that you're making a pizza and need mozzarella cheese. So you go to the store and buy the cheapest mozzarella cheese you can find. The decision of which brand to buy is simple since it depends only on cost.

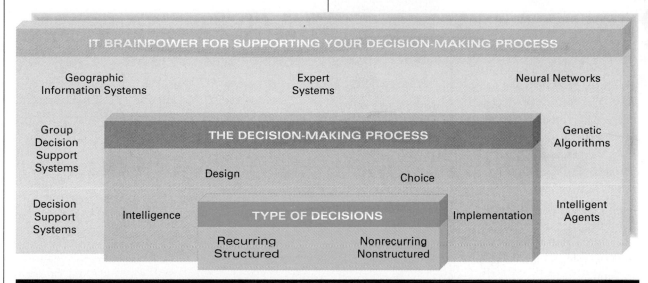

FIGURE 5.1

Your Focus for This Chapter

Now contrast buying cheese with the decision you would face if you were offered four jobs that were equally attractive for different reasons. Which one do you choose? How do you decide? No doubt you'll base your decision, in part, on the salary. A salary offer below a certain threshold knocks the job out of contention. On the other hand, if it is within an acceptable salary range, less tangible criteria become important. If the jobs are in different cities, you'll weigh your personal preferences for each place. You'll also want to consider other intangible aspects of each job, such as opportunities for advancement and personal growth prospects. These characteristics are harder to quantify and compare.

Choosing the right job is definitely more complex than buying mozzarella cheese because it has multiple decision criteria and not all of them are quantifiable. So it's much more difficult to select the "best" of the alternatives. Buying cheese is an example of a structured decision, whereas choosing the right job is an example of a decision with nonstructured elements.

A ***structured decision*** involves processing a certain kind of information in a specified way so that you will always get the right answer. No "feel" or intuition is necessary. These are the kinds of decisions that you can program—if you use a certain set of inputs and process them in a precise way, you'll arrive at the correct result. Calculating gross pay for hourly workers is an example. If hours worked is less than or equal to 40, then gross pay is equal to hours times rate of pay. If hours worked is greater than 40, then gross pay is equal to 40 times rate of pay plus time and a half for every hour over 40. You can easily automate these types of structured decisions with IT.

A ***nonstructured decision*** is one for which there may be several "right" answers and there is no precise way to get a right answer. No rules or criteria exist that guarantee you a good solution. Deciding whether to introduce a new product line, employ a new marketing campaign, or change the corporate image are all examples of decisions with nonstructured elements.

In reality, most decisions fall somewhere between structured and nonstructured, and you can still use IT to facilitate the decision-making process. The job choice decision is an example (see Figure 5.2). In choosing the right job, the salary part of the decision is structured, whereas the other criteria involve nonstructured aspects (for example, your perception of which job has the best advancement opportunity). Stock market investment analysis is another example of "somewhere in between" because you can easily calculate financial ratios and use past performance indicators. However, you still have to consider nonstructured aspects, such as projected interest

WHAT JOB DO I TAKE?

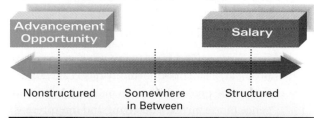

FIGURE 5.2

Viewing Structured versus Nonstructured
Decision Making as a Continuum

rates, unemployment rates, and competition.

Another way to view decisions is by the frequency with which the decision has to be made. The decision of which job to take is the sort of decision you don't make on a regular basis—this is a nonrecurring, or ad hoc, decision. On the other hand, determining pay for hourly employees is a routine decision that businesses face each week. Therefore determining pay for hourly employees is a recurring decision.

A *recurring decision* is one that happens repeatedly, and often periodically, whether weekly, monthly, quarterly, or yearly. You will usually use the same set of rules each time. When you calculate pay for hourly employees, the calculation is always the same regardless of the employee or time period. A *nonrecurring*, or *ad hoc*, *decision* is one that you make infrequently (perhaps only once) and you may even have different criteria for determining the best solution each time. A company merger is an example. These don't happen often—although they are becoming more frequent. And if the managers of a company need to make the merger decision more than once, they will most likely have to evaluate a different set of criteria each time. The criteria depend on the needs of the companies considering the merger, the comparability of their products and services, how they choose to structure debt, and so on.

How You Make a Decision

When you make a decision—whether you realize it or not—you go through four distinct phases (see Figure 5.3):[6]

■ *Intelligence* (find what to fix): Find or recognize a problem, need, or opportunity (also called the diagnostic phase of decision making). The intelligence phase involves detecting and interpreting signs that indicate a situation which needs your attention. These "signs" can come in many forms: consistent customer requests for new-product features, the threat of new competition, declining

sales, skyrocketing costs, an offer from a company to handle your distribution needs, and so on.

■ *Design* (find fixes): Consider possible ways of solving the problem, filling the need, or taking advantage of the opportunity. In this phase, you develop all the possible solutions you can.

■ *Choice* (pick a fix): Examine and weigh the merits of each solution, estimate the consequences of each, and choose the best one (which may be to do nothing at all). The "best" solution may depend on such factors as cost, ease of implementation, staffing requirements, and timeliness of the solution. This is the prescriptive phase of decision making—it's the stage at which a course of action is prescribed.

■ *Implementation* (apply the fix): Carry out the chosen solution, monitor the results, and make adjustments as necessary. Simply implementing a solution is seldom enough. Your chosen solution will always need fine-tuning, especially for complex problems or changing environments.

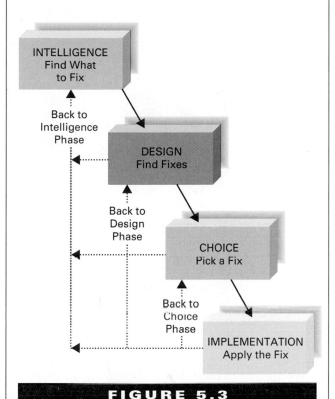

FIGURE 5.3

Four Phases of Decision Making

These four phases are not necessarily linear—you'll often find it useful or necessary to cycle back to an earlier phase. When choosing an alternative in the choice phase, for example, you might become aware of another possible solution. Then you would go back to the design phase, include the newly found solution, return to the choice phase, and compare the new solution to the others you generated.

Decision Support Systems

Help in Deciding What to Do

In Chapter 4, you saw how data mining can help you make business decisions by supporting your ability to slice and dice your way through information. Decision support systems are similar in concept to data mining. Like data mining, they allow you to locate and use information effectively.

A *decision support system (DSS)* is a highly flexible and interactive IT system that is designed to support decision making when the problem is not structured. A DSS is an alliance between you, the decision maker, and specialized support provided by IT (see Figure 5.4). IT brings speed, vast amounts of information, and sophisticated processing capabilities to help you create information useful to making a decision. You bring know-how in the form of your experience, intuition, judgment, and knowledge to the decision-making process. IT provides great power, but you—as the decision maker—must know what kinds of questions to ask of the information and how to process the information to get those questions answered. In fact, the primary objective of a DSS is to improve your effectiveness as a decision maker by providing you with assistance that will complement your insights. This union of your know-how and IT power makes you better able to respond to changes in the marketplace and to manage resources in the most effective and efficient ways possible. Following are some examples of the varied applications of DSSs:

- Baylor University Medical Center uses a DSS called MediSource which analyzes the interaction between drugs that are prescribed for a patient. This DSS covers about 98 percent of the most commonly prescribed drugs in medicine.[7]

- The First Coast Guard District, based in Boston, uses a DSS to assign 16 cutters to patrol areas where they respond to calls for search and rescue, law enforcement, and pollution control.[8]

- United Airlines uses a DSS to schedule flights. Since the DSS has been in operation, United Airlines has seen its flight delays reduced dramatically.[9]

Components of a Decision Support System

DSSs vary greatly in application and complexity, but they all share specific features. A typical DSS has three components (see Figure 5.5): data management, model management, and user interface management.

What You Bring	Advantages of a DSS	What IT Brings
Experience	Increased productivity	Speed
Intuition	Increased understanding	Information
Judgment	Increased speed	Processing capabilities
Knowledge	Increased flexibility	
	Reduced problem complexity	
	Reduced cost	

FIGURE 5.4

The Alliance Between You and a Decision Support System

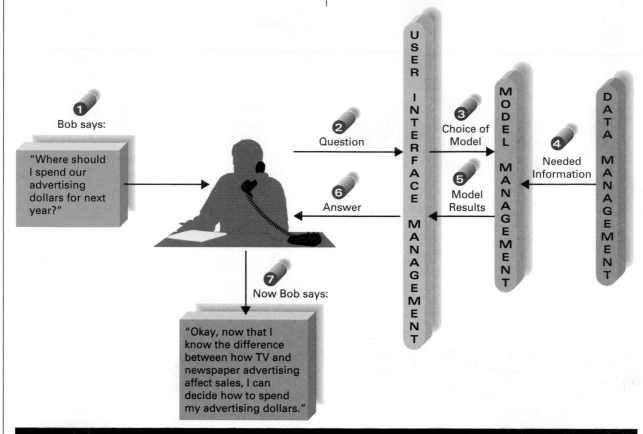

FIGURE 5.5

Components of a Decision Support System

Before we look at these three components individually, let's get a quick overview of how they work together. When you begin your analysis, you use the user interface management component to tell the DSS which model (in the model management component) to use on which information (in the data management component). The model requests the information from the data management component, analyzes that information, and sends the result to the user interface management component, which in turn passes the results back to you.

The **data management** component performs the function of storing and maintaining the information that you want your DSS to use. The data management component, therefore, consists of both the DSS information and the DSS database management system (see Figure 5.6). The information you use in your DSS comes from one or more of three sources:

■ You may want to use virtually any *information available in the organization* for your DSS. What you use, of course, depends on what the decision is and what information you need and whether it's available. You can design your DSS to access this information directly from your company's databases and data warehouses. However, specific information is often copied to the DSS database to save you time in searching through the organization's databases and data warehouses.

■ Some decisions require input from *external sources* of information. Various branches of the federal government, Dow Jones, Compustat data, and the Internet, to mention just a few, can provide additional information for use with a DSS.

■ You can incorporate your own insights and experience—your *personal information*—into your DSS. You can design your DSS so that you enter this personal information only as needed, or you can keep the information in a personal database that is accessible by the DSS.

The **model management** component consists of both the DSS models and the DSS model management system. A model is a representation of some event, fact, or situation. Because it's not always practical, or wise, to experiment with reality, people build models and use them for experimentation. Models can take various forms. Consider these examples:

■ The police force uses cardboard cutouts to represent criminals and bystanders in a crisis

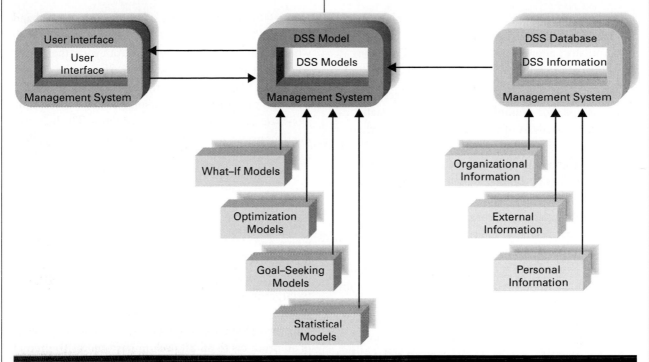

FIGURE 5.6

Inside Decision Support System Components

situation to train police officers to react appropriately and not shoot the good guys. Thus, the cutouts form a model that represents a real-life situation.

■ Your local video arcade most probably has a race-car game, which is a simulation (or model) of real race car driving. You can experiment with this

representation of reality without exposing yourself to the hazards of the Indy 500.

■ Airlines use sophisticated flight simulators to train pilots to fly passenger planes. Commercial pilots have to periodically undergo testing in a simulator. The simulator artificially creates loss of engine power, fire in the cabin, and other crisis situations

INDUSTRY PERSPECTIVE

Food

Hormel Foods Beefs Up Sales

Hormel Foods Corporation tracks 20 brands in 9 categories with UPC codes so that it can evaluate the sales by brand and measure the success of marketing efforts. To achieve this, Hormel has installed a decision support system, which primarily serves the market research, product, and sales

departments. Using this system, Hormel can effectively analyze trade promotions and measure incremental sales in one-fourth the time it used to take.

The impact of the decision support system was dramatically evident in an in-store promotion that increased Hormel's sales by 46 percent, from $1.3 to $1.9 million. Brent Payne, product manager of Hormel Micro Cup Meals and Kid's Kitchen Microwave Meals,

firmly believes, "We can quickly pinpoint the quality and depth of merchandising support that is achieved, as well as gauge consumer takeaway."

The system even allows managers to determine which of their distribution outlets is most effective and evaluate what the competition is doing.[10, 11] ❖

to ensure pilots are able to deal with such problems before lives are at stake. Again, a model (the simulator) allows experimentation and provides information without risk to life or limb.

Businesses use models to represent variables and their relationships. For example, you would use a statistical model called analysis of variance to determine whether newspaper, TV, and billboard advertising are equally effective in increasing sales. DSSs help in various decision-making situations by utilizing models that allow you to analyze information in many different ways. The models you use in a DSS depend on the decision you're making and, consequently, the kind of analysis you require. For example, you would use what-if analysis to see what effect the change of one or more variables will have on other variables, or optimization to find the most profitable solution given operating restrictions and limited resources.

The model management system stores and maintains the DSS's models. Its function of managing models is similar to that of a database management system. The model management component can't select the best model for you to use for a particular problem—that requires your expertise—but it can help you create and manipulate models quickly and easily.

The **user interface management** component allows you to communicate with the DSS. It consists of the user interface and the user interface management system. This is the component that allows you to combine your know-how with the storage and processing capabilities of the computer. The user interface is the part of the system

you see—through it you enter information, commands, and models. This is the only component of the system with which you have direct contact. So, from your (the knowledge worker's) point of view, the interface *is* the system. If you have a DSS with a poorly designed user interface—if it's too rigid or too cumbersome to use—you simply won't use it no matter what its capabilities. The best user interface uses your terminology and methods and is flexible, consistent, simple, and adaptable.

For an example of the components of a DSS, let's consider the DSS that Lands' End, a catalog sales company, uses.[12] Lands' End has 20 million names in its customer database. It sells a wide range of women's, men's, and children's clothing, as well as various household wares. To match the right customer with the right catalog, Lands' End has identified 20 different specialty target markets. Customers in these target markets receive catalogs of merchandise that they are likely to buy, saving Lands' End the expense of sending catalogs of all products to all 20 million customers. To predict customer demand, Lands' End needs to continuously monitor buying trends. And to meet that demand, Lands' End must accurately forecast sales levels. To accomplish these goals, it uses a DSS which performs three tasks:

- *Data management:* The DSS stores (or cradles) customer and product information. In addition to this organizational information, Lands' End also needs external information, such as demographic information and industry and style trend information.

Hallmark Stocks While the Craze Is Hot

Lion King, Pocahontas, and Mulan were enormous hits for a while. And with hit movies comes merchandising, when fast-food restaurants, toy stores, and greeting card stores sell products related to the movie. This is a window of

opportunity that closes quickly, so the party plates, action figures, and Christmas tree ornaments have to be in the stores while the craze lasts.

Hallmark Cards, Inc., of Kansas City, is acutely aware of the cost of lost sales and shipping mistakes. For many years Hallmark has captured TPS (transaction processing system) information from its point-of-sale scanners into its DSSs to

analyze sales trends and forecast demand. To further strengthen its distribution, Hallmark now adds its distribution information to the mix. Decision makers can analyze what went wrong with delivery in the past, and try to avoid future problems, thus ensuring that orders arrive at the stores when demand begins.[13] ❖

Pizzeria Decisions

When you go into a pizzeria, you have to decide what to order. This is not a structured decision—unless you like only one flavor of pizza. But you get a menu full of information to help you make your decision. When restaurant managers have to decide how many employees the restaurant requires, what kinds of pizza to offer, when to make entrees, how much of the pizza raw materials to order, they need information too—and they need to analyze it.

California Pizza Kitchen solved the problem by using a DSS to help it decide these issues. All 77 restaurants in the chain are connected and transmit information to corporate offices continuously. District managers visit three or four restaurants daily and they are connected to the main system with notebook computers and can access the food cost system from the road. Thus they can keep up with inventory levels, recipes, sales, and personnel schedules. The DSS allows the district managers to analyze the information they access. The combination of increased access to information and a well-designed DSS has led to a profit increase of 5 percent in many of the restaurants.[14] ❖

■ *Model management:* The DSS has to have models to analyze the information. The models create new information that decision makers need to plan product lines and inventory levels. For example, Lands' End uses a statistical model called regression analysis to determine trends in customer buying patterns and forecasting models to predict sales levels.

■ *User interface management:* A user interface enables Lands' End decision makers to access information and specify the models they want to use to create the information they need.

Decision Support Systems

To Build or Not to Build

The power of a DSS lies in its (1) ability to analyze information and (2) ease of use. A DSS creates new information on demand to help you make decisions of different types. A DSS can help with decisions that are nonstructured or somewhere between structured and nonstructured. You can develop a DSS for your own use or be part of a team of experts that develop a DSS for numerous people. In either case, the procedure for developing a DSS involves four steps that parallel the decision-making process.

Step 1: Intelligence

In this step, you need to answer the following questions:

■ Do you need a DSS?

■ If the answer to the first questions is *yes*
  ◆ What do you want the DSS to do?
  ◆ What information and models do you need?

The first step is to examine the problem and consider whether you need a DSS or whether you could more effectively solve the problem with some other IT system, such as an MIS report or an EIS. If you choose DSS support, then carefully consider what it will take to support your decision making process. If the problem is complex and has several parts, the best strategy is to "divide and conquer." In other words, decide on a portion of the problem and construct your DSS to help with that portion first. Give careful thought to the information you'll use, where it will come from, and what models you'll need to process the information.

If many knowledge workers will use the DSS, or if the DSS is very complex, then you'll have to invest a lot of time and effort in a formalized approach to planning, organizing, and coordinating the development process. Say, for example, you need to develop a DSS that financial consultants will use for the recurring decision of advising clients on retirement portfolios. This DSS would have to fit the needs and styles of all the financial consultants using it, and the development team would have to spend lots of time in deliberation and discussion with all the people who will use it. If, however, you're the only one who will use the DSS, you could simply build one yourself or seek the advice of a DSS builder. The development process can be much less rigorous; however, you still must be specific about what you want to do with your DSS and how you want to do it.

Step 2: Design

This step requires you to answer the following questions:

- What's available to you commercially?
- What can you build?

You can buy specialized DSSs for particular types of problems. There are, among others, financial modeling packages, statistical packages, inventory control packages, and project management packages. Commercial packages have the models already built and provide an interactive user interface that allows you to enter the information you need to analyze and access the right models.

If you don't find a fully developed DSS to fit your needs, you can develop your own. You can build your own models, use models already available, or opt for a combination. A DSS generator like Excel or Quattro Pro simplifies the building of a DSS (see Figure 5.7). A **DSS generator** is software that enables you to develop a DSS for a specific task. The menu system serves as the user interface. So the DSS generator provides a user interface management system that you can enhance with macros. The spreadsheet page holds the information. You can build your own models using formulas and functions, or you can use the predefined analysis models. You could have several models on different pages of the spreadsheet and move information between them.

You can integrate many commercially available models into spreadsheets or combine them to fit your needs. For example, if you're constructing a DSS to evaluate a proposed investment, you could use a financial modeling package like PC EXPRESS to make return on investment calculations. You could add a regression model that you created in Quattro Pro showing projected sales based on pertinent variables. Then you could formulate a decision tree using ARBORIST, which is a graphic decision tree module that links to spreadsheets.

Step 3: Choice

This step involves answering the following questions:

- What will you buy?
- What will you build?

Now it's time to decide what you're going to buy and what you're going to build. When considering commercially available packages, pay special attention

to the flexibility of the user interface. If you're combining models, consider compatibility. If you don't do your homework first, you might find yourself entering the same information multiple times.

Step 4: Implementation

This step involves the following:

- Build or install the DSS.
- Learn, test, and evaluate your DSS thoroughly.

This step involves making your DSS operational and testing it. If you buy a DSS, you'll have to install it and learn to use it properly. If you build your own, you'll have to put together the information, models, and possibly, the user interface. Then you test the DSS. The testing will ensure accuracy and indicate the benefit of the system to you. It's very important to verify the results of the analysis you run on your DSS. You should test the DSS thoroughly with as much and as varied information as possible.

If you follow these four steps, you'll have a working DSS. But you'll have to fine-tune and improve it continually, especially if you use it often. The purpose of a DSS is to provide you with decision-making support, and because your decision-making approach changes with time, your DSS must change too.

Ethical Questions in Decision Support Systems

Ethical behavior means that you consider the results of your actions—this is called *accountability*. The higher the risk of potential damage, the more important accountability becomes. Consider this hypothetical situation.

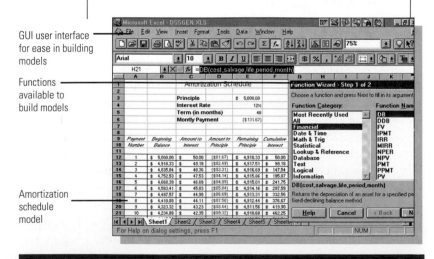

GUI user interface for ease in building models

Functions available to build models

Amortization schedule model

FIGURE 5.7

A DSS Generator Up Close

Let's say a small town used a DSS to plan fire protection for its inhabitants. Using a commercially available DSS, the town council projected the number of fire trucks the town would need, the location of the fire stations and hydrants, and so on. The town council believed that the system would be wholly adequate because the DSS software had been used correctly. However, one day, a little boy was playing with matches and set a sheet of paper on fire. He heard his mother coming and quickly hid the burning paper under the bed. The house was rapidly engulfed in flames. Firefighters were dispatched. When they arrived at the site, however, the nearest hydrant was out of reach of their hoses. By the time they retrieved extra hoses and started the water flowing, the little boy's house and those on either side were gutted. Whose fault was it that the fire department was unable to render adequate assistance? Do the DSS developers bear any responsibility for creating a faulty program? Should the city administrators have relied on the results they obtained from the DSS? Should they have cross-checked their results?

Consider another situation. A social club for retired railroad workers and surviving spouses has extensive information on members, including age, address, phone number, income level, and number of people in the household. Using a DSS, the officers of the organization generate a list containing the names of potentially gullible people and sell the list to a shady insurance company, knowing that the insurance company plans to take advantage of club members. The social club does not tell its members that it has sold the list. This is perfectly legal because, in general, private organizations are not bound by any laws concerning the use of the information they collect (as long as the information is not copyrighted or otherwise protected), only government agencies are. Of course, being legal is not the same as being ethical.

"Legal" means that a law doesn't prohibit an action. "Ethical" means that your concept of what is right will dictate an action. Because the law offers little or no direction, how you use information pertaining to clients and customers depends on your ethics and your organization's ethical culture. You're accountable ethically, if not always legally, for information that customers and clients give you. In the absence of legal guidelines, many professional organizations, including the legal and medical professions, have adopted strict ethical guidelines on the use of client information. The Association of Information Technology Professionals (AITP) is among several organizations that have established guidelines for IT specialists. To be an ethical decision maker, you must consider how information is collected and how it will be used.

Group Decision Support Systems
IT Power for Team Meetings

Let's say you and nine classmates in an archeology class are planning a field trip to a dig site. Each of you has a computer and individually considers alternative sites, analyzing cost and time demands, transport considerations, and so on. After that, you get together and discuss your ideas, narrowing the alternatives. Then you return to your computers and analyze the revised list of possibilities.

CAREER OPPORTUNITY

Many claims are made about DSSs. It's important that you understand not only the benefits of DSSs but also their limitations. A little skepticism is often a good thing. Some early research will save you lots of time and trouble later on. If you're considering buying a fully developed DSS or a DSS generator, find other people who are already using the system and ask their opinion. You can find interest groups all over the country that specialize in one type of software or problem. Contacting one of these groups is a good way to get information. The Internet is a good place to start looking.

Let's revisit this scenario, but this time we'll augment your IT with telecommunications and specialized groupware. Now you and your team(classmates) are connected by a computer network, and everyone can view everyone else's suggestions. Furthermore, you have software to help the team gather, consolidate, analyze, and rank the suggestions. You can now collectively suggest dig sites, keep the suggestions that have promise, analyze the cost and benefit of each one, and form a plan of action.

In this revised scenario, you and your team used a group decision support system. A ***group decision support system (GDSS)*** is a type of decision support system that facilitates the formulation of and solution to problems by a team. A GDSS facilitates team decision making by integrating (1) groupware, (2) DSS capabilities, and (3) telecommunications (see Figure 5.8).

The more complex and the less structured the decision a team has to make, the more a GDSS can help. For example, the Department of Energy's Emergency Preparedness Team uses a GDSS to develop a strategic defense plan against nuclear bomb threats. Working in the desert near Las Vegas, the team uses its GDSS to pool ideas to generate the most effective disaster plan.[15]

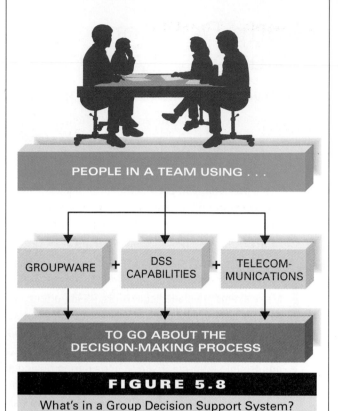

PEOPLE IN A TEAM USING . . .

GROUPWARE + DSS CAPABILITIES + TELECOM-MUNICATIONS

TO GO ABOUT THE DECISION-MAKING PROCESS

FIGURE 5.8

What's in a Group Decision Support System?

In our discussion of GDSSs and how they can help you and your organization, we'll explore the team decision-making process, the components of a GDSS, and the types of team meetings a GDSS can support.

The Team Decision-Making Process and You

You can use a GDSS to support a team engaged in any one or more of the first three phases of decision making: intelligence, design, or choice. But, whatever the objective of the meeting, you usually go through three distinct steps (see Figure 5.9).

❶ *Brainstorming:* Your team members generate ideas in this step. Your team could be identifying the strengths, weaknesses, opportunities, or threats faced by your organization. Or you could be considering or choosing possible solutions to a problem. Avoid discussing the merits or drawbacks of the ideas that other team members contribute at this stage, simply note them.

❷ *Issue categorization and analysis*: During this step, you and your team members arrange ideas into manageable classifications. Then you further

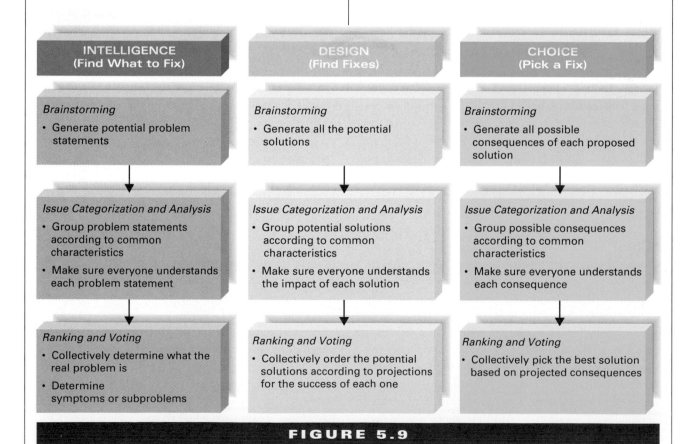

INTELLIGENCE (Find What to Fix)	DESIGN (Find Fixes)	CHOICE (Pick a Fix)
Brainstorming • Generate potential problem statements	*Brainstorming* • Generate all the potential solutions	*Brainstorming* • Generate all possible consequences of each proposed solution
Issue Categorization and Analysis • Group problem statements according to common characteristics • Make sure everyone understands each problem statement	*Issue Categorization and Analysis* • Group potential solutions according to common characteristics • Make sure everyone understands the impact of each solution	*Issue Categorization and Analysis* • Group possible consequences according to common characteristics • Make sure everyone understands each consequence
Ranking and Voting • Collectively determine what the real problem is • Determine symptoms or subproblems	*Ranking and Voting* • Collectively order the potential solutions according to projections for the success of each one	*Ranking and Voting* • Collectively pick the best solution based on projected consequences

FIGURE 5.9

Team Decision-Making Steps for Intelligence, Design, and Choice

discuss those ideas, clarify any unresolved issues, and evaluate the worth of each idea.

❸ *Ranking and voting:* When your team has seen, discussed, and analyzed the ideas, each member assigns weights to each idea. After prioritizing them, the team votes on the final ranking.

These three steps constitute the process of team decision making. In GDSS-enhanced meetings, existing IT is combined with specialized groupware to improve productivity by helping team members simultaneously contribute and view suggestions and ideas, review the ideas, and reach a consensus.

Key Components in a Group Decision Support System

Like all IT systems, a GDSS is an important alliance between people and IT tools.

People in a GDSS	IT Tools in a GDSS
Team	Groupware
Facilitator	DSS capabilities
	Telecommunications

People in a GDSS

People have one of two roles in a GDSS. The first role is a member of the team working on a problem. The team consists of people united by a common goal. This goal may be solving a problem or taking advantage of an opportunity—either of which involves making a decision. It's important that the team members willingly work together and exchange ideas. As with all IT systems, if the people who are supported by the system are uncooperative, the outcome will be less than optimal. A GDSS is simply ineffective when team members don't want to work together.

The second role is that of the facilitator who helps the team reach its goals. A group facilitator has two roles, one nontechnical and one technical. The nontechnical role involves planning and running the meeting, providing advice on the formulation of a meeting agenda, determining the format of the meeting, and conducting the meeting without participating in the discussion. The facilitator's nontechnical skills often affect the outcome of a GDSS meeting. The facilitator's technical role involves handling the administrative and technical details of GDSS meetings. These include responsibility for the operation of the computers and the network, the DSS capabilities, and the groupware. The facilitator's technical skills enable the team to be efficient and productive.

IT Tools in a GDSS

IT tools are a very important part of a GDSS. These tools consist of groupware, DSS capabilities, and telecommunications. As you saw in Chapter 2, groupware is the umbrella term for any kind of software that allows teams to communicate and share documents. GDSS groupware is a special kind of groupware specifically designed to accommodate team decision making. It has capabilities that support the three phases of team decision making:

■ *Brainstorming:* This part of GDSS groupware allows you and your team members to enter comments and suggestions simultaneously and anonymously. The GDSS groupware then collects the various contributions and displays them either on a viewing screen or on the individual team members' computers.

■ *Issue categorization and analysis:* Based on key words, the GDSS software sorts and classifies the team's ideas. Each set of ideas then goes into a separate electronic folder. You can then open any or all of the folders and add your comments. You can also refine and reorganize the topics in the folders.

■ *Ranking and voting:* You assign weights to the various ideas, and then the GDSS groupware calculates the outcome and shows these results numerically or graphically to the team.

GDSS groupware was originally developed for meetings in which all participants are in the same room. Today, however, GDSS groupware supports other types of meetings. Team members need not be in the same room, or even in the same building. Later in this chapter, we'll discuss the various types of meetings made possible by IT.

Specialized GDSS groupware is not the only kind of groupware you can use to improve your team meetings. You can, in fact, use any type of groupware that facilitates communication and decision making including, but not limited to, electronic mail, electronic bulletin boards, videoconferencing, and language translation groupware. Document management groupware is particularly helpful because it allows the team to collaborate on documents, spreadsheets, and other projects.

The DSS capabilities that you use depend on the type of decision you're making. So you must consider which method of analysis—whether statistical, what-if, or another—must be applied to your information to render the most informed decision. Each member of your team must be able to formulate suggestions and analyze those of others. Without the ability to analyze alternatives, you can't adequately assess them and, therefore, cannot contribute fully to the meeting.

The cornerstone of a GDSS-enhanced meeting is a telecommunications network—the hardware and software that connect computers. The type of network you use depends on the type of meeting. For example, a local area network connects team members in the same room, but teams dispersed in different geographic locations need a wide area network, and might also use videoconferencing. In Chapter 6, we'll discuss networks and telecommunications in depth.

The GDSS concept supports many different types of meetings. In addition to improving the productivity of traditional meetings, IT can also provide new, more flexible meeting formats. Let's now consider the nature of meetings and how the GDSS concept can help.

Meetings: A Fact of Life in Business

A large part of business involves decision making; and a large part of decision making involves groups of people working collaboratively. Cooperation is the keystone to innovation and creativity in business. Cooperation, however, involves meetings, and meetings consume a large proportion of work time—35 percent for tactical management

and between 50 and 80 percent for strategic management. Thus meetings use two of the most valuable assets an organization has—time and people.

Because IT systems save time and increase employee productivity, the most effective organizations in the information age will be those that use IT systems to connect people and their ideas. A GDSS is one such IT system. A GDSS will help your organization get the most from its meetings by directly addressing the two biggest problems associated with meetings—too much time spent and too little productivity achieved. GDSSs exist to maximize the positive effects of team decision making—the synergy of collective effort—and minimize the negative effects of wasted time and energy.

Traditional face-to-face meetings are notoriously time-inefficient. Meetings without IT support are sequential—everyone takes a turn speaking—and that takes a lot of time. A GDSS changes the form of the meeting so that participants can offer their contributions simultaneously. A GDSS-enhanced meeting reduces the likelihood of detouring into less important or irrelevant topics. And a GDSS-enhanced meeting allows you to access needed information during the meeting.

The effectiveness, or productivity, of meetings also declines with an increase in the size of the team. Meetings

INDUSTRY PERSPECTIVE

Manufacturing

Finding What to Fix at IBM

"What's the problem?" It was asked time and time again by IBM's manufacturing shop floor manager. Everyone seemed to have a different idea—poor equipment maintenance, low-quality raw materials, inadequate communication with production planning, lack of sufficient shop floor space, and so on.

This is a problem all businesses face—not why shop floor control has gone haywire —but rather what problem is causing **any** malfunction. This is the

first stage in decision making—finding what to fix (intelligence).

To find the exact problem (and not simply the symptoms), IBM's shop floor manager worked with a group facilitator to develop an agenda, announced the upcoming meeting, and gathered key personnel in a GDSS decision room for some serious and productive brainstorming. The meeting proceeded as follows:

1. The team spent 35 minutes offering 635 ideas and insights.

2. The team spent the next 30 minutes consolidating those ideas and insights into a list of key issues.

3. During the last 45 minutes of the meeting, the team ranked the key issues and voted on their relative importance.

After just 2 short hours, IBM's shop floor manager had a complete report of the team's comments, consolidated and prioritized.

In decision making, the most important stage is intelligence—finding what to fix. That's probably why it's the first step. One of the most wasteful activities in business—and one of the most costly—is fixing the wrong problem.[16, 17] ❖

of 3 to 5 people work well but, after that, the more people participating in a meeting, the less productive the meeting becomes. Decisions are often biased by the presence of influential members, conflict between members, and groupthink. *Groupthink* arises when individual members of the team are discouraged from thinking independently. A GDSS-enhanced meeting induces a greater level of independent thought and a greater degree of anonymity, minimizing the unwillingness of many people to express or support controversial opinions.

Meetings When and Where You Want to Be

Because IT connects people and computers, it supports not only traditional face-to-face meetings that occur in the same place at the same time, but also a wide variety of other meeting formats. We can classify meetings into two main categories: Same-time meetings and different-time meetings. The GDSS concept adjusts groupware, DSS capabilities, and telecommunications components to the meeting type (see Figure 5.10).

Same-Time Meetings Can Be	Different-Time Meetings Can Be
In the same room	
In the same city	In the same city
On the same planet	On the same planet

Same-Time Meetings (Synchronous Meetings)

Same-time, or *synchronous*, meetings require team members to interact directly with one another simultaneously. Such meetings can occur while participants are in the same room, the same city, or scattered around the planet.

Same Room A *same-room* meeting implies that all the team members meet in the same room. Most GDSS groupware has been developed for same-room meetings where project teams get together to solve a problem or make a decision. This type of team often consists of representatives from several areas of responsibility within the organization. For example, if your organization is considering the introduction of a new product, the project team might consist of representatives from strategic management, marketing, engineering, and accounting.

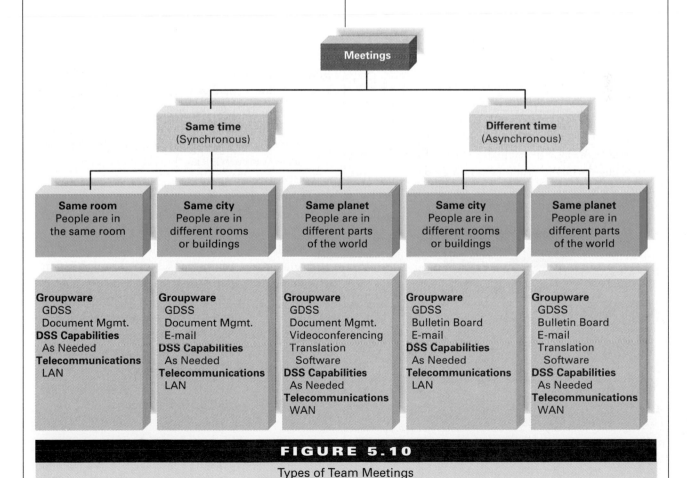

FIGURE 5.10

Types of Team Meetings

Bank Executives Don't Get Out Much These Days

The executives of the Inter-American Development Bank, based in Washington, DC, are busy folks who have to make many team decisions that are not structured, for example,

- Which software to buy for the financial department
- Which external auditors to hire for the bank

- Which satellite communications providers to choose
- Which health insurance program to furnish to its employees

Using a GDSS incorporating videoconferencing together with Lotus Notes groupware, the executives manage to come to speedy decisions on all of these matters, without having to spend time and money traveling. The decision makers at Inter-American found that the GDSS concept greatly

enhances their decision process because they can address each decision systematically, weighing the risks and benefits of each component of the decision. They found that the GDSS helped them focus on the issues pertaining to the decision and allowed each member of the team to offer input in an orderly and complete manner.[19] ❖

Same-room GDSS meetings usually take place in a GDSS *decision room*, which has telecommunications in the form of a local area network that connects the team members. The network might also be connected to the organizational databases, making organizational information available to the team. Each computer in the room is equipped with GDSS groupware and DSS capabilities. You and your team members enter your ideas at your computers and your comments are displayed on a public viewing screen, making them visible to the entire team (see Figure 5.11). The facilitator is particularly helpful in running the GDSS groupware. Using a decision room equipped with GDSS groupware, IBM has been able to

reduce meeting times by over 50 percent; Boeing has managed an impressive 90 percent decrease in meeting times and estimates a savings of nearly $7,000 in employee time.[20]

Same City In *same-city* meetings, team members are located within a small geographic area, like a building, block, or city. They do not meet in the same room. They may choose to participate in the meeting from their respective offices rather than gather in a decision room. For example, a team composed of stockbrokers may want to meet and discuss market trends to identify potential threats or opportunities. But they don't want to have to get together in one room. Travel takes time and is often stressful. And while in transit, stockbrokers can't watch stock movements and may miss important calls from clients. So they agree to meet electronically. They use the organization's telecommunications network to connect electronically; and, using document management groupware that allows them to share all kinds of documents, they have their meeting. As well, more than 200 state courthouses use videoconferencing for proceedings involving prisoners. The practice not only cuts costs by reducing the need to transport inmates to courthouses but also reduces the opportunity for escapes and injuries to guards.[21]

Same Planet A *same-planet* meeting takes place when the team members are dispersed geographically and meet electronically. As companies spread across the country

Viewing Screen

Facilitator

FIGURE 5.11

Model of a GDSS Decision Room[18]

How Can a GDSS Help?

Look at the five scenarios below, and identify the most important benefits that a GDSS would provide. What phase (or phases) of the decision-making process would each situation call for?

1. A team of engineers within a company is trying to create a more fuel-efficient automobile.

2. Marketing representatives located in various parts of the world want to develop a strategic marketing plan for a new product line.

3. You and your fellow students are planning to make a presentation in a management class and you meet to consider how best to organize it.

4. A fast-food franchiser is meeting with its franchisees to determine pricing for a new sandwich.

5. A steering committee in an organization is trying to determine why customer satisfaction levels have dropped. ❖

and around the world, face-to-face meetings become more difficult, but the pressure to reach decisions quickly in an increasingly competitive world becomes more intense. The more dispersed the team members, the more costly and inconvenient it is to bring them together in a single room. A same-planet meeting can make use of three types of IT support. First, the meeting can be similar to a same-city meeting, using telecommunications and groupware. Second, it can resemble a same-room meeting if it uses videoconferencing, which allows team members in each location to see and hear the other teams. Desktop videoconferencing can turn your monitor into a TV set, showing your discussion partners. Sun Microsystems even uses desktop videoconferencing to meet with its customers.[22] Third, another form of videoconferencing can connect decision rooms with video screens or TV sets. For example, if four teams were meeting in different cities, each decision room would have three TVs, one showing each of the other teams. Then, by using telecommunications to connect the decision rooms, all the participants could send suggestions back and forth.

Some GDSS groupware includes language translation software to accommodate meetings whose participants speak different languages. This is of great benefit to transnational firms. You should be cautious, however, about language translation software, because it's very difficult to translate one language into another. A statement may make sense to the original speaker but make no sense whatsoever to the listener after it's translated. The box below illustrates this point. The package that generated this strange version of English is supposed to help Japanese- and English-speaking financial specialists communicate. It sells for about $2,000.

Different-Time Meetings (Asynchronous Meetings)

Teams whose members are located in the same city (or even the same building) may not find it convenient or efficient to meet at the same time. When team members are dispersed around the planet, same-time meetings may be even more difficult to achieve. For example, time differences mean that daytime in the United States is nighttime in Asia.

I Beg Your Pardon, What Did You Say?

Before translation: Most business people settle accounts by check, the use of cash is rare.

After translation: It is settled an account between each other's checking account with transaction of business fellow, and it is rare to use cash.

Before translation: Current policy stipulates that living expenses, including residence, car, utilities, and phone, are not subject to reimbursement.

After translation: We don't pay the purchase of residence and automobile, fare of electricity/gas/water service/telephone in cash usually currently. ❖

However, the dispersed team members can still meet in a *different-time* or *asynchronous* meeting that could last days, weeks, or even months. In this type of meeting, a viewing screen would not be a feasible way of displaying comments. Here your team would use an electronic bulletin board, a central database, or e-mail. In different-time meetings, the schedule is flexible, and each team member can contribute as appropriate and feasible. A different-time meeting would have all the elements of a same-time meeting, but it would take longer to complete the meeting. For example, you could send the agenda to your team members through e-mail; then members could post suggestions to an electronic bulletin board, or they could distribute them to the other members through e-mail. At a later stage, they could explore and clarify issues to reach a consensus. It's also difficult to include a facilitator in different-time meetings. However, the duties of the facilitator are still crucial to the success of a meeting; and where a facilitator is unavailable or impractical, the duties are distributed among team members.

Geographic Information Systems

Words and Pictures

Suppose you've decided to go on a 2-week vacation that will include camping, sightseeing, and mall touring in Minnesota (after all, Minneapolis boasts the largest shopping mall in the United States—The Mall of America). What maps should you buy? Some will show roads for traveling from one place to another; others will show campgrounds in the state that boasts 10,000 lakes; others will pinpoint historic landmarks; and still others will detail hotels around The Mall of America as well as the locations of the hundreds of stores in the mall.

To get a truly comprehensive picture of your proposed vacation, you'd have to buy each map, redraw them to make a single map, then note on it where you'll go and how you'll get there. Of course, you could choose to carry all the maps and use them only when needed. But what about a business that needs to analyze different maps with geographic, demographic, highway, and other information to decide where to build a new distribution facility?

Fortunately there's a special type of DSS for just this kind of problem—it's called a geographic information system. A ***geographic information system (GIS)*** is a decision support system designed specifically to work with spatial information. Spatial information is any information that can be shown in map form, such as roads, the distribution of bald eagle populations, sewer systems, and the layout of electrical lines. Today GISs are helping businesses perform such tasks as

- Identifying the best site to locate a branch office based on number of households in a neighborhood
- Targeting pockets of potential customers in a particular market area
- Repositioning promotions and advertising based on sales
- Determining the optimal location of a new distribution outlet

Directions in Cyberspace

Would you like to find out where a movie is playing? Would you also like to know before you arrive whether there is a restaurant to your liking nearby? You can do this for 15,000 theaters nationwide by accessing the *Playbill Magazine* Web site at www.playbill.com. You also get access to local maps to find out where the theater is and what businesses are nearby.

Playbill didn't build this system itself. It uses GeoSystems' service which has GIS databases with the locations of more than 12 million businesses nationwide. A business signs up for GeoSystems' service (which costs between $6,000 and $20,000 per year). Then potential customers send queries about a business's location by accessing its Web site. The query is passed on to the GeoSystems server which builds a map of the location and sends it back to the querying customer. The map incorporates graphics from the business's Web site, making it appear that the site visited generated the map.[23] ❖

GISs Take a Bite out of Crime in England

The Leicestershire Constabulary, like all the other police forces in the world, spends long, laborious hours collecting details about crimes, and then even more hours trying to make sense of the data collected. The latter task has become considerably easier, however, since the Leicestershire police began using a GIS. Now investigators feed massive amounts of information about the location, time, and method of crimes into their GIS. Then the GIS produces colorful displays of maps and diagrams. With the GIS, the police can replicate events on maps and plot scenarios based on the sightings of suspects or vehicles in different places. As the story evolves, the picture changes. The GIS also allows officers to draw links on-screen to connect suspects to events.

The GIS helps investigators see patterns in the time, location, and method of crimes. For years the police have used text-based systems to search for such patterns. For example, an officer can search for a particular time, place, or method. The advantage of the GIS is that the officers can see the various kinds of information in overlays giving the whole picture at once instead of in pieces. This makes it easier to see whether a particular crime is being committed at a particular time or place, allowing the police to intervene by being there to catch the criminal or by beefing up police presence to deter the crime.

Another advantage of the GIS is that police decision makers can easily track the effectiveness of deploying officers in a particular area by measuring the crime clean-up rate. This allows police chiefs to make better decisions concerning when and where to position their forces.[25] ❖

THE GLOBAL **PERSPECTIVE**

When businesses combine textual information and spatial information, they are creating a new type of information called *business geography*. GISs are well-suited to storing, retrieving, and analyzing business geography to support the decision-making process. Healthdemographics, a San Diego–based company, sells such a business geography–based GIS to nursing home providers.[24] Using Healthdemographics' GIS system, nursing home providers can store, retrieve, and analyze information from many external databases containing national demographic information, along with information from operational databases within nursing home organizations.

For example, all nursing home providers make decisions based on supply and demand. Supply is the nursing home providers serving the area. Demand is simply those geographic areas that have populations in need of long-term care and assisted living. Healthdemographics' GIS system helps nursing home administrators visually correlate and analyze these supply-and-demand characteristics.

If you need spatial information for a GIS, you can obtain that information from a variety of sources, including government agencies and commercially available spatial information databases. For example, the U.S. Census Bureau can provide you with demographic information, the Bureau of Labor Statistics can give you employment information, and polling companies such as Scarborough Research Corp. have consumer-habit information.

A GIS is actually a combination of sophisticated graphics and database technology. Using a GIS, you can logically link textual and spatial information. For example, you could gather geographic information about the distribution of customers who buy yachts (spatial information). You could also gather information about their color preferences (textual information) and link it to the spatial information. Then, using queries similar to those illustrated in Chapter 4, you could analyze both the spatial and textual information, generating output in the form of maps, graphs, or numeric tables.

A GIS database represents information thematically. That means that a GIS map is composed of many separate, overlapping information layers, each of which has its own theme. For example, the first layer might be roads, the next might be utilities (water, electricity, etc.), the third school-age children, and the fourth homes within a certain price range. In reviewing Figure 5.12, notice how the information structure resembles a cube much like the multidimensional nature of a data warehouse. You can use a GIS to slice and dice information as you need it, in the same way you'd use data mining.

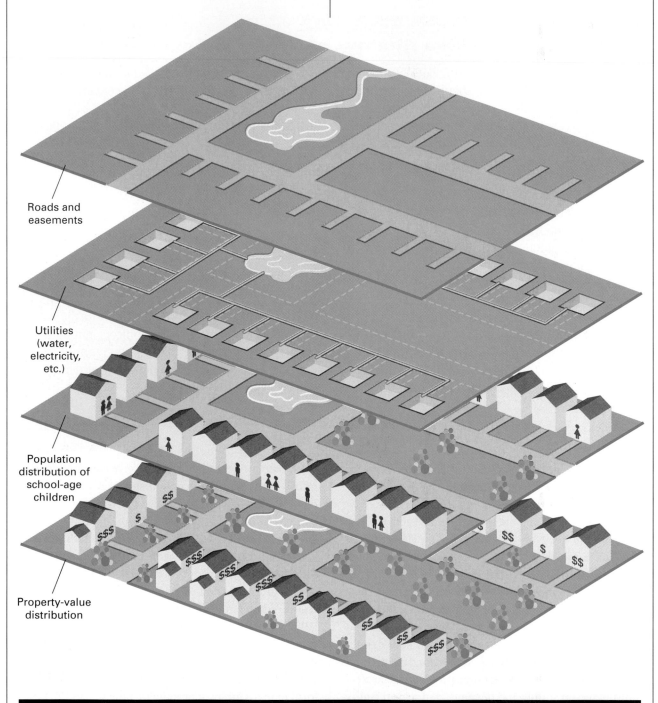

Roads and easements

Utilities (water, electricity, etc.)

Population distribution of school-age children

Property-value distribution

FIGURE 5.12

Thematic Mapping in a Geographic Information System

A GIS not only processes spatial information, but also presents information spatially. To understand the importance of this feature, imagine asking a friend for directions to a mall. If the directions are given to you in an oral or written form, you probably won't find the mall as readily as you would have if you'd been given a map complete with landmarks and compass directions. Business geography is no different—a picture is still worth a thousand words. Figure 5.13 is a map of toxic release sites and schools in Bronx County, New York City. Thus, the possible exposure of school children is clear. For other such maps look at Mapinfo's Web site at www.-mapinfo.com. Following are some other examples of GIS applications:

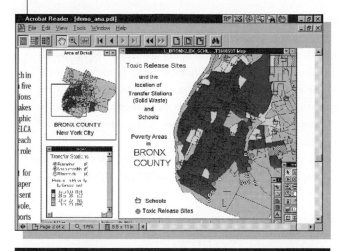

FIGURE 5.13

Are the Children in Danger?

- Scars uses a GIS to plan the daily routes that Sears drivers nationwide must take when delivering appliances and other merchandise to customers' homes. Scars saves millions of dollars annually on its 4 million home deliveries with its GIS. The 52 distribution centers use the GIS to reduce the time it takes to map out a delivery route from 2.5 hours to about 20 minutes.[26]

- Relocate, a real estate service firm in Manhattan, uses GIS maps to analyze the real estate market. For example, to determine why an office building remains vacant at $25 per square foot, Relocate asks the GIS to display a map showing all the buildings in that class. If the average rent is $23, it becomes instantly obvious why the $25-per-square-foot building remains vacant.[27]

- Boise, Idaho, has grown rapidly over the last several years. The sheriff's office maintains a 900-page map book which department dispatchers on the 911 lines use to help police officers, firefighters, and paramedics locate emergency scenes. The county sheriff's department used to update the map book every 2 years by drafting and copying updated pages individually. The map sections have very detailed information including street names, rights of way, address ranges, and hydrants. Since installing a GIS, the sheriff's department can plot a page within 15 minutes, or the whole map book within a few weeks. Updates are now made every 2 weeks, keeping the maps current, which is crucial for this fast-growing urban area. Each department can also get a specialized map. For example, the fire department needs the location of hydrants, but the paramedics don't.[28]

Artificial Intelligence
Where No Machine
Has Gone Before

DSSs, GDSSs, and GISs are IT systems that augment business brainpower. IT can further expand business brainpower by means of artificial intelligence—the techniques and software that enable computers to mimic human behavior in various ways. Financial analysts use a variety of artificial intelligence systems to manage assets, invest in the stock market, and perform other financial operations.[29] Hospitals use artificial intelligence in many capacities, from scheduling staff, to assigning beds to patients, to diagnosing and treating illness.[30] Many government agencies use artificial intelligence, including the IRS and the armed forces. Credit card companies use artificial intelligence to detect credit card fraud, and insurance companies use artificial intelligence to ferret out fraudulent claims.[31] Artificial intelligence lends itself to tasks as diverse as airline ticket pricing, food preparation, oil exploration, and child welfare.

Artificial intelligence (AI) is the science of making machines imitate human thinking and behavior. For example, an expert system is an artificial intelligence system that makes computers capable of reasoning through a problem to reach a conclusion. We use the process of reasoning to find out, from what we already know, something that we don't know. The Marion County Department of Public Welfare uses an expert system to help evaluate cases of child abuse, standardizing the set of questions and relative importance of the answers so that critical aspects of the situation are not neglected.[32] With 600 cases a month and an 80 percent employee turnover rate (because of the low pay and nature of the work), consistency is a problem. Now when a complaint is called in the caseworker asks pertinent questions, then feeds the answers into an expert system. The system applies reasoning techniques to reach a conclusion, then makes a recommendation on what action the caseworker should take.

Today computers can see, hear, smell, and, important for business, think—in a manner of speaking. Robots are a well-known form of AI. A **robot** is a mechanical device equipped with simulated human senses and the capability of taking action on its own (in contrast to a mechanical device like an automobile which requires direction from the driver for its every action). Robots are in use in many industries. For example, Piedmont Hospital's Pharmacy Dosage Dispenser is a robotic prescription-filling system. Using bar code technology, this pharmaceutical robot receives medication orders online, retrieves prepackaged doses of drugs, and sends them to hospital patients.[33] One of the most exciting new areas of research in robotics is the development of microrobots that can be introduced into human veins and arteries to perform surgery.

A recent U.S. Commerce Department survey reported that 70 percent of the top 500 companies use artificial intelligence as part of decision support, and the sale of artificial intelligence software is rapidly approaching the $1 billion mark. The artificial intelligence systems that businesses use most can be classified into the following major categories:

- Expert systems, which reason through problems and offer advice in the form of a conclusion or recommendation

- Neural networks, which can be "trained" to recognize patterns

- Genetic algorithms, which can generate increasingly better solutions to problems by generating many, many solutions, choosing the best ones, and using those to generate even better solutions

- Intelligent agents, which are adaptive systems that work independently, carrying out specific, repetitive or predictable tasks

Expert Systems
Following the Rules

Suppose you own a real estate business, and you generate over 40 percent of your revenue from appraising commercial real estate. Consider further that only one person in your firm is capable of performing these appraisals. What if that person were to quit? How do you replace that expertise? How fast can you find someone else? How much business would you lose if it took you a month to find a suitable replacement?

In business, people are valuable because they perform important business tasks. Many of these business tasks require expertise, and people often carry expertise in their heads—and often that's the only place it can be found in the organization. AI can provide you with an expert system that can capture expertise, thus making it available to those who are not experts so that they can use it, either to solve a problem or to learn how to solve a problem. An *expert system*, also called a *knowledge-based system*, is an artificial intelligence system that applies

reasoning capabilities to reach a conclusion. Expert systems are excellent for diagnostic and prescriptive problems. Diagnostic problems are those requiring an answer to the question "What's wrong?" and correspond to the intelligence phase of decision making. Prescriptive problems are those that require an answer to the question "What to do?" and correspond to the choice phase of decision making.

An expert system is usually built for a specific application area called a *domain*. You can find expert systems in the following domains:

- Accounting—for auditing, tax planning, management consulting, and training

- Medicine—to prescribe antibiotics where many considerations must be taken into account (such as the patient's medical history, the source of the infection, and the price of available drugs)

- Process control—for example, to control offset lithographic printing

- Human resource management—to help personnel managers determine whether they are in compliance with an array of federal employment laws

- Financial management—to identify delinquency-prone accounts in the loan departments of banks

- Production—to guide the manufacture of all sorts of products, such as aircraft parts, and so on

- Forestry management—to help with harvesting timber on forest lands

A DSS sometimes incorporates expert systems, but an expert system is significantly different from a DSS. To use a DSS, you must have considerable knowledge or expertise about the situation with which you're dealing. As you saw earlier in this chapter, a DSS *assists* you in making decisions. That means that you must know how to reason through the problem. You must know which questions to ask, how to get the answers, and how to proceed to the next step. However, when you use an expert system, the know-how is in the system—you need only provide the expert system with the facts and symptoms of the problem for which you need an answer. The know-how, or expertise, that actually solves the problem came from someone else—an expert in the field. What does it mean to have expertise? Well, when someone has expertise in a given subject, that person not only knows a lot of facts about the topic, but also can apply that knowledge to analyze and make judgments about related topics. It's this human expertise that an expert system captures.

Let's look at a very simple expert system that would tell a driver what to do when approaching a traffic light. Dealing with traffic lights is the type of problem to which an expert system is well-suited. It is a recurring problem, and to solve it you follow a well-defined set of steps. You've probably gone through the following mental question-and-answer session many, many times without even realizing it (see Table 5.1).

When you approach a green traffic light, you proceed on through. If the light is red, you try to stop. If you're unable to stop, and if traffic is approaching from the left or right, you'll probably be in trouble. Similarly, if the light is yellow, you may be able to make it through the intersection before the light turns red. If not, you will again be faced with the problem of approaching traffic.

Let's say that you know very little about what to do when you come to a traffic light, but you know that there are experts in the field. You want to capture their expertise in an expert system so that you can refer to it whenever the traffic light situation arises. To gain an understanding of what's involved in the creation and use of an expert system, let's now consider the components of an expert system individually with the traffic light example in mind.

Components of an Expert System

An expert system, like any IT system, combines information, people, and IT components.

Information Types	People	IT Components
Domain expertise	Domain expert	Knowledge base
"Why?" information	Knowledge engineer	Knowledge acquisition
Problem facts	Knowledge worker	Inference engine
		User interface
		Explanation module

These components and their relationships are shown in Figure 5.14. Dotted lines enclose the expert system's IT components.

Information Types

The traffic light *domain expertise* is the core of the expert system, because it's the set of problem-solving steps—the reasoning process that will solve the problem. You'll also want to ask the expert system how it reached its conclusion, or why it asked you a question. The *"Why?" information* included in the expert system allows it to tell you such things. It's information that's provided by the expert—the traffic expert in our example. With the domain expertise and the "Why?" information, the expert system is now ready to solve traffic light problems. So now you need to enter the *problem facts*, which are the

	TABLE 5.1 Traffic Light Expert System			
Rule	**Symptom or Fact**	**Yes**	**No**	**Explanation**
1	Is the light green?	Go through the intersection.	Go to Rule 2.	Should be safe if light is green. If not, need more information.
2	Is the light red?	Go to Rule 4.	Go to Rule 3.	Should stop, may not be able to.
3	Is the light likely to change to red before you get through the intersection?	Go to Rule 4.	Go through the intersection.	Will only reach this point if light is yellow, then you'll have two choices.
4	Can you stop before entering the intersection?	Stop.	Go to Rule 5.	Should stop, but there may be a problem if you can't.
5	Is traffic approaching from either side?	Prepare to crash.	Go through the intersection.	Unless the intersection is clear of traffic, you're likely to crash.

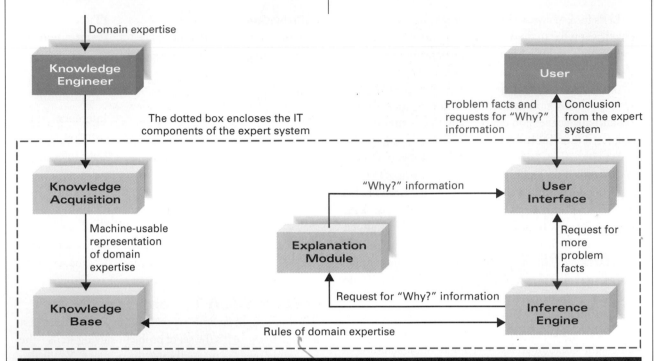

FIGURE 5.14

Expert System Components

specifics of your traffic light situation. Problem facts are the symptoms of and assertions about your problem. You'll enter these problem facts as answers to the expert system's questions during your consultation.

People

Three separate roles must be filled in the development and use of an expert system. The first role is that of the domain expert, who knows how to solve the problem. The *domain expert* provides the domain expertise in the form of problem-solving strategies. In our traffic light expert system, the domain expert could be an official from the department of motor vehicles. This official, turned domain expert, would also be able to indicate where to gather further domain expertise, and might direct you to the local police station or give you a booklet with the rules of

the road. Eventually, the combination of these sources will produce the five steps that you saw in Table 5.1.

The domain expert usually works with an IT specialist, a *knowledge engineer*, who formulates the domain expertise into an expert system. In this case, the knowledge engineer might consider it best to represent the five steps in the form of rules, making a *rule-based expert system*. The knowledge engineer will see to it that the rules are in the correct order and that the system works properly. See the box below for an example of how the knowledge engineer might formulate the rules.

The *knowledge worker* or user—that's you—will then apply the expert system to the problem of what to do when approaching a traffic light. When you face the traffic light problem, you would run a *consultation* (see Figure 5.15) and provide the expert system with the problem

Domain Expertise Captured as Rules by the Knowledge Engineer

Rule 1: IF The light is green
   THEN Go through the intersection.
   REASON If light is green, should be safe. If not, need more information.

Rule 2: IF The light is red
   THEN Go to Rule 4 else go to Rule 3.
   REASON Should stop, may not be able to. ❖

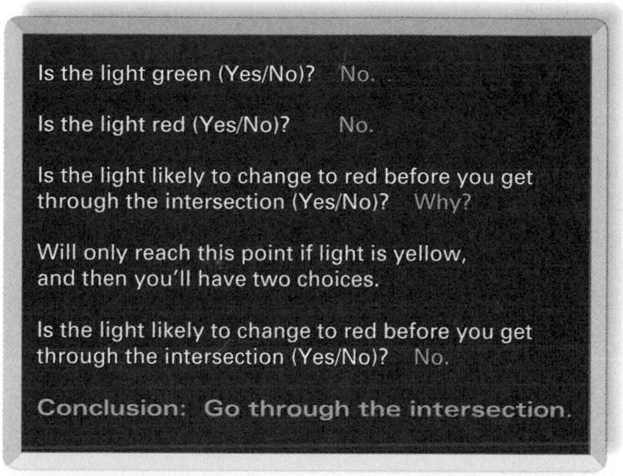

Is the light green (Yes/No)?   No.

Is the light red (Yes/No)?   No.

Is the light likely to change to red before you get through the intersection (Yes/No)?   Why?

Will only reach this point if light is yellow, and then you'll have two choices.

Is the light likely to change to red before you get through the intersection (Yes/No)?   No.

Conclusion: Go through the intersection.

FIGURE 5.15

Running a Consultation

facts. You would answer the questions as they appear on the screen, with the expert system applying the appropriate rules and asking you more questions. This process continues until the expert system presents you with a conclusion (telling you what to do) or indicates that it can't reach a conclusion (telling you that it doesn't know what you should do).

IT Components

When the knowledge engineer has converted the domain expertise into rules, the *knowledge base* stores the rules. All the rules must be in place before a consultation, because the expert system won't be able to offer a conclusion in a situation for which it has no rules. For example, if the traffic light is broken and has been replaced by a four-way stop sign, the expert system, as it stands, would not be able to reach a conclusion. The knowledge engineer could, of course, go back to the domain expert and enter rules about four-way stops. The knowledge engineer uses the *knowledge acquisition* component of the expert system to enter the traffic light rules. The domain expertise for the rules can come from many sources, including human experts, books, organizational databases, data warehouses, internal reports, diagrams, and so on.

The *inference engine* is the part of the expert system that takes your problem facts and searches the knowledge base for rules that fit. This process is called *inferencing*. The inference engine organizes and controls the rules—it "reasons" through your problem to reach a conclusion. It delivers its conclusion or recommendation based on (1) the problem facts of your specific traffic light situation and (2) the rules that came from the domain expert about traffic light procedures in general. The *user interface* is the part of the expert system that you use

United Nations Employees Are "Expertly" Paid

You might think that automating a payroll is a relatively simple process. After all, it's just the type of TPS that computers have been handling since their inception. However, not all payroll calculations are simple. Take the United Nations for instance. Based in New York City, the United Nations employs 15,000 people in 100 locations worldwide using dozens of currencies. But that's only part of the story. What the United Nations pays its employees is determined by a base salary plus entitlements. The entitlements, which constitute a significant portion of an employee's income, are based on the employee's location and contract. These rules and regulations of entitlements are explained in three volumes of several hundred pages each.

To try and cope with these complications, a payroll expert system was begun in 1990 as part of a 5-year, $70 million project to develop an integrated system for accounting, payroll, human resource management, procurement, property management, travel, and transportation functions. One of the early problems that knowledge engineers encountered was lack of consistency across locations. United Nations offices in different places interpreted the rules differently. Additionally, when building their expert system, the UN knowledge engineers had to allow for regulations to change. The payroll expert system was completed successfully, despite the difficulties, and is used by more than 2,000 knowledge workers in Amman, Jordan; Bangkok, Thailand; Geneva, Switzerland; Nairobi, Kenya; Santiago, Chile; and Vienna, Austria. UN sister agencies, like the International Labour Organization, have also implemented the expert system.[34] ❖

THE GLOBAL PERSPECTIVE

to run a consultation. Through the user interface, the expert system asks you questions, and you enter problem facts by answering the questions. In the traffic light expert system, you would enter "yes" or "no." These answers are used by the inference engine to solve the problem.

The domain expert supplies the "Why?" information, which is entered by the knowledge engineer into the *explanation module,* where it is stored. During a consultation, you—as the knowledge worker or user—can ask why a question was posed and how the expert system reached its conclusion. If you're using the expert system as a training tool, then you'll especially want to know how it solved the problem.

In Figure 5.16 you can clearly see the distinction between the development and use of an expert system. The domain expert and the knowledge engineer develop the expert system, then the knowledge worker can apply the expert system to a particular set of circumstances.

You, Too, Can Have an Expert System

You can acquire an expert system in three ways. You can buy a complete, off-the-shelf expert system; develop an expert system using an expert system shell; or build an expert system from scratch. The required components will vary, depending on your approach (see Table 5.2).

If you want to buy an off-the-shelf expert system, you can choose from several hundred which are commercially available. These expert systems act as advisers in specialized domains. You do not need a knowledge engineer or domain expert for such a system because the domain expertise has already been captured. A few examples of commercially available expert systems are

- *Mudman,* which helps geologists analyze soil for oil drilling purposes
- *Financial Advisor,* which analyzes investment opportunities
- *Loanprobe,* which banks use to audit loan loss evaluations and to determine necessary bank reserves

Having bought it, you must learn to use your expert system. Then, when you face a problem, simply run a consultation and answer questions as they are posed.

If an off-the-shelf system is not available or does not appeal to you, the least troublesome way of developing your own expert system is with an expert system shell. An *expert system shell* is a software package designed to facilitate the development of an expert system. An expert system shell functions rather like Quattro Pro and Microsoft Excel (which provide you with an easy way

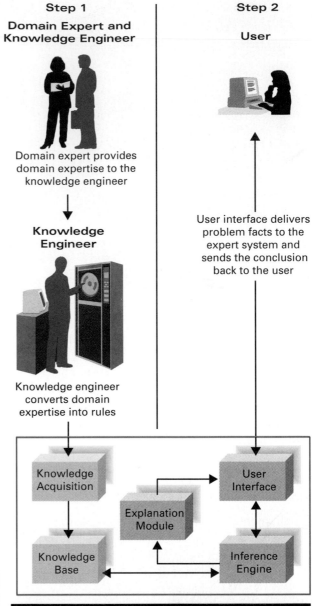

FIGURE 5.16

Developing and Using an Expert System

of developing a DSS). An expert system shell makes the development of an expert system much easier by providing an inference engine, explanation module, user interface, and knowledge acquisition module. You, or the knowledge engineer, can enter the appropriate rules and "Why?" information to suit the purpose of the expert system you're developing.

One example of an expert system shell is *Exsys,* which is available in two levels: professional and entry level. The entry-level version is a scaled-down package for beginners. *Exsys* uses menus to allow the knowledge worker to enter rules and run a consultation. *VP-Expert* is another expert system shell. It includes commands to

TABLE 5.2   What Components of the Expert System Do You Need to Provide?

Necessary Components	Off-the-Shelf Expert System	Expert System Shell	Expert System Developed from Scratch
Information			
Domain expertise	No	Yes	Yes
"Why?" information	No	Yes	Yes
Problem facts	Yes	Yes	Yes
People			
Domain expert	No	Yes	Yes
Knowledge engineer	No	Yes	Yes
Knowledge worker or user	Yes	Yes	Yes
IT Components			
Knowledge base	No	Yes	Yes
Knowledge acquisition	No	No	Yes
Inference engine	No	No	Yes
Explanation module	No	No	Yes
User interface	No	No	Yes

create a knowledge base from a table contained in a text, database, or worksheet file. *VP-Expert* will let you see how the inference engine navigates a problem to arrive at a solution.

If you can't find a ready-made expert system and don't want to use a shell, you can enlist a knowledge engineer to build an expert system to fit your specific needs. The knowledge engineer would interview the domain expert and then transform the domain expertise into computer code, using a programming language like Lisp, Prolog, or C. To build an expert system, the knowledge engineer must construct the inference engine, explanation module, knowledge acquisition module, user interface, and the knowledge base.

Whether you use an expert system shell or build an expert system from scratch, you must consider two things. First, you must make certain that the problem you're trying to solve is amenable to an expert system solution. That means that the solution to the problem must have a concrete, logical, and well-defined solution process. Second, you must have a domain expert who is willing and able to communicate the solution process.

What Expert Systems Can and Can't Do

An expert system uses IT to capture and apply human expertise. For problems with clear rules and procedures, expert systems work very well and can provide your company with great advantages. An expert system can:

- Handle massive amounts of information
- Reduce errors
- Aggregate information from various sources
- Improve customer service
- Provide consistency in decision making
- Provide new information
- Decrease personnel time spent on tasks
- Reduce cost

You can, however, run into trouble in building and using an expert system.

1. Transferring domain expertise to the expert system is sometimes difficult because domain experts cannot always explain how they know what they know. Often experts are not aware of their complete reasoning processes. Experience has given them a feel for the problem, and they just "know."

2. Even if the domain expert can explain the whole reasoning process, automating that process may be impossible. The process may be too complex, requiring an excessive number of rules, or it may be too vague or imprecise.

3. In using an expert system, keep in mind that it can solve only the problems for which it was designed. It cannot deal with inconsistency or a newly encountered problem situation. An expert system can't learn from previous experience and can't

Playing Traffic Cop in Crowded Skyways

Fifty thousand flights per day from 300 major airports are under the jurisdiction of air traffic controllers all over the country. The air traffic controllers must keep certain details in mind like the fog in San Francisco that usually lifts by 10 A.M. and the runway at Boston's Logan International Airport that is not lighted, so no planes can use it after dark. Believe it or not, only 40 traffic management specialists are responsible for the entire national airspace system and must decide what to do in the case of problems such as storms, accidents, and closed runways. They must do all of this hours in advance. And a bad decision can be very expensive for the airlines.

For example, when air traffic controllers diverted numerous flights heading to Chicago to other airports as a thunderstorm raged, at least one airline lost millions. This was because so many of its airplanes, which were needed in Chicago, had to be brought back.

The FAA now has an expert system called *Smartflow* which contains 15,000 rules supplied by FAA veterans. The system helps the traffic management specialists make the best decisions possible. In the case of Chicago, the expert system would recommend that the aircraft be held at the point of origin and not flown elsewhere.

Smartflow is capable of predicting problems 8 hours ahead and suggesting ways of coping, such as slowing aircraft down, increasing aircraft spacing, rerouting planes to alternate airports, or delaying takeoffs. The user interface provides color-coded maps at three levels. The first shows the entire U.S. airspace, the next shows 20 regional FAA air traffic centers, and the last shows individual airports, complete with the location of runways, towers, and terminals. Air traffic controllers can select key objects at any level to show more detail and current information.[35, 36] ❖

---

apply previously acquired expertise to new problems the way humans can.

❹ An expert system has no common sense or judgment. One of the early expert systems built into an F-16 fighter plane allowed the pilot to retract the landing gear while the plane was still on the ground and to jettison bombs while the plane was flying upside down, both highly dangerous actions.

Ethical Questions in Expert Systems

Expert systems can diagnose mechanical problems with automobiles and suggest scheduling plans for production, but they can just as easily be developed to provide conclusions that affect lives. An expert system can recommend that someone get a loan from a bank or be admitted to a university. For any IT system that affects people, we must consider the ethical dimension. Let's examine three questions:

❶ Will an expert system act ethically?

❷ What kind of decisions should you let an expert system make for you?

❸ Should you accept the decision of an expert system without question?

You already know the answer to the first question! An expert system will act the way it's programmed to act. So, if a system was programmed with domain expertise that was biased in some way, then the expert system's conclusion will be biased too. The question becomes whether the decisions you're making using an expert system reflect your ethical standards. You will especially want to know this if your decisions will affect lives.

For the second question—What decisions should an expert system make?—let's exemplify with an expert system that processes job applications and makes recommendations as to whether an applicant is suitable. One advantage of an expert system is that it is consistent (which can be helpful if you find yourself called upon to defend your decision by the legal system). The consistency of an expert system ensures that criteria are not weighed differently for different applicants. For example, an expert system will not, cannot, give preference to a lower GPA because the applicant is better looking. Choosing an employee, like many decisions you make in business, is one of those complicated tasks that requires a choice, not between "good" and "bad" but between "good" and "better," and "better" is a matter of judgment. You have an ethical responsibility to your

organization and its shareholders to choose the most qualified person, and you have a responsibility to the applicants to treat them fairly. Therefore, when you're considering which decisions to allocate to an expert system, you would do well to keep in mind the ethical implications of your decision and whether an expert system can adequately consider every aspect of the problem.

Our third question asks whether you should question the conclusions of an expert system. An expert system (or any IT system) is only as good as the people who developed it. Always view any computer-generated results carefully and critically.

Neural Networks
They Learn by Example

Suppose you see a breed of dog you've never encountered before. Do you know it's a dog? For that matter, do you know it's an animal? Probably so—in both instances.

Credit Card Companies Watch the World with Neural Networks

Financial institutions are the heaviest users of neural networks. For example, Merrill Lynch & Co. and Shearson Lehman Brothers, among other financial giants, use neural networks to help traders forecast market patterns and predict which stocks will perform well. Chase Manhattan Bank uses a neural network internally to evaluate commercial loans. Banks also use neural networks to decipher the numbers at the bottom of checks which are often blurred, off-center, or incomplete.

Fraud detection is one of the fastest growing application areas of neural networks. Suppose you use a MasterCard credit card. You go on vacation and, so you don't have to constantly worry about carrying cash around in a strange place, you use your credit card, and you use it, and use it. Then the credit card company calls your home to ask if everything is all right because there is "unusual activity" on the credit card. How come? MasterCard, along with many other credit card companies, uses a neural network to detect fraud, which cost credit card companies $680 million in 1995 alone. MasterCard trains its neural network to spot peculiarities in individual accounts. This "spotting of peculiarities" saved MasterCard over $50 million per year.

Credit card companies aren't the only targets of fraud. Health insurance companies have to be on guard too. Cigna Corp. Healthcare Group Inc., in conjunction with IBM, has developed a Fraud and Abuse Management System that uses a neural network to identify variations among physicians in order to find anomalies. The system searches for patterns in such activities as billing charges, laboratory tests, and frequency of office visits. For instance, if the stated diagnosis were a sprained ankle, and the tests included an electrocardiogram, the neural network would detect the anomaly and flag it for the account manager.[37–40] ❖

You know from experience that it's an animal that's classified as a dog. A neural network simulates this human ability to classify things. A *neural network* is an artificial intelligence system which is capable of learning because it's patterned after the human brain.

Neural networks are useful to a variety of applications. For example, many airports use a neural network called SNOOPE to detect bombs in luggage. Because chemical compounds have distinct patterns, SNOOPE can easily detect the compounds inside the luggage as they pass through a checking system.[41] In medicine, neural networks check 50 million electrocardiograms per year, check for drug interactions, and detect anomalies in tissue samples that may signify the onset of cancer and other diseases. In business, neural networks are very popular for securities trading, fraud detection, credit evaluation, real estate appraisal, and even handwriting recognition. Neural networks are most useful for identification, classification, and prediction where a vast amount of information is available. By examining hundreds, or even thousands of examples, a neural network detects important relationships

INDUSTRY PERSPECTIVE

Health Care

Doctor, It Only Hurts When I Laugh!

In medicine, patterns of symptoms are what clue the physician to what's wrong. And pattern recognition is the forte of the neural network. Neural networks diagnose illnesses by comparing patient symptoms to those of known diseases and illnesses. Horus Therapeutic Inc. is a company that trains neural networks to find tumors. The neural network looks for the distinctive patterns left in the blood when tumors invade healthy tissue. This neural network can make very accurate diagnoses based on blood tests. Neural networks are also used to analyze pap smears. The process involves finding a

few abnormal cells on a slide with about a half million cells.

The symptoms of a heart attack are many and vary in intensity from patient to patient; they are also different in men and women. Many a person has mistaken a heart attack for heartburn. Because the best chance of recovery comes from immediate medical intervention, it's very important to establish early on whether a patient is actually suffering a heart attack. But that's often difficult to determine quickly. Doctors use the patient's serum CK levels, or ECG results to diagnose a heart attack (or myocardial infarction, if you want to be technically correct). Doctors use several diagnostic aids, including biochemical tests, expert systems, and statistics. So far, none of these methods has provided totally dependable diag-

nostic accuracy. The University of California's San Diego Medical Center, however, is reporting much better results when doctors use a neural network to make the initial diagnosis. The neural network looks at the patient's pattern of symptoms and can predict, to an extraordinary degree of accuracy, which patients are having (or had) a heart attack. The researchers who developed this diagnostic neural network stress that it's not meant to replace the physician's opinion but to complement it. The researchers hope that the neural network will highlight relationships in the heart attack information that may have been heretofore overlooked.[42–44] ❖

TEAM WORK

What Input Would You Have to Provide the Neural Network?

Each of the five situations below would be well suited for a neural network. Identify the output that will be expected from each application, and identify what input the neural network would need.

1. When students apply for admission to a university, they will be admitted, rejected, admitted on probation, or admitted as continuing education students until they have sufficient prerequisites for admission. Name 10 student characteristics that would need to be considered.

2. A concert hall owner wants to determine ticket prices for musical events. The output would be the prices of $12, $18, or $50. What aspects of the town where the concert hall is located would be relevant? Name 10 characteristics of the visiting act that should be included.

3. An airline wants to decide whether to add flights to its roster for a particular city. The criterion for the decision will be the comparison of this city to other similar cities. The outputs will be no flights, one flight, or two flights. Name 10 aspects of the cities that the airline would be interested in.

4. A company wants to choose suppliers from a long list. A particular supplier will be examined by the neural network and a recommendation of acceptance or rejection will result. Name 10 characteristics that should be fed to the neural network about the suppliers.

5. A grocery chain wants to determine which breakfast cereal products to carry. Given the brand name of a cereal, the neural network will decide whether to carry it or not. Describe information about the cereal cost and price, customers, and store location that you would input to the neural network. ❖

and patterns in the information. For example, if you provide a neural network with the details of numerous credit card transactions and tell it which ones are fraudulent, eventually it will learn to identify suspicious transaction patterns.

Training a Neural Network

Bradford Lewis, a stock fund manager for Fidelity Investments, manages a fund that is consistently one of the best performing in the industry. Using a neural network, Bradford feeds 180,000 attributes (profits, per share earnings, book value, and so on) of 2,000 stocks into a neural network to look for patterns. He is "trying to capture as much of the historical cause and effect of the stock markets" as he can.[45] His first step is to show the neural network examples of "good" stocks. From these, the neural network "learns" the characteristics of a good stock. The neural network then practices identifying examples of good and bad stocks. The characteristics that repeatedly appear in the good stocks are assigned more weight by the neural network. For example, suppose

that the stocks of businesses that have been in operation for more than 10 years always appear as good stocks. The neural network will assign this characteristic more weight than, say, the current price of the stock, which fluctuates. After lots of practice, the neural network can recognize good stocks on its own.

Citibank uses neural networks to find opportunities in financial markets.[46] Using a neural network to carefully examine historical stock market data, Citibank financial managers learn of interesting coincidences or small anomalies (called market inefficiencies). For example, it could be that whenever IBM stock goes up, so does Unisys stock. Or it might be that a U.S. Treasury note is selling for 1 cent less in Japan than it is in the United States. These snippets of information can make a big difference to Citibank's bottom line in a very competitive financial market.

Would You Like to Have a Neural Network?

More than 200 neural network packages are on the market today, many of which will run on a personal computer

IBM's Antivirus Warriors Are Armed with Neural Networks

Every day about 200 computer vandals devise up to 10 viruses, carefully and deliberately aiming them at innocent software and information. A midwestern bank with about 200 servers and 10,000 desktop computers had to close for 4 days when a virus froze its network. It could not process wire transfers or access customer accounts. No branch offices could access the central system. *Forbes* magazine's computer network was out of commission for an entire day because of a virus.

Is anyone doing anything about this? Fortunately, the answer is yes. Every day about 30 antivirus researchers go to work to analyze these viruses and construct antidotes. The job is becoming ever more difficult because of the explosive growth of corporate networks, many of which are connected to the Internet. IBM is a leader in virus detection and removal. Researchers at IBM are now using neural networks to automatically detect boot-sector viruses—the most prevalent type of viruses.

Neural networks work well in this situation because they can learn what to look for and can adapt to new viruses. IBM's neural network virus detector learned on virus particles. Researchers fed it 3-byte chunks of code likely to be found in virus programs, but not in legitimate applications.

One drawback with antivirus software is the problem of false positives. Antivirus software that falsely detects a virus can cause as much trouble as an actual virus, because the company usually shuts down its network while it tries to find a nonexistent problem. The neural network virus detector has proved to be very reliable, giving only three false positives in millions of trials. IBM provides this antivirus software to its customers over the Internet.[48] ❖

and cost less than $100. There are two major categories of neural network products—those that stand alone and those that work in conjunction with a spreadsheet.

The stand-alone neural networks tend to run faster, speeding up training and processing. Sometimes you really need this extra speed—a Colorado physician did when using a neural network to detect early signs of trouble in patients under anesthesia.[47] The neural network he developed analyzes the amount of carbon dioxide in the airways of a patient. Furthermore, most stand-alone neural networks will read spreadsheet data.

Spreadsheet neural networks are activated by a menu command in the spreadsheet. You build and train the neural network by using the neural network menu. Many people find spreadsheet neural networks very convenient because they are already familiar with spreadsheets and spreadsheet operations. For example, Twenty-First Securities Corporation uses spreadsheets in combination with an off-the-shelf neural network package to manage corporate cash. Twenty-First Securities credits this neural network/spreadsheet combination with helping the company make substantial gains during the October 1987 stock market crash. In fact, its assets went from $750 million before the crash to about $2 billion afterward.[49]

Ethical Questions and Neural Networks

Neural networks pose an interesting ethical problem because you can apply pattern recognition just as easily to other human behavior as to credit card use. For example, the Chicago Police Department uses a neural network to analyze information pertaining to its 12,500 person police force to identify officers who may be prone to misconduct.[50] So far, the neural network has identified 91 officers, half of whom were already enrolled in misconduct counseling programs. Is this reasonable? Are police officers different from civilians because they are the guardians of society and have powers that ordinary citizens do not possess, such as the power to enforce search and arrest warrants? Is it necessary, desirable, ethical, or even legal to monitor them more closely?

Even more disturbing is a case in England where neural networks are analyzing the behavioral patterns of children in the hope of forecasting potential criminals.[51] The implications of such a system are of great concern to civil liberties activists. Should a child be classified early in life as a potential troublemaker? Many experts believe that a child will meet the expectations of adult guardians. Is it better to identify troubled children early in an effort to help them, or is it detrimental to label them so early?

Genetic Algorithms

It's a Matter of Breeding

Have you ever wondered how chefs around the world create recipes for great-tasting foods? For example, how did the Chinese discover that cashew nuts and chicken taste good when combined? How did Mexican chefs arrive at combining tomatoes, onions, cilantro, and other spices to create pica de gallo? How did British chefs decide to combine lamb and mint jelly? All those great recipes came about through *evolutionary processes.* Someone literally decided to put together a few ingredients and taste the result. Undoubtedly, many of those combinations resulted in unpalatable concoctions that were quickly discarded. Others were tasty enough to warrant further experimentation of combinations.

Today significant research in AI is devoted to creating software capable of following similar evolutionary processes. This software is called a genetic algorithm. A *genetic algorithm* is an artificial intelligence system that mimics the evolutionary, survival-of-the-fittest process to generate increasingly better solutions to a problem. Genetic algorithms use three concepts of evolution:

Selection—or survival of the fittest. The key to selection is to give preference to better outcomes.

Crossover—or combining portions of good outcomes in the hope of creating an even better outcome.

Mutation—or randomly trying combinations and evaluating the success (or failure) of the outcome.

Genetic algorithms are best-suited to decision-making environments in which thousands, or perhaps millions, of solutions are possible, and each of those solutions must be carefully evaluated. As you might imagine, businesses face decision-making environments such as these every day. Genetic algorithms are good for these types of problems because they use selection, crossover, and mutation as methods of exploring countless solutions and the respective worth of each. For example, US West uses a genetic algorithm to determine the optimal configuration of fiber-optic cable in a network that may include as many as 100,000 connection points. By using selection, crossover, and mutation, the genetic algorithm can generate and evaluate millions of cable configurations and select the one that uses the least amount of cable. At US West, this process used to take an experienced design engineer almost 2 months. US West's genetic algorithm can solve the problem in 2 days and saves the company $1 million to $10 million each time it's used.[52]

In a genetic algorithm, there is really no "intelligence" behind selection, crossover, and mutation. Genetic algorithms simply use these concepts to produce and evaluate numerous solutions. You have to tell the genetic algorithm what constitutes a "good" solution. That could be low cost, high return, etc., since many solutions are useless or absurd. If you created a genetic algorithm to make bread, for example, it might try to boil flour to create moistness. That obviously won't work, so the genetic algorithm would simply throw away that solution and

continued on page 208

Planning the Olympics

Large international sporting competitions involving many events cause nightmares for planners. Some events are indoor, some are outdoor; some are team events and others are individual events; and then there is the problem of scheduling men's and women's events separately, and it all has to take place within a set period of time. This is a good problem for a genetic algorithm because there are many possible combinations, some good, some not so good.

Consider which features of a plan generated by a genetic algorithm for scheduling Olympic events would disqualify it from selection for the next generation of solutions. For example, you wouldn't want two decathlon events scheduled simultaneously or the 200-meter and the 400-meter sprints run at the same time. ❖

Artificial Intelligence Systems in Action

Expert Systems for Medicine

Qual-Med HMO wants its clients to get the correct medical help as fast as possible. So it uses an expert system to field medical emergency calls. Say you're out walking and twist your foot. Later the same evening your ankle starts to swell and hurt badly. It's too late to call your primary-care physician so you call Qual-Med's 24-hour medical hotline staffed by nurses. When you call, your call and your complete medical history are transmitted to a nurse who uses an expert system to determine your course of action. If you need to see a specialist, the nurse can direct you to an authorized orthopedist who specializes in ankle injuries.[53]

Expert Systems for Credit Cards

American Express uses expert systems to better serve its customers and manage its credit business. Expert systems help process credit applications, authorize credit, and collect overdue accounts. One of the most famous expert systems, called *Authorization Assistant,* was developed by American Express and does the work of 700 authorization employees. It decides whether to allow a customer charge. American Express has no limit on credit cards, and this makes the decision challenging. *Authorization Assistant* saves the company many millions of dollars per year. When problems arise in a customer account, another expert system pulls together all the information needed to analyze the account. Previously, employees had to make an average of 22 calls to straighten out problems—it now takes a single call. This leaves the staff with more time to devote to the customer.[54, 55]

Expert Systems for Foreign Law

The more companies expand beyond domestic borders, the greater their need for support in those areas that make operating outside the country more complex. Legalities can be particularly perplexing. Large companies have legions of experts in international law, but many smaller organizations do not. Contracts with foreign distributors, suppliers, and customers can be minefields for the inexperienced. An expert system called *Expert System* is commercially available and helps in the drafting of agreements with non-U.S. parties. It is not meant to replace lawyers, but is a useful training tool to help knowledge workers master the complexities of international trading.

Another package helpful for global companies is *Origin,* which is an expert system to help with exporting and importing issues. Under NAFTA, certain products have preferential tariff rules. The most complex sets of rules pertain to the Rules of Origin. Customs authorities in the three NAFTA countries can impose stiff penalties for infractions of the rules. Because the risk is significant, companies want to play by the rules.[56, 57]

Neural Networks for Sales

Sales generate vast quantities of information, and all businesses want to capitalize on that information. Many businesses—such as General Motors, Blockbuster Entertainment Corp., Kraft General Foods, Inc., and Harley-Davidson Inc.—store sales information in huge data warehouses and then use neural network software to identify patterns that help them predict sales better. Marketing analysts

have found that past customer behavior, as recorded in actual business transactions, is by far the best indicator of future buying patterns. Great Universal Stores, whose 11 million customers generate 50 million phone calls a year, uses neural networks to help its 200-strong tele-marketing team maximize results. The neural network continuously monitors the relative success of various sales scripts and learns which work best.[58, 59]

Neural Networks for Defense

The U.S. Navy uses neural networks to detect sub-marines underwater by reading the pattern of radar waves bounced off the vessels. The North American Radar Air Defense also uses a neural net-work to identify threats in the sky. The tricky part is to determine which flying objects spell danger—like hostile fighter planes—and which are harmless, like a flock of geese.[60]

Neural Networks for Utilities

The utility industry was one of the first to embrace neural networks. The power companies turn to neural networks to find electricity usage patterns so that

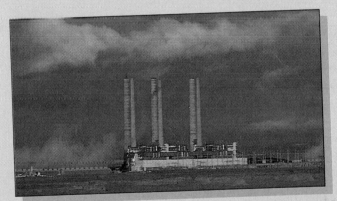

they can analyze rate structures and forecast demand. Of course, utility companies have always paid special attention to forecasting and rate structures. Before neural networks were available they used regression analysis models but they now find that neural networks work much faster.[61]

Genetic Algorithms for Suspect Identification

The psychology department at New Mexico State University has developed a genetic algorithm to draw a suspect's face from the description supplied by a witness. The usual way of doing this is for an artist to draw and redraw the face. However, witnesses cannot always recall facial features exactly, but can often recognize a whole face. The system presents 20 faces and the witness rates them on a 10-point scale. The genetic algo-rithm uses that information to generate additional faces by the processes of selection, crossover, and mutation.[62]

Genetic Algorithms for Finance

Many companies are applying genetic algorithms to financial problems. Citicorp is experimenting with genetic algorithms in stock market trading. Interestingly, at the beginning of the simulation the computer traders acted in an apparently rational and simple way. But, as more complex circumstances arose, the computer traders behaved more like people traders. As patterns of price movements appeared, the computer traders that had learned to exploit them were able to profit.[63]

Genetic Algorithms for TV Advertising

When the salespeople talk to their customers and fill orders for TV advertising at the UK's Channel 4, they offer clients a choice of position in the lineup, a time of airing, and the regions to which the ad can be transmitted. The country is broken down into regions, and an advertiser can choose to have the ad shown in any one or combination of these regions. Or the advertiser can choose to run different ads in

different regions. But if the same ad runs in a combination of regions, it must be transmitted simultaneously to all of them. With all these constraints, each 4-minute break can have as many as 50 commercials in various combinations. So schedulers now use genetic algorithm software to generate random solutions, evaluate these solutions, and recombine the best of those for several generations. Eventually a good solution is reached. This application of IT has saved the TV station four positions in its scheduling department, reducing costs considerably.[64] ❖

try something else. Other solutions would eventually be good, and some of them would even be wonderful. According to David Goldbert, a genetic algorithm pioneer at the University of Illinois at Urbana-Champaign, evolution is the oldest and most powerful algorithm there is, and "three billion years of evolution can't be wrong!"[65]

Intelligent Agents

Tireless Assistants

"Agents" are an integral part of the business world. There are insurance agents, real estate agents, and travel agents. Human agents are people who perform a service at your bidding, and bring to their work specialized knowledge and ability. The more your agent knows about you and your tastes, the better able that agent is to provide you with a product or service that appeals to you. A relatively new AI technique, called an intelligent agent, performs much the same function, but in an IT environment. An *intelligent agent* is an artificial intelligence system which can move around your computer or network performing repetitive tasks independently, adapting itself to your preferences. Intelligent agents usually work in the background, so your computer is still available to you for use. For example, your intelligent agent might search the Internet every morning for information about your state senators, your favorite sports team, the comic strip you like the most, and so on, presenting you with a customized newspaper to read with your morning coffee.

An intelligent agent is constructed from one or more of the most modern software technologies including expert systems, neural networks, genetic algorithms, and object-oriented programming. Intelligent agents can (1) act as personal assistants, (2) find and retrieve information from your company's database, or (3) find and retrieve information across networks.

Act as a Personal Assistant An intelligent agent can help you with routine computer tasks in a manner that accommodates your individual habits. For example, you could instruct your intelligent agent to send an e-mail to someone. You could also tell it to check in 1 hour to see if the recipient picked up the message and, if not, to fax the message at that time. The intelligent agent would be able to look up the e-mail address, find the fax number, and if you didn't already have the fax number in your phone book, would insert it. In other words, personal assistant intelligent agents act, to a limited degree, like good assistants. Intelligent agents can sort and prioritize e-mail, schedule meetings, and make travel arrangements. They are called "intelligent" because they not only perform all these tasks, but also take your preferences (which they learn on the job) into account. For example, your intelligent agent might notice that you never schedule meetings early in the morning, or that you always want to travel in the middle of the day, and arrange things accordingly.

Today's knowledge worker can access vast amounts of information from many sources, and it is becoming increasingly difficult to separate the essential information from the less important. An intelligent agent for document management would help you control business documents by finding what you need, and filtering out what you do not.

Find and Retrieve Information from Your Company's Database Of great interest to business is the data mining potential of intelligent agents, which can access data warehouses quickly and intelligently with very little intervention from you. For example, a lawyer's intelligent agent could search a legal data warehouse to find cases that meet certain criteria. The intelligent agent, after some experience, would know that if the lawyer were searching for cases pertaining to divorce, for example, it would need to find only cases in a particular state. Nabisco, Inc., a $7.7 billion processed-food company, needs similar information filtering for its 300 executives, and employs intelligent agents to find, filter, and automatically forward relevant information.[66]

Find and Retrieve Information Across Networks An intelligent agent is not limited to one database. It can traverse databases on different types of computers and operating systems. That means it can cruise the Internet for you day and night without your intervention. For example, you could send your intelligent agent out to check on financial Internet sites so that you can stay current with investment opportunities. Hertz Corporation uses intelligent agent software to look for predetermined changes in the pricing structure of competitors. The intelligent agent alerts Hertz decision makers when competitive prices exceed preset levels.[67] Commercial intelligent agents are available from several companies. For example:

■ Andersen Consulting has an Internet intelligent agent called BargainFinder that searches through online music CD shopping services to find availability and pricing for any CD title that you choose.[68]

■ Firefly Network Inc. has an intelligent agent (called Firefly, as in "bright bug") that builds profiles of the people who use its Web site. Then it sorts them to recommend new selections for its visitors based on the likes and dislikes of each person's nearest psychographic neighbors.[69]

Combining IT Brainpower Systems
Attacking the Problem on Multiple Fronts

Every IT system that offers you support in your decision making has its own particular strengths. DSSs, GDSSs, and GISs all require that you know which steps to take to solve the problem and that you execute them. That is, you have the know-how and can direct the computer at each step of the process. In AI systems, the know-how is in the system. You provide the problem, and the system takes care of solving it. See Table 5.3 for an overview of the AI systems we have discussed in this chapter. Clearly, many business problems would benefit from the combination of two or more approaches.

Decision Support Systems and Artificial Intelligence

Many problems are such that you would like to be able to hand over part of a problem to an AI system, and then use the results from that system as part of your decision-making process. Many companies are doing just that. For example, people are combining DSSs with expert systems, and GISs with neural networks for even better results. A DSS that incorporates expert systems is called an *intelligent DSS*, a *DSS/ES*, or a *knowledge-based DSS*.

TABLE 5.3   AI Systems Compared

AI System	Problem Type	Based on	Starting Information
Expert systems	Diagnostic or prescriptive	Strategies of experts	Expert's know-how
Neural networks	Identification, classification, prediction	The human brain	Acceptable patterns
Genetic algorithms	Optimal solutions	Biological evolution	Set of possible solutions
Intelligent agents	Specific and repetitive tasks	One or more AI techniques	Your preferences

Expert systems, used in conjunction with the usual DSS components, solve an aspect of a problem or provide information to other DSS components. An intelligent DSS, in addition to the usual data management, model management, and user interface management components, has a fourth component called a "knowledge management component." This component allows the DSS to maintain the expert systems, and to access them as needed in the decision-making process. Following are two examples of intelligent DSSs:

- Household Finance Corp. (HFC) uses an intelligent DSS to expedite home mortgage loans. The HFC DSS has an expert system that performs real estate evaluation in a couple of hours—a task that used to take 18 days. The expert system contains the expertise it takes to appraise a house and the results are then analyzed in combination with the other DSS-generated information to help loan officers reach a decision on whether to grant a loan.[70]

- The German Air Force is experimenting with a "cockpit assistant" to help its pilots determine whether their flying skills are up to par on a particular day, and to assist in complex situations. The cockpit assistant monitors and analyzes the pilot's performance, comparing it to standard operating procedure in the pilot's handbook. The DSS thus gives pilots the information they need to decide whether they ought to be flying that day. By monitoring the pilot's eye movement, the cockpit assistant can assess the pilot's behavior and tell whether the pilot is focusing on the most appropriate instrument at a particular time. The expert system component can then offer advice on what instruments to check and what to do in emergencies.[71]

When you combine a GIS with a neural network, you get a huge amount of information, displayed in a pattern, which your neural network can analyze. Both private and governmental institutions have found this combination very valuable. Here are two examples:

- The United States currently has about 2.2 million hazardous waste sites which are tracked by 700 different governmental agencies. To help it oversee its 11 million records, the government has developed a neural network that works with a geographic information system containing information from the Census Bureau. This system supplies individuals and businesses with valuable information that is useful when purchasing property or conducting business. The system is updated when sites are cleaned up.[72]

- There is no Nielsen rating system for billboard posters. So it's hard for companies to measure the impact of billboard advertising. In England, a company called Poster Audience Research combines demographic information from a GIS with a neural network to estimate the traffic passing posters and the relative visibility of different sites, giving the industry a credible measurement system, and allowing salespeople to provide potential advertisers with hard evidence.[73]

Hybrid Intelligent Systems

A new type of AI system is a *hybrid intelligent system*, which incorporates two or more AI techniques. All sorts of combinations are possible. In Chapter 4 you learned about data mining and intelligent agents. Data mining uses a combination of AI systems to detect trends and patterns with an extraordinary degree of accuracy. Intelligent agents are another example of blending AI systems. Consider two others.

Neural Networks and Expert Systems One of the most challenging problems with an expert system is the enormous effort it takes to change and adapt it. And, because the strength of neural networks is their ability to learn, the integration of neural networks and expert systems gives rise to a "trainable" expert system. Thus the tedious task of adaptation of the expert system can be automated with considerably less intervention from the knowledge engineer. Another example of combining an expert system and a neural network is intelligent help desk software. When a question arrives at the help desk, the help desk software can look for the pattern of symptoms of the problem, and then apply the rules from the expert system to assist the help desk operator in giving advice to the caller.

CAREER OPPORTUNITY

The future holds many innovations that will be useful for business, but keeping track of all the new developments is a daunting task. You need a plan. For example, read technology-based publications on a regular basis. Many good publications are available in varying degrees of specialization. *Informationweek* is a good magazine that focuses on technology in business. Most business-related publications such as *Newsweek, Time,* and *The Wall Street Journal* have technology sections.

Neural Networks and Genetic Algorithms A neural network is first provided with test patterns; then it can recognize patterns by itself. However, a neural network can provide you with misleading results if it is run with incomplete information. Genetic algorithms can provide millions of combinations of variables allowing the neural network enough information to work with. First of America Bank Corp. uses an AI system consisting of a neural network, a genetic algorithm, and expert system techniques to sift through its customer records to find those people most likely to respond to credit card offers and those least likely to default.[74] Another use for genetic algorithms lies in training neural networks. Genetic algorithms generate hundreds or even thousands of new solutions or patterns from old ones. If you combine the two, you get a genetic algorithm that can train neural networks with far more examples than would be feasible for a human trainer.

CLOSING CASE STUDY: CASE 1

Milk Collection in Rural India

What's the best way to collect milk from far-flung villages in tropical heat when refrigeration is erratic or unavailable, and you don't own any trucks? A dairy in India faced just such a problem, and solutions reached manually proved to be unreliable. But Etah found a reliable solution using IT support. Today Etah Dairy uses a decision support system called CARS to find the most cost-effective schedule and routes for its milk collections. Using CARS, Etah has reduced transportation costs and the loss of milk because of curdling (which used to be as high as 11 percent during the hottest months).

Every day, Etah Dairy collects milk from a portion of its 70 milk collection centers (MCCs) in different villages within a 150-kilometer radius of Etah. Which MCCs are operational depends on the seasonal milk supply forecast. Each morning the milk producers deliver milk to the local MCC, which stores the milk in special tanks. Some MCCs have refrigerated tanks; others add ice to the milk to keep it cold. Each day the dairy dispatches tankers to collect the milk from the MCCs and deliver it to the dairy for processing. The tanker drivers generally work from 6:00 A.M. to 8:00 P.M. and make one or more trips. Some of the work time is used in weighing the milk, filling the tanks, and emptying them again at the other end.

Every effort is made to collect all the milk during the morning trips. Evening trips are made only if necessary because: First, even though many MCCs have refrigerated storage, the electricity supply is unreliable and power outages for up to 12 hours per day are usual. When the power is off, ice has to be added to the milk, but the tropical climate melts the ice quickly, so morning collections are essential. Second, Etah found that milk picked up in the evening is often hijacked en route to the dairy.

Etah's objective in using CARS is to minimize its cost per ton of milk. Cost is affected by the availability of milk and the expense of leasing trucks. When the dairy does not collect a sufficient milk supply from the MCCs, a third-party supplier provides the balance, which costs more than the milk from Etah's MCCs. The season determines how much milk is available and, consequently, which of Etah's MCCs remain operational. The supply of milk varies from 45 to 170 tons, depending on the season. The leasing fees depend on which trucks Etah leases—the larger the tanker, the greater the cost. So, on a daily basis, management must make decisions about which MCCs should remain operational and how many vehicles should be leased to keep the cost as low as possible.

Etah uses both seasonal and daily information. The seasonal information includes MCC details, distance information, data about vehicles available for lease, and so on. The daily information includes the amount of milk available at the various MCCs and whether Etah has currently leased vehicles. The DSS analyzes both types of information and generates reports on routes for the vehicles, transportation costs, and other details.

Using CARS, Etah dairy found that it could reduce transportation and loss of milk costs. With the added efficiency of the CARS system, distant MCCs, which were often simply omitted from the manual schedule, are usually included in the route. This reduces Etah's cost of purchasing milk from third parties.[75, 76] ❖

◄ Questions ►

1. Which of the four phases of decision making does CARS support? Explain your answer.

2. List the decisions supported by CARS. For each one, explain whether and why it is structured, nonstructured, or somewhere in between.

3. Based on your answer to question 2, describe the types of information that CARS must supply to allow Etah's decision makers to achieve their goals.

4. What are the ethics involved in deciding which MCCs should remain operational? Should Etah worry about the livelihood of employees in smaller dairies? Why or why not?

KNOWLEDGE WORKER'S -LIST

Categories of Decisions and the Process of Decision Making. Decisions can be categorized as structured or nonstructured and recurring or nonrecurring. A *structured decision* involves processing a certain kind of information in a specified way so that you will always get the right answer. A *nonstructured decision* is one for which there may be several "right" answers, and there is no precise way to get a right answer. Most decisions have structured and nonstructured elements.

A *recurring decision* is one that happens repeatedly, and often periodically, whether weekly, monthly, quarterly, or yearly. A *nonrecurring decision* is one that you make very infrequently (perhaps only once) and you may even have different criteria for determining the best solution each time.

The decision-making process follows four steps.

Intelligence (find what to fix) is the first stage, and this is where you establish the nature of the problem or opportunity.

Design (find fixes) is the next step, and here you find all the solutions you can.

Choice (choose a fix) is the third step and the one where you decide on a plan to address the problem or opportunity.

Implementation (apply the fix) is the final stage where you put your plan into action. These steps are not always sequential. You often cycle back to earlier steps.

The Various Types of Decision Support Systems and Their Respective Roles in Effective Decision Making. A *decision support system (DSS)* is a highly flexible and interactive IT system that is designed to support decision making when the problem is not structured. A typical DSS has three components: data management, model management, and user interface management. The development and use of a DSS usually require your active participation.

For making decisions as part of a team you would utilize a *group decision support system (GDSS)* which consists of groupware, DSS, and telecommunications to help teams formulate and solve problems. The groupware, DSS, and telecommunications vary according to the nature of the meeting. The three phases of team decision making are brainstorming, issue categorization and analysis, and ranking and voting.

Meetings belong to one of two major categories. A *same-time meeting (synchronous meeting)* is a meeting where the team members interact, offering ideas and suggestions during an appointed time period. They may be in a decision room where they can see each other, or they may be in different locations, perhaps connected by videoconferencing. The type of IT support varies depending on the situation.

A *different-time meeting (asynchronous meeting)* takes place over a period of days or weeks. Team members do not interact directly but exchange ideas and suggestions by sending them to some central location like a bulletin board or database to be reviewed as the schedules of the team members allow.

A *geographic information system (GIS)* is a decision support system designed specifically to work with spatial information. Spatial information is any information that can be shown in map form. A GIS helps your decision making by making it easy to manipulate spatial information and display results graphically.

The Different Types of Artificial Intelligence Systems and How They Contribute to Better Decision Making. *Artificial intelligence (AI)* is the science of making machines mimic human thought processes and behavior. Four types of AI systems are widely used in business: expert systems, neural networks, genetic algorithms, and intelligent agents.

An *expert system* is an artificial intelligence system that applies reasoning capabilities to reach a conclusion. An expert system captures and makes available to you

5. Could Etah incorporate any AI systems to improve its decision support? If so, cite examples of where AI could be applied and describe the benefits that Etah would derive. What additional information, if any, would Etah have to provide for the AI-enhanced support system?

CLOSING CASE STUDY: CASE 2

Australia Uses an Expert System to Evaluate Worker Injuries

The Government Insurance Office of Australia (GIO), the largest general insurance company in the country,

the expertise of a human expert. Expert systems solve problems by mimicking the reasoning process of a human expert to reach a conclusion. The problem-solving strategy of a *domain expert,* the *domain expertise,* is transferred to the **knowledge base** by the **knowledge engineer** using the **knowledge acquisition** component. Then you, the **knowledge worker** or user, supply the *problem facts* using the **user interface,** and the **inference engine** reasons through your problem facts and the domain expertise in the knowledge base to reach a conclusion. If you have a question about how the expert system reached its conclusion, you can ask for the *"Why?" information* from the **explanation module.**

A **neural network** is an artificial intelligence system that is capable of learning because it's patterned after the human brain. After lots of practice, a neural network can recognize patterns without human intervention. You develop and train a neural network for a specific problem area. When the neural network has been trained, you provide it with a new pattern and it can give you information about that pattern.

A **genetic algorithm** is an artificial intelligence system that mimics the evolutionary, survival-of-the-fittest process to generate increasingly better solutions to a problem. It uses the evolutionary concepts of selection, crossover, and mutation to generate new solutions or strategies. **Selection** is the process of choosing good solutions, **crossover** is the process of combining portions of good solutions, and **mutation** is the process of randomly changing parts of a solution. When fed a set of possible solutions, a genetic algorithm can generate many, many more solutions.

An **intelligent agent** is an artificial intelligence system that can move around your computer or network performing repetitive tasks independently, adapting itself to your preferences. An intelligent agent is a combination of the most modern software technologies.

How to Choose an IT System to Suit a Particular Decision. In order to find the right kind of decision

support for your problem, you must know which IT systems support decision making, what they can do, and what you have to do.

A **DSS** is used to analyze information for problems that are not structured, either recurring or nonrecurring. You must have the expertise to solve the problem, know which model to use, and be able to interpret the results. A DSS can be used for any or all of the first three stages of decision making—intelligence, design, and choice.

A **GDSS** exists to help teams meet more efficiently and effectively by providing an integration of groupware, DSS, and telecommunications. A GDSS-enhanced meeting is especially helpful for nonstructured decisions and can benefit any or all of the first three phases of decision making.

A **GIS** is helpful for generating, analyzing, and displaying spatial information.

AI systems provide you with software that has know-how of its own. You don't have to do the problem solving yourself; you provide the AI system with information and let it carry on from there.

The most widely used AI system in business is an **expert system,** which is well-suited to recurring diagnostic and prescriptive problems in which the solution process is well-defined and concrete.

A **neural network** works well for identification, classification, and prediction problems. A neural network is good for problems where lots of information must be integrated to produce an overall pattern.

A **genetic algorithm** will generate an optimal solution from generations of solutions. A genetic algorithm must be given criteria specifying what constitutes a "good" solution.

An **intelligent agent** is helpful in performing repetitive, predictable tasks, like sending faxes or e-mail, or searching networks and retrieving items of interest.

The various types of decision support systems (DSS, GDSS, and GISs) can be combined with AI systems. Two or more AI systems can also be combined giving **hybrid intelligent systems.** ❖

uses an expert system called EcoLoss to predict future economic loss and assess compensation for claimants. The system, which GIO has used since 1988, was developed by Continuum Australia, a unit of Texas Continuum Co. EcoLoss performs four major tasks for GIO:

- It helps the insurance knowledge worker determine the claimant's work capacity. This is achieved

by analyzing a series of medical reports, the circumstances surrounding the case (like other benefits being received by the claimant), the recency of the reports, and investigations into the circumstances of the injury.

- If the claimant is unfit to return to preaccident duties, EcoLoss recommends a list of occupations that the claimant could work at. This is important in judging the amount of compensation due to the worker.

- The third task of EcoLoss is to calculate a lump sum assessment, taking into consideration the list of recommended occupations and the claimant's likelihood of finding a job in one of them, based on qualifications, experience, age, and gender.

- The last task that EcoLoss performs is to present information on job availability for each of the recommended occupations. This assessment takes into consideration the claimant's residence, employment offices, public transport facilities, and travel time.

EcoLoss uses a database of 1,600 occupations covering almost 6,500 job titles. EcoLoss can match similarly phrased titles efficiently and can also correct misspelled words. Medical reports are captured and analyzed by the expert system's rules to arrive at a prognosis of work capacity. EcoLoss also has other applications. For example, lawyers use the expert system in developing third-party bodily injury cases. Four states in Australia use EcoLoss to assess workers' compensation awards and rehabilitation plans.[77] ❖

◄ Questions ►

1. The discussion of the EcoLoss system did not mention an explanation module. Do you think it has one? If certain jobs are recommended for a claimant, would it be helpful to know how EcoLoss reached its decision? Why or why not?

2. Which experts, do you think, were consulted to develop the EcoLoss expert system? What sort of educational and work backgrounds would they have to have? Do you think they had to explain a lot of procedures and terms to the knowledge engineers?

3. Consider the decisions that EcoLoss makes. Are those decisions structured or nonstructured? Are EcoLoss's decisions recurring or nonrecurring?

4. EcoLoss provides what kinds of advantages to GIO?

5. Could EcoLoss be used as a training tool for novice insurance claim processors? What stengths and weaknesses might an expert system have compared to a human trainer?

6. There are many variables involved in any injury insurance claim. Would it be better for GIO to use a neural network instead of an expert system? Why or why not?

REAL [H·O·T]

Electronic Commerce
Business and You on the Internet

Starting Your Own Business

You saw in the Real HOT Electronic Commerce section at the end of Chapter 1 how to use the Internet to find a job. Perhaps you'd rather run your own business. Well, you can use the Internet to do that too, since it's replete with terrific resources that you can use to focus your dream of a new business, implement your dream, keep it alive, and help it thrive.

No matter how many reputable experts you ask or good books you read on starting a new business you'll find some common threads of advice. These include the importance of stamina, persistence, self-discipline, and a liking for the business you're in. Stephen King, the best-selling author of scary stories, is an excellent example of someone who has these qualities. He works at

writing *every* day except his birthday, Christmas day, and the Fourth of July. If you own your own business, you'll probably have the same demanding schedule.

Another very important ingredient in the recipe for success is the ability to make decisions. (See our discussion of an information-literate knowledge worker in Chapter 1.) Because finding and assessing information on starting your own business is so important, let's see how the Internet can help.

In this section we've included a number of Web sites about starting your own business. On the Web site that supports this text (http://www.mhhe.com/business/mis/haag, select "Electronic Commerce Projects"), we've provided direct links to these Web sites as well as many more. This is a great starting point for completing this Real HOT section. We encourage you to search the Internet for others.

Advice on All Aspects of Starting a Business

Whether or not you have a particular type of business in mind, you can find many Web sites that will help you get started. Some sites contain general advice and some are specific to groups, industries, or regions. For example, the Minority Business Development Administration at http://www.mbda.gov is designed for minority group members seeking to start a business. And Dun & Bradstreet's site (http://www.dnb.com) has information on the best cities in the United States to start a business.

Many organizations exist to help you get started and to promote successful small businesses of all types. These organizations should be your starting point.

- **SBA** (Small Business Administration) is an umbrella organization for SBDCs and SCORE, organizations that offer free advice nationwide.
- **SBDCs** (Small Business Development Centers) are usually attached to universities and are staffed by people who have extensive experience helping people to choose and start businesses.
- **SCORE** (Service Corps of Retired Executives) is an organization of experienced businesspeople who hold seminars and provide one-on-one consulting services. ACE (Active Corps of Executives) has a similar program. The difference is that the counselors are still active in business.
- **Your state commissioner of commerce/economic development** can help you with start-ups, particularly with aspects unique to the state in which you intend to operate.
- **Your local chamber of commerce** has information on small business programs and sources. For opportunities abroad, start at the ICBB-Net Consortium (http://www.icc-ibcc.org/cgchp.html), which is an international business network for the global business community. It is comprised of chambers of commerce from all over the world along with many public and private international trade facilitation organizations.

In the table on page 218, we've listed some organizations and their Web addresses; and on the Web site that supports this text, you'll find many others. Choose five of these and determine the following:

A. Does the organization's site state a fee, if any, for any services rendered?

B. Does the site offer information on government regulations?

C. Is this site designed to help a specific group of people or industry?

D. Does the site offer financing in any form? If so, what form (i.e., grant, loan, award, and so forth)?

E. Are seminars available?

F. Does the site offer help in recruiting personnel?

G. Is this organization publicly or privately funded?

H. Does this site list any success stories?

Franchising

When you start a new business from scratch, you're inventing your business as you go along. Your methods and innovations might be very successful or they might not. Estimates on the failure rate of new businesses vary, but all agree that a large proportion fail. In contrast, over 90 percent of franchisees are still in business after five years. So, franchising might be a good business opportunity for you.

Franchise Solutions at http://www.fransol.com has a list of franchise opportunities. In the table on page 218, you'll see a list of franchise sources and their Web sites. Additional sites can be found on our Web site. Look at five of these and answer the questions below.

A. What is the franchiser looking for in an investor?

B. Does the site state how much you'll be expected to invest?

C. How much of your investment may be borrowed?

D. Will the franchiser finance any part of the cost of the franchise?

E. Will you have to pay royalties?

F. Do you need to buy or lease a building or equipment?

G. Do you have a say in the location of the business?

H. Is training provided? What is the duration and fee?

Let Your Customers Ride the Internet to Your Company

Smart businesspeople today make the Internet an integral part of their business. The Internet is the perfect

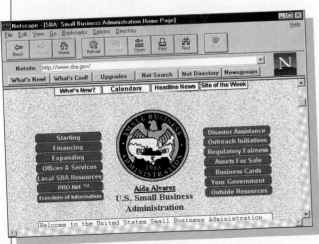

marketing tool. It's very inexpensive compared to other media, such as TV advertising or telemarketing, response is instant, and its reach is worldwide. You can use the Internet in any one of the three following levels:

- **Advertising presence**   At this level, you simply advertise to your customers through the Internet. The advertising can take one of many forms:
  - A Web site where visitors leave a trail of statistics that you can use in marketing plans.
  - E-mail to connect you to customers and prospects. The cost of these mass mailings is low and the amount of work involved is minimal.
  - Electronic press releases to reporters to enable you to reach an even larger audience.
  - Advertisements in dozens of electronic publications, sending your message to both the general population and special-interest groups.

- **Customer support**   You can use the Internet for customer support, customer service, and customer retention programs. Customers can send questions and comments, or even register, thereby augmenting your marketing information.

- **Store front**   Like many companies today, you can use the Internet to sell your goods and/or services either as a supplemental access for customers or as your whole store. This involves a much deeper commitment in that you'll have to consider many complex issues like designing and accessing databases, methods of payment, security, and so on, depending on the extent of your Web service.

Check out our Web site at http://www.mhhe.com/business/mis/haag and select "Electronic Commerce Projects" for tips on how to design and develop a Web site. At the end of Chapter 9 in the Real HOT section, you'll find great design tips for building your Web site.

If you'd prefer to get help designing and building your site, you can call in expert Web site developers. They can help you to make your Web site attractive and, more important, make it profitable. In the table on page 218 you'll find addresses of Web site development companies.

Whatever level of Web usage you choose, remember that the work does not end when you have the site up and running; in fact, that's when the trouble and expense really begin in earnest. Your Web site is your showcase for the whole world to see. Your site should give customers the impression that you're on top of things and are consistent in your excellence.

Choose three business sites for each of the three levels listed above (advertising presence, customer support, store front) and compare the sites as follows.

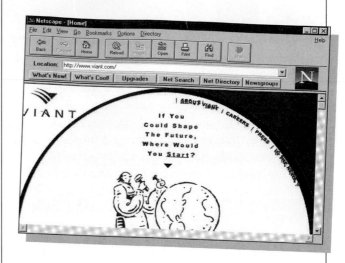

A. Which sites are better from a customer point of view, and why?

B. Do they all give you precise information about the products and services of the company (price, cost of shipping, and so on)?

C. Was any information left out that you think ought to be included?

D. Consider the advertising presence level sites you chose. Could or should each of these three sites be upgraded to a customer-support site? Why or why not?

E. What sort of contact information do the "customer support" level sites give you (e-mail, phone number, and so forth)?

F. Do the store front level sites promise secure transfer of credit card information?

G. Do the store front level sites require you to enter all your demographic and credit card information the next time you visit

Who and Where Are Your Customers?

One of the cardinal rules for succeeding in business is that you must know your customers. How can you get to know your customers and their preferences? One way is to hire a market research supplier. Good market research will help prevent you from spending time, money, and energy in ineffective efforts.

Some market research suppliers—A.G. Nielsen, for example—collect data and sell it to whoever wants to pay for it. Others tailor research to the customer's specific needs. Some do both. Most companies specialize in a product area such as pharmaceuticals or supermarket products. Five of the larger market research suppliers are listed in the table on page 218. Look at three of these sites and three others (remember, our text's Web site has lots of appropriate sites), and for each, note the goods or services they specialize in. Where does each company collect data? What products and services does the company offer? How is the data collected (survey, phone, and so on)? Do any of the sites collect data through the Internet?

Another great source of information for marketing purposes on the Internet are online demographic databases. At the end of Chapter 4, the Real HOT section has a module with lots of demographic database sites.

Business Plans, Financing, Accounting

The financial aspect of a business is extremely important. You need money to get started and to expand. You need to keep track of money coming in and going out and you also need to inform various branches of government about all this money.

Business Plans

Before you go in search of funding to start your business, you need a well-developed business plan. No self-respecting investors or bankers will even consider handing over large sums of money unless you convince them that it makes sense to trust their money to you and your business. The generally accepted way of formally demonstrating your competence is by producing a well-written business plan.

Generally a business plan will consist of (1) detailed descriptions of your business, product, market, competition, and so forth; (2) financial statements, including sales forecasts, break-even analysis, and balance sheet; and (3) any other supporting evidence, such as letters of commitment, brochures, or resumes of key personnel. You can obtain sample business plans and pointers on how to develop your own business plan at the SBA site (http://www.sba.gov/starting/businessplan.html). You can also find companies that will help you write a business plan or sell you business plan software. In the table on page 218, you'll see five sites that offer help with business plans, and our text's Web site has many more. Find five of these Web sites and note which sites offer sample business plans, which offer software, and which offer consulting on the preparation of a business plan.

Financing

Once you have your business plan in hand, you can begin seeking start-up funds. Two of the major sources are loans and venture capital. Loans can come from a bank or from an organization like the SBA, which is the largest single source of federally assisted financing for small businesses. To compare loan rates, check out at http://www.bankrate.com/brm/biz_home.asp and http://www.hsh.com.

Venture capital comes in many varieties. Some venture capital is restricted to a particular industry, region, or group. At http://www.quicken.com, you'll find general information and comparisons on venture capital. The table on page 218 lists five sites that deal with venture capital, and our text's Web site has many more. Choose five to review, and for each, consider whether the site offers venture capital or will find a source for you. Is it clear whether a fee will be expected, and if so, when will it be due? If the site offers financing, does it tell you what the investors expect in return for their investment? Is the capital restricted to a particular industry, region, or societal group?

Accounting

Accounting expertise is a must when you start up. You'll need to decide what sort of organization you want to have—sole proprietorship, partnership, C corporation, S corporation, limited liability partnership, and so on. Then, your business will need good bookkeeping practices, including journalizing cash receipts, financial statements, bill paying, income tax planning for yourself, and payroll and taxes for your employees. Public accountants provide various accounting services and often financing and start-up advice. Public accounting firms come in all sizes, from the large national firms like Arthur Andersen (http://www.arthurandersen.com) to regional firms like Baird, Kurtz and Dobson (http://www.bkd.com), to local independent firms or individuals. For a list of over 3,000 offices of 1,800 CPA firms, see the CPA Firms site at http://www.cpafirms.com. In the table on page 218, you'll see the Web site addresses for five CPA firms. Find five more (more CPA sites are available on our Web site), and compare all 10 on the basis of whether each specializes in some aspect of accounting such as tax or environmental accounting. Also, check out whether the CPA firm offers simple bookkeeping or additional services such as financial planning, retirement planning, and disaster planning.

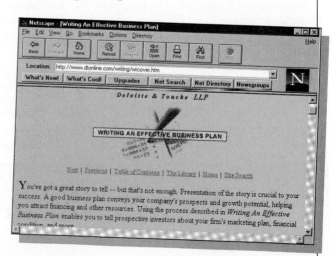

Web Sites for Starting Your Own Business

Advice on Starting a Business	Address
Small Business Administration	http://www.sba.gov
Small Business Development Center	http://www.smallbiz.suny.edu
SCORE	http://www.score.org
National Association of Entrepreneurs	http://nae.org
YoungBiz	http://youngbiz.com

Franchise Opportunities	Address
McDonald's	http://www.mcdonalds.com/corporate/franchise/index.html
TruServ	http://www.truserv.com/home.index.asp
Motel 6	http://www.motel6.com/franchising/franchise.html
Steak-Out	http://www.steakout.com
Blimpie	http://www.blimpie.com/frame_franchise.htm

Web Developers	Address
Viant	http://www.viant.com
Scient	http://www.scient.com
IXL	http://www.iXL.com
US Interactive	http://www.USInteractive.com
Proxicom	http://www.proxicom.com

Market Research Suppliers	Address
AG Nielsen	http://www.nielsenmedia.com
IMS	http://www.ims-global.com
Arbitron	http://www.arbitron.com
Burke	http://www.burke.com
Market Facts	http://www.marketfacts.com

Business Plans	Address
Palo Alto Software	http://www.pasware.com/sample.htm
A Business Plan Software Company	http://www.a-businessplan.com
BizProWeb	http://www.bizproweb.com/pages/shareware/win95_bizplan.html
Entrepreneurial Edge	http://www.edgeonline.com/main/bizbuilders/biz/sm_business/busplan.shtml
Deloitte & Touche	http://www.dtonline.com/writing/wrcover.htm

Venture Capital	Address
Alaska Division of Trade & Development	http://www.state.ak.us/local/akpages/COMMERCE/dced.htm
Mid-Willamett Valley Council of Governments	http://www.open.org/sedcor/mwv_cog.htm
LMT Financial	http://www.loftusweb.com/bizloan.html
Aabaar Venture Capital	http://www.vcap.com
Coral Ventures	http://www.coralventures.com/frame.html

Accounting Firms	Address
Pricewaterhouse Coopers	http://www.pwcglobal.com
KPMG	http://www.us.kpmg.com
Mayer Hoffman McCann	http://www.mhmlc.com
Ernst & Young	http://www.ey.com
Mitchell & Titus	http://www.mitchelltitus.com

Go to the Web site that supports this text:
http://www.mhhe.com/business/mis/haag
and select "Electronic Commerce Projects."

We've included links to over 100 Web sites for starting your own business, and a section on government agencies dedicated to starting and running small businesses.

KEY TERMS AND CONCEPTS

Ad Hoc Decision
Artificial Intelligence (AI)
Choice
Crossover
Data Management
Decision Support System (DSS)
Decision Support System (DSS)
   Generator
Design
Domain Expert
Expert System
Expert System Shell
Explanation Module

Genetic Algorithm
Geographic Information System
   (GIS)
Group Decision Support System
   (GDSS)
Hybrid Intelligent System
Implementation
Inference Engine
Intelligence
Intelligent Agent
Knowledge Acquisition
Knowledge Base
Knowledge-Based System

Knowledge Engineer
Model Management
Mutation
Neural Network
Nonrecurring Decision
Nonstructured Decision
Recurring Decision
Robot
Rule-Based Expert System
Selection
Structured Decision
User Interface
User Interface Management

SHORT-ANSWER QUESTIONS

1. What are the four types of decisions discussed in this chapter? Give an example of each.
2. What are the four steps in making a decision?
3. What is a DSS? Describe its components.
4. What are the problems that arise when more than five people meet to make a decision?
5. What different types of meetings can you have involving time and place?
6. What is a geographic information system used for?
7. How is information represented in a geographic information system?

8. What is artificial intelligence? Name the artificial intelligence systems used widely in business.
9. What are the components of an expert system?
10. What are five advantages of an expert system?
11. How does a neural network work?
12. What three concepts of evolution are used by the genetic algorithm?
13. What are intelligent agents? What tasks can they perform?

DISCUSSION QUESTIONS

1. Some experts claim that if a business gets 52 percent of its decisions right, it will be successful. Would using a decision support system guarantee better results? Why or why not? What does the quality of any decision depend on?
2. Early systems researchers called expert systems "experts in a box." Today, in most situations, people who consult expert systems use them as assistants in specific tasks and not to totally replace human experts. What sorts of tasks would you feel comfortable about having expert systems accomplish without much human intervention? What sorts of tasks would you *not* be comfortable having expert systems handle independently? Give examples.
3. Consider the topic of data warehouses in Chapter 4. Many people believe that, in the future, AI systems will be increasingly applied to data

warehouse processing. Which AI systems do you think might be helpful? For which tasks, or situations, might they best be applied?
4. Consider the differences and similarities among the four AI techniques discussed in this chapter. Name some problems that might be amenable to more than one type of AI system.
5. AI systems are relatively new approaches to solving business problems. What are the difficulties with new IT approaches in general?
6. Neural networks recognize and categorize patterns. If someone were to have a neural network that could scan information on all aspects of your life, where would that neural network potentially be able to find information about you? Consider confidential (doctor's office) as well as publicly available (department of motor vehicles) information.

CASE STUDY

Using Networks to Eliminate Paper in the Pulp and Paper Industry

Suppose you were in an industry and figured out a way to eliminate the need for the primary product you produce? Would you hide your idea hoping no one else would discover it or would you champion the idea and encourage your organization to exploit it fully? Those are the type of questions Fletcher Challenge Canada, a $2.5 billion paper and pulp giant in Canada, faced. It seems that Fletcher determined that the sharing and communication of information by means of paper documents just wasn't

IN THE NEWS

Networks
Technologies for Electronic Commerce
Networks
Networks

working. Too many people complained that they never had access to the right information at the right time.

So Fletcher decided to create an extensive computer network that would give its employees electronic access to needed information, in essence abandoning the use of paper to distribute information. That sounds like a great idea and computer networks certainly support the electronic movement of information, but there were other obstacles to overcome. With the home office located in Vancouver, British Columbia, the primary sales office located in San Francisco, and three mills located in remote areas that could only be accessed by helicopter or ferryboat, there was the problem of how to connect such geographically dispersed sites. To overcome this problem, Fletcher turned to the Internet. After all, the Internet connects some 75 million people all over the world, so why not use it to connect Fletcher's five locations?

Using the Internet created another problem. The Internet is a public network, which essentially means that anyone can use it. It only makes sense that, if Fletcher were to use the Internet to post strategic and sensitive information on Web sites, other organizations (potentially competitors) could access it as well. To overcome this problem, Fletcher created an **intranet**, a form of an internal

IN THE INFORMATION AGE, KNOWLEDGE WORKERS UNDERSTAND...

1. Client/server as the emerging blueprint for organizational networks

2. Network-enabling technologies and concepts that support electronic commerce

3. Key external electronic commerce aspects that networks support

4. Key internal electronic commerce aspects that networks support

5. Network perfect service as it relates to network range, reach, and responsiveness

organizational Internet guarded against outside access by special security software called a **firewall**.

Today, Fletcher uses its intranet to distribute all types of information throughout the organization, including customer information, product specifications, and employee newsletters. And the firewall security software prohibits outside organizations from gaining access to the intranet-stored information.[1] ❖

Introduction

Fletcher's story is not an uncommon one—all organizations today are struggling with how to use technology to support the sharing and communicating of information among employees. And, like Fletcher, many organizations are sectioning off a portion of the Internet for their own specific use. In doing so these organizations are creating intranets, which include security software to prohibit outside organizations from gaining access to intranet-stored information.

Other organizations are using technology and computer networks to extend beyond organizational boundaries to reach customers and work with suppliers, distributors, and retailers who may be located all over the world. For these organizations, the solution is the same as for those seeking to internally share and communicate information—computer networks that support the electronic movement of information from one location to another. By way of introduction, let's formally define two terms:

Computer network (which we simply refer to as a **network**) is a connection of two or more IT (information technology) components (typically computers) that gives people the ability to share software, share information, share peripheral devices, communicate with each other, and share processing power.

Telecommunications is the electronic movement of information from one location to another.

As you can see, networks and telecommunications go hand in hand. Networks support telecommunications because networks connect IT components so that people can share and communicate information.

Therefore a network can be as simple as two desktop computers connected to the same printer (peripheral sharing) or as complex and far-reaching as the Internet—a collection of computers all over the world that supports the sharing and communicating of information (telecommunications). Networks are perhaps the most important aspect of IT in business today because they support telecommunications. According to one survey of 22 large transnational organizations, networking accounted for almost 33 percent of their entire IT budgets.[2] Using networks, organizations all over the world are electronically moving information (telecommunications) to reach hundreds of millions of customers and form business partnerships with other organizations that may not even speak the same language.

When we talk about interacting with customers or other organizations through IT, we refer to it as *electronic commerce*. But electronic commerce is more than just interacting with the marketplace. It includes using technology to electronically perform internal processes as well. In this chapter, we want to alert you to many of the exciting types of electronic commerce that networks support. In fact, in the first five chapters of this text, you've already learned about many types, such as virtual organizations, data warehouses, group decision support systems, customer integrated systems, and many more. In this chapter, we'll revisit some of those aspects of electronic commerce and introduce you to many new ones.

As this chapter unfolds, we'll first introduce you to client/server—the emerging blueprint for organizational networks (see Figure 6.1). As a network blueprint, client/server addresses both the technology-independent workings of your organization as well as five models for implementing the most appropriate network. With that in mind, we then discuss various network-enabling technologies and concepts. That section provides you with an overview of networks from a technological viewpoint and introduces you to many network technology terms. In the section that follows, we focus on the real advantages of networks—that is, electronic commerce, both external and internal. Finally, we want to introduce you to network perfect service so that you'll understand the range, reach, and responsiveness of a network. If your organization can build a network that encompasses perfect service, you'll be able to meet the customer's moment of value.

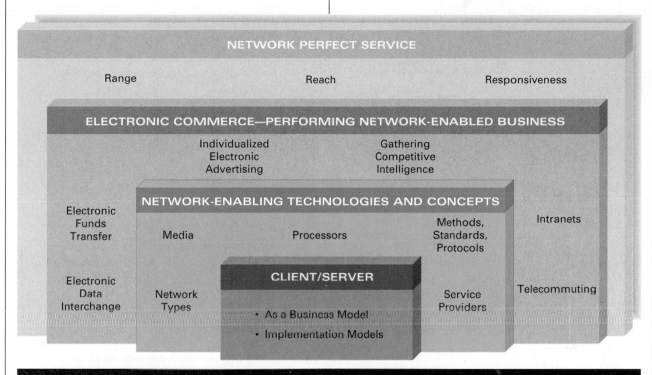

FIGURE 6.1

Your Focus in This Chapter

Client/Server

The Emerging Blueprint for Networks

As we've already stated, a network connects various IT components to allow you to share software, share information, share peripheral devices, communicate with other people, and to share processing power. The extent to which these five objectives are met really determines the true nature of a network. The most basic form of a network is a *peer-to-peer network*, which provides only two abilities—the ability to communicate with other people and the ability to share peripheral devices (see Figure 6.2*a*). Peer-to-peer networks are typically small, not exceeding 25 computers. These types of networks work well in small office environments in which the primary objective of the network is simply to connect people so that they can communicate with each other and share peripheral devices such as printers and scanners.

Today's organizations also require knowledge workers to share software, information, and—most important—processing power. To facilitate this, organizations are creating networks based on a client/server model. A *client/server network* is a network that contains one or more host computers (called "servers") that provide some type of service to the other computers (called "clients") in the network (see Figure 6.2*b*). Client computers are almost always personal computers or workstations; servers, on the other hand, range from powerful workstations to mainframe computers. The services that a server provides include (1) maintaining information and software that people in a network can access and work with and (2) actually performing processes that a client workstation may need to do.

The key difference between a peer-to-peer network and a client/server network is the *network operating system (NOS)*—the system software that determines how a network functions. The NOS is responsible for managing (1) the communications within a network, (2) the sharing of peripheral devices such as printers, (3) the sharing of information, (4) the sharing of software, and (5) any coordinated processing that takes place between the server and the clients. Peer-to-peer NOSs support only the first two—the communications within a network and the sharing of peripheral devices. Client/server NOSs, on the other hand, support all five functions. For example, Figure 6.2*b* shows a client/server network in which the server is responsible for managing access to shared information and software. In this instance, the server is often called a "file server." Figure 6.2*a* also

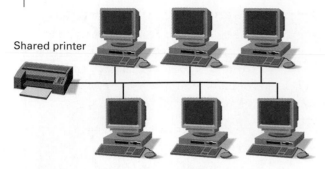

Shared printer

(a) Peer-to-peer networks support your ability to communicate with other people in the network and share peripheral devices.

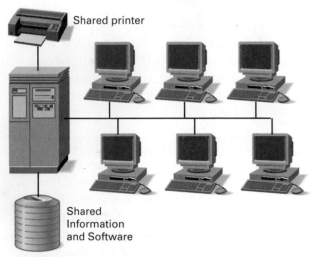

Shared printer

Shared Information and Software

(b) Client/server networks possess servers that support your ability to share software, share information, share peripheral devices, communicate with other people, and share processing power.

FIGURE 6.2

Peer-to-Peer and Client/Server Networks

shows that peer-to-peer networks don't have file servers that manage access to shared information and software.

Client/Server as a Business Model

Although many people use the term client/server to describe a specific network or network structure, client/server is actually a *business model*. As a business model, client/server requires that the processing be distributed to the exact place in a network where the processing needs to be performed. As such, client/server is the foundation of decentralized computing, which we discussed in Chapter 2. The client/server business model focuses on building an IT infrastructure that suits your organization's operations. Client/server is composed of the following types of information, software, and processing power:

■ **Information**
 ◆ *Local* Information that is unique to a particular organizational function
 ◆ *Global* Information that spans the entire organization

■ **Software**
 ◆ *Local* Processes that work with local information
 ◆ *Global* Processes that work with global information

■ **Processing power**
 ◆ *Local* Processing power that executes local software to work with local information
 ◆ *Global* Processing power that executes global software to work with global information

In this instance, we use the terms *local* and *global* synonymously with client and server, respectively. So client workstations maintain all information and software and possess processing power for working with local information. Servers, on the other hand, maintain all information and software and possess processing power for working with global information (organizationwide information).

Buehler Foods, a 30-store retail chain, is using client/server to take advantage of this separation of global and local processing and to realize other benefits.[3] At each store, registers are connected to a server that contains pricing and inventory information. This serves two purposes. First, if a price must change, the change can be made in a matter of seconds on the server. Second, as registers scan products, that information is immediately used to update inventory levels on the server.

These advantages (such as the ability to change a price quickly) are common in most retail stores. But Buehler Foods hasn't stopped there. Each store server is connected to larger servers at the home office. Through this connection, debit and credit processing and check verification occur. The home office servers also maintain vitally important customer purchasing profiles. That way, customers can shop at any of Buehler's 30 stores, and the home office servers can update their profiles and generate customer-specific coupons. After all, pricing and inventory information is store-specific or local, whereas customer purchasing profiles are not store-specific and must be maintained organizationally. Buehler Foods is just one of many organizations that have benefited from a client/server business model. A few other organizations are listed below:

■ *Fannie Mae*, the nation's largest issuer of mortgage-backed securities, had some real problems.[4,5] When a loan request came in, it often had to be rekeyed 12 times and took as long as 60 days to close. Fannie

Mae solved the problem with a client/server network that places the right information in the hands of the right people at the right time (giving employees the ability to provide customer moment of value). Fannie Mae hopes to use its client/server network to approve loans in a matter of hours and cut loan origination costs by $1,000 to $1,500.

- *Connecticut Mutual Life* found that customer requests for financial products sometimes backed up by months.[6] To eliminate this problem, Connecticut Mutual implemented work flow automation software on a client/server network to electronically move customer requests to one of 500 service representatives. In just 2 years, Connecticut Mutual realized a 35 percent return on investment, reduced annual operating costs by $4 million, and increased policy retention.

- *Ertl Toys* recently implemented an international client/server network.[7] On it, Ertl placed vitally important information concerning customers, competitors, and consumer buying trends. With access to this information, marketing specialists can more easily and accurately predict how many of which products to manufacture for any given holiday season.

- *Bank of Boston* needed a system that would allow all of its employees to instantly call up an entire portfolio history of any of its 100,000 customers or sales prospects.[8] By going with a client/server network, Bank of Boston has realized over $700,000 in profits and reduced administrative costs by $200,000.

Client/server sounds great as a business model and, when implemented correctly, offers your organization many internal benefits and significant advantages in the marketplace. However, how to implement the client/server business model is another issue altogether. Many organizations that have embraced the client/server business model have found it very difficult to implement. As your organization considers implementing client/server, you must keep in mind how your organization works, what information would be considered global and local, and what software and processing power must be distributed for working with global and local information. In the following section, we address these issues, as well as the five client/server implementation models.

Types of Client/Server Implementations

When you choose to implement client/server, you can follow one of five basic client/server implementation

models (see Figure 6.3 on page 226). Which you choose depends on the nature of your business environment and the type of information processing the client/server implementation will support. As you can see from Figure 6.3, the five client/server implementation models differ according to several factors:

1. Where the processing for the presentation of information occurs
2. Where the processing of logic or business rules occurs
3. Where the data management component (DBMS) and information (database) are located

In these implementation models, you should always focus on **where** the software is executed. In any client/server implementation, the software is split by three levels—presentation, logic, and data management. *Presentation* deals with the formatting of information as it's displayed or printed and the editing of information as you enter it. *Logic* deals with the actual business rules that are implemented as software. For example, in a payroll environment, logic includes how to handle overtime, sick leave, and vacation accumulation. Finally, *data management* deals with the retrieval and storage of information in a database. This is essentially the DBMS (database management system) engine we discussed in Chapter 4. Below we provide a brief description of each client/server implementation model.

Client/Server Model 1: Distributed Presentation In the first model, the server handles almost all functions, including a major portion of the presentation. In this particular instance, both the client and server share in the duties of formatting information for screen or printer output and the editing of information as you enter it.

Client/Server Model 2: Remote Presentation In the second model, the server handles all logic and data management functions, and the client handles all presentation functions.

Client/Server Model 3: Distributed Logic In this model, the server handles the entire data management function, the client handles the entire presentation function, and both share in processing the logic or business rules.

Client/Server Model 4: Remote Data Management In the fourth model, the server handles only the data management function, whereas the client is responsible for all logic and presentation.

Client/Server Model 5: Distributed Data Management In the final model, the client handles all

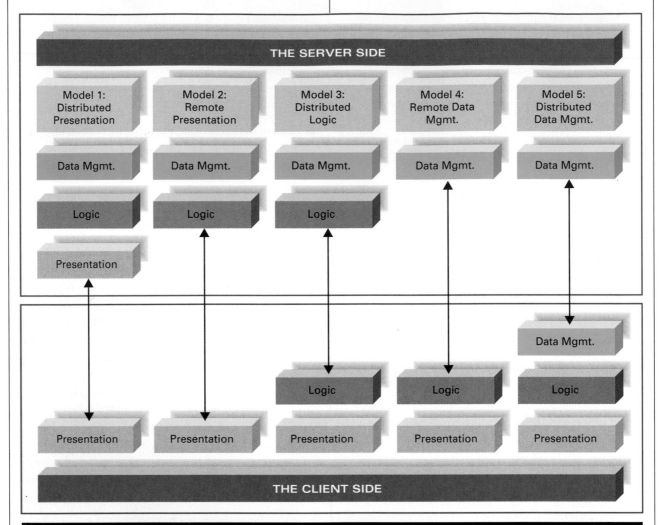

FIGURE 6.3

The Five Implementation Models for Client/Server[9]

logic and presentation processing and shares the data management function with the server.

The implementation model you choose depends on how your business works and where processing must occur. To help you understand these various implementation models, let's consider two examples—one for model 3 and one for model 5.

Model 3 Client/Server Implementation

In model 3—distributed logic—the server handles the entire data management function, the client handles the entire presentation function, and both share in processing the logic or business rules. Suppose you are the manager of the manufacturing division of an organization and need to give pay raises to each of your employees. You use the following divisional and organizational rules for determining pay raises:

Divisional Rules

❶ Each manufacturing employee begins with a base raise of $2,500.

❷ No manufacturing employee can receive less than $2,000 as a pay raise.

❸ If loss of time because of injury is greater than 3 days, then deduct $500 from the pay raise.

❹ If overtime hours worked is less than 5 days, then deduct $500 from the pay raise.

Organizational Rules

❶ No employee with less than 5 years of experience can receive a pay raise that exceeds $2,500.

❷ The pay raise you award must be within 20 percent of last year's for each employee.

❸ For each employee that has taken at least three business-related trips in the last year, add $500 to the pay raise.

As you begin to determine pay raises, the following steps would occur (see Figure 6.4):

❶ You would request information for a given manufacturing employee.

❷ Your client workstation would send that request to the server.

❸ The server would retrieve the employee information from the employee database.

❹ The server would return the employee information to your client workstation.

❺ Your client workstation would execute the divisional manufacturing business rules or logic relating to how you determine pay raises for manufacturing employees.

❻ Your client workstation would format and present to you the employee's information and proposed pay raise.

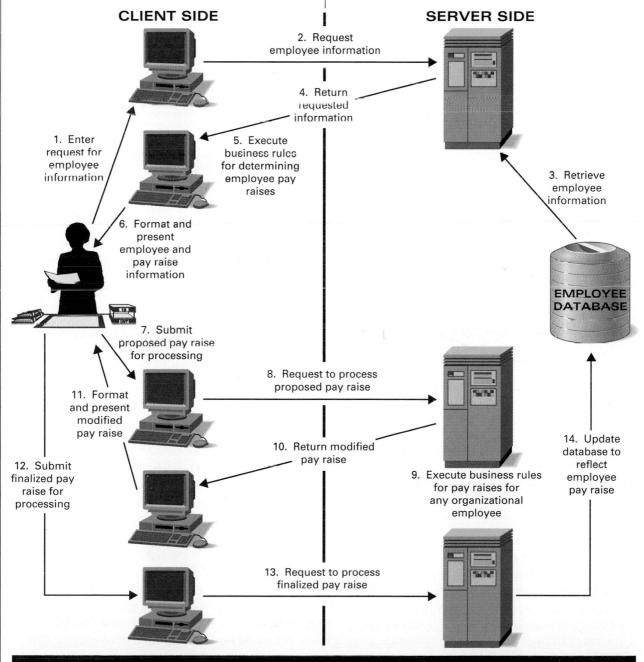

CLIENT SIDE

SERVER SIDE

2. Request employee information

4. Return requested information

1. Enter request for employee information

5. Execute business rules for determining employee pay raises

3. Retrieve employee information

6. Format and present employee and pay raise information

EMPLOYEE DATABASE

7. Submit proposed pay raise for processing

11. Format and present modified pay raise

8. Request to process proposed pay raise

10. Return modified pay raise

12. Submit finalized pay raise for processing

9. Execute business rules for pay raises for any organizational employee

14. Update database to reflect employee pay raise

13. Request to process finalized pay raise

FIGURE 6.4

Model 3 Client/Server Implementation for Employee Pay Raises

⑦ You would submit the proposed pay raise for processing.

⑧ Your client workstation would send that information to the server.

⑨ The server would execute the organizational business rules or logic relating to pay raises for all employees.

⑩ The server would return to your client workstation the pay raise (modified according to the organizational business rules) for the employee.

⑪ Your client workstation would format and present to you the modified pay raise.

⑫ You would submit the finalized pay raise for final processing.

⑬ Your client workstation would send that information to the server.

⑭ The server would update the employee database to reflect the employee's pay raise.

In the instance of a model 3 implementation of client/server in determining pay raises, the server is responsible for data management (retrieving and updating employee information) and executing the business rules or logic that apply to all employees for pay raises. Your client workstation is responsible for editing your entry of information, formatting the presentation of information to you, and executing the business rules or logic that apply to pay raises for manufacturing employees only.

When presented step-by-step, the implementation of client/server may seem complex and tedious. And indeed it is from a software perspective. But to you, as a knowledge worker, the process is totally transparent. As you work in any client/server environment (regardless of the implementation model), you don't know how the

INDUSTRY PERSPECTIVE

Financial Services

Distributing Data Warehouses in a Client/Server Environment

In Chapter 4 we looked at data warehouses—collections of information in an organization that support online analytical processing (OLAP). Data warehouses give people the ability to slice and dice their way through information structures with many dimensions as they make decisions. Considering data warehouses and the variety of decisions that people make every day, it only makes sense that different people have different OLAP information needs. So, instead of just creating one large data warehouse that everyone uses, many organizations are creating smaller data warehouses—called *data marts*—that satisfy the information and OLAP needs of a group of people.

Such is the case at First Interstate Bankcorp in Los Angeles. First Interstate built a corporatewide data warehouse for those people who need corporatewide information, but it also built department or division data warehouses (data marts) for those people who need only the information that relates to specific aspects of their business. For example, loan departments and various cash management departments have their own specialized data marts.

Distribution is the key here. How do you distribute these various data marts across a large network? First Interstate uses a client/server concept. In the client/server environment, the corporatewide data warehouse is placed on a separate server that anyone using a client workstation can access. Additionally, all the smaller data marts are placed on department or division servers—these data marts are only accessible by the appropriate department or division employees.

Why create these separate, smaller data marts? Well, you'll recall from Chapter 4 that organizations build data warehouses because people need to create complex queries that sometimes slow operational databases. The same is true for corporatewide data warehouses—the more people using the data warehouse, the slower the response time. So it only makes sense that smaller data marts can ease the processing burden on larger data warehouses. And behind literally any type of data warehouse— whether a corporatewide data warehouse, a data mart for a division, or your own personal data warehouse—stand the client/server concepts that place processing exactly where it needs to take place.[10] ❖

data management, logic, and presentation are distributed. And you don't really care—as long as the processing that you need takes place.

If you think about our example of a client/server implementation for handling employee pay raises, you can see one of the many advantages of client/server. In our example, your client workstation processes the business rules or logic only for employees of the manufacturing department, whereas the server processes the business rules or logic for all employees. And, as you determine pay raises for manufacturing employees, the manager of distribution could be doing the same for distribution employees. In that instance, his or her client workstation would process the business rules for pay raises of distribution employees, while the server performs the same processes it carries out for you. In this way, the server handles business rules common to all organizational employees, whereas respective clients handle only business rules for their particular division.

Model 5 Client/Server Implementation

Let's consider another example of a client/server implementation, this time for model 5, where the server acts only to help the client in accessing information stored on the server. The client is then responsible for presentation and logic, as well as data management for local information. To illustrate model 5, let's assume that you have a decision support system (DSS) on your client workstation and need to work with a personal data warehouse of information that describes sales over the past 5 years (see Figure 6.5). The servers in this case—and there may be many—are responsible for executing the OLTP (online transaction processing) software and extracting the information you require for your data warehouse. That information is passed to your client workstation. Once there, your client workstation builds the data warehouse according to your logical information requirements and allows you to perform a variety of queries as you use your DSS. This separation of duties between the servers and your client workstation makes business sense. The servers process OLTP software where the transaction processing needs to take place and perform the necessary extraction of information from the operational databases; your client workstation is then responsible for creating your data warehouse and executing your queries.

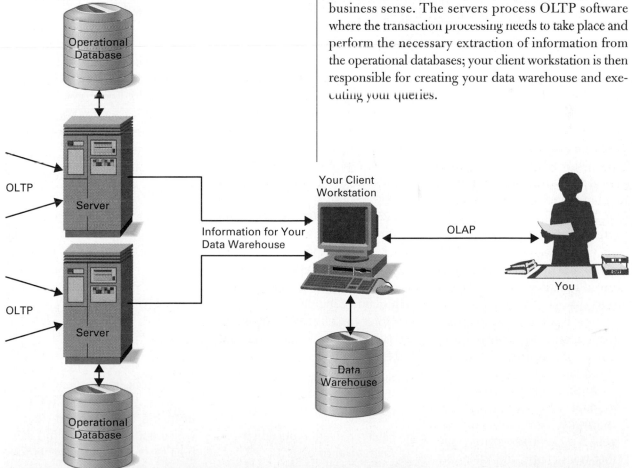

FIGURE 6.5
A Personal Data Warehouse in a Client/Server Implementation

The Advantages and Disadvantages of Client/Server

Client/server—whether you consider it a business model or a network implementation model—is critical to the success of most businesses today. And, as with all types of technology, client/server has both advantages and disadvantages that you must consider. We discuss many of these below.

Advantages

- **Distribution of processing mirrors organizational workings** Most important, client/server allows you to develop a technological structure that mirrors your organizational operations. This is key—IT is simply a set of tools for working with information and performing tasks related to information

processing. Because you can choose from a variety of implementation models, client/server networks help you build the technology structure best suited to your organizational demands.

- **Distribution is transparent** Regardless of the implementation model you choose, the distribution of information, software, and processing power is transparent. That is, as knowledge workers perform their information-processing tasks, they need not be concerned with the location of information and software or on which computer (client or server) the processing takes place. Because of this advantage you may be asking, "Then why am I learning about client/server? If the distribution of information, software, and processing power will be transparent to me, why should I care about which of the five client/server

INDUSTRY PERSPECTIVE

Health Care

Client/Server Helps Eliminate the Patient Paper Chart

If you've ever been to a doctor's office or a hospital, you've witnessed the "great paper chase." No matter what you have done—from a routine physical to a CAT scan—volumes of paper follow you everywhere you go. Not only is much of your information duplicated in different areas, physicians have a difficult time tracking down all your information which they need to provide you with the best possible health care.

At Staten Island University Hospital in New York all that is changing. And the ultimate goal is a client/server network that will capture and maintain a paperless patient chart that will follow you electronically throughout your visit. With

the new system, hospital workers and even off-site physicians will be able to quickly gain access to any patient record. According to Katherine Kania, Staten Island's coordinator of applications development, this will be a substantial improvement over the old system. As she explains, "It would take you 25 to 30 minutes to get all the information you needed for a patient's complete health record. On the client/server system, you'll be able to access all the pieces of the record in five minutes."

Other benefits and aspects of the client/server paperless patient system include

- An annual savings of over $1 million in information-processing costs
- Fifteen percent reduction in manual labor costs
- Reduction in patient stays by a half day (a $1.1 million savings for patients)

- A doctor's ability to use automatic speech recognition to enter bedside notes
- A simple and easy-to-use graphic user interface

The complete computerized patient record is a long-term goal for all health care providers. At Staten Island, part of the solution is a client/server network. That solution is equally applicable to most hospitals, doctor's offices, and clinics around the country. For example, the Red Cross uses a client/server network that has no physical connections. Using wireless communications technologies, the Red Cross can instantly pick up its client/server network, move it to the location of a disaster, and never worry about having to run cables to connect the clients to the server.[11, 12] ❖

implementation models is used?" Well, it's important for you to understand client/server because you're one-half the client/server equation—you are the *client*. Your ability to very clearly express your information, software, and processing power needs and distinguish them as local or global will enable your organization to define which client/server implementation model is best.

- **Software reuse** In our example of a model 3 implementation, we demonstrated a key benefit of client/server networks. That benefit is the client/server's ability to reuse software in many different locations. This software reuse ultimately reduces software development costs and increases programmer productivity.

- **Servers can control information use** Giving the right people access to the right information is a goal of today's information-based business environment. And controlling which people have access to what information is equally important. In a client/server environment, the server contains the necessary security features for controlling who has access to information and how they can use that information.

- **Flexibility on the client side** By distributing processing to its exact location, client/server networks provide complete freedom and flexibility to knowledge workers as they use client workstations to work with local information and software.

- **Scalability** One of the great advantages of client/server is *scalability*. That is, as your organization changes in size, scope, and information and information-processing requirements, you can change the scale of your client/server implementation. For example, it's relatively easy to add additional client workstations; add another server and split functions between the existing and the new server; and add additional internal memory, processing speed, and information storage to servers.

- **Support for electronic commerce concepts** You can sum up all the above advantages by simply saying that client/server supports electronic commerce concepts. Business today is definitely moving toward complete electronic commerce, both internally and externally.

Disadvantages

- **Existence of non-client/server-oriented software** Client/server software is distributed according to presentation, logic, and data management. Most non-client/server software has been developed without this in mind. So many organizations are facing a critical question—"How do we take advantage of client/server when our software is not designed to distribute processing according to presentation, logic, and data management?" The answer, in many cases, is to rewrite the old software—and that costs money.

- **Hidden costs** As with all types of technology, client/server networks cost money, and many of these costs are hidden. Unfortunately, many people look at a network and equate costs with new hardware acquisition, hardware upgrades, wiring, and so on. But, according to the Gartner Group, over 70 percent of client/server implementation costs may be tied up in labor and spread across both IT professionals and knowledge workers.[13] Those costs include application development labor (8 percent), server operation and other miscellaneous labor (8 percent), knowledge worker support labor (15 percent), and knowledge worker labor time spent by people learning and operating their client workstations (41 percent).

The Keys to Client/Server

Client/server really is the emerging blueprint for networks in organizations today. Most organizations realize—and rightfully so—that the advantages of client/server far outweigh the disadvantages. So how does your organization use client/server to realize the advantages while minimizing the disadvantages? Below we discuss three issues that might help.

- **Knowing how your organization works** First and foremost, client/server will only work if you know how your organization works. Why? Because the best client/server implementation is one that mirrors how your organization works. To determine the "best" client/server implementation, you must understand how your organization works, including where processing needs to occur and whether information and information processing are local or global.

- **Choosing the appropriate implementation model** Once you understand how your organization works, you must define the correct client/server implementation model. That means you must understand how to distribute presentation, logic, and data management across the network. And the best implementation model may be different for different areas of your organization.

- **Implementing client/server with object-oriented techniques** In Chapter 4 we briefly introduced you to object-oriented concepts when we discussed object-oriented databases and database

TEAM WORK

Defining Client/Server Implementation Models

A key to your success in using client/server is your ability to select the most appropriate implementation model for your organization. Choosing the right model depends on the business situation at hand. Below we describe several business situations. For each choose the most appropriate client/server implementation model.

Same-Time, Same-Room Group Decision Support System (GDSS) Figure 5.11 (p. 188) in Chapter 5 diagrams a GDSS decision room for same-time, same-room meetings. In this instance, a client/server network would support such functions as the collective generation of ideas, organization and categorization of ideas, and ranking of and voting on ideas.

Configurations for Operating Internationally Photo Essay 3-1 (p. 104) in Chapter 3 discusses the three configurations for operating

transnationally. For each, choose the most appropriate client/server implementation model.

Global Distribution System Closing Case Study, Case 1, of Chapter 2 (p. 74) discusses Marriott's global distribution system. As you choose the most appropriate client/server implementation model for this situation, consider travel agents as well.

Groupware Figure 2.12 in Chapter 2 (p. 59) diagrams a group document manufacturing database shared by production and distribution employees. In this instance, a client/server network must support capturing, updating, and querying information stored in the group document database.

To choose the most appropriate client/server implementation model for each of the above situations, it will be helpful if you first describe what information is used, what people use the information, how those people use the information, and where they are located. ❖

---

management systems. Most people believe that a successful client/server implementation begins with the use of objects. Texas Instruments (TI), for example, created an object-oriented computer-integrated manufacturing (CIM) system on a client/server network.[14] Because its client/server is object-based, TI can easily shut down production, swap new manufacturing objects (which contain both information and processes) for old ones, and quickly change the entire manufacturing process. TI believes its object and client/server–based system will deliver annual returns in excess of $60 million.

Network-Enabling Technologies and Concepts

The technical side of networks is perhaps the fastest-moving, most confusing, and most complex aspect of information technology. The area of networks is so littered with acronyms that many people refer to it as "the alphabet soup of technology." Nonetheless, you need to understand many of the terms associated with network-enabling technologies and concepts. By understanding these, you'll be able to better communicate with network specialists, who ultimately will provide you with a network that supports all your information-processing and communications needs. And, equally important, you'll be better prepared to take full advantage of all aspects of electronic commerce.

To introduce you to the technical and often confusing side of networks, we've grouped network-enabling technologies and concepts into five categories. These include the following:

❶ **Types of Networks**—There are many types of networks. Some cover small areas, such as an office or building, whereas others cover large geographic areas. Other networks, such as peer-to-peer networks, support only communication and the sharing of devices, whereas client/server networks support much more.

❷ **Communications Media—The Paths over Which Information Travels** Telecommunications implies that information must travel from one place to another, and that information must travel over some path.

❸ **Communications Processors—The Connections Within a Network** For computers and other devices to communicate in a network, they must be connected to the network in some way.

❹ **Communications Methods, Standards, and Protocols—The Manner in Which Information Is Communicated** For network telecommunications to be possible, there must be predefined methods, standards, and protocols by which information will be communicated from one place to another.

❺ **Communications Service Providers—The Issue of Network Ownership** Networks are expensive—sometimes too expensive for a single organization to build and maintain alone. In this instance, you can use the services of other organizations to build your network.

Over the next several pages, we use photo essays to introduce you to the first four categories of network-enabling technologies and concepts—types of networks (Photo Essay 6-1); communications media (Photo Essay 6-2); communications processors (Photo Essay 6-3); and communications methods, standards, and protocols (Photo Essay 6-4). The last category deserves special attention, so let's take some time to explore communications service providers.

Communications Service Providers
The Issue of Network Ownership

Network ownership is important in today's networked business world. This issue deals with everything from who has the right to use the communications media that make up the connections between components in a network to security and privacy. In its simplest form, ownership boils down to two choices—public and private. In either case, your choice will affect cost, availability, services provided, speed, and security.

Our following discussions on network ownership focus primarily on networks that cover great distances and require the use of the communications media provided by *communications service providers*. Smaller networks—such as LANs within an office building—are almost always private. That is, if your organization builds a LAN, then your organization would purchase, install,

and maintain the communications media. This is an example of a private network—your organization owns the exclusive rights to use the communications media.

Public Networks

A *public network* is a network on which your organization competes for time and use with other people and organizations. The most common example of a public network is the telephone system. As an individual, you compete with other people for use of the telephone system. In other words, you have no guarantee that lines will always be open and available to you. For example, if you've ever tried to call someone on a holiday, you may have received a very fast busy signal or a recording that told you all lines into that region were busy.

You can easily extend that example to dialing into your school's computer system from home. You are essentially using a public network to gain access to your school's computer. The Internet is also an example of a public network. As an Internet user, you are competing with other people for time and use—that's why connecting to Web sites may be slow at certain times and fast at others.

In a public network system, your organization typically (see Table 6.1 on page 242)

❶ Operates on a pay-as-you-go basis for time (cost)

❷ Competes for time and use (availability)

❸ Communicates only information from one place to another (service)

❹ Communicates more slowly than private networks (speed)

❺ Doesn't guarantee privacy (security)

For example, if you use a modem and the public telephone network to transmit information from your office in New York to another office in Phoenix, then you would

(continued on page 236)

6-1 # Types of Networks: Different Networks You'll Find in Use Today

There are many types of networks in existence today. Earlier in this chapter, we discussed two types of networks—peer-to-peer and client/server. Peer-to-peer networks support basic communications between people and the sharing of peripheral devices, whereas client/server networks support basic communications between people and the sharing of peripheral devices, software, information, and processing power. You can distinguish among types of networks in other ways. Two such ways are by geographic distance and by physical structure.

Networks by Geographic Distance

There are two basic types of networks by geographic distance:

Local area networks (LANs) cover a limited geographic distance, such as an office, office building, or a group of buildings within close proximity.

Wide area networks (WANs) cover large geographic distances, such as a state, a country, or even the entire world.

To understand networks by geographic distance, let's consider the case of Metropolitan Life Insurance Co., which uses a WAN to connect its LANs.[15] At Metropolitan, connecting its LANs by means of a WAN for the pension department was the only way to stay competitive in the marketplace. As Paula Medina, technical project manager for MetLife, explained, "We saw a need to gather more competitive information and to provide our sales associates with more meaningful information about prospects and client history. We realized that technology would be a powerful enabler for this process." MetLife's technology includes a WAN that connects a central server at the home office to five LANs, two in offices in New York and three in offices elsewhere in the United States (see Figure 6.6).

The central server provides access to the organizational pension database. That database contains information on all current and prospective clients, as well as vitally important information about competitors. Each LAN site also contains its own server with a database of client and product information for that particular site. As updates are made at each LAN site, the LAN servers communicate those updates to the central WAN server. Likewise, the central server nightly updates all appropriate information on the LAN site servers. And when sales associates are on the road, they can dial into the central server to receive whatever updates they need.

At MetLife, each LAN provides information-processing capabilities for a specific office location, and each office location covers a limited geographic distance. And, by connecting all the LANs to cover a large geographic distance, MetLife has created a WAN. Besides geographic distance, this is another good way to distinguish between LANs and WANs. WANs are typically large networks that connect multiple, smaller networks. The Internet is another great example of a WAN that connects many LANs. If you consider all the schools in the country that are connected through the Internet, the Internet is a WAN that connects the LANs of all the schools.

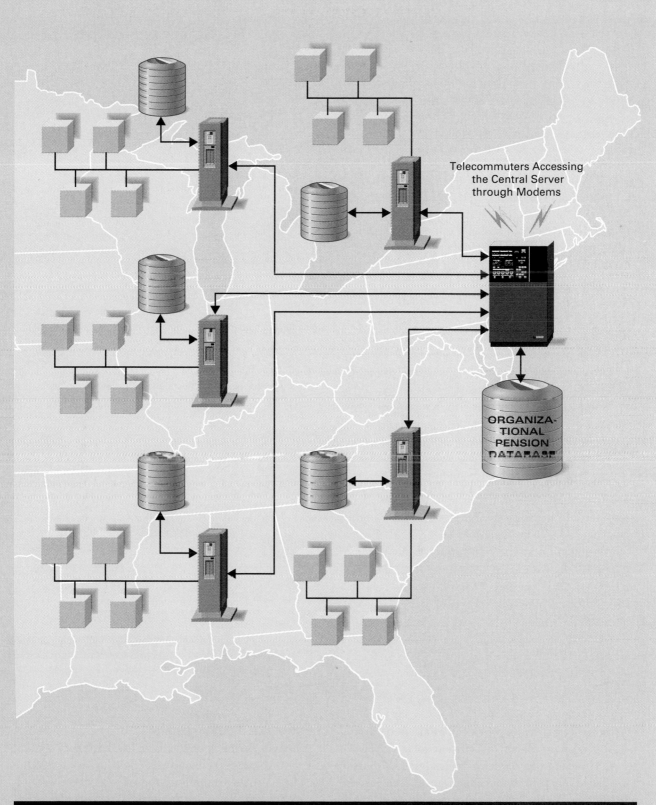

FIGURE 6.6

Local and Wide Area Networks at Metropolitan Life Insurance Co.

Networks by Physical Structure—Topologies

Regardless of your choice of a LAN or WAN, you must also decide how to physically structure or arrange the computers in a network. **Network topology** refers to the physical arrangement of computers in a network. Types of networks according to topology include bus, ring, and star (see Figure 6.7).

- **Bus topology** All computers are connected to a single communications medium over which all communications travel (see Figure 6.7a). The common communications medium in a bus topology is called the "bus." If you send a message to another person in a bus topology, that message (along with a unique address for that person) travels the entire bus. Each computer reads the address and determines if it's the intended recipient. If it is, it accepts the message; if it isn't, it simply disregards the message.

- **Ring topology** All computers are connected to a single communications medium (similar to a bus), and that communications medium is connected at both ends to form a closed loop (see Figure 6.7b). As with the bus topology, all communications travel the entire communications medium, and each computer must read the address and determine if it is the intended recipient.

- **Star topology** This arrangement has a central computer from which all other computers radiate (see Figure 6.7c). In this instance, if you send a communication to another person, that communication must pass through the central computer, which, in turn, interprets the address and sends the communication appropriately. ❖

(a) A bus topology connects all computers to a single communications medium over which all communications travel.

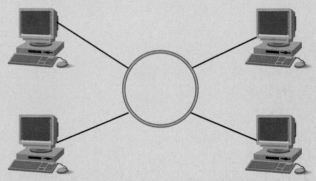

(b) A ring topology connects all computers to a single communications medium that is connected on both ends to form a closed loop.

(c) A star topology connects all computers to a central computer.

FIGURE 6.7
Bus, Ring, and Star Network Topologies

(1) pay the long-distance provider for time used; (2) compete with other people and organizations for availability and use; (3) have only the service of transmitting information provided to you; (4) transmit information at a slower speed, as determined by the long-distance provider; and (5) have no guarantee of security or privacy. In the latter point, if you wanted some sort of security, you would have to provide security measures (such as data encryption) yourself.

Private Networks

A *private network*, on the other hand, is a network that your organization either owns or exclusively leases the right to use the communications media to connect network components. For example, if your organization creates a LAN within an office building, then your organization would purchase, install, and maintain the communications media. For networks that cover a greater

(continued on page 243)

PHOTO ESSAY 6-2 Communications Media: The Paths over Which Information Travels

A key aspect of networks and telecommunications is the movement of information electronically from one place to another. It may be as simple as sending information from one office to another in the same building, or it may be as far-reaching as sending information around the world. Whatever the case, information must travel over some path from its source to its destination. **Communications media** are the paths, or physical channels, in a network over which information travels from one place to another. All communications media are either guided or unguided. **Guided communications media** transmit information over a closed path (such as a wire). **Unguided communications media** (which are also referred to as *wireless communications media*), on the other hand, transmit information through the air—in much the same way as radio stations broadcast their programming. Forms of guided and unguided communications media include:

Guided	Unguided
Twisted-pair cable	Microwave
Coaxial cable	Satellite
Optical fiber	Broadcast radio
	Infrared

Bandwidth

Before we discuss the various media, we should address an important consideration for communications media—bandwidth. For our purposes, **bandwidth** refers to the range of frequencies available on a communications medium. Bandwidth is important because it determines the capacity of the communications medium. In general, the greater the bandwidth, the greater the capacity. *Capacity* for a communications medium refers to the amount of information (given in bits per second) that can be transmitted in a single second. For example, if a particular communications medium has a maximum capacity of 16 megabits per second (mbps), up to 16 million bits of information can be transmitted in a single second.

Guided Communications Media

The most popular form of communications media is **twisted-pair cable**, two insulated copper wires twisted in a spiral (see Figure 6.8). Twisted-pair cable makes up the bulk of the world's public telephone communications system. That's also the reason twisted-pair is the most commonly used communications medium; it's already in place and it's relatively simple for your organization to set up a network using twisted-pair cable. Although it's the most commonly used medium, twisted-pair cable is also the slowest and least reliable of the guided communications media. A single twisted-pair cable is capable of providing a capacity of up to 16 mbps for short distances (typically not more than 1 to 2 miles). More realistically for network communications though, twisted-pair cable can handle up to 64 kilobits per second (kbps). Distance, noise on the line, and interference tend to limit its reliability.

For human speech communication, this is not much of a problem; if there's a crackle on the line, you can still understand what your friend is saying. Information communication across a network, however, requires much greater accuracy. For example, a crackle that changes a credit card number from 5244 0811 2643 741 to 5244 0810 2643 741 is more than a nuisance; in business it means retransmitting the information or applying a charge to the wrong person's credit card.

A faster and more reliable alternative to twisted-pair cable is **coaxial cable**, one or more central wires surrounded by thick insulation (see Figure 6.8). In fact, coaxial cable is probably what connects your television set to a cable TV service provider. Coaxial cable is capable of carrying 500 mbps, or about 15,000 voice calls, simultaneously. Because of its particular construction, coaxial cable is much less susceptible than twisted-pair cable to outside interference and information damage.

The fastest and most reliable guided communications media is **optical fiber**, which uses a very thin glass or plastic fiber through which pulses of light travel (see Figure 6.8). Optical fiber is similar to flashing Morse code

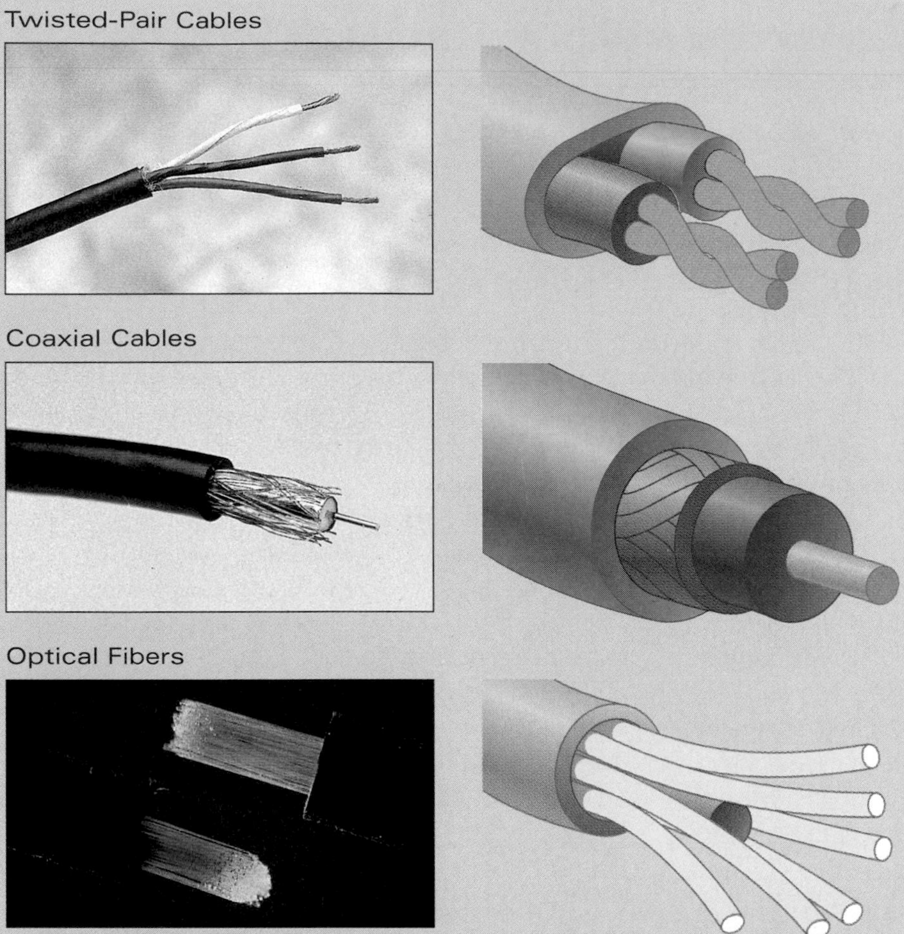

Twisted-Pair Cables

Coaxial Cables

Optical Fibers

FIGURE 6.8

Forms of Guided Communications Media

with a light through a hollow tube or fiber. Optical fiber has advantages in size (one fiber has the diameter of a strand of human hair), capacity (exceeding 1,400 mbps), and quality (much greater transmission reliability).

Unguided Communications Media

For many networks, guided communications media are simply unfeasible, especially for telecommunications across rugged terrain or great distances. For whatever reason, if guided communications media do not offer your organization what it needs, unguided communications media may be a possibility. Unguided communications media are called "unguided" because they broadcast (or radiate) information in many directions rather than through an enclosed path.

Microwaves are unguided communications media that use a high-frequency band of radio broadcast transmission and dish-shaped antennae for sending and receiving information. Microwaves are called "line-of-sight" media because the microwave signal cannot bend around the surface of the earth (see Figure 6.9). So to send information using microwaves for distances exceeding about 20 miles intermediate antennae must receive the information and retransmit it around the surface of the earth.

Satellites are basically microwave transmission systems in space. A satellite is an amplifier, or repeater, that receives information from one location on earth, repeats the data, and sends it to one or more receiving locations on earth (see Figure 6.10). Satellite communications media are very cost effective for moving large amounts of information, especially when there are many receiving locations. Again, satellites are unguided, meaning that many locations can simultaneously receive the same transmission. For example, Kmart and other retailers place very small aperture terminal (VSAT) satellite dishes on the roofs of their stores. The VSATs allow individual stores to transmit sales information to

FIGURE 6.9

Unguided Microwave Communications Media

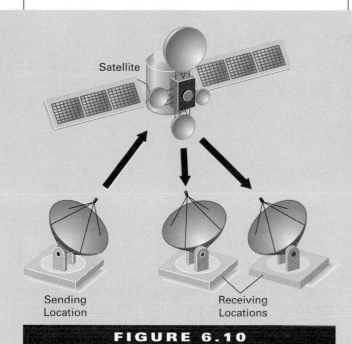

Satellite

Sending
Location

Receiving
Locations

FIGURE 6.10

Unguided Satellite Communications Media

the home office, and the home office can transmit information to all the stores simultaneously.

Broadcast radio is an unguided communications media similar to microwaves and satellites, except that the receiving locations needn't be in line-of-sight or have a dish-shaped antenna to receive information transmissions. Broadcast radio media are popularly used for digital pagers, cellular phones, and wireless local area networks within a building or limited geographic area. Broadcast radio waves, however, are very susceptible to reflections from buildings and other physical structures and interferences from other signaling devices. You've probably discovered this if you've ever used a cellular phone and had a call "dropped" when you passed under an overpass or walked into the basement of a building.

The final type of unguided communications medium is that of infrared. **Infrared** is an unguided communications medium that uses a red light (below the visibility of the human eye) to transmit information. The most common application of infrared is for controlling televisions and VCRs with a remote control device. In the area of networking, infrared is used to connect wireless local area networks in the same room and connect computers to peripheral devices, such as keyboards and printers. However, infrared typically has a low capacity (about 1 mbps) and is susceptible to line-of-sight interference.

Key Considerations for Communications Media

Communications media technology is vitally important in a network. To determine the most appropriate communications media, you must consider the capacity, reliability, cost, and distance of your network as well as the mobility of your network users. Let's consider each of these.

- *Capacity* In its simplest form, network capacity determines (1) how much information can simultaneously travel over the communications media and (2) how fast that information will travel. Determining capacity is rather like determining how much *horsepower* you need for your network. That is, the amount of information you need to communicate (force) and the speed with which you need to communicate that information (speed) will determine which communications media you require.

- *Reliability* Reliability really addresses the guarantee of *perfect service* of your network. For example, if you require a network with a great guarantee of perfect service, you probably won't choose infrared or twisted-pair as the communications media because they are susceptible to outside interference and noise.

- *Cost* Cost is always an overriding consideration in building a network, and your choice of capacity and reliability will affect cost the most. Communications media with greater capacity and reliability will cost more than those with less capacity and reliability.

- *Distance* Knowing the extent of geographic distance that your network must cover will also help you determine the most appropriate communications media. Some communications media—such as infrared and broadcast radio—really only work well over small distances, whereas optical fiber, microwave, and satellite communications media work well over great distances.

- *Mobility* Finally, you need to consider the mobility of network users. Many organizations today are equipping telecommuters with cellular phones so that they can work anywhere without proximity to an actual phone line. Other organizations are building LANs based on wireless technologies, so the entire network becomes mobile. ❖

PHOTO ESSAY 6-3 Communications Processors: The Connections Within a Network

In a network, **communications processors** are the hardware devices that unite the various communications media and computers and route communications throughout a network. The most simple and common form of a communications processor is a modem. A **modem** is a device that converts the digital signals of your computer into an analog form that can be transmitted over a telephone line and then converts the analog signal back to digital signals at the other end of the transmission (see Figure 6.11). Communications media, like the standard telephone system, pass signals in analog mode; computers, however, work in digital mode. So a modem converts digital signals into analog signals for the sender and then

Digital	Digital-to-Analog Conversion	Analog	Analog-to-Digital Conversion	Digital
Digital uses discrete electronic pulses to represent information.		Analog uses a continuous electronic stream to represent information.		

Telephone Line

In a network that exclusively uses digital signal communications, a modem isn't required. However, a communications processor must still be present to connect your computer to the communications medium. One such device is a *network interface card*—a special network card that fits into one of the expansion slots in the back of your workstation.

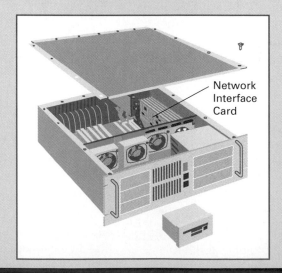

Network Interface Card

FIGURE 6.11

Making the Network Connection

converts analog signals to digital signals for the receiver.

In most networks, you'll also find a variety of other, more complicated, communications processors that perform a wide range of functions. These communications processors include multiplexers, cluster controllers, front-end processors, and internetworking units.

Multiplexers

Multiplexers aggregate several communications media and allow them to share a single communications medium that operates at a much higher capacity (see Figure 6.12). Multiplexers are used in pairs; one multiplexer combines communications at one site and the other separates the communications at the other site. Multiplexers are extremely cost effective if there are many computers in one geographic area that need to communicate with a computer in another geographic area.

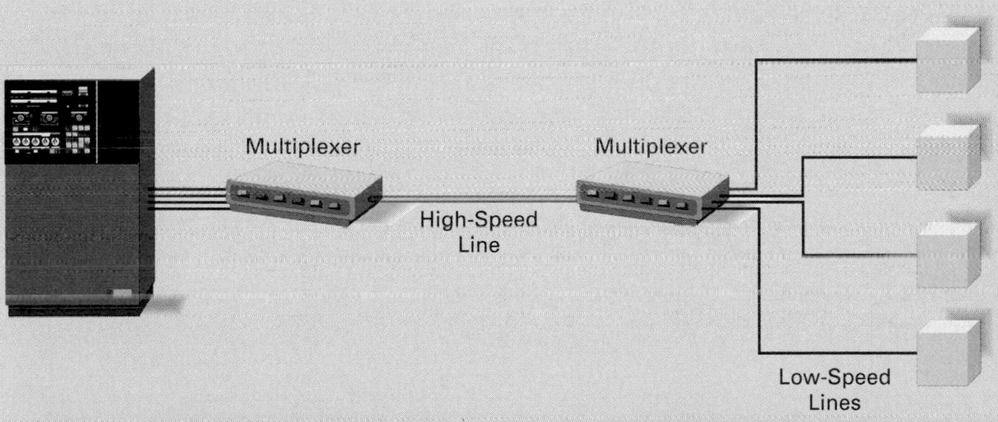

Front-End Processors

Front-end processors are special computers that handle the communications function for a host computer or server in a network (see Figure 6.14). In a network without a front-end processor, the host computer or server is responsible for handling information-processing tasks (data management, logic, and presentation) and communicating with all the other computers. This communication responsibility can lead to greatly decreased processing performance. If this is the case, a front-end processor is used to relieve the host computer of its communications responsibility.

Internetworking Units

Most networks of any size are actually combinations of smaller networks. And many of these smaller networks may be of the same type; others may have different topologies, communicate using different methods (discussed in a moment), and come from different vendors. Whatever the case, **internetworking units** are special hardware devices that connect two or more networks. The three common types of internetworking units include bridges, routers, and gateways (see Figure 6.15 on p. 243). The choice of which internetworking unit to use depends on the similarities and differences of the networks you need to connect.

Multiplexer   Multiplexer

High-Speed Line

Low-Speed Lines

FIGURE 6.12

Multiplexing Communications

Cluster Controllers

Cluster controllers also manage a group of devices that share a single high-speed communications medium connected to another location (see Figure 6.13). Cluster controllers, however, differ from multiplexers in that they do not combine and separate communications. They merely handle the communication congestion and competition for the single high-speed communications medium the devices share.

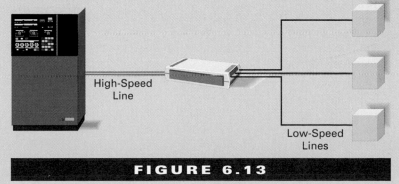

High-Speed Line

Low-Speed Lines

FIGURE 6.13

Cluster Controller

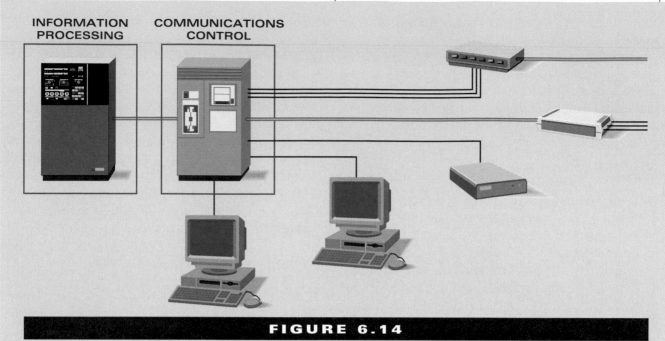

INFORMATION PROCESSING   COMMUNICATIONS CONTROL

FIGURE 6.14

Separating the Processing and Communication Workload

A **bridge** connects two networks of the same kind, such as two IBM networks that use a ring topology. Because the networks are the same, the bridge acts only to pass communications between the networks. A **router** connects networks that are somewhat dissimilar with respect to certain communications aspects, such as how computers are addressed and the size of messages sent. A router, for example, may be used to connect star and bus topology networks.

Finally, **gateways** connect networks that are completely dissimilar with respect to how they work and communicate internally. For example, a gateway would be used to connect an Apple LAN to an IBM LAN. In fact, the Internet—which gives anyone, regardless of chosen technology, the ability to see and work with the same information in the same format—connects networks all over the world using gateway internetworking units. ❖

TABLE 6.1 Public and Private Network Issues

Cost	Availability	Services	Speed	Security
Private				
Own—acquisition, installation, and maintenance Lease—fixed rate per time period (usually monthly)	No competition for use	Can have additional services beyond simply communicating information	Typically faster than public networks	Higher than that of public networks
Public				
Pay-as-you-go basis for time and use	Must compete for use	Only the ability to communicate information from one place to another	Typically slower than private networks	Little or no guarantee of privacy

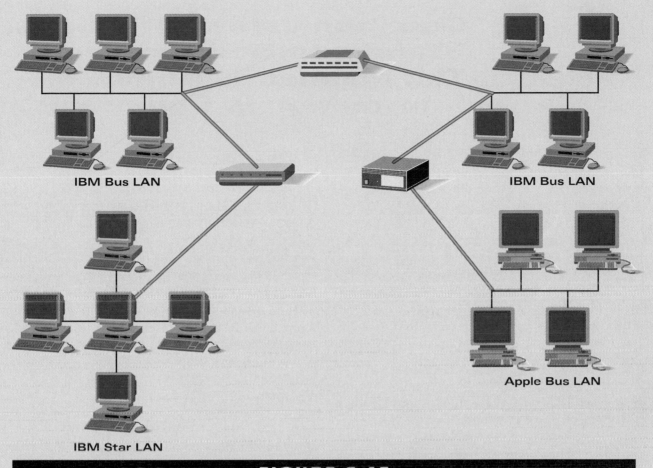

IBM Bus LAN

IBM Bus LAN

IBM Star LAN

Apple Bus LAN

FIGURE 6.15
Connecting Networks with Internetworking Units

distance, your organization may still need exclusive rights to use communications media but doesn't want to actually own them. In that case, you can lease dedicated lines from a communications service provider. Thus you're guaranteed to always have that line available to you. When leasing dedicated lines to support a private network, your organization (see Table 6.1)

1. Pays a flat fee per month for the leased line (cost)

2. Is guaranteed time and use of the line (availability)

3. Can typically request additional communications services beyond just moving information from one location to another (service)

4. Communicates information at a higher speed as compared to public networks (speed)

5. Has a higher guarantee of privacy as compared to public networks (security)

The issue of network ownership, however, grows ever more confusing and vague as each day passes. It once was a simple matter of choosing between (1) owning or exclusively leasing the communications media used to connect network components or (2) using public network systems and competing for time and use with all organizations using the same network. Today, however, choosing between private and public network ownership is not so simple. Now your organization can also choose from value-added networks and virtual private networks. Each of these—in some form or fashion—resembles aspects of both private and public networks and offers additional communications services.

Value-Added Networks
A *value-added network (VAN)* is a semipublic network that provides additional services beyond the simple communication of information from one place to another.

(continued on page 246)

Communications Methods, Standards, and Protocols: The Manner in Which Information Is Communicated

In a network environment, rules must be established for governing the manner in which information moves from one place to another. We group these rules into the general category of *communications methods, standards, and protocols.* Communications methods, standards, and protocols constitute the most technically complex aspect of telecommunications and networks. Here we simply provide a broad overview of some of the more important and widely used methods, standards, and protocols.

Ethernet and Token Ring

Ethernet Ethernet is a communications standard for connecting components in a LAN. It uses a shared communications medium (such as a bus topology). In an Ethernet environment, each network component constantly monitors the communications medium for traffic. When a transmission is broadcast throughout the network, each component determines whether it is the intended recipient. If it is, it accepts the transmission; if it's not, it disregards the transmission. When a network component must send a transmission, it first listens to the communications medium for traffic. If the communications medium is idle, the network component broadcasts its transmission. If the communications medium is busy, the network component waits until the medium is available.

Token ring Token ring is another communications standard for LANs. In a token ring environment, a single electronic token or "clipboard" is passed among the network components, with each component taking its turn to use the token. If the token contains a transmission, the receiving network component determines whether it is the intended recipient. If it is, it accepts the transmission and passes on the token with a receipt acknowledgment. If it's not, it passes the token on around.

FDDI

Fiber distributed data interface (FDDI) FDDI is a communications standard for connecting high-speed LANs or links among geographically dispersed LANs. FDDI incorporates a ring topology, token passing, and two communications media that transmit in different directions (see Figure 6.16). One ring provides the primary communications path; the second ring is used in case the first ring fails. FDDI most often uses optical fiber as the communications medium, making it extremely fast.

ATM

Asynchronous transfer mode (ATM) ATM is a transmission method for sending information that divides a long transmission into smaller units (called "packets"). These packets are then sent over the network (often traveling different paths) and reassembled at the destination. For example, if you're using a multimedia application stored on a server, the server might break the multimedia application into packets containing video, text, and sound. The server would transmit them over the network to you, where your client workstation would reassemble the application and present it to you (see Figure 6.17).

ISDN, TCP/IP, and X.12

Integrated services digital network (ISDN) ISDN is both the plan and the international communications standard for the transition of the world's public telephone system from analog to digital for the purpose of transmitting all formats of information (voice, video, text, and so on) simultaneously over twisted-pair telephone lines. Most current telephone systems are severely limited in the amount of information they can transmit, the speed of the transmission, their reliability,

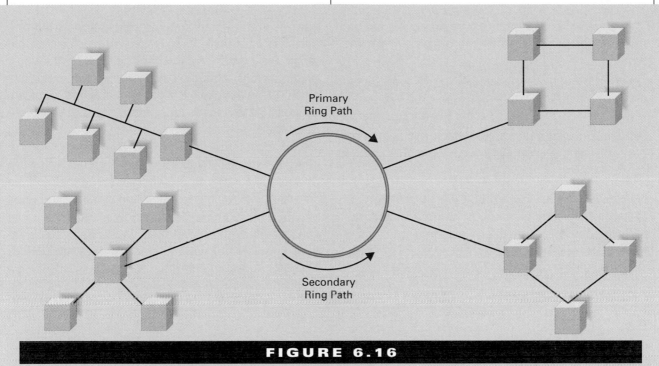

FIGURE 6.16

Fiber Distributed Data Interface (FDDI) to Connect Local Area Networks

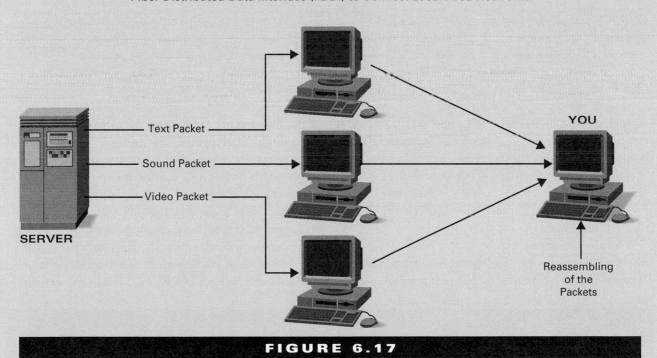

FIGURE 6.17

Asynchronous Transfer Mode (ATM) for Networking Multimedia

and the services they provide. ISDN is the blueprint for transmitting all forms of information 10 to 30 times faster than today's speeds and handling multiple applications simultaneously on the same line.

Transmission control protocol/Internet protocol (TCP/IP) TCP/IP is actually the standard by which the Internet works today. Developed originally to work on the predecessor to the Internet—the ARPANET—TCP/IP today enjoys wide acceptance and support as the primary method for transmitting information over the Internet.

X.12 X.12 (sometimes represented as X12, without the period) is the standard for transmitting common-formatted information during electronic data interchange (EDI). When we discuss electronic commerce in an upcoming section, we'll focus on EDI as well as how X.12 fits in.

We could fill an entire book with discussions of other communications methods, standards, and protocols. Among those, we might include discussions of CSMA/CD, OSI, SNA, X.400, X.25, X.12 Edifact, SONET, CDDI, RS-232, ISO 7498, and ADSL. So what does all this mean to you? Why is it important to know that various communications methods, standards, and protocols exist? Why exactly are you reading this material? The answer is quite simple. It's not so that you'll memorize the "alphabet soup" of telecommunications or be able to define which standard, method, or protocol you'll need. What's most important is that you understand that there are a variety of ways to send information across a network. The best choice depends on your ability to effectively communicate your business needs. If you can do that, then a networking specialist will be able to determine whether you need an Ethernet, token ring, or some other standard. If you can't clearly communicate your business needs, then who knows what will happen? Always remember, business needs should drive the technical specifications of networks, not vice versa. ❖

Similar to a public network, a VAN is owned and operated by a communications service provider and is used by many organizations. Similar to a private network, a VAN provides services beyond the communication of information, typically operates at a greater speed than public networks, and offers higher security than public networks.

Valued-added is the most important aspect of a VAN. For example, if your organization needs EDI capabilities with various suppliers and customers around the world, you can choose to create your own network by purchasing all the necessary network hardware and software, leasing private lines from various communications service providers, and developing the software for handling the necessary conversions associated with the EDI transmission of information (most likely in the X.12 format). If you require this capability, then you've chosen to create a private network.

However, your organization may find that this is simply unfeasible—economically, technically, or otherwise.

So you can choose to pay for the services of a VAN. For example, you might choose to use General Electric Information Services' value-added network. GE created this VAN several years ago and already has in place the necessary communications media and software for handling the EDI transmission of information. It's really just a simple matter of developing interfaces between (1) your system and GE's VAN and (2) your customers' and suppliers' systems and GE's VAN. GE takes care of all the rest—always assuring that you have communications capability among various countries' communication services providers (if you need international communications capabilities), establishing mail boxes for EDI transmissions, and so on.

When you choose to use a VAN, your organization will most often pay for the service according to the amount of information it sends. This is another significant advantage of VANs. Instead of paying for the guarantee of the availability of a dedicated line, as you would

TABLE 6.2 Value-Added and Virtual Private Network Issues

Cost	Availability	Services	Speed	Security
Value-Added Network				
Pay-as-you-go basis for time and use	No competition for use	VAN owner provides additional services	Typically faster than a public network	Higher than that of public networks
Virtual Private Network				
Flat fee per month plus fee for time used	No competition for use	VPN owner provides limited additional services	Typically faster than a public network	Higher than that of public networks

in a private network, you essentially work on a pay-as-you-go basis, as in a public network. Table 6.2 summarizes the characteristics of a VAN according to cost, availability, services, speed, and security.

Virtual Private Networks

Virtual private networks are a relatively recent addition to the ownership issue of networks. A *virtual private network (VPN)* is a public network that guarantees availability to your organization, but does not provide you with a dedicated line or with communications media. Instead, your information travels with a myriad of other information from other organizations. In this instance, the VPN provider offers your organization the services of data encryption to provide a guarantee of privacy. When using a VPN, your organization (see Table 6.2)

❶ Pays a flat fee per month plus a fee for time used (cost)

❷ Is guaranteed availability, but not in the form of a dedicated line (availability)

❸ Typically receives some additional communications services, such as data encryption (service)

❹ Communicates information at a higher speed compared to public networks (speed)

❺ Has a higher guarantee of privacy compared to public networks (security)

VPNs are becoming particularly prevalent on the Internet as organizations attempt to perform electronic commerce functions across the Internet. Most important, an *Internet virtual private network (Internet VPN)* provides your organization with a way of establishing a *virtual* Internet network that consists of only you, your customers, and suppliers. Additionally, Internet VPNs provide security measures, which make transmissions such as credit card information more secure across the Internet. Internet VPNs will become increasingly important in the coming years. According to one survey, the number of Internet-based business transactions is expected to double every year for the next several years.[16] And 75 percent of the Fortune 1,000 companies have said that they plan to extend their use of the Internet from a simple extension of the marketing department to a medium for conducting real business. Figure 6.18 also shows the projected revenues for all VPN providers through the year 2005.

Almost every national telephone service provider (Baby Bells, AT&T, MCI, Sprint, and so on) offers domestic VPN services. But many organizations have communications needs that extend beyond domestic boundaries. If your organization is one of these, then you can use the service of an *international virtual private network (international VPN)*—virtual private networks that combine the capabilities of telephone service providers around the world.

International VPNs are not the offering of a single organization. Rather, international VPNs are offered by alliances of several organizations that have telecommunications interests in various countries around the world. The three most dominant alliances include Concert, Phoenix, and Worldpartners.[17] Concert Communications Co. is an alliance that includes British Telecom and MCI Communications. Phoenix is an alliance of three major telecommunications providers—Deutsche Telekom AG (Germany), France Telecom, and Sprint. Finally, Worldpartners is the largest international VPN provider and includes AT&T, Kokusai Denshim Denwa (Japan), Singapore Telecom, and Unisource, which itself is an alliance of telecommunications providers from the Netherlands, Spain, Sweden, and Switzerland.

International VPNs are particularly important for transnational operations. Organizations that are transnational and need international communications capabilities previously faced the challenge of dealing with numerous phone service providers in different countries and receiving bills in many forms of currencies. Today, transnational companies simply

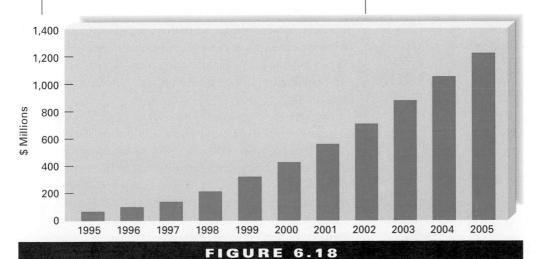

FIGURE 6.18

Projected Revenues for All Virtual Private Network Providers[18]

Assessing the Benefits of Networks by Ownership

Complete the table below by rank ordering private, public, value-added, and virtual private networks according to cost, availability, services, speed, and security. For example, identify the network that provides the greatest security with a "1" and the network that provides the least security with a "4." In some instances, your answers will depend on the particular business function the network will support. In these instances, be prepared to justify your answers with a real or hypothetical business example. ❖

Networks	Cost	Availability	Services	Speed	Security
Private					
Public					
Value-Added					
Virtual Private					

use the services of a single international VPN provider. In this way, the international VPN provider performs all the negotiating across international boundaries and bills organizations in the currency of their choice.

Electronic Commerce
Performing Network-Enabled Business

Electronic commerce is all about performing business functions electronically or with the aid of technology. In fact, this whole book is about electronic commerce. That is, all our discussions have focused on how to use information technology to support functions that occur in business. Consider these examples:

- Transaction processing systems
- Executive information systems
- Interorganizational systems
- Databases and database management systems
- Data warehouses and data mining tools
- Neural networks
- Group decision support systems

Each technology-related topic we've discussed focuses on how to use that technology to support electronic commerce.

Let's now consider electronic commerce within the context of networks, network technologies, and network concepts. After all, we are in the information age, and networks support telecommunications—the electronic movement of information from one location to another. First, let's review our definition of electronic commerce from Chapter 1.

> **Electronic commerce** is a modern methodology that addresses the use of information technology as an essential enabler of business. Electronic commerce supports both internal and external business functions. That is, **external electronic commerce** addresses the use of information technology to support how a business interacts with the marketplace, and **internal electronic commerce** addresses the use of information technology to support internal processes, functions, and operations.

This definition encompasses two themes: (1) information technology in support of how a business interacts with the marketplace and (2) information technology in support of internal processes, functions, and operations (see Figure 6.19).

So electronic commerce *really* is all about performing business functions electronically or with the aid of technology. It doesn't matter whether you're processing payroll checks or setting up a Web site on the Internet. If you're using technology to do business, you're performing electronic commerce. From your organization's point of view, it also means being able to electronically order products and services from other organizations, give other organizations the ability to electronically order products and services from you, move money electronically, reach

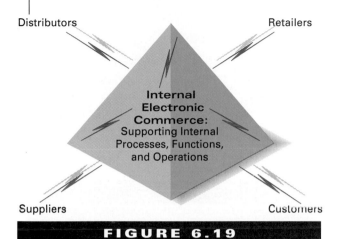

External Electronic Commerce:
Interacting with the Marketplace

Distributors

Retailers

Internal Electronic Commerce: Supporting Internal Processes, Functions, and Operations

Suppliers

Customers

FIGURE 6.19

External and Internal Electronic Commerce

customers through electronic advertising, have employees work together while in different locations, use technology to aid in designing and producing products, and perform a host of other business activities using technology.

Unfortunately, we can't cover every aspect of electronic commerce in this text. However, we do want to alert you to some key aspects of electronic commerce—both internal and external—that offer your organization a real competitive advantage, including the following:

- Ordering products and services ————
- Moving money without handling it
- Reaching the exact customer
- Gathering competitive intelligence ————
  External electronic commerce
- Intranets ———— Internal electronic commerce
- Telecommuting ————

In previous chapters we've already introduced ordering products and services through electronic data interchange and the concept of telecommuting. These two topics deserve a second look within the context of networks, while we introduce you to several other aspects of electronic commerce.

Electronic Data Interchange

Ordering Products and Services Electronically

One of the most important and widely used forms of electronic commerce is that of moving information electronically between two organizations as one organization orders products and services from another

organization. In Chapter 2 we introduced this electronic movement of information as an interorganizational system (IOS). In this type of IOS, two organizations use electronic data interchange to electronically move information. ***Electronic data interchange (EDI)*** is the direct computer-to-computer transfer of transaction information contained in standard business documents, such as invoices and purchase orders, in a standard format.

Using EDI, organizations simply eliminate the flow of standard business paper documents between them. This reduces the time it takes to move information and the cost associated with handling paper documents. The most important aspect of EDI is that of developing a standard format by which information will be transferred. This is true because EDI can transfer information directly from one computer to another without human intervention. Earlier, we introduced you to the X.12 standard, and X.12 is the standard format used today for EDI.

Suppose, for example, that your organization uses EDI to order raw materials from a supplier. Internally, your IT systems (such as order processing, material requirements planning, and production scheduling) would capture, process, and determine your raw materials needs (see Figure 6.20). When communicating that information to your supplier, you would first convert it into the X.12 standard, then send it electronically to your supplier. The supplier's system would accept the information (in X.12 format), convert it into the appropriate form for internal use, and distribute that information to such departments as accounts receivable, warehousing, and distribution.

EDI is of fundamental importance to your organization. Not only does it save time and money, it's also becoming the standard for interorganizational transactions. Most businesses today—regardless of size—have EDI links with suppliers, customers, retailers, and distributors. Many of these organizations have so fully embraced EDI that they won't do business with an organization that doesn't have similar EDI capabilities. EDI is also important to your organization because it supports many of the strategies for achieving a competitive advantage, which we discussed in Chapter 3. For example, most organizations that use a JIT (just-in-time) approach incorporate EDI when ordering from suppliers. In the instance of JIT, EDI reduces the amount of lead time associated with ordering from other organizations. Additionally, most virtual organizations use EDI to electronically move information between the partnering organizations. In fact, the ability to move information electronically from one place to another—of which EDI is a part—is the foundation on which many virtual organizations are built.

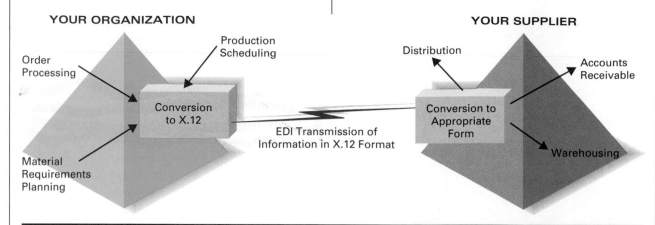

YOUR ORGANIZATION

Order Processing

Production Scheduling

Conversion to X.12

Material Requirements Planning

EDI Transmission of Information in X.12 Format

YOUR SUPPLIER

Distribution

Accounts Receivable

Conversion to Appropriate Form

Warehousing

FIGURE 6.20

Electronic Data Interchange (EDI) and X.12

Electronic Funds Transfer

Moving Money Without Handling It

Electronic funds transfer (EFT)—also called "financial EDI"—refers to the electronic passing of funds (money) between businesses and banks and their customers. EFT is the same day, almost instantaneous, electronic movement of money between banks that represents financial transactions between organizations. To better understand the benefits of EFT and how it works, let's look at how labor-intensive it is to handle your personal checks without EFT. As a customer, suppose you write a check to Dillard's department store when you purchase a new pair of shoes (see Figure 6.21). Dillard's deposits your check at its bank (which we'll call First Bank); First Bank

INDUSTRY PERSPECTIVE

Retail

Peapod Gets Customer Integrated with Electronic Commerce

Ordering products electronically sometimes makes great sense. It's relatively straightforward and simple to order music CDs, clothing, or a variety of other products electronically. But what about ordering ice cream, frozen pizzas, or near-ripe bananas from a local grocer?

For most of us, grocery shopping tends to be very personal. We want a certain kind of cereal, we buy only fat-free hot dogs, we buy chips only when they're on sale, and so on. These personalized buying habits have led many to believe that most people aren't willing to buy groceries electronically. But Andrew and Thomas Perkins—the founders of Peapod—think otherwise, and they've set up a customer integrated system (CIS) for grocery shoppers who would rather stay at home.

Peapod's customers pay a $6.95 monthly fee to access Peapod's online grocery network. Then they pay another $6.95 for delivery, plus a 5 percent premium over the cost of the groceries. And how does Peapod maintain "personalized" grocery buying habits? Well, customers can set up regular shopping lists and simply check off what they want. While online, customers browse stores by aisle, check the nutritional information on each product, and find special offers. Customers can even request three extremely ripe bananas, two near-ripe bananas, and two pounds of green bananas.

Is it working? Absolutely. Peapod now has 8,000 regular customers in Chicago and 2,000 in the San Francisco Bay Area. Peapod also guarantees delivery within 90 minutes, which means the pizza and ice cream will still be frozen.[19, 20] ❖

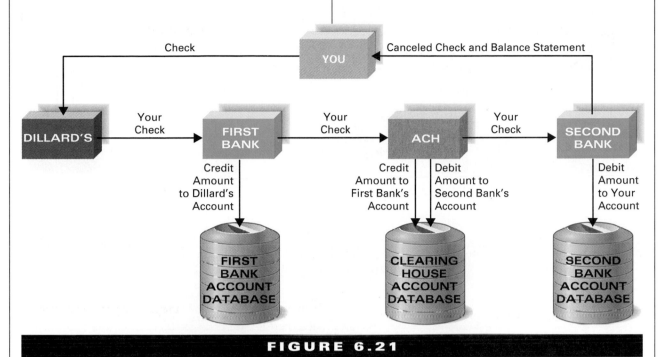

FIGURE 6.21

Your Check as It Travels

processes the check internally—crediting Dillard's account for the appropriate amount—then forwards your check to an automated clearinghouse.

An *automated clearinghouse (ACH)* is an intermediary organization that handles the electronic movement of money between two banks. Within the ACH, each bank (that subscribes to its service) pledges collateral to ensure the settlement of money transfers. In our example, the ACH would electronically credit the collateral account of First Bank and debit the collateral account of your bank—Second Bank. The ACH then forwards your check to your bank. Second Bank debits your account for the appropriate amount and then sends you your canceled check with a balance statement at the end of the month. If you don't have enough money in your account, your bank will assess you an overdraft charge and return your check to the ACH. The ACH reverses its previous process, credits your bank's (Second Bank) account, debits First Bank's account, and returns the check to First Bank. First Bank then must debit Dillard's account and return the check to Dillard's, which is then responsible for collecting its money from you.

This process is time and labor intensive. Your check, throughout the process, must be handled by many people in different organizations. This process is **not** an example of EFT between you (as the customer) and Dillard's. The goal of EFT is to eliminate this movement of physical instruments (your check in this case) between banks, automated clearinghouses, organizations, and

customers. This obviously will eliminate much of the time and labor involved in processing a check.

Now, let's revisit the same process using for our example General Motors, one of its parts suppliers, EDI, EFT, and a VAN (see Figure 6.22). Since 1982, GM has been using a VAN, EDI, and EFT to collect payments from dealers and make payments to its suppliers.[21] In 1993 alone, GM made over 700,000 EFT payments to its suppliers, valued at over $38 billion. When GM needs parts from a supplier, it sends the appropriate request information in EDI format through a VAN. Once the supplier receives the information, it begins the process of moving the parts to GM and sends GM information in EDI format back through the VAN verifying the parts shipped and the amount GM owes.

GM then submits an electronic payment authorization to one of its banks (we'll call it First Bank). First Bank debits GM's account and forwards the electronic payment authorization to an ACH. The ACH debits First Bank's account and credits Second Bank's account (the supplier's bank). The ACH then forwards the electronic payment authorization to Second Bank, which credits the supplier's account and sends an electronic payment settlement notice to the supplier.

The GM example is one of *true* electronic commerce. Information pertaining to requested parts, parts shipped, amount owed, payment authorization, and payment settlement notice is all moved electronically between organizations—absolutely no paper is used. And the transfer

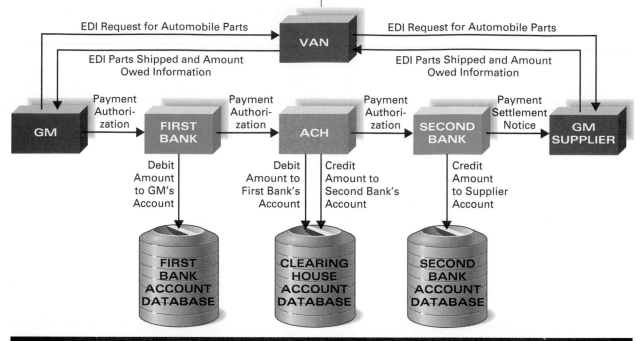

FIGURE 6.22
General Motors and Electronic Funds Transfer

of money between those involved is handled electronically through EFT.

Individualized Electronic Advertising

Reaching the Exact Customer

Imagine this scenario. Several years from now, you get up in the morning, start the coffee, and, instead of going outside to get your paper, you turn on your computer to read the morning news. Your electronic version of a newspaper appears on the screen with highlights of topics you're interested in. You've programmed your electronic newspaper to display only those articles of interest by topic, scores and stories of the NFL and not college football, and any articles relating to Little League baseball games in your part of town. What you also get is a special individualized advertising section. In it you find several ads for new cars because yours is 5 years old. You also find advertisements for products you commonly purchase at the grocery store, and those advertisements are all for the grocery stores within a 5-mile radius of your home.

The Toronto Stock Exchange Gets "Virtual" with EDI and EFT

In an effort to create the first worldwide virtual trading floor, the Toronto Stock Exchange is embracing technology, specifically electronic data interchange and electronic funds transfer. Under a proposed system called the Canadian Automated Trading System (CATS), electronic data interchange will be used to receive stock-trading information from and transmit verification information to trading firms all over the world. No longer will trading firms have buyers and sellers on the floor who negotiate prices and deals.

At the end of each day, CATS will reconcile the financial position of each trading firm and notify firms of the balance they owe or the balance they are to receive. Then CATS will use EFT to transfer money to or receive money from each firm, depending on its respective financial position. All information will be electronically moved, as will all money.[22] ❖

THE GLOBAL PERSPECTIVE

Seem odd or even astounding? Not really. Many people predict that newspapers will appear this way in the near future. You'll be able to customize your newspaper so that it shows only stories you want to see, and your newspaper will contain only advertisements that are pertinent to you. Let's think about this type of advertising for a moment. Why would you receive car ads? Well, your car is 5 years old, and car dealers know that people typically purchase a new automobile every 5 years. And why did you receive ads from grocery stores within only a 5-mile radius? Well, grocery stores know that people shop for groceries at stores located in close proximity. This is a form of ***individualized electronic advertising***—using technology to determine who gets what advertisements and electronically sending those advertisements to only those people.

Individualized electronic advertising differs radically from other forms of advertising, such as television and radio. Suppose you own a pizza delivery operation. You can, for example, advertise on TV during a football game (more pizzas are purchased during football games than any other televised sporting event). But what you can't do is customize that advertisement for people who prefer vegetarian-style pizzas. With real individualized electronic advertising, however, you can electronically send ads for vegetarian-style pizzas to those homes occupied by vegetarians. How would you know where to send those ads? It's simple—you've got a record of all pizzas ordered by household in your database.

Individualized electronic advertising is basically a two-step process (see Figure 6.23). First, an individualized advertising system sifts through databases—containing customer, sales, and product information—to determine individual customers and their exact buying

habits. Second, the system electronically distributes individualized advertisements to those people through the Internet. The real keys to your organization's ability to perform individualized electronic advertising are (1) extensive databases that contain customer buying habits and (2) the presence of computers in the households of people to whom you want to send individualized advertising. The first key is already a reality for most organizations: today organizations track a variety of information pertaining to their customers. The second key—computers in every household—will probably not become a reality for several years. But that doesn't mean organizations should postpone planning for this type of electronic commerce activity.

In business, advertising can result in either a huge increase in sales or static sales (which means that your advertising efforts were a failure). Your organization's success in advertising depends on what you know about your market and how effectively you can reach different segments within the market. As businesses begin to more fully exploit electronic commerce, knowing customers and reaching them without paper (individualized electronic advertising) will surface as a key business and strategic issue.

Knowing More Than Your Competitors
Gathering Competitive Intelligence

In today's information-based environment, knowledge is a key to success. Knowing who your customers are and what they want, knowing what your products cost to make, and knowing what your competitors are doing (or

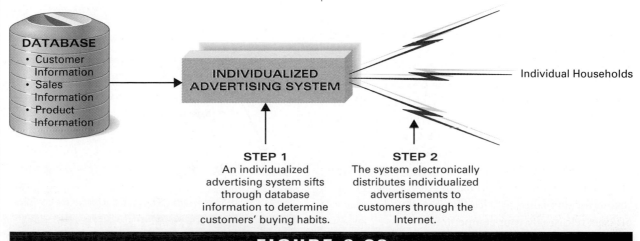

DATABASE
• Customer Information
• Sales Information
• Product Information

INDIVIDUALIZED ADVERTISING SYSTEM

Individual Households

STEP 1
An individualized advertising system sifts through database information to determine customers' buying habits.

STEP 2
The system electronically distributes individualized advertisements to customers through the Internet.

FIGURE 6.23

The Two-Step Process to Performing Individualized Electronic Advertising

Inns & Outs Is the Internet Source for Bed & Breakfast Information

In 1995, Eric Goldreyer recognized the Internet as an excellent place to conduct electronic commerce. But Eric didn't want to sell a product. He used the Internet to provide an advertising service for bed and breakfast inns all over the United States (including Hawaii and Alaska), Canada, Mexico, and the Caribbean. With Eric's service, bed and breakfast inns can advertise on the Internet and instantly reach the 40 million plus people cruising the Internet every day.

For you, Eric's service (http://www.innsandouts.com) is completely free. Once there, you can obtain vacation information on more than 15,000 bed and breakfast inns. For each inn, you can find photos, price ranges, pet policies, and current information on area attractions, special events, and sightseeing opportunities.

You'll also have real-time chatting capabilities and be able to register to win an all-expenses-paid bed and breakfast vacation getaway. Check it out and sign up for your free vacation. You might just win.

Eric's site is a special form of individualized electronic advertising that many organizations are performing on the Internet. Like Eric, these organizations offer one-stop electronic advertising for common products and services. ❖

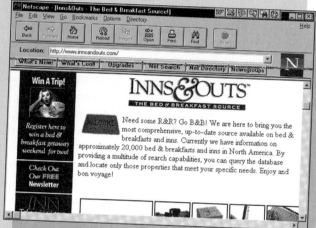

planning to do) are all keys to success in business. All this information is part of competitive intelligence. ***Competitive intelligence*** is simply information about the internal workings of your organization as well as the external market surrounding your organization. For external market information, most organizations focus a great deal of their efforts on gathering competitive intelligence about their competitors.

So how do networks enable you to gather this type of competitive intelligence? In many ways. Consider this. If your organization is concerned that a competing organization is about to introduce a new product, you can access external databases that contain information about patents pending with the federal government. In those databases, you can search information to learn whether your competitor has applied for a patent on a new product in the last 6 months. You can also access Lexis-Nexis (an electronic database provided by Reed Elsevier) and search for published articles that may detail any new product releases by your competitor.

Another great way to gather competitive intelligence using networks is to access your competitors' Web sites.

Many organizations today are using the Internet to inform their customers of upcoming product releases (see Figure 6.24). It might surprise you that many of these

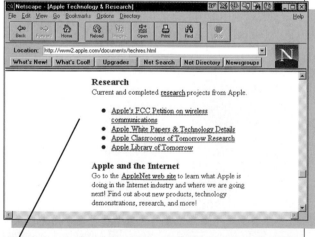

Like many organizations, Apple publishes much of its work in progress on the Internet. Sites like these are great places to gather competitive intelligence.

FIGURE 6.24

Learning about Your Competition on the Internet

organizations are so excited about letting customers know what's upcoming that they sometimes publish very sensitive information on the Internet. This method of gathering competitive intelligence has given rise to a new job in business—*Internet cruisers*. Organizations are now paying people to cruise the Internet every day to learn what the competition is doing and saying.

Many organizations have come up with even more interesting ways of using technology to gather competitive intelligence. Frito Lay is a good example. When Frito Lay's stockers enter a retail store to replenish shelf supplies, they use a handheld computer to record what the competition is doing—the amount of shelf space, the number of products, any new products, and the total number of items on the shelf. This information is then transmitted by way of technology to the home office, where marketing specialists attempt to determine exactly what the competition is doing and to develop strategies for beating the competition in the marketplace.

Whether you're gathering competitive intelligence about your competitors, customers, or internal processes, it falls within the category of electronic commerce if you do it by way of technology. And gathering competitive intelligence today is an important business activity. Remember, what you don't know can put you out of business.

Intranets
The Internet Within

For many organizations, the Internet represents a great way to easily, quickly, and inexpensively connect to customers, suppliers, distributors, and retailers all over the world. By simply setting up a Web site full of advertisements, product information, and product ordering capabilities, your organization can reach millions of people and organizations around the world. But you can also use the Internet to connect people within your organization, no matter where they are.

And many organizations today are doing just that. To do so, these organizations are developing intranets. An *intranet* is an internal organizational Internet that is guarded against outside access by special security software (see Figure 6.25). We call the special security software that protects against outside access a *firewall*. In Chapter 2 we introduced US West's intranet, the *Global Village*. US West's intranet allows 15,000 employees to meet in online chat rooms, exchange documents, discuss ongoing projects, and conduct virtual meetings with staff located in remote geographic areas.

US West, and hundreds of other organizations, have created intranets for several reasons. First and most notably, the Internet already connects millions of people all over the world, so why not internalize the Internet for internal connectivity? Second, firewalls provide vitally important security measures to prevent people outside the organization from accessing strategic and sensitive information that may be placed on an intranet. You can also set up firewall software so that employees within your organization can't gain outside Internet access. In fact, many organizations have done this to keep employees from checking out cool Web sites instead of performing their real job responsibilities. On the following page we've listed a few organizations and what they're doing with intranets.

ON YOUR OWN

Gathering Competitive Intelligence for a New Business

Suppose you want to open a restaurant and need to know what the competition is like. Well, it's simple enough to find out. There are a variety of sites on the Internet that describe restaurants and favorite dining spots in most major cities.

Choose the type of restaurant you'd like to open (for example, Cajun or Chinese), choose a city with at least 500,000 people, and explore on the Internet to gather competitive intelligence. As you do, answer the following questions:

1. Why type of restaurant did you choose?
2. What city did you choose?
3. What Web sites did you find for gathering competitive intelligence?
4. Did you find enough information to make a decision?
5. What other forms of competitive intelligence would you probably need to gather besides a list of competing restaurants?

Don't give up if you initially don't find any Web sites that offer the information you want. The information is somewhere—keep surfing. ❖

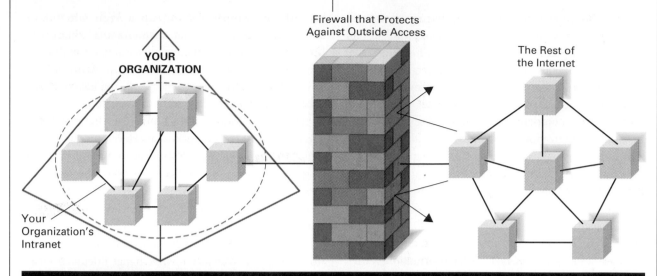

FIGURE 6.25

An Organizational Intranet—the Internet Within

- The Los Alamos National Laboratory set up an intranet for only $250,000.[23] On the intranet, Los Alamos publishes some 10 million internal classified, technical, and administrative documents. Los Alamos estimates that it will save over $500,000 per year in printing and distribution costs by making this information available electronically.

- Bechtel Group, a $7.9 billion architecture giant, has created an intranet called the Global Knowledge Network (GKN).[24] On the GKN, Bechtel posts mission-critical, organizationwide information, including three-dimensional designs of proposed facilities that anyone (internally) can access as a virtual reality simulation, walking through virtual corridors, climbing virtual stairs, and taking rides on virtual elevators and escalators.

- At Tyson Foods, cooking up an intranet makes simple business sense.[25] Donny Drummonds, Tyson's Internet administrator, created an intranet that over 5,000 employees with Web browser software access to see phone directories, lists of employees in each department, e-mail address books, and an MIS training schedule for knowledge worker classes.

Providing Outsiders with Access to Internal Intranets

Many organizations are setting up intranets, just like Los Alamos, Bechtel, and Tyson, to give employees the ability to access organizationwide information and to communicate with each other. But many other organizations are actually allowing outside people and organizations to access internal intranets. Visa International Inc. is an example of an organization opening up its intranet to outside organizations.[26] Previous to providing outside intranet access, Visa sent over 19,000 member banks diskettes containing fraud alert and marketing information. Now each member bank is given a password that bypasses the firewall security system. Once in, a bank can check the status of a transaction electronically or access certain customer information. Many of these processes once took more than a day to complete manually. Today, banks can perform them in a matter of seconds.

When your organization provides outside access to an intranet, you've created an *extranet*—a special application that allows other organizations and people access to information published on an intranet. Extranet applications are becoming particularly prevalent on the Internet as organizations attempt to capitalize on the worldwide connectivity to customers and suppliers. Besides the necessary passwords to protect against unauthorized outside access, most organizations employ the services of an Internet VPN provider when setting up extranet applications. The Internet VPN provider basically (1) guarantees the availability and speed of an Internet connection from one place to another and (2) provides vitally important data encryption software to ensure the privacy and security of the Internet-traveling information.

Other organizations are creating extranet applications to support the concept of a virtual organization. One such virtual organization is the Direct Marketing Resource Collaborative (DMRC), a virtual division of direct-mail specialist WA Wilde Inc.[27] DMRC's goal is to connect freelance marketing specialists with clients requiring marketing expertise. By setting up an extranet,

DMRC gives the freelance marketing specialists access to client information. In secure chat rooms, freelancers can have virtual meetings with clients to discuss marketing promotions, advertising media, and campaign costs. Creating an extranet application like this has given DMRC the ability to create a virtual organization of freelance marketing specialists who may work on many projects but are never really employees of DMRC.

What's So Great about Intranets?

If you step back and think about organizational intranets, you may think, "Wow—intranets are great! They let an organization securely communicate information among employees, and they even provide for controlled outside access." Indeed, these are important reasons why intranets are becoming so popular. But to understand the true allure of intranets, you first need to understand why the Internet is so great. If you ask people, they'll offer many reasons— the ability to share information, connectivity among 75 million people worldwide, cool Web sites, and numerous others. But the real reason the Internet is so popular is

because it's completely *platform independent*. It doesn't matter what kind of hardware you have (IBM, Apple, DEC, or UNISYS), what kind of operating system you're running (Windows NT, System 7, UNIX, OS/2, VMS, or Windows '98), or even what size of computer you have (laptop, desktop, workstation, minicomputer, mainframe, or even super computer), you can still use the Internet.

That's a substantial advantage for businesses today. In the past, organizations wrestled with how to connect different hardware and how to get different operating systems to work together. The Internet has eliminated most of those obstacles. With its relatively simple technology, based on open systems connectivity and TCP/IP, the Internet has become a way to connect all people, regardless of the technology platform. The same is true for intranets. Anyone who has a Web browser can access intranet-stored information—even people outside your organization (if they have password access). So intranets are a great way to easily, quickly, and inexpensively communicate information. But the real reason intranets are so great is because they work on Internet-based technologies, something most people and organizations already have.

INDUSTRY PERSPECTIVE   **Entertainment & Publishing**

Geffen Records Rocks and Rolls on the Internet and Its Intranet

Can you imagine an organization spending 100 percent of its IT budget on just the Internet and an intranet? That's what Geffen Records has done— its entire IT budget is earmarked for supporting its Internet Web site and an internal company intranet.

If you visit Geffen's Web site (http://www.geffen.com), you can read about your favorite artists and bands, sample new releases of albums, and even send fan mail to your favorite band. That's exactly what Geffen was hoping to do with

its Web site—attract potential customers. But Geffen also realized an unanticipated benefit. It seems that many artists began to visit Geffen's Web site, noticed the extent to which Geffen was using innovative technology, and are now beating the door down to sign recording contracts with Geffen.

Internally, Geffen chose to create an intranet for communicating and sharing information among its employees. Those employees— about 225 total—are located in 30 field offices in Atlanta, Chicago, New York, and London. By employing firewall security, Geffen can post sensitive information on the intranet and guarantee that only employees will be able to access it—even if those employees are half way around the world.

The benefits of the intranet are extraordinary. As Doug Fenske, assistant vice president of the technology department, explains, "Finding stuff on paper is really hard, but on the intranet it's a lot easier. You know where the information is without having to go through lots of people."

Organizations today are desperately seeking to exploit all types of technologies, especially networks. And some organizations—like Geffen Records— have decided to base their entire business operations on networks. These organizations realize that all commercial activities can be performed electronically.[28] ❖

Intranets Offer a Worldwide Solution for Sharing Information

THE GLOBAL PERSPECTIVE

Sharing information is fundamental to the success of today's organizations. But many hurdles exist. Thousands of employees, operations dispersed all over the world, and a variety of hardware and software platforms make it seemingly impossible to connect everyone to every information resource in an organization. An intranet, or internal company Internet, solves such a problem.

Deere & Co. has some 34,000 employees using different hardware and software throughout 10 countries. Thus Deere faced the problem of efficiently disseminating strategic information. Upon initial investigation, Deere discovered more than 50 different software tools—such as Lotus Notes and e-mail—were being used among its employees to share information. It was literally impossible to find a single tool that every business unit used. To solve this problem, Deere turned to an intranet. As Karen Lekowski, senior systems analyst for Deere, explains, "Internet technology was the easiest, quickest, and cheapest way to solve our problems."

Today, Deere employees use the intranet to view electronic phone books, read the latest information on pensions and benefit plans, review Deere's financial position, and work on vitally important strategic projects. Of course, security is a major consideration. Thanks to firewall software and other measures, Deere doesn't worry about security.[30] ❖

Telecommuting

Empowering Employees to Work Regardless of Location

Imagine that you awaken one morning and dress for an important interview. You carefully think about every question that could be asked of you and try to formulate the most appropriate responses. You arrive at the interview and things seem to be going well; your qualifications meet the job description. Then comes the big question, "We have a telecommuting program. How would you feel about working at home 4 days a week instead of coming into the office?" What would your response be?

CAREER OPPORTUNITY

So what's the future for intranets? In a word—**big**. In the next 5 years, you can expect that almost all organizations will set up intranets. Many of these intranets will simply support employee access to internal information. Others will support extranet applications. In Figure 6.26, you can see projections for intranets, why organizations are setting up intranets, and who has access to them. And here are a few more statistics for you to consider: It's estimated that intranets already connect some 15 million knowledge workers, and that 50 percent of large organizations will have intranets by the year 1998.[29]

If it sounds too good to be true, think again. Today, over 15 million people in the United States telecommute, and that figure is expected to grow by 20 percent in the next several years.[31] In Chapters 1 and 3 we discussed *telecommuting*—using communications technology to work in a place other than a central location. And that "other place" for many telecommuters is their home, an airplane, a hotel room, or even the offices of customers. You can divide telecommuters into two groups. The first group includes those people required to work outside the office because that's where the real work is. For example, many salespeople need to be in the offices of their customers instead of waiting for a call in the home office. The second group includes those people who can work away from the home office because it doesn't matter where they perform their work.

A good example of this second group of telecommuters is insurance claims processors who work for Federated Department Stores.[32] Federated has sent home about one-half its claims processors, allowing them to do their work without first driving through traffic. When a Federated employee submits an insurance claim for processing, another employee scans in the document and sends it by way of communications technology to a telecommuter working at home. The telecommuting employee processes the claim at home and retransmits the finished claim to the home office. Are there any benefits to the company? You bet. Throughout the process, the claims system tracks the time it takes to process a claim and keeps a record of which claims are processed by

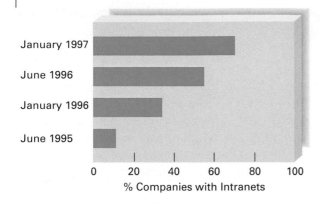

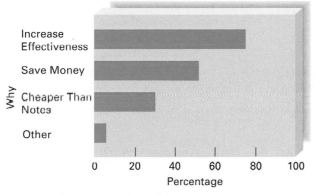

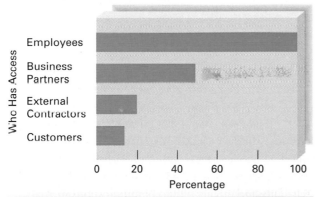

FIGURE 6.26

The Rise of Intranets—Who and Why[33]

each telecommuter. As a result of telecommuting, processing claim productivity has increased by approximately 50 percent, from 7 days to just 3 days.

For most organizations, telecommuting is not a fad—it's rapidly becoming a business standard. Consider these few examples of the many organizations undertaking telecommuting programs:

■ J. C. Penney has taken telecommuting so far that it's sent home its catalog order-entry specialists.[34] By setting up a network that routes telephone calls to the homes of telecommuters, J. C. Penney's catalog order-entry specialists handle telephone orders while working at home.

■ Aegon USA Inc. is setting up a telecommuting program that will eventually include several hundred employees.[35] At a total cost of $6,000 to $8,000 per worker and $300 in monthly communications expenses, Aegon figures it will save so much money that it's buying home office furniture for each employee.

■ Provident Mutual Life Insurance is even sending its programmers home to work.[36] Using relatively simple communications technologies, programmers can write software at home, upload it to the central computer, and run it to see if it works correctly. Currently, 30 percent of Provident's IT staff work at home at least 1 to 3 days a week.

Network Technologies That Support Telecommuting

The list of organizations with telecommuting programs is almost endless. For most of these organizations, the real question is not who should telecommute or what jobs are ideally suited for telecommuting, but rather which technologies are needed to support telecommuting. And the general answer is networking technologies; specific answers, however, depend on which applications you're trying to support.

We refer to this support as *network range*—the variety of information and transactions that must occur across the network (see Figure 6.27). On one end of network range is simple communications that can be easily facilitated by e-mail and other forms of communications software. This type of network range for telecommuters is most often supported by modems that support the transfer of information across standard telephone lines at generally acceptable speeds. At the other end of network

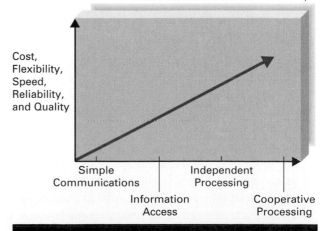

FIGURE 6.27

Network Range in Support of Telecommuting

AT&T Tells Employees to Stay Home and Phone in for Work

Four days of every week John Coughlin, account executive and consultant for AT&T, gets up in the morning at his Manhattan Beach house and stays there to do his work. And when he's not at home working, he's on the road meeting with customers. Only 1 day a week, John makes the boring commute to the AT&T office.

John is part of the growing population of telecommuters at AT&T. In fact, in a 2-year period, the number of AT&T telecommuters grew from 5,000 to 12,000—that's almost 10 percent of salaried U.S. workers for AT&T. At home, AT&T equipped John and the other telecommuters with laptop computers, printers, cellular phones, and two additional phone lines each—one for phone and fax and one for 24-hour-a-day connectivity to AT&T's internal computer network.

AT&T's telecommuting program had three goals, and they've all been met. First, AT&T wanted to provide every incentive possible to get account executives and consultants in the offices of customers. So it eliminated more than one-half its office space when it told employees to work somewhere else, preferably face-to-face with customers. Second, AT&T wanted to reduce real estate costs. That's happened too—last year AT&T saved almost $80 million. Finally, AT&T had heard that telecommuting increases the productivity of workers. And it has—many AT&T telecommuters report that their productivity has increased by more than 40 percent.

If your organization happens to be a phone company like AT&T, why not tell employees to stay at home and phone in for work? You'll save money and increase productivity; you also probably own the phone lines your employees will use.[37, 38] ❖

range are transactions that require cooperative processing between the telecommuter's computer (client) at home and a computer (server) at the home office. In this particular instance, network technologies may include the use of dedicated lines, value-added network providers, and communications media and standards (such as ISDN) that support the high-quality transmission of information at great speeds.

CAREER OPPORTUNITY

Telecommuting is quickly becoming a standard in business, and telecommuting is only possible because of network technologies. That doesn't mean, however, that telecommuting is for every employee or equally supports each business process. In the box at the top of page 261, we've highlighted many of the reasons organizations are choosing to establish telecommuting programs. But there are many downsides to telecommuting. Before you decide that telecommuting is better than sliced bread, read in Chapter 10 about how to choose the best employees and business processes for telecommuting and some of the pitfalls you may encounter if you make the wrong choice.

Determining network technologies needed to support telecommuting always goes back to one fundamental question: "What business process are you trying to support?" If you can answer that question, you'll be able to determine such issues as the extent to which you need cooperative processing (level of client/server implementation), speed of the communications media, and the reliability and quality of the communications media. And, as we've stated before, increased network capabilities always entail more cost, flexibility, speed, reliability, and quality of your network technologies.

How Electronic Commerce Will Affect the Business World

Electronic commerce is here to stay. In spite of the fact that a relatively small portion of households in the United States currently have computers, businesses will continue to push all aspects of electronic commerce. In the coming years, you can expect electronic commerce to affect the business world in the following ways.

EDI Will Become a Requirement EDI will become the standard by which all organizations (and potentially individual customers) will transfer

Why Organizations Are Developing Telecommuting Programs

The benefits of telecommuting for both the organization and employees are abundant. Below are just a few of the many benefits of a telecommuting program.

- **The 1990 Federal Clean Air Act** This act requires that organizations with more than 100 employees in one location reduce commute times by at least 25 percent.

- **Reduce facilities costs** According to Allen Baldridge, senior manager for Northern Telecom's real estate and facilities division, a typical 8-by-8 foot cubicle space costs more than $2,000 per year in just rental and operating costs.

- **Place workers nearer work** For many telecommuters, being nearer the real work makes them more productive, especially knowledge workers such as sales representatives.

- **Increase quality of life** Many telecommuters experience a greater quality of life by working at home.

- **Reach a larger labor pool** Organizations can reach a larger labor pool of part-time employees if employees can work from home instead of slogging through traffic for a 4-hour work shift.

- **Improve recruitment and retention** Today's job seekers place a high priority on finding an organization that will allow them to telecommute.

- **Decrease absenteeism** By working at home, most telecommuters can still perform some duties if they have the flu or have to be at a PTA meeting in the middle of the day.[39] ❖

INDUSTRY PERSPECTIVE Food

Pepsi's Real Thing Is Wireless Telecommuters

Have you ever seen large Pepsi trucks drive up to a local grocery store and begin unloading products to replenish shelf supplies? Most people have, and they think the trucks simply load up every morning with a variety of products and stock whatever the stores need. But that's not true—not for Pepsi at least. Before the truck is even loaded, sales reps enter stores armed with handheld computers, check store inventory levels, and use wireless communications to send information about the store's needs to various distribution centers.

Even before Pepsi used wireless communications, its sales reps entered stores before the trucks arrived, but then the sales reps called in their order requests on public pay phones. "It got to the point where the reps were standing at pay phones for 15 to 20 minutes," says Paul Contois, MIS manager at Pepsi Cola Allied Bottlers. Paul went on to explain, "There were plenty of cold, rainy days when our reps were standing at a phone booth, balancing the phones on their shoulders. They had to look at the paper order in one hand and try to dial 15 to 30 six-digit product numbers and quantities with the other."

Not so anymore. Whenever a sales rep completes an order using a handheld computer, it takes only the touch of a button to wirelessly communicate the order to the distribution center. It takes only about 45 to 75 seconds to transmit the order and receive an acknowledgment. Paul estimates that this saves the reps about 1½ hours daily.

Telecommuting through wireless communications technologies is becoming big for most businesses today. And that's important, because, as Paul says, "That means we can do more business with fewer people."[40] ❖

Combining Organizational Strategies and Electronic Commerce

In Chapter 3 we introduced seven strategies for generating organizational force, speed, and horsepower. Many of these strategies rely heavily on your organization's ability to perform electronic commerce activities. Below, identify the two or three most important electronic commerce activities that would provide the greatest support for each strategy. Think carefully about each strategy and its focus on force, speed, or both. ❖

Organizational Strategy	Electronic Data Interchange	Electronic Funds Transfer	Individualized Electronic Advertising	Intranet	Telecommuting
Just-in-Time					
Teams					
Information Partnerships					
Timeless and Locationless Operations					
Transnational Firm					
Virtual Organization					
Learning Organization					

standard business document information. In fact, many organizations today will not do business with suppliers or customers who are not linked to them electronically. Don't underestimate the significance of this move—it will require that some organizations invest heavily in technology to support EDI (or use the services of a VAN).

Disintermediation Will Displace Many Organizations Electronic commerce will make winners of many organizations, but by its very nature, it will also make losers of many more. Most significantly, electronic commerce will eliminate many "middle men" or intermediary organizations. Eliminating intermediary organizations in the chain of providing goods and services is called *disintermediation*. Consider two simple examples. First, if you can

order any product or service (a car, shoes, or CDs) over the Internet, where does that leave retail organizations? Second, as organizations begin to electronically advertise, where does that leave organizations that make catalogs or organizations in television or radio? If you get your newspaper every morning electronically, what happens to paper-delivery people?

EFT May Mean the End of Cash and Checks as We Know Them Right now, EFT is handled almost exclusively between two organizations. But, in the coming years, you can expect individual customers to begin using EFT. In some form or fashion, we already are—through direct deposit and the electronic payment of bills to utility companies, phone companies, and so forth. You'll also see the

Chrysler Doesn't Want Ford to See Its Intranet

Intranets certainly support the internal sharing and communication of information. But, because intranets are actually smaller portions of the much larger Internet, outsiders can potentially bypass your firewall and access your most vital and strategic information.

That's first and foremost on Chrysler's mind as it uses an intranet to design better cars. Chrysler's intranet-stored information includes estimates of what other automobile manufacturers, such as Ford, are spending on particular parts. But you won't find Chrysler-specific part cost information on its intranet. Why not? As Susan Unger, executive director of information systems at Chrysler, explains it, "The last thing I want is that [Chrysler part cost information] getting into competitors' hands."

If your organization is considering using an intranet, don't underestimate the importance of firewall security measures. Those measures ensure that your competitors can't access vital and strategic intranet-stored information.[41] ❖

---

emergence of digital cash, which is nothing more than an electronic representation of money. We cover digital cash and its potential in Chapter 7.

Individualized Electronic Advertising Will Require More Focused Market Information An important aspect of individualized electronic advertising is knowing specific characteristics about specific customers. In most business environments today, advertising is targeted at market groups—by location, by age, by income level, and so on. The real winners in electronic advertising will be those organizations that are able to distinguish their respective markets right down to the individual customer level. This will require even more capturing, tracking, and processing of customer information.

Intranets Will Become the Standard for Communicating Internal Information Intranets are a great way to internally communicate information for two reasons. First, they offer protection through firewalls from outside access. Second, intranets are based on Internet technologies, which most organizations already have in place.

Telecommuting Will Allow Everyone to Stay at Home More Telecommuting is not the "business fad of the month." Most organizations are specifically targeting telecommuting as a way to do business anywhere.

Network Perfect Service
Range, Reach, and Responsiveness

Throughout this text, we explore the concept of perfect service as it relates to customer moment of value. *Network perfect service* simply occurs at the customer's moment of value—where the customer wants it (location), how the customer wants it (form), and when the customer wants it (time). And business is all about providing perfect service at the customer's moment of value. The same is definitely true of networks. For networks, perfect service is the delivery of networking capabilities where, how, and when they are wanted. With respect to network perfect service, we refer to where as *network reach*, how as *network range*, and when as *network responsiveness* (see Figure 6.28). Let's explore how perfect service relates to networking.

For range, we identify groupings of information and transactions according to the following questions:

- Does your network need to support only basic communications between people through e-mail and the use of shared peripheral devices such as printers and scanners?
- Does your network need to enable shared information access, whether in a file, database, or data warehouse?
- Does your network need to support various computers that process transactions independent of each other? That is, will there be computers in the network that completely process transactions without sharing in the processing?
- Does your network need to support various computers as they process transactions in cooperation with each other?

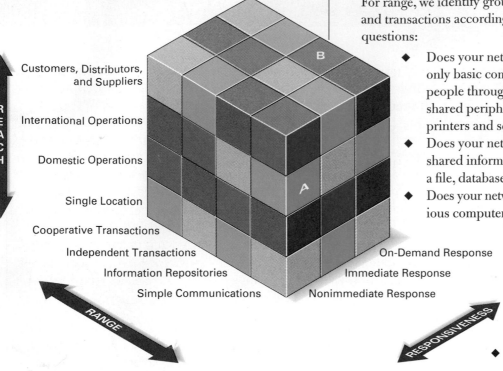

REACH
- Customers, Distributors, and Suppliers
- International Operations
- Domestic Operations
- Single Location

RANGE
- Cooperative Transactions
- Independent Transactions
- Information Repositories
- Simple Communications

RESPONSIVENESS
- On-Demand Response
- Immediate Response
- Nonimmediate Response

Point A: Simple communications across international operations that do not require immediate responses.

Point B: The ability of your customers, distributors, and suppliers to access your organization's information whenever they need to.

FIGURE 6.28

Network Perfect Service—Reach, Range, and Responsiveness[42]

Network reach addresses the people, organizations, and business processes that your network should include. As you consider network reach, you should answer the following questions:

- Will the network be limited to a single location, such as an office building or city?
- Will the network support the people and business processes throughout your organization's domestic operations?
- Will the network support your organization's international activities?
- Will the network connect you to your customers, distributors, and suppliers?

Answers to these questions will help you determine certain physical network requirements. For example, network reach that spans the world will require a wide area network, perhaps a virtual private network, satellite communications media, and internetworking units.

Network range addresses the information and transactions that must travel across your network.

Answers to these questions will help you determine whether you need a peer-to-peer network or a client/server network and which communication services the network operating system must support. For example, a network that needs to support just basic communications and peripheral sharing may be implemented as a peer-to-peer network, whereas cooperative transaction support will require a client/server network.

Network responsiveness addresses the level of service—speed, reliability, and security—your network must provide. In this particular instance, you should address the following questions:

- Does your network need to support information processing and communications that do not require an immediate response? For example, payroll processing can occur at the end of the week or month.
- Does your network need to support information processing and communications that require an immediate response? For example, a POS system that retrieves pricing from a server requires an immediate response.

Transportation

FedEx Takes Shipping to a Whole New "Value-Added" Dimension

If your primary business is parcel delivery like FedEx, who are your customers? Actually there are two groups—customers for whom you're delivering and customers you're delivering to. So how can you take advantage of that situation? How can you bring both customer sets closer to each other and create a powerful alliance between yourself and the customers you're delivering for? That's the question FedEx wrestled with and eventually answered. Its answer was to become a value-added network (VAN) provider that would act as an intermediary between its two customer sets.

FedEx's VAN service is called *BusinessLink.* Here's how it works.

- FedEx provides businesses with software to create Internet catalogs:

  Businesses create their catalogs by entering product information and pricing.

  FedEx places the catalogs on the Internet and incorporates security features for credit card transactions.

- Customers use Web browser software to access an Internet catalog:

  When an order is placed, FedEx electronically transmits the order to the appropriate business, along with a FedEx tracking number for shipment.

  FedEx picks up the parcel at the business warehouse and delivers it to the customer.

The benefits for all involved are enormous. Businesses win because they get 24-hour-a-day product ordering, an association with a large organization, and an Internet presence. Customers win because they can order products anytime they want and track incoming deliveries by the FedEx tracking number. Most important, FedEx wins because it creates a close relationship between itself and the businesses it serves and because it generates revenues from the actual delivery process.

Today's networks—including the Internet—have limitless possibilities for obtaining competitive advantage. For FedEx, its new *BusinessLink* program includes connecting customers all over the world (range), cooperative transactions (reach), and on-demand responses (responsiveness). Who would have thought that a parcel delivery organization like FedEx would have become a VAN provider? The answer is no one, and that's why FedEx now has a competitive advantage through networking.[43] ❖

- ◆ Does your network need to support on-demand responses to information processing and communications? For example, if your organization is connected to customers through EDI, your customers should be able to order products and services whenever they want.

Answers to these questions will help you determine several network issues, including the necessary speed of the communications media and the extent to which you must have backup and recovery systems in place.

Perfect Delivery

The Relationships Among Reach, Range, and Responsiveness

The extent to which your organization can meet the where, how, and when characteristics of the network,

and the extent to which your organization can guarantee those characteristics determine your level of *network perfect delivery.* And guaranteeing network perfect delivery is elusive. For example, in late 1996, America Online failed in the area of perfect delivery when its Internet-accessing system went down for almost 24 hours.

You should understand, however, that network perfect delivery is not always about guaranteeing availability 24 hours a day. Consider ATMs as an example. The worldwide ATM network has the following characteristics:

- *Reach* Customers around the world
- *Range* Cooperative transactions
- *Responsiveness* On-demand response

But is the ATM network always available? The answer is no. ATMs are periodically shut down early Monday mornings for routine maintenance on the network. ATM

Defining the Relationship Among Reach, Range, and Responsiveness

In Figure 6.28 on page 264, we identified two points and the relationships among range, reach, and responsiveness. For example, point A is for simple communications (range) across international operations (reach) that do not require immediate responses (responsiveness).

For the opening case study, the nine industry perspectives, and the two global perspectives in this chapter, plot the relationships among range, reach, and responsiveness. You may need to plot some organizations in several areas of the cube because their networks support varying degrees of reach, range, and responsiveness. ❖

---

providers have determined that the fewest ATM-based transactions occur during that time. And as customers, we're willing to accept that we may not be able to get cash at 3:30 A.M. on Monday morning. So, perfect delivery is still achievable, even when a network is not always available.

On the other hand, some networks must work all the time. For example, when the air traffic control network fails for 15 minutes, catastrophic results for air travelers and airports are likely. So how do you determine the extent to which the guarantee of network perfect delivery deals with 24-hour-a-day availability? You guessed it—it all goes back to understanding your business needs and letting those needs drive your network perfect delivery requirements.

CLOSING CASE STUDY: CASE 1

Promina Health Systems Treats the Paper Disease with an Intranet

When most people think of hospitals, they envision people in white uniforms, expensive equipment, medications and pharmaceutical drugs, and massive amounts of information flowing everywhere. Indeed, when you're in a hospital, a number of paper-based documents—including an admittance form, an insurance form, nurse station orders, pharmacy orders, radiology analyses, meal requests, lab results, a doctor's clipboard, and many other forms of information—follow you wherever you go. At Promina Health Systems, CIO Bill Dotson

had one goal in mind—do whatever it takes to get rid of the paper.

On the surface, the solution seemed simple—set up a network that would enable the electronic flow of information throughout the hospital. But that was only one piece of the puzzle. Bill was responsible for creating a paperless environment not only for one hospital, but also for all nine hospitals in Promina Health Systems. That meant linking nine accounting departments, nine human resource departments, nine lab departments, nine pharmacies, and more than 300 doctors who had offices outside the hospital system but used the system to perform surgeries.

To create a paperless environment for the nine hospitals, Bill decided to go with groupware and an intranet. Groupware, as it turns out, is the solution for internal electronic commerce. Groupware tools, including work flow automation, group scheduling, and videoconferencing software, support Promina's efforts to electronically move information among its employees and associates. The intranet is the solution for internal electronic commerce. By using simple Internet-based technologies, Bill created an intranet to support the sharing of information among the nine hospitals.

To start Bill chose several simple projects. He first put Promina's procedures and policy manuals on the intranet for everyone to access. This alone eliminated the need to pass around and keep several copies of hundreds of pages of manuals. Then Bill began implementing human resource applications on the intranet. All employees can now electronically access phone books, calendars of events, and a list of continuing education courses. Employees can even electronically submit requests for travel. To do this they simply complete an electronic travel request that's immediately routed to the appropriate person for approval.

Bill's goal of using groupware on the intranet will eventually support all 300 doctors and over 13,000 hospital employees as they go paperless. In health care, this represents a substantial savings in cost, which Promina will pass on to patients in the form of better health care at a more affordable price.[44] ❖

◄ Questions ►

1. How would you characterize the type of network that connects the nine hospitals in Promina Health Systems by geographic span? How would you characterize each network within each hospital?

2. According to ownership, what type of network does Promina Health Systems have? What potential role do public, value-added, and virtual private network providers play in Promina's network?

3. What specific functions does groupware support for Promina? Which groupware software applications could Promina use to facilitate the flow of information among the various hospitals?

4. What security concerns does Promina have for electronically moving information from one hospital to another? What precautions has Promina taken? What other security measures might Promina employ to ensure the privacy of confidential patient information?

5. According to network reach, range, and responsiveness, how would you categorize Promina's complete network? Do some applications fall into different categories of network perfect service? What would they be?

6. With respect to network perfect delivery, does Promina's network include 24-hour-a-day availability? Is there a specific time period in which Promina could take its network down for routine maintenance? If so, how would communications be handled during that period?

7. Why did Promina choose to use groupware and an intranet to create a paperless environment? What specific business issues led Promina to create a paperless environment? Besides using groupware and an intranet, what other electronic commerce concepts could Promina employ to further a paperless environment?

Avex Electronics Wants to Go Web Wild with Electronic Data Interchange

What would you do if you wanted to extend your business hours, reduce errors that occur when entering transactions, and step up communications between your organization and your business partners? The task doesn't necessarily seem overwhelming, but many people would employ a combination of tactics to achieve all three goals. But not Mike Gordon, manager of electronic commerce at Avex Electronics. He's even figured out a way to achieve all three goals without a substantial investment in any new technology. His solution is simple—begin performing electronic data interchange (EDI) over the Internet. Besides achieving those three goals, Mike sees some additional benefits of performing EDI on the Internet as follows:

- Unlike traditional value-added network (VAN) providers who charge a fee per EDI transaction, Internet service providers charge a flat fee for monthly usage. This represents substantial savings.

- Because most organizations now have access to the Internet, Mike hopes to create more trading opportunities. With a simple connection to the Internet as opposed to developing interfaces to VAN providers, potential Avex business partners will have an easier time establishing EDI links with Avex.

Nonetheless, many organizations are skeptical of Mike's idea for many reasons. Most notably, those wary of EDI on the Internet point out that

1. Security of information traveling on the Internet is less than that of going through a VAN provider

2. Reliability of the Internet always working at an acceptable speed is questionable

3. VAN providers do offer additional communications services that you can't get through the Internet

4. When using the Internet, you have no one to blame but yourself if something goes wrong.

And these are all valid points. The EDI transmission of information—because it includes information contained in standard business documents—needs to be reliable

Client/Server as the Emerging Blueprint for Organizational Networks. As the emerging blueprint for organizational networks, client/server addresses the technology-independent workings of your organization and five models for implementing the most appropriate network. A *client/server network* is a network that contains one or more host computers (servers) that provide some type of service to the other computers (clients). As a business model, client/server requires that the processing be distributed to the exact place in a network where the processing needs to be performed. As such, client/server networks distinguish information, software, and processing power as either global or local.

The five implementation models of client/server split presentation, logic, and data management responsibilities between the server and clients in a network. These models range from splitting the presentation function between the server and clients while the server handles data management and logic (model 1) to splitting the data management function between the server and the clients while the clients handle logic and presentation (model 5).

Network-Enabling Technologies and Concepts That Support Electronic Commerce. You can group network-enabling technologies and concepts into five categories. These include

1. *Types of networks* According to functionality (client/server or peer-to-peer), geographic distance (local or wide area network), and physical structure or topology (bus, ring, or star).

2. *Communications media—the paths over which information travels* Telecommunications implies that information must travel from one place to another, and that information must travel over some path. Communications media are either guided and transmit information over a closed path (twisted-pair, coaxial cable, or optical fiber) or unguided and transmit information through the air (microwave, satellite, broadcast radio, or infrared).

3. *Communications processors—the connections within a network* For computers and other devices to communicate in a network, they must be connected to the network in some way. Communications processors include modems, multiplexers, cluster controllers, and internetworking units (bridges, routers, and gateways).

4. *Communications methods, standards, and protocols—the manner in which information is communicated* For network telecommunications to be possible, there must be predefined methods, standards, and protocols by which information will be communicated from one place to another. Some of these include Ethernet, token ring, fiber distributed data interface, asynchronous transfer mode, integrated services digital network, transmission control protocol/Internet protocol, and X.12.

5. *Communications service providers—the issue of network ownership* Networks are expensive—sometimes too expensive for a single organization

and secure. If your organization uses a VAN provider, then you're guaranteed reliability and security. And, equally important, if something does go wrong, you can hold the VAN provider responsible.

But that hasn't stopped Mike in his push to perform EDI on the Internet. Mike has already convinced some of Avex's larger trading partners—including Texas Instruments, Marshall Industries, and National Semiconductor—to send and accept EDI transactions over the Internet. But, unless he convinces all of Avex's 80

business partners to do the same, he may have to abandon his idea.[45] ❖

◄ Questions ►

1. How do you think Mike could convince Avex's other business partners to begin performing EDI over the Internet? What could he do to convince them that the Internet is secure and reliable?

2. Could Avex use an Internet virtual private network to handle its EDI transactions over the Internet?

to completely build and maintain. In this instance, you can use the networks of other organizations to build your own network. Networks according to ownership include private, public, value-added, virtual private, Internet virtual private, and international virtual private.

Key External Electronic Commerce Aspects That Networks Support. External electronic commerce is all about doing business electronically in the marketplace—communicating with suppliers, distributors, retailers, and customers. Key external electronic commerce aspects include

- *Ordering products and services* Using ***electronic data interchange*** to directly transfer transaction information in standard business documents from computer to computer

- *Moving money without handling it* Using ***electronic funds transfer*** to eliminate the movement of physical instruments such as payment authorizations and checks

- *Reaching the exact customer* Using ***individualized electronic advertising*** to determine who receives which advertisements and sending those advertisements to those people electronically

- *Knowing more than your competitors* Using a variety of network technologies to gather ***competitive intelligence***—information about the internal workings of your organization as well as the external market surrounding your organization

Key Internal Electronic Commerce Aspects That Networks Support. Internal electronic commerce is all about electronically supporting internal processes, functions, and operations. Organizations perform internal electronic commerce by using such network-enabled tools and concepts as interorganizational systems, virtual organizations, paperless offices, online transaction and analytical processing, groupware, and group decision support systems. Internal electronic commerce also involves intranets and telecommuting.

- ***Intranets*** are internal organizational Internets that can be protected against outside access by firewalls.

- ***Telecommuting*** allows employees to use communications technology to work in a place other than a central location.

Network Perfect Service as It Relates to Network Range, Reach, and Responsiveness. ***Network perfect service*** is the ability to provide networking capabilities where (range), how (reach), and when (responsiveness) they are wanted. ***Network reach*** addresses the people, organizations, and business processes that a network includes. ***Network range*** addresses the information and transactions that must travel across a network. ***Network responsiveness*** addresses the level of service—speed, reliability, and security—a network must provide. The extent to which your organization can meet the where, how, and when characteristics of the network and the extent to which your organization can guarantee those characteristics determine your level of ***network perfect delivery***. ❖

What would be the advantages and disadvantages of using an Internet virtual private network?

3. An important service that most VAN providers offer is that of security software such as data encryption to ensure the security of EDI information as it travels. How could Mike incorporate security software into his idea? How would this affect his desire to limit his investment in technology?

4. Many organizations today simply won't do business with organizations that don't have EDI capabilities. What if Avex took a similar step with

respect to performing EDI on the Internet? What if you were a business partner of Avex and were told that you had to perform EDI on the Internet? What would be your response? Would your response differ if Avex accounted for a large portion of your business?

5. How could Mike alter his idea to include an intranet as well as EDI and the Internet? Would this potentially persuade some of Avex's business partners to begin actively performing EDI on the Internet? Why or why not?

REAL [H·O·T]

Electronic Commerce
Business and You on the Internet

Getting Health Care Information on the Internet

When most people think of performing electronic commerce on the Internet, they immediately think of ordering products and services, buying plane tickets, making hotel reservations, purchasing concert tickets, and performing a host of other activities. What you may not realize is that you can use the Internet as a valuable resource for health and medical purposes. It seems almost strange, especially considering that most medical help requires one-on-one interaction with a member of the medical profession, but you really can find valuable medical help on the Internet. In many instances, you can even order medical and health-related products on the Internet.

However, as you search the Internet for medical help, you need to keep in mind that all of the persons or organizations posting information may not be qualified to do so. Don't simply connect to an online first-aid Web site and follow whatever advice is given without carefully checking who posted that information and what his or her qualifications are. It may surprise you to find that many unqualified people are posing as medical experts on the Internet. On the other hand, there are a variety of well-qualified organizations, such as the Mayo Clinic and the MS foundation, setting up Web sites in the interest of your medical well-being. Just as we encouraged you in Chapter 3 ("Finding Investment Opportunities Using the Internet") to carefully weigh the credibility of investment recommendations on the Internet, we also encourage you here to even more carefully scrutinize any medical information you find on the Internet (http://www.quackwatch.com may be of help).

In this section, we've included a number of Web sites related to getting health care information on the Internet. On the Web site that supports this text (http://www.mhhe.com/business/mis/haag, select "Electronic Commerce Projects"), we've provided direct links to all these Web sites as well as many, many more. These are a great starting point for completing this Real HOT section. We would also encourage you to search the Internet for others.

Diet and Nutrition

Of great interest to almost everyone today is diet and nutrition. We have simply become a more health-conscious society concerned with how our intake of food affects our health. Important issues in this area include the times of the day to eat (the most or least), consuming enough fiber, avoiding foods with certain sweeteners or produce that has been exposed to certain pesticides, and creating a delicate balance between fat and sugar intake.

In the table on page 272, we've provided a list of sites on the Internet devoted to nutrition and diet (many more are included on the Web site that supports this text). Connect to several of these and see what they have to say. As you do, consider the following. What organization or person supports each site? Is the site really concerned with your physical well-being or is it perhaps a for-profit organization seeking your money? Are you eating properly according to each site? Are you going to alter your diet in light of any information you read?

If you're interested in what the government has to say concerning what's good and bad for you, we recommend that you connect to two different sites. The first is for the U.S. FDA Center for Food Safety and Applied Nutrition at http://vm.cfsan.fda.gov/list.html. The second is for the National Food Safety Database at

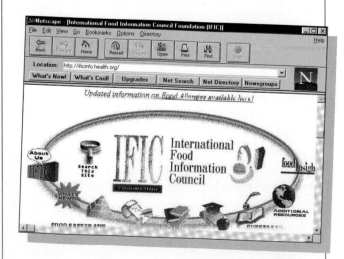

http://www.foodsafety.org/. Both of these provide excellent, up-to-date nutrition and diet information.

Health and Fitness Magazines

As you work through the electronic commerce projects at the end of the chapters in this text, you'll notice many common threads, one of which is online versions of many printed magazines and newspapers. For example, in working through Chapter 3, concerning investing on the Internet, you probably connected to the online version of *The Wall Street Journal* to obtain financial news and information. And in Chapter 7, on news, weather, and sports, you'll find a variety of sites for such magazines and newspapers as *Sports Illustrated, Business Week,* and *USA Today.*

Likewise in the area of health and fitness, you can find numerous online versions of printed magazines. In the table on page 272, we've provided a list of sites for online versions of health and fitness magazines. And don't forget to connect to the Web site that supports this text for direct links to these magazines as well as many others. Connect to several of these sites, review the online versions of the magazines, and answer the following questions for each.

A. Is the site for an online health and fitness magazine that also exists in printed form, or is it purely online?

B. Must you pay a subscription fee to view the entire magazine?

C. Does the site contain only an electronic version of the magazine, or does it include additional features and late-breaking news?

D. How does the site categorize its articles?

E. What mechanisms does the site provide for you to search for specific information?

F. Does the site provide additional links to online versions of other health and fitness magazines?

G. Does the site provide graphics or animation with movement to demonstrate such things as exercises?

Alternative Medicine

Today, a variety of alternative medical resources is available on the Internet. This includes information on such treatments as acupuncture, chiropractic, meditation, Tai Chi, yoga, and vibrational medicine. Of course, you can't actually receive an acupuncture treatment over the Internet, but you can find out about acupuncture and acupuncture practitioners on the Internet.

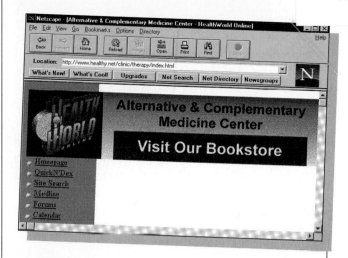

In the table on page 272, we've listed some alternative medicine sites on the Internet and where you can find them. We've also listed several others on the Web site that supports this text. And if you're really interested in learning more about this topic, we recommend that you connect to http://www.noah.cuny.edu/alternative/alternative.html (Ask Noah: Alternative Health), a great site for exploring alternative health issues on the Internet.

Connect to at least five alternative medicine sites. For each, answer the following questions.

A. What organization or person supports the site?

B. What is the major focus of the site?

C. Must you pay a subscription fee to access the full site?

D. Does the site provide additional links to related sites?

E. Can you request that printed material be sent to you?

F. Can you order products such as dietary supplements? If so, how do you pay for them?

G. Can you order books and pamphlets?

H. Overall, how do you feel about exploring alternative medicine through the Internet?

Hospitals and Clinics

Sites for hospitals and clinics provide another valuable source for medical and health information on the Internet. Today, it's estimated that over 30,000 hospitals and clinics worldwide have set up shop on the Internet. But these sites differ from a lot of other medical and health sites. As you've already explored, there are a large number of sites that actually offer medical advice—how to eat nutritionally, home remedies for the common cold, and even perhaps some rather unbelievable cures for what ails you.

Most hospital and clinic sites are different. At a hospital or clinic site, you can typically read its mission statement, obtain physical characteristics (e.g., number of beds, number of attending physicians, directions), and learn about what services are offered. But what you probably can't do is obtain recommendations concerning how to cure yourself.

In the table below, we've provided a list of hospitals and clinics and where you can find them on the Internet. On the Web site that supports this text, we've included direct links to these and many others. And if you're interested in finding hospitals and clinics in your area, we recommend that you connect to http://www.doctorline. com/hbstate.htm (Hospitals by State), which contains a database of over 28,600 hospitals arranged by state.

Connect to five different sites for hospitals and clinics on the Internet and answer the following questions.

A. What organization owns or sponsors the hospital/clinic?

B. Is the hospital/clinic a part of a nationwide network of medical facilities? If so, what is that network?

C. Can you read about the various services offered?

D. Is the hospital/clinic for-profit or not-for-profit?

E. Can you read profiles of attending physicians?

Web Sites for Health Care Information

Diet and Nutrition	Address
Arbor Nutrition Guide	http://www.arborcom.com
International Food Information Council	http://ificinfo.health.org
You Are What You Eat	http://library.advanced.org/11163/gather/cgi-bin/wookie.cgi
American Dietetic Association	http://www.eatright.org
Ask the Dietitian	http://www.dietitian.com

Health and Fitness Magazines	Address
Runner's World Online	http://www.runnersworld.com
Men's Fitness	http://www.mensfitness.com
Ability Magazine	http://www.abilitymagazine.com
Go Girl!	http://www.gogirlmag.com
Maxim	http://www.maximmag.com/2.3

Alternative Medicine	Address
Alternative & Complementary Medicine Center	http://www.healthy.net/clinic/therapy/index.html
Get Well	http://www.moreinfo.net/getwell
Healing Heart Center	http://www.talamasca.org/avatar
Office of Alternative Medicine (NIH)	http://www.altmed.ad.nih.gov
LifeMatters	http://lifematters.com

Hospitals/Clinics	Address
Virtual Hospital (Iowa)	http://www.vh.org
Bethany Hospital (Chicago)	http://www.advocatehealth.com/sites/bethany.html
New England Medical Center (Boston)	http://www.nemc.org/home
Children's Hospital of Philadelphia	http://www.chop.edu
Columbia Providence Hospital (South Carolina)	http://www.provhosp.com

Pharmaceutical Organizations	Address
Abbott Laboratories	http://www.abbott.com
Allergan	http://www.allergan.com
Bayer	http://www.bayerus.com
Bristol-Myers Squibb	http://www.bms.com
Eli Lilly and Company	http://www.lilly.com

F. How much help can you find concerning physical well-being?

G. Why do you think hospitals and clinics fail to offer much medical advice on the Internet?

Pharmaceutical Organizations

If you're interested in learning about specific pharmaceuticals, drugs, and pharmaceutical supplies, one of the best places to visit on the Internet is the manufacturer of the product. These pharmaceutical organizations are just like most other organizations on the Internet. They've established Web sites to tell you about the company and its range of products. Of course, most pharmaceutical organizations have very rigorous ordering procedures to protect themselves from liability.

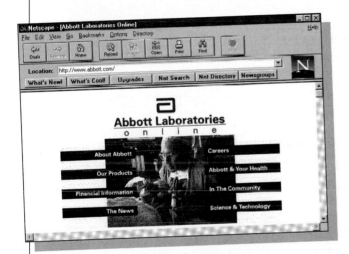

Many pharmaceutical organizations also post "white papers" on the Internet. These white papers detail current research in progress. You can, for example, read about the latest research into cures for cancer, hair loss, and arthritis. Some discussions of the research probably won't make much sense, and you can certainly expect to read only an overview of the research, not a detailed analysis of it. As we discussed in this chapter, many organizations are performing competitive scanning by visiting the Web sites of their competitors. And pharmaceutical organizations do the same.

In the table on page 272, we've provided a list of several pharmaceutical organizations and where you can find them on the Internet (you'll find many others on the Web site that supports this text). And, if you'd like to view a fairly comprehensive site that contains hundreds of pharmaceutical links, we recommend that you connect to http://pharminfo.com/pin-hp.html (Pharmaceutical Information Network).

Visit at least five different Web sites for pharmaceutical organizations and answer the following questions.

A. What sites did you visit?

B. Can you readily find a list of pharmaceutical products offered by the organization?

C. Does the site list any prices for products?

D. Can you in fact order some products? If so, what are they?

E. Does the site contain research in progress in the form of white papers?

F. Does the site provide links to other pharmaceutical-related sites?

 Go to the Web site that supports this text: **http://www.mhhe.com/business/mis/haag** and select "Electronic Commerce Projects."

We've included links to over 100 Web sites concerning getting health care information on the Internet, including support organizations such as the American Cancer Society.

KEY TERMS AND CONCEPTS

Asynchronous Transfer Mode (ATM)
Automated Clearinghouse (ACH)
Bandwidth
Bridge
Broadcast Radio
Bus Topology

Client/Server Network
Cluster Controller
Coaxial Cable
Communications Media
Communications Processor
Communications Service Provider
Competitive Intelligence

Data Mart
Disintermediation
Electronic Commerce
Electronic Data Interchange (EDI)
Electronic Funds Transfer (EFT)
Ethernet
External Electronic Commerce

Extranet
Fiber Distributed Data Interface
 (FDDI)
Firewall
Front-End Processor
Gateway
Guided Communications Media
Individualized Electronic Adver-
 tising
Infrared
Integrated Services Digital
 Network (ISDN)
Internal Electronic Commerce
International Virtual Private
 Network (International VPN)
Internet Virtual Private Network
 (Internet VPN)

Internetworking Unit
Intranet
Local Area Network (LAN)
Microwave
Modem
Multiplexer
Network (Computer Network)
Network Perfect Delivery
Network Perfect Service
Network Range
Network Reach
Network Responsiveness
Network Topology
Network Operating System (NOS)
Optical Fiber
Peer-to-Peer Network
Private Network

Public Network
Ring Topology
Router
Satellite
Star Topology
Telecommunications
Telecommuting
Token Ring
Transmission Control
 Protocol/Internet Protocol
 (TCP/IP)
Twisted-Pair Cable
Unguided Communications Media
Value-Added Network (VAN)
Virtual Private Network (VPN)
Wide Area Network (WAN)
X.12

SHORT-ANSWER QUESTIONS

1. What is a network? What are the tasks that a network supports?
2. What two tasks are supported by a peer-to-peer network? How does that differ from a client/server network?
3. What is network topology? What are the three network topologies?
4. What is the difference between guided and unguided communications media?
5. Why is bandwidth an important consideration for telecommunications?
6. What is a fiber distributed data interface? What are its advantages over other forms of communications methods, standards, and protocols?

7. What is a value-added network? How is it a combination of a public and private network?
8. Why are Internet virtual private networks becoming important?
9. Why is electronic data interchange of fundamental importance to any organization today?
10. What two steps are involved in performing individualized electronic advertising?
11. What is competitive intelligence?
12. How does an intranet differ from the Internet? How are extranets related to an intranet?
13. What is network reach, range, and responsiveness? How do they relate to the guarantee of network perfect delivery?

DISCUSSION QUESTIONS

1. How is the Internet a form of client/server network? What client/server implementation model supports the Internet, or are there many? If there are many, describe specific Internet applications and the client/server models that would support them.

2. Higher-education facilities seek to exploit telecommuting specifically for faculty. What aspects of a faculty member's job are suited to telecommuting? How would you feel if your classes were offered through videoconferencing so that faculty members could stay at home instead of coming to school? What types of communications media would be most appropriate for offering classes through communications technology?

3. Intranets provide an easy and inexpensive way an organization can make sensitive and strategic information available to all employees while controlling (or eliminating) outside access. But what about controlling internal access to information? For example, does the human resource department need access to diagrams of products under development? In what ways can organizations still realize the advantages of intranets while controlling internal access to intranet-posted information?

4. Many people believe that someday we'll live in a completely "wireless" society, without cables to connect anything except appliances to electrical outlets. What are the current major obstacles of unguided communications media that will have to be overcome for that to happen? Can you actually see a time when that will happen? Can you name some specific instances of when it will always be necessary to have cables for connections?

5. What are the ethical issues related to gathering competitive intelligence pertaining to your customers and competitors? What about Frito Lay? Does it act ethically in sending employees into stores to record what its competitors are doing? What about an organization that regularly checks its competitors' Web sites for product release information? What about an organization that has its employees call a competing organization for product information, while posing as potential customers? What about a car dealership that—while a salesperson is showing you a new car—runs a check on your current car to see whether it's been paid for? These are all ways of gathering competitive intelligence—but are they ethical?

6. In Figure 6.4, p. 227, we illustrated how determining pay raises for employees in different divisions would work in a client/server network. What other typical business processes can you identify that would benefit from splitting the logic or business rules between a server and a client workstation? What about any other business processes that would benefit from one of the other four client/server implementation models?

7. Many people believe that individualized electronic advertising is just around the corner. This form of electronic commerce has many advantages. From a consumer point of view, what do you see as the major disadvantages of receiving individualized electronic advertisements? Are there ways to potentially overcome these disadvantages?

8. Does society have any responsibility toward intermediary organizations that go out of business because disintermediation occurs as we realize the full potential of electronic commerce? Many organizations are attempting to retrain individual workers who lose their jobs to technology or downsizing, but what about **entire** organizations that go out of business?

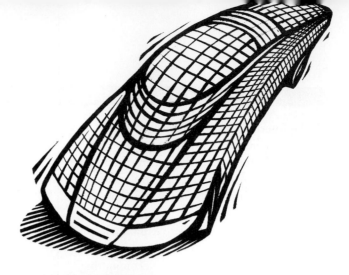

CASE STUDY

Hollywood Goes High Tech to Create Sensation on the Screen

What do all these movies have in common—*Broken Arrow, Terminator 2: Judgment Day, Casper, Toy Story, Free Willy, Apollo 13, Jumanji, Forrest Gump, Braveheart, Die Hard 3*, and *Roger Rabbit?* Well, other than the fact that they were all Hollywood blockbuster movies, they all contained footage that was computer-generated or enhanced. It's true—many of the scenes you saw were never really filmed with a camera.

And that's true for almost all Hollywood movies today. Instead of actually filming scenes, producers capture certain images and use computer technology to enhance the scenes or combine portions of several scenes. In Hollywood today, screen sensation is all about visual effects. Of the over

IN THE NEWS

Emerging Technologies

Innovations for Tomorrow

$1 billion spent on production costs for movies in the summer of 1995, $150 million of that went to visual effects costs. According to Greg Estes, product and technical marketing manager at Silicon Graphics, "Visual effects have become one of the main drivers in the business." Think about these scenes from some of the movies mentioned above:

■ *Terminator 2: Judgment Day* In this movie, producers used a technique called "morphing" to transform the bad terminator into different people—a woman, a police officer, and a security guard.

■ *Free Willy* and *Apollo 13* In these movies, a technique called "transparency" was used to create Willy's huge splashes in the water and the beautiful sunset view from the Apollo 13 capsule.

■ *Die Hard 3* If you think Bruce Willis was lying on the street when a car nearly hit him, think again. Using a technique called "digital recasting," producers were able to combine two scenes: (1) Bruce as he lay on the ground and (2) a car in the middle of the street just inches away from where Bruce wasn't.

■ *Casper, Toy Story,* and *Roger Rabbit* In these movies, producers developed *three-dimensional* characters and scenes to combine real people and animated characters.

FEATURES

IN THE INFORMATION AGE, KNOWLEDGE WORKERS UNDERSTAND...

1. Why some technologies are categorized as "emerging"

2. How emerging technologies are beginning to incorporate more of the senses

3. The dramatic changes occurring as a result of and on the Internet

4. The role of the wireless revolution in mobilizing people and technology

5. How emerging technologies will affect their personal lives

CHAPTER 7

Creating visual effects is not cheap. Many scenes that incorporate visual effects cost as much $10,000 per second to create. Couple that with the fact that desktop graphics workstations capable of performing such techniques as morphing and digital recasting cost as much as $60,000 apiece, and you can see that Hollywood is spending a lot of money to get you into a movie theater.

Hollywood isn't satisfied with just creating visual effects on the big screen. Today you can buy multimedia CD-ROM versions of many movies, take them home, and actually control how the movie plot unfolds. You can also buy the technology for making your own visual effects. For about $60, you can own a package called Morph that will help you recreate the morphing process used in *Terminator 2: Judgment Day*.[1,2,3] ❖

Introduction

Hollywood truly has embraced high tech; for that matter, so have most businesses around the world, regardless of industry. Hollywood's high-tech focus includes some relatively new technologies, or what we refer to as ***emerging technologies***. For example, digital recasting, morphing, and transparency are all important components of multimedia. You may be wondering why multimedia would be called an "emerging technology," especially when you can go to virtually any grade school anywhere in the country and see hundreds of young children learning to read, spell, and perform arithmetic using multimedia applications. Well, the term "emerging" doesn't necessarily mean brand new. We call a technology emerging if it falls into one of two categories:

- It is a technology that is so new that most businesses haven't exploited it.

- It is a technology that is fairly well-established, but businesses haven't fully exploited it.

In the first instance, we include such technologies as electronic cash, which facilitates Internet cash transactions. This is a very new technology. In fact, it's so new that many organizations still aren't certain how it will work or whether they even want their customers to make electronic cash purchases. These types of emerging technologies, for the most part, really are **new** technologies.

In the second instance, we include technologies such as multimedia. Schools may be using multimedia applications, but few organizations are exploiting the full benefits that multimedia offers, most notably those of enhancing presentations with visual and sound effects. We refer to these types of technology as *emerging* because the business world in general has yet to exploit their full potential.

Regardless of which technologies we describe as emerging or why, it's important for you to learn about them so you can determine how best to use them. And that's the focus of this chapter—emerging technologies, what they are, how they are being used, and how they may be used in the future. To facilitate our discussion of emerging technologies, we've grouped them into four categories (see Figure 7.1):

- **Emerging technologies for all the senses** These include applications that incorporate one or more of the following features: three-dimensional images, automatic speech recognition, multimedia, and/or virtual reality. These emerging technologies enhance the presentation of information to you.

- **Emerging technologies for the Internet explosion** You may think that the Internet is a standard technology, but many new technologies for the

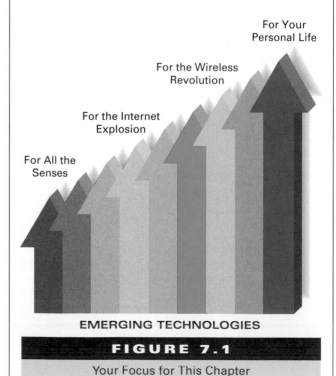

For Your Personal Life

For the Wireless Revolution

For the Internet Explosion

For All the Senses

EMERGING TECHNOLOGIES

FIGURE 7.1

Your Focus for This Chapter

Internet are emerging. These include electronic cash and converging technologies for communicating through and accessing the Internet, such as Internet telephones and Internet PCs.

- **Emerging technologies for the wireless revolution** These include smart phones, global positioning systems, and wireless local area networks. In Chapter 6 we discussed unguided, or wireless, communications media; here we look to new technology applications in the wireless revolution.

- **Emerging technologies for your personal life** These include intelligent home appliances and smart cards. You probably won't find these in the business environment, but these emerging technologies will definitely make your personal life easier.

As you explore the emerging technologies we present in this chapter, you should constantly ask yourself two questions. First, are these technologies still emerging or have they become standard? After all, this book was available in 1999—maybe things have changed since then. Second, have other technologies surfaced that could be classified as emerging? Information technology is one of the most rapidly changing and dynamic aspects of the business world. How many new technologies have you seen in the last 6 months? What are they? Which of the four categories would you place them in? Or do you need to create a new category?

Emerging Technologies for All the Senses

Throughout this text we've described information technology as a set of tools that helps you work with information and perform tasks related to information processing. It's a simple and accurate description, but some people forget that there are many types of information and that information can be presented in numerous different forms. Until recently, people working with technology have been content to work with information in traditional ways—entering text on a keyboard, viewing a graph on the screen, printing a document, and so on. But there are several emerging technologies that promise to radically change that. Those emerging technologies allow you to work with information that appeals to the senses. This group of emerging technologies includes three-dimensional imaging, automatic speech recognition, multimedia, and virtual reality.

3-D
Technology for Real Sight

Traditionally, we have viewed information displays in two dimensions or pseudo three dimensions. In two dimensions, you see only length and width—for example, the first graph in Figure 7.2 is two-dimensional. In pseudo three dimensions, shades and shadows are added to create a display that is somewhat realistic (second graph in Figure 7.2). Because it's not truly three-dimensional, it's called "pseudo." Most personal productivity software packages available today are capable of producing pseudo three-dimensional views of graphs, photos, and artwork. But what they can't do is generate real three-dimensional images.

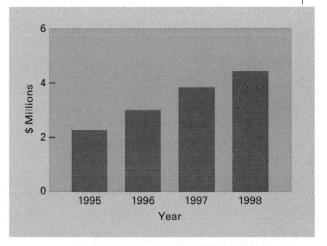

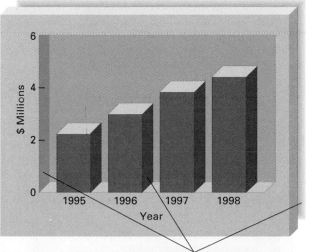

In pseudo three-dimensional views, shades and shadows are added to images.

FIGURE 7.2
Two Dimensions and Pseudo Three Dimensions

Real ***three-dimensional (3-D)*** technology presentations of information give you the illusion that the object you're viewing is actually in the room with you. You can see the depth of the image, turn it to reflect different angles to see its various perspectives, and in some ways understand the density of the object. Although 3-D technology is still in its infancy, it's already turning up in a number of areas—medicine, movies, video games, data visualization, science, education, and many others (see Figure 7.3). In fact, in the opening case study you saw how Hollywood is incorporating 3-D technologies into movies such as *Toy Story* and *Casper*.

3-D technology is not really a stand-alone technology; instead, it's incorporated into other types of technology and IT systems. For example, a number of Web sites include 3-D representations of photos (see Figure 7.4), and the number is growing to the extent that many people believe we'll all be surfing the Internet in 3-D in just a few short years. This, of course, would increase the allure of the Internet for electronic commerce. 3-D will allow consumers to get a great real-life view of products before they buy them. 3-D technologies are also showing up in multimedia and virtual reality applications (which we'll discuss later in this chapter).

The Future of 3-D Technologies

It's really only a matter of time before 3-D technologies become commonplace. In the past, capacity and speed constraints of other technologies (hard disks, internal memory, CPUs, and monitors) made 3-D very expensive and slow. As Dan Mapes, president of SynergyLabs, explains, "3-D was always seen as a very specialized, high-cost option, like an expensive spice from China. That day is passing fast." [4] Even today's inexpensive home computers have sufficient capacity and speed to generate 3-D images. It's just a matter of time before 3-D becomes a standard technology.

Automatic Speech Recognition
Conversing with Your Computer

People and computers have been engaging in normal conversation for many years now—in the movies. First, the computer captures and understands the words of the person; second, the computer generates speech in response to the words spoken by the person. For this to occur, two IT systems are needed, one for each phase. We refer to the first phase as automatic speech recognition

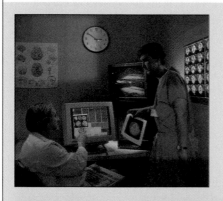

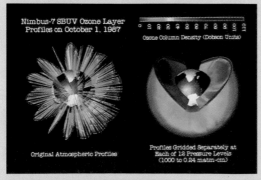
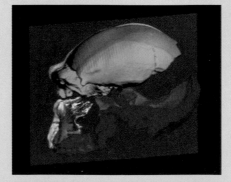

FIGURE 7.3

Three-Dimensional Applications

Like many Web sites, Lightscape (http://www.lightscape.com) generates 3-D images for your viewing. Soon all Web sites (even your personal one) will make use of 3-D technologies.

FIGURE 7.4
3-D Technologies on the Internet

and the second phase as speech synthesization. Of the two, automatic speech recognition is the real emerging technology that promises to forever change how people enter information and commands.

An ***automatic speech recognition (ASR)*** system not only captures spoken words but also distinguishes word groupings to form sentences. We refer to ASR as a system

because it contains a number of IT components that work together. For example, an ASR system contains an input device (a microphone), software to distinguish words, and databases containing words to which your spoken words are matched. To distinguish words and sentences and match them to those in a database, an ASR system follows three steps (see Figure 7.5).

■ **Step 1: Feature Analysis** The first step of ASR is called ***feature analysis***. Feature analysis captures your words as you speak into a microphone, eliminates any background noise, and actually converts the digital signals of your speech into phonemes. A phoneme is simply the smallest unit of speech, something most people equate with syllables. In Figure 7.5, you can see that the ASR system distinguished two phonemes in the word "tonight": "tə" and "nīt." This is exactly what you would see if you looked up the word "tonight" in the dictionary to determine how to pronounce it. The feature analysis step then passes the phonemes to step 2.

■ **Step 2: Pattern Classification** The second step is called ***pattern classification***. In it, the ASR system attempts to recognize your spoken phonemes by locating a matching phoneme sequence among the words stored in an acoustic model database. The acoustic model database is essentially the ASR

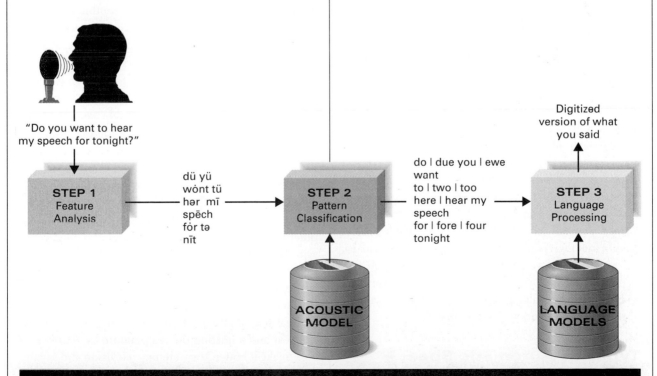

FIGURE 7.5
The Three Steps in Automatic Speech Recognition

system's vocabulary. In doing so, the ASR system is attempting to determine if it recognizes the words you spoke. Figure 7.5 shows that the system found two possible matches for "dü," the words "do" and "due." It also found multiple matches for "tü," "hər," and "fȯr." So, it sends all these possibilities to language processing—step 3.

■ **Step 3: Language Processing** The third step is called *language processing*. In it, the ASR system attempts to make sense of what you're saying by comparing the possible word phonemes (generated in step 2) with a language model database. The language model database includes grammatical rules, task-specific words, phrases, and sentences you might frequently use. If a match is found, what you said is stored in digital form.

Step 3—language processing—is by far the most complicated step, because the ASR system must attempt to determine your exact words. For example, did you begin your sentence with the word "do" or "due," was your second word "you" or "ewe," and so on. This is definitely not a simple process for a computer; it may be for you, but it's not for a computer. Throughout this process, the ASR system must perform a number of tasks, including evaluating the inflection of your voice. In our example, you're asking a question. So the ASR system recognizes the inflection for a question and, thus, determines that your first word is "do," rather than "due."

Our example illustrates why ASR systems are called "recognition" systems instead of "understanding" systems. While conversing with another person, you can easily distinguish "do" from "due," "you" from "ewe," and so on, according to the context of the sentence in which the word is used. However a computer has a difficult time with this because it possesses limited interpretative capabilities. Consider this sentence: "Fruit flies like a banana." What does it mean? Well, in the context of gardening Olympics, it implies that if you were to toss a piece of fruit into the air, it would "fly" through the air in the same way a banana would if you were to throw it. More realistically, though, it means that a winged insect called a fruit fly is particularly fond of the taste of a banana. So, while an ASR system would be able to correctly recognize your words, it certainly couldn't determine whether you were talking about the gardening Olympics or the taste preferences of certain insects.

Types of Automatic Speech Recognition Systems

If you survey the current ASR systems that are available today, you'll find four different types—discrete, continuous, speaker-independent, and speaker-dependent. *Discrete ASR* systems require you to pause between each spoken word. This may seem a bit cumbersome, but even with pauses, speaking is faster than typing, and most people adapt quickly to providing a pause between each word. *Continuous ASR* systems can process continuous streams of words—that is, normal speech patterns. Of these two, discrete ASR systems are the most prevalent. Continuous ASR systems have a long way to go before they can distinguish individual words in rapid, continuous speech.

Speaker-independent ASR systems can be used by anyone, but their vocabularies are often limited, and some lack expansion capabilities. For example, a number of speaker-independent ASR systems work in conjunction with personal productivity software such as word processing applications. They allow you to speak, rather than type or point at, certain commands (such as file, save, print, and so on). However, you can't use these systems to actually enter text by speaking. Finally, a *speaker-dependent ASR* system lets you "train" it to recognize your voice. You train these systems by reading a lengthy text, such as a Mark Twain novel, into a microphone. As you read, the system begins to recognize your voice and build its vocabulary. However, a speaker-dependent system recognizes only the speech of the person who trained it.

Ultimately, everyone would like ASR systems to be continuous and a combination of both speaker-dependent and speaker-independent. That is, the best ASR system would allow you to speak normally (continuous), allow you to expand its vocabulary (speaker-dependent), and allow multiple users (speaker-independent). Such a system is in the future—perhaps 5 years—but ASR systems are definitely moving in that direction. If you'd like to learn more about today's ASR systems, connect to the Web site for this text at http://www.mhhe.com/business/mis/haag, select "Emerging Technologies," and then choose "ASR Systems."

Some Interesting Uses of Automatic Speech Recognition

Can you imagine that one day you'll sit in front of a computer to type a term paper, and instead of typing, you'll actually speak your paper? That possibility is just around the corner. In fact, many people believe that ASR systems will be standard technology on home computers within the next few years. That's only a small portion of the real potential of ASR systems. Imagine driving in your car and adjusting the temperature by simply saying, "make it hotter," or watching television and saying, "ESPN," to switch the channel. This will become a reality in your lifetime. Not to be outdone, businesses are seeking innovative ASR implementations to gain advantage in the marketplace. Some of those organizations are listed below:[5]

- Sprint, US West, Southwestern Bell, and many other telephone service providers already offer voice dialing to their customers. By simply saying "dad" or "pizza," your telephone will automatically dial the number from a list of predefined numbers.

- KitchenAid recently demonstrated voice-controlled refrigerators, ovens, dishwashers, washing machines, and dryers. With a voice-controlled oven, for example, all you have to say is "prime rib, 8 pounds," and the oven will automatically set the temperature and notify you when dinner is ready.

- Thomas Cook Travel is working on a voice-controlled travel agency system that you can use over the phone. When you call for plane reservations, a computer will ask you for your destination and decipher your response to determine where and when you want to go and when you want to return.

Many organizations are even exploring "interviewerless interviews." With this type of system, marketing research firms will be able to perform telemarketing activities without human operators.[6] The possibilities really are limitless—anything you can communicate by typing, pointing, or speaking, can probably benefit from an ASR system.

The Future of Automatic Speech Recognition

ASR is an emerging technology because it has a long way to go before it becomes a standard business application. Nonetheless, the ASR market was expected to exceed $751 million in revenue by the end of 1997, up from $189.3 million in 1992.[7] ASR will not become a standard business technology until the following conditions are met.

- **Greater Storage for an Expandable Vocabulary** Sounds, even when phonetically digitized, require more storage space than a word in text form. If you need an ASR system with a large vocabulary, you'll need more storage for an acoustic model.

- **Better Feature Analysis to Support Continuous Speech** The most notable drawback to continuous ASR systems is their limited ability to distinguish words that are quickly and continuously spoken. One of the problems is that we tend to drop consonants when we speak, making it

If You Can't Speak It, Write It

One possible alternative to automatic speech recognition is *automatic handwriting recognition.* With handwriting recognition, you use a special pen or stylus to write words on a screen that captures your handwriting and converts it into editable text. Apple's Newton portable computer, for example, made use of handwriting recognition for several years. Unfortunately, Apple's Newton wasn't a big success in the United States because it made too many mistakes that users had to eventually correct.

But, in other countries, handwriting recognition technologies are almost an absolute necessity. In China, for example, users must type in YUYTU to designate the Chinese character for "race." Consider even further that there are some 6,000 widely used characters in the Chinese language and you can see why someone wouldn't want to memorize the equivalent English codes for each Chinese character. And, because ASR is still not perfect in its capturing and separation of words, many Chinese (and Japanese) users of technology are turning to automatic handwriting recognition systems. These systems capture Chinese or Japanese characters written on the screen and then compare them to a database of almost 20,000 conceivable characters.

New technologies for capturing information are emerging every day. And their success definitely depends on the country in which the technology is used. Handwriting recognition technologies were never really successful in English-speaking countries; in other countries, these same technologies are extremely successful and beneficial. As ASR systems continue to increase in effectiveness, it will be interesting to see if the language used determines how successful they are.[8] ❖

THE GLOBAL PERSPECTIVE

difficult for an ASR system to determine where one word ends and another begins. This process is handled by feature analysis (step 1), which must become more sophisticated, because some people don't want to pause between each spoken word (as a discrete ASR system requires).

- **More Dynamic Language Models to Support Speech Understanding** Speech recognition is great, but true speech understanding would be much better. For this to happen, language models that understand words in context must become more dynamic, understanding your words not only within the context of a sentence, but also in a paragraph or even in an entire conversation.

- **More Flexible Pattern Classification to Support Many People** For ASR to become truly viable in the workplace, a given system must be usable by anyone, in the same sense that anyone can use a keyboard or mouse. With the exception of speaker-independent systems, which usually have a limited vocabulary, ASR systems lack this quality. The proliferation of ASR systems that can interpret the speech of anyone—even those suffering from a head cold or speaking in a dialect—will define the true success of automatic speech recognition in business.

Multimedia
A Gold Mine of Information in Sight and Sound

If you think about it, we communicate using a variety of media forms. Teachers in classrooms speak, write on the board, and perhaps show slides from a presentation graphics software package. Books communicate with you through written words, photos, graphs, and drawings. Movies communicate with you through video and sound. The list is endless. Each of these examples is actually a form of multimedia because each one communicates with you through many (*multi*) forms (*media*).

Multimedia, one of the latest and most dynamic trends in technology, however, does more than present many forms of media. We define ***multimedia*** as the simultaneous presentation of information through many forms of media that you can control (see Figure 7.6). This definition has several implications. First, multimedia is a combination of content (information) and software (how you control the presentation of the information). Second, multimedia encompasses many forms of media for presenting information—text, graphic images, sound, and video (which can be animated). Third, multimedia can present information through various forms of media simultaneously. That is, you can look on the screen and potentially read text, watch a video, and see a drawing—all while listening to some form of narration.

ON YOUR OWN

Understanding the Speed of Automatic Speech Recognition

Consider the following paragraph:

There truly will come a time when knobs and dials are no longer present on any home appliance. Instead, people will simply speak commands and the appliance will respond appropriately. For couch potatoes, this represents a real problem. The only exercise for most couch potatoes occurs while operating the remote control—with automatic speech recognition, their thumbs won't even get a workout.

Now time yourself while you type that paragraph using word processing software and compare that time to those listed below:

- How long does it take you to say that paragraph using a continuous flow of words?

- How long does it take you to say that paragraph if you pause after each word?

What were your results? How much time did you save by speaking the paragraph instead of typing it? Based on the length of the typed paragraph, how much time would you save if you spoke a 10-page term paper instead of typing it? By the way, how many spelling errors did you make while typing the paragraph? ❖

PC Magazine publishes each issue as a multimedia application. Above, you can see that a narrator is explaining how to use various features.

FIGURE 7.6

A Sample Multimedia Application

Most important, multimedia is a presentation that you can control. This *interactivity* is a key component of today's multimedia applications. Without interactivity, multimedia is really nothing more than a movie. When you watch a movie, you may be able to rewind or fast forward, but you can't really control how the sequence of events (information) is presented.

In a multimedia application, a presentation of information is stored in the form of an **object**—a combination of information and procedures for presenting that information. If you're watching a multimedia presentation and see planets revolving around the sun while you're listening to a narrative on the solar system, the information contained in that object includes the planets (their size and color) and the recorded narration. The object also contains procedures that determine when the narration begins and how the planets revolve (their speed and their size change as they move nearer or farther from you). The procedures would also describe how you could move from that object to another object. For example, there may be a procedure that determines which planets you can click on and the links to obtain information about other planets. This linking of multimedia objects is what really allows you to control how you navigate through a multimedia application.

To this point, multimedia has been exploited mostly for personal applications such as encyclopedias and certain forms of video games. But the business world isn't far behind. In 1993 revenues of multimedia business applications were estimated at $554 million. By the end of 1997 that figure soared to almost $3.5 billion. For the business world, multimedia represents a whole new way of storing, accessing, and presenting information in a variety of environments. Multimedia applications offer a number of benefits: (1) they can store information in a wide variety of forms in an object, (2) they allow you to logically link those objects in any way you wish, and (3) they convey the stored information to you through a variety of media. Let's take a look at areas in which businesses currently use multimedia.

Where Is Business Using Multimedia?

The business world is currently using multimedia in three different ways: (1) to support internal processes, (2) to inform customers about products and services, and (3) to enhance products and services. In support of internal processes, most organizations are using multimedia for training. Multimedia training applications allow organizations to teach employees about new topics, products, or procedures without employing instructors or conducting formal training classes. Multimedia training may not seem like a big deal, but consider this: according to The American Society for Training and Development, over $210 billion is spent each year on employee training.[9] Furthermore, approximately 78 percent of that amount represents time and money lost while employees attend training sessions. If multimedia can reduce training expenses by as little as 5 percent, the business world would save almost $11 billion annually. That makes multimedia training support worth looking into. Some specific examples of multimedia training systems follow:

- Union Pacific uses multimedia to train new railroad traffic controllers, who eventually must be able to route 700 trains daily over 23,000 miles of track.

- AT&T uses multimedia to train employees to handle communications blackouts. Obviously, multimedia works well here because AT&T can't very well shut down parts of its network as a training exercise just to teach its employees how to handle different situations.

- Many insurance companies have sales training multimedia applications. In these applications, insurance agents meet a potential customer and then must choose from a variety of strategies to sell insurance to that customer.

Many organizations have also determined that multimedia is a great method for advertising products and services. And, when you think about it, multimedia advertising makes perfect sense. With a multimedia

Showing Products Through Multimedia in the Grocery Store

Many people get lost in a grocery store. Where are peaches—the canned fruit section, the dried fruit section, or the produce section? Where are artichoke hearts in vinegar—the canned vegetable section or the pickle and condiment section? Where is bulgur wheat—the organically grown section or the baking section? What's even worse is that most grocery stores group products into different categories, which means that the same products will be located in different areas of different stores.

Nature's Fresh, in Portland, Oregon, is hoping to alleviate some of those shopping worries by installing multimedia displays throughout the store. So, if you need to find peaches, you use a touch-sensitive multimedia kiosk and choose peaches and then the type you want. The multimedia system will display not only the store location of peaches, but also other information such as nutritional content, price, and whether they're organically grown.

You've probably seen such multimedia kiosks in shopping malls that provide you with directions. But what about grocery stores? Have you ever wanted to find toothpicks and didn't have the slightest idea where they would be? With the simple touch of a multimedia screen at Nature's Fresh, you'll never have to wander up and down aisles again—unless you want to.[10] ❖

advertising system, customers need only view the products and services that most interest them. Additionally, while "viewing" those products and services, customers can watch video clips, hear stories from other customers who use those products and services, and even see statistics and graphs concerning the life or safety of a product or service. Below are several uses of multimedia as a method of advertising.

- Florsheim Shoes has placed multimedia kiosks in its 400 stores nationwide and also in about 100 Sears department stores. Using Florsheim's kiosk, you can shop for shoes by style, color, and size and see high-quality photos as well. You can even enter your name, address, and credit card number to have a pair of shoes delivered directly to your home.

- Blockbuster has developed in-store video game kiosks that are essentially multimedia applications that let you try hundreds of different video games before you decide which one to buy. Once you make your choice and enter your credit card number, a system within the kiosk downloads the game from the home office and stores it on a game cartridge for you.

- Many airlines are installing flight-booking multimedia kiosks in airports all over the world. Now, instead of standing in line to buy a ticket, you enter the kiosk and choose the exact flight you want from options displayed on a screen. You can even view diagrams of planes and the airport itself so you'll know where your gate is located.

Finally, many organizations are actually incorporating multimedia into products and services for retail sale. Our opening case study about Hollywood's use of multimedia in movies is an excellent example of this. By using such techniques as morphing (transforming images) and digital recasting (inserting images into already-produced movie scenes), Hollywood has dramatically increased the real-life nature of movies and, at the same time, decreased costs.

Education provides another example. Many textbooks come with some form of a multimedia presentation on CD-ROM. Many such multimedia presentations can bring a textbook "to life" with video, animation, and sound. In the near future, you may not even buy textbooks for classes; instead you'll simply pay for the right to use a multimedia presentation of the textbook on your school's network. This is a form of *electronic publishing*, which takes advantage of multimedia to publish items such as books, magazines, newspapers, and advertising flyers in an electronic format rather than in the print-on-paper format associated with traditional publishing processes.

What Does It Take to Build a Multimedia Application?

Building a multimedia application is not actually that difficult. Many of today's authoring tools provide easy-to-use graphic interfaces that support your ability to quickly design, build, and link a series of multimedia objects. Other required functions such as capturing video, scanning graphic images, and inserting the images into a multimedia application are also relatively simple. So why isn't everyone building multimedia applications? Two reasons—*cost* and *creativity*.

A complete multimedia application development environment can be costly—especially for an individual. Besides a computer with ample RAM and disk storage, you'll need additional capturing (input) and conveying (output) technologies (see Figure 7.7). Some of the input technologies include an audiocassette player, a VCR, a camcorder, and a scanner. Output technologies include a set of speakers, a printer, and a high-resolution monitor or screen.

Creativity plays a significant role in the development of effective multimedia applications as well, and it may be the most important feature **you** bring to the multimedia application development environment. Developing a multimedia application of prewritten material may not require much creativity, but developing a sales training multimedia application for the insurance industry will certainly require a great deal of creativity on your part. That's why you'll find that the best multimedia application developers tend to be graphic artists who learned to apply their skills in a technology environment.

INDUSTRY PERSPECTIVE

Entertainment & Publishing

Paper and Ink May Be in the Past for the Chicago Tribune

Chicago Tribune Co., a classic publishing and broadcasting company, has decided to shed its paper and ink and become one of America's most aggressive multimedia players. After relying on papers and TV stations for most of its revenues over the past 25 years, it now wants to distribute products—everything from children's books, news, and country-and-western TV shows—through CD-ROM, online computer services, and interactive cable.

To position the company for this bold move, CEO Robert McCormick has been selling and buying right and left. First, he unloaded the *Daily News*. Then he sold 41 percent of the Tribune's newsprint operation. With money from those sales

and over $100 million in annual operating revenues, McCormick went on a buying spree that included

- *Education* $197 million for three publishers—Compton's Multimedia, Contemporary Books, and Wright Group
- *Television Food Network* 20 percent ownership of the cable network
- *ChicagoLand Television News* 24-hour news channel
- *America OnLine* 11 percent stake in the information service
- *The Road* Produces country music shows for TV and home video
- *WB Network* Links eight TV stations to Time Warner's fifth network

Before making these sales and acquisitions, Tribune obtained 65 percent of its revenues (over $1.9 billion in 1993) from its six newspapers, with the remaining 35

percent coming from its eight TV stations and six radio stations. Now McCormick hopes his new ventures will contribute at least 25 percent of operating revenue. For example, he hopes that Compton's Multimedia will reach several hundred million in sales in just 2 years.

The Chicago Tribune isn't the only publishing giant shedding its paper and ink and opting for electronic publishing media. R. R. Donnelley & Sons Co., also located in Chicago, is on a bold mission to rid itself of paper and provide information content in any electronic form that the customer wants. Its electronic arm, *Global Software Services,* now contributes 23 percent of total sales, up from a modest 8 percent only 5 years ago.

Technology is changing, and so must business. For the newspaper business that means shedding paper and ink and moving to multimedia.[11, 12] ❖

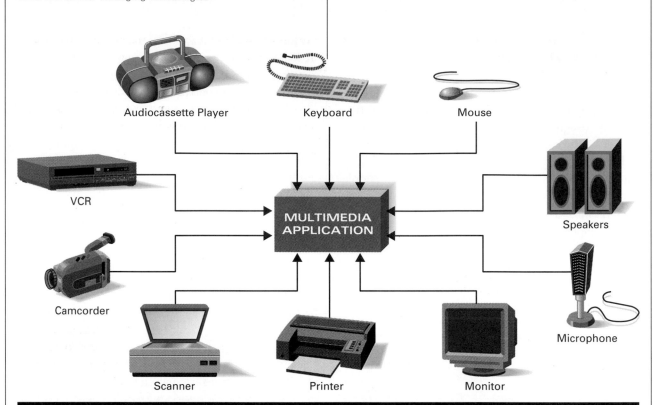

FIGURE 7.7
The Multimedia Application Development Environment

So, if your organization has the money and you possess the creativity, what are the steps you would go through to develop a multimedia application? In general, most multimedia application developers follow six phases (see Figure 7.8):

① Analysis

② Design

③ Programming

④ Production

⑤ Testing and documentation

⑥ Delivery

As with all types of application development, the process of developing a multimedia application is largely iterative rather than sequential. For example, programming will occur before, during, and after production and often during testing and documentation. Let's briefly consider the important aspects of each phase.

Phase 1: Analysis
During the analysis phase of multimedia application development, you lay the groundwork for your multimedia application by addressing five important issues.

What is the subject matter? This is obviously the first and most important question. What message are you trying to convey? Is the subject matter instructional, sales-oriented, entertaining, technical? Which types of subject matter are best conveyed visually? Which are best conveyed in audio form? Answering these questions will give you a better idea of the focus and direction of your multimedia application.

Who is the target audience? Good multimedia applications are always developed with people in mind. Who is the typical person that will use the multimedia application? What is his or her level of computer literacy, or does computer literacy even matter? To what types of media will the typical person most likely respond? For example, if you're developing a multimedia application to teach 6-year-olds how to perform addition, then you'll want to incorporate a large amount of sound and graphic images to hold their attention.

What is the setting? Setting refers to where and how the multimedia application will be used by the target audience. Will the multimedia application be used on a trade show floor, on a personal computer, over a network, in a business setting, or perhaps in an industrial setting?

Why multimedia? If there's a second most important question to answer, this is it. In other words, what problems are involved in conveying information currently? How will a multimedia application help solve those problems? Do the benefits of a multimedia application outweigh the costs associated with its development?

What other developers need to be involved? Finally, you need to assess your own development skills. For example, if you find that you'll need a great deal of video production, are you the best person to develop the video? Should you consider hiring someone to develop high-quality video?

Phase 2: Design

During the design phase, you concentrate on the content of the multimedia application and the way people will navigate it. As you concentrate on the content of the multimedia application, you'll create storyboards to develop the multimedia objects you'll use in your presentation. A *storyboard* is a visual representation of your multimedia objects. Most multimedia application developers first create a storyboard as a simple pencil sketch, then further refine its features (see Figure 7.9).

During the design phase, you also focus on how you'd like users to navigate the multimedia application. This is perhaps the most important aspect of the design phase because it determines how, and the order in which, the user will view the multimedia application. You can lay out the navigation of a multimedia application in five ways—linear, menu, hierarchy, network, and hybrid (see Figure 7.10). We briefly describe each of these next.

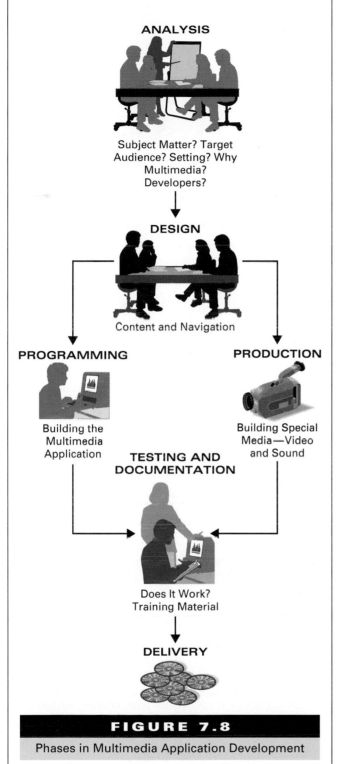

ANALYSIS

Subject Matter? Target Audience? Setting? Why Multimedia? Developers?

DESIGN

Content and Navigation

PROGRAMMING

Building the Multimedia Application

PRODUCTION

Building Special Media—Video and Sound

TESTING AND DOCUMENTATION

Does It Work? Training Material

DELIVERY

FIGURE 7.8

Phases in Multimedia Application Development

How will the multimedia application be used? Will it be used as a quick presentation, such as an information kiosk in a shopping mall? Or perhaps it will be used in a classroom setting in which students will interact with the multimedia application over long periods of time to learn about a particular topic.

Need three icons here for sound, video clips, and graphs. Each should be a button.

Storyboards often start as simple drawings and descriptions of which features are needed (left). Later the drawings and descriptions are further refined (right).

FIGURE 7.9

Creating and Refining Storyboards

(a) Linear

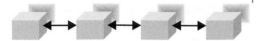

(b) Menu

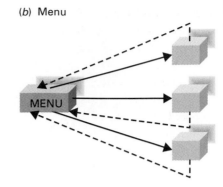

(c) Hierarchy

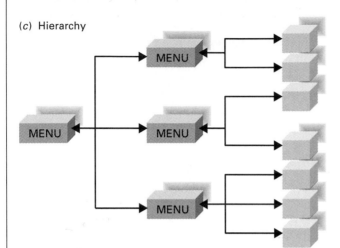

(d) Network

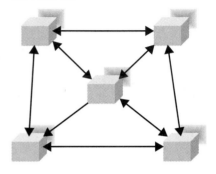

(e) Hybrid

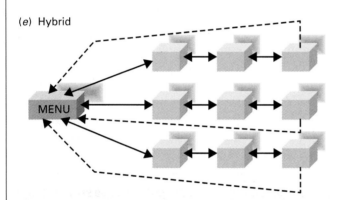

FIGURE 7.10

Methods of Navigating Through a Multimedia Application

- *Linear* Allows users to move forward to view new material or backward to review previous material.

- *Menu* Allows users to choose from a list of available topics and returns them to the menu once they've reviewed the requested material.

- *Hierarchy* Allows users to choose from a list of available topics, which in turn include menus to allow users to further refine their viewing choices.

- *Network* Allows users to jump from any given presentation to another, whether related or unrelated. This is probably the most complex and interesting design.

- *Hybrid* Allows users several navigation options, because it combines any of the other four navigation forms. For example, it might combine linear and menu navigation forms.

Your choice of navigation method will be influenced by the decisions you made in phase 1. That is, if you correctly define the subject matter, the target audience, the setting, and the reasons you want to use multimedia, you'll be able to identify the most effective navigation method or methods for your presentation.

Phase 3: Programming

In the programming phase, you choose the appropriate multimedia authoring software, convert your storyboards (created in phase 2) into multimedia objects on the computer, and build your multimedia application by creating the links that will allow people to navigate through it. ***Multimedia authoring software*** (sometimes called "authoring software") is software specifically designed to help you create a multimedia application. Authoring software can include simple presentation graphics software, such as PowerPoint and Harvard Graphics, or full-fledged authoring software, such as Authorware, Quest, Icon-Author, and Macromedia Director. Your choice of multimedia authoring software is critical. It's important that you choose authoring software that not only supports all your multimedia development needs, but also is easy to use. For a complete list of today's newest and best authoring software, connect to the Web page for this text, and select "Multimedia."

Phase 4: Production

The production phase is most often performed in conjunction with phase 3 (programming). In the production phase, you concentrate on building special forms of media—usually sound and video. If you incorporate sound, you can record it yourself or use prerecorded sound elements from cassette tapes and CDs. Be careful here—using a popular song from a CD may enhance your presentation, but you may have to obtain permission from the recording artist to use it, which can be extremely costly.

Phase 5: Testing and Documentation

During phase 5, you document how the multimedia application works and test the application by allowing potential users to experiment with it. While doing this, you'll obviously find yourself returning to phases 2 through 4 to define additional navigational paths, design new objects, make any corrections to the existing objects, and capture more special media.

You should plan to spend a great deal of time on testing and documentation. It's critical that you create a multimedia application that works correctly and satisfies all the information and navigational needs of your target audience. You'll also want to create good documentation, so people can quickly learn how to use your multimedia application.

Phase 6: Delivery

Once you've completed the testing and documentation, you're ready to deliver your multimedia application. Most multimedia applications today are delivered on CD-ROM (with DVD on the rise) because it's durable and has ample storage space. You must have a recordable CD drive to store your multimedia application on a CD-ROM. This is an additional expense to your multimedia application development environment. Recordable CD drives cost between $700 and $3,000. Couple that with the $7 cost of a blank CD, and you can see how your expenses can quickly multiply. Consider even further that once you "burn" (the term associated with writing to a CD-ROM) a CD, you can never change its

content. So make sure you're completely happy with your multimedia application **before** preparing it for delivery.

So Why Isn't the Business World Using More Multimedia?

Multimedia is a very effective method of communicating information because it enriches presentations, retains audience attention, and often eliminates the need for one-on-one interaction. Why, then, isn't the business world more fully embracing multimedia? There are two answers: one is related to network issues and the other to business process issues.

CAREER OPPORTUNITY

Some organizations would like to develop multimedia applications, but their employees lack multimedia development experience. Developing multimedia applications is quite different from developing other, more formal business applications, such as payroll and order entry. In addition to requiring creativity, multimedia application developers must also know how to use and program objects; how to capture and manipulate special forms of media, such as voice and video; and how to use multimedia authoring software. This is a substantial career opportunity for you—organizations desperately need good multimedia applications developers. According to *USA Today,* multimedia application development is one of the 10 hot jobs of the future, with salaries approaching and exceeding $100,000.[13] You should give this some serious thought.

All organizations use networks to electronically move information. Those same networks must also support the movement of multimedia information. And video and sound clips—important parts of a multimedia application—take up a lot of space. For example, 1 second of television-quality video can take up an amazing 1 million bytes. So organizations must have networks that can accommodate the electronic movement of both traditional and multimedia information. That can be a real problem, one you've probably experienced if you've tried to access a multimedia-intensive Web site. Undoubtedly, you had to wait several minutes or more for the document to load the graphics, video, and sound.

Also, many organizations don't support internal processes with multimedia because some processes are not well-suited to multimedia. Consider a payroll system as an example. If you were a payroll clerk, would you really need voice and animated presentations of information and the ability to jump around all over the payroll application? The answer is no, and that same answer holds true for many business processes. This all goes back to the analysis phase of multimedia development and answering, "Why multimedia?" Many organizations have answered this question by determining that many business processes simply don't need multimedia support.

Virtual Reality

Making You Feel Like You're There

Imagine a time when you can experience a roller coaster ride, snow skiing, and sky diving without ever going to a theme park, visiting the slopes of Colorado, or getting in an airplane. Sound too good to be true? Not actually. On the horizon is a new technology that will virtually place you in any experience you desire. That new technology is *virtual reality*—a three-dimensional computer simulation in which you actively and physically participate. Let's look again at that definition and note several key features of virtual reality.

- Virtual reality incorporates 3-D technologies to give you a real-life illusion.

- Virtual reality creates a simulation of a real-life situation.

- In virtual reality, special input devices capture your physical movements and special output devices send physical responses back to you.

That last feature is what truly distinguishes virtual reality from other types of technology. For example, multimedia incorporates many media such as sound, video, and animation. So does virtual reality. But virtual reality

FIGURE 7.11

Input and Output Devices in Virtual Reality

goes one step further by incorporating physiological input and output (the sense of touch). In fact, taste and smell are the only senses that aren't usually represented in virtual reality; and even those might one day be incorporated.

To incorporate physiological input and output, virtual reality makes use of several special input and output devices—most commonly gloves, headsets, and walkers (see Figure 7.11). A *glove* is an input device that captures and records the shape and movement of your hand and fingers and the strength of your hand and finger movements. A *headset* is a combined input and output device that serves two purposes. As an input device, a headset captures and records the movement of your head—side to side, up and down. As an output device, a headset contains a screen that covers your entire field of vision and displays various views of an environment, based on your movements. Finally, a *walker* is an input device that captures and records the movement of your feet as you walk or turn in different directions. In some virtual reality systems, walkers also act as output devices by changing the tension of the rollers, to simulate walking through sand or mud, or even changing their angle, to simulate walking up or down a hill.

To illustrate how these work, consider a virtual reality environment in which you're trying to shoot monsters in a swamp. When you put on your headset, you see the swamp in front of you. As you move your head, you see different views of the swamp. Don't forget—your views of the swamp would be in 3-D, giving you the illusion that you're really in a swamp. As you begin to walk on the walker, the headset adjusts your view so that it looks like you're walking into the swamp. And, as you proceed into a marshy bog, the walker adjusts its tension to make it more difficult for you to walk. There's a glove on your hand and a gun in the glove. As you move your hand, the headset adjusts its view so you can virtually see your hand and the direction in which you're pointing the gun. So, when you finally see a monster, you move your hand in the appropriate direction and squeeze the trigger. On your screen you see the gun fire and, you hope, vaporize the monster.

Applications of Virtual Reality

In 1995 revenues for virtual reality were estimated at $275.8 million, which is not really that much.[14] Nonetheless, virtual reality applications are popping up everywhere, sometimes in odd places. One of the more common applications of virtual reality is found in the entertainment industry. For example, there are a number of virtual reality games on the market, including downhill Olympic skiing, race car driving, golfing, air combat, and marksmanship (similar to our example of monsters in a swamp). Some require special input and output devices (more than just gloves, headsets, and walkers). For example, virtual reality race car driving uses a clutch, brake, gas pedal, and gear shift; and virtual reality skiing uses a huge fan to give you the illusion of wind blowing in your face as you race down a ski slope.

Also in the area of entertainment, virtual reality is appearing in many movies. For example, in *Disclosure* Michael Douglas enters a virtual reality environment that simulates a large room with filing cabinets full of information. In *Virtuosity* virtual reality gets so real that Denzel Washington must track down a virtual reality killer who figured out how to exit the virtual environment and enter the real world. And, if you saw the movie *Congo,* you might have noticed that Amy (the gorilla) uses sign language and virtual reality gloves to communicate with humans.

In business, many organizations are exploring virtual reality to create numerous simulated environments. Consider these examples:

■ Matsushita Electric Works has devised a virtual reality system to help you select new kitchen appliances. You simply provide Matsushita with the layout of your kitchen, which is scanned into a virtual reality system. Once you enter the virtual reality environment, you can change your refrigerator or dish washer, see how they fit, and even request color changes.

■ Volvo has a virtual reality system to demonstrate the safety features of its cars. In this virtual reality system, you virtually experience a car wreck to learn how air bags work.

■ Many airlines use virtual reality to train pilots how to effectively react in adverse conditions. In this environment, pilots are faced with bad weather, defective engines, and malfunctioning landing gear.

Think about the last example. Is it really possible for airlines to provide anything but a simulation of real-life conditions? Not really—and that's one of the greatest advantages of virtual reality. It can create simulations of

INDUSTRY PERSPECTIVE   **Health Care**

Virtual Reality Simplifies Patient's World

Imagine a world in which the color blue feels like sandpaper, a world in which the only furniture you can sit on must be green, or a world in which the sound of a pin dropping on the floor sounds like the cracking of thunder. Most of us can't. Unfortunately, that's the real world for a person with autism. Autism is a disease that interferes with the development of the part of the brain that processes sensory perceptions. And, in many instances, autistic people may feel sandpaper grinding across their skin when they see a color or they may be unable to correlate similar objects, such as chairs, bar stools, couches, and love seats (all items on which you can sit).

For autistic people, the world is a mishmash of objects that makes no sense to them when they have to deal with them all at once. That makes teaching autistic people very difficult. For example, if you place two differently colored chairs in front of an autistic person and tell him or her that they are both chairs, that person may become confused and disoriented.

A simple world is the best world for individuals suffering from autism. Unfortunately, the real world is not simple. So Dorothy Strickland and many others are researching ways to use virtual reality to teach people with autism. In a virtual reality simulation, researchers can eliminate all forms of background noise, colors, and objects, except those that they want the autistic person to focus on. As the autistic person becomes comfortable with the virtual reality simulation, new objects or colors can be introduced without the usual adverse effects.

Technology is really great—it can help an organization gain a competitive advantage in the marketplace or help you get a job in the future. But the greatest uses of technology may never make anyone rich; instead those uses will allow many mentally and physically challenged individuals to cope with daily life.[15] ❖

environments without the presence or incorporation of physical objects. Thus pilots can virtually crash a plane while they learn to cope with adverse conditions. Yet no one is injured, no planes are lost.

Motorola also discovered this benefit of virtual reality when training assembly line workers.[16] Traditionally, Motorola had spent hundreds of thousands of dollars to build replica assembly lines to facilitate training. With virtual reality assembly line training, however, Motorola simply created a "virtual" assembly line that presents different situations to each worker with the press of a button. By using virtual reality, Motorola has realized a tenfold increase in savings. But it doesn't stop there—Motorola has found that virtual reality–trained employees learn more efficiently than employees who were trained on real assembly lines. As Art Paton, instructional design manager at Motorola, explained, "They [employees] become totally immersed in the virtual environment and seem to absorb concepts much faster." That, coupled with cost savings, is a substantial advantage of virtual reality training.

The health care industry, likewise, is exploring virtual reality for a variety of applications. Using virtual reality, doctors can now practice surgery, explore the human body, and diagnose diseases, all without touching a cadaver.[17] Some doctors are even using virtual reality to perform long-distance triage. In this instance, a doctor in one location slips into virtual reality gloves and a special head-mounted camera to examine a patient. Another doctor—who can be located half way around the world—also wears virtual reality gloves and a headset.

Whatever the first doctor sees and feels is electronically communicated to the second doctor who, in turn, sees and feels the same thing. This health care application of virtual reality will soon be widely used for disaster area triage when it's impossible to transport doctors quickly to the location.

Cybersickness
The Downside of Virtual Reality

Every coin has two sides. Virtual reality, like all technologies, has associated disadvantages as well as advantages. People who participate in virtual reality environments sometimes experience *cybersickness*, including eyestrain, simulator sickness, and flashbacks.[18] You may experience eyestrain if you remain too long in a virtual reality system that uses a low-resolution headset for displaying views. Because of the low resolution, your eyes must work harder to distinguish images. Some people experience simulator sickness when the physiological inputs and outputs of the system are out of sync. For example, if you move your head and the headset takes an extra second to adjust your view, you may experience nausea or dizziness. Finally, some people experience virtual reality flashbacks several hours after using virtual reality. This occurs because virtual reality systems cannot yet provide you with a wholly "virtual" physical experience. So your brain must compensate for this while you use virtual reality. Later, your brain may also try to compensate while you're experiencing real life. This may cause you to experience déjà vu or a temporary disassociation with reality.

HERE'S AN
IT TWIST   Controlling a Computer with Your Mind

For many people, believing in new technology advances such as automatic speech recognition and virtual reality is hard to do. Even more people have a really difficult time believing that we'll someday be able to control a computer with our minds. Well, how about this—a small firm recently introduced a product called *The Mind Drive*. And it does just what its name says. It lets you control movements on the screen without ever touching an input device.

The Mind Drive actually does have an input device, but it works like no other. The input device for *The Mind Drive* is a sensor that slips over your finger. It measures very, very small physiological responses through your skin and sends them to the CPU. The CPU interprets your physiological responses and causes movement on the screen. And you never lifted a finger—literally. Applications that will use *The Mind Drive* include action video games, art and music software (think, and the orchestra changes tempo), lie detector games, and learning enhancement software.

In the movie *Field of Dreams,* the big catch phrase was, "If you build it, they will come." With *The Mind Drive,* the catch phrase will be, "If you think it, it will happen."[19] ❖

Piping Virtual Reality Through an Intranet

In Chapter 6 you learned about the many advantages of intranets, such as the ability to utilize existing Internet technologies and the ability to protect against outside access to an internal intranet. Indeed, intranets are a great way for organizations to provide employees with access to information, while ensuring that outsiders can't gain access to it.

Most organizations today are using intranets to provide access to mainly text and graphic information. But, Bechtel Group Inc., a $7.9 billion construction, architecture, and engineering giant, wants more than just text and graphic information on its intranet—it wants to create virtual reality systems on its intranet and allow any of its 20,000 worldwide employees to actively and physically participate in the virtual reality systems.

In doing so, Bechtel can create virtual reality environments of proposed building and construction designs. Then Bechtel employees anywhere in the world will be able to use the intranet to see and feel the proposed designs. All they have to do is put on their virtual reality gear (gloves, headsets, and so on), connect to the intranet, and have virtual reality piped directly to their computer. No longer will designers from all over the world have to meet in the same room to experience virtual reality.[22] ❖

The Future of Virtual Reality

Virtual reality is part of your future, regardless of its disadvantages. Researchers are working daily to solve the problems that produce cybersickness. Further, researchers are suggesting innovative uses for virtual reality—some that may dramatically alter both your business and personal life. In business, for example, some people are exploring virtual reality as a tool to illustrate corporate downsizing.[20] In this instance, a CEO can define the new structure of an organization (fewer employees, new business processes, and less building space) in virtual reality. Other top managers can then virtually view and experience the effects of the proposed organizational changes. One day, virtual reality may be the first tool individuals and groups reach for when they want to create or reorganize a business—and it may simulate the fact that you no longer have a job.

On the home front, you may soon be able to experience the company of friends and family members through virtual reality piped over the Internet.[21] These types of virtual reality applications make use of *Cave automatic virtual environments (CAVEs)*, which are special 3-D rooms spread across the world. You enter a CAVE, as would your friends or family members in another location. Once inside, your image (including sound and movement) would be projected into the other CAVE; likewise, the images of the people in the other CAVE would be projected into your CAVE. All of you would simply have the illusion of carrying on a conversation while sitting in the same room. Someday, grandparents may be able to enjoy their distant grandchildren in a playground through the use of CAVEs.

Some Final Thoughts About Emerging Technologies for All the Senses

Emerging technologies such as automatic speech recognition and virtual reality encompass most of the senses except taste and smell. Smell may be incorporated sooner than you think. Researchers are already working on special aroma-producing systems that use combinations of perfume-like substances to create virtually any smell. Just think about it—while using virtual reality to surf the waves of Hawaii, the system may also produce a salt smell (and splash water in your face when you fall).

Taste, unfortunately, has a long way to go. Although researchers can reproduce literally any taste, most people are wary of placing something in their mouths and swallowing any residue. If we do get to the point where IT systems actually reproduce tastes for us, one question will be on everyone's mind: "If it's a virtual taste, does that mean the calories are also virtual?" It'll be interesting to see (or rather taste).

The Internet Explosion

Emerging All Around You

Undoubtedly, the Internet is the most visible, rapidly changing, dynamic, mind-boggling, and exciting emerging technology. Perhaps we shouldn't just say "the Internet." More appropriately, what's really most exciting and emerging about the Internet is the way in which the business world and individuals are exploiting it. For example, in Chapter 6 we explored how organizations are establishing their own private Internets, called "intranets." We also looked at other topics such as extranet applications, Internet virtual private networks, individualized electronic advertising, and competitive intelligence gathering—all of which have something to do with exploiting the Internet and its worldwide connectivity.

In this section we want to look at two more emerging aspects of the Internet: (1) electronic cash, which you can use to purchase products on the Internet; and (2) the convergence of your telephone, television, computer, and cable TV service as a way of communicating through and accessing the Internet.

Electronic Cash

Virtual Money on the Internet

Currently, we have three major methods of paying for products and services—cash, debit card or check, and credit card. For every purchase you make, you use one of these methods of payment. The same will be true when you make purchases over the Internet. Let's briefly explore these methods of payment, and then we'll see how they'll work on the Internet, especially Internet cash transactions. Everyone is familiar with *cash transactions*. You buy a product or service in exchange for real cash, either folding or coins. Cash is a tender backed by the federal government. So we all know that we can accept a $10 bill from someone today and that it will be worth $10 tomorrow when we use it to make purchases.

Debit and credit transactions are different. Like cash, *debit transactions* require that you gather money in advance and then spend it. When you make a purchase using a personal check or your checking account debit card, you complete a debit transaction. That is, you build up a pool of money in your checking account, and then you spend it. *Credit transactions*, on the other hand, give you the ability to make purchases first and pay for them later. When you charge products on a store charge account or your credit card, for example, you're creating a balance that you must later pay.

On the Internet, debit and credit transactions occur similarly. For example, you can use your checking account debit card or credit card to make purchases on the Internet. When you locate a product you'd like to purchase, you simply provide the merchant with your account number. If you use a debit card, the merchant will notify your bank of the transaction. Your bank simply debits your account and credits the account of the merchant. If you use a credit card, the merchant will notify your credit card issuer of the transaction. The credit card issuer will pay the merchant for the transaction and bill you for the transaction amount.

Internet cash transactions, however, are very different from real-life cash transactions. When you cruise the Internet in search of products to buy, you can't carry around or use hard cash—you need electronic cash. *Electronic cash* (also called *e-cash* or *digital cash*) is exactly what its name implies—an electronic representation of cash. This electronic representation of cash is nothing more than a file (similar to a word processing or spreadsheet file) that says you have a certain denomination of money in electronic form. You can then buy products and services on the Internet by sending the e-cash file to a merchant. It may sound simple (and it is in theory), but e-cash is the subject of much debate.

Figure 7.12 demonstrates how e-cash will someday work on the Internet. To use e-cash to make purchases on the Internet, the first thing you have to do is obtain e-cash from an electronic bank on the Internet. You can buy e-cash in a variety of ways—you can send real cash through the mail, provide your debit or credit card number as if you were making a regular product purchase, or actually open an account with an electronic bank and request that an amount of e-cash be deducted from your account balance and sent to you. Whatever the case, the electronic bank will electronically send you e-cash files. For example, you could request $100 in e-cash in $20 increments. What you would end up with is 5 e-cash files, each representing $20 on your hard disk.

Once you have your e-cash, all you have to do is find a product to purchase on the Internet and send the appropriate number of e-cash files to the merchant (for example, a $40 purchase would require two e-cash files). In turn, the merchant can use the e-cash to purchase products and services from other merchants or return it to the electronic bank for real money.

What's Holding Up Electronic Cash?

E-cash is deceivingly simple—instead of using real money, you simply use an electronic form of money. And indeed, someday it will be simple and commonplace. First,

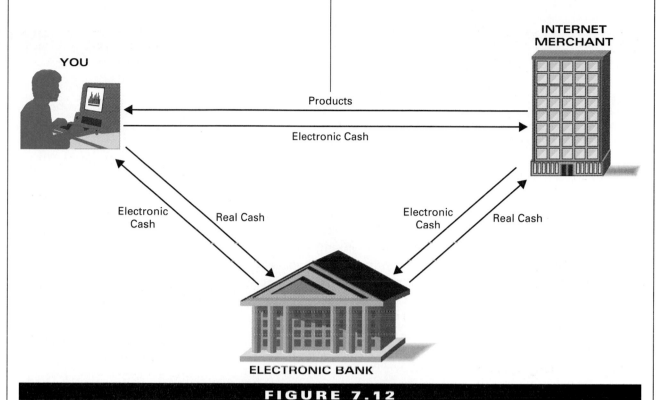

FIGURE 7.12

How Electronic Cash Will Work on the Internet

however, there are many hurdles to overcome. We describe some of these below.

- **Anyone Can Be an Electronic Bank** Currently, there are no governmental regulations defining who can become an electronic bank. In fact, you as an individual can open your own electronic bank on the Internet. You don't need the government's permission, and you don't need to be backed by the FDIC or FSLIC.

- **There Are No Standards for How E-Cash Should Look** Many electronic banks are surfacing on the Internet, and none of them agree on what an e-cash file should look like. So e-cash from one electronic bank doesn't necessarily look like e-cash from another electronic bank. This has many merchants wary—dealing with different forms of e-cash is almost like accepting different forms of international currency.

- **Merchants Must Have Accounts with Electronic Banks** Most electronic banks require that merchants establish accounts with them to facilitate real-money and e-cash exchange. For example, the Mark Twain Bank in St. Louis is an electronic bank from which you can purchase e-cash.[23] Unfortunately, a merchant to whom you send

e-cash must also have an account with the Mark Twain Bank in order to convert your e-cash into real money.

- **E-Cash Makes Money Laundering Easy** E-cash is completely anonymous. It contains no information about you—only about the denomination and electronic bank provider. Thus e-cash can easily be used for money laundering. Illegally obtained real cash can easily be traded in for e-cash; the owner of the e-cash can then spend it without anyone knowing its origination.

- **E-Cash Is Easy to Lose** E-cash is simply an electronic file on your hard disk; so, if your hard disk crashes, you may lose your money, and it is unlikely that your electronic bank will replace it. Likewise, you could accidentally erase your e-cash files, or they could be destroyed by some glitch that occurs while you transmit them to an Internet merchant.

What Will It Take for Electronic Cash to Become a Reality?

In spite of its drawbacks, e-cash is coming and it will be widely used in a matter of a few years. For e-cash to become a reality, two major things must happen. First,

Creating an Internet-Exclusive Bank

There are currently many obstacles to overcome before electronic cash is widely accepted over the Internet. But banks haven't hesitated to exploit the Internet to provide financial products and services. Many "traditional" banks today offer some services on the Internet; others have chosen to use the Internet as the sole distribution channel for financial services.

In Atlanta, a group of bankers and entrepreneurs are creating one such Internet bank called the Atlanta Internet Bank (AIB). The AIB will have no drive-up windows and no lobbies in which you can get a bank representative's help. Instead, you'll perform all your banking transactions through the Internet. Initially, the AIB plans to offer checking and money market accounts and bill payment services; later it will add brokerage services and credit products.

The jury is still out concerning how successful Internet-only banks will be. According to Don Shapleigh, AIB's president, "This is a new venture that is plowing uncharted ground, so it's going to be an extremely interesting process. We are looking forward to trying it out in Atlanta and, after that, taking on the world." Can you imagine that? Someday you may never see a bank building. Instead, all banks will exist in virtual cyberspace on the Internet.[25] ❖

standards are needed to define how e-cash will look and work. One organization working on these standards is the Joint Electronic Payments Initiative (JEPI), headed by such businesses as Cybercash, IBM, and Microsoft.[24] Several other organizations are also working on standards. All these organizations will have to unite and agree on a common standard. Second, the federal government must become involved in developing regulations for electronic banks. Most merchants are wary of electronic banks because there are no formal rules governing their operation or liquidity. You should be wary as well. Research an electronic bank before you send it money; you may be sending your money to a "mom and pop" shop that runs away with it.

CAREER OPPORTUNITY

Is there a career opportunity associated with e-cash? You bet. Now it's easier than ever to open your own business on the Internet. You'll reach millions of people daily by setting up shop on the Internet, and e-cash will soon be an easy, convenient method for your customers to make purchases.

Once these two problems are solved, e-cash will become a standard Internet technology. As merchants gain confidence in and begin accepting e-cash, more consumers

will use it. Acceptance of e-cash will follow the same pattern as the recent and increasing acceptance of non-Visa or non-MasterCard credit cards; as more merchants accept them, more consumers will use them.

Converging Technologies for Communicating Through and Accessing the Internet

Let's stop and think for a moment about the many ways information comes into your home or apartment and the many ways you transmit information. The postal service shows up every day to deliver and pick up your mail. A newspaper-delivery person throws you a newspaper at 6:00 A.M. every morning. You use the telephone to receive incoming calls and call other people. You use your computer to connect to the Internet or your school's network. You use your television (most likely connected to a cable TV service provider) to watch the news, sporting events, and your favorite shows.

Basically, information flows in and out of your home every day through a variety of channels. Now, let's focus on just your telephone, computer, television, and cable TV service provider. What do all of these have in common? In short, they all support the electronic movement of information. And that has led many people to ask some obvious questions: "Why not combine some or all

Finding Electronic Cash on the Internet

Do a little cruising around the Internet to find electronic banks that provide e-cash and merchants who accept e-cash. To find electronic banks, you might want to start at the sites for the Mark Twain Bank and Cybercash. Those sites will probably provide you with a list of additional sites that accept e-cash for purchases.

How many electronic banks did you find? Are some of these "real" banks or simply organizations that convert your hard money into electronic money? Did you happen to find any electronic banks that looked a little "shady," as though you couldn't trust them?

What about merchants who accept e-cash—how many of those did you find, and what type of merchandise are they selling? Do these merchants offer payment forms other than e-cash? ❖

---

of these devices? After all, I have a digital alarm clock that always displays the time, wakes me up in the morning, and plays music. Why can't I have a *cable-vision-phone-computer*?" Well, in some form or fashion you can. And what's really great is that these devices also give you access to the Internet. So they essentially become *Internet-accessing-cable-vision-phone-computer* devices. That's a mouthful and obviously not the real name for any such device. But it does convey the appropriate message—some sort of device that combines many of the features of a telephone, television, computer, and cable TV service provider, all the while giving you access to the Internet.

Let's take a look at a few of these emerging devices or technologies that support your electronic movement of information and access to the Internet.

Internet Telephones
Almost-Free Long-Distance Calls

One of the great advantages of the Internet is worldwide connectivity, which allows you to access information resources and communicate with people all over the world (for example, through e-mail or in chat rooms). What's even better, these communications are paid for

---

International Electronic Cash

Two ways to predict the potential success or failure of emerging technologies is to (1) look at the organizations who are pushing the use of such technologies and (2) evaluate the worldwide acceptance of such technologies. Those ways certainly hold true for electronic cash. If big financial institutions don't support e-cash, it probably won't succeed. And, if the worldwide financial community does not support e-cash, its acceptance and use in only the United States may not be enough to define it as a truly standard technology.

With those issues in mind, it seems that e-cash will someday become a standard technology. Currently, organizations such as Citibank,

THE GLOBAL PERSPECTIVE

Wells Fargo, MasterCard International, and Deutsche Bank (in Germany) are actively pursuing the use of e-cash on the Internet. Those organizations are definitely big, and they have a tremendous worldwide presence and influence. With support from those organizations, e-cash does indeed seem destined to become a standard technology.

However, one major obstacle still exists. Many of these organizations are working independently, often offering e-cash that looks and works differently. For e-cash to become standard, agreements will have to be made among these organizations concerning how e-cash will look and work.[26, 27] ❖

through the monthly fee you pay your Internet service provider, such as America Online. In other words, these connections are made without long-distance charges accruing to your monthly phone bill. Most people understand these advantages, so they quickly began taking advantage of the Internet as a communication tool to make almost-free long-distance calls all over the world.

This emerging technology is called an ***Internet telephone***, which provides you with the technology tools required to carry on a phone conversation over the Internet. An Internet phone is not simply a telephone; it is a collection of technology tools that support Internet telephone calls. In fact, an Internet telephone system doesn't even include a traditional telephone. To demonstrate how an Internet telephone works, let's consider making a phone call using VocalTec's Internet Phone (see Figure 7.13). Basic requirements include a personal computer equipped with a sound card (obviously for generating

THE BASICS

A Computer with a Sound Card, Microphone, and Set of Speakers

GETTING STARTED

Software to Make an Internet Phone Call

VocalTec's Web Site

Registration and One-Time Fee

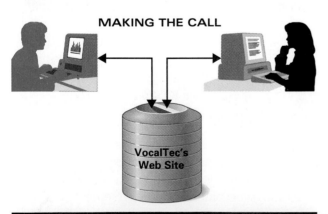

MAKING THE CALL

VocalTec's Web Site

FIGURE 7.13

Making an Internet Phone Call

sound) and a microphone and set of speakers connected to the sound card. Fortunately, most personal computers manufactured today contain this equipment. If you have the required technology, you can connect to VocalTec's Web site at http://www.vocaltec.com and download the necessary software for making Internet phone calls. You'll also be asked to register as an Internet phone caller. When you register, VocalTec will charge you a small one-time fee, probably less than $50.

When you want to make a phone call over the Internet, you go through a series of simple steps. First, you connect to the Internet through your Internet service provider. Then you connect to VocalTec's Web site, where you browse through a listing of people who are currently on the Internet and also have Internet phone-calling capabilities. From the list, you click the name of the person you want to speak with, then speak into the microphone. You'll hear the other person's voice through your speakers.

You should know, too, that making an Internet phone call could require some coordination. For example, if you want to talk to a friend in the Philippines, you'll each have to agree on a time when the phone call will occur. That way, your friend's name (usually a nickname) will appear on the list of people currently on the Internet who also have Internet phone-calling capabilities.

Cable-Ready Computers
For Watching TV While You Work

Most of you are probably familiar with cable-ready TVs. These types of TVs basically need no special cable box for you to connect to your local cable TV service provider. With them, you connect your TV directly to the cable TV outlet. You may be able to do the same with your computer. If you can, your computer is called a ***cable-ready computer***, which is a computer that you can connect directly to a cable TV outlet to receive programming you can watch on your monitor (see Figure 7.14).

You simply need a computer that contains a special video and sound card that connects to a cable TV outlet and the software necessary to display cable TV programming on your monitor. You can even purchase special software that enables picture-in-picture technology. With this technology, you can work on a word processing document while watching television on a smaller picture located in the corner of your monitor. And, if you have video capturing and editing software, you can even capture clips of your favorite show and store them on your hard disk.

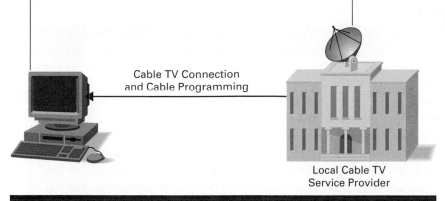

Cable TV Connection and Cable Programming

Local Cable TV Service Provider

FIGURE 7.14
Getting Your Computer Cable Connected

Compared to traditional computer modems, cable modems are extremely fast. For example, most cable modems operate at speeds around 10 million bits per second, whereas most traditional computer modems operate at speeds around 56,000 bits per second. That means you'll be able to receive and send transmissions 150 times faster with a cable modem. Cable modems also support bidirectional flows of information between you and your cable TV service provider. Traditional cable boxes, on the other hand, support the flow of information in only one direction, from your cable TV service provider to you. Because you also need to send Internet destination information to your cable TV service provider, cable modems support the incoming flow of information to you as well as the outgoing flow of information to your cable TV service provider, who transmits information to the Internet.

Cable Modems
Your Cable TV Service Provider as an Internet Service Provider

Most cable TV service providers aren't content just to pipe cable programming into your computer. They would also like to provide you with Internet-accessing capabilities through a cable modem. A *cable modem* is a special communications processor that connects your television to a cable TV service provider. With it, you can access through your TV not only cable programming, but also the Internet (see Figure 7.15). In addition to the cable modem, your cable TV service provider will also provide you with a special combined keyboard and mouse that you use to cruise the Internet. What's even better is that these special devices use an infrared technology, so you can relax in your favorite chair as you navigate or view the Internet or TV channels.

Cable modems are quite different from both traditional computer modems and cable TV reception boxes.

Internet PCs
Just What Some People Need

Some people, as odd as it may sound, really don't require information-processing capabilities in their homes. It's true, there will always be people who don't need word processing, spreadsheet, or any of the many other capabilities that technology provides. That doesn't mean, however, that those same people won't want to access the Internet. For these individuals, it doesn't make financial sense to invest thousands of dollars in a home computer

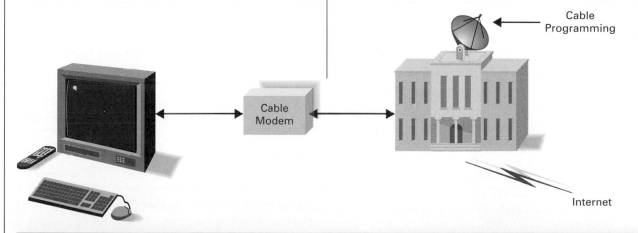

Cable Programming

Cable Modem

Internet

FIGURE 7.15
Connecting to the Internet Through a Cable TV Service Provider

I Want My WebTV

Even if you can't get a cable modem from your local cable TV service provider, you can still use your television to view the Internet. One of the many products available today to help you do this is offered by Phillips Magnavox (a subsidiary of Microsoft), and it's called WebTV. WebTV contains a special box that you connect to your television and to a phone line.

When you turn on WebTV, it will use your phone line to connect to the WebTV Internet Network provided by Phillips Magnavox.

Once you're connected, the Internet will appear on your television screen. WebTV also comes equipped with a keyboard you use for entering commands and an infrared remote control you can use to click on buttons at different Web sites. WebTV also comes with various safeguards, so you can perform such functions as

prohibiting access to adult-oriented sites.

The cost of a WebTV system is about $100, but that's only the initial cost. You also have to pay $20 a month to use the WebTV Internet Network. That's a small price, considering you have to pay the $20 monthly fee to subscribe to an Internet service provider anyway. So for about $100 you get all the necessary hardware and software to see the Internet on TV. ❖

---

just to access the Internet. Today, however, those people can purchase an *Internet PC*—a computer that supports only Internet access.

Internet PCs look just like other desktop machines, but they lack many of the internal bells and whistles associated with conventional PCs. For example, Internet PCs have limited storage space, internal memory, and CPU (central processing unit) speed. Because of their limited capacity, Internet PCs are often called "hollow PCs." This type of emerging technology is designed specifically for cruising the Internet and little else. Price is the allure of these machines—you can purchase one for as little as $300.

The All-Purpose Home Computer

Finally, many of today's home computers are actually *Internet-accessing-cable-vision-phone-computer* devices. It's true—many of today's home computers (that sell for less than $1,500) come equipped with all the necessary gadgets to allow you to (1) access the Internet (a simple modem and browser software), (2) watch TV and cable programs (cable-ready cards), and (3) make phone calls (a microphone and speakers). All you really have to do is figure out how to take advantage of each feature. And don't forget, with technologies such as e-mail, desktop videoconferencing, individualized electronic advertising, and electronic newspapers, in the future you may never encounter a postal service worker or newspaper-delivery person.

So What Does the Future Look Like for Converging Technologies and the Internet?

That's a really great question and, if you can come up with the right answer, you'll be rich. We can make some general predictions about the future of converging technologies and the Internet, but who knows what will really happen. First, over the next several years, there'll be enormous positioning in markets that support the electronic creation and movement of information, namely in the areas of telecommunications, Internet service providers, and cable TV service providers. Already companies such as US West are buying cable TV service providers all over the country in the hope of someday combining your telephone and cable service. Other companies, such as AT&T, offer their customers value-added services such as free access to the Internet. This

---

HERE'S AN IT TWIST A Virtual Pet Cemetery

You don't have to spend much time cruising the Internet to come across some very interesting and weird Web sites. One such site is the Cyberspace Pet Mall (http://net-mar.com/mall/). What may surprise you is that you'll find a virtual pet cemetery there. That's right—for a small price, you can leave a photo and short story of your pet in the virtual pet cemetery. Some people obviously have a strange definition of doggie heaven.[28] ❖

prediction of the future will materialize; unfortunately, it makes other trends difficult to predict.

Second, the consumer market is now demanding all-in-one integrated devices; someday, however, it will do a partial "about face" and begin purchasing dedicated devices. Why? Because an all-in-one device can certainly handle all your communication needs, but it probably won't perform all of them extremely well. It is likely, then, that the consumer market will often opt for quality over integration. You should understand, however, that the consumer market will continue to demand *connectivity*, which is something entirely different from all-in-one integration. This demand for connectivity means that people will still want access to the Internet and will want to view it on their TV screens. But that's not the only way they'll want to access and view the Internet.

Third, and almost the exact opposite of the second prediction, many dedicated devices simply will not survive. Think about Internet PCs. These devices provide Internet access but lack real computing capabilities such as word processing, spreadsheet, and presentation graphics. Consider, too, those individuals who want Internet access. Wouldn't they also want other information-processing capabilities—those that require storage devices and a fast CPU? It's almost like assuming that people who drive convertible cars don't ever want a top, which simply isn't true—those people don't want a top when the weather is nice, but they certainly do when it's raining or snowing.

Finally, as access to the Internet and its vast information resources becomes cheaper, faster, easier, and more reliable through a variety of emerging technologies, you'll probably see the end of read-only storage devices such as CD-ROM. If you think about it, CD-ROM disks just hold information (even if that information is a game) that you need to access. Well, what happens to CD-ROM when you can find that same (and even more) information on the Internet and can access it so quickly that you believe it's really a part of your home computer? If you're interested, you can read Appendix A, which includes a discussion of magneto-optical storage devices and digital video disks—a new type of storage technology that has marked the end of CD-ROM.

The Wireless Revolution

Virtual Connectivity

In Chapter 6 we introduced you to unguided communications media, which are also called wireless communications media. These communications media connect people and technology without physical cables—what you might refer to as "virtual connectivity." For the most part, these types of communications media are fairly well established, but the business world has yet to truly exploit their full potential or use them in innovative ways. In the future, however, you can expect organizations and people everywhere to join the wireless revolution, using wireless technologies for virtually all their connectivity needs.

As you view wireless technologies now and in the future, think of them from two points of view: (1) those technologies for mobilizing people and (2) those technologies for mobilizing technology itself. Both uses of wireless technologies are definitely on the rise and show no sign of ending.

Wireless Technologies for Mobilizing People

You're probably familiar with several types of wireless technologies for mobilizing people, namely digital pagers and cellular phones. But are you familiar with all their uses? For example, today you can get a digital pager for about $150 that is capable of displaying up to 240 characters of an e-mail message. You can even set up your e-mail system so that it will page you when you receive an e-mail message. And what about those cellular phones? Sure it's nice to be able to call anyone no matter where you are without having to find a pay phone. Now you can purchase a cellular modem for about $200 for your laptop computer so you can communicate with another computer or connect to the Internet without a telephone line.

Those are just a few examples of some innovative uses of seemingly simple communications devices such as digital pagers and cellular phones. And other communications devices—based on wireless technologies—are emerging, including smart phones and the global positioning system. Let's take a more detailed look at these technologies.

Smart Phones
All Your Communication Needs in a Portable Phone

In recent years, the use of portable technologies, from digital pagers and cellular phones to laptop computers and portable printers, has definitely increased. If you had to carry all those devices they wouldn't seem very portable. Individually they may be easy to carry around; but, if you want to carry several items, you may want to consider investing in a luggage porter. That may soon change with the emergence of a wireless technology that combines many features of other portable technologies.

That new technology is called a *smart phone*, which is a cellular phone that also acts as a transmittal and reception station for digital page messages, e-mail messages,

A Texas rancher recently equipped his cattle with digital pagers. Now, when it's feeding time, the rancher simply picks up the phone and sends the cattle a digital page. Weird or wired farm animals?[29] ❖

and faxes and also has Internet access capabilities. A smart phone is not only powerful, but also compact—it fits easily in the palm of your hand or inside your coat jacket. Like a cellular phone, you use a smart phone to send and receive calls. The other features are enabled by an intelligent keyboard and a small screen. Using the keyboard, you can compose short messages, up to 160 characters in length, and send them as a fax, an e-mail message, or a digital page. The screen also displays incoming faxes, e-mail messages, and digital pages. You can even use the keyboard to navigate Web sites, which are displayed on the screen.

AT&T PocketNet Phone

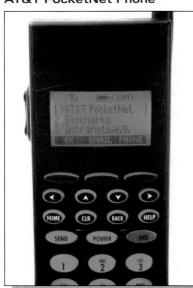

PocketNet Phone is a smart phone offered by AT&T. Its price tag is about $350, plus a monthly airtime charge of $40. The price certainly seems right but, before you leap, ask yourself whether you really need another portable technology. A smart phone can replace your cellular phone and digital pager and provide you with access to the Internet, but you certainly can't use it for spreadsheet work or for seeing and hearing a multimedia presentation. Nonetheless, many people will opt for smart phones because they're equipped with more capabilities than a standard cellular phone.

Global Positioning System
Knowing Where You Are While You Roam

Wireless technologies, such as digital pagers, smart phones, and laptop computers with cellular modems, indeed seem to solve many problems. These technologies allow you to contact friends, family members, and offices, regardless of your proximity to a phone line. But "where

you are" could still present problems. You've undoubtedly encountered this problem while traveling a lonely stretch of highway —what highway you are on, where the nearest town is, and many other questions have probably crossed your mind. You've got a road map, but it doesn't show farm-to-market road 358 near Boise, Idaho.

Well, fortunately, a new technology—the global positioning system—is available that will help you always know where you are. The *global positioning system (GPS)* is a collection of 24 earth-orbiting satellites that continuously transmit radio signals you can use to determine where you are (see Figure 7.16). A GPS receiver— a small handheld device—picks up the radio signals from four of the satellites and can pinpoint your exact position within a few hundred feet. The GPS receiver also contains maps that you can then use to determine where that nearest town is or on what road you're traveling.

For many years, GPS receivers have been used commercially. Airplane pilots, sea captains, and military personnel constantly use GPS receivers to determine their

Wherever you are, your GPS receiver will pick up the transmissions from four of the satellites to determine your exact location.

FIGURE 7.16

Knowing Where You Are with the Global Positioning System

location and the distance to certain destinations. That same technology is also available to you. A personal GPS receiver costs only about $300. If you're an airplane pilot, you can order a special GPS receiver that includes maps of air spaces and airports. Many people have found interesting and innovative applications of GPS receivers, including Doug Hartford, who uses a GPS receiver to monitor crop yields (see "Food Industry Perspective").

Wireless Technologies for Mobilizing Technology

In our previous discussion, you've seen some emerging technologies for mobilizing people. But wireless technologies can do more than just make people mobile, they can also make technology itself mobile. One such wireless technology that's emerging is a *wireless local area network (wireless LAN)*—a network that covers a limited distance in which all components or computers are connected without physical cables. In a wireless LAN, a central access point is established through which all wireless communications travel (see Figure 7.17). This access point is usually physically connected to a LAN server that provides information and software to all the wireless clients. Peripheral devices, such as printers and scanners, can also be wirelessly connected to the central access point. What's really great about wireless LANs is that they allow you to easily move computers or peripheral devices without worrying about moving a cable (pulling cable for a network is a major business expense). So, if you were to rearrange your office, you could move your computers without concern for cable outlets.

Listed below are several organizations that have realized benefits from wireless networks.

■ IBM has developed a new wireless service for real estate agents. For only $210 a month, real estate agents gain wireless access to a Multiple Listing Service (MLS) database. The monthly fee includes the lease of modem, laptop computer, and software, which allow agents instant access to sales listings.[30]

CENTRAL ACCESS POINT

Information and Software

FIGURE 7.17
A Wireless Local Area Network

■ Karolinska Hospital (Stockholm, Sweden) is using a wireless LAN to mobilize nurses in an effort to increase the efficiency of patient prescription distribution.[31] Nurses move through the hospital with a wireless laptop computer and prescription drugs. In each room, they simply access the network to determine the patient's medication. They can then administer the prescription and use a bar code scanner to instantly update the information on the network's database.

HERE'S AN IT TWIST   Wireless Mouses and Keyboards

Today it's not really even necessary that you be anywhere near your personal computer to do your work. That's right—now you can purchase wireless mouses and keyboards and be up to 50 feet away from your computer while still controlling what you do. Of course, if you were 50 feet away, you probably couldn't read what's on the screen. But you can use a wireless keyboard to lean back and relax in your favorite chair and not have to worry about the keyboard cable length. ❖

Global Positioning System Helps Harvest Crops

Many people, unfortunately, have a very simplified view of farming requirements. They see farming as plowing, sowing, and harvesting. Once harvested, the farmer takes the crop yield to the local grainery, then waits for the next crop, right?

In its simplest form, that may be a somewhat accurate representation of the farming business. But farming is really all about yield management—taking whatever steps are necessary to ensure the largest crop harvest. And that's not simple. You can't simply manage crop yields by sections or even by acre. Instead, you really need to measure the crop yield every few feet and compare it to other measures such as soil type, seed variety, field and planting geometry, tillage practices, drainage, pest populations, and organic matter density.

Measuring crop yield every few feet is an almost insurmountable task, but not for Doug Hartford, a farmer in Grundy County, Illinois. His combine (a piece of farm equipment that harvests grain) is really high tech. Immediately below the chute through which the grain feeds, Doug has installed a sensor plate that measures the crop yield every foot and sends that information to a computer. The computer is connected to a GPS receiver that pinpoints the exact location. When Doug is finished combining, he can print a two-dimensional map that plots his exact crop yield on a foot-by-foot basis.

GPS receivers are great if you need to know where you are because you're lost. But Doug is never lost in his own fields—he uses his GPS receiver to measure crop yield for every foot of soil that he plants.[35, 36] ❖

- Hertz Corp. is using a wireless LAN to speed up development of car rental contracts.[32] Shuttle bus drivers are now equipped with handheld computers, which allow them to gather necessary information from customers while transporting them to their rental cars and electronically transmit the information to the office. So, when customers arrive at the office, their contracts have already been written.

- The Indiana State Legislature had a real problem—Senate and House of Representative members needed to communicate with each other, but the state didn't want to tear up its recently refurbished 108-year-old capitol building to set up a wired LAN.[33] The solution was simple—equip everyone with portable computers and access to a wireless LAN. The state of Indiana expects paper expenses to drop by 50 percent, which will easily pay for the cost of the wireless LAN.

- At Stanford University, students no longer go to labs to use computers.[34] Instead, they can access them wirelessly, regardless of whether they're in the student union building, sitting on the lawn, or eating in the cafeteria. Indeed, Stanford's students can access the wireless network from anywhere within a 15-mile radius of the campus.

- Outboard Marine is using wireless networks and portable computers to gather and track statistical operational information for its quality improvement program.[37] Using portable computers, production line personnel can move through eight manufacturing lines, a distance equal to four football fields.

Addressing the "Ility" Issue of Wireless Technologies

In business, communication by means of wireless technologies—whether for people or technology—addresses the key "ility" issue. That is, portab**ility** and mob**ility.** Just think about it—if you require a mobile workforce, you must provide them with portable technologies connected to a network. If your employees are meeting in a hotel room, network connections can be achieved through the phone line. But what about line personnel on a factory floor (Outboard Marine)? They can't very well stop what they're doing and find the nearest phone line. These people require the portability and mobility of wireless technologies.

In Figure 7.18, you can see that wireless LAN revenues are expected to increase by almost 250 percent from 1995 to 1997. This is only for wireless LANs—it

WIRELESS LAN REVENUES ON THE RISE

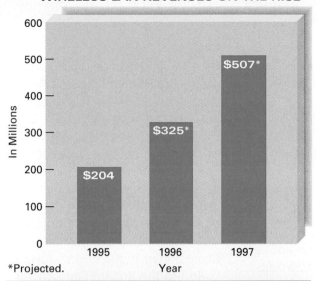

*Projected.

FIGURE 7.18

Wireless LAN Revenues on the Rise[38]

doesn't include cellular phones, digital pagers, smart phones, microwaves, or satellites. If you include these, total wireless revenues will probably exceed $10 billion in 1997. It all goes back to the "ility" issue—making your workforce mobile with portable technologies that allow them to communicate with others, regardless of location.

CAREER OPPORTUNITY

Wireless technologies give people the ability to work anywhere anytime without accessing telephone lines or cables. The use of these technologies is definitely on the rise—revenues for wireless office products (simple digital pagers and cellular phones) are expected to exceed $3.3 billion in 1998, up from $394 million in 1995.[39] Your career opportunity lies in determining if, how, and where wireless technologies can increase your productivity in more places. If they can, join the wireless revolution.

Emerging Technologies for Your Personal Life

Many of the emerging technologies we've discussed will significantly affect not only your personal life, but also your internal business operations and market interactions.

The business world is also producing technologies that simplify your personal life. And where's the competitive advantage in developing emerging technologies that make your personal life easier? Think about it for a moment. You've probably purchased such items as an answering machine, a digital alarm clock, and a microwave oven just because they make your life easier. These purchases generate revenues for the product manufacturer. Of the many emerging technologies that will make your personal life easier, we highlight two in this section—smart cards and intelligent home appliances.

Smart Cards
Electronic Cash in Your Wallet

Many people are predicting that paper currency and metal coins will become obsolete with the growing acceptance and use of electronic versions of money. In the previous section, we explored the use of electronic cash on the Internet. Another form of electronic cash is the *smart card*—a small plastic card (about the size of a credit card) that contains a memory chip on which a sum of money can be recorded and updated (see Figure 7.19). It's really just a simple matter of buying a smart card for a certain denomination and then using it for buying clothes, paying for gas, making long-distance calls on pay phones, or even riding on public transportation.

To make a purchase with a smart card, you insert the card into a card reader device that (1) reads the amount of money you have stored on your card, (2) deducts the amount of your purchase, and (3) tells you your balance. When you've spent the balance, you can take the smart

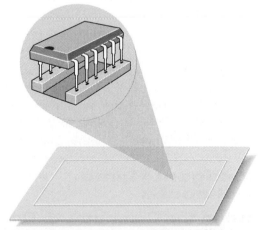

A smart card contains a memory chip on which electronic money can be stored and updated.

FIGURE 7.19

The Anatomy of a Smart Card

Wireless LANs—A Competitive Necessity or a Life Saver?

At J. B. Hunt Transport wireless local area networks are both a competitive necessity and a life saver. As George Brooks explains it, "In our business, wireless is a competitive necessity. A lot of shippers won't do business with you if you don't have it." That's why J. B. Hunt outfitted its 8,300 vehicles with wireless onboard computers that use satellites to link them with the home office. J. B. Hunt's system, *Road-riders,* has helped to

- Book up to 10 percent more road miles per day
- Increase fleet manager productivity by 20 percent
- Reduce driver-dispatch phone contact from 2 hours to 15 minutes
- Reduce transmissions from $1 (for a phone call) to 20 cents

Those benefits, along with the fact that many shippers won't do business with you if you don't use wireless technologies, certainly make wireless LANs a competitive necessity in the transportation industry. But how do wireless LANs save lives? Consider this example. Several years ago, a J. B. Hunt truck driver suffered a heart attack while making deliveries and nearly died. Thanks to the onboard wireless computer, the driver was able to notify the home office of his condition. Within minutes, the home office faxed a map of the driver's location to the Royal Canadian Mounted Police, who were able to save the man's life.

You be the judge—are wireless LANs a competitive necessity, a life saver, or both?[41] ❖

card back to where you bought it and purchase more electronic money to replenish it.

Smart cards have been around for several years in a variety of forms. For example, toll road administrators have made them available to commuters in an effort to relieve congestion at toll booths. And the sponsors of the 1996 Summer Olympics experimented with smart cards, allowing people to use them for purchasing soft drinks, food, and Olympics-related items such as clothing. The Tran$cash Consortium is even developing a public transportation smart card that can be read while still in your wallet.[40] The Tran$cash system uses a wireless technology that will communicate with your smart card when you board the bus. The wireless technology emits a signal that locates your card, deducts the fare, and updates your balance—you never have to present your card to the driver.

Intelligent Home Appliances

Getting the Computer to Do Your Work (Almost)

Wouldn't it be great to have a full-time maid to cook your meals, wash the dishes, and launder your clothes? You'd probably pay dearly for such a service; unfortunately, your budget probably won't allow such an expenditure.

And don't expect a computer robot to show up at your doorstep that will perform all those functions. In spite of what you may have seen on *The Jetsons* or *Lost in Space,*

TEAM WORK

Finding Home Appliances with a Brain

Visit several local appliance stores, find intelligent home appliances, then answer the following questions:

1. What intelligent home appliances did you find?
2. What was the cost of each appliance?
3. What functions do the appliances perform?
4. Which, if any, are voice-controlled?
5. Is there a difference between the cost of the intelligent appliance and the same appliance with no intelligence? ❖

HERE'S AN IT *TWIST*   **Your Very Own Decoder Ring**

For years now, people have been researching ways to make business computer systems secure—to keep the wrong people from gaining access to important information. But what about at home? How can you stop people (family members, friends, or even a burglar) from firing up your system and going through your files, copying your programs, or damaging the data?

Well, the answer may be a personalized decoder ring. Each ring has a unique chip that a sensor attached to your computer will read to determine if you're the owner of the computer. If you're not, the system will shut down. If you are, the system will come on and allow you to use the computer. The really good thing is that these rings cost only about $50. And that's a small price to pay for security.[43] ❖

it'll be a long time before the technology industry develops a robot to take over your household chores. But don't despair. There is a growing number of home appliances that can ease your burden. These appliances are called *intelligent home appliances*—appliances that contain an embedded IT system that controls numerous functions and is capable of making some decisions. Consider these examples:

■ Smart vacuum cleaners that automatically adjust settings based on naps or densities of your carpet, varying densities and weights of dirt, and collection bag fullness.[42]

■ Handheld camcorders that make sure your movie never jumps around. For example, Matsushita has developed a camcorder that compares each frame to the previous one, determines if the movement of objects is due to hand movement jitters, and, if so, eliminates the problem.[44]

■ Gas ranges that detect when water is about to boil, regulate simmering, and adjust temperature settings for a variety of cookware and foods.[45]

■ Clothes washers that automatically balance loads to avoid stoppage, determine dirt content to add detergent, determine type of clothes for the

INDUSTRY PERSPECTIVE   Hospitality & Leisure

Taco Bell and Pizza Hut Use Fuzzy Logic to Make Decisions

Fuzzy logic systems are definitely not limited to intelligent home appliances. Most organizations have found that almost all types of decision making must handle fuzzy information. That simply means that artificial intelligence techniques, such as neural networks and expert systems (systems that can aid an organization in decision making), must be able to work with fuzzy information.

For Taco Bell and Pizza Hut, divisions of PepsiCo, this means combining fuzzy logic with a neural network to create a new technique called "hybrid modeling." A **hybrid model** combines two or more artificial intelligence techniques to help you solve complex problems more effectively than you could with the help of any one AI technique. Taco Bell and Pizza Hut's hybrid models combine fuzzy logic and neural networks to help planners determine where to open new sites.

Pizza Hut, for example, uses the hybrid model to determine which type of restaurant to build

in a new location. Types of Pizza Hut restaurants include dine-in, carry-out-only, delivery-only, or some combination of the three. For some sites, a dine-in restaurant may be a miserable failure, whereas a delivery-only restaurant would do very well. And when you consider that as much as $1 million may be invested in a new restaurant, a hybrid model that can increase the effectiveness of the decision will provide a healthy return and easily pay for itself.[46, 47] ❖

TWIST   Robots That Check the Refrigerator for Old Food

For years, robots with eyes and ears have been detecting sounds and images. Now there's a robot with a nose that can detect odors. Many appliance manufacturers plan to add these robots to refrigerators. The robots can then tell you when perishable food is going bad—even if it's a closed milk container.[51] ❖

appropriate cycle, and determine clothes weight for the amount of water.[48,49]

- Dishwashers that can save you as much as $44 annually in electricity and water consumption by evaluating dirt content and shutting off the wash cycle when your dishes are clean.[50]

You, in fact, may be using many intelligent appliances and not even know it. As each day passes, home appliances with embedded IT systems are becoming more commonplace. Many of these intelligent appliances make use of automatic speech recognition. So, when you say "boil water," an intelligent gas range will adjust its settings based on the amount of water you have to boil and the type of cookware you're using. You may even be able to tell your microwave oven to "pop popcorn." It will adjust the settings and even shut itself off when all the kernels are popped—no more burned popcorn in the microwave.

Behind these new types of intelligent home appliances is an emerging technology called fuzzy logic. *Fuzzy logic* is a method of working with "fuzzy" information;

KNOWLEDGE WORKER'S -LIST

Why Some Technologies Are Categorized as "Emerging." Categorizing a technology as emerging doesn't necessarily mean that it's brand new. Technologies can be called emerging because

- The technology is so new that most businesses have really yet to begin using it
- The technology is fairly well-established, but businesses have yet to fully exploit it

In the first instance, you can include such technologies as electronic cash. In the second instance, you can include such technologies as multimedia.

How Emerging Technologies Are Beginning to Incorporate More of the Senses. Emerging technologies that are beginning to incorporate more of the senses include

- *3-D* Technologies that present images realistically enough that you may believe the object is in the room with you
- *Automatic speech recognition* Technologies that can capture what you say and distinguish between words and sentences

- *Multimedia* Technologies that simultaneously present information through many forms of media that you can control
- *Virtual reality* Technologies that present a three-dimensional computer simulation in which you actively and physically participate

The Dramatic Changes Occurring as a Result of and on the Internet. Changes surrounding the Internet are undoubtedly the most visible, rapidly changing, dynamic, mind-boggling, and exciting of all the emerging technologies. Two such changes include

1. *Electronic cash*—An electronic representation of cash that you can use to make purchases on the Internet
2. Converging technologies for communicating through and accessing the Internet, including
   - ◆ *Internet telephones* The technology tools necessary for carrying on a phone conversation over the Internet
   - ◆ *Cable-ready computers* A computer that you can connect directly to a cable TV outlet to

that is, information that is incomplete, ambiguous, or imprecise. For example, fuzzy logic can analyze information such as *hot, cold, tall, short, medium, reasonable,* or even *somewhat.* As opposed to most types of IT systems that require crisp, discrete information (such as a specific number or measurement), fuzzy logic systems work with information that is often a matter of interpretation. For example, if you were describing professional basketball players, would you describe a 6-foot 5-inch player as "tall"? What about a 6-foot 4.5-inch player—would that person be "short"?

Fuzzy logic is actually a subfield of artificial intelligence (AI), which we discussed in Chapter 5. Recall that AI is the science of making machines imitate human thinking and behavior. That human thinking and behavior almost always deal with a type of fuzzy information. Intelligent home appliances must incorporate fuzzy logic (such as determining the boiling point of water) to make decisions.

Airlines Are Using Technology to Make Your Traveling Easy

You probably enjoy flying—it usually means that you're taking a vacation to get away from it all. But there are a number of things about vacations that we all hate, including working with a travel agent to find the best ticket prices, going to the airport and standing in long lines to check luggage, standing in another long line to check in at the gate, and then standing in yet another long line to actually board the plane. For many people, it's a turnoff—and it costs airlines a lot of money to run you through all those hurdles.

In the future, you can expect that to change. Almost all airlines are currently experimenting with emerging technologies to make your travels easier than ever before.

receive programming that you can watch on your monitor

◆ *Cable modems* Special communications processors that connect your television to a cable TV service provider to receive cable programming on and Internet access by means of your TV

◆ *Internet PCs* A "hollow" computer that supports only Internet access and use

◆ **The all-purpose home computer** What you find in retail stores today that lets you do all of the above

The Role of the Wireless Revolution in Mobilizing People and Technology. Wireless communications media connect people and technology without physical cables—what you might refer to as *virtual connectivity.* You can consider wireless technologies from two points of view

1. **For mobilizing people** New emerging technologies in this area include

    ◆ *Smart phones* Cellular phones that also act as a sending and receiving station for digital page

messages, e-mail messages, and faxes and also give you the ability to connect to the Internet

◆ *Global positioning system* 24 earth-orbiting satellites that continuously transmit radio signals that you can use to determine your location

2. **For mobilizing technology** Most notable here are *wireless local area networks*—networks that cover a limited distance in which all components or computers are connected without physical cables

How Emerging Technologies Will Affect Their Personal Lives. Many emerging technologies will simplify your personal life. Two such emerging technologies include

■ *Smart cards* A small plastic card that contains a memory chip on which a sum of money can be placed and updated

■ *Intelligent home appliances* Appliances in your home that contain an embedded IT system that controls numerous functions and are capable of making some decisions ❖

These emerging technologies include electronic ticketing or e-ticketing, self-check-in machines, Web sites for online reservations, and smart cards. Let's take a look at each.

- **Electronic Ticketing** Electronic ticketing, or e-ticketing, replaces the physical ticket you would receive after you make a reservation. The electronic ticket you purchase through the airline or a travel agent is a confirmation number stored in a database. When you arrive at the gate, you give the agent either the confirmation number or your name. You don't have to worry about losing your ticket, and airlines can board passengers faster. Most airlines—including ValuJet, Southwest, United, and Continental—already use some form of e-ticketing and estimate that they save an average of $25 million annually. US Air even estimates that it may save as much as $1 billion through e-ticketing.

- **Self-Check-In Machines** Many airlines have installed multimedia kiosks at airports. Once inside the kiosk, you can select your flight, buy a ticket, reserve a seat, pay by credit card, and obtain a receipt and boarding pass. And you do all of this without ever talking to a travel or reservation agent.

- **Web Sites for Online Reservations** Most airlines also have Web sites on which you can view flight schedules, make reservations, and pay for tickets. You can do all this from the comfort of your home.

- **Smart Cards** Delta Airlines is currently experimenting with a special type of smart card to help passengers. Your smart card would contain all the necessary information for purchasing a ticket—your name, credit card number to which you want the flight billed, and even your frequent flier number. Once you select your flight, all the information is transferred in a matter of seconds from your smart card to the airline's computer.

Airlines haven't stopped there. Once you're on the plane, you may find that your reserved space is equipped with a private television screen, so you can watch whatever you want (including pay-per-view movies). Many newer airplanes are even equipped with a local area network to which you can connect your laptop computer and print documents on a high-quality laser printer.[52-54] ❖

◄ Questions ►

1. Try connecting to the Web sites of various airlines. What type of support do they provide for making online reservations? Do they provide a way for you to actually pay for the ticket over the Internet? If they do, would you feel comfortable with your credit card number traveling across the Internet? Why or why not?

2. Airlines save money through e-ticketing because fewer people are needed to check and track passenger tickets. Do airlines have any social or ethical responsibilities to provide these displaced workers with other jobs? If they do, can airlines expect to save as much money through e-ticketing?

3. Delta's use of a smart card for ticketing is actually a variation of a smart card we discussed in this chapter. How could airlines use real smart cards to help passengers during check-in? Some people would have to store several thousand dollars on a smart card. Would you feel comfortable with that much money on a smart card? Is it any different than having a credit card with a large credit line?

4. What about people with computer phobias? If all airlines use technology for ticketing and boarding, what will happen to people who don't want to use technology? Will airlines always have to have mechanisms in place for boarding passengers with physical tickets?

5. Do you think Internet reservation sites could negatively impact travel agents? Visit a local travel agency and see what its employees think the future is for Internet online reservations. Also ask them how they plan to stay in business as more travelers use the Internet to purchase airline tickets.

6. What other forms of emerging technologies could airlines use to make traveling easier for you? For example, could airlines use some sort of scanning technology to make sure your luggage arrives at the same destination as you? Do they already do this?

CLOSING CASE STUDY: CASE 2

Do-It-Yourself Scanning at the Grocery Store

Perhaps emerging technologies of the future will most affect customer integrated systems (CIS). Recall from Chapter 2 that a CIS places technology in the hands of customers and allows them to do their own processing. In this chapter, we've already looked at several emerging examples—smart cards, electronic ticketing, and many others. Well, grocery stores are not to be outdone—they're creating do-it-yourself scanning systems based on wireless technologies and advanced scanning technologies.

In the future, when you enter a grocery store, you'll insert your credit card into a slot and receive a handheld bar code scanner. As you move through the grocery store, you'll pick up the products you want, scan them yourself, and then place them in your cart. You can even scan a product, press a key, and see the price of the product. You'll receive the price display through wireless technologies that transmit information from a server to wherever you are in the store.

When you finish shopping, you simply return your bar code scanner—its content will determine your bill, which will be charged against the credit card you originally used to obtain the bar code scanner.[55,56] ❖

◄ Questions ►

1. As grocery stores begin to adopt do-it-yourself scanning, what security issues will they have to consider? For example, what happens if you leave the store with a bar code scanner or place something in your shopping cart without scanning it?

2. All grocery stores include fresh produce—vegetables and fruits. Those products obviously don't have UPC symbols stamped on them. How will this problem be overcome?

3. How many people do you actually think will use do-it-yourself scanning devices in grocery stores? What about people with a handicap? Would you use one? Why or why not? If shoppers don't use them, how will the cost savings of grocery stores be affected?

4. With this type of technology, grocery stores will be able to track even more information about your shopping habits. For example, they'll know in which order you buy your products and the time that elapses between your selection of milk and your selection of breakfast cereal. As a manager of a grocery store, would this type of information be useful? How would you use it? Might it lead you to rearrange products by location and shelf space?

5. Related to the previous question, are there any ethical concerns surrounding the amount of information a grocery store knows about your buying habits? For example, what if a grocery store determines that you buy bread only after you buy lunch meat and, based on this knowledge, decides to send you coupons for lunch meat, assuming that you'll also buy bread? Do you find it somewhat unsettling that a store may know so much about you? Why or why not?

6. If do-it-yourself scanning does become common practice in grocery stores, can you see a time when you'll do the same in a video rental store? A hardware store? A department store? Create a list of retail stores for which do-it-yourself scanning is and is not well-suited. What are the distinguishing characteristics of the retail stores on each list?

Electronic Commerce
Business and You on the Internet

Finding News, Weather, and Sports Information

Many people believe that, besides worldwide connectivity, one of the greatest benefits of the Internet is its ability to provide up-to-date information. For example, you can connect to the U.S. Census Bureau to learn the population of the United States or connect to the New York Stock Exchange to receive up-to-the-minute stock quotes. No matter what type of timely information you require, you can probably find it on the Internet.

The same is true for getting the latest news, weather, and sports information. On the Internet, you'll find millions (really) of sites that provide information on world news events, local happenings, worldwide weather information forecasts, and scores and statistics for almost every conceivable sporting event. And many of these sites even incorporate multimedia to present information through sight, sound, and video.

A caveat must be made here. As we discussed in the Electronic Commerce sections for Chapter 3 ("Finding Investment Opportunities Using the Internet") and Chapter 6 ("Getting Health Care Information on the Internet"), you should carefully weigh the credibility of all information you find on the Internet. Anyone can publish anything on the Internet—there is no review process and no guarantee of the correctness or reliability of that information.

In this section, we've included a number of Web sites related to finding news, weather, and sports information on the Internet. On the Web site that supports this text (http://www.mhhe.com/business/mis/haag, select "Electronic Commerce Projects"); we've provided direct links to all these Web sites as well as many, many more. These are a great starting point for completing this Real HOT section. We would also encourage you to search the Internet for others.

News Information

News information has always come to us in a variety of ways—newscasts on television, the daily newspaper, news talk shows on the radio, and so on. While you may think that many of these are up-to-date, they're actually not. When you watch the news on a local television station, for example, you get what has happened in the last several hours, but perhaps not what happened 15 minutes ago. But with the Internet, you can read about the most recent events, much of which may have occurred in the last 10 minutes. And that's one of the great advantages of the Internet over other, more-traditional media for distributing news information. As soon as news occurs (of course, you may not really consider it newsworthy), that news is being posted on a variety of sites.

In the table on page 316, we've listed some sites on the Internet where you can go to learn about the latest news happenings around the world. On the Web site that supports this text, we've provided direct links to these sites as well as many other news-related sites.

Choose a current news event, connect to five different news-related Web sites, and answer the following questions.

A. What current event did you choose?

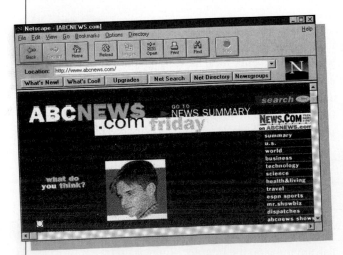

B. What organization or company sponsors each site?

C. Which Web sites contain information related to your chosen event?

D. What is the time of last update for each Web site?

E. Are you able to find an unbiased presentation of your current event or are you also able to read commentaries?

F. Which Web sites provide links to other Web sites containing related information?

G. How credible do you think the site is in terms of the information provided and the sponsors of the site?

Sports Information

Let's face it—some sports enthusiasts are more aptly referred to as sports *fanatics.* And up until a few short years ago, these enthusiasts were most often males between the ages of 12 and 40 who read sports magazines, watched every hour of televised sports they could on the weekends, and participated in a variety of community and school-sponsored athletic programs.

But not anymore. Sports—participating in, watching, and collecting memorabilia—is now a worldwide pastime. Women's athletics is on the rise; people over the age of 50 have their own softball leagues and professional golf tours; children as young as four participate in summer soccer and winter hockey; there are more sold-out attendances of college football games than there are sold-out attendances of some academic classes. In general, the whole world has jumped on the sports bandwagon, and we've all realized that our quality of life increases with our physical fitness.

And the Internet has certainly enjoyed more acceptance because of sports. We did a simple search on "sports" and found over 17 million Web sites—everything from *Sports Illustrated* magazine to bowling tournament results for a town in Ohio. It seems the whole world wants to read about sports, and there are just as many people posting sports information on the Internet. In the table on page 316, we've listed some popular sports sites on the Internet. We've also included numerous others on the Web site that supports this text.

To explore sports information you can find on the Internet, choose a favorite sports topic. That could perhaps be snow skiing, children's weekend leagues, sports memorabilia, college basketball, women's platform diving, or rugby—whatever you want. Search for information on the Internet and answer the following questions.

A. What topic did you choose?

B. How many sites did the search engine return?

C. What kind of sites are available—sports companies, magazines, television stations, personal pages, college sites, professional team sites, and so forth?

D. Did you find sites that were unrelated to your original search? If so, why do you think this happened?

E. Which sites do you consider to be the best? Why?

F. How up-to-date are the sites?

G. Are the sites devoted to just a particular time period or to covering the latest events?

Weather Information

The world at large has also become increasingly interested in the weather—current happenings, tomorrow's forecast, the forecast for the weekend, the movement of the latest hurricane in the Gulf Coast region, and snow skiing conditions in Colorado. If you don't believe it, think about the Weather Channel. It's a 24-hour-a-day, seven-day-a-week weather program on cable television.

As well, you'll find tens of thousands of sites on the Internet that provide up-to-the-minute weather information. In the table on page 316, we've listed some weather sites and where you can find them on the Internet. And don't forget to connect to the Web site that supports this text for a list of other weather information sites. You might also want to check the list of sites in the Real HOT section of Chapter 10 ("Making Travel Arrangements on the Internet").

Choose five weather sites, connect to them, and answer the following questions for each.

A. What is the name and address of the site?

B. Who supports the site?

C. When was the site last updated?

D. How often is information updated?

E. What geographical areas are covered (e.g., local, U.S. only, worldwide, and so forth)?

F. Is information in both text and graphic form?

G. Is the graphic information static, does it move, or is it 3-D?

H. Is video provided?

Interpreting Weather Information

Although everyone is interested in the weather on a daily basis, very few people actually understand the vast majority of weather-related terms. And even fewer people understand how the weather affects their daily lives. Consider these questions. Does the fishing get better as the barometric pressure rises or falls (and are there other factors)?

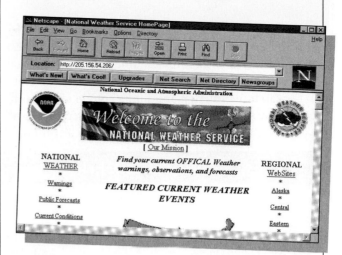

What's the difference between a low-pressure and high-pressure system? What is humidity a measure of? How do you calculate the heat index? What is a trough?

Many of the weather terms in the above questions you hear almost everyday. You could better understand the weather and how it affects your life if you understood those terms. In the table on page 316, we've provided a list of sites on the Internet that will help you develop a better understanding of weather terms and the weather in general (there are also a number of others on the Web site that supports this text). At your leisure, we suggest that you explore several of these sites. We haven't provided any particular questions for you to answer or projects to complete for interpreting weather information; but understanding weather terminology is just as important as understanding computer terminology.

Your Local Television Stations

In some of the previous sections, we listed many national television stations such as CNN, ABC, and CBS. Your local stations also probably have Web sites. There, you'll find the latest happenings in the news, weather, and

sports for your area of the country. In the table below, we've listed several television stations in different cities and their Web site addresses. You'll also find a list of numerous others on the Web site that supports this text.

Search the Internet and find a couple of the local television stations that service your area. Were they easy or hard to find? How does the information at their Web sites compare to their broadcast news programs? Do you think there will ever come a time when television broadcast news is completely replaced by Internet-based news distribution? If not, then why are both national and local television stations creating Web sites?

Web Sites for News, Weather, and Sports Information

News	Address
ABC News	http://www.abcnews.com
CNN Interactive	http://www.cnn.com
CBC Newsworld Online	http://www.newsworld.cbc.ca
CNBC	http://www.cnbc.com
FOX News	http://www.foxnews.com

Sports	Address
	http://channel.cnnsi.com
	http://www.sports.at
	http://www.indysports.com
	http://www.sportinggreen.com
	http://www.amateur-sports.com

Weather	Address
The Lighthouse	http://www.weather24.com
National Weather Service	http://205.156.54.206
Tracking El Nino	http://www.pbs.org/wgbh/nova/elnino
The Weather Channel	http://www.weather.com/homepage.html
Weather Underground	http://www.wunderground.com

Interpreting Weather	Address
	http://www.itl.net/Education/online/weather
	http://ddi.digital.net/~rothertj/u_do_it.htm
	http://208.134.241.150/glossary
	http://208.134.241.150/learn_more/dave/index.html
	http://208.134.241.150/breaking_weather/encyclopedia

Local Television Stations	Address
KHON in Honolulu	http://www.khon.com/news
KUSA in Denver	http://www.9news.com
KATU in Portland	http://katu.citysearch.com/local
WXIN in Indianapolis	http://www.wxin.com
KUHT in Houston	http://www.kuht.uh.edu

 Go to the Web site that supports this text: **http://www.mhhe.com/business/mis/haag** and select "Electronic Commerce Projects."

We've included links to over 100 Web sites for finding news, weather, and sports information on the Internet, including online newspapers and magazines.

KEY TERMS AND CONCEPTS

Automatic Speech Recognition (ASR)

Cable Modem

Cable-Ready Computer

Cave Automatic Virtual Environment (CAVE)

Continuous Automatic Speech Recognition

Cybersickness

Discrete Automatic Speech Recognition

Electronic Cash (E-Cash; Digital Cash)

Electronic Publishing

Emerging Technology

Feature Analysis

Fuzzy Logic

Global Positioning System (GPS)

Glove

Headset

Hybrid Model

Intelligent Home Appliances

Internet PC

Internet Telephone

Language Processing

Multimedia

Multimedia Authoring Software

Pattern Classification

Smart Card

Smart Phone

Speaker-Dependent Automatic Speech Recognition

Speaker-Independent Automatic Speech Recognition

Storyboard

Three-Dimensional (3-D)

Virtual Reality

Walker

Wireless Local Area Network (Wireless LAN)

SHORT-ANSWER QUESTIONS

1. Why are some technologies considered to be "emerging"?

2. What three steps are involved in automatic speech recognition?

3. How do the four types of automatic speech recognition systems differ?

4. In what ways are multimedia applications different from a movie?

5. What are the five different navigation methods for a multimedia application?

6. What is virtual reality? What are the key features of virtual reality?

7. What type of cybersickness sometimes occurs when people use virtual reality?

8. How does electronic cash work on the Internet?

9. What are the types of emerging technologies that give you the ability to communicate through and access the Internet?

10. What are the emerging technologies for mobilizing people? Technology itself?

11. What are the key "ility" issues that wireless technologies address?

12. What are intelligent home appliances? What can they do for you?

DISCUSSION QUESTIONS

1. For each emerging technology we've presented in this chapter, which do you consider to be emerging and which do you now consider to be standard? Also, make a note of any emerging technologies we discussed that simply fizzled out and never became a reality.

2. What new emerging technologies have you noticed in recent months that we did not include in this chapter? Are they considered emerging because the technology is so new that most businesses have really yet to begin using them, or are they fairly well-established but businesses have yet to fully exploit them?

3. As we discussed in Closing Case Study, Case 2, many emerging technologies will have a significant impact on customer integrated systems. Which emerging technologies in this chapter do you believe will have the greatest impact on customer integrated systems? Why and how? Which emerging technologies do you believe will have the least impact on customer integrated systems? Why do you believe this?

4. Based on the emerging technologies in this chapter, what do you believe the "home of the future" will look like? Think about every facet of a home, from lawn and garden sprinklers to garbage disposals and trash compactors.

5. For the emerging technologies we discussed, how do you think they will impact organizational horsepower—through speed, force, or a combination of the two? As you consider this question, order the emerging technologies sequentially from those that will have the greatest impact on organizational horsepower to those that will have the least.

CASE STUDY

Chaos in California

In 1996 the state of California was in a state of IT chaos. At the Department of Motor Vehicles, antiquated systems failed 32.8 percent of the time, leaving customers waiting for hours while $25 million in newer computers sat idle, awaiting software to be written for them. Down the hall at the Department of Social Services, millions were paid out in fraudulent benefits because the state had no system to check for duplicate benefits in more than one county. Possibly the most painful blunder occurred in a revenue-generating operation—the state's lottery. While spending over $57 million to create a new lottery system, delays cost the state over $100 million in potential lottery revenue. Clearly the state was in need of a systems plan that met the needs of the state.

To ensure that state goals were aligned with the goals of any new IT system, the state created the position of *chief information officer (CIO)* and appointed John Flynn to the position. Megan Cotter, an industry analyst at

IN THE NEWS

Planning for IT Systems

Knowing Where You're Going

G2 Research in Mountain View, California, explained, "The creation of the CIO position, whose role is to set a strategic direction for IT that the state has never had before, clearly is an effort on the governor's part to set things straight." The state had to, first, understand its needs at the strategic planning level and, then, plan for just those IT systems that met the needs. One method of meeting the needs is focusing on the identification of specific information requirements.

In 1 year, California spread $2.5 billion in IT systems funding across 125 agencies. Every agency had its own priorities and made systems requests to support those priorities. As the state's CIO, however, John's job was to make sure all these agencies' systems helped the state reach its goals. So John identified a *critical success factor* *(CSF)* for the state—cut costs by eliminating fraudulent benefit claims. The next step was to identify the information required to support that CSF. "One of the problems in the state is that agencies don't talk to each other," says Debra Bowen, former head of the state's IT budget subcommittee. Payment of welfare benefits alone required 58 separate county-operated systems. The state proceeded with a new Statewide Automated Welfare System (SAWS) that uses fingerprint imaging to ensure that no one receives duplicate benefits. This system will save the state millions by communicating to all counties information about who received what benefit and when—eliminating fraud. This system meets both the identified information requirements and the economic goals of the state.[1] ❖

FEATURES

IN THE INFORMATION AGE, KNOWLEDGE WORKERS UNDERSTAND...

1. The importance of IT systems planning as well as a systems plan

2. How to ensure IT systems alignment with the organizational goals and strategies

3. How to identify specific processes and information needs that require IT systems support

4. How to evaluate IT systems for development

5. How to plan for what you can't live without

CHAPTER 8

Introduction

The state of California learned the importance of IT systems planning after several expensive missteps. Identifying the right IT systems for your organization can be confusing unless you begin that selection process at the strategic level. Using his chief information officer position, John Flynn ensured that new systems—like SAWS—supported the state's goals of cutting costs by eliminating fraudulent benefit claims. In this way, John's organization found and developed only those systems it truly needed.

Finding the best IT systems for your business is a little like purchasing missing pieces to a puzzle (see Figure 8.1). The pieces have to fit just right. Finding that fit

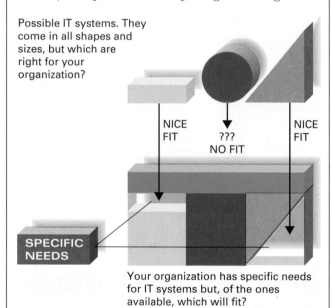

Possible IT systems. They come in all shapes and sizes, but which are right for your organization?

NICE FIT ??? NO FIT NICE FIT

SPECIFIC NEEDS

Your organization has specific needs for IT systems but, of the ones available, which will fit?

The whole point of the IT systems planning process is to find IT systems that enable the business to go where it needs to go. The systems plan provides a road map for IT to support your business.

FIGURE 8.1
Systems Planning: Testing for Fit

is a process called IT systems planning. ***Information technology systems planning (IT systems planning)*** is the process that uses the goals, strategies, objectives, processes, and information requirements of your organization as a foundation for identifying and selecting which IT systems to develop and when to develop them. You document the results from this planning in the ***information technology systems plan (IT systems plan)***. This systems plan then becomes the basis for your organization's systems development. Considering one system at a time from the systems plan, you'll first define the scope of that project. Then you'll define the system requirements, design the system, and implement and support it. With systems planning, these steps comprise the *systems development life cycle*, which we'll discuss in detail in Chapter 9.

The systems planning process involves five steps, depicted in Figure 8.2. The first step, aligning organizational goals and IT, ensures that your business succeeds because of IT, not in spite of it, and produces a view of how IT fits within your organization. You use methods such as IT fusion, the competitive forces model, and competitive intelligence to focus the IT effort within the organization. The second and third steps identify specific processes and specific information that require IT systems support by using such methods as the value chain, an information architecture, critical success factors, and business systems planning. These methods may be used alone or in conjunction with one another. Identifying both specific processes and specific information results in a list of possible IT systems that require development.

Once you have this list of systems, your fourth step is to evaluate the IT systems for organizational fit using such methods as cost-benefit analysis, risk analysis, and capital investment analysis. This evaluation reduces the list of possible IT systems to those your organization's limited resources can afford. The fifth and final step is to decide which IT systems you can't live without. You

Aligning Organizational Goals and Information Technology

Purpose	■ To ensure that the IT goals and strategies of your organization are in harmony with its business goals and strategies
Useful Methods	■ IT fusion ■ Competitive forces model ■ Competitive intelligence
Result	■ A clear view of how IT systems support your organization's goals and strategies ❖

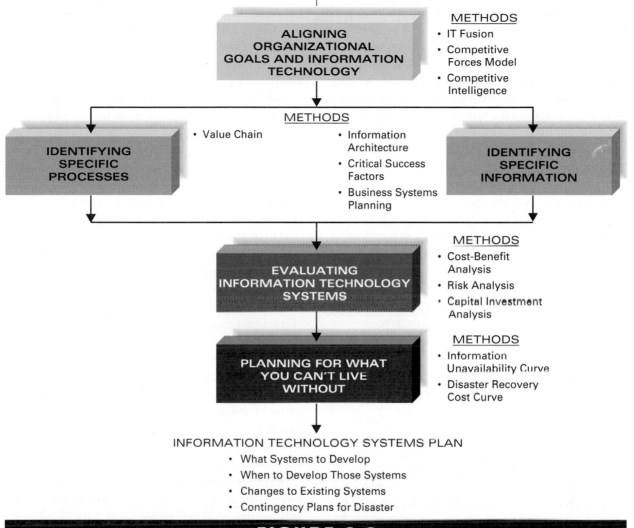

FIGURE 8.2

The Systems Planning Process

look at the cost to your organization of losing any existing or proposed system to a disaster, using an information unavailability curve, while balancing the cost of quickly recovering those systems, using a disaster recovery cost curve. Within each of these five steps, you must continually evaluate existing IT systems for modification or replacement. It's important to remember that IT systems are by no means permanent and have a life like any other business asset. These steps, however, as well as this chapter, focus on new systems planning.

The five systems planning steps generate a comprehensive list of new systems to develop, a timetable for developing them, recommended changes to existing systems, and contingency plans for disaster. All this information is documented in a formal IT systems plan. The plan is your map for the use of IT in your organization.

This chapter takes you through each of the steps in systems planning. You'll examine some possible methods for accomplishing each step, as well as creating an IT systems plan. The plan itself makes up the first, and most important, step in systems development, which you'll examine in Chapter 9.

Aligning Organizational Goals and Information Technology

Isn't It Too Late?

Today, many businesses *require* IT to meet their goals and so it's important to include IT in their business planning. For these businesses, you must consider IT as you formulate organizational strategy. Otherwise IT is relegated to a supporting role, that is, supporting goals that were made long before anyone even considered IT. For example, a bank may formulate an organizational strategy with or without IT. Without IT, the strategy might be providing superior service with traditional tellers. As an afterthought, the bank might consider developing a system to assist these tellers, but the organizational strategy remains the same. Formulating a strategy with IT, the bank might question the necessity of tellers when ATMs can provide 24-hour service. When considered at the time a strategy is conceived, the impact of IT is quite startling.

Selecting IT systems after you create organizational goals misses a strategic opportunity—and it creates a problem. Imagine creating the system to support the bank tellers. What kinds of functions and features should you include? Once you begin deciding how to support the tellers, do you think you'll ever ask the question, "Should this teller function even exist in the first place?" Or the bigger question, "Is this the best way to provide perfect customer service?" It's unlikely that you'd ask these questions.

CAREER OPPORTUNITY

IT fusion is easily visible to workers and customers at all levels. When you telephone a company with a question, can you tell whether the rep is using IT? How? Does the rep make remarks like, "Sorry, the system's slow today—we'll have to wait"? Or even, "Could I have your address again? I keyed it into a different system earlier." Such highly visible examples of the lack of IT fusion are high-priority targets for improvement. As a knowledge worker, you should always be alert to examples of businesses succeeding in spite of IT instead of because of it. Your ability to spot these alignment troubles and suggest solutions will make you a valuable addition to any organization.

One approach to integrating IT into the business involves *aligning* business and technology goals within an organization. So let's take at close look at the concept of alignment. What does alignment really mean anyway? Webster defines alignment as "a forming in line" or "an arrangement of groups or forces in relation to one another."[2] Closer to home, checking your car's front-end alignment might come to mind. And what is that all about? It's about ensuring that the two front wheels point in the same direction or work harmoniously. Still, when we speak of alignment, we're struggling with a fundamental problem. To align, you must take two separate entities and make certain they are in a line, or if that's not possible, you must at least point them in the same direction.

Suppose you had just one front wheel? Would your car still require a front-end alignment? Of course not. And what does this have to do with IT? Well, if you have one set of business goals and another set of IT goals, you must constantly struggle to align these two separate sets of goals. Why not end the struggle and bring them together somehow so that you have only one set of goals for the organization? It's sort of like having only one front wheel to steer your organization. That seems like such a simple concept but, of course, it's not. To develop one set of organizational goals requires considering IT from the start, just as the bank considered IT when formulating the idea for automated customer service using ATMs.

Organizations deal with this alignment struggle in many different ways. One solution is to elevate the most senior IT manager to the organizational planning level, thus ensuring IT input when the business plan is formulated. Many organizations have created the position of chief information officer. The ***chief information officer (CIO)*** is the strategic-level IT manager who directs all IT systems and personnel while communicating directly with the highest levels of the organization. Whatever the title, the purpose is to allow the business to incorporate IT within the business goals and enable the greatest use of IT. An IT professional at this organizational level can help the organization see the IT possibilities, like our bank ATM.

Let's take a look at one more example of what we mean by IT alignment with organizational goals. Imagine that your credit card organization currently approves your transactions without verifying credit status and that it takes its reps about 20 minutes to process the transaction approval decision. Then suppose that you find a way to reduce the decision-making time to 10 minutes by introducing an IT system that would streamline the information-gathering process and quickly display it to the approval reps. That would be quite an improvement, but could more have been done? Well, suppose that someone with knowledge of the possibilities of IT systems contributed to the plan when the business goal to reduce the transaction approval time was first considered. That person could have suggested automating the entire approval process, which would eliminate the approval rep position and reduce approval time from 20 minutes to 20 to 30 seconds. This is precisely the logic behind the creation of a high-level CIO position.

In addition to moving IT management up to the business planning level, your organization may also apply a method called IT fusion to align IT with business goals. To ensure defense of your organization's current competitive position, you may examine the competitive environment with a method called the competitive forces model. Gathering information about how your competition is using IT to support its business goals also helps focus your planning efforts. Whatever method you choose to align IT and the business, this first step in the systems planning process should result in a clear view of how IT supports the goals and strategy of your organization. From this view, you can identify specifics about IT systems that you might consider developing in your organization. But before we get ahead of ourselves, let's examine IT fusion, the competitive forces model, and competitive intelligence as a way of aligning the business and IT.

IT Fusion

Bringing Business and Technology Together

As organizations struggle to integrate business and IT, some no longer think of the two separately. For these firms, IT is such an integral part of business that it's impossible to imagine the business without IT. They want the same to be true for their customers. That is, they want to provide customer service with *transparent* technology.

When was the last time you used IT without noticing the technology? It's hard to think of such an example, isn't it? Look at a device you may use quite frequently, your VCR. Most people never really figure out how to program the VCR to record a television show—and if we do, learning how to use the technology requires a great deal of effort. If you do succeed in programming your VCR, it seems as if you're succeeding in spite of the technology rather than because of it (see Figure 8.3). Say you want to record the *Seinfeld* show, for example, and your VCR is capable of recording for a specified time period, on a certain date, and on a certain channel. To use the VCR technology, you must restate your goals in terms the VCR can understand, for example, "I want to record from 7 P.M. to 7:30 P.M. on 08/12/97 on channel 7." Does that seem like a transparent use of technology? As simplistic as this example may seem, businesses worldwide struggle daily with using technology. When these businesses hear IT spoken of as a tool for competitive advantage, they simply chuckle. They can't even get their IT to support their day-to-day business without great effort.

You can also think of transparent technology as *fusing* together all parts of the business with IT, an idea originally developed by Peter G. W. Keen.[3] ***Information technology fusion (IT fusion)*** occurs when the information technology within your organization is indistinguishable from the business processes and the people who exploit the information technology. So if you don't even know you're using IT, your organization has

achieved IT fusion. What would a process that achieved IT fusion look like? Remember our VCR example? Let's apply IT fusion to that simple process.

Many VCRs today are equipped with VCR Plus technology, which is one step closer to IT fusion (see Figure 8.3). With this technology, you enter a code (up to five digits) for the television show you wish to record. The time, date, and channel information are contained in the code, so they are automatically programmed. Relatively invisible isn't it? Of course, you still have to find that five-digit code in your weekly television guide. And what happens if the time and date change at the last minute? Maybe the baseball World Series goes to seven games, and your favorite show isn't on that night. So real IT fusion hasn't arrived yet.

With this VCR version, however, you can see how transparent the technology becomes. You're aware of, but aren't concerned by, its capabilities and don't need

NONTRANSPARENT TECHNOLOGY: SUCCEEDING IN SPITE OF TECHNOLOGY

Record Program:

TRANSPARENT TECHNOLOGY: SUCCEEDING BECAUSE OF TECHNOLOGY

Record Program:

FIGURE 8.3
Creating Transparent Technology

Accumulating Frequent Flier Miles "Transparently" at US Air

As the decision of which airline to fly becomes increasingly price-based, US Air, of Arlington, Virginia, strives to add new value for its customers. Frequent flier programs are a long-standing customer perk with most major airlines. US Air's program has more than 17 million members, generating as much as 20,000 pieces of mail daily. You see, US Air customers accumulate frequent flier miles not just when they fly US Air but also when they patronize US Air

program partners, including hotels, car rental agencies, and other businesses. To claim miles for some of these program partners, members must mail receipts to US Air. And, of course, once members mail these receipts, they want credit for their miles. The result has overwhelmed US Air. "The program has been getting so big, . . . " says Dan Block, vice president of marketing services, "We simply couldn't handle it. So we are using technology to improve productivity and enhance customer service."

In the past, when anxious customers called about the status of their mileage awards, a US Air rep might have answered, "I don't know. The system shows no new mileage awards." Now that does

not sound like transparent technology, does it? Using a work flow and imaging IT system, customer reps can now view all of a customer's correspondence on the screen while still on the phone with the customer. And if the rep must transfer the customer call to another rep, the customer's information is transferred with the phone call. The result—customers are more satisfied and feel US Air cares about them. To the customer, all of this is accomplished with essentially transparent information technology. Wouldn't you rather the customer appreciate your employee's rather than your technology efforts?[5] ❖

to be. You succeed because of, not in spite of, the technology. It's easiest to see the effect of transparent information technology from an external organizational view, as a customer for example. Federal Express offers its customers a money-back guarantee on overnight package delivery and 30-minute tracking.[4] How is this possible? Where does the technology leave off and the people take over? As a customer, it's really hard to tell. These capabilities require IT systems, and Federal Express succeeds *because* of them.

Porter's Competitive Forces Model

Fighting Back with IT

As your organization struggles to integrate IT into the business, it will also search for basic IT strategies. In Chapter 3, we explored seven OHP (organizational horsepower) strategies to create a competitive organization using IT. These strategies allow your organization to base its competitive efforts on its strengths while using IT to innovate. And these strategies must be integrated into

the IT systems plan. There are times, however, when your organization must use IT simply to defend its position in the marketplace. At the very least, your organization should carefully examine all its interactions within the competitive environment to eliminate any opportunity for the competition.

One method of exploring your organization's competitive environment is Porter's competitive forces model.[6] The ***competitive forces model*** is a tool to formulate strategy by examining the environment in which your organization competes (see Figure 8.4). In the model, five forces found in most industries are identified:

■ *Customer force* A strong customer force is generated by a well-informed buyer, a price-sensitive buyer, and similar product/service alternatives.

■ *Substitute force* A strong substitute force is generated by the existence of price-competitive product/service alternatives.

■ *Supplier force* A strong supplier force is generated by suppliers with necessary, unique products/services and a concentrated supplier market.

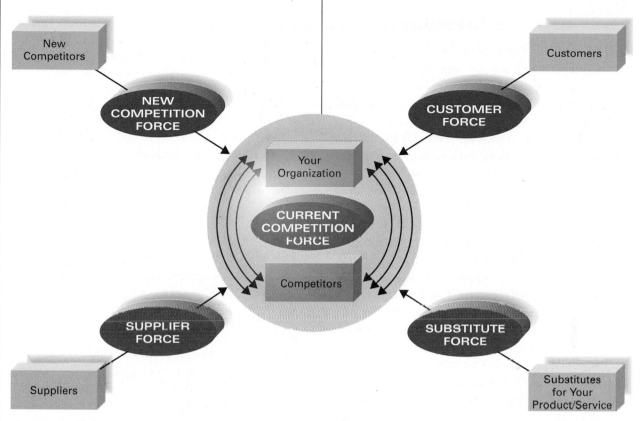

Your organization must react to competitive forces from its competition. Likewise, your organization together with its competitors are subject to customer, substitute, supplier, and new competition forces. All of these competitive forces shape your organization's business and IT strategy.

FIGURE 8.4

Five Competitive Forces That Shape Strategy

- *New competition force* A strong new competition force is generated by low barriers to market entry, nonproprietary products or raw materials, and little government regulation.

- *Current competition force* A strong current competition force is generated by low brand identity, product/service similarity, slow industry growth, and industry overcapacity.

To use the model, you begin by determining the strength of each force and then look for opportunities to effect beneficial change. The opportunities for changing competitive forces with IT form the basis of a defensive competitive strategy. Porter suggests choosing from three basic strategies as a result of using the model:

- *Low-Cost Producer* Your organization produces its product/service at the industry's lowest cost to combat competition. This strategy requires a weak supplier force to strengthen the bargaining power of your organization. The use of just-in-time purchasing and inventory management IT systems supports the transaction volume necessary for this strategy.

- *Differentiation* Your organization produces a product/service that customers purchase because of its unique characteristics. This strategy reduces the customer and substitute force by reducing competitive alternatives for customers. The use of IT systems to support the customer service process is just one of the possible methods IT systems may incorporate to help differentiate an organization.

- *Focus* Your organization targets a small market niche for its product/service. This affects all market forces by effectively changing focus from an entire industry to a portion of that industry where forces may differ significantly in favor of your organization. The use of databases, data warehousing, and decision support IT systems supports discovering and exploiting a unique market niche.

Critical to identifying the appropriate strategy is the appropriate application of IT. So identifying a strategy simultaneously with the identification of a supporting IT system is recommended to facilitate the alignment of IT with the business.

Competitive Intelligence
What Are They Up To?

An integral part of IT systems planning is understanding how your systems strategy compares to your competition. Knowledge of your competition also supports the competitive forces analysis. Remember, when your customers make the decision to purchase from you, they are saying that your firm offers them perfect service, or the closest thing to perfect service they can find. In many cases, the customer's concept of perfect service is framed by what's possible. For example, if no one in your industry offered 24-hour customer service, customers would consider service at 8 A.M. the closest thing to perfect service, even if they wanted service at 2 A.M. on that morning. However, the first competitor who begins to meet that 24-hour need redefines the closest thing to perfect service for all customers and competitors. If you were unaware of this service change, you'd actually lose some understanding of your customers because you failed to monitor your competition. *Competitive intelligence*, as discussed in Chapter 6, involves more than just monitoring what your competition does. It also involves examining what your competition hopes to do and how IT systems support its business strategy.

Gathering competitive intelligence provides many other benefits to organizations as well. A formal competitive intelligence process can

- Help you anticipate changes in your customer market
- Help you anticipate actions by your competitors
- Alert you to new or potential competitors
- Allow you to learn from the successes and failures of other organizations
- Allow you to learn about regulatory changes that can affect your organization
- Allow you to compare your business processes to others

Although the organizational needs for competitive intelligence are strong, gathering competitive intelligence is a relatively new process at most companies. Less than 7 percent of large American companies have their own full-blown competitive intelligence divisions. Eighty percent of those are less than 5 years old.[7]

INDUSTRY PERSPECTIVE | **Retail**

Schwab Eliminates the Middleman

Charles Schwab & Co., a discount stock broker, competes by keeping its costs down —a low-cost producer strategy. Sometimes this involves rather sophisticated technology. For example, to provide up-to-the-minute stock quotes, Schwab has applied speech-recognition software. A customer calls a toll-free number, recites an eight-digit account number and the name of a stock, and instantly receives a current stock price. All this without a single employee's intervention. And that translates into significant savings for the firm.

The aspect that's so unusual about Schwab's use of technology is how tightly integrated this IT system is with Schwab's business processes. Most firms, when faced with an expensive customer service process, simply apply technology to the problem with little thought given to how the process might be changed. A common result is customers forced to navigate their way through long menus of keypad options. So, instead, Schwab created a system where customers continued doing what they always did—verbally request information. The computer does the work of finding the information rather than forcing the customer to do so with keypad options. This required careful planning. "It seems so simple, but it really is rocket science," said Bob Morgen, the project manager in charge of implementing the system. "We sat around a table for months sifting through all of the things a person might say," Bob explained. When the project team was done, it had discovered 2 million permutations to identify 13,000 stocks and mutual funds. In the end, Schwab had a system that kept costs down and that customers hardly noticed. Truly a great application of (pehaps transparent) technology.[8] ❖

What Is the Competitive Intelligence Process?

The competitive intelligence process consists of the four steps detailed in Figure 8.5: planning, gathering, analysis, and integration. The process begins with planning and ends with integration into the IT systems plan. The four steps are as follows:

❶ *Planning* Before beginning the process, your organization must define the *purpose*, *scope,* and *timing* of its competitive intelligence. Most often the purpose will be to augment IT systems planning, and you'll define the scope of the intelligence as including customers as well as competitors. The timing may require a one-time process or a continuous process. Continuous competitive intelligence is called **competitive scanning**.

❷ *Gathering* You may gather intelligence directly from the source, called **primary intelligence**. This is certainly the best source of information and the rawest or most unaltered form of intelligence, if what you need is available. You may also gather information indirectly from a source other than the primary one—called **secondary intelligence**. Secondary intelligence is usually information that has been altered and/or has an opinion added to the primary intelligence. You may gather intelligence in *electronic* form, generally enabled by networks (as discussed in Chapter 6). Or you may gather paper or spoken intelligence in *nonelectronic* form. Information gathered electronically is much easier to analyze in the next step of the process.

❸ *Analysis* As a knowledge worker, you play a significant role in analyzing competitive intelligence. You apply your knowledge in your field to make sense of the intelligence that has been gathered. Your expertise is so important because it's unlikely that complete information will be available, so it will be up to you to close the gaps.

❹ *Integration* The analyzed competitive intelligence is integrated into the business and IT goals. There, planners decide what response, if any, is appropriate to new business and IT strategy.

What Can You Contribute to Competitive Intelligence?

Knowledge workers contribute to all steps of the competitive intelligence process. You'll help plan the purpose, scope, and timing of the process. You'll also assist in gathering intelligence, especially electronic intelligence. Once the intelligence has been analyzed, you'll

also assist in applying the intelligence to the IT systems plan. Perhaps your most time-consuming role, however, will be analyzing the competitive intelligence. As a knowledge worker, you'll analyze the competitive intelligence using your specific expertise in your chosen field, gained in college and in the workplace. Let's illustrate with a possible scenario.

PLANNING

Planning for the competitive intelligence process involves establishing the *purpose, scope,* and *timing.*

GATHERING

Intelligence gathering is from *primary* and *secondary* sources and in *electronic* or *nonelectronic* form.

ANALYSIS

Knowledge worker experts perform the analysis of intelligence.

INTEGRATION

The results of the intelligence analysis are integrated into the business and IT systems goals. Knowing how IT systems support a competitor's business affects your organization's goals.

FIGURE 8.5

The Four Steps in the Competitive Intelligence Process

Motorola Had More Intelligence Than It Knew

When Motorola, the computer chip manufacturer based in Schaumburg, Illinois, decided competitive intelligence could be helpful, no one dreamed it already possessed such information. In the mid-1980s, Motorola was in the middle of a heated computer chip battle. Naturally, competitive intelligence is helpful in such a situation, so Motorola hired Jan Herring, formerly an intelligence officer with the Central Intelligence Agency. Jan first examined the information already within Motorola and determined which types of intelligence-gathering networks already existed. This is standard operating procedure for an intelligence audit and precedes formal intelligence gathering.

What did Jan find? He found what he suspected he'd find in a firm the size of Motorola. Competitive intelligence was gathered through informal networks, but a system for sharing the information was lacking. No one had ever considered a collaborative effort of all these informal networks to support the strategic business plan. Once Jan unified the informal networks and formalized the gathering process, information contributions jumped from 2 to 20 percent. The system Jan created ensures that Motorola won't operate in a competitive information void anytime in the future. Remember, sometimes your organization may know more than you think. So just ask around; like Motorola, you may discover competitive intelligence right under your nose.[9] ❖

Suppose you work for a paper manufacturing firm, and it has gathered intelligence about a new system at your largest competitor. This new system allows your competitor to communicate with a large market of possible suppliers of recycled paper raw materials. Analyzing this intelligence requires expertise from several different fields. The finance expert determines if the potential supplier agreements required for such a system would make it cost effective. The marketing expert determines if the market for recycled paper would support increased production. And the manufacturing expert determines if the sources of materials with whom the system connects have supplies that meet your organization's quality standards. All these knowledge workers contribute to the analysis of competitive intelligence. This, in turn, provides your organization with ideas for effective use of its IT systems.

Both IT fusion and competitive intelligence help your organization define how IT systems can support the organization. IT fusion identifies areas for improvement and where business, people, and technology may not be well-aligned. Competitive intelligence keeps you in touch with how your customers see the competitive market and focuses your efforts on areas that seem to be successful in the market. The result of both alignment methods is a clear view of how IT can support the goals and strategy of the organization. With this view, you can begin to plan specifics about IT systems, which you'll examine in the next few planning steps.

Identifying Specific Processes

Building Better Processes with Information Technology

Once your organization has a clear view of how IT can support the business, you can use that view to identify specific areas of opportunity or need within the business. Two key areas are business processes and information needs, both of which IT can support. The identification of processes and information needs can be performed together or individually in systems planning. Either way, they both consider how IT supports the business and both result in a preliminary list of the IT systems your organization needs. We'll first examine methods of identifying specific processes that need support and then examine methods of identifying specific information needs within the organization.

The business processes within your organization are simply the groups of activities that you use to accomplish the organization's work. Today, many of these

Identifying Specific Processes

Purpose	■ To identify specific business processes within the organization that require IT systems support
Useful Methods	■ Value chain
Result	■ A preliminary list of the IT systems your organization needs ❖

processes require IT systems support. Few of us could imagine a grocery store, for example, that sells products without a bar code scanning checkout system. So you identify those processes that require IT support to create a list of systems your organization requires. One method of identifying specific processes that require IT support is the *value chain* method, which examines how your organization adds value to its products and services. More specifically, you can see which business processes either add or reduce value for the customer. Both types of processes identify areas where IT systems can help. When you support a process with IT that already adds value, you're adding additional value where it's most visible to your customers. Supporting a process with IT that reduces value to your customer can turn that process around by becoming more efficient or better addressing customer needs.

The Value Chain Method
Searching for Specific Processes

Once you have a general view of how IT can support your business, it's important that you reinforce this view by ensuring IT support for all important business processes. But what processes are important, and how do you find them? One graphic tool that helps you identify those important processes is called the value chain, developed by Michael Porter.[10] The *value chain* views the organization as a chain—or series—of processes, each of which adds value to the product or service for the customer. Customers patronize your organization because of the value that it adds to products and services. It's what your organization does to deliver more perfect service. If you view your organization as a value chain, you can identify the important processes in adding value for customers and, thus, identify IT systems that support those processes.

INDUSTRY PERSPECTIVE

Hospitality & Leisure

Finding a Way to Add Value

Do consumers make travel purchases in much the same way as businesses? For the most part, an individual business makes many more travel purchases than an individual consumer. And businesses usually have strict guidelines for employee travel—no first-class tickets or no full-fare coach tickets, for example. So businesses rely on travel agents to remember all their specific travel guidelines and ensure that all purchases adhere to those guidelines.

American Express and Microsoft have teamed up to create a customer integrated system that capitalizes on adding value to corporate travel purchases. An Internet-based system (http://www.americanexpress.com) offers a customizable interface for each organization. Employers have tight control over their employees' travel including such options as preferred airlines and spending ceilings. Other online travel services target consumers. In creating a business-targeted service, American Express and Microsoft needed to differentiate their business services from the consumer services. They did this by identifying what processes added the most value for the business customer, which made identifying the needed IT support easy.[11] ❖

Figure 8.6 depicts the components of a value chain. The chain of primary value processes along the bottom half takes the raw materials and makes, delivers, markets and sells, and services your organization's products or services. Processes along the top half of the chain, such as management, accounting, finance, legal, human resources, research and development, and purchasing, support the primary value processes. Your organization requires these support value processes to ensure the smooth operation of the primary value processes. All value chain processes possess an individual value. However, these processes combined have a total value greater than the sum of their individual values. We call this additional value value-added, and it's depicted on the far right of the value chain. The larger the value-added, the more value customers place on an organization's product or service. To the organization, this can mean a competitive advantage and often greater profits. Let's look at how a firm might use the value chain to identify both value-added and value-reducing processes.

If you've ever purchased a necktie, you may have heard of the Robert Talbott company of Carmel Valley, California.[12] Talbott is the premier necktie manufacturer in the United States, providing one of every two ties sold in a Nordstrom department store. Talbott has always shunned technology—all of its tie orders, historically, were written on paper forms. That used to work fine, because Talbott has always ensured added value by utilizing high-quality workmanship, unique designs, and fabrics. However, as you've already read, customer "wants" now drive their demands, and those demands are always changing. Today customers want constantly updated styles and more of them. In fact, Talbott now creates four neckwear lines for Nordstrom each year with up to 300 designs per line. Keeping up with all those necktie designs has become increasingly difficult for Talbott. Given this situation, how could the value chain help Talbott plan for a better way of meeting customer demands? Well, it would begin by identifying both value-added and value-reducing processes. Let's look at the identification of value-added processes first.

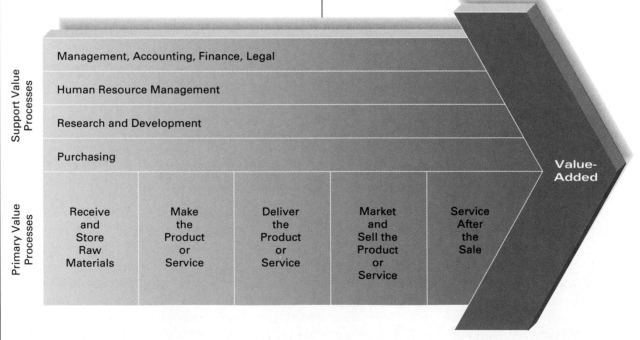

The value chain is composed of primary value and support value processes. From left to right, and along the bottom half of the chain, the organization creates its product or service through primary value processes. Along the top half of the chain, the support value processes provide the organization support in performing those primary value processes. When all processes are combined they have a total value greater than the sum of their individual values, called "value-added," and it's depicted on the far right of the value chain. Greater value-added means a competitive advantage and, often, greater profits.

FIGURE 8.6

The Components of a Value Chain

Identifying Processes That Add Value

Talbott should begin by looking at the firm's processes and identifying, with help from customers, those processes that add the most value. These include manufacturing high-quality ties and purchasing quality materials at Talbott. Then Talbott should graphically depict the customer responses on a value chain. Figure 8.7 is one possible result. Notice how the processes are sized to represent the value that customers attribute to those processes. The largest source of value-added is the high-quality manufacturing process. Still, a close second is the purchasing process that provides access to high-quality sources of silks and other fabrics. As these processes are the ones most visible to customers, they will quickly add even more value when supported by new IT systems. Therefore Talbott created a computer-aided design system to reduce the time it takes to create and manufacture new ties.

Identifying Processes That Reduce Value

In addition to identifying value-added processes, it's important to identify those processes that reduce the value for the customer. Using the same technique to gather this information from customers, Talbott should create a value-reducing value chain. Talbott identified the sales process as the process that reduced value the most, as shown in Figure 8.8. It found sales were lost because salespeople were promising neckties that were out of stock. It often took up to 3 days to discover the out-of-stock status and communicate that fact to the customers. Customers were beginning to lose faith in Talbott's ability to deliver high-quality ties. They saw this process failure as one that reduced Talbott's value to them as customers.

To correct their sales process deficiencies, Talbott implemented a new IT system to get timely product information to the sales force. Using laptop computers, the sales force now carries product-line custom CD-ROMs

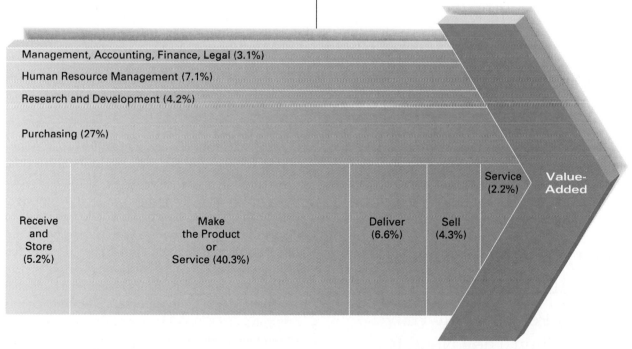

Talbott asked its customers to quantify how much value each process added to the products and services they received. Using a total of 100 points for the value chain, each customer distributed those points among Talbott's processes. The results from all customers were tallied and used to size each process in the value chain. Process percentages total 100 percent for the value chain.

The results showed that the high-quality production process (Make the Product or Service) adds the most value for the customer at 40.3 percent. Also highly valued is the process that purchases unique, high-quality fabrics (Purchasing, 27%). As these processes are most visible to customers, they will quickly add even more value when supported by new IT systems.

FIGURE 8.7

The Value-Added View of a Necktie Manufacturer

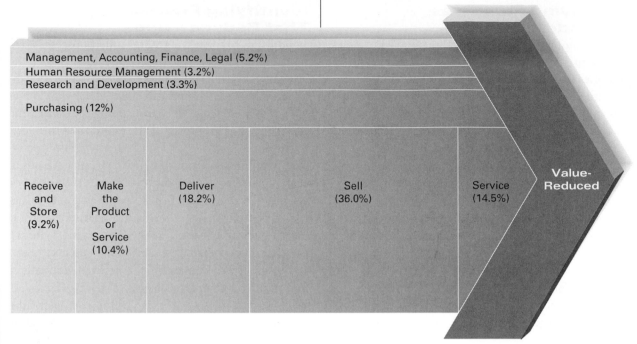

Management, Accounting, Finance, Legal (5.2%)
Human Resource Management (3.2%)
Research and Development (3.3%)

Purchasing (12%)

| Receive and Store (9.2%) | Make the Product or Service (10.4%) | Deliver (18.2%) | Sell (36.0%) | Service (14.5%) | Value-Reduced |

Talbott asked its customers to quantify how much each process reduced the value of the products and services they received. Using a total of 100 points for the value chain, each customer distributed those points among Talbott's processes. The results from all customers were tallied and used to size each process in the value chain. Process percentages total 100 percent for the value chain.

The results showed that the selling process (Sell) reduces the value for the customer the most at 36.0 percent. Any process that significantly reduces value to customers is a target for improvement and support by IT systems. For most firms, including Talbott, they just cannot afford to allow a process to endanger their relationships with customers.

FIGURE 8.8

The Value-Reduced View of a Necktie Manufacturer

on the road with them. They place orders over their computers from their hotel rooms and receive inventory updates at the same time. As a result, customers have new faith in an old friend who adds more value than ever.

Identifying Specific Information

Getting People What They Need, When They Need It

As you've seen in this textbook, MIS is all about using IT to put the right information in the hands of the right people at the right time. But to do that you have to identify the information those people need before you can determine which IT systems to build. This is the next step in systems planning, and it is a significant one. Remember, information is a resource upon which you build an organization. Carefully planning for and managing the use of information supports everything an organization does.

To identify your organization's information needs, you can employ a variety of methods; in this section, we'll look at three. You may create an *information architecture* that matches the people who need information with the information they need. Another choice is to identify your organization's *critical success factors* and the supporting information those factors require. You may also choose to use *business systems planning* to identify both users and creators of organizational information. Identifying your organization's information needs gives you a preliminary list of the IT systems that your organization requires.

An Information Architecture

Uniting People and Information

Everything your organization does must be supported by an information base. You'll find, therefore, that planning to create an IT system that supports competitive analysis, for example, is useless without knowledge workers to apply that analysis. Likewise, if you lack a source of

Finding Value at Your Bookstore

When you are performing a value chain analysis, customer input is critical. One organization with whom you've had experience as a customer is your school bookstore. Every semester or quarter you grab what you need, stand in line, and pay the price for the written word.

As a team, construct a value chain using the value-added perspective discussed in this chapter. Using Figure 8.7 as a guide, poll your team members for their opinions about the processes that have the most value for them, allocating 100 points total for all processes. You'll have your percentages after you average the numbers for each process from each team member. Last, construct the value chain using the percentages to estimate the size of each process. Use the table below to help you understand how each process affects you as a customer. How do the responses within your own team compare? If you were preparing an IT systems plan for the next year at the bookstore, how would this information affect your decisions? If others in your class do this exercise as well, how do their results compare?

Value Chain Process	Impact on You
Management, accounting, etc.	Have you ever had to deal with management?
Human resource management	Ever heard employees complain about the work benefits?
Research and development	Has the bookstore ever had special events or attractions?
Purchasing	Ever sold a book back?
Receive products	Ever had to ask for books not yet on the shelves?
Make the product/service	How do employees help you with what books you'll need?
Deliver the product or service	Does the bookstore deliver?
Market and sell	How does the bookstore market its books and merchandise?
Service after the sale	Ever had to return anything? ❖

competitive intelligence, an IT system created to compile that information would starve from lack of input. To model the use of information in an organization, you can construct an information architecture. This architecture provides a solid base for identifying needed IT systems.

An information architecture unites two of your organization's most important resources—information and people. You see, the ***information architecture*** for an organization describes what *information* your organization needs and which *people* within your organization

Identifying Specific Information

Purpose	▪ To identify specific information needs within the organization that require IT systems support
Useful Methods	▪ Information architecture
	▪ Critical success factors
	▪ Business systems planning
Result	▪ A preliminary list of the IT systems your organization needs ❖

Obtaining the Information Wherever, Whenever

For many firms, identifying information requirements is much more than just identifying needs. They must consider also when and where the information is required. That's certainly the case for the Bank of America, based in San Francisco. Bank of America fields 350 service technicians who maintain 5,000 automatic teller machines and 100,000 PCs throughout California, Arizona, Nevada, New Mexico, and Texas. When repair calls reach the communications system, Bank of America needs to know the address of the malfunctioning device, the type of equipment in question, and the nature of the problem; and all this information must be delivered immediately to the appropriate field technician.

That informational need spelled out the need for a wireless information delivery system for Bank of America's field technicians. The system now in use includes a wireless radio network that takes advantage of handheld computing devices. When a repair call is received, it is relayed to the geographic area in which a technician lives, along with the repair information. Once the repair has been made, the technician transmits the information over the air to Bank of America's central computer system in California. Implementing this system allowed Bank of America to reduce call center personnel by 25 percent and saved service technicians about 20 to 60 minutes daily. All this has been achieved by asking the right questions—what information is needed, when it is needed, and what form is needed.[13] ❖

need that information. You may describe the people by categories of workers, their departments, or the business processes they support. You may describe the information by classes of information or even its sources.

Information for the Moment of Value

To use information effectively within an organization, you must be able to get the information you need, when you need it, and in the form you need. Maybe that sounds trivial, or you might think that ensuring information access, timing, and form is the job of the information professional, not the knowledge worker. The trouble is that IT professionals don't know the *what, when,* and *how* of your information requirements unless you tell them. Let's look at a simple information scenario.

Imagine that one day you receive a call from your globe-trotting sister. She's calling from Norway and is in desperate need of cash to continue her travels, so she would like you to wire her some money from your bank account in Dallas, Texas. She gives you the name and phone number of a bank in Oslo, Norway, where she can pick up the cash tomorrow. You have the money, and although you've never wired money overseas, you tell your younger sister you'll do what you can to help. Then you call the bank in Oslo to see what is required for the wire transfer and someone answers on the phone who doesn't even speak your language. You struggle with the words until you get what you think is the right transfer information. Then you call your bank and discover that no one there has ever wired money to Norway and they aren't sure that the branch can do it. This is rapidly becoming more than you bargained for, you think.

What has this to do with the use of information within your organization? Well, imagine that the money is important information. It's certainly in the wrong place. In this case, the money is in your bank instead of the Oslo bank. It's also unavailable when your sister needs it. And it's definitely in the wrong form—American instead of Norwegian currency. Actually, the mechanics of handling such a money transfer are not that difficult, but the system must be in place to do so. The same would apply if the money were information. You must ask ahead of time, who needs what and when so that you can build the IT systems to ensure timely information delivery.

Figure 8.9 depicts a basic information architecture framework. This two-dimensional view adequately identifies the information required in an organization and who needs it. However, as you learned in Chapter 1, information really has three dimensions—time, content, and form. And each of these information dimensions differs for the people requiring that information. Let's look at an example.

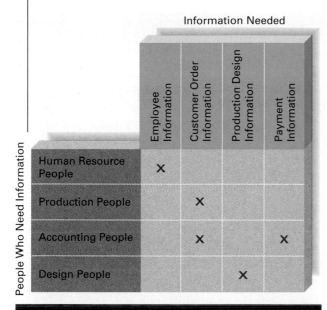

FIGURE 8.9
A Basic Information Architecture Framework

- Will the organization support corporatewide information networks to facilitate information sharing?
- Which organizational processes should be centralized and which should be distributed to operational locations?
- Will any network used for information sharing be secure, or will only nonsensitive information be communicated?
- What is the most efficient distribution of information, local or global, for each process?
- What is the most flexible distribution of information, local or global, for each process?
- Do your answers to all of the above questions support the organizational strategy? If not, reconsider your response.

Answering these questions will help you identify the IT systems that will most appropriately deliver the required organizational information.

Critical Success Factors
Supporting Your Goals with Information

When most of us consider something that needs to be done, we focus on the first goal we wish to accomplish rather than what we need to do the job. Once we have a goal in mind, we think about how we'll go about achieving it. This is certainly true in organizations as well. A

Imagine that the production people require customer order information as soon as the order is placed (time), with products ordered by part number (content) and each individual customer order sheet separated (form). The accounting people also require customer order information, but of a different nature. In accounting, they may require customer order information on a weekly basis (time), with sales tax information included (content), and presented as an electronic spreadsheet (form). With information described along each of these three dimensions of time, content, and form for all people who need that information, our view of the information architecture takes on new dimensions as well. In Figure 8.10, you can see the relationships among the information needed, the people who need the information, and the three dimensions for all information identified.

The last aspect of an information architecture that you must consider may be the most difficult to determine. Once you decide who needs what information and you express that need in terms of information time, content, and form, you still must decide where you will maintain that information. In Chapter 6, you learned about networks and how the client/server blueprint supports either local or global information. Although one advantage to using a client/server network is that distribution of information is transparent to knowledge workers, where you'll place this information must be considered when planning for new systems.[14] The information architecture must address information distribution concerns, including the following:

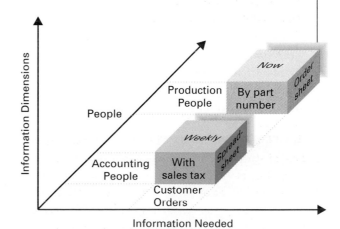

This multidimensional information architecture allows you to represent the three dimensions of information for each user of that information.

FIGURE 8.10
The Multidimensional Information Architecture Framework

INDUSTRY PERSPECTIVE   **Manufacturing**

Does It Matter Where You Keep Your Information?

Satisfying information requirements across a large organization is challenging. But does it matter where you keep the information? For Lockheed Martin Corp., the answer is yes—and no. No, because it doesn't matter where you locate the information, so long as it's accessible. Yes, because

it's less expensive to "do it from a sophisticated central site," says Paul Strassman, the former chief information officer at the Department of Defense.

Lockheed hoped to cut its help desk costs by centralizing 13 geographically dispersed help desks into one central location. The challenge for Lockheed was to not sacrifice help desk responsiveness during the consolidation. A help desk satisfies computer end users' information needs by resolving

their computer problems over the phone. And it's 30 percent cheaper to resolve a systems problem over the phone than it is to dispatch a technician to fix it. So failing to provide adequate help desk service might have cost Lockheed millions. As it was, Lockheed successfully completed its consolidation and is anticipating savings of $7 million over 5 years on an investment of $12 million.[16] ❖

---

discount store would first set a goal of being the lowest-priced retailer in the area and *then* determine how it's going to achieve that goal.

As a knowledge worker, you'll require large amounts of information to perform your job. How can you be assured you'll have what you need to accomplish your goals? One method for addressing a knowledge worker's information requirements is the critical success factors method developed by John Rockart.[15] Using this method, managers and knowledge workers identify a small number of critical success factors for their own area of responsibility. A *critical success factor (CSF)* is a factor critical to organizational success. Table 8.1 provides some examples of CSFs in various organizations. By identifying CSFs, knowledge workers help define information requirements and, in turn, IT systems that support those information needs.

AT&T used the CSF method to help its long-distance service business.[17] AT&T's customer reps had found it difficult to communicate the advantages of using AT&T over the competition as small-business owners complained of increasingly complicated rate structures. As a result, the reps simply weren't making sales, a CSF for the firm. So AT&T examined the sales process and found that its rate information was not in a form that was helpful to its customers. AT&T then created a new system called 1-800-COMPARE after the phone number it hoped potential new customers would call. AT&T implemented an IT system that used data mining technology to search through a caller's phone records and provide a side-by-side rate comparison of the caller's current carrier to AT&T. All this while the prospective customer was still on the phone with the rep. This information was all the reps needed to succeed and execute a CSF for the firm.

TABLE 8.1   Critical Success Factor Examples

Type of Organization	Critical Success Factors	Type of Organization	Critical Success Factors
Start-up engineering firm	Designs that meet standards All engineer-certified	Discount retail chain	Fully stocked shelves Qualified suppliers
Bank	Low transaction costs 24-hour customer account access	Shipping firm	On-time package delivery Accurate package tracking
Ice cream manufacturer	Fresh product on store shelves Innovative flavors		

Consider how you might assist your school in identifying information needs using CSFs. Graduating students in, on average, 4 years by ensuring sufficient class availability might be a CSF. What kind of information would be required to meet this CSF? To determine how large classes *have to be* you might require current and projected enrollment numbers. To know the maximum size a class *could be*, you'd need to count the number of seats in each classroom. To know how many sections of a class *you could offer* you'd need to know how many faculty are available to teach those classes. The list of information requirements could go on and on. Once you compile these needs, you can see immediately which type of IT system your school requires to satisfy these information needs. For example, your school might require an IT system that captures all the needed information from the different systems around the school and calculates a master class schedule.

Aligning organizational goals and IT systems planning is a constant challenge using the CSF method. Because you gather CSFs from many workers, the CSFs may represent conflicting goals. This is especially true in organizations that don't effectively communicate their strategic vision. For these organizations, knowledge workers and managers may be unclear about how their contributions fit into the organization's strategy. That means you'll end up with individual CSFs that may not support the business direction and could result in IT systems that don't either.

Business Systems Planning
Supporting Current and Future Information Needs

Using critical success factors is problematic because they support only existing information requirements. Business systems planning was designed and developed by IBM to address both existing and future information requirements. *Business systems planning (BSP)* identifies information requirements by documenting the relationships between business processes and information classes. You'll remember from Chapter 3 that the definition of a process is a sequence of activities that takes raw materials from a supplier and serves outcomes to a customer. One of the outcomes of most processes is newly created information. For example, when you hire a new employee, you create an employee file containing information about that new employee. So the process of hiring employees creates employee description information. Once

INDUSTRY PERSPECTIVE   **Food**

What's Critical to H. J. Heinz's Success? It Depends on Whom You Ask

When you work for a company as large and diverse as H. J. Heinz Co., of Pittsburgh, Pennsylvania, identifying critical success factors (CSFs) can become quite a challenge. That's because Heinz is not just the food company best known for ketchup. Heinz also owns Ore-Ida Inc., one of the world's largest producers of frozen potato products, as well as tuna packager Starkist Foods Inc. In fact, Heinz owns 16 different food companies, or operating units, worldwide. So how does a firm with such diverse products and locations decide what's critical to its success? The key is ensuring that the IT strategy supports the business strategy before gathering critical success factors.

You see, at H. J. Heinz the corporate strategy doesn't support mixing the strategies of the various operating units. Each unit operates independently and according to its own strategic plan. Therefore, the information requirements of each operating unit must reflect that unit's business strategy. Philip Lichtenfels, the senior executive who oversees all of Heinz's information gathering, summarizes the corporate strategy nicely: "Every year, each IT organization does a strategic plan that reflects the business needs of that operating unit." So, although most organizations combine information requirements from all of the organization's divisions, it's not always appropriate. Just make certain that the method by which you define the organization's information requirements parallels the way you define the organization's business needs.[18] ❖

Defining Information Requirements with Critical Success Factors

When knowledge workers identify their critical success factors, they really just summarize what's important to their success. In doing so, they simplify the job of identifying what information they need to support those important processes. Below is a table of critical success factors and the information required to support those critical success factors for obtaining a good job after graduation. Imagine that you are looking ahead to graduation and creating a strategic business plan for you personally. To get you started, the information required to support the first CSF is provided. ❖

Critical Success Factor	Information to Support the Critical Success Factor
Take appropriate courses	Course catalogs, job listings, and degree requirements
Develop good study habits	
Maintain awareness of job openings	
Nurture time management skills	
Make relevant business contacts	
Understand career objectives	
Develop a job search plan	

created, this employee information can be used by the payroll process to access an employee's pay status. Notice that the employee information contains many pieces of information about employees. This grouping of related information is referred to as an **information class** instead of a piece of information, such as an employee's name.

The BSP method documents the creators and users of information, forming the basis of an information architecture illustrated in Figure 8.11. The resulting matrix uses a "C" or a "U" to represent processes that create or use, respectively, a particular information class. One key advantage to this process/information matrix is the identification of the information creator. All information systems require a supplier for their information and the CSF method identifies only information users, not suppliers.

When you apply any matrix approach to identifying information requirements, the question of granularity always arises. That is, in how much detail do you describe information and processes? Let's take a look at the three steps of creating the BSP matrix to answer that question:

❶ Senior management defines the business processes. Taking this top-down approach to process definition allows the BSP method to include future goals and requirements derived from the direction defined by senior management.

CAREER OPPORTUNITY

As a knowledge worker you'll find it advantageous to always ask yourself *who* created the information you require. That person, or department, is a wonderful source of additional supporting information as well as insight into how the information originated within your organization. The information creator can communicate how the information was created, its limitations, and even its intended use. You may discover that you have been using information in ways the information creator never intended.

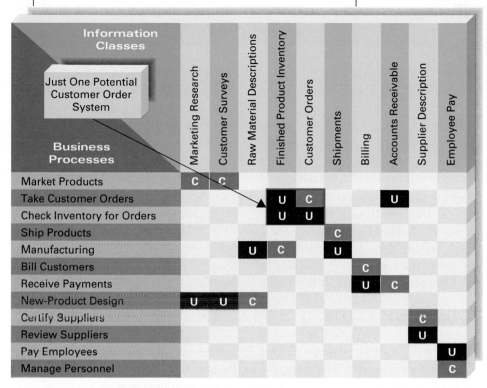

The relationship between business processes and information classes is designated by either a "C" for processes that create those information classes or a "U" for processes that use those information classes. The matrix identifies a potential customer order IT system.

FIGURE 8.11

Relating Business Processes and Information Classes

information classes as well as the processes at the appropriate level of detail.

The BSP method identifies information ownership. Much later, when you develop the IT systems that the BSP method identifies, information ownership will ensure information integrity in those systems.

The BSP method identifies IT systems as well as the information they support. First, you identify logical groupings of process/information relationships to determine potential systems projects. Graphically, you look for groups of Cs and Us in the BSP matrix and draw a box around them. It may be necessary to rearrange the process or information-class orders. The box of grouped relationships represents a potential systems project. The matrix in Figure 8.11 identifies a potential customer order IT system.

❷ Process experts define the information classes needed to support each process. The process experts' definition of information classes is driven by the requirement that each information class may be created by only one process.

❸ Process experts relate the information to the processes using the *create* and *use* criteria. In the matrix depicted in Figure 8.11, this means each vertical column for an information class may contain only one "C." This helps define the

Evaluating Information Technology Systems

Selecting from the Possibilities

At this point in the systems planning process, you've identified potential IT systems that fit within the organizational goals, support processes, and information

Evaluating Information Technology Systems

Purpose	■ To evaluate the preliminary list of IT systems your organization needs, based on the application of organizational criteria
Useful Methods	■ Cost-benefit analysis ■ Risk analysis ■ Capital investment analysis
Result	■ A final list of which IT systems your organization must develop and when it must develop them ❖

Using Technology So Customers Make the CardinalChoice

Cardinal Health Inc., a $9 billion pharmaceuticals wholesaler in Dublin, Ohio, represents a growing trend in the health care field—using information to reinvent processes aimed at controlling costs and providing better service. Its new IT system, CardinalChoice, supports that effort. Cardinal knows its customers (pharmacies and hospitals) are feeling the cost squeeze from *their* customers (patients and their insurance companies). So Cardinal has established a business strategy of providing the right pharmaceuticals at the right price. It hopes, further, to influence the customer's idea of the "right price" by adding information through technology to the purchasing decision.

Improving customer service with information is nothing new at Cardinal. Since 1988, it has made its corporate network available to customers to provide the best pricing information and allow them to place orders in 5 minutes or less. It's all about giving customers the information they require. William Bottlinger, VP of MIS at Cardinal, explains, "It helps our customers buy the right drugs at the right price so they can better manage their inventories." Originally, the network required customers to have special hardware and software. Now customers can use their own PCs to access Cardinal's network—through their extranet CardinalChoice system (extranets are discussed in Chapter 6). Matching key processes with information using IT supports better customer service and is helping Cardinal Health lead the way in the health care field.[19] ❖

needs. However, some of the systems you identify may be inappropriate for your organization because, for one reason, every firm operates with limited resources. You simply can't do everything you want or need to do. So now's the time to take a hard look at which systems you can afford to develop as well as when.

Your organization has various analysis methods available for this evaluation process. You may employ a cost-benefit analysis, a risk analysis, and a capital investment analysis. You can use each method alone or in combination. Table 8.2 contains a summary of each method. Let's review each analysis option with an eye toward deciding how best to determine which systems to develop and when.

Cost-Benefit Analysis Method

Bad News, Good News

All IT systems identified to this point in the systems planning process will benefit the organization. Still, they each carry an associated cost. And you must weigh both the benefits and the costs. The *cost-benefit analysis* is the process of evaluating IT systems for development by comparing systems costs with systems benefits. At this point, the cost and benefit figures you arrive at are clearly estimates. For many projects, you perform a more thorough cost-benefit analysis at the end of the systems

TABLE 8·2 Information Technology Systems Evaluation Methods

Evaluation Methods	Analysis Characteristics	Evaluation Methods	Analysis Characteristics
Cost-benefit analysis	• Costs described monetarily • Includes intangible benefits • Most comprehensive analysis	**Capital investment analysis**	• Communicates in business terms • Quantifies selection guidelines • May oversimplify the selection
Risk analysis	• Identifies business dangers • Risks may be hard to quantify • Ignores the benefits		

design phase of systems development when costs and benefits are more certain.

Proposed Systems Costs

The proposed systems costs are calculated from several sources. Systems costs should include

- Cost estimates for systems development
- Cost estimates for systems operation and maintenance
- Cost estimates for systems adoption at different times in the future
- Costs for the organizational change required

Gathering these cost estimates can be quite a challenge. Especially difficult is estimating the cost of adopting a system at different times in the future. You'll use these costs to schedule systems development. The last cost you must gather captures the cost of the change within your organization. For example, your system may require user training to be effective. You might need to reengineer some business processes, which is an expensive endeavor. In gathering these costs, you'll make some assumptions. Be conservative and estimate costs on the high side. Your objective here is not to justify a proposal. Rather it is to ensure that the proposal is right for your organization.

Proposed Systems Benefits

Besides costs, you must identify systems benefits. IT systems benefits fall into two categories—tangible and intangible. *Tangible benefits* are systems benefits that can be monetarily quantified. *Intangible benefits* are systems benefits that cannot be monetarily quantified. Examples of tangible and intangible benefits are shown in Table 8.3.

It's best to make every effort to quantify all benefits for a proposed system. Intangible benefits make the

systems selection process just that much more difficult. So, to be sure, include intangible benefits as required, but exercise caution.

Comparing Costs and Benefits

Typically, you compare costs and benefits by charting the quantifiable costs and benefits over time. The example shown in Figure 8.12 reflects high costs during systems development while benefits remain at zero. Once the system is operational, benefits surface and costs drop to a level required to maintain the system. The greater the difference between the curves as time goes on, the more advantageous the system.

Risk Analysis Method
Will It Succeed?

All IT systems involve a degree of risk. *Information technology systems risk* is the possibility that a system will not

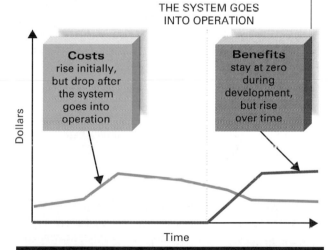

FIGURE 8.12

Comparing Costs Versus Benefits over Time

TABLE 8.3	Tangible and Intangible Benefits for IT Systems
Tangible Benefits	**Intangible Benefits**
Increased profits	Improved customer satisfaction
Increased market share	Enhanced employee morale
Reduced product/service costs	Higher-quality corporate image
Lower supply costs	Regulatory requirements satisfied
	Better decisions

Everyone Benefits from GE's Information Technology

It's late at night and a young boy with very serious head injuries arrives at San Francisco General Hospital. Surgeons rush the boy in and order a CAT scan, only to discover the scanner won't work. A call goes out to General Electric, the maker of the CAT scan device, but GE's medical-system technicians in Milwaukee are gone for the night. So the alert GE staffer in Milwaukee taking the call contacts colleagues in Paris, France, who are just beginning the next day's work. But what can technicians from France do? The answer is quick in coming. Within 15 minutes, the Paris engineer has the trouble identified online and the equipment up and working to perform the CAT scan for the young boy in San Francisco.

Sound fanciful? It's not. Not for General Electric Co., a $70 billion diversified multinational firm. You see, when GE first designs a product, it searches for ways to add value for customers while adding benefits for GE. The software-driven CAT scan device is a great example. It's easy to repair remotely, making it more attractive to hospitals. That same feature reduces the support costs for the product. The costs to add such a feature are far less than this tangible benefit. To integrate such systems benefits, GE stays focused on the business of profitably producing products rather than becoming enamored with the technology. Just ask Gary Reiner, chief information officer. As Gary puts it, "People responsible for IT should be more business-oriented than technology-oriented. The critical thing is knowing how to leverage IT for business purposes." Keeping IT systems aligned with the business keeps IT systems benefits high and costs low at GE.[21] ❖

THE GLOBAL **PERSPECTIVE**

---

achieve the predicted benefits. You may express this risk as a probability of success or failure. Generally, systems risk is expressed *qualitatively* with high risk defined as a system that stands a good chance of failing to achieve the predicted benefits. The qualitative risk analysis framework in Figure 8.13 identifies general categories of systems that you want to develop and ones you might avoid, based on the degree of risk compared to the magnitude of benefit.

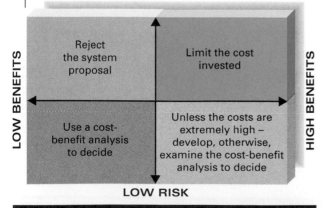

HIGH RISK

LOW BENEFITS

Reject the system proposal

Limit the cost invested

Use a cost-benefit analysis to decide

Unless the costs are extremely high – develop, otherwise, examine the cost-benefit analysis to decide

HIGH BENEFITS

LOW RISK

FIGURE 8.13

Evaluating Systems Risk[20]

The source of systems risk offers some opportunity for you to reduce the risk through systems design or alternative implementation strategies. Sources of risk include the following:

- The technology may not yet be proven.

- The projected costs did not include all factors.

- The market or economy adversely affected estimated costs.

- The existing technology within the organization is incompatible with the new systems technology.

- Excessive time elapsed from the time of selection to implementation, causing cost or benefit estimates to become unreliable.

- Significant organizational change can occur and affect all estimates.

- Poor or too many assumptions.

Avoiding some of the listed sources of risk is straightforward, once you see the list. For example, avoiding making assumptions when collecting the cost and benefit information is not too difficult, once you're aware of the dangers.

Capital Investment Analysis Method

Is It Worth It?

The most quantitative of the evaluation methods is *capital investment analysis*, which calculates a quantitative measure of IT systems value. A number of different financial models may be used to generate a quantitative measure of value-added. In Table 8.4 you'll find a list of these different capital investment models, along with directions on how to perform the calculations.

Calculating the value of a system using a financial model is as simple as learning the equation. Although some may seem complex to you, they are all just numerical calculations. In fact, it is that straight-forward feature of the financial models that warrants caution. Calculating the return on investment for a proposed system, for example, yields a number, say 12 percent. Many organizations will set goals for investment returns and limit funding for any project with returns less than the stated goal. So, if your organization has an investment return goal of 13 percent, the 12 percent return on a systems proposal would be grounds for rejection. Suppose, however, that the system created an extranet with your customers so that they could receive products in 3 days instead of 2 weeks? Is it still a poor investment? You can see that the decision is more difficult than that. More than anything, the challenge in using financial models for systems evaluation is not to forget what's behind those numbers—support for the business goals. Avoid using financial analysis as your sole evaluation tool, and consider all variables in your "equation."

CAREER OPPORTUNITY

Although many of the financial models in Table 8.4 may seem daunting, calculations such as net present value and internal rate of return are used widely for capital budgeting project evaluations as well as investment securities evaluation. Whether you invest in a friend's hot business idea or recommend that your firm invest in some project, you do both hoping for something in return. Best of all, most financial calculators have buttons on them that calculate NPV and IRR. Pull your calculator out and take some time to discover how those functions work. The return on that investment of time will be great!

TABLE 8.4 Capital Analysis Financial Models

Financial Model	Formula	Type of Result
Payback method (in years)	$\dfrac{\text{Original investment}}{\text{Annual net cash flow}}$	= time to pay back
Cost-benefit ratio (as a factor)	$\dfrac{\text{Benefits}}{\text{Costs}}$	= cost-benefit ratio
Return on investment (ROI, as a percent)	$\dfrac{(\text{Benefits} - \text{cost} - \text{depreciation})}{\text{useful system life}}$	= net benefit
Net present value (NPV, in \$)	Total net present value of all cash flows[*]	= value today of return in future
Internal rate of return (IRR, as a percent)	The NPV represented as a percentage return[*]	= expected return

[*]The net present value and internal rate of return calculation are too complex to summarize above. So both are defined completely below:

Net present value = sum of the present value of all future payments less the initial cost

$$= -CF_0 + \sum \left[CF_t / (1 + r)^t \right] \quad \text{where } CF_0 = \text{the initial cost}$$
$$CF_t = \text{each future payment}$$
$$r = \text{the discount rate}$$
$$t = \text{the number of the time payment}$$

Internal rate of return = the rate that completes the following summation equation

$$\text{Cost} = \sum \left[CF_t / (1 + IRR)^t \right] \quad \text{where } CF_t = \text{the future payments}$$
$$IRR = \text{the internal rate of return}$$
$$t = \text{the number of the payment}$$

Contingency Planning

Planning for What You Can't Live Without

The last step in systems planning involves looking beyond which systems your organization requires. You must look to see how dependent your organization is on your existing IT systems and how badly your organization would be affected if those systems were unavailable for some reason. Essentially asking yourself, "What systems can't I live without?" If you have systems subject to unavailability, your organization might lose revenue owing to system loss.

Planning for Disaster

What You Can't Live Without

When the World Trade Center in New York was damaged by a bomb in February 1993, the world reacted with shock and surprise. There was one more sad surprise few heard about. Of the 350 businesses operating from the building on the day of the bombing, 150 were out

of business a year later.[22] Why? No, it wasn't because their offices were damaged by the bombing. Most were simply unprepared for the disruption that for days prevented them from entering the building and accessing their computer systems. If those businesses had planned for such a disaster, they might not have lost their businesses. In fact, 90 percent of businesses whose computers are down for more than 5 working days will be out of business within a year.[23] But would you have imagined such a sequence of events? Most of us would not. At least not without some framework of consideration.

Potential Opportunities for Disaster

It may be difficult to anticipate all the possibilities of disaster. Some possibilities you should consider include

■ *Weather-related disasters such as floods, lightning strikes, hurricanes, and tornadoes* How would you plan for a tornado ripping through your $1.2 billion retail distribution outlet in the midwest, which recently happened to an industrial manufacturer?[24]

■ *Earthquake disasters* How would you prepare for facility destruction and loss of electrical, gas, and water services from an earthquake? Broken water

Planning for the Inevitable at John Wiley & Sons

The workday at publisher John Wiley & Sons, Inc., seemed uneventful right up until the alarms sounded. Within minutes, everyone evacuated the entire midtown Manhattan skyscraper—fleeing an electrical fire. Fortunately, no one was hurt, although one ominous thought did come to everyone. Were the critical information systems damaged? As Leslie P. Shenkler, manager of technical planning, recalled, "Everyone's hearts were palpitating, and it

reminded our executives how important disaster prevention and disaster recovery is."

So what did John Wiley do as a result of that fire? It reinforced its commitment to planning for disasters. Every 6 months, Wiley's IT systems in New York undergo tests to ensure that a disaster recovery plan is in place for systems such as order entry, warehousing, financial systems, and even lowly e-mail. Why e-mail? Well, as Richard Walker, a network services manager, states, e-mail "has become a critical part of our business." Over 10,000 messages move across Wiley's networks daily, supporting communications among editors,

authors, and literary agents. You see, in publishing, prepress communications among the players is critical to publishing success.

The important message here is not that all businesses should test their e-mail systems. Actually, organizations should identify their own mission-critical systems and see to it that they test them regularly. It's just a matter of time before they'll need those tests. By the way, Wiley & Sons survived its Manhattan fire without suffering systems downtime. Do you think your organization will be as well-prepared?[25] ❖

Planning for What You Can't Live Without

Purpose	■ To examine the possibilities of losing an IT system and formulating procedures to minimize the damage
Useful Methods	■ Information unavailability curve ■ Disaster recovery curve
Result	■ A list of IT systems critical to your organization and a contingency plan based on how quickly you can afford to recover those systems ❖

pipes and electrical or gas fires all can result from an earthquake. Packard Bell, the computer manufacturer, lost its headquarters, manufacturing facility, and service center in Chatsworth, California, to one of the worst earthquakes in California's history in January of 1994.[26]

■ *Loss of system and information access* Sure the system's fine, but that does you no good if you can't access it. That certainly was the case for the

businesses unlucky enough to have offices in the World Trade Center. Simple but rigorous procedures can avoid an all too common scenario. Often users remember to make copies of their information on diskettes but leave the diskettes on their desk, irretrievable in the event of a disaster.[27]

■ *Technology failure* All of us who use computers have experienced a computer failure. Simple, nondisaster-related hardware failures occur

Betting on Disaster

As a group of sharp financial analysts with IT systems knowledge, your group has been given the task of evaluating several different disaster recovery plans created by your organization's contingency planning group. Your task is to take the information unavailability costs and balance them against the disaster recovery costs for three different implementation proposals. You'll select a proposal based on which proposal costs the least while taking the least time to recover. Based on the table below, the information unavailability curve has been plotted. Add the plots for the recovery cost curves for each proposal. As a group, discuss the alternatives

and recommend one proposal for adoption. Be certain you can justify your recommendation. ❖

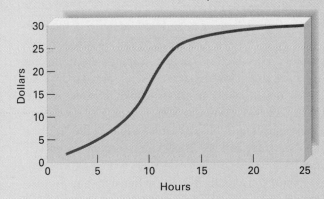

Information Unavailability Cost Curve

	Time from Disaster in Hours					
Costs	**2**	**4**	**8**	**12**	**16**	**24**
Information unavailability costs (in thousands of dollars)	$2	$4	$10	$24	$28	$30
Recovery proposal 1 costs (in thousands of dollars)	30	22	15	10	7	5
Recovery proposal 2 costs (in thousands of dollars)	26	16	10	7	6	5
Recovery proposal 3 costs (in thousands of dollars)	28	18	11	10	10	10

frequently and are not completely unavoidable, but information backups and recovery procedures can reduce the damage.

Given these ever-present opportunities for disaster, how does an organization protect itself? You begin with *contingency planning*—the process of examining the possibilities of losing an IT system and formulating procedures to minimize the damage. Once you've documented the results of your contingency planning in a contingency plan, you make decisions about how specifically you'll implement this plan. We'll cover those implementation issues in Chapter 10. The contingency plan becomes part of your IT systems plan as a system to implement just like any other. Let's examine the three steps of contingency planning.

CAREER OPPORTUNITY

Think of this contingency planning as risk assessment. We all deal with risks throughout our lives. You risk your health and automobile whenever you drive, so you reduce the risk by buying health and automobile insurance. The risk is reduced because the potential harm (at least financially) is reduced. Consider this mental model of risk assessment whenever you purchase technology for yourself or the organization. Consider what risk you incur if you lose the use of the technology, and consider insurance (in the form of backup technology or power supplies) as a risk reducer.

Step 1: Discovering What's Really Important

Contingency planning begins with identifying the functions or processes in your business that are critical to your success. The tough part here is to apply a discriminating eye to all areas of your business. When asked individually, few departmental managers would likely suggest that their particular function is unimportant. Therefore senior management must be involved to reinforce the organization's strategy and vision. As you'll see, this step is crucial, because preparing for disasters is quite expensive.

Once you identify the critical functions and processes, you identify the IT systems that support those functions and processes. You examine how information flows in and out of each system as well as where that information resides. You examine all documentation for the IT systems and any procedures that might be in place for backup and recovery of information. Finally you gather managers' estimates of losses associated with the unavailability of key IT systems and information. With this information, you move to step 2.

Step 2: How Much Does It Cost to Have Information Unavailable?

Once you know which processes are critical to your organization and which systems support those processes, you estimate the cost of the unavailablility of critical information. Managers will have provided perceptions supporting an estimate that is formulated into the *information unavailability cost curve*, or a depiction of the cost to the organization of the unavailability of information.[28] An example of one such curve is shown in Figure 8.14. You can see from the cost curve that, typically, the cost to the organization is quite low during the initial hours following a disaster. How long this cost remains low varies from organization to organization. A grocery store that loses the use of its point-of-sale checkout system would incur costs quite rapidly. Nevertheless, for all organizations, the curve tilts upward rapidly at some point within hours of the loss. This jump in cost reflects lost business revenues.

Finally, the cost levels again at a high level and remains there until the information is restored. The longer an organization endures the loss at this point, the more likely it is to go out of business. Creating such a cost curve places a monetary value on the information loss and can be balanced with the cost of recovery in step 3, the final step.

Step 3: Balancing the Cost of Unavailability with the Cost of Recovery

Do you own any insurance? Insurance is really what contingency planning is all about. You realize a disaster could occur and that the disaster would hurt you financially. So you purchase insurance to cover that financial loss in the event the disaster does occur. But how much should you pay for insurance? Suppose nothing ever happens? Was

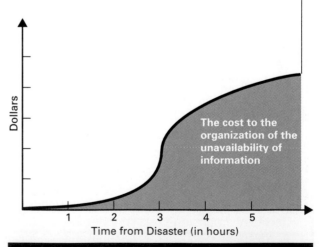

The cost to the organization of the unavailability of information

Time from Disaster (in hours)

FIGURE 8.14

A Typical Information Unavailability Cost Curve

that a good investment? These are tough questions. One way of looking at this cost is to develop a ***disaster recovery cost curve*** that depicts the organization's disaster recovery costs based on how quickly you wish to recover.

As you can see, in a typical recovery cost curve (see Figure 8.15), the cost to recover very quickly is quite high but drops fairly rapidly until the cost remains quite low for recovering very slowly. The cost of rapid recovery is high because recovering quickly usually means maintaining standby or even concurrent systems resources. You will develop a recovery cost curve for each possible implementation of your recovery plan (see Chapter 10). To choose the best recovery implementation, you overlay the recovery cost curve on the information unavailability curve, as seen in Figure 8.16. The best recovery plan, in cost and time, is determined by the intersection of the two cost curves.

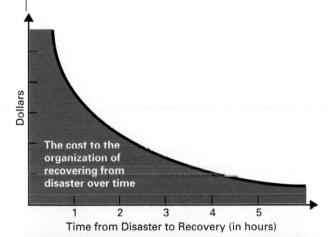

FIGURE 8.15

A Typical Disaster Recovery Cost Curve

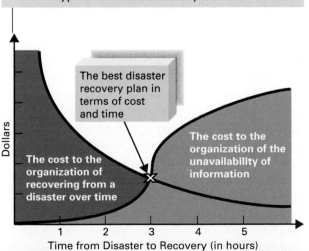

FIGURE 8.16

Deciding How Much to Spend on Disaster Recovery

The Information Technology Systems Plan

Putting It All Together

The culmination of all your systems planning efforts is the IT systems plan. The systems plan provides concrete direction to the systems development process (discussed in Chapter 9) and documents which systems will be developed and when. An example outline for an IT systems plan is shown in Figure 8.17, posed as a series of questions that the plan should answer.

If you examine the example plan carefully, you'll see that the plan includes all that we've discussed in this

❶ **Business Vision and Strategy**

Where is your organization going?

How does it intend to get there?

❷ **IT Support for the Business Vision and Strategy**

How will IT support the business direction?

What part did IT play in formulating the business direction?

When was the last IT systems plan developed?

When will the next IT systems plan be developed?

❸ **Existing IT Systems**

What systems currently exist?

How do they support the business?

Are the existing systems still appropriate?

What changes are proposed?

❹ **Proposed IT Systems**

What IT systems have been selected for development?

What business processes are supported by these systems?

What information needs are supported by these systems?

How have these systems been evaluated?

❺ **IT Systems Contingency Plan**

What plan is there to protect the systems from disaster?

How were the protected systems selected?

❻ **IT Systems Budget**

What is the cost of the IT systems plan?

What are the benefits of the IT systems plan?

❼ **IT Systems Development Time Frame**

When will the selected systems be developed?

FIGURE 8.17

An Information Technology Systems Plan

Answering *When* at Pratt & Whitney

Implementing IT systems globally makes answering the question of *when* to implement particularly challenging. Pratt & Whitney, a $6.2 billion aircraft manufacturer based in East Hartford, Connecticut, operates 86 support engineering offices in 48 countries around the globe. So when the firm's business plan called for more complete and consistent customer service, the IT group knew it would face a big challenge. They knew from experience the complications with global implementation. It could take years to put a system in place that was planned years before. Joe Muldoon, an IT field-support team leader, still remembers when a new PC on its way to the firm's Rome office fell off the delivery truck, smashing into the middle of the street. And it got worse. The PC vendor had no dealership in Rome, so the Pratt & Whitney local employees had to box up the pieces and ship the PC back to headquarters in Connecticut for repair. Joe knew that because of complications and delays like that one, global deployments stretched out until they were years behind schedule.

Management at Pratt & Whitney began its customer service planning with these considerations in mind. But they weren't willing to accept a system that, once deployed, was almost obsolete. So, they *outsourced* the deployment to another firm with more resources and global expertise (see Chapter 9 for a discussion on outsourcing). What kinds of goals did the planners set? The plan involved creating a global customer service network for field reps. Reps could look at up-to-the-minute design and specifications for all engine products. But this involved upgrading both software and PCs in 86 offices in 48 countries. Joe had estimated that his group could do the job in 12 to 18 months. But the IT planners knew this was unacceptable. This schedule meant that global customers would receive grossly varying levels of service over as much as 2 years in their different locations. So how quickly do you think the outsourcer projected complete global deployment? Just 6 months for all 86 offices. The more remarkable goal was that of converting individual offices in just 48 hours. This greatly reduced operational impact—an important business goal. Pratt & Whitney understood that all good plans are helpful only while they're relevant. And it's just as important to implement those plans quickly. So move quickly—your customers certainly do.[29] ❖

---

chapter. The order and format differ from the steps in the systems planning process, though. And that's appropriate. When you create any plan for management, you always summarize your plan first. In this plan, you describe the business and how IT fits into that business, quickly followed by current and proposed systems. Only then can you provide contingency, budget, and development detail that supports these systems.

Although the systems plan document is the end result of the systems planning process, it is not the end of the process. One failing of any planning document is that it implies some finality to the process. As a consequence, many planning documents never see the light of day, they simply gather dust on a bookshelf. A plan must be more than a document if it's to be effective. Think of the plan as a map to which you must refer frequently as you travel the road to business success. And if the map seems to be taking you away from your destination, revisit the

planning process and discover if the map is still accurate. The competitive environment changes quickly. This is even more true in the world of IT systems. With so much change around your organization, it's not a question of *if* your systems plan will become obsolete, but *when*. Take Fannie Mae, the nation's largest source of home mortgage loans, as one example.[30] Over the past 3 years, Fannie Mae has created 130 client/server applications and 15 object-oriented ones, while planning for 40 more applications in 1996. What's the hurry? Fannie Mae's approach is to crank out IT systems that support the organization's strategies and tactics *before those plans are out of date*. In Chapter 9, you'll examine methods to accelerate the systems development process. But nothing replaces up-to-date planning. So, if your organization ever has any question at all as to whether its systems map is still accurate, don't hesitate to stop and ask for directions and draw a new map.

ON YOUR OWN

Is This the Right System for You?

Most of us will buy quite a few personal computers in our lives, yet most of us don't know how to select one. There are hundreds of models to choose from, many brands to consider, and options galore. Let's take the cost-benefit IT systems evaluation option and apply it to a personal computer purchase. You may find the process enlightening and even one you'll use at work.

Use the chart below as your guide through the analysis. For a personal computer purchase, you'll identify many intangible benefits. That's okay, just

be certain to link those benefits to specific computer features. For example, one computer system might include a telephone answering machine. What's the benefit to you? Well, if you already have a telephone answering machine, there is none. If, however, you don't have one, you might use the machine to ensure that college recruiters can leave a message for you. That's a clear benefit and worth something to you. Fill in all the costs and benefits for three systems you've examined. You can get the information from newspaper or magazine ads, or you can visit a store. Take all the information as a whole and make a systems decision. Does the answer surprise you? Would it help to have other impartial individuals do the analysis? ❖

System Name	Costs	Benefits, Tangible and Intangible
1.		
2.		
3.		
And the winner is:		

CLOSING CASE STUDY: CASE 1

Getting Everyone on the Same Page at NationsBank

When the third largest commercial bank in the United States thinks about what it can do for customers, auditing is not the first task that comes to mind. But when managers at NationsBank looked at its audit process (the process of ensuring the validity of financial information) and saw that it took 350 people several months and mountains of paper to complete, they knew it was time for a new IT systems plan.

They began by examining a value chain for processes that added value to customers. They also looked at the

costs of these various processes. They discovered that audits, though important processes at banks, added little value to customers. They also discovered that the audit process consumed a large amount of NationsBank's resources. Many more resources, as it happens, than at other banks. You see, competitive intelligence told NationsBank that other banks were more efficient auditors. So managers began to explore various options. One collaborative solution was to change how individual sites were audited. "Auditing is done on a team basis," explains John Curry, senior vice president of NationsBank. Those teams move from site to site to perform audits. NationsBank began to imagine what the process would be like if teams could perform site audits concurrently instead of sequentially. To do so, the various audit teams would need the ability to communicate large amounts of information on an ad-hoc basis. The IT systems professional involved in this

KNOWLEDGE WORKER'S ✓-LIST

The Importance of IT Systems Planning as Well as a Systems Plan. *Information technology systems planning (IT systems planning)* is the process that uses the goals, strategies, objectives, processes, and information requirements of your organization as a foundation for identifying and selecting which IT systems to develop and when to develop them. Systems planning answers the questions concerning *what* IT systems should be developed in your organization and *when*. The process has five steps: (1) aligning organizational goals and information technology, (2) identifying specific processes, (3) identifying specific information, (4) evaluating information technology systems, and (5) planning for what you can't live without. These five steps create an *information technology systems plan (IT systems plan)* that documents the results of this planning. The IT systems plan document is the key end result from the IT systems planning process. It provides a map that will tell you how IT supports the business and furnishes input into the systems development process (discussed in Chapter 9).

How to Ensure IT Systems Alignment with the Organizational Goals and Strategies. Planning for IT systems should occur at the same time as business planning, so you can exploit the full possibilities of IT systems.

Two methods to facilitate organizational alignment are information technology fusion and competitive intelligence. *Information technology fusion (IT fusion)* occurs when the information technology within your organization is indistinguishable from the business processes and the people who exploit the information technology. Using the *competitive forces model*, a tool to formulate strategy by examining the environment in which your organization competes, your organization ensures IT strategies that defend its competitive position. Knowledge about the competition is gathered through *competitive intelligence*—a process used to analyze the competitive environment using four steps: planning, gathering, analysis, and integration. The result of this process is a better understanding of what IT systems opportunities or threats exist.

How to Identify Specific Processes and Information Needs That Require IT Systems Support. One method for identifying specific processes is the *value chain*, which views the organization as a chain—or series—of processes, each of which adds value to the product or service for the customer. The value chain is used to identify the top value-adding processes, as well as the top value-reducing processes. Both of these process types require IT support.

---

planning suggested that groupware software (discussed in Chapter 2) and client/server technology (discussed in Chapter 6) might support the concurrent audit process.

Before actually developing an IT system to support this new process, NationsBank had to document the information requirements of the audit teams and others who relied on this information. These requirements formed the basis of an information architecture for the organization. And the proposed IT system had to be compared with other systems competing for development resources.

In the end, NationsBank developed a groupware system, based on Lotus Notes software, that supported concurrent site audits nationwide. Now audit documents move through the process electronically with two or three auditors at different locations reviewing each audit report. Using these electronic document links, auditors can access supporting documentation for any transaction with the click of a mouse button. Previously auditors had to dig through reams of paper to find supporting documents. The new system at NationsBank has produced many benefits. As John puts it, "The ability to communicate—for people to have this multiple access and do work concurrently vs. a very sequential operation—is a tremendous advantage."[31,32] ❖

◄ Questions ►

1. How did NationsBank ensure that its IT strategy supported its business strategy? Can you think of any other way it might have aligned the strategies?

2. What method of identifying information needs did NationsBank use? Was this a good choice? What other methods might it have used to identify information needs? Support your choice.

3. In addition to identifying information needs, what else did NationsBank identify as needing IT support? What method did it use for this identification? Why?

4. What role did knowledge workers play in the IT systems planning process at NationsBank? Do you think this role is typical or unique? Why or why not?

Three methods of identifying information needs are an information architecture, critical success factors, and business systems planning.

- An *information architecture* for an organization describes what information your organization needs and which people within your organization need that information. The architecture should reflect the time, content, and form dimensions of information.

- A *critical success factor (CSF)* is a factor critical to organizational success. Identifying information required to support CSFs identifies required IT systems.

- *Business systems planning (BSP)* identifies information requirements by documenting the relationships between business processes and information classes.

All of these methods help you identify information needs that require IT systems support.

How to Evaluate IT Systems for Development. Three methods of evaluating IT systems for development are (1) a cost-benefit analysis, (2) a risk analysis, and (3) a capital investment analysis.

- A *cost-benefit analysis* is the process of evaluating IT systems for development by comparing systems costs with systems benefits. Benefits may be tangible or intangible.

- A risk analysis method examines the *information technology systems risk*, which is the possibility that a system will not achieve the predicted benefits. You compare high and low risk to high and low benefits to select a system for development.

- A *capital investment analysis* calculates a quantitative measure of IT systems value. Financial models used in this analysis include the payback method, the cost-benefit ratio, the return on investment, the net present value, and the internal rate of return.

How to Plan for What You Can't Live Without. You evaluate current and proposed systems for the cost associated with the loss of information balanced against the cost to recover quickly. *Contingency planning* is the process of examining the possibilities of losing an IT system and formulating procedures to minimize the damage. Selecting a disaster plan involves comparing the information unavailability cost curve with the disaster recovery cost curve. ❖

5. What change in external factors could require NationsBank to revisit the systems planning process? How might NationsBank ensure that it will know when this occurs?

6. How do you think NationsBank went about discovering that its competitors were more efficient at auditing? Do you think the information gathered was electronic or nonelectronic? Why?

CLOSING CASE STUDY: CASE 2

Competitive IT

Environments change quickly in business and that means your IT systems plan must change just as quickly. Volkswagen AG (VW) began manufacturing its Jetta and the legendary Beetle model in Mexico in August of 1996. That's the same year that the North American Free Trade Agreement began breaking down trade barriers between Mexico and the rest of North America.

Managers at VW knew that the agreement was both good and bad news. The good news was that sales were forecast to increase from 1,000 to 1,700 cars per day in 1997. The bad news was that increased competition—from Toyota Motor Corp., Daimler-Benz AG, and BMW NA—was also forecast and meant VW had to respond. "We're expecting a lot more competition in Mexico over the next year, so we've got to have the best technology and the best response times that we can," explained Jaime Flores, a software manager at VW in Puebla, Mexico.

Using IT to reduce a business's response time to the market is a common strategy; however, VW had to identify key areas for such an application. Examining its value chain, VW spotted one area where value was increasingly reduced—spare parts. As sales and production rose, demand for spare parts did as well. The system VW had in place to order spare parts lagged far behind the demand, however. Most of the 200 Mexican dealerships had to enter spare parts orders on diskettes, ship them to manufacturing, and wait more than a week for parts to arrive. The only alternative was stocking excess inventory in anticipation of demand, and that was expensive.

Based on the identified requirements, VW created an Internet–based spare parts ordering system. Why the Internet? "There are some real advantages for companies like Volkswagen to use the Internet to connect smaller dealerships that can't otherwise play in the [electronic data interchange] space," remarks Waverly Deutsch, an analyst at Forrester Research, Inc., in Cambridge, Massachusetts, and an expert in the EDI field. VW knew its technological limitations, especially with small dealerships in Mexico. That didn't mean they wanted anything less than a state-of-the-art ordering system. Using the Internet, dealers are now able to receive shipments within 24 hours. This quick response time translated into new value for customers as well as a defensive strategy to combat increased competition.

The new spare parts system made economic sense to VW as well. The system, which is part of a $35 million investment in manufacturing and distribution software and related hardware, is expected to deliver $50 million in cost savings over the next 3 years. The savings will come from both lower inventory levels at dealers and reduced labor requirements to manage those inventories. Through careful application of IT systems planning methods, VW has created a system that supports its business.[33] ❖

◄ Questions ►

1. Did VW plan for "transparent technology"? Would users agree with your assessment? Why or why not? What might VW have done to increase the transparency of the technology?

2. What process did VW identify that required IT support? Might there have been other processes that required support?

3. Did VW identify any specific information as required? If not, what technique might it have applied to identify information? What do you think VW would have discovered?

4. What type of competitive intelligence did VW gather when making its decision? In what form do you think the intelligence was gathered, electronic or nonelectronic? Can you think of other intelligence that VW could have gathered?

5. How did VW evaluate the new IT system? Did the system make economic sense? Why or why not?

6. Perform a risk analysis on the spare parts ordering system for VW. Use the analysis framework from Figure 8.13 as a guide. How did you evaluate the risk of the system, high or low? How did you evaluate the benefits of the system, high or low? Based on this analysis, would you have recommended that VW invest in the system?

7. Did VW perform any contingency planning for the new system? What specific factors might place the new system in danger? Would rapid recovery of the system be a priority? How long do you think might be an acceptable "downtime"?

Electronic Commerce
Business and You on the Internet

Finding Freeware and Shareware on the Internet

When you buy your first computer, the software you use seems like a secondary decision as most computers come preloaded with an abundance of software. But after a while you begin to see a need for different software, and that's when sticker shock sets in. Even upgrading to the latest version of your existing software can make a real dent in your pocketbook. And after installing new software, you may find it simply doesn't meet your needs. That's when you notice you can't return opened software; you can only exchange it for a new copy. So if it doesn't meet your needs you're out of luck with retail software.

An alternative to retail software that you might consider is shareware or freeware. Shareware is sometimes called "try before you buy" software because users are permitted to try the software on their own computer system (generally for a limited period of time) without any cost or obligation. Then you make a payment if you decide you want to keep using the software beyond the evaluation (trial) period.

Freeware is software available at no charge to people for as long as they choose to use it. Of course, freeware developers provide no support or updates to the software, whereas shareware developers often provide printed manuals, technical support, bonus or additional software, or upgrades. Whether you take the shareware or the freeware approach you'll find games, screen savers, antivirus software, messaging software, and much more. If you'd like more information about shareware look up the Association of Shareware Professionals at http://www.asp-shareware.org/searchsites.html/. Likewise, the Freeware Central site at http://freebie.cfcl.com/free/ will provide you with more information about freeware.

In this section, we've included a number of Web sites related to downloading freeware and shareware. On the Web site that supports this text (http://www.mhhe.com/business/mis/haag, select "Electronic Commerce Projects"), we've provided direct links to all these sites as well as many, many more. These are a great starting point for completing this Real HOT section. We would also encourage you to search the Internet for others.

Protecting Your Computer Investment

Have you ever been frantically typing away on your computer, desperately trying to make an assignment deadline,

when all of a sudden something goes wrong with your computer? If you're lucky the problem is easy to identify. So you correct the problem and go on about your work. Other times the solution eludes you. Most of the time these problems have nice logical explanations like hardware or software conflicts or failures of some kind. In a few rare instances, the problem may have been caused intentionally—by a computer virus, a program that someone develops with malicious intent to harm an IT system.

So how does a computer virus get into your system? Anytime you download software, open a file attachment to an e-mail, or read a file off a diskette from another computer you stand the chance of contracting a computer virus. And access to the Internet increases your opportunity of downloading files from many different sources. So virtually every company installs antivirus protection software (that scans new files for known viruses and purges them from every computer). The catch is that traditional antivirus software can only find viruses it knows about. As new viruses come along, antivirus software must be updated. And the devious minds that develop viruses seem to find more and better ways to infiltrate your system every day.

In the table on page 356 you'll find a list of antivirus software. And on the Web site that supports this text, you'll find a list of many others. Find at least two of these, download the software, and answer the following questions.

A. Is the antivirus software shareware, freeware, or traditional retail software? *free ware*

B. What are some of the viruses the software detects? *short*

C. Does the software remove the virus as well as detect it? *yes   removes and detect*

D. Are updates available for the software to detect new viruses? How often are they available? At what cost? *yes daily , free*

E. Does the software detect viruses not yet created? *no* Does it say how it performs this detection? *no*

F. Does the software site offer recommendations to reduce your chance of contracting a virus? *yes*

G. Does the site tell you what to do if you've already contracted a virus? *yes*

Throughout this section, you'll find instructions to download software from many different Web sites. And, as you've just learned, doing so can greatly increase the chance that your computer will become infected with a computer virus. Viruses can tag along within downloaded files, within attachments to e-mails, or on diskettes traded with classmates. And new viruses are being created every day, making detection difficult. Still you must do all you can to prevent a virus from damaging your computer, so before you proceed any further in this section, you need to ensure you have antivirus software installed and running on your computer. Use the exercise you've just completed to find one of the many available titles. Then be certain you scan your computer hard drive and any new files you download. It's a good idea to use this same procedure for any files you bring home from other students or ones that you modified in your school's computer laboratory. So, get your copy of antivirus software now. Otherwise, you're computing on borrowed time!

Using Your Computer for More Than Work

By far the most popular freeware/shareware applications are games. The quality of these games is truly amazing for software that is free to download and begin playing immediately whenever you want. Shareware/freeware games are so numerous on the Internet that you'll often find games grouped by categories. Common categories are action/adventure, board, card, casino, educational, role-playing, simulation, sports, strategy and war, and word games.

When you're looking over the games available, remember that you should first ascertain whether the software is shareware or freeware. In some cases the Web site is not really clear on this issue. For example, some game descriptions make no mention of money, yet after you've downloaded the game it talks about registering your game for a price. At the other end of the spectrum, you'll also encounter traditional software that lists a price next to the description and requires a credit card to download and purchase. And often these games will describe themselves as shareware. Remember though, true shareware permits you to download the software and try it for free. So, in this case, the term shareware is a bit of a misnomer.

In the table on page 356, we've provided a list of games available on the Internet and where you can find them. And on the Web site that supports this text, you'll find a list of many others. Choose two games, navigate to their location, download the games, and answer the following questions.

A. Is a description of the game provided?

B. Are system requirements listed?

C. Can you tell if the game is freeware or shareware without downloading it?

D. Are any of the games you selected really commercial software that requires a purchase before you download the game?

E. If the game is shareware, how long may you use it until registration is required?

F. If the game is shareware, does the game cease to function after the free period is over? How can you tell without waiting that long?

G. How long does it take to download the game? Is it worth it?

Animating Your Computer Screen

Wander through most any office or even your school computer lab and you'll see a variety of screen savers in action. Screen savers—the software that occupies your screen when the computer is unused for a period of time—are very common utilities. Sometimes the screen saver provides a beautiful scene with a recurring action. Others provide a different look every time they activate. Microsoft Windows 98 includes several standard screen savers. *Desktop themes* are now common on most operating systems. In addition to providing software that activates when your computer is inactive, desktop themes alter the look of the basic screen you see when you're working. Borders, standard application icons, and even the cursor are changed with desktop themes.

If there is a downside to all this beautification it must be the amount of processing time that these software applications consume. If you have an older computer with limited memory, you may find that a sophisticated screen saver affects the performance of other applications. Or, when you return to your computer and move the mouse,

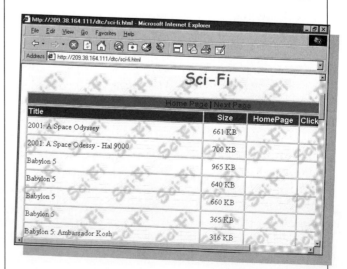

you may find that your computer takes a while to drop the screen saver and return to your application. But that's a small price to pay for such beautiful screens—isn't it?

In the table on page 356 you'll find a list of screen savers (some include desktop themes). And on the Web site that supports this text, you'll find a list of many others. Connect to at least two of these, download the software, and answer the following questions.

A. Is a description of the screen saver provided?

B. Is the screen saver available for different operating systems?

C. Are any of the screen savers you selected retail software that requires a purchase before you download it?

D. Do any of the screen savers include desktop themes for Windows?

E. Can you tell if the screen saver is freeware or shareware without downloading it?

F. Are any other screen savers or desktop themes available at the site?

G. In what form does the software arrive?

H. Does it work as advertised?

Searching for Shareware and Freeware

So maybe you'd like to be able to try the software before you buy. Then the shareware/freeware software concept appeals to you. And you're in luck if you want applications like screen savers or antivirus software. Just look through the tables provided here or go to the Web site that supports this text. But what if you want some shareware to help you compose music or to keep track of your soccer team's schedule? Well then you'll have to go searching for that software. You could use a general-purpose search engine like Yahoo! and type in "shareware" and "music" or "soccer." If you do this, you will find a few shareware software titles to download. But suppose those few titles don't meet your needs?

Finding shareware/freeware titles can be daunting for two reasons. First, currently there are over one million shareware and freeware titles available to you. And unless a search engine is designed specifically for this type of software, you'll likely miss many of these titles. Second, most shareware/freeware developers don't have their own Web sites. To address both of these challenges, Web sites have been created that maintain databases of thousands of shareware/freeware software titles. Most also include a search engine to help you navigate through these thousands of titles.

In the table on page 356, we've provided a list of sites that store shareware/freeware titles. And on the Web site that supports this text, you'll find a list of many others. Select two of these, access the sites, search for some titles that would be of interest to you, and answer the questions that follow.

A. How does the site group the software?

B. Can you search by operating system or platform?

C. Does the site provide descriptions of the software?

D. Can you search by file size?

E. Are screen captures from the software provided?

F. Are reviews and/or ratings of the software provided?

G. When was the last update for the site?

Communicating over the Internet

Have you ever sent an e-mail to a friend and had him or her respond right away? It's often a little surprising and raises another question. Wouldn't it be great if you always knew just which of your friends were on the Internet at the same time as you? One way to accomplish this is to always check a predesignated chat room somewhere on the Internet for your friends. But that's a bit cumbersome. There's a better way. Instant messaging freeware applications allow you and your friends to watch for each other and tell instantly when each other logs onto the Internet. Once you see them, you can send them messages (that arrive faster than e-mail and need not be opened), request real-time chats with them, include more than one friend in these chat sessions (they are private), and make friends with people who are on the Internet when you are. Instant messaging applications do require you to register yourself and receive either a "handle" (a name

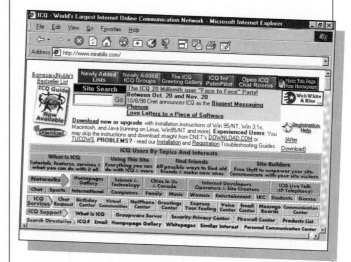

you pick for yourself) or a registration number. Your friends will look for your handle or number to tell if you are on the Internet when they are.

If you decide that e-mail is what most of your friends wish to use or you're using it to communicate with potential employers, you may still have a problem. If you use your school or company's e-mail system, you'll find that when you travel or are away from school or work you must dial back into the school or work system to retrieve your e-mail. If you travel this can mean long-distance charges. Or maybe the number of phone lines to dial into the system is not sufficient for the traffic. Either way, retrieving your e-mail can be a hassle. Enter browser-based *free* e-mail. A number of companies now offer free e-mail accounts that can be accessed through your Web browser just by accessing the Internet. And many of the larger Internet service providers offer toll-free phone numbers for Internet access. This means that no matter where you are you have quick, cheap access to your e-mail.

Web Sites for Downloading Freeware and Shareware

Antivirus Software	Address
F-Prot	http://www.datafellows.com
ViruSafe	http://www.virusafe.com
Anyware Anti-Virus	http://www.helpvirus.com
All Macro Anti-Virus	http://www.ffg.com
Sophos Anti-Virus	http://www.sophos.com

Games	Address
Champions of Zulula—Elite Edition	http://freespace.virgin.net/jeremy.m/games/zulula.zip
Monopoly	http://www.gamersinn.com/library_files/download/m/monogl11.zip
WinChess	http://www.channel1.com/users/pmeas/winchess
Doom—shareware version	ftp://ftp.thevrsource.com/thegames/doom19s.zip
Planet Blupi	http://hotfiles.zdnet.com/cgi-bin/texis/swlib/hotfiles/getit.bin?fcode=000HPF
Share the Earth 2	http://www.gamesdomain.co.uk/directd/pc/win95/adventures/earth2.html

Screen Savers and Desktop Themes	Address
Bouncing Bones	http://wkweb5.cableinet.co.uk/brilliant/free.htm
Star Trek	http://209.38.164.111/dtc/sci-fi.html
Corporate Comedy	http://www.screamsavers.com
Audubon Birds	http://www.bonanzas.com/ssavers/windows95.html
The Simpsons Theme	http://www.klotsnet.com/themes/tvthemes.htm

Shareware/Freeware Search Resources	Address
ZDNet Software Library	http://www.zdnet.com/swlib
Free Games Online	http://surf.to/freegames
The Gamer's Inn	http://www.gamersinn.com/tavern
C/Net Shareware.com	http://www.shareware.com
Only Freeware	http://freeware.intrastar.net

Messaging and E-Mail Software	Address
ICQ	http://www.mirabilis.com
MIRC	http://www.geocities.com/~mirc
AOL Instant Messenger	http://www.aol.com/aim
Yahoo! Mail	http://mail.yahoo.com
Microsoft Hotmail	http://www.hotmail.com

In the table on page 356, we've provided a list of both instant messaging software sites and free e-mail providers. And on the Web site that supports this text, you'll find a list of many others. Pick one instant messaging software site, download the software and have a classmate do the same, register with the service, and try communicating. Pick one free e-mail provider, register with the company, notify a classmate, and practice sending and receiving e-mail through this service. Then answer the questions that follow for the messaging software and the free e-mail provider.

A. How easy is the messaging software to download, install, and register?

B. Are you able to determine if your classmate is online? Can you communicate with him or her?

C. How quickly do the instant messages arrive using the messaging software?

D. Are you able to find new friends on the messaging software? Can you qualify them by similar interests?

E. What other services does the messaging software offer? Are any of interest to you?

F. How easy is it to register and use the free e-mail? Is it completely free?

G. Does the free e-mail service allow you to attach files to your e-mail messages? If so, does the service limit the size of these files?

 Go to the Web site that supports this text: **http://www.mhhe.com/business/mis/haag** and select "Electronic Commerce Projects."

We've included links to over 100 Web sites for downloading freeware and shareware as well as running your Web site with freeware.

KEY TERMS AND CONCEPTS

Business Systems Planning (BSP)
Capital Investment Analysis
Chief Information Officer (CIO)
Contingency Planning
Competitive Forces Model
Competitive Intelligence
Competitive Scanning
Cost-Benefit Analysis
Critical Success Factor (CSF)
Disaster Recovery Cost Curve
Information Architecture
Information Technology Fusion (IT Fusion)

Information Technology Systems Plan (IT Systems Plan)
Information Technology Systems Planning (IT Systems Planning)
Information Technology Systems Risk
Information Unavailability Cost Curve
Intangible Benefit
Primary Intelligence
Secondary Intelligence
Tangible Benefit
Value Chain

SHORT-ANSWER QUESTIONS

1. What is information technology systems planning?
2. What is an information technology systems plan?
3. What are the five steps in information technology systems planning?
4. What are three methods of aligning organizational goals and information technology?

5. What is IT fusion? What is the goal of IT fusion? How is it used?
6. What is the competitive forces model? How is it used?
7. What is competitive intelligence? Why is it used?

8. What are the four steps in the competitive intelligence process?

9. What is the value chain? How is it used?

10. What is an information architecture? What does it identify?

11. What is a critical success factor? How is it applied in the critical success factor method? What step in the IT systems planning process does it support?

12. What is business systems planning? What step in the systems planning process does it support?

13. What are three IT systems evaluation analysis methods?

14. What are tangible IT systems benefits? What are intangible IT systems benefits? Which are best avoided?

15. What is capital investment analysis? How is it used?

16. What is information technology systems risk?

17. What is the information unavailability cost curve?

DISCUSSION QUESTIONS

1. What is the purpose of IT systems planning? What product is produced at the end of the process? What process begins at the end of IT systems planning?

2. Should IT systems planning occur before, at the same time, or after business planning? Why? Justify your response.

3. How do you know when you have fused organizational and information technology goals? Can you think of any examples that you have observed? Do you think it is feasible?

4. What is the role of the knowledge worker in competitive intelligence? How would the knowledge worker utilize value chain analysis for competitive analysis?

5. Which is more reliable, primary or secondary intelligence? Name three sources of both for a large industrial company. Do you think this information is easy or difficult to gather?

6. Which systems planning step should be performed first: identifying specific processes or identifying specific information? Which of these steps is best for identifying IT systems needs? Which do you think is the most widely accepted?

7. Can you think of why a process in the value chain would be value-reducing? Do you really think that organizations operate with processes that are value-reducing? How could that happen?

8. How difficult do you think it is to create an information unavailability cost curve? Compare that with the difficulty of creating a disaster recovery cost curve. Which is easier or more difficult and why?

9. How do you decide which disaster recovery plan to use? Explain all the steps in the process and justify how you would select a plan.

10. When is systems planning complete? Many businesses operate without a written business plan. Do you think many organizations also operate without a systems plan? Why or why not? What are the dangers of not having a systems plan?

CASE STUDY

Programmers Get One Slice of Pizza for Every Nine Lines of Code

In late 1995, Microsoft finally released its long-awaited new personal computer operating system—Windows '95. For 3 long hard years, Microsoft worked diligently to create Windows '95. And all that work has definitely paid off: According to one survey in 1996, 36 percent of IT managers planned to upgrade to Windows '95. Three years, however, seems like a long time just to develop a personal computer operating system—doesn't it? Well, if it does, consider these even more startling statistics that appear at right.

IN THE NEWS

363 Systems development is a function of *what, when, who,* and *how.*

365 Asking the right questions can help you answer the *who* question.

376 Ninety-five percent of all projects incur cost and time overruns. And 65 percent of those eventually incur costs two to three times greater than originally planned.

378 Selfsourcing—developing systems for yourself as a knowledge worker—is one more aspect of knowledge worker computing.

386 Revenues from IT-related outsourcing are expected to exceed $120 billion in the year 2000.

386 Forty-five percent of businesses have outsourced some major portion of their IT environment.

389 Duke Power Co. officially "turned the lights out" on a systems development project after spending over $12 million.

397 Bell & Howell uses joint application development to reduce the delivery time of an electronic catalog from 60 days to just 2 days.

Developing IT Systems

Bringing IT Systems to Life

Windows '95 Is 11,236,344 Lines of Code

- It took 9,234,455 hours of work.
  Or **49 minutes** per line of code.
- It took 2,333,345 hours of testing.
  Or **12.5 minutes** per line of code.
- Programmers consumed 126,237 pizzas.
  Or **one slice of pizza** for every 9 lines of code.

During those millions of hours and years of work, over 10,000 people were involved in the creation of Windows '95. Most of those people were employees of Microsoft. In some instances though, Microsoft hired outside people to help with the work. When an organization does this, it's called *outsourcing*.

Microsoft also released thousands of copies of Windows '95 early all over the world and asked key users to review the product for completeness and working accuracy. Why? Because the eventual buyers of Windows '95 are Microsoft's customers, and customers are the most important people in the development process of any product or service.

Sometimes Microsoft worked closely with potential users to develop the look, feel, and layout of screens. Initially, no one really knew what the screens should look like or which icons to include, so Microsoft built several mock screens and asked users to suggest improvements or changes. When you build models to determine

FEATURES

IN THE INFORMATION AGE, KNOWLEDGE WORKERS UNDERSTAND...

1. Why their participation is important in the development of IT systems

2. How organizations traditionally develop IT systems through insourcing and their role during that process

3. What selfsourcing and outsourcing are and how they affect the way organizations develop systems

4. Various tools and methods that can increase the efficiency and effectiveness of the systems development process

characteristics of a product, the process is called *prototyping*.

Outsourcing, end-user reviewing, and prototyping are just three of the many methods your organization can use to develop any product or service. In this chapter, we focus specifically on developing IT systems and how organizations go about the development process. Most important, we discuss your role as a knowledge worker during the development of IT systems.[1,2] ❖

Introduction

Microsoft's development story is similar to that of most organizations. Today organizations all over the world are spending millions of hours and billions of dollars to develop IT systems. As a knowledge worker in today's information age, IT systems will definitely affect your work. Those systems that effectively meet your needs will help you be more productive and make better decisions. Those systems that don't meet your needs may have a damaging effect on your productivity. So it's vitally important that you help your organization develop the best systems possible.

That also means you can expect to deal with systems development in your job, regardless of your chosen field of study. If you major in MIS, you'll take many courses relating to systems development including systems analysis, systems design, programming (in several languages), and many others. And even if your chosen area of study is not MIS, the process of systems development will definitely affect you.

Even more important, how well you participate in the systems development process will affect you. As we discuss systems development in this chapter, we focus specifically on what, exactly, your role is as a knowledge worker during systems development. That is, what tasks and functions are you responsible for while your organization develops IT systems? Again, it's important that you understand what functions and tasks you need to perform, because the systems you help develop will affect your productivity, and ultimately have an impact on the success of your organization.

Systems Development Is a Question-and-Answer Session

When people approach systems development, they do so mainly by asking questions. Some of these questions include: "*What* systems should we develop?" "*When* should we develop those systems?" "*Who* should develop systems?" and "*How* should we go about developing systems?" The most important question people always ask is, "*Why* is my participation important during the systems development process?" These are all great questions and your answers to them will determine the success of the systems development process. Let's start by addressing *why* your participation is important, and then we'll look at the *what, when, who,* and *how* aspects of systems development.

Why Is Your Participation Important?

Many people who have come before you and undoubtedly many who will follow also ask another question: "I'm not going to be an IT specialist—so why should I learn about the systems development process?" If you're asking that same question, congratulations—you're well on your way to becoming an information-literate knowledge worker. Why? Because you're simply asking, "Why is this material important to me? What does it mean? How can I use it?"

Your participation in the systems development process is vitally important because you are (or will be)

❶ A business process expert

❷ A liaison to the customer

❸ A quality control analyst

❹ A manager of other people

First and foremost, in business you **are** the business process expert. For example, if you're an administrator at a hospital and the development of a new nursing allocation system is under way, who knows best how nursing allocation should occur? That's right—you do. During systems development, business process experts (which we refer to as knowledge workers throughout this text) know how things should work, what things should happen, how to handle exceptions, and so on. It would be ludicrous to tell a group of IT specialists to develop a new nursing allocation system without telling them how nurses should be allocated according to certain criteria, such as expertise, overload hours, and time of year. In business, you are a business process expert. Without your input, the new system will never meet your needs.

Second, your knowledge of and participation in the systems development process is vitally important because you're a liaison to the customer. That is, you know what a certain customer segment wants, and you can relay that information to the project team. For example, if you work for a telephone company and manage a call center that fields billing questions, aren't you qualified to provide information pertaining to the appearance and content of new phone bills? Of course you are. And, if you want to make your customers happy, you have to act as a liaison between them and the project team.

Third, your participation is important because you'll act as a quality control analyst during the systems development process. Once you help define the logical requirements of a new system, you can't simply walk away and expect a system that meets your needs. For example, you still need to help review alternative technical solutions, acting as a quality control analyst to assure that the chosen technical alternative meets your logical needs.

Finally, your participation in the systems development process is important because you have ultimate responsibility for the work and productivity of others. In short, you will be a manager of other people, and it's your responsibility to see that new systems will improve the productivity of those you manage.

Systems Development
What, When, Who, and *How?*

In viewing systems development as a question-and-answer session, you also need to ask *what, when, who,* and *how.* In Chapter 8, we dealt with the *what* and *when* questions of the systems development process during the planning step. These two questions always come first because they are the most important and they deal with all proposed systems development projects in your organization. Your organization should always determine *what* systems to develop and *when* to develop those systems within the strategic direction and goals of your organization.

In this chapter, we focus on the *who* and *how* questions of systems development. That is, (1) *who* will be responsible for the development of a specific system and (2) *how* or what tools and methods should you use to develop a specific system? You should notice that these two questions deal with a specific system. Your organization must consider each of these questions for each new systems development project. Many organizations today choose different *who*'s and different *how*'s for different projects.

Answering the *Who* Question of Systems Development

When approaching systems development as a knowledge worker, you have three choices for answering the *who* question—IT specialists within your organization, knowledge workers such as yourself, and another organization (see Figure 9.1). First, you can choose IT specialists within your organization to develop a new system. If this is your decision, you're choosing to *insource* the development of a new system. Second, you can ask knowledge workers (one of which may be you) to develop their own respective systems, which is *selfsourcing*. This is becoming quite common in most organizations and is part of the overall concept of knowledge worker computing. Finally, you can choose another organization to develop a new system, which is *outsourcing*.

Determining *who* is critical in systems development. In the box to the right, we've highlighted important issues to help you make the *who* decision. As we explore the various *who*'s throughout this chapter, we'll discuss these issues in more detail.

Answering the *How* Question of Systems Development

The *how* question of systems development relates to the tools and methods you choose for the development of a new system. The *how* question has numerous alternatives.

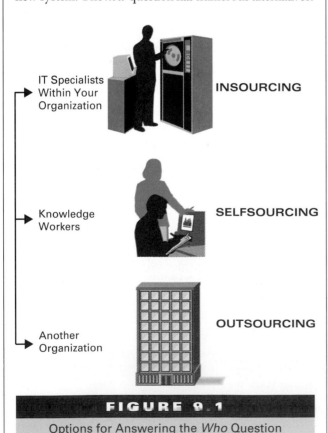

FIGURE 9.1

Options for Answering the *Who* Question

For example, in Chapter 2, we introduced groupware; and in Chapter 4, we looked at how to develop a system using a personal productivity software package (a DBMS package for creating a personal database). In this chapter, we want to look at five more *how* options, which include the following:

- *Traditional systems development life cycle* A structured approach to systems development in which you, as a knowledge worker, tell IT specialists within your organization what you want

- *Prototyping* The process of building models of systems to determine requirements and express functionality

- *Application software packages* Prewritten software packages that automate common business functions, such as payroll and inventory control

- *Computer-aided software engineering* Software tools that automate some or all steps in the traditional systems development life cycle

- *Joint application development* Workshops that unite knowledge workers and IT specialists to increase the effectiveness of communicating requirements and solutions

As we explore various *how*'s throughout this chapter, we'll discuss issues that will help you decide which *how* is best for a given systems development project.

Combining *Who* and *How*

The *who* and *how* answers to the systems development questions are definitely interrelated. For example, if you choose IT specialists within your organization (insourcing), they'll most often use the traditional systems development life cycle. If you choose to develop your own system (selfsourcing), you'll most often use prototyping. Whatever the case, decisions that you'll face during systems development are not simple, and making the wrong decision can cost your organization millions of dollars and a strategic or competitive advantage in the marketplace.

As this chapter unfolds, we'll focus on the *who* of systems development and, in that context, what tools and methods are most commonly used by those people. In the next section, for example, you'll learn about insourcing and the traditional systems development life cycle; following that discussion, you'll learn how to perform selfsourcing using prototyping; next, you'll learn about outsourcing; and, finally, we cover two additional *how*'s (computer-aided software engineering and joint application development), both of which can be invaluable to the systems development process.

To help you better understand the process of systems development and the relationship between *who* and

Asking Questions to Make the *Who* Decision

	Answer	Choices		
		Insource	Selfsource	Outsource
1. Will the system support a unique core competency?	Yes	Yes	Maybe	No
2. Is cost an overriding consideration?	Yes	No	Maybe	Yes
3. Is time critical?	Yes	No	Maybe	Yes
4. Do you possess the necessary technical expertise?	Yes	Yes	Maybe	No
5. Is organizational control of the system critical?	Yes	Yes	Maybe	No
6. Will the system support a common business or industry function?	Yes	Maybe	No	Yes
7. Is gaining or having the necessary technical expertise part of your strategic plan?	Yes	Yes	Maybe	No
8. Will the system support only a small number of knowledge workers? ❖	Yes	Maybe	Yes	Maybe

how, we introduce each discussion with a table illustrating the relationship.

Insourcing and the Traditional Systems Development Life Cycle

Separating Duties Among IT Specialists and Knowledge Workers

Most organizations today still choose insourcing as the *who* and the traditional systems development life cycle as the *how* for systems development. Recall that insourc-

ing involves choosing IT specialists within your organization to develop the system. The *traditional systems development life cycle (traditional SDLC)* is a structured step-by-step approach to developing systems that creates a separation of duties among IT specialists and knowledge workers. In the traditional SDLC (which we'll simply refer to as the SDLC), knowledge workers are the business process experts and quality control analysts, whereas IT specialists are responsible for the actual design, implementation, and support of the system. Using the SDLC, your organization follows six steps (see Figure 9.2), including

❶ *Planning* Establish an IT plan to meet the strategic plans of the organization.

❷ *Scoping* Define the scope of the proposed system.

❸ *Analysis* Determine the logical requirements for the proposed system.

	How				
Who	Traditional SDLC	Prototyping	Application Software Packages	CASE	JAD
Insource	✔				
Selfsource					
Outsource					

When you choose the traditional systems development life cycle as the *how,* you have also chosen insourcing as the *who*. Read on to learn why.

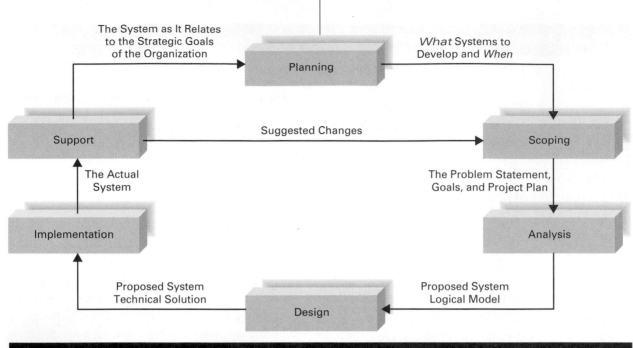

The System as It Relates
to the Strategic Goals
of the Organization

What Systems to
Develop and *When*

Planning

Suggested Changes

Support

Scoping

The Actual
System

The Problem Statement,
Goals, and Project Plan

Implementation

Analysis

Proposed System
Technical Solution

Proposed System
Logical Model

Design

FIGURE 9.2

The Six Steps in the Traditional Systems Development Life Cycle

Matching IT Planning with Business Planning

IT planning should always come first because it lays the foundation for all proposed systems development efforts; and these systems development efforts are aimed at helping your organization realize its business goals. Unfortunately, IT planning is seldom in sync with business planning. There are many reasons for this, including the fact that technology is changing so fast and many organizations do not perform IT planning in conjunction with developing the organization's overall goals and strategies.

Another reason IT planning and business planning seldom match is because of what we call the "applications development backlog," which represents all requested systems development efforts that cannot be carried out because of limited resources, usually money and IT specialists. This backlog is a real problem. If your organization needs a new system soon to take advantage of an opportunity in the marketplace, that proposed system may very well join the growing number of other projects that can't be implemented because of the applications development backlog.

Wal-Mart, the $100 billion retail giant headquartered in Bentonville, Arkansas, faced the same problem in early 1996; that is, how can IT planning be in sync with business planning when we're years behind in developing systems? Wal-Mart's solution was to aggressively pursue whatever means necessary to cut the applications development backlog to just 12 months, the same time frame for its business planning cycle. For example, Wal-Mart increased its IT budget by 10 percent and hired 240 new IT specialists, increasing its IT staff by over 50 percent.

Fusing IT planning with business planning can fail for many reasons. The most important of which, perhaps, is the growing applications development backlog. If this is true in your organization, you must first take action to eliminate that backlog.[3] ❖

④ *Design* Convert the logical requirements into a technical system design.

⑤ *Implementation* Create the new system.

⑥ *Support* Provide ongoing support.

In the rest of this section, we briefly review the planning step and thoroughly explore scoping through support steps of the SDLC. For a more in-depth explanation of the planning step, we encourage you to review Chapter 8.

Throughout this section, we also highlight ITW Enterprises as it proceeded through the SDLC. ITW Enterprises (ITW) serves the metropolitan area of Detroit by assisting business executives in finding temporary apartment housing while they work in Detroit. In late 1999, ITW found itself in somewhat of a dilemma. Business was booming, which was good. Unfortunately, ITW found that it had quickly outgrown its supporting IT infrastructure. The IT systems at ITW simply could not handle the huge volume of information that flowed through the organization. ITW had a real problem; without access to timely and correct information, employees couldn't perform their jobs effectively, which meant that customers were unhappy and revenues were lost. The owner of ITW, Abigail Green, recognized that a new system was badly needed.

Photo Essay 9-1 details ITW prior to the new system, including customers, the organizational structure, how processes worked, and the supporting IT infrastructure.

Step 1: Planning

Establishing an IT Plan to Meet the Strategic Plans of the Organization

Planning is the first step in any systems development process—regardless of your answer to *who* or *how*. During the planning step of systems development, your goal is to forge an important alliance between the strategic direction of the organization and the IT systems plan (what we referred to as "fusion" in Chapter 8). Again, we cannot stress enough the importance of the planning step in systems development. Proper planning not only helps your organization define new systems but also helps align the IT systems plan with the strategic organizational plan; aids in determining whether the development of systems should be insourced, selfsourced, or outsourced; and

(continued on page 370)

 We've Got a Problem . . .

No Wait—We've Got Many Problems!

Abigail Green started ITW 3 years ago from her home to supplement her income. "Supplement" is no longer the correcct term. Abigail's business now represents over 50 apartment complexes, works with over 300 business executives per month, and generates almost $250,000 in profit annually. So what's the problem? Business is great, and the money is even better. How could there be a problem? Let's listen to what some employees (and a customer) have to say.

"One of my biggest jobs is to find new apartment complexes to represent. But I never know what type of apartment complexes we need to represent. I can go look in the master client workbook, but it takes me hours to determine that we need more apartment complexes with workout facilities or more complexes with three-bedroom apartments."

—Mark from Apartment Services

"The daily reports we receive from Apartment Services were okay when I was only working with a few clients. Today I worked with over 40 clients, all of whom had different desires. I'm tired of requesting 40 different reports every day. Besides, by the end of the day many units in some apartment complexes are gone. Too much information—much of which is already old—does me no good."

—Nash from Client Services

"Last week I received a folder from Client Services that didn't include the name of the apartment complex a client had chosen. I spent almost an hour tracking down the right person who could tell me a simple apartment complex name. I lost valuable time and had to come in on the weekend to make it up."

—Julia from Finance

"I really appreciate the service you provide. But I asked to see several photos of each apartment complex before making my decision. It took several days for those photos to arrive. When I finally chose an apartment complex, it was already full."

—Rhonda (an unhappy customer) ❖

ITW Enterprises at Work

OVERVIEW

ITW Enterprises (ITW) serves the metropolitan area of Detroit by assisting business executives (*clients*) in finding temporary apartment housing. ITW generates cash flow by charging a fee to each apartment complex in which it places a client. Clients are not charged for the services ITW provides.

Each apartment complex that ITW represents provides information concerning available apartments for rent and general information about amenities, including swimming pools, workout facilities, on-site security, and so on. When ITW places a client with an apartment complex, ITW generates a fee for services statement for that apartment complex.

When a client contacts ITW, a client profile is built that details client requirements and projected length of stay. ITW then matches the client with the apartment complex that meets most—if not all—of his or her needs. Again, clients are not charged a fee.

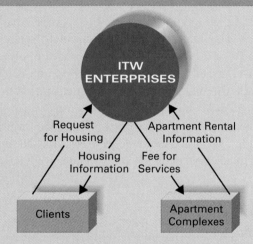

ITW has two sets of customers—apartment complexes and business executives who need temporary housing. People who need temporary housing are called "clients."

ITW represents apartment complexes to clients. When a new apartment complex is signed, information concerning location, rental price, size, furnished or unfurnished, leasing price, and so on, is gathered. This information can be changed at any time. Also, ITW can terminate its relationship with any current apartment complex, at which time the information is removed.

Clients of ITW fall into one of two categories:

1. Business executives who need temporary housing while they work in Detroit for 6 months or less. These executives then return to their permanent residences in other cities.

2. Business executives who have been permanently transferred to Detroit and need temporary housing while they find permanent housing.

ORGANIZATIONAL STRUCTURE*

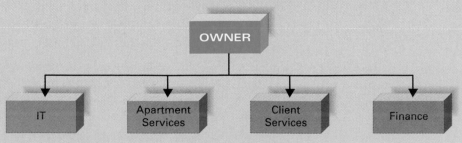

*Description of the organizational structure is at the top of the next page.

- The IT Department—manager and 5 staff members—responsible for all systems development and support.
- The Apartment Services Department—manager and 4 staff members—responsible for acquiring and maintaining information concerning apartment complexes.
- The Client Services Department—manager and 6 staff members—responsible for working with clients to find the appropriate housing. This includes gathering a profile of each client and matching him or her to the appropriate apartment complex.
- The Finance Department—manager and 3 staff members—responsible for generating invoices for and collecting money from apartment complexes represented by ITW.

HOW PROCESSES WORK AND THE IT INFRASTRUCTURE

APARTMENT SERVICES DEPARTMENT

FINANCE DEPARTMENT

FOLDER

Once a fee for services statement has been generated, the Finance Department passes the folder (client profile and apartment complex information) to Apartment Services. Apartment Services, in turn, updates the apartment complex database.

Apartment Services considers itself completely automated. It utilizes a multiuser database spread across a local area network that any Apartment Services employee can use to add, change, delete, or query any information concerning any apartment complex.

APARTMENT DATABASE

The Finance Department creates fee for services statements for the various apartment complexes based on the folders received from Client Services. The Finance Department uses special software that accesses the apartment complex database (shared by Finance and Apartment Services) to obtain the appropriate fee. Then the Finance Department must manually type each fee for services statement.

MIS Reports by Apartment Criteria

CLIENT SERVICES DEPARTMENT

FOLDER

Client Services is currently paper-based. When a prospective client first contacts ITW, Client Services builds a client profile and places it in a master client workbook. This way, any Client Services employee can work with any client by simply retrieving the appropriate profile from the workbook.

MASTER CLIENT WORKBOOK

When a client is matched to a specific apartment complex, Client Services creates a folder that includes the client profile and information concerning which apartment complex that client has chosen. That folder is then sent to the Finance Department for fee processing.

Each day, the employees in Client Services split the workbook equally and work with several clients. Apartment Services also generates daily reports for Client Services concerning available apartment housing. These reports are really MIS reports because they can be generated by specific criteria. For example, if a client needs a two-bedroom furnished apartment, Client Services can request that type of report from Apartment Services.

these models should deal only with logical aspects, not physical. Creating logical models, however, is not simple. You must detail each piece of information carefully and define each process in excruciating detail. To help with this, the consultant introduced the project team to a number of modeling tools, one of which was flowcharting—a graphic tool for depicting the steps in a process. The project team first tackled the process of what happened after a match was found. This process included completing the folder, generating the fee for services statement, and updating the apartment database to reflect that a specific unit was no longer available at an apartment complex. Figure 9.4 shows the project team's flowchart for this process.

Although everyone knew what happened, it was alarming to see it laid out step-by-step. The seemingly simple process involved all three departments and 12 steps. The next task facing the project team was to create the best way the process should occur. And it didn't take long. After a few attempts at a drawing board, the team came up with a new process (see Figure 9.5).

The analysis step results in a complete logical model of how the proposed system will work and an updated project plan (which includes a new justifiable feasibility review). The complete logical model of the proposed system must include a step-by-step description of the processes as well as thorough documentation of all the information the proposed system will work with.

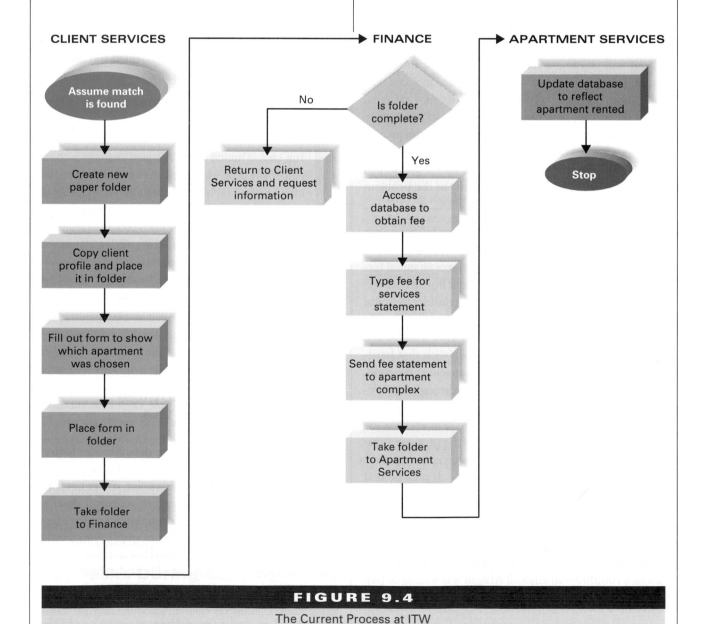

CLIENT SERVICES　　　　　　　**FINANCE**　　　　　**APARTMENT SERVICES**

Assume match is found

Create new paper folder

Copy client profile and place it in folder

Fill out form to show which apartment was chosen

Place form in folder

Take folder to Finance

Is folder complete?　　No → Return to Client Services and request information

Yes

Access database to obtain fee

Type fee for services statement

Send fee statement to apartment complex

Take folder to Apartment Services

Update database to reflect apartment rented

Stop

FIGURE 9.4

The Current Process at ITW

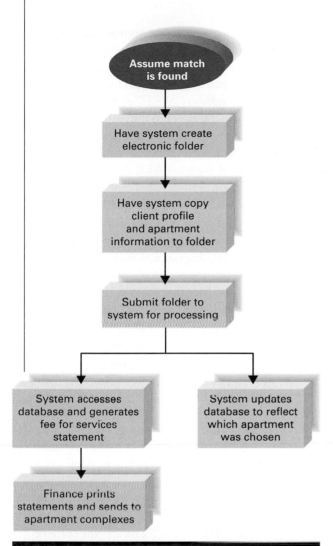

FIGURE 9.5

Proposed Process at ITW

Key Tasks During Analysis

Model, study, and analyze the current system and business processes Before you can develop a new system, you must first understand how the current system and business processes work. Although you've already defined the problem in scoping, in analysis you explore it in more detail. This includes modeling in detail each process step-by-step and each piece of information you work with. As the project team at ITW found out, modeling the current system prior to creating the proposed system can be an eye-opening experience.

Define new information and processing requirements The goal of any systems development effort is to create a system that works with new information and/or performs new processes. As with the current system model, you must define each of these in great detail.

Model the new system Once you've defined the current system and new processes and information, it's time to combine the two to create a new system model. This new model will be created from a logical point of view and will provide the foundation for developing a technical model in step 4.

Update the project plan and scope Once you perform all tasks in analysis, you must revise the project plan and scope. This involves updating the preliminary budget, the feasibility review, and the time frame for development. It may also involve adding new people to the project team and revising the problem scope.

Your Role During Analysis

Provide information concerning how the system currently works You're the business process expert—that means you know how current processes and the system work. It's vitally important that you provide this information as the current system model will become the foundation for developing the new system model.

Provide information concerning new information and processing requirements You're still the business process expert. You know how things need to change—what new business processes and information you need. At ITW, the members of the project team from the various departments played a key role in providing information concerning how the current system worked and what new information and processing were needed.

Monitor and justify the new feasibility review Again, much of the money for the new systems development will come from your budget. It's your responsibility to justify the expenditure.

Step 4: Design

Convert the Logical Requirements into a Technical System Design

The goal of step 4—*design*—is to build a technical blueprint of how the proposed system will work. In this step, your role becomes that of quality assurance. IT specialists complete most of the tasks in design, but you must still review their recommendations and assure that the proposed technical solution meets your logical requirements. The recommendations of the IT specialists will address hardware, software, telecommunications, information, people, and procedures, as well as user interfaces (screens, reports, and so on).

At ITW, the IT specialists spent 2 months exploring many options, evaluating their worth, and determining their cost. Their final recommendation to the team seemed to satisfy everyone's needs and meet the stated goals. Let's review their recommendations for the hardware, software, telecommunications, and information building blocks of the system.

Hardware The new system would require a local area network on which each employee had a workstation (see Figure 9.6). This would involve purchasing workstations for each person in Client Services. The local area network would contain two important features: first, a server on which apartment and client information would reside; and second, an all-important connection to the Internet that would allow the clients of ITW to view apartment information, including photos and complex layouts.

Software For an operating system, the IT specialists recommended using Windows NT. This would provide security features that would limit access to information to only those who required it. For example, when a Client

Services employee logged on, the security features of Windows NT would allow them view and query access only to apartment information, but it would also allow them to add, change, and delete client profile information.

For application software, the IT specialists determined that necessary interfaces to the two existing systems would not be required. The application software currently used for those two systems would continue to be used without modifications for the new system. In fact, the IT specialists even decided that the software used to create and maintain the database for the apartment complexes could also be used to create and maintain the client profiles. The proposed system, however, included requirements for matching a client profile to a list of potential apartment complexes. The IT specialists determined that they would have to write special application software to do this. This new application software would take a specific client profile and query the apartment database to create a list of potential complexes, based on ranking criteria that the client provided.

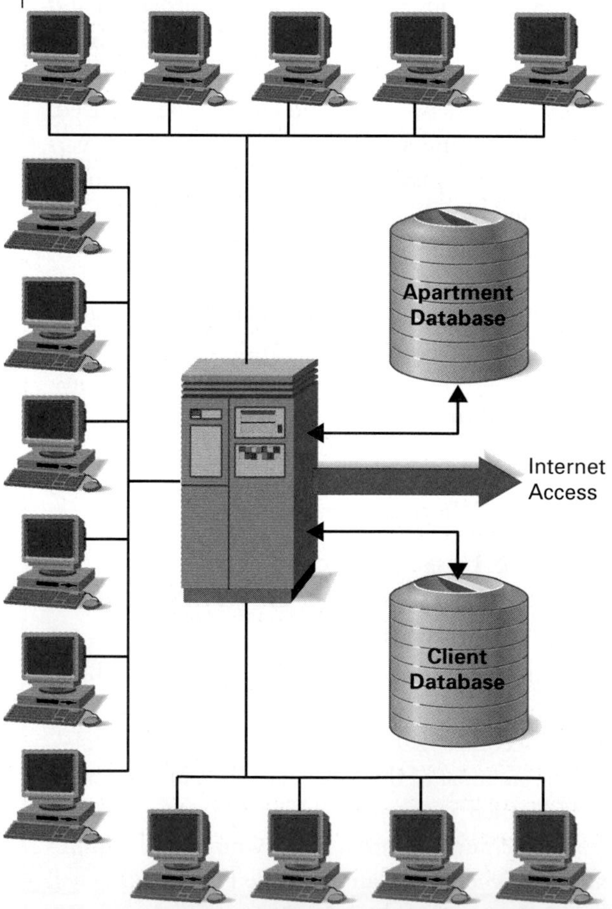

Telecommunications The link to the Internet would create a substantial marketplace advantage. If clients wanted to see information concerning specific apartments, they could simply access ITW's Web site and query available apartments based on key field information that Client Services would provide. Some people initially thought that would mean creating two copies of all apartment information—one for the apartment database and one for the Web site. The IT specialists explained, however, that they could easily write utility software that would extract information from the apartment database and place it on the Web site every hour. The system would handle everything.

Information Information is at the center of ITW's proposed system. More important, the ability to freely access and communicate information is vital. The proposed system included two databases—apartment and client— that would reside on the local area network. For determining the exact content of these databases and their structures, the IT specialists created E-R diagrams, employed normalization, and created a data dictionary that specified the attributes. They also built sample screens and reports for the rest of the project team to review. During its review, the project team requested a few changes and added an additional query screen.

Key deliverables of design include a recommended technical model of how the proposed system will work and function and an updated project plan. As with all steps, the updated project plan may include new project milestones and an updated and justifiable feasibility review.

FIGURE 9.6

The Proposed Hardware Solution at ITW

Key Tasks During Design

Identify alternative technical solutions Because the goal of design is to build a technical blueprint of how the proposed system will work, you'll probably have to explore many different options. Technology today offers a variety of hardware and software platforms. It's important that you explore all of them. At ITW, the IT specialists explored a number of alternative technical solutions and evaluated the worthiness of each.

Analyze the alternative solutions and choose the best Once you've developed several technical alternatives, you must analyze each in terms of time, cost, and technical feasibility. This will allow you to recommend the best solution. Again, IT specialists, for the most part, perform this function, but it's still your responsibility to analyze and question various technical alternatives.

Update the project plan and scope Once you've chosen the best technical solution, you have to update the project plan. Again, this will include revising the time frame, performing an updated feasibility review, and identifying new project team members to carry out step 5.

Your Role During Design

Ensure that the recommended technical solution meets the logical requirements During design, your role decreases as a business process expert and increases as a quality control analyst. The IT specialists will develop several alternative technical solutions. It's your job to analyze each and ensure that the recommended solution best meets your logical requirements.

Monitor and justify the project plan Again, at the end of each step you must update and justify the project plan, including the new time frame and the feasibility review.

Step 5: Implementation

Creating the New System

The goal of step 5—*implementation*—is to bring the proposed system to life and place it in the organization. This step involves writing and testing any necessary software and acquiring and installing any new hardware. IT specialists perform most of these tasks, but quality assurance is still a key role for you. The IT specialists involved in implementation are charged with delivering an operational system complete with documentation. Your organization will use this documentation during support if any changes are necessary.

Key Tasks During Implementation

Programming Programming involves writing any necessary software. IT specialists perform this function and may take months or even years to write the software. At ITW, the programming was relatively simple—the IT specialists had to write only the software that matched clients to apartment complexes and the utility software that extracted apartment information from the apartment database and loaded it into ITW's Web site.

Hardware acquisition and installation Most new systems require new hardware. It may be as simple as adding internal memory to workstations or as complex as setting up a wide area network across several states. Whatever the case, the IT specialists, for the most part, are responsible for hardware acquisition and installation. At ITW, the IT specialists purchased and installed workstations for each Client Services employee and connected everyone by way of a local area network.

Testing Once the new hardware and software are in place, your responsibility increases dramatically. It's now time for you to test the new system to ensure that it works correctly and meets your logical needs. Many people overlook testing or do it hurriedly. Never sacrifice the time it takes to test the system completely. At ITW, for example, the project team loaded the new databases with fictitious information, generated hundreds of queries, and created numerous fee for services statements to ensure that the new system worked perfectly.

Training Once you determine that the new system works correctly, you must provide training for the people who will use it.

Conversion Conversion is simply moving from the old system to the new system. There are a variety of conversion methods, including

- *Parallel conversion* Using both the old and new system until you're sure that the new system performs correctly
- *Plunge conversion* Discarding the old system completely and immediately using the new system
- *Pilot conversion* Having only a small group of people use the new system until you know that it works correctly and then adding the remaining people to the system
- *Piecemeal conversion* Converting to only a portion of the new system until you're sure that it works correctly and then converting to the remaining portions of the new system

At ITW, the project team chose to use a parallel conversion method for moving Client Services from the old system to the new system. This gave them a backup if the new system failed.

Your Role During Implementation

Determine the best training method All knowledge workers must learn how the new system works, and you can train those people in a variety of ways, including classes and one-to-one training.

Determine the best method of conversion Conversion is critical. Parallel conversion is the safest, but most expensive, method because it may require that some people perform the same task on two systems. Plunge conversion, on the other hand, is the quickest and cheapest, but the most dangerous, method. If the new system fails, your organization is without an operational backup system. Your choice is critical and will depend on the nature of the system and its importance to daily operations.

Provide complete testing of the new system Testing is critical. You must thoroughly test each portion of the system as well as the entire system. Never sacrifice testing time or your system may not work correctly all the time.

Monitor the budget and schedule and look for "runaway" projects Most systems development projects become "runaway" projects during implementation because not enough time or money was allocated to the programming function. Programming is not a simple task, and it can become even more difficult if some requirements weren't defined. You should monitor the programming function carefully and ensure that programming dates are met.

Runaway projects are a serious problem in today's business environment. According to a *Computerworld* survey, 95 percent of all projects incur costs and time overruns.[4] And 65 percent of those eventually incur costs two to three times greater than originally planned.

Step 6: Support

Providing Ongoing Support

Support is the final sequential step of any systems development effort. The goal of this step is to ensure that the system continues to meet stated goals. Once a system is in place, it must change as your business changes. Constantly monitoring and supporting the new system involves making minor changes (for example, new reports or information capturing) and reviewing the system to ensure that it continues to move your organization toward its strategic goals.

Key Tasks During Support

React to changes in information and processing needs As changes arise in the business environment, you must react to those changes by assessing their impact on the system. It might very well be that the system needs to

---

INDUSTRY PERSPECTIVE

Transportation

When Runaway Projects Affect Your Life

The Federal Aviation Administration (FAA), the government arm in charge of monitoring and promoting aviation safety, is stuck in implementation. In 1983, the FAA set out on a 5-year mission to replace its automated air traffic control facilities. After spending an amazing $7.6 billion on development, the system—which was to be completed in 1988—is still unfinished. That means that the system is now about 11 years behind schedule.

What's even worse is the cost associated with maintaining the old system while attempting to complete the new project. The FAA estimates that it spends $19 million annually on just replacement parts for the old system. And those replacement parts are vacuum tubes. If you've never heard of vacuum tubes on a computer, there's a good reason for it. In the late 1940s and early 1950s, the primary technology base for computers was vacuum tubes. Since then, we've moved through transistors and integrated circuits to our current technology base—the microprocessor and very-large-scale integrated (VLSI) circuits.

How safe do you feel flying through the air, knowing that the FAA is controlling your aviation safety with a computer system based on 1940s technology?[5] ❖

INDUSTRY PERSPECTIVE

Food

Planning for Change with Object-Oriented Technologies

The business environment is certainly changing, and IT systems must change as well to match new business goals and processes. But changing IT systems and how they work (the major tasks of step 6, "Support") is very time-consuming and difficult. Therefore many organizations are developing new systems today, focusing specifically on using technologies that will support faster and easier changes tomorrow.

One such technology involves objects, which we've briefly discussed in numerous previous chapters and describe in some detail in Appendix C. PepsiCo, for example, is installing an object-based production and inventory system in 65 bottling plants and 240 distribution centers throughout North America. PepsiCo's desire to make changes quickly to the system was a key factor in its decision to use objects. As Mark Arsenault describes PepsiCo's decision, "Its business changes rapidly, and the company felt that the adaptability and flexibility inherent with our object architecture would make it easier for them to reflect these changes in the system."

Change is a natural part of life, even the life of an IT system. In today's fast-paced, ever-changing business environment, you must plan for change. Change is very necessary, and your success depends on your ability to (1) recognize that change must occur and (2) plan for that change.[6] ❖

---

change to meet the ever-changing needs of the business environment. If so, you need to notify the IT specialists of those changes.

Assess the worth of the system in terms of the strategic plan of the organization After several years, it's entirely possible that an existing system may no longer meet the strategic needs of your organization. In this instance, the system may require a major overhaul, or you may have to scrap it in favor of a new system.

Your Role During Support

Provide a mechanism for people to request changes To create the best support environment, you need to provide a way for knowledge workers to request changes. You could develop a form that knowledge workers could fill out to request changes or have weekly meetings to discuss any needed changes.

Assess the worth of proposed changes before passing them on to the IT specialists Once you receive requested changes, you must assess their worth before passing them on to the maintenance team. Again, changes cost money that will probably come from your departmental budget. You must carefully weigh each requested change for merit and monetary worth.

As you can see, the SDLC is a structured, step-by-step process that creates a separation of duties among knowledge workers and IT specialists. In design, for example, IT specialists are responsible for developing several alternative technical solutions. Your responsibility is to evaluate the alternative solutions. And, in implementation, the IT specialists are responsible for programming, while you're responsible for testing the software to make sure it works correctly.

Insourcing (as the *who*) and the SDLC (as the *how*) are among the many ways to develop IT systems and offer your organization many advantages. But, as with everything, each advantage can also be a disadvantage. Table 9.1 highlights many of the advantages of insourcing and the SDLC and points out how these advantages can sometimes be disadvantages.

Ongoing Support

"Today, we couldn't survive without our new system. And we realize that, as our business changes, the system must change as well. So, we created a project maintenance team that meets every Friday to evaluate the effectiveness of the system, identify any changes, and assess whether the changes are worth making."

—Abigail Green ❖

TABLE 9.1 The Pros and Cons of Insourcing and the SDLC

Advantages	Disadvantages
Allows your organization to tailor a system to your exact needs.	It takes time to get exactly what you want.
Uses a structured step-by-step approach.	Some smaller projects suffer from a structured approach.
Creates a separation of duties among IT specialists (technical responsibility) and knowledge workers (business process responsibility).	IT specialists and knowledge workers speak different languages, which can create a communications gap.
Requires key deliverables before proceeding to the next step.	If you omit a requirement early, it can be costly to correct that mistake later.

Does that mean your organization should abandon insourcing and the SDLC and find better ways to develop systems? Absolutely not. In many instances, the best way to develop systems is to allow your organization's IT specialists to use a structured step-by-step approach. In other instances, though, alternative *who*'s and *how*'s are more appropriate.

CAREER OPPORTUNITY

In the remainder of this chapter, we explore two alternatives to the *who* question—selfsourcing and outsourcing. We also explore a number of alternatives to the *how* question. For you, the real key to success is the ability to determine which *who* and which *how* is most appropriate for a given systems development project.

Selfsourcing and Prototyping

Empowering Knowledge Workers to Develop Their Own Systems

Throughout this text, we've elaborated on the concept of knowledge worker computing—knowledge workers taking an active role in developing and using their own systems to support their efforts in personal and workgroup environments. What we want to look at now is how you, as a knowledge worker, go about developing systems, which we call selfsourcing. **Selfsourcing** (also called **knowledge worker development**) is the development and support of IT systems by knowledge workers with

Who	*How*				
	Traditional SDLC	**Prototyping**	**Application Software Packages**	**CASE**	**JAD**
Insource		✔			
Selfsource		✔			
Outsource					

*When you choose selfsourcing as the *who*, you'll most often employ a technique called prototyping as the *how*. So we introduce both in this section. You'll also find that prototyping is an excellent tool for insourcing. Read on to see how prototyping differs for insourcing and selfsourcing.

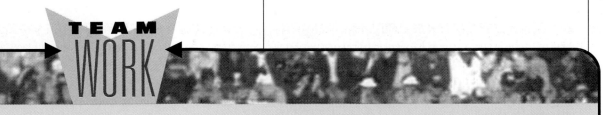

little or no help from IT specialists. So selfsourcing is simply one more aspect of knowledge worker computing.

You should understand that some selfsourcing projects still involve support from IT specialists. For example, Eaton Corp., located in Minnesota, actively encourages the selfsourcing of systems development in Lotus Notes by providing training classes to knowledge workers.[7] In these training classes knowledge workers learn how to set up a document database; use built-in templates to develop applications quickly; and create customized forms, views, and macros. And, when Eaton's knowledge workers actually begin creating their own systems, IT specialists are available to answer questions and handle more complicated technical issues, such as installing software on a client/server network or creating a local area network from scratch.

When a group of knowledge workers decides to create an IT system through selfsourcing, they most often employ a technique called prototyping, or building a model of the system before creating the final system. You'll also find that prototyping is a popular technique when IT specialists in your organization follow the SDLC. So, before we explore the steps in selfsourcing, let's take a look at prototyping.

Prototyping
Building Models

Prototyping is the process of building a model that demonstrates the features of a proposed product, service, or system. A ***prototype***, then, is simply a model of a proposed product, service, or system. If you think about it, people prototype all the time. Automobile manufacturers build prototypes of cars to demonstrate safety features, aerodynamics, and comfort. Building contractors construct models of homes and other structures to show layout and fire exits. Your instructor may give you sample test questions for an upcoming exam. These sample questions are a model of what you can expect.

In systems development, prototyping can be a valuable tool to you. Prototyping is an iterative process in which you build a model from basic requirements, have other knowledge workers review the prototype and suggest changes, and further refine and enhance the prototype to include suggestions. Most notably, prototyping is a dynamic process that allows knowledge workers to see, work with, and evaluate a model and suggest changes to that model to increase the likelihood of success of the proposed system.

You can use prototyping to perform a variety of functions in the systems development process. Some of these include the following:

Gathering requirements Prototyping is a great requirements gathering tool. You start by simply prototyping the basic systems requirements. Then you allow knowledge workers to add more requirements (information and processes) as you revise the prototype. Most people use prototyping for this purpose.

Helping determine requirements In many systems development processes, knowledge workers aren't sure what they really want—they simply know that the current system doesn't meet their needs. In this instance, you can use prototyping to help knowledge workers determine their exact requirements.

Proving that a system is technically feasible Let's face it, there are some things to which you cannot apply technology. And knowing whether you can is often unclear while scoping the proposed system— that's why scoping includes a technical feasibility review. If you're uncertain about whether

something can be done, prototype it first. A prototype you use to prove the technical feasibility of a proposed system is a **proof-of-concept prototype**.

Selling the idea of a proposed system Many people resist changes in IT. The current system seems to work fine and they see no reason to go through the process of developing and learning to use a new system. In this case, you have to convince them that the proposed system will be better than the current one. Because prototyping is relatively fast, you won't have to invest a lot of time to develop a prototype that can convince people of the worth of the proposed system. A prototype you use to convince people of the worth of a proposed system is a **selling prototype**.

The Prototyping Process

Prototyping is an excellent tool in systems development, as Thai Airways (discussed below) learned. However, who uses prototyping and for what purpose determines how the prototyping process occurs. Most often, IT specialists use prototyping in the SDLC to form a technical system blueprint. In selfsourcing, however, you can often continue to refine the prototype until it becomes the final system. The prototyping process for either case is almost the same; only the result differs. Figure 9.7 illustrates the difference between insourcing and selfsourcing prototyping. Regardless of *who* does the prototyping, the prototyping process involves four steps:

Thai Airways Uses Prototyping to Compete for International Flights

Two factors changing the landscape of business today are competition and globalization. Many organizations have more competition than ever before because competitors are emerging from countries across the world. For the airline industry, this simply means using technology in every way possible to compete effectively.

At Thai Airways, competing effectively with the larger, international airlines is always a key business goal. So, when several airlines introduced frequent flier programs and began taking business away from Thai Airways, it had no choice but to develop a frequent flier program of its own. The only problem was that Thai Airways needed the new system fast.

To develop the system quickly, IT specialists at Thai Airways built models, or prototypes, of the proposed system that demonstrated user interfaces, system functionality, and the information the new system would handle. After a few review sessions, Thai Airways had a working prototype of the system and was able to quickly develop the full system. Thanks to prototyping, Thai Airways is now using its frequent flier program to take customers away from larger airlines.[8] ❖

THE GLOBAL **PERSPECTIVE**

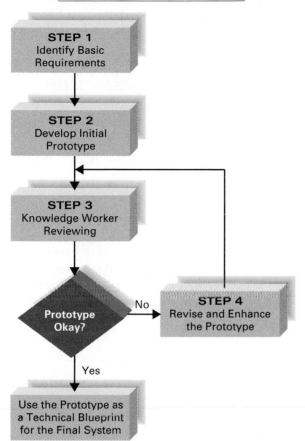

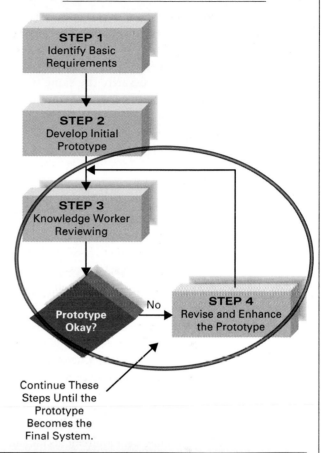

FIGURE 9.7

Prototyping Steps for Insourcing and Selfsourcing

❶ *Identify Basic Requirements* During the first step, you gather the basic requirements for a proposed system. These basic requirements include input and output information and, perhaps, some simple processes. At this point, however, you're typically unconcerned with editing rules, security issues, or end-of-period processing (for example, producing W-2s for a payroll system at the end of the year).

❷ *Develop Initial Prototype* Based on the basic requirements, you then set out to develop an initial prototype. Most often, your initial prototype will include only user interfaces, such as data entry screens and reports.

❸ *Knowledge Worker Reviewing* Step 3 starts the truly iterative process of prototyping. When knowledge workers first enter this step, they evaluate the prototype and suggest changes or additions. In subsequent returns to step 3 (after step 4), they evaluate new versions of the prototype. It's important to involve as many knowledge workers as possible during this step. This will help resolve any discrepancies in such areas as terminology and operational processes.

❹ *Revise and Enhance the Prototype* The final sequential step in the prototyping process is to revise and enhance the prototype according to any knowledge worker suggestions. In this step, you make changes to the current prototype and add any new requirements. Next, you return to step 3 and have the knowledge workers review the new prototype.

For either insourcing or selfsourcing, you continue the iterative processes of steps 3 and 4 until knowledge workers are happy with the prototype. What happens to the prototype after that, however, differs.

During selfsourcing, you're most likely to use the targeted application software package or application development tool to develop the prototype. This simply means that you can continually refine the prototype until it becomes the final working system. For example, if you choose to develop a customer service application using

Lotus Notes, you can prototype many of the operational features using Lotus Notes development tools. Because you develop these prototypes using the targeted application development environment, your prototype can eventually become the final system.

That process is not necessarily the same when insourcing. Most often, IT specialists develop prototypes using special prototyping development tools. Many of these tools don't support the creation of a final system—you simply use them to build prototypes. Therefore, the finished prototype becomes a blueprint or technical design for the final system. In the appropriate stages of the SDLC, IT specialists will implement the prototypes in another application development environment better suited to the development of production systems.

The Advantages of Prototyping

Encourages active knowledge worker participation First and foremost, prototyping encourages knowledge workers to actively participate in the development process. As opposed to interviewing and the reviewing of documentation, prototyping allows knowledge workers to see and work with working models of the proposed system.

Helps resolve discrepancies among knowledge workers During the prototyping process, many knowledge workers participate in defining the requirements for and reviewing the prototype. The "many" is key. If several knowledge workers participate in prototyping, you'll find it's much easier to resolve any discrepancies the knowledge workers may encounter.

Gives knowledge workers a feel for the final system Prototyping, especially for user interfaces, provides a feel for how the final system will look, feel, and work. When knowledge workers understand the look, feel, and working of the final system, they are more apt to determine its potential for success.

Helps determine technical feasibility Proof-of-concept prototypes are great for determining the technical feasibility of a proposed system.

Helps sell the idea of a proposed system Finally, selling prototypes can help break down resistance barriers. Many people don't want new systems because the old one seems to work just fine, and they're afraid the new system won't meet their expectations and work properly. If you provide them with a working prototype that proves the new system will be successful, they will be more inclined to buy into it.

The Disadvantages of Prototyping

Leads people to believe the final system will follow shortly When a prototype is complete, many people believe that the final system will follow shortly. After all, they've seen the system at work in the form of a prototype, how long can it take to bring the system into production? Unfortunately, it may take months or years. You need to be sure that people understand that the prototype is only a model—not the final system missing only a few simple bells and whistles.

Gives no indication of performance under operational conditions Prototypes very seldom take all operational conditions into consideration. This problem surfaced for the Department of Motor Vehicles in a state on the East Coast.[9] During prototyping, the system—which handled motor vehicle and driver registration for the entire state—worked fine for 20 workstations at two locations. When the system was finally installed for all locations (which included over 1,200 workstations), the system spent all its time just managing communications traffic—it had absolutely no time to complete any transactions. This is potentially the most significant drawback to prototyping. You must prototype operational conditions as well as interfaces and processes.

Leads the project team to forgo proper testing and documentation You must thoroughly test and document all new systems. Unfortunately, many people believe they can forgo testing and documentation when using prototyping. After all, they've tested the prototype, and why not use the prototype as the documentation for the system? Don't make this mistake.

Again, prototyping is most probably a tool that you will use to develop many knowledge worker computing systems. Let's now take a look at the set of steps you would go through to develop a knowledge worker computing system using prototyping.

The Selfsourcing Process

You can probably create most smaller knowledge worker computing systems in a matter of hours, such as interfacing a letter in a word processing package and a customer database. More complicated systems, however, require that you follow some sort of formal process during development. Next we describe the steps for the selfsourcing process of more complicated systems (see Figure 9.8), and in the box on page 383 we summarize the key tasks

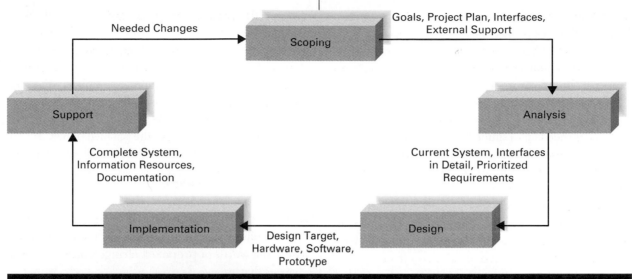

FIGURE 9.8

The Selfsourcing Process

within each selfsourcing step. As you will see, selfsourcing is very similar to the steps of the SDLC.

Step 1: Scoping

During step 1 of selfsourcing—*scoping*—you perform many of the same tasks as in the SDLC. These tasks include defining the problem and the goals of the new system, identifying any systems that require an interface,

and creating a project plan. You must also determine what type of external support you need. In spite of the fact that you believe you (or your group) won't need any help from IT specialists, that may not be true. This, especially, may not be true if you're developing an application that must run across a network. If you can clearly define what external support you need now, you can probably find IT specialists to help.

Key Tasks in Selfsourcing

Step 1: Scoping

- Define the goals of the new system
- Create a project plan
- Identify any systems that require an interface
- Determine what type of external support you will require

Step 2: Analysis

- Study and model the current system
- Understand the interfaces in detail
- Define and prioritize your requirements

Step 3: Design

- Select a design target (hardware and software)
- Acquire the necessary hardware and software
- Develop an initial prototype

Step 4: Implementation

- Fully develop the prototype into a complete system
- Test the new system
- Train
- Convert to the new system
- Completely document the system

Step 5: Support

- Provide ongoing maintenance ❖

Step 2: Analysis

In step 2 of selfsourcing—*analysis*—your tasks remain similar to those while using the SDLC. That is, you must still study and model the current system and explore any necessary interfaces in great detail. At this point, you should also prioritize your requirements for the new system. Most selfsourcing systems do not and cannot meet every single need. It's a simple fact—although tools, such as Lotus Notes and other groupware packages, are quite powerful, they may not be able to do everything you need. Additionally, you may not have the time to spend on the development of a new system that meets your every need. If you carefully prioritize your requirements now, you'll be better prepared to make trade-offs later.

Step 3: Design

During step 3—*design*—you begin the prototyping process. But first you need to select the software you'll use to create your system and the hardware on which it will reside. This may, of course, involve purchasing, installing, and testing new hardware. Once you've done this, you begin the prototyping process. At this point, you simply create a working model to assure that you can develop the new system.

Step 4: Implementation

During step 4—*implementation*—you continue the prototyping process by allowing other knowledge workers to review the prototype and make suggestions or changes. You then incorporate those changes into the prototype and go through the review process again. Once everyone is completely happy with the new system (which is the prototype in its final form), you must completely test and document the new system, as well as provide training and convert to the new system. As in the SDLC, you can convert to the new system using the parallel, plunge, piecemeal, or pilot methods or some combination of the four.

Step 5: Support

The final step of selfsourcing is *support,* which is the same for the SDLC. During this step, it's your sole responsibility to continually monitor the new system, assess the worth of proposed changes, and make any changes that are necessary.

The Advantages of Selfsourcing

Improves requirements determination During insourcing, knowledge workers tell IT specialists what they want. In selfsourcing, knowledge workers essentially tell themselves what they want. This greatly improves the effectiveness of capturing requirements, which helps ensure the success of the new system.

Increases knowledge worker participation and sense of ownership No matter what you do, if you do it yourself, you always take more pride in the result. The same

Time Warner Lets Knowledge Workers Develop Property Tax Returns

Like many organizations, Time Warner Cable operates in almost every state in the United States. Within each state, Time Warner also operates in numerous counties. For each county within each state, Time Warner has different requirements for filing property tax returns. For example, some counties charge fees that increase with property utilization per square foot; other counties charge according to levels of revenues; and still other counties require quarterly or yearly tax returns. And, as you might well guess, property tax return requirements change almost every year for each county.

To stay on top of its property tax return system, Time Warner has turned over development and support to knowledge workers. Using Lotus 1-2-3 (with templates and macros), knowledge workers develop and support a property tax return system unique to the county for which each worker is responsible. For Time Warner, the most important step is to regularly review these spreadsheets to make sure they work correctly and file tax returns according to new county codes.

If your organization has a system that changes frequently or contains unique features (such as different requirements according to counties within states), you might want to consider letting knowledge workers develop and support it. Often, selfsourcing can react to changes much more quickly than insourcing. ❖

is true when developing an IT system through selfsourcing. If knowledge workers know that they own the system because they developed and now support it, they are more apt to actively participate in its development and have a greater sense of ownership.

Increases speed of systems development Many small systems do not lend themselves well to insourcing. These smaller systems may suffer from "analysis paralysis" because they don't require a structured step-by-step approach to their development. In fact, insourcing may be slower than selfsourcing for smaller projects.

Potential Pitfalls and Risks of Selfsourcing

Inadequate knowledge worker expertise leads to inadequately developed systems Many selfsourcing systems are never completed because knowledge workers lack the real expertise with IT tools to develop a complete and fully working system. It may seem like no big deal. The system couldn't have been that important if the people who needed it never finished developing it. But that's not true. If knowledge workers choose to develop their systems, they must spend time away from their primary duties within the organization. This diverted time may mean lost revenue.

Lack of organizational focus creates "privatized" IT systems Many selfsourcing projects are done outside the IT systems plan of an organization. This simply means that there may be many "private" IT systems that do not interface with other systems and possess uncontrolled and duplicated information. These types of systems serve no meaningful purpose in an organization and can only lead to more problems.

Insufficient analysis of design alternatives leads to subpar IT systems Some knowledge workers jump to immediate conclusions about the hardware and software they should use without carefully analyzing all the possible alternatives. If this happens, knowledge workers may develop systems that are processing inefficient.

CAREER OPPORTUNITY

Managing selfsourcing when other knowledge workers perform it is vitally important. But so is managing selfsourcing when you're the knowledge worker doing the developing. Make sure that **you** follow a good set of steps and the guidelines set forth by your organization. No matter what you think, you are not immune to the potential pitfalls and risks of selfsourcing.

Lack of documentation and external support leads to short-lived systems When knowledge workers develop systems, they often forgo documentation of how the system works and fail to realize that they can expect little or no support from IT specialists. All systems—no matter who develops them—must change over time. Knowledge workers must realize that those changes are their responsibility. They also need to realize that making those changes is easier if they document the system well.

Outsourcing
Going Outside for Technology and Systems Development

In 1995, Merrill Lynch hired Sybase Inc. for $10 million to overhaul its IT infrastructure.[10] Sybase's recommended system, Trusted Global Advisor (TGA), allows

	How				
Who	**Traditional SDLC**	**Prototyping**	**Application Software Packages**	**CASE**	**JAD**
Insource					
Selfsource					
Outsource			✔		

*When you choose outsourcing as the *who,* you're not really concerned about *how* that organization develops a system, even if it has to develop the system from scratch. When outsourcing, however, you can find prewritten application software packages that automate common business functions.

Merrill Lynch's 25,000 retail brokers to sell small customers sophisticated financial products that have previously been available only to large financial traders. The new system lets the brokers access all subsystems, including client profiles, financial planning tools, and order entry. The new system even supports fax and e-mail capabilities, so Merrill Lynch can automatically send copies of research reports to all its clients.

Merrill Lynch's choice of *who* to develop an IT system is an example of outsourcing. Simply put, ***outsourcing*** is the delegation of specific work to a third party for a specified length of time, at a specified cost, and at a specified level of service. In the case of Merrill Lynch, it chose to outsource the overhaul of its IT systems to Sybase. IT outsourcing today represents a significant opportunity for your organization to capitalize on the intellectual resources of other organizations by having them take over and perform certain business functions in which they have more expertise than you. Outsourcing is becoming so big in the IT area that revenues from IT-related outsourcing are expected to exceed $120 billion in the year 2000 (up from $80 billion in 1995).[11] According to a 1996 Yankee Group survey of 500 companies, 90 percent have outsourced at least one major business function and 45 percent have outsourced some major portion of their IT environments.[12]

As your organization considers the possibility of outsourcing in systems development, you'll find that outsourcing takes on one of three forms (see Figure 9.9). First, many organizations will simply choose to purchase existing application software packages that automate common business functions instead of developing them through insourcing. These types of application software packages may differ from what you think. In this particular instance, we're not talking about personal productivity software or accounting software you can buy at a local computer store. We're talking about large software packages that may cost as much as a half million dollars.

Second, some organizations may find that existing application software packages meet only some of their requirements. In this instance, these organizations will ask the software manufacturer to make certain modifications. Finally, other organizations will outsource the development of entirely new systems for which no application software currently exists. Whatever the case, outsourcing is an integral part of the strategic plan of most organizations today, and much of this future outsourcing will take place in systems development.

The Outsourcing Process

The outsourcing process is similar to the SDLC, except that you turn over much of the design, implementation, and support steps to another organization. As with all other systems development efforts, your organization begins with planning (step 1), in which you identify what systems need to be developed and their respective time

1. Purchase an existing application software package.

2. Purchase an existing application software package and request modifications.

YOUR ORGANIZATION

3. Outsource the development of an entirely new system for which no application software package exists.

FIGURE 9.9

Major Forms of Outsourcing Systems Development

Want to Reduce Your Inventory? Buy Software

In manufacturing, the cost of inventory is much more than just a simple summation of the parts you have on hand multiplied by their value. Inventory costs also include *carrying costs*—the cost to order inventory, the cost to move inventory, the cost of warehouses, the cost of utilities and insurance, and so on. And those carrying costs can represent as much as 25 percent of your total inventory costs.

That's a real problem for most manufacturers, even further compounded by the fact that manufacturing processes—which include material requirements planning and production scheduling—often have a difficult time maximizing on the order in which production should occur. So, many manufacturers are turning to complex computer programs that optimize production processes. But those manufacturers aren't developing their own systems; instead, they're purchasing software from outside vendors.

One such vendor is i2, a company that has developed a $500,000 software package called Rhythm. Solectron Corp., for example, purchased Rhythm and credits it with moving inventory 30 percent faster and reducing carrying costs by 25 percent. Timken Steel is another company that purchased the same software. For Timken, Rhythm has cut inventory levels by 30 percent, cut production cycle times in half, and improved on-time delivery of finished products by 25 percent.

If your organization needs new software for whatever reason, seriously search the software market for what you need. You might just find it, and it might save your organization a lot of money.[13] ❖

---

frames for development. Below, we describe the remaining steps of the outsourcing process.

Select a Target System

During step 2 of the SDLC—*scoping*—your goal is to lay the groundwork for the development of a proposed system. During that time, your project team performs an initial feasibility review, looking to assess the proposed system in terms of time, cost, and technical feasibility. If you find that a proposed system is unfeasible for some reason, then it becomes a possible candidate for outsourcing. For example, if you determine that your organization doesn't possess the necessary technical expertise for a proposed system or that time doesn't permit insourcing its development, outsourcing may be a possibility. You may also find that it's simply cheaper to outsource than it is to insource the development of a proposed system. You may also know of application software packages that perform the same functions as your proposed system. Whatever the case, during this step in the outsourcing process you select a target system for potential outsourcing.

Establish Logical Requirements

Regardless of your choice of insourcing or outsourcing, you must still perform step 3 of the SDLC—*analysis*—or establishing the logical requirements for the proposed system. If you choose to outsource, the statement of your logical requirements becomes the foundation of your request for proposal.

Develop a Request for Proposal

Outsourcing involves telling another organization what you want. *What you want* is essentially the logical requirements for a proposed system, and you convey that information by developing a request for proposal. A *request for proposal (RFP)* is a formal document that outlines your logical requirements for the proposed system and invites outsourcing organizations (which we'll refer to as "vendors") to submit bids for its development. An RFP is the most important document in the outsourcing process. For systems of great size, your organization may create an RFP that's literally hundreds of pages long and requires months of work. It's vitally important that you take all the time you need to create a complete and thorough RFP. Eventually, your RFP will become the foundation for a legal and binding contract into which your organization and the vendor will enter. At a minimum, your RFP should contain the elements in Figure 9.10. We briefly describe some of the important aspects of an RFP below.

Problem statement Why your organization wants a new system, including why the current system does not meet your needs.

Description of current system Underlying business processes that the current system supports, the current hardware and software, information that the current system works with, and a description of the systems to which the new system must interface.

Description of proposed system A logical (as opposed to physical) description of the system you want—what new processes the system must support and what information the system must be able to work with.

Request for support plan How and when you want the vendor to perform software and hardware maintenance.

Request for development time frame A detailed time frame showing when the vendor will complete various portions of the development. You would also include a statement of when your organization needs the development completed.

Request for statement of outsourcing costs A detailed and thorough statement of the outsourcing costs.

How RFP returns will be scored How you'll score the RFP returns in terms of what new processes and information are most important. Here you can simply list what processes and information are required, which ones would be nice, and those that are optional.

Deadline for RFP returns A final date by which you will accept RFP returns. In most instances, you'll want to give vendors anywhere from 60 to 180 days to provide a response.

All this information is vitally important to both your organization and the vendors. For your organization, the ability to develop a complete and thorough RFP means that you completely understand what you have and what you want. For the vendors, a complete and thorough RFP makes it easier to identify a proposed system that will meet most, if not all, your needs.

Evaluate Request for Proposal Returns and Choose a Vendor

Your next task in outsourcing is to evaluate the RFP returns and choose a vendor. You perform the evaluation of the RFP returns according to the scoring method you identified in the RFP. Evaluating RFP returns is seldom a simple process. No two vendors will ever provide RFP returns in the same format. And the RFP returns you receive will almost always be longer than the RFP itself.

Once you've thoroughly analyzed the RFP returns, it's time to rank them and determine which vendor to

❶ Organizational overview

❷ Problem statement

❸ Description of current system
    3.1 Underlying business processes
    3.2 Hardware
    3.3 Software (application and system)
    3.4 System processes
    3.5 Information
    3.6 System interfaces

❹ Description of proposed system
    4.1 New processes
    4.2 New information

❺ Request for new system design
    5.1 Hardware
    5.2 Software
    5.3 Underlying business processes
    5.4 System processes
    5.5 Information
    5.6 System interfaces

❻ Request for implementation plan
    6.1 Training
    6.2 Conversion

❼ Request for support plan
    7.1 Hardware
    7.2 Software

❽ Request for development time frame

❾ Request for statement of outsourcing costs

❿ How RFP returns will be scored

⓫ Deadline for RFP returns

⓬ Primary contact person

FIGURE 9.10

Outline of a Request for Proposal (RFP)

use. Most often, you rank RFP returns according to cost, time, and the scoring mechanism you identified. Again, ranking RFP returns is not simple. One vendor may be the cheapest, but requires the longest time to develop the new system. Another vendor may be able to provide a system quickly, but without some of the features you identified as critical. Other important factors to consider when choosing a vendor relate to the vendors themselves. That is, you'll want to consider how long they've been in business, quality of references from other companies for whom the vendors have worked, and how many projects they've completed that relate to yours. You must carefully weigh these intangible considerations when choosing a vendor.

A Request for Proposal and the Systems Development Life Cycle

If you review Figure 9.10 on the previous page closely, you'll notice that an RFP looks very similar to the steps of the SDLC. In the table below, identify which steps of the SDLC correspond to each element of an RFP. ❖

Elements of a Request for Proposal	Step(s) of the SDLC
1. Organizational overview	
2. Problem statement	
3. Description of current system	
4. Description of proposed system	
5. Request for new system design	
6. Request for implementation plan	
7. Request for support plan	
8. Request for development time frame	
9. Request for statement of outsourcing costs	
10. How RFP returns will be scored	
11. Deadline for RFP returns	
12. Primary contact person	

Once you've chosen the vendor, a lengthy and legal process follows. Outsourcing is serious business—and serious business between two organizations almost always requires a lot of negotiating and the use of lawyers. Eventually, your organization has to enter into a legal and binding contract that very explicitly states the features of the proposed system, the exact costs, the time frame for development, acceptance criteria, and criteria for breaking the contract for nonperformance or noncompliance.

Test and Accept Solution

As with all systems, testing and accepting the solution is vitally important. Once a vendor installs the new system, it's up to you and your organization to thoroughly test the solution before accepting it. This alone may involve months of running the new system while operating the old one (the parallel conversion method).

When you "accept" a solution, you're saying that the system performs to your expectations and that the vendor has met its contract obligations so far. Accepting a solution involves "signing off" on the system, which releases the vendor from any further development efforts or modifications to the system. Be careful when you do this—modifications to the system after sign-off can be extremely expensive. In 1996, Duke Power Co., a utility company based in Charlotte, North Carolina, continually tested but never accepted an outsourced system.[14] Duke officially turned the lights out on a $23 million customer information systems project after investing over $12 million in its development. Duke Power outsourced the development of the customer information system and had no choice but to terminate the project when the vendor requested an additional 2 years to make necessary modifications.

Monitor and Reevaluate

Just like systems you develop using the SDLC, systems you obtain through outsourcing need constant monitoring and reevaluation. In outsourcing, you also have to reassess your working relationship with the vendor. Is the vendor providing maintenance when you need it and according to the contract? Does the system really perform the stated functions? Do month-end and year-end processes work according to your desires? Does the vendor provide acceptable support if something goes wrong? These are all important questions that affect the success

Creating Outsourcing Alliances to Avoid Finger-Pointing

THE GLOBAL PERSPECTIVE

It happens all the time—someone always blames someone else for the problem. If you've ever purchased a computer and had a problem with a piece of application software that wouldn't print correctly, you've probably encountered this. The application software manufacturer may tell you it's a printer problem. The printer manufacturer may tell you it's a problem with your operating system. And the operating system manufacturer may very well tell you that the application software is to blame.

This type of problem is common for organizations that outsource different functions to different vendors—especially for IT systems development. J. P. Morgan, a worldwide investment banking organization, didn't want that to happen.

So it entered into a 7-year, $2 billion outsourcing agreement with Pinnacle Alliance. What's really interesting is that Pinnacle Alliance is a combination of Computer Sciences Corp., AT&T Solutions, Andersen Consulting, and Bell Atlantic Network Integration. Each of these organizations brings special expertise to the alliance and promises not to do any finger-pointing when a problem occurs.

The four organizations in Pinnacle Alliance will work together to develop new systems for J. P. Morgan. In the outsourcing environment, these organizations compete head-to-head for outsourcing contracts. For J. P. Morgan, however, they've pooled their resources to take part in one of the richest outsourcing deals ever.[15] ❖

of your outsourcing efforts. The most important question, though, is, "Does the system still meet our needs and how much does it cost to update the system?" In many outsourcing instances, if the system needs updating you must contract with the original vendor. This is potentially one of the greatest drawbacks to outsourcing. When you outsource a system, you create a heavy dependency on that vendor to provide updates to the system, and updates are not inexpensive.

The Advantages and Disadvantages of Outsourcing

Throughout our discussions of outsourcing, we've directly or indirectly described many of the advantages and disadvantages of outsourcing. Below we summarize the major advantages and disadvantages of outsourcing the systems development process.

■ **Advantages: Allows your organization to**

Focus on Unique Core Competencies By outsourcing systems development efforts that support noncritical business functions, your organization can focus on developing systems that support important, unique core competencies.

Exploit the Intellect of Another Organization Outsourcing allows your organization to obtain intellectual capital by purchasing it from another organization. Says John Halvey, a partner specializing in outsourcing deals at the law firm Millbank, Tweed, Hadley, and McCloy, "People want to buy knowledge, not develop it themselves."[16]

Better Predict Future Costs When you outsource a function, whether systems development or some other business function, you know the exact costs. Zale Corp., a discount jewelry store, outsourced some of its IT systems and tied payments to the vendor according to how well Zale's stores perform.[17] After all, the new IT systems will affect a store's performance, so why not tie a vendor's payment to it?

Acquire Leading-Edge Technology Outsourcing allows your organization to acquire leading-edge technology without technical expertise and the inherent risks of choosing the wrong technology.

Reduce Costs Outsourcing is often seen as a money saver for most organizations. And, indeed, reducing costs is one of the important reasons organizations outsource.

Improve Performance Accountability Outsourcing involves delegating work to another organization at a specified level of service. Your organization can use this specified level of service as leverage to guarantee that it gets exactly what it wants from the vendor.

- **Disadvantages: Your organization may suffer from outsourcing because it**

Reduces Technical Know-How for Future Innovation Outsourcing is a way of exploiting the intellect of another organization. It may also mean that your organization will no longer possess that expertise internally. If you outsource because you don't have the necessary technical expertise today, you'll probably have to outsource for the same reason tomorrow.

Reduces Degree of Control Outsourcing means giving up control. No matter what you choose to outsource, you are in some way giving up control over that function.

Increases Vulnerability of Strategic Information Outsourcing systems development involves telling another organization what information you use and how you use that information. In doing so, you could be giving away strategic information and secrets.

Increases Dependency on Other Organizations As soon as you start outsourcing, you immediately begin depending on another organization to perform many of your business functions. For example, GE was set to introduce a new washing machine—but it didn't happen on time.[18] It seems that GE outsourced some of its parts development and the vendor was late, resulting in a delayed product introduction that cost GE money.

CAREER OPPORTUNITY

Why is it important for you to understand the outsourcing process? Two reasons. First, outsourcing is a part of most organizations today, including yours. Second, outsourcing probably means more work for you, and you should be aware of this. If you choose outsourcing, you'll still be responsible for tasks such as providing key information about the current system and the requirements of the new system. You'll also be responsible for outsourcing-related tasks such as creating an RFP, evaluating RFP returns, and choosing a vendor.

INDUSTRY PERSPECTIVE **Financial Services**

Outsourcing the Availability, Speed, and Security of a Network

In Chapter 6 we discussed a vitally important aspect of network technologies—ownership. Within network ownership, your organization can choose from a variety of options, including public, private, value-added, and virtual private. With the exception of a private network, all these options

basically amount to outsourcing some or all your networking and telecommunications needs.

And, no matter how big or small, most organizations are choosing to outsource their telecommunications needs. Consider MasterCard International. MasterCard's network supports the following astounding numbers:

- 22,000 financial institutions in 30 countries
- Settlement of $500 million per day on the average in credit and debit card transactions

- Over 16 million transactions on its busiest days during December
- Almost 11 million transactions on a typical day

But MasterCard's primary business isn't telecommunications, so it has outsourced the development and maintenance of its network to AT&T Solutions. MasterCard's network is thus a *virtual private network,* one on which AT&T always guarantees availability, speed, and security.[19] ❖

Other Tools and Methods for Supporting the Systems Development Process

Up to this point, we've looked at three of the many *how*'s for developing systems—the traditional SDLC, prototyping, and application software packages. And, indeed, these are just three of the *how*'s for developing systems. No matter the group of people responsible for the development of a system, there are a variety of other tools and methods that they can use. In this section, we highlight two new *how*'s—computer-aided software engineering tools and joint application development. Both are widely used in many organizations today and deserve some explanation.

Computer-Aided Software Engineering

Software for Automating the Development of Software

Suppose you're required to create a graph. Could you do it yourself with pencil and paper? Certainly. And, if you did, you would be creating a graph *manually*. Most people, however, would prefer to use spreadsheet software, such as Lotus 1-2-3 or Excel. Spreadsheet software basically makes you more efficient by automating the tasks or sets of steps you must perform. Consider these examples of efficiency:

- By organizing your information in cells, you can quickly reference those cells to specify the graph parameters.

- If you find that your graph doesn't contain the correct information, you don't have to change the graph. You simply change the information, and the spreadsheet software automatically regenerates the graph for you.

- With a few clicks of the mouse, you can easily change the graph type, its appearance, and rotation.

- Because you save the information in a file, you can easily use it for other purposes, such as including it in a budget proposal.

Now think about the SDLC. That process is nothing more than a set of steps. It starts with determining the problem and developing a plan for proceeding; moves through gathering logical requirements and converting them into a technical design; converts the technical design into software (part of implementation); and, finally, supports the system. Until recently, developing systems using the SDLC was a manual process. Today, however, ***computer-aided software engineering (CASE) tools*** are available that automate some or all steps in the SDLC.

CASE tools support your systems development efforts in two major ways. First, they help you model and store information pertinent to a specific system. This gives you the flexibility to easily change the information if changes occur in the business environment. Second, CASE tools help you perform the systems development tasks of converting information to a new form. For example, once you've built the technical design for a new system (including screen and report layouts, the data dictionary and database E-R diagram, and the processes the software must perform), CASE tools can automatically create the software and information resources that support those elements. Many CASE tools can perform these conversions in a matter of minutes, and the software contains no bugs and works exactly as you specified. Of course, you still have to test the software to make sure it meets your logical requirements.

Your organization can use CASE tools to develop a variety of systems. For example, Cinergy Corporation

| | How | | | | |
Who	**Traditional SDLC**	**Prototyping**	**Application Software Packages**	**CASE**	**JAD**
Insource				✔	
Selfsource					
Outsource					

*When you choose a computer-aided software engineering tool as the *how*, you've also chosen insourcing as the *who*. Read on to learn why.

(a utility company in the midwest) recently used a CASE tool to develop a system to help manage its coal-purchasing activity.[20] Cinergy's coal-purchasing system is a client/server system, supports managers as they make decisions regarding coal-purchasing contracts (which means it's a decision support system), and supports online transaction processing (which also means it's a form of a transaction processing system).

Categories of CASE Tools and Their Components

You can categorize CASE tools in three ways. These categories include

- *Integrated CASE tools,* which support the entire SDLC
- *Upper CASE tools,* which support the front-end steps of the SDLC, including planning, scoping, analysis, and design
- *Lower CASE tools,* which support the back-end steps of the SDLC, including design, implementation, and support

As you can see, integrated CASE tools contain six components, one for each step in the SDLC. Upper CASE tools contain four components that support the planning,

INTEGRATED CASE TOOLS HELP YOU

1. Model your entire organization
   - Structure
   - Divisions and departments
   - Goals
   - Processes and information

2. Generate systems based on your organizational model

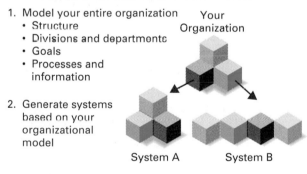

3. Make changes to your organizational model

4. Regenerate systems based on your new organizational model

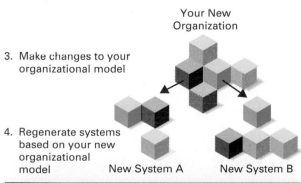

FIGURE 9.11
Integrated CASE Tools Focus— Your Entire Organization

scoping, analysis, and design steps. Lower CASE tools contain three components that support design, implementation, and support. Regardless of the CASE tool your organization chooses, it will always contain one other significant component—a project repository. A ***project repository*** is a database that contains information pertaining to all the systems development projects that your organization has undertaken using the CASE tool. This information can include project plans, logical systems requirements, proposed technical solutions, and any other form of documentation relating to systems development projects.

The goal of an integrated CASE tool is to support your systems development efforts as your organization changes (see Figure 9.11). It's simple—if your organization changes, you use an integrated CASE tool to make changes to your organizational model. The CASE tool then uses those changes to help you create new systems or make changes to existing systems. So, as your organization changes, you don't simply react by changing a single system or developing a specific new system. Instead, you use an integrated CASE tool to model your organizational changes and then allow it to help you make modifications to systems across your organization. Let's briefly examine how an integrated CASE tool supports all the steps in the SDLC (see Figure 9.12).

Step 1: Planning
During planning, CASE tools help you model information concerning the goals and objectives of your organization, the current IT infrastructure, the IT systems plan, the structure of your organization, and current information and processes within your organization. Many CASE tools specifically support one of the many planning methodologies we introduced in Chapter 8. Once you've defined all this information, the CASE tool stores it in the project repository, allowing you to work with that information for any specific systems development project.

Step 2: Scoping
During scoping, CASE tools help you capture and work with any information relating to the groundwork for the development of a specific system, including the problem statement, goals of the new system, required interfaces, the feasibility review, project team members, and the project plan. Later, if you find that a project is going to cost more than originally proposed, you can return to the feasibility review (in the project repository), provide the new costs, and reevaluate the project. CASE tools are also particularly helpful in building a project plan by offering you many different automated project planning and management tools.

- Goals and Objectives of Your Organization
- Current IT Infrastructure
- IT Systems Plan
- Organizational Structure
- Current Information and Processes

- Problem Statement
- Goals of the New System
- Interface Requirements
- Feasibility Review
- Project Team
- Project Plan

- Model of Current System, Processes, and Information
- New Information and Processes
- Model of New System, Processes, and Information

- Technical Alternatives of the System
- Detailed Specifications of How the Software Should Work
- Screen and Report Designs
- Database and File Layouts

- Generate Software Automatically from Detailed Design Documents
- Generate Test Data
- Debug a System and Find Mistakes

- Regenerate Software After Changing Design Specifications
- Reverse-Engineer Old Systems to Support Changes

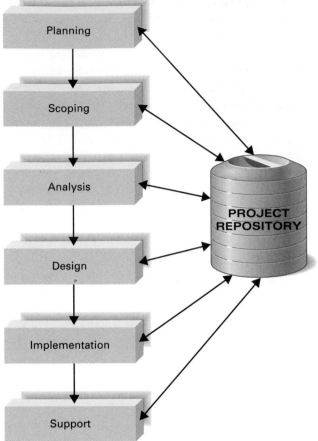

FIGURE 9.12

CASE Tool Support for the Systems Development Life Cycle

Step 3: Analysis

During analysis, CASE tools help you model and capture the logical requirements for a proposed system and any new information and processes that must be present. The advantage of using CASE tools at this point is that many of them provide analytical capabilities for evaluating the completeness and correctness of your models. For example, if you define a process that retrieves a part cost from a database, the CASE tool will verify that you have created a data dictionary for that element.

Step 4: Design

In this step, CASE tools help you model and capture technical alternatives for the proposed solution and generate detailed specifications concerning how the software should work. As in analysis, CASE tools provide capabilities to help you ensure that a proposed technical solution meets the logical requirements. During design, CASE tools also have facilities that help you build sample screens and reports and documentation concerning database and file layouts.

Step 5: Implementation

During implementation, organizations spend more time and money on programming than on any other task. Fortunately, most CASE tools use detailed design documents to automatically generate software. This alone substantially reduces the time it takes to complete the systems development process. And, if you find that a certain detail was omitted or incorrectly defined, you simply change the design specification and let the CASE tool regenerate the software (similar to using a spreadsheet to regenerate a graph with new information). CASE tools will also help you generate test data and provide mechanisms that support a programmer's need to debug a system and find mistakes.

Step 6: Support

In the final step, CASE tools help during the support step in two ways. First, if your organization developed an existing system using a CASE tool, it becomes relatively simple to react to changes. All that's necessary is to change the design specifications and then regenerate the software. Second, if an existing system was not developed using a CASE tool, you can still use a CASE tool to make modifications. First, the CASE tool will perform *reverse engineering*, or analyze the existing software and create design specifications from it. Second, you then make changes to the design specifications. Finally, you have the CASE tool regenerate the software.

The Advantages of CASE Tools

CASE tools, regardless of category, offer significant advantages over the manually performed SDLC. Some of these advantages follow.

Increased speed and efficiency of SDLC First and foremost, CASE tools increase the speed and efficiency of the SDLC. Many organizations have been able to dramatically reduce systems development time by using CASE tools. For example, once you develop the design documents for a system, some CASE tools can automatically generate the software. This alone may save thousands of hours of programming and debugging.

Repository of project information By creating a repository of project information, CASE tools help you completely capture and record all information concerning a system. Not only that, you can use information concerning a previous system when developing a new one. That way, you don't have to "reinvent the wheel" each time.

Valuable control checking Because CASE tools automate much of the SDLC, they also provide many valuable control mechanisms. As we discussed earlier, CASE tools can ensure that you have defined information in a data dictionary if a certain process uses it.

Deployment of systems across multiple platforms Most CASE tools can help you develop systems that work on a variety of platforms. For example, you can document a single system and then have the CASE tool generate the software for a UNIX-based operating environment on Apple Macs and for a Windows-based operating environment on IBMs. Most CASE tools will generate software in a variety of programming languages, including C, C++, FORTRAN, and COBOL.

The Reality of CASE Tools

Your organization will realize many benefits from using CASE tools. Nonetheless, you need to understand that CASE tools are not a systems development panacea. They work well only if your organization uses them correctly. Below is a list of things you should keep in mind when using CASE tools.

You must still have a solid background in analysis and design Using a CASE tool doesn't mean that you don't need essential skills in systems analysis and design. As Maurice Frank puts it, "A CASE tool is like a word

---

processor. If you don't know how to write, not even the richest feature set will turn you into a Shakespeare. Even the best CASE tool cannot turn you into a great systems designer if you don't understand the basics of analysis and design."[22]

CASE tools are not for knowledge workers CASE tools are quite complicated to use and quite complicated to learn. As a result, your organization should leave the use of CASE tools to IT specialists. That's why we say that CASE tools as the *how* goes with insourcing as the *who*.

CAREER OPPORTUNITY

Your role as a knowledge worker during the SDLC does not change just because IT specialists choose to use a CASE tool. Your roles are essentially the same as they would be if your organization were following the manual SDLC. You're still a business process expert, liaison to the customer, quality control analyst, and manager of other people. It's difficult to comprehend the true function and performance of CASE tools unless you see them in action. If you'd like to learn more about CASE tools, including some of the more popular ones and their capabilities, connect to our Web site. Select "Systems Development," and choose "CASE Tools."

You must spend more time in front-end processes CASE tools offer significant time savings in the latter steps of the SDLC. However, you will only realize those time savings if you're willing to spend more time during analysis and design. CASE tools cannot generate software from incomplete, ambiguous, or incorrect specifications. You must be willing to spend the time up front during the SDLC to realize the benefits later.

Integrated CASE tools require a detailed organizational understanding Integrated CASE tools require that you have a complete, detailed, and thorough understanding of your entire organization. Not only that, they require that you constantly update your organizational model as changes occur.

Joint Application Development
Defining and Building Systems as a Team

In many systems development projects, you'll hear knowledge workers say, "Computer people simply don't understand business processes. How can they develop an IT system for me if they don't understand what I do?" You'll also hear IT people say, "Knowledge workers simply don't understand how technology works. It's impossible to design a system for them when they don't even understand how it will work." Sounds like some pretty harsh statements. Unfortunately, you all too often hear those when organizations use the SDLC (and insourcing) to develop systems. This communications gap between knowledge workers and IT specialists is perhaps the single most important reason the SDLC produces incorrect systems. Just think about this: If you tell an IT specialist what you want and that person doesn't understand you, can you expect a system that meets your needs? If the system doesn't meet your needs, how much more time and money will your organization spend to correct the system? If you've been burned once by this communications gap, how excited will you be to actively participate in the SDLC again?

Is there a solution to this communications problem? What can you do to communicate more effectively with IT specialists? One potential answer is joint application development. *Joint application development (JAD)* is

	How				
Who	**Traditional SDLC**	**Prototyping**	**Application Software Packages**	**CASE**	**JAD**
Insource					✔
Selfsource					✔
Outsource					

*When you choose joint application development as the *how*, you haven't eliminated either insourcing or selfsourcing as the *who*. Most often, you'll use joint application development when choosing insourcing as the *who*. Read on to learn why.

a workshop that unites management, IT specialists, and knowledge workers to define and specify the logical requirements and technical alternatives for a proposed system. A JAD workshop is highly structured in how it works but creates a relaxed and informal environment in which the project team gathers to (1) break down their communication differences, (2) work as a team to define the logical requirements for a new system, and (3) explore several technical alternatives for the new system. As Doug Smith, CFO of American Management Systems, explains, when you use JAD "you get all the stakeholders together, come to a consensus, and get a common vision of where you want to go."[23]

A JAD workshop often lasts several days. This may seem like a long time. But a JAD workshop is extremely short when you compare it to the time it takes to individually interview numerous knowledge workers, document those interviews, and meet again with them to determine whether the documentation is correct. Bell & Howell's Industrial Data Solutions unit, for example, used JAD workshops to reduce the delivery time of an electronic catalog from 60 days to just 2 days.[24] And, although the time savings is important, George Langan says, "Everybody talks about reengineering—do more with less people. What we're accomplishing is we're truly rethinking the way we do things, and we're letting the people who do it do the thinking." So JAD provides an excellent medium for breaking down communication barriers and identifying requirements, and it also acts as a valuable front-end tool for business process reengineering.

The success of JAD depends on the willing and open-minded participation of many people who bring special expertise and knowledge to a JAD workshop. These people include

Facilitator The person who actually runs the JAD workshop. ***Joint application development facilitators*** do not have any decision-making power in the workshop—they simply run the workshop, keep the participants moving forward through the agenda, and resolve conflicts between participants.

Executive Sponsor The management person within your organization who ensures that your organization completely supports the JAD process and the proposed system.

Project Manager Manager of the proposed system who brings project management expertise and information concerning the plan for the proposed system to the JAD workshop.

Scribe The person who is responsible for recording all conversations, discussions, and decisions in the JAD workshop.

Knowledge Workers Those people in your organization who will use the proposed system and possess business process expertise.

IT Specialists The IT people who will eventually participate in the development of the proposed system. This group provides information concerning the feasibility of potential technical alternatives.

The Joint Application Development Process
1. Establish the JAD Project
The first step in JAD is to establish the JAD project. This includes scoping the proposed system and formulating the guidelines for the JAD workshop. You've probably already gathered much information relating to the scope of the proposed system, but the facilitator also

TEAM WORK

Automating Joint Application Development

If you think about JAD, it closely resembles two topics we've discussed in previous chapters. First, JAD workshops consist of a group of people working together, which groupware (Chapter 2) supports. Second, JAD workshops consist of a group of people making decisions together, which group decision support systems (GDSSs) (Chapter 5) support.

Identify the various software components of groupware and a GDSS that can automate a JAD workshop. How would your organization benefit from automating a JAD workshop? Can you see any potential disadvantages or pitfalls? How would you overcome them? ❖

Combining Prototyping and JAD—It's RAD

The prototyping process closely resembles that of joint application development—getting knowledge workers and IT specialists together to determine logical requirements and explore several technical alternatives for a proposed system. The only real difference is that you perform JAD in a highly structured workshop. The goal, however, remains the same. So the question is, "Why not combine prototyping and JAD?"

Well, you can, and the process is called rapid application development. ***Rapid application development (RAD)*** is a systems development method that combines prototyping and joint application development to increase the effectiveness of the systems development process. RAD simply states that you carry your prototyping tools into a JAD workshop and work with all participants to perform the prototyping process. Let's consider the use of RAD in the health care industry.

Normally, when doctors need special customized spinal implants, they must go to great lengths to draw and describe every dimension and detail from many angles. These descriptions and drawings are often easily misinterpreted, resulting in delays and increased development costs. Today, however, that's all changing. Companies that produce implants are performing JAD workshops, in which doctors participate, and using special prototyping software to develop models in a matter of hours.

One such company is Danek Medical Group in Memphis, Tennessee. Danek's prototyping software is a combination of Pro/Engineer and Fused Deposition Modeling (FDM). These software pieces allow Danek to quickly build three-dimensional CAD drawings of a spinal implant model. Several doctors then review the models on screen and suggest changes. The advantages are overwhelming. As Larry Gause, Danek engineering technician, explains, "Using FDM allows us to respond to customers' needs immediately, a valuable advantage in today's competitive market. Using our old methods, getting approval on a finished design could take several weeks. We can now provide a finished model in a matter of hours."

At the very heart of the company's RAD approach are powerful prototyping tools and JAD workshops that help designers and doctors communicate effectively.[25] ❖

---

helps you scope the project properly. To do this, the facilitator interviews the project manager and executive sponsor to gain an understanding of the proposed system. The facilitator then develops and documents his or her own view of the system. In subsequent meetings, the facilitator, project manager, and executive sponsor revise this documentation. During this step, you also choose the appropriate participants for the JAD workshop. The facilitator may help in this process by identifying the areas from which participants are needed.

2. Introduce Participants to the Project and JAD Workshop

A preworkshop meeting always precedes the actual JAD workshop. In it, the facilitator introduces the proposed system, its scope, and the agenda for the workshop. At this point, participants freely critique the material, offer suggestions, and fine-tune any necessary information. This first meeting mainly acts to ensure that the actual JAD workshop will start off on the right foot with the right information.

3. Prepare JAD Workshop Materials

After the preworkshop meeting, the facilitator revises the scope of the proposed system and develops the JAD workshop agenda. He or she also prepares any necessary audiovisual presentations, such as slide shows and flip charts. Once that is completed, the JAD workshop begins.

4. Perform the JAD Workshop

In an actual JAD workshop, participants meet 4 to 8 hours for 3 to 5 days. The goal of the JAD workshop is to reach a consensus on the logical requirements of the proposed system and explore many technical alternatives.

As the group proceeds through the agenda, the knowledge workers provide ideas for solutions to the business problem. The IT specialists then provide advice on technical alternatives to support the various proposed business solutions. As a cohesive team, the participants work through their communication differences, resolve any issues, share ideas with each other, and eventually reach a consensus.

The facilitator's role is critical to the success of the JAD workshop. The facilitator must ensure that (a) the participants follow the agenda, (b) the group doesn't get side-tracked, and (c) any conflicts between specific participants are resolved. Although the facilitator is not directly involved in any decision making, he or she is responsible for seeing that the group meets its ultimate goal—defining the logical requirements for the proposed system and exploring several technical alternatives.

The result of the JAD workshop is a document that describes the logical requirements for the proposed system and suggests several alternative technical solutions.

CAREER OPPORTUNITY

The success of JAD depends on many factors—one of which is how well you perform your role as a knowledge worker in a JAD workshop. If you choose to use JAD, put on your casual clothes, open your mind to new ideas, and prepare to actively participate in the JAD workshop. Also, don't limit JAD to just the systems development process. In both your business and personal life, you can use JAD to address any number of problems, from building a new home to deciding on a new product distribution system.

ON YOUR OWN

Matching IT Systems to the *Who* of Systems Development

In this chapter, we discussed three alternative *who*'s for systems development—IT specialists within your organization (insourcing), knowledge workers (selfsourcing), and another organization (outsourcing). In Chapter 2, we looked at seven different types of IT systems that support your organization's business processes and how they work with information.

Complete the table below by identifying which of the alternative *who*'s are most appropriate for developing the seven different types of IT systems. In some instances, you may find that different groups of people can develop these systems. For each that you identify (even if it's only one), be prepared to give a business example. ❖

IT Systems	Insourcing	Outsourcing	Selfsourcing
TPS			
CIS			
MIS			
WSS			
DSS and AI			
EIS			
IOS			

The Advantages of Joint Application Development

Joint application development, as a team-oriented approach, is a great method for bringing people together and letting them define and build a system as a group. And most people have found that there are no real disadvantages to JAD, with the exception of the costs associated with performing a JAD workshop and hiring a facilitator. This cost, however, is offset by many advantages, including the following.

Improved systems design that better meets the needs of knowledge workers Because JAD breaks down communications barriers, knowledge workers are better able to express their requirements and IT specialists are better able to understand those requirements.

Reduced delivery time for the new system JAD improves the delivery time of a new system in two ways. First, JAD is faster than traditional interviewing techniques for gathering requirements. Second, because IT specialists can more effectively gather requirements, they don't have to spend as much time "backtracking" to gather previously undefined or ambiguous requirements.

KNOWLEDGE WORKER'S ✓-LIST

Why Knowledge Worker Participation Is Important in the Development of IT Systems. No matter *what* systems your organization chooses to develop, *when* it chooses to develop those systems, *who* will develop those systems, or *how* your organization will develop those systems, your participation is important because you are

- *A business process expert* who possesses knowledge concerning how business processes work and how they need to change
- *A liaison to the customer* who understands how your customers interact with the organization and what information they need
- *A quality control analyst* who is responsible for ensuring that the final system meets your logical requirements
- *A manager of other people* who is responsible for the work and productivity of your employees.

How Organizations Traditionally Develop IT Systems Through Insourcing and Their Role During That Process. Insourcing involves using IT specialists within your organization to develop a system. In this case, the *how* is the **traditional systems development life cycle**—a structured step-by-step approach to developing systems that creates a separation of duties among knowledge workers and IT specialists. In the six steps of the SDLC, your roles are outlined in the table at the bottom of the next page.

What Selfsourcing and Outsourcing Are and How They Affect the Way Organizations Develop Systems. *Selfsourcing* (or *knowledge worker development*) is the development and support of IT systems by knowledge workers with little or no help from IT specialists. So selfsourcing is an important aspect of *knowledge worker computing*—knowledge workers taking an active role in developing and using their own systems to support their efforts in personal and workgroup environments. During selfsourcing, knowledge workers basically forgo IT specialists and the use of the SDLC in favor of developing and supporting their own systems. IT specialists still provide support for technical assistance.

Outsourcing is the delegation of specific work to a third party for a specified length of time, at a specified cost, and at a specified level of service. In systems development, your organization can outsource literally everything, with the exception of planning. In outsourcing, the most important document is a request for proposal. A *request for proposal (RFP)* is a formal document that outlines your logical requirements of a proposed system and invites outsourcing organizations or vendors to submit bids for its development.

Various Tools and Methods That Can Increase the Efficiency and Effectiveness of the Systems Development Process. Besides the SDLC, other tools and methods your organization can use during the systems development process include

Improved relations among management, IT specialists, and knowledge workers Breaking down communications barriers definitely improves the relations among management, IT specialists, and knowledge workers. Because they can now communicate more effectively they feel more at ease when working with one another.

Increased sense of ownership by management and knowledge workers JAD is an active participation process. And when management and knowledge workers more actively participate in the systems development process, they develop more of a sense of ownership for the eventual system.

AT&T Goes Global with CASE

AT&T's Easylink Services faced a monumental systems development challenge. Because of major restructuring of three business units, Easylink Services needed to create a system that merged multiple systems and databases to handle customer accounts worldwide. Each of the three business units had different business rules that needed to be consolidated so that a single system supported each of them across multiple hardware and

Computer aided software engineering (CASE) tools Tools that automate some or all steps in the SDLC. *Integrated CASE tools* automate the entire SDLC; *upper CASE tools* automate the planning, scoping, analysis, and design steps; *lower CASE tools* automate the design, implementation, and support steps.

Joint application development (JAD) A workshop that unites management, IT specialists, and knowledge workers to define and specify the logical requirements and technical alternatives for a proposed system. ❖

Your Roles During the SDLC

Planning (from Chapter 8):

- Understand how the strategic direction of the organization will affect your area.
- Provide information requirements for your area.
- Identify proposed IT systems needed in your area.
- Participate in developing an IT systems plan.

Scoping:

- Define the exact problem or opportunity.
- Participate in developing a plan for proceeding.

Analysis:

- Provide information concerning how the system currently works.
- Provide information concerning new information and processing requirements.
- Monitor and justify the new feasibility review.

Design:

- Ensure that the recommended technical solution meets the logical requirements.
- Monitor and justify the project plan.

Implementation:

- Determine the best training method.
- Determine the best method of conversion.
- Provide complete testing of the new system.
- Monitor the budget and schedule and look for "runaway" projects.

Support:

- Provide a mechanism for people to request changes.
- Assess the worth of proposed changes before passing them to the IT specialists.

software platforms. As Susan Olszewski said, "We needed a tool that would allow us to develop applications on one platform and then deploy on multiple platforms."

The answer for Easylink Services was Texas Instruments' CASE tool called Composer. Composer, an integrated CASE tool, allowed the development team to model, consolidate, and capture business rules without regard to any specific technology environment. Then the team used Composer's powerful back-end support tools to generate the needed software for different platforms. As Jack Wojciechowski explained, "In a relatively short time, we developed a large UNIX-compatible system written in C, with a development team who had previously never worked in either UNIX or C!"

Today, the Easylink system runs under many different operating systems and on different types of hardware. All over the world, the system supports such functions as ordering, billing, technical services, and accounts inquiry. From the customer's perspective, the new system has dramatically reduced the time it takes to complete an order. For AT&T, it means rapid systems generation for a variety of software and hardware platforms.[26] ❖

◄ Questions ►

1. Why do you think AT&T chose an integrated CASE tool for its Easylink system instead of an upper or lower CASE tool? Could AT&T have chosen an upper or lower CASE tool and achieved the same results? Why or why not?

2. Composer helped AT&T develop a UNIX-compatible system written in C. However, as Jack explained, the development team had no experience in either UNIX or C. Could this be a potential problem later when the development team needs to make changes? After all, they're not really experts in either UNIX or C.

3. How did AT&T's use of a CASE tool aid in business process reengineering? Does this one isolated example mean that CASE tools can offer support for reengineering certain business processes?

4. Could AT&T have used joint application development, prototyping, or rapid application development to aid in creating the new Easylink system? What role would each have played? What additional benefits do you think AT&T would have realized had it used some of these other tools and methods?

5. Apparently, AT&T gave little thought to outsourcing. Why do you think it chose not to outsource?

Do you think it considered and rejected the idea? How might it have answered the questions in the box on p. 365 to reach that conclusion?

box on p. 365

CLOSING CASE STUDY: CASE 2

Deregulation in Utilities Stirs Up Systems Development

For many years, utility companies have enjoyed monopolistic economic conditions in their markets. It was very simple—you had no choice but to use the utility provider in your area. But not so anymore. The government has deregulated most utility environments, not only encouraging the entrance of new competitors, but also forcing existing utility companies to provide better services to retain old customers and attract new ones. And that's not easy. If you lose an old customer to a new competitor, you essentially have to raise the rates of existing customers to offset the revenue loss. As Steven Drenker, a business unit manager at Electric Power Research Institute, explains it, "For the utility, that's called a death spiral."

To increase their competitive positions, most utilities are revamping old IT systems to provide their customers with better service. For example, most large and commercial users of utilities are now demanding real-time usage quotes, energy management summaries, and lump sum billing for multiple sites. The older IT systems of utilities, unfortunately, don't support these features. So systems development projects are underway all over the country for almost every utility provider.

But many utility providers have found their new systems development efforts to be extremely difficult. Many of them have already spent millions of dollars on new systems, only to abandon their development efforts because of cost and time overruns. For example, Pacific Gas & Electric and Duke Power—two of the country's largest electric companies—scrapped systems development projects after spending somewhere between $50 million and $70 million.[27] ❖

◄ Questions ►

1. Of the three *who*'s of systems development, which would you recommend that utility providers primarily use for developing new systems and why? Which would you recommend that they use the least and why? For the other *who* alternative, in what instances would you recommend that it be used?

2. When creating project teams, how important is it that utility providers include customers? What types of customer should be on the project teams—household users, commercial users, or perhaps a combination of the two?

3. Many utility providers are turning to CASE tools to support their development efforts. For the short term, what category of CASE tool would you recommend that they use and why? What about the long term—is your answer the same or would you recommend a different category of CASE tool?

4. What do you think is the major reason utility providers are having such a difficult time developing these new systems? Do you think the magnitude of this reason or problem will increase or decrease over time? Why?

5. What is the role of prototyping while utility providers develop these new systems—proof-of-concept or selling? Perhaps some combination of the two? Does the role of prototyping differ according to which group of internal users or external customers are seeing, using, and evaluating the prototype? Why or why not?

6. Most older systems for utility providers use a centralized concept with a mainframe computer, whereas new systems development efforts are targeted for a client/server environment. How does the development of systems for client/server differ from centralized environments? How are they the same?

REAL [H·O·T]
Electronic Commerce
Business and You on the Internet

Building the Perfect Web Page

Almost everyone's doing it—some are doing it better than others, but the simple fact is that almost every business you can name is building a Web page. Businesses are building Web pages for a variety of reasons—to create a presence on the Internet, to provide an electronic storefront for displaying products and services, and to give customers the ability to order those products and services.

And, about one of every fifty people is doing the same. Some want to because it's the "in thing," others want to show off their pets, and still others build Web pages in the hope of meeting people (called *e-friends*) around the world. Whatever the reason, building a Web page is actually a process of building something, just as we discussed building IT systems in this chapter. You have a variety of building tools (called Web development tools) available to you; you must consider the target audience for whom you're building your Web page; there are good ways and bad ways to build a Web page; and Web pages always require maintenance and updating.

In this electronic commerce section, we'd like to alert you to the many facets of building a Web page. These facets include:

- HTML—the language for creating a Web page.

- Web development tools for accelerating the process of creating a Web page.

- Online references and books for creating a Web page.

- Free images and backgrounds you can find on the Internet.

- Counters for keeping track of "hits" to your Web page.

- Dos and Donts of building a good Web page.

- Service provider requirements.

What we can't do is take you through a step-by-step process for building a Web page (although we will point you toward some great references, one of which is the Web site that supports this text). But what you will gain by reading this section is insight into the process of building a good Web page. Because of that, this electronic commerce section differs from those in other chapters. You won't find a lot of exercises to complete or questions to answer. But we do hope that you'll be excited about building your very own Web page after reading this section.

In this section, we've included a number of Web sites related to building the perfect Web page. On the Web site that supports this text (http://www.mhhe.com/business/mis/haag, select "Electronic Commerce Projects"), we've provided direct links to all these Web sites as well as many, many more. These are a great starting point for completing this Real HOT section. We would also encourage you to search the Internet for others.

HTML—The Language of Web Pages

Hypertext markup language (*HTML*) is the language used to create Web pages on the Internet. Using HTML, you simply specify (1) what information you want on your Web page, such as your name or a photo of your pet, and (2) how that information is supposed to look. And, like all other programming languages and software such as Word or Excel, new versions of HTML become available from time to time, with the most recent versions offering you more capabilities and flexibility.

In HTML you specify how information is supposed to look by using tags. A tag in HTML is (for the most part) a formatting statement. For example, consider the following HTML statement:

<CENTER><B><I>Web Page Heading</I></B></CENTER>

That HTML statement contains some information for a Web page ("Web Page Heading") along with three tags that determine how the information will be displayed.

In this instance, the three tags are CENTER, B, and I. The CENTER tag will display the information centered on the screen, the B tag will bold the information, and the I tag will italicize the information.

Notice also that these tags have a beginning and ending point. For the CENTER tag, <CENTER> starts centering information and </CENTER> stops centering information. So, all information between the beginning and ending CENTER tag is centered. The same is true for the bold tag (<B> and </B>) and the italicize tag (<I> and </I>). Most, but not all, tags in HTML have a beginning and ending point.

So, to create a Web page using HTML you simply need to learn the tags in HTML (there are several hundred). Then, you determine what information you want your Web page to contain and what tags you need to use to affect the presentation of that information when someone accesses and views your Web page.

By the way, if you find a really great looking Web site and wonder what HTML code created it, you can easily find out. From your browser's menu bar, choose "View" and then "Source" or "HTML Source." What you'll then see is the exact HTML code used to create that site.

Web Development Tools

There are a variety of ways in which you can build your Web page. Most notably, you can (1) write your own HTML code, (2) use a word processing package, (3) purchase and use a Web development tool, or (4) download and use a free Web development tool. Of course, many issues will affect your decision. If you want a really elaborate Web page, you should write your own HTML code or purchase a Web development tool. If price is a concern, then purchasing a Web development tool may not be an option. And if you're just interested in getting a simple Web page up and running, you should probably consider using a word processing package or downloading a free Web development tool.

If you choose to write your own HTML code, then you'll need to become very familiar with HTML and its tags. You may also need to be prepared to learn and use a graphics package such as PhotoShop or CorelDraw. Writing your own HTML code requires the most expertise (and usually time), but it also gives you the greatest flexibility and capability. And, if you really become an HTML expert, you can expect to get a job writing HTML and make a salary in excess of $50,000 per year in many cases.

Perhaps the simplest way to create a Web page is to use a word processing package such as Microsoft Word. To do so in Word, create a document that represents

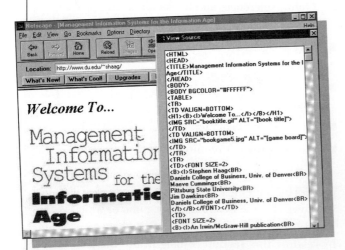

what you want your Web page to look like. As you do, add all the necessary formatting (color, bolding, centering, and the like), make use of tables and lists, and insert any clip art you want. When you're done, choose "File" from the menu bar and then "Save as HTML." Word will automatically generate the HTML code necessary to produce a Web page just as your document looks. Afterward, you can choose "View" from the menu bar and "HTML Source" to see what the code looks like (you can also change the code at that point, which will automatically change the look of your Web page).

Your third option for creating a Web page is to purchase and use a Web development tool (some people refer to these as Web authoring tools). A Web development tool is simply a piece of software that facilitates your building a Web page. Using one of these tools—most of which come with easy point-and-click interfaces—you define what you want your Web page to look like (much as you would using Word). Then the software takes over and generates the HTML code for you.

The real advantage of Web development tools lies in Web site management. Most Web sites actually contain more than one Web page. For example, once you connect to the main page of a Web site, it will probably contain links or buttons that you click on to view additional information or explore other parts of the Web site. Each part is actually called a *Web page,* with all the Web pages making up a *Web site.* And using a Web development tool, you can easily create, manage, and maintain a huge Web site that may have as many as a thousand separate pages.

In the table on page 407, we've listed some of the more popular Web development tools, their manufacturers, and the manufacturer Web sites you can visit to gather additional information on these tools. And you can connect to the Web site that supports this text to see a list of several others, as well as a brief review of each of these tools and any new tools that have been recently released. If you're going to purchase a Web development tool, you should make your decision carefully. We recommend you consider the following issues:

- How much will it cost?
- How widely is the product used?
- How easy is it to create a simple Web page?
- How easy is it to create a complex Web page?
- Does the product support good site management?

As a final alternative, you may want to consider using a free Web development tool. This category of software is often called freeware (which typically is free) or shareware (which may require you to pay a nominal fee). For more on freeware and shareware, revisit the Real HOT

electronic commerce section for Chapter 8. Of course, many people will tell you that you get what you pay for. So if it's free, don't get your hopes too high that you'll be able to do everything you want using one of these tools. Indeed, many of these free Web development tools don't support easy point-and-click interfaces; rather, they are simply text editors that help you write HTML code.

If you're interested in obtaining a list of freeware/shareware Web development tools (as well as a fairly extensive list of tools for which you must pay), connect to http://www.cpcug.org/user/mohnkern.htmled.html. That site contains a list of well over 50 Web development tools, many of which are freeware or shareware.

References for Creating a Web Page

What do you do when you want to learn how to do something? You take a class, perhaps buy a book, or even ask a professional. As you consider building a Web page, you'll need to learn how to write HTML or use a Web development tool. And, if you're really serious about building a great Web site, you should probably do all of the above. Perhaps your school offers a course in building Web pages or you can enroll in a weekend conference on building Web pages taught by a professional.

If you're interested in purchasing some books, we've provided a recommended list below, separated into two categories—one for designing Web pages and one for writing HTML. If you choose to use a Web development tool, you'll be able to find a variety of books devoted to the software of your choice.

Designing Web Pages:

- *Guide to Web Content & Design* (Roger Parker)
- *Creating Killer Web Sites* (David Siegel)

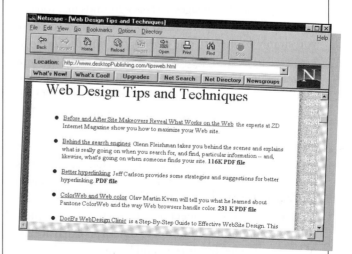

CASE STUDY

To Whom Do Doctors Go for Help?

How do doctors keep track of all the new medications and treatments available for what ails you and still have time to see patients? Pharmaceutical reps help make it possible by providing a wealth of information to doctors worldwide. Pfizer, a company that sold $10 billion worth of pharmaceutical products in 1995, is a leader in using IT to enable its 2,700 sales reps to customize their sales pitches. Because of its IT system, Pfizer reps can quickly provide doctors with highly detailed information about each product's effectiveness, side effects, and cost. Having complete information quickly is the key to the success of Pfizer reps because

- The average sales call to a doctor is less than 5 minutes
- Doctors have different prescribing patterns

IN THE NEWS

Managing IT Systems

Staying on Track

- Medical solutions and approaches change rapidly
- Insurance company policies differ and are constantly changing
- Government-sponsored health insurance programs, like Medicare and Medicaid, are a maze of rules, regulations, and exceptions
- Pressure is growing to contain costs in the field of medicine.

When planning the new automated system, Vita Cases, vice president of business technology and marketing research at Pfizer, said, "with a customer-focused strategy in a rapidly changing health care environment, we need to better coordinate information between headquarters and the field." To that end, Pfizer hired Dendrite International, a developer of pharmaceuticals sales territory management systems. Together they developed Sherlock, which pooled the information of three systems. In addition, the new system was designed to incorporate, on an ongoing basis, the information in the files and heads of individual sales reps, making it available to the rest of the sales force.

After the pilot program proved successful, Pfizer issued notebook computers and modems to all sales representatives. Now all sales reps can access information as they need it and input new or updated information to the central database. This means that if a sales rep has visited a doctor, other reps can learn about the visit and the details of the conversation.

FEATURES

IN THE INFORMATION AGE, KNOWLEDGE WORKERS UNDERSTAND...

1. The nature of management
2. The role, access to, and protection of information
3. The control and protection of IT components
4. The importance of providing a work environment that accommodates diversity and encourages ethical behavior

Sales reps say that the additional information provides them with a better understanding of the environment and customers. This is evidenced in the bottom line—within a year, sales were up 26 percent to $10 billion.

This dramatic improvement was due in large part to Pfizer's excellent management of its IT system. Specifically, Pfizer

- Recognized that information is not just a frill—it's part of the product

- Listened to its knowledge workers, who said they needed more information and better access to it
- Realized that much valuable information was being carried around in its sales reps' heads
- Planned its IT system, then tested the plan before releasing it to everyone
- Standardized the hardware and software, keeping costs and knowledge worker frustration low[2] ❖

Introduction

You may not realize it, but you're a manager. Perhaps you don't have the title, but at the very least, you manage your life. Along with your schoolwork, you may have a job, extracurricular activities, even children. You have to organize, coordinate, and control all these parts of your life with limited resources and conflicting objectives. You also play different roles in the management of your life. You connect with other people and respond to and handle problems and pressures; you're a leader and a negotiator; you allocate resources. These are some of the traditional activities and roles of a manager. The modern view of management also addresses its *purpose*. Management's basic purpose is to provide stability while accommodating change.[1] The more complicated and dynamic your environment, the more complex the job of managing becomes. The management of IT systems is a case in point.

The **management of IT systems** means providing an environment of stability without stagnation and change without chaos for information, information technology, and knowledge workers. Managing an IT system is a very delicate balancing act (see Figure 10.1). You have to sustain your current IT system components (the balls in the air) while adjusting them to the forces of change (the shifting blocks underneath) and simultaneously protecting your IT system from harm, both internal and external (the threats flying overhead).

A stable IT system provides consistency and predictability, which are vital for the effective functioning of an organization. You expect a particular version of your word processor to look the same on any PC you use. (Neither automobiles nor computers were widely used until they were perceived as having a certain level of dependability and consistency.) However, stability can become restrictive and actually obstruct effectiveness if it is oppressive. For example, keeping all computers in one room, instead of on the desks of individual knowl-

edge workers, may ensure a stable environment but will not encourage knowledge worker productivity.

All change, even change for the better, is stressful. But change is not a choice—it will happen regardless of

FIGURE 10.1

Managing IT Systems Is a Balancing Act

whether you want it or not. However, the way you handle change *is* a choice. If you're smart, you'll accept it, integrate it, and make it work for you. If you're *very* smart, you'll initiate change in the direction that's beneficial to you. For example, if you're advancing your education, you're embracing change and pursuing continuous improvement.

In a business environment, continuous improvement (see discussion in Chapter 3) is the vehicle that advances your ability to deliver the customer's moment of value. You must plan for and manage change. In the current dynamic environment of IT, that's quite a challenge. You don't want change to happen so quickly that you not only can't keep up, but also can't even perform routine operations. For instance, you wouldn't want to learn how to use a new version of a spreadsheet every week.

In the opening case study, Pfizer changed its IT system to better meet its customers' needs. There is no better reason for change in a business organization. Note how Pfizer approached the change in a systematic way. First came the planning stage where the company sought the help of experts, planned extensively, and tested its new plan thoroughly—a process you studied in Chapter 8. Second, Pfizer developed the IT system for companywide use. You saw in Chapter 9 how to do that. Third, Pfizer made certain that its knowledge workers had the IT components they needed to access and use the information they required to serve their customers. But the job is not yet done: the company must make sure that the system continues to be dependable, but also that it can adjust to changes in the organizational and business environment. That's what this chapter is about—the management of IT systems.

IT systems are composed of knowledge workers who use information technology to generate and access information. Therefore, managing IT systems involves managing these three critically important components of business—information, IT, and knowledge workers (see Figure 10.2). In today's information-based business environment, well-managed IT systems are no luxury; they form the life-support system of your organization.

Managing Information

In considering the management of information we'll

- Examine the role of information in an organization
- Discuss the management of access to information
- Address the protection of information from loss and damage (security) and from abuse (privacy)

The Role of Information
Raw Material and Capital

Nothing else is as universal or as versatile as information. What else can you sell or lease to someone else—and retain for yourself? This unique resource called "information" has two functions in an organization—as raw material and capital.

Information as Raw Material

Raw materials are the components from which a product is made. For example, the raw materials of a chair might be wood, glue, and screws. But almost anything you buy also has information as part of the product. If you doubt this, wander through a store and see how many products incorporate absolutely no information. The amount of information varies, of course. You get a lot more information if you buy a 747 jet airplane than if you buy a cake mix. Sometimes it's the information that makes a product particularly valuable. Take the example of two identical pairs of sports shoes that were originally made by the same company but sold under different logos. It is very likely that the shoes with the more widely known or prestigious logo will sell for a higher price than those with the lesser-known logo. The more desirable logo doesn't increase the functional value of the shoes. They're the same shoes. But the information (the logo) that is part of the shoes sends a statement to the customer's peers: "The wearer is cool!" This is the part of the product for which the customer is prepared to pay extra. Here we have an example of the wants-driven

FIGURE 10.2
Your Focus for This Chapter

Hyatt Offers More Than a Room and a Bed

Information is business capital, and so is an IT system. And information and IT systems are different from other capital in that you can lease them to other businesses without depriving yourself of their use. If you rent out a building, you can hardly expect to continue using it. If you develop an IT system, however, you can lease it to others and still use it.

The Hyatt Hotel group is doing just that. When you book a hotel that belongs to a chain, you usually don't call the specific hotel to make the reservation. Rather, you call a central toll-free number to reserve a room at one of the chain's hotels. It takes a pretty sophisticated IT system to handle all that. The Hyatt Hotel group's reservation staff of about 1,000 people use the Spirit Hospitality Reservation system to place the bookings.

Having gone to all the trouble of developing this system, the Hyatt Group added greatly to its investment return by making the Spirit system available to other hotel chains. Spirit can handle up to 3,500 hotels at once. Among Hyatt's first customers were Sceptre Hospitality, Southern Pacific Hospitality Corp., La Quinta Inns, and Hawthorne Suites.[5] ❖

---

consumerism that you read about in Chapter 1. The information part of the product often constitutes a portion of the customer's moment of value.

Because IT systems generate and deliver information, the most successful firms no longer view IT systems as optional but as a required business function. This type of company is not satisfied with the traditional user's manual type of information content. Several instances come to mind. You already read the Pfizer example. United Parcel Service's (UPS) $1 billion budget for IT is second only to its expenditures on aircraft.[3] This is because UPS is selling not only a shipping service, but also information. For example, you can connect to the UPS Web site and track your package. As UPS CIO Frank Ergbrick puts it, "a package without information has no value."

General Motors doesn't just sell vehicles. Its Cadillacs feature an option called OnStar that combines a global positioning system (GPS)—which identifies your position anywhere on earth—with networked sensors, a cell phone, and a link to customer support centers. If the car's air bag inflates, the sensor sends a signal to the customer support center, which tries to contact you on the cell phone. If there is no response, the support center uses the GPS to locate your car, then alerts the emergency service nearest you.[4]

Information as Capital

Capital is the type of asset you use to produce a product or service. Buildings, trucks, and machinery are examples of capital. For our chair manufacturer, the capital would be the factory building, the saw, the glue dispenser, screw

drivers, and so on. These items are not part of the chair, but they're necessary to build it. You incur a cost in acquiring capital, and you expect a return on your investment. You can sell or lease capital assets.

Information can also be thought of as capital. It is used by companies to provide a product that meets a customer's moment of value. For example, think back to the case in Chapter 1 where the store manager acquired information that led her to move beer next to diapers for Friday evening customers. That information didn't go into either the diapers or beer, but it indirectly contributed to the customer's moment of value, not to mention this store's profit margin.

Information capital is one of the most important and universal types of capital in an organization. Not every organization has a building or a truck, but every organization has information. We cannot state the case too strongly: Information and, consequently, the IT systems that provide it are as important to business as breathing is to you.

Access to Information

You saw in Chapter 1 that information has three dimensions: content (what), time (when), and form (how). Managing information means providing your organization with the most effective means to access the right information, at the right time, in the right form.

Access to the Right Information

If you wanted to fly from Los Angeles to New York, you'd need flight timetables from the airlines that service that route. But when acquiring that information you need to be able to depend on its accuracy. An inaccurate timetable would be worse than not having one at all because you would make plans based on erroneous information. In any situation the information you need is, of course, dependent on what you're doing. But the issue of accurate and consistent information is universal.

Capturing accurate and consistent information is becoming increasingly challenging. With the trend toward CISs (customer integrated systems), companies must be doubly vigilant about information entry. For example, the American Airlines SABRE reservations system allows corporate customers to access airline schedules and make reservations. When your customers input information it's hard to assure its quality. You can set up procedures and rules for your own employees, but it's much more difficult to do that for customers. One way to monitor information is to use software packages that help you clean up "dirty" information. How does it work? The software looks at all name fields, for example, for those that are near matches (such as William Jones and Wm. Jones). Then it checks the customer's social security number or date of birth. If they match, the software consolidates the records.

As data warehouses become more popular and important, the issue of quality information becomes increasingly important. In the past, inaccurate information may not have created problems. It does create problems, however, with data warehouse technology. For example, an insurance company was creating a data warehouse to analyze medical diagnosis codes for which it was paying claims. The company found that there was an unusually high incidence of "hemorrhoid" diagnosis in one region.[6] Upon further investigation it was discovered that claims processors used that code to identify difficult customers. In this case the diagnosis was irrelevant to paying claims, but it was very important when assessing overall risk to the company. This example illustrates an important point: Information of poor quality cannot be used for decision making, even if the information is acceptable for operational processing. Many organizations are finding that before they set up data warehouses, they have to spend a lot of money and time (sometimes years) cleaning up dirty information.

INDUSTRY PERSPECTIVE   Health Care

A Prescription for Good Health Care

What do health care providers need to ensure quality health care? The right information, that's what! And they need it at the right time and in the right form. To achieve this goal, the health care industry is switching from paper-based patient records to electronic records, and thus its reliance on IT is growing by leaps and bounds. St. Alphonsus Regional Medical Center in Boise, Idaho, in the patient care business since 1894, is a case in point. Some of "St. Al's" patient information was computerized, but much of it was stored on microfiche. When a health provider needed patient information, someone would have to pull the film, make paper copies, and deliver them. It took from 2 to 4 days for doctors to get reports. This was indeed the right information, but hardly timely or in the right form! And patient records were increasing at a rate of 1.5 million per year.

As Debra Harris, the director of medical information services at the hospital, said, "In a managed care environment, information is vital to your financial success." Thus, the hospital embarked on an ambitious plan to improve things. First on the agenda was an IT system using optical character recognition (OCR) to convert paper records into electronic form, which could then be linked to information in the centralized IT system. An AI-based retrieval system allows health care providers to access records using plain English commands. Included in the move to electronically capture information is a system which enables physicians to deliver their reports to a dictation system on the central computer system. Transcriptionists (some of whom are telecommuters) retrieve the digitally recorded words and store them in a searchable database. Ultimately, a multimedia system will provide video, physicians' recorded voice notes, photographs of patients and staff, signatures, and any other form of information that is required.[7, 8] ❖

Training a Revolving Workforce

You've heard of CD-ROM technology. A related system is CD-i which stands for compact disk instruction. The system consists of a CD placed in a VCR-like player which you then hook up to a TV set and control with a mouse, keyboard, or other input device.

CD-i has full-motion video without videodisk players or high-end computers. CD-i systems are also compatible with European as well as U.S. TV standards, and the multiple tracks can accommodate several language versions of instruction.

PFS, the Dallas-based supply arm of PepsiCo, Pizza Hut, Kentucky Fried Chicken, and Taco Bell, chose a CD-i system to train its workers. With a global workforce spread over 22 sites, PFS was looking for a way to deliver standardized training that met federal requirements. The company wanted a way to deliver training information to new employees or to experienced employees when procedures changed. Having looked at computer-based training and finding it to be very expensive, PFS decided on CD-i training because of its effectiveness, flexibility, and low cost.[9] ❖

Having taken steps to ensure the accuracy and consistency of the information you capture and store, you now have to decide how long to retain information. Some of it doesn't have to be kept forever; for example, item numbers of discontinued parts. Other information requires long-term storage, like customer account histories. In the past, most companies kept records for time periods specified by regulatory agencies such as the IRS. However, now that you can use data mining and AI systems to analyze information, these time limits may be inappropriate. For example, you might want to analyze customer buying patterns over the previous 10, or even 20, years.

Access to Information at the Right Time

Information is worthless if it's not available when you need it. Sales reps won't sell much if they can't immediately quote prices to their customers, and customers won't buy your product if they don't know about it. The job of managing information includes making it available to knowledge workers and customers when they need it. Knowledge workers should be able to access complete customer information at every point of contact. They should have organizational and external information available as they need it. Many companies, like Pfizer in the opening case study, provide notebook computers and modems to sales representatives so that they can get the information they need immediately. Similarly, your customers should be able to access information pertaining to you and your product or service whenever they want it (the perfect service concept). That may

mean Internet access, toll-free numbers, or personal calls from reps.

Access to Information in the Right Form

If you've ever tried to read an indecipherable owner's manual in tiny print with no pictures or diagrams, or if you've wondered what your normally placid dog is trying to tell you when it becomes agitated and barks incessantly, you know the importance of the presentation of information. Information should be available in a form that's understandable, consistent, logical, and as easy to manipulate as a pencil. It should be produced in the format that's the most appropriate—words, graphs, tables, sound, or video. Presenting information in a familiar format helps increase its usefulness. The real estate company of Cushman & Wakefield recognized that fact when deciding on an interface for its intranet-based human resource and real estate information. Its employees were comfortable accessing information on the Internet, so the company decided to present information on an intranet with a Netscape Navigator interface. Using this system, 2,000 knowledge workers in 40 locations have access to corporate policies and human resource information, as well as detailed information on thousands of commercial properties worldwide.[10] Because staffers were familiar with the Netscape browser, Cushman & Wakefield didn't have to spend as much time and money on training as it would have if it had chosen a completely new and unfamiliar interface. The employees also make fewer mistakes because they're accessing information through an easy-to-use, familiar interface. They're able to concentrate more on the task, and the IT they're using is so comfortable it becomes almost invisible (the concept of IT transparency).

Security

Is Your Information Safe?

What do you need *information security* for? Well, now that you've spent huge amounts of time, money, and energy on capturing, generating, and providing access to the information that's so vital to your organization, you'll want to protect it from loss and damage. In this case, the management responsibility focuses on preventing change rather than enabling it. Hard disks can crash, computer parts can fail, hackers can gain access and do mischief, and thieves can steal your organization's information. The proliferation of client/server technology has resulted in the distribution of mission-critical information throughout the company, increasing the likelihood of misuse or damage. Estimates for the cost of recreating lost information range between $2,000 and $8,000 per megabyte.

A lost tape could cost up to $500,000 to replace. Many companies use data compression to increase the storage capacity of their disks, making the loss of a disk even more serious.

Back Up or Die

As always, an ounce of prevention is worth a pound of cure. The easiest and most basic way to prevent loss of information is to make backups. There's no action you can take that's more rudimentary or essential than making copies of important information methodically and regularly (at least once a week). Employee carelessness and ignorance cause about two-thirds of the financial cost of lost or damaged information.[11] Take the example of one company whose accounting server went down the day that paychecks should have been distributed. The crisis arose during a transition of administrators. The people who had been temporarily running the system thought that backup occurred automatically. It didn't, so all payroll information was lost. To get the system up and running again, the company had to pay thousands of

Get Your Information While It's Hot!

Organizations that provide products and services usually incorporate information into the product or service. For the organizations listed below, state the *what, when,* and *how* of the product's information, as well as whether information is the most or least important part of the product or service. ❖

Organization	What	When	How	Most Important	Least Important
Library					
Psychic Friends Network					
Legal firm					
Candy store					
Airline					
Elementary school					
Department store					
Movie theater					
TV station					
Antique store					
Mountain bike store					
Jewelry store					
Internal Revenue Service					
Stockbroker firm					
Air Force recruiting office					

Service That Fits

Do you hate it when you pick up something in a store and, as you walk toward the checkout, find that you can't remember the price and that it's not displayed on the product? Unlike many retailers, Sports Authority, Inc., attaches a price label to every item on its shelves because "the customer wants to see a price sticker on every piece of merchandise." So says Joe Crenshaw, vice president of MIS at Sports Authority, the largest retailer selling only sporting goods.

Another unusual aspect of Sports Authority's business practice is that it doesn't warehouse the goods it sells. Instead, products are shipped directly from suppliers to the chain's 145 outlets. This requires increased efficiency in information transmission, and the company places great emphasis on its telecommunications infrastructure for e-mail and other information transmission. To collect a different kind of valuable information, managers installed Lotus Notes in all stores so that employees could send suggestions to headquarters.

Sports Authority, Inc., is using IT for three kinds of information. First, the company delivers price information to the customer where the customer wants to see it. Second, Sports Authority is sharing information with its suppliers to avoid warehousing costs (just-in-time). Third, the company is practicing an information-sharing philosophy by encouraging employees to offer suggestions, essentially employing a learning organization strategy as detailed in Chapter 3.[13] ❖

dollars to consultants to restore the network application, and it had to pay 4 people for 300 hours of overtime at $10 an hour to reenter information. In addition, it cost $48,000 for a disk-recovery company to retrieve the information from the damaged disk drive. And all this could have been avoided.[12]

Your backup plans should include your applications software too. Unless you can combine it with your applications, your information is of limited use. Make sure that you back up ALL information. It's easy to forget about the information that is not stored in the main computer system or network, like correspondence and customer information kept by administrative assistants and receptionists, and private information not kept in the main organizational databases or data warehouses.

Backups can be made on floppy disks, removable hard disks, CD-ROMs, DVDs, or tape. You can store the backups in a safe, in a different location, or in a televault.

- *Safe* Should you choose to store your backups in a safe, make sure that it is not only fireproof, but also heatproof. Floppy disks and CD-ROMs suffer damage at temperatures above 125 degrees. Also remember that water damage is possible (perhaps from a burst water pipe), so get a safe that is waterproof, too.

- *Different location* Most experts recommend that you store your backups in a separate building in case anything happens that affects the entire building.

- *Televault* You can store your backups with a security company that specializes in storing information from many organizations. This is known as *televaulting*. Such a company encrypts your information and stores it for you.

Information Theft
Don't Make It Easy

Law enforcement officials say that mostly employees, rather than outsiders, tamper with information. They often steal it to sell to other organizations. Some of the more popular targets of information theft are customer information, new-product plans, company financial information, and legal records. Mostly the victim doesn't even know it happened because making a copy of information doesn't alter the original in any way. The cost of information theft is very hard to quantify, but most people recognize it as a serious problem that is aggravated by the fact that existing federal laws don't specifically cover the theft of proprietary information, making prosecution particularly difficult.

Your safest bet is to prevent the problem in the first place. Measures that you can take include encrypting information and restricting access to files. Encryption makes it very difficult for anyone who steals corporate information to read it. Encryption is particularly important for very vulnerable information, like that which is stored on notebook computers, because it can be snatched by a thief in the blink of an eye. You can restrict access to files by using one or more of three levels of applications security:

- You can impose log-in passwords at the operating system level, but make sure you change passwords frequently.

- You can purchase add-on utilities that restrict access.

- You can apply application-level security. For example, you can lock an MS-Word document with a password.

Viruses
A Sick Idea

A *computer virus* is a program which someone develops with malicious intent to harm an IT system. A computer virus can cause damage when it finds its way into a set of instructions like an .EXE file or an MS-Word macro. Thousands of different types of viruses exist and the number is increasing every day. Viruses can destroy the operating system, destroy information, slow down processing, turn off the printer, and so on. Your computer can get a virus if it executes a program that contains that virus. For example, say you find a game that you like on the Internet and that game has a virus. If you download and run the game, your computer will have the virus too. For this reason, it's a good idea to carefully control programs and information that are loaded onto your

company's computers. As an added precaution, keep an antivirus program RAM resident so that it can check any file that you load into memory from a disk or download from another computer. But don't forget to update your antivirus programs so that you can catch newly invented viruses.

Internet Loopholes

We all know how convenient and easy to use the Internet is. Fully one-third of the companies that use the Internet exchange important correspondence. The risk in connecting computers to the Internet to give knowledge workers better access to information is that unauthorized people (called hackers) can gain access too. Perhaps even worse, they can break into other parts of your system. It is estimated that 20 to 90 percent of the organizations using the Internet suffer such break-ins. No one is immune: even the Department of Justice and CIA sites have been invaded. Some hackers try to get into your system just for the thrill of it, others want to steal credit card numbers or trade secrets. But what you want is to keep them out. A firewall can help.

A *firewall* is a barrier that prevents an outsider from accessing your organization's system (see Chapter 6 for a more extensive discussion). A firewall is usually placed between internal networks and the Internet. It's a border-crossing checkpoint where knowledge workers stop to

---

GONE...

. . . But Not Forever

If your disk has been damaged, you can take it to a data-recovery company, which perhaps can retrieve your information. Some data-recovery companies claim that unless your information is gone because the SAVE command did not work properly, they can retrieve your information. First, you submit your disk for appraisal; then the company examines the damage and gives you an estimate of how much it will cost to recover the information.

Recovering information from a hard disk is not a simple process. It requires the use of a clean room, which is about 50,000 times cleaner than the air we breathe, because opening a hard disk can let in particles of dust. The tiniest particle of smoke or a fingerprint can prevent a disk from operating. In the clean room, the disk is removed from its housing and put into a special machine to rotate it so that the data signals can be read. The information is then copied to a new hard disk.

Data-recovery companies keep their methods secret. Some data-recovery software packages are available commercially, but they don't fix serious problems like head crashes, or wet or melted disks.

. . . And Forever

Although most people worry about losing information, some people worry that it can't be erased. They fear that it will fall into the wrong hands. Knowledge workers can't completely clean disks themselves—it takes an expert. The same experts who retrieve information from damaged disks can also fix it so that no one else can retrieve information from a disk. Government departments, hospitals, and other organizations which store information that must be kept safe are the major customers for this search-and-destroy service.[14] ❖

have their credentials checked. An IT specialist writes and maintains the internal rules identifying the types of people, addresses, or applications that are allowed or excluded.

Privacy

Is It an Invasion or Just Good Business?

The issue of privacy is a vexing one for businesses. Companies need information about their employees and customers to be effective in the marketplace. But people often object to having so many details about their lives in the hands of others. We'll examine this topic in the context of both employer-employee and business-customer relationships.

Employer and Employees
It's Personal

Most job applicants fill out a job application, but what else can an employer find out about a potential employee? The answer is "pretty much anything the employer wants to know." Here's a partial list of databases available for perusal:

- Motor vehicle records
- Criminal reports
- Insurance coverage
- Credit reports
- Telephone usage patterns
- Medical histories

The employer can also ask the potential employee to take drug and psychological tests, the results of which are the property of the company. Once the employee has been hired, the employer can monitor him or her using methods not available to the police without a court order:

- An "active badge" allows employers to track workers as they move around the organization. Ceiling-mounted sensors intercept an infrared signal emitted from the badge. This badge will tell your employer exactly where you've been and how long you were there.[15]

- At the touch of a button a supervisor can tell what's on a knowledge worker's screen, catching employees who surf the Internet on company time visiting sports sites and such. Supervisors can monitor and examine e-mail at will. (Remember that deleting a message does not necessarily get rid of it.) *Macworld* magazine estimates that about 20 million Americans work for companies that inspect their employees' voice mail, e-mail, or computer files. If you count video camera and telephone monitoring, the number is closer to 50 million.[16]

- Many freight trucks are equipped with miniature computers attached to the engine, which record speed, length of rest periods, distance traveled, and so on.

Businesses have good reasons for seeking and storing personal information on employees: First, they want to hire the best people that they can, and then they want to ensure that staff members are conducting themselves appropriately and not wasting or misusing company resources. Second, businesses can be held liable for the actions of employees, and can even be sued for failing to adequately investigate the backgrounds of employees. Third, legislation affecting benefits requires that businesses record extensive information on employees' dependents, marital relationships, and so on.

Clearly, we have two conflicting goals: the right of employees to privacy and the needs of companies to have information. There is no magical solution. The best hiring and monitoring policies and procedures will strike a balance between the rights of the employer and those of the employees. Following are some guidelines.[17]

- Inform prospective employees of the background checks you're making and allow them the opportunity to correct mistakes in the information.

- Allow the employee to be part of the checking process where possible. For example, you could allow the person to secure a credit report and attach explanations of any problems. This approach may save you time and trouble because half of all credit reports contain errors. The Federal Trade Commission reports more complaints about the accuracy of credit reports than any other consumer issue.[18]

- Collect only relevant information. For example, a credit report may be relevant when hiring a bank employee but not a receptionist or carpenter.

- Make sure that policies and guidelines are spelled out so that employees know what to expect. Be explicit about when and how they're being watched or listened to, and whether it's routine or only undertaken when a problem is suspected.

- Make it clear that e-mail and voice mail are company resources and should be used as such. However, keep in mind that you're dealing with human beings, so a certain amount of flexibility is a must.

- Keep personnel files private. Using an identifying field other than the employee's social security number will help.

- To keep discarded personnel information safe from prying eyes, destroy it completely by shredding or burning it. Also be careful about throwing away tapes, diskettes, and CD-ROMs with personnel information. Much personal information is retrieved from dumpsters by the wrong people.

Business and Customers
How Much Privacy and How Much Service?

What kinds of information can a marketer (or anyone else) find out about you, your socioeconomic status, and your preferences? Again the answer is "just about anything they want." One journalist discovered this fact when he asked a trained investigator to have a quick look around databases that are publicly available for a small fee. Here's what the investigator found in a few minutes:

- The places the journalist had lived for the last 10 years
- The names of his neighbors
- An accurate estimate of his household income
- His age, height, weight, and eye color
- His social security number
- His wife's name and evidence of his past divorce
- Confidential information about his mortgage

- A detailed description of his home, complete with the number of bathrooms and fireplaces, and the type of siding
- Information on the bankruptcy of a relative
- The absence of a criminal record in his home state

How is all this information so readily available? Every time you use a credit card, fill out an application for a job, enter a drawing for free groceries, or give your medical history to the admissions department of a hospital, someone records information about you. Your utility and phone usage records tell a story about you, as does your car's license tag. This information collection is not new, but what is new is that database and data warehouse technology make the storage of huge amounts of information possible. Data mining tools allow the slicing and dicing of that information to an extent heretofore only dreamed about. IT also provides new ways of collecting information. For example, if you buy a GM car with an OnStar system as described earlier in this chapter, then information on the whereabouts of your car is being transmitted to the support center. Is this good or bad? The answer may depend on what happens as a result of personal information in the hands of decision makers. Take the case of a woman whose child has leukemia. It's one thing if this information is used to offer the woman a special vacation package for sick children. But it's quite another if a company uses the information to deny a job

What Does the Law Say?

When a company collects or buys information, that information belongs to the company to use or sell. This is true even for medical records. Some legislation is on the books:

- The Privacy Act of 1974 was passed to give everyone the right to access and correct personal records and explicitly prevents information from being used for any purpose other than that for which it was collected. But this law applies only to federal agencies. Car registration and license information, being state-administered, are widely accessed by marketers. For example, the Marriott Hotel chain matches the names of its guests with motor vehicle and property records. This information then becomes the basis for deciding which customers to include in mailing campaigns.

A patchwork of other legislation targets specific industries, for example,

- The Cable Communication Policy Act of 1984 requires prior written or electronic consent from viewers to release viewing choices, retail transactions, or "other personally identifiable information." Summary information is excluded from these requirements.
- The Bork Bill (officially known as the Video Privacy Protection Act of 1988) was passed after a Washington, D.C., weekly published a list of Robert H. Bork's videotape rentals. At that time Bork was the subject of Supreme Court confirmation hearings. The Bork Bill prohibits the use of video rental information on customers for any purpose other than that of marketing goods and services directly to the customer.[19, 20] ❖

Who Owns Personal Information in Other Parts of the World?

THE GLOBAL PERSPECTIVE

Not all countries see information as the property of the collector. In 1995 the European Parliament announced a directive stipulating that individuals on whom information is collected be made aware of the users of the information, the purpose for the collection, to whom the information may be disclosed, right of access, correction, and so on.

Holland, Germany, and many other countries have similar legislation, which views personal information as the property of the individual. But New Zealand has the most stringent rules. New Zealand's Privacy Act requires that information a company collects must be relevant and essential for the business purpose of the company. Going even further, the law demands that personal information be collected directly from the individual, and that individual authorization must be given first. Companies in New Zealand are also required to take reasonable steps to inform the individual about any information being collected, the purpose of the collection, and the name and address of any organization collecting and storing it; companies must also allow individuals to access and correct any personal information.[21] ❖

to the woman because her special medical needs might cause the company's premiums to rise.

As was the case with the employer-employee relationship, a company has good reasons to have and use information about consumers: First, companies need to identify potential customers, then they need to know about customers so that they can tailor their goods and services accordingly. Second, companies need to be able to access information easily to provide ongoing good service. So businesses collect this information themselves and/or buy it from other businesses. For example:

- Mailing list companies routinely offer information on millions (80 or more) of families that can be accessed by income, age, credit card use, mail-order buying, number and age of children, and so on.[22]

- MasterCard OnLine provides a 1.2 terabyte database of credit card transaction information to its 22,000 members. This information includes account numbers, but not names or addresses.[23]

- ShopKo Stores, Inc., a retailer in Green Bay, Wisconsin, allows its suppliers to access and analyze information in its data warehouse through

While You're Looking at the Internet, It's Looking at You

When you sit in your own home or college lab and surf the Internet, you have the impression that your travels are private and anonymous. That's not so! You'll have noticed that a Web site can record the number of its visitors. It can also track what files, graphics, sound, or video visitors access. You also know that some sites request that you identify yourself and ask for some details. But many Web sites go beyond these tracking methods with **cookies**, which are little chunks of information about you that the Web site stores on *your* hard disk.

The type of information that is stored in a cookie varies; some just record your site of origin and your e-mail address, others keep detailed information on where you visited and for how long. Some Web sites use the information to allow you to revisit a site without reregistering, or to bring you directly to some part of the Web site, based on the previous visit. To find out if there are cookies on your hard disk look for files called "cookies.txt." You can prevent cookies from being deposited on your disk by configuring your browser to inform you before a cookie is made, or you can visit a Web site that shields your identity and allows you to travel to other sites anonymously. Of course, your identity is still only as safe as the shielding site. ❖

Responsibilities in the Management of Information

	Stability	Change
Access	Provide a predictable, accurate, and reliable information base.	Adjust to business needs, for example, • Provide CISs for customer input. • Give knowledge workers notebooks with modems for better access. • Change the form of information for a more transparent interface.
Security	The focus is stability, to prevent unwelcome intrusion and unauthorized access.	Change tactics to meet new dangers; for example, update your antivirus software regularly.
Privacy	Prevent unwelcome change in the lives of your employees and customers.	Change the policies and procedures to fit changes in how information is accessed. For example, formulate policies for information that leaves the building.

browser software. ShopKo's goal is to enhance vendor partnerships, thus bringing value to customers by allowing suppliers to analyze daily sales of 200,000 items in 130 stores. Here we have an example of an information partnership of the kind you saw in Chapter 3.[24]

■ Ticketmaster Corp. provides information gleaned from the cash registers of 2,700 Blockbuster video rental, Dayton Hudson, Marshall's, and Tower Records stores along with 15 telemarketing centers that handle 4 million inbound calls annually.[25]

Consumers benefit greatly as the recipients of goods and services because of the easy availability of information. They can buy large ticket items like cars and furniture immediately with instant credit. Special car alarm systems locate their cars within a large area. They get more comfortable chairs, better pizza, easier access to stores selling specialty goods like ski equipment or baseball card collections. However, people are becoming increasingly concerned about the unbridled distribution of personal information. More and more people are refusing to provide personal information. In fact, 80 percent of Americans believe they have lost control over how information about them is used. As many as 60 percent reported having refused to give information to a business because they thought it was not needed or was too personal.[26] Many provide fictitious information. This is because they have no trust that the information they give will be treated with care. What most people would like to have is a measure of control over their personal information, its disclosure, and its use.

The worst-case scenario outcome of consumers' ambivalence about providing personal information is a protracted tug-of-war between consumers and businesses with legislation and lawsuits aplenty. Several cases have already been litigated and many more have been filed. For example, in a case against Radio Shack, Robert Beken won $1,000 in damages for misuse of his personal data. When he paid his bill by check, he wrote a contract on the back committing the company to refrain from sending him advertisements or mailings. Radio Shack's position was that the store clerk had no authority to enter into such a contract on behalf of the store.

The best course of action would be to recognize that both businesses and consumers benefit greatly from the availability of information and, therefore, the best interests of both would be served by viewing information as partnership property.[27] Then consumers would feel comfortable about providing information, and businesses could use it to their mutual benefit. This approach would require procedures and guidelines that address the types and uses of personal information and the exercise of great care when passing on information that identifies individuals.

Managing Information Technology

Now that we've considered the management of information itself, we'll turn to managing the IT components that help generate and deliver it. Managing IT components means

- Having control of your IT components
- Arranging IT components to preserve the health of knowledge workers
- Taking steps to guarantee that a sudden disaster doesn't sever your information flow and shut you down

Control
Taking Charge of Components and Costs

Advances and breakthroughs are daily occurrences in the IT industry. Better, faster, easier-to-use hardware and software, along with new approaches to generating and delivering information appear constantly. Having control means (1) integrating IT components into your organization so that the technology is as invisible as possible and (2) keeping track of the costs involved.

Interoperability
Making It All Work Together

Interoperability, also known as standardization, refers to the extent to which IT equipment and software components are compatible. When you buy a phone, a phone jack, or an answering machine, it doesn't occur to you to ask whether the device will work with the phone system to which you're connected. That's because the phone system has interoperability.

This level of interoperability is the goal of IT systems everywhere. Your IT systems should be as integrated as the phone system. However, because an IT system is often much more complex than a phone system, integration is seldom simple to achieve. There are different types of computers and several brands each of supercomputers, mainframes, minis, and microcomputers. The biggest problems arise when connecting IT components in a network. Computer trade journals are full of sad stories about the perils of making a large number of computers, printers, routers, and so on, work together.

It's not just a question of hardware either. There are different operating systems (Unix and Windows for example). There are different network protocols. Many application software packages are available for almost every business task. Information has different formats—it can be text, sound, graphics, or video. Information, even text information, can be stored in multiple ways. All these differences cause major problems when you're trying to connect knowledge workers to information. The best approach is to consider interoperability whenever you're deciding to add equipment or software. If you already have different systems in place, you can purchase hardware adapter components and software that will bridge the incompatibility.

You can overdo standardization, though. Say you have standards in place governing the type of computers that you buy for knowledge workers. It may well be the case that some knowledge workers need a different type of system, perhaps a more powerful workstation. Standardization should always move your organization in the direction of better customer service.

Cost Control

Once upon a time, when all IT systems were managed exclusively by IT specialists, and computers cost upwards of hundreds of thousands of dollars, companies kept careful track of their investments in IT components. But since the advent of PCs, when the control and use of IT components began to spread beyond the walls of the computer center, many companies are finding, to their dismay, that they don't really know what they have or how much it's costing them. Organizations often buy IT components such as PCs, printers, and the like on an ad hoc basis, and many companies don't even know how many PCs they have, like the large organization that could only estimate that it had between 50,000 and 90,000 PCs. A

Cost Savings of Standardization

- You'll spend less on training when knowledge workers can transfer knowledge about equipment and interfaces.
- Knowledge workers will make fewer mistakes if computers and software are familiar.
- You can move replacement knowledge workers into the positions of absent ones more easily

- You can stockpile fewer replacement parts for networks and other IT equipment.
- You have fewer software packages to back up and store in preparation for emergencies.
- You can benefit from economies of scale in purchasing IT components if you buy a large quantity of the same item. ❖

IBM Goes for Interoperability Gold

Probably the biggest job of interoperability of IT components was undertaken by IBM for the 1996 Olympic Games. For this $40 million project IBM had to coordinate

- 300 LANs
- 7,000 PCs
- 80 minicomputers
- 3 mainframes
- 10,000 voice lines
- 500 data lines
- 9,000 radios
- 6,000 pagers
- 2,000 wireless devices

And integrate their systems with

- Timing devices by Swatch
- Imaging systems by Eastman Kodak Co.
- Printing systems by Xerox Corp.

To run more than 100 applications that served

- 130,000 knowledge workers
- 16,000 athletes and officials
- 15,000 journalists
- 25,000 relatives of athletes and coaches
- 75,000 volunteers, contractors, and staff members.

IBM had to keep several distinct IT systems up and running to serve various stakeholders:

- The Commentators Information System provided live feeds to the broadcast, print, and radio press. The reporters received scores and statistics in real time.

- The INFO96 information system offered e-mail, news, local weather information, schedules, and athletes' biographies to spectators by way of PC kiosks equipped with touch screens. Spectators were able to print information on any one of several thousand printers.
- IBM's Web site offered scores, commentary, and other sports information, and had 189,000,000 hits.
- The Games Management System served the Olympics management team, staff, and volunteers providing logistical, financial, and personnel information.[30] ❖

---

report in *Infoworld* says that failure to track equipment costs U.S. companies $20 billion a year in unaccounted hardware, inaccurate software licenses, and, in some locales, even property taxes.[28]

The initial outlay for individual IT components is, comparatively speaking, not very large, but it's only the beginning. Estimates vary on how much it costs to own, manage, and support each employee's computer, but most studies suggest a range between $8,000 to $12,000 per year, depending on the type of company and its needs. The lifetime cost greatly exceeds the initial cost because of ongoing repair, the inventory of spare parts, software updates, upgrades of RAM, and so on. Because large companies usually have upwards of 2,500 PCs, failure to control IT equipment costs can seriously impact investment plans and profit margins. By developing and maintaining effective standards for tracking and managing their IT components, most companies could save about 13 percent of their IT budgets.[29]

Ergonomics
Are You Sitting Comfortably?

Having IT components that work together is very important, but the physical arrangement of IT components in relation to knowledge workers impacts their health and well-being. Thus we need to consider ergonomics. *Ergonomics* is the study of how to design and arrange your workplace so that you can achieve maximum productivity and reduce discomfort and adverse health effects. Microsoft Corp.'s Bill Gates and other celebrities use chairs designed to position their bodies at the same angle that the body naturally assumes in a zero-gravity environment.[31] The chairs have 10 different adjustments geared to align your spine at a 128-degree angle. The design of the chairs is based on NASA studies showing the relaxation posture that astronauts assume when floating around in gravity deprivation. Ergonomics actually involves much more than having a good chair.

Chevron Becomes Cost Conscious

For Chevron, with about 40,000 PC-type computers worldwide, the cost of maintaining IT equipment is quite an investment. Estimates of the lifetime cost of PCs range from $8,000 to $12,000 per year, depending on the company. To keep costs at a minimum,

the company decided on a plan of standardization. The major part of the plan is to ensure that almost all Chevron knowledge workers have common hardware and operating system platforms. The exceptions are those people who need a different system to maximize their productivity.

As well as exercising its buying clout to reduce the cost of new IT equipment, Chevron is requiring

vendors to install Chevron's own application software on new computers prior to delivery. This saves installation time for Chevron knowledge workers and IT specialists. In order to speed up distribution of software, Chevron sends new versions of software through e-mail to its knowledge workers across the world, reducing mailing costs.[33] ❖

It deals with all types of work areas and machinery, but we will limit the discussion here to IT equipment.

Improperly arranged computer components can cause physical injuries. **Repetitive strain injury (RSI),** also referred to as cumulative trauma disorder (CTD), is characterized by headache, neckache, eyestrain, wrist pain, fatigue, and stress caused by repetitive actions. RSI, known as "the industrial disease of the information age," is the leading cause of injury, productivity loss, and financial strain on small businesses, costing hundreds of thousands of dollars a year in work-related injuries.[32] Some victims even become disabled, temporarily or permanently. The U.S. Bureau of Labor Statistics says that, nationwide, the number of RSI-related illnesses and injuries was 22,600 in 1982 and 332,000 in 1994. These figures correspond to the tremendous increase in the use of computers during that period. Remember that it was in 1982 that the IBM PC was introduced. An estimated 4.4 million people in the United States suffer from various computer-related disorders. When an employee is out with an injury, the company may have to pay overtime for workers to assume the job of the absentee and, perhaps, train someone else.

So how can you, as a knowledge worker or a manager of IT systems, avoid becoming part of the RSI statistics? Basically, your computer system should be an extension of your body as you perform the task. Certain guidelines have been developed by experts who have studied the problem for years. Note in Figure 10.3 the posture of the person and how the keyboard and mouse are positioned to keep the arms parallel to the floor.

Disaster Recovery
Murphy's Law Applies

So far we have considered management of information and purchase and arrangement of IT components. But what if the unthinkable happens? What if a flood or storm or earthquake wipes out our carefully constructed and beautifully managed IT system? Annually, about 250 natural disasters occur around the world. This number remains relatively stable, but the economic loss seems to be increasing. Between 1980 and 1984 about $15

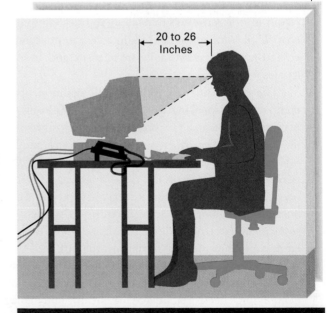

20 to 26 Inches

FIGURE 10.3

What the Experts Say

Carpel Tunnel Syndrome: A Painful Ailment

The government reports that carpel tunnel syndrome requires a longer recovery period than any other work-related illness or injury. *Carpal tunnel syndrome* is a type of RSI in which the wrist becomes inflamed and swells when the median nerve is pinched where it passes through the bones of the wrist. First you experience a loss of feeling in the hand and then a loss of strength. In severe cases, even simple tasks become difficult and extremely painful to perform. On average, a knowledge worker with this condition requires 32 days away from work.[35] ❖

---

billion was lost annually. But from 1990 to 1992 the loss was $40 billion per year.[34] Unfortunately, natural disasters aren't the only danger on the IT system horizon. Fires, burst water pipes, and gas leaks can all cause serious damage to an IT system. You need to be prepared. Banks are required by law to have a disaster recovery plan. A *disaster recovery plan* is a plan of how you will carry on business if a major catastrophe occurs and knocks out your IT system. General Motors demands that its dealers have one. Your business should have one too. A disaster recovery plan is aimed at anticipating and recovering from change—the undesirable kind. A well-managed disaster recovery plan focuses on business recovery and on computer operations as a necessary part of getting your business going again.

Here's the Plan

You saw in Chapter 8 how to formulate a contingency plan—the strategic plan that determines what information is crucial to the survival of the organization and the resources that will be devoted to its protection. A disaster recovery plan details the implementation of that contingency plan. A good disaster recovery plan will take the following into consideration: customers, facilities, knowledge workers, business information, computer equipment, and communications infrastructure (see Figure 10.4).

Customers Your customers, however patient, cannot wait indefinitely for you to get back on your feet—they have troubles of their own. Customers will be reassured if you inform them of what is happening so that they can plan accordingly. If you have a short customer list, you can inform each one individually. If you have many customers, you should consider using radio, TV, and/or newspaper advertisements to notify them of the current situation, alternative arrangements, and when you expect to be back in operation. This will not only reduce their uncertainty, but also leave them with increased confidence in your company (which means you could actually benefit from a disaster). While you're making alternative arrangements, greet callers with a message that informs them of your current status; or, even better, make arrangements for a person to do the job. If your business involves taking phone orders, have forms on hand that duplicate the screens that would normally be used.

ON YOUR OWN

Is Your Computer a Health Hazard?

Find five computers in different places and measure

- The distance from your eyes to the monitor
- The angle of your hands when they're on the keyboard
- The height of the mouse in relation to the keyboard

1. When you work at a computer for a long time, do you ache in any particular spot? If so, where?

2. If you feel discomfort, are the keyboard and monitor arranged according to the guidelines in Figure 10.3?

3. Do you take a rest periodically? Experts recommend that you do so about once every hour. ❖

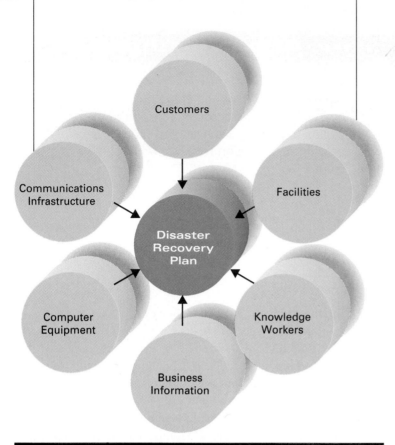

FIGURE 10.4

The Six Prongs of a Disaster Recovery Plan

across the United States, and it has sites in 40 other countries around the world that offer facilities and equipment, and even teams of specialists who will help restore operations.[37]

Knowledge Workers Your knowledge workers must know beforehand when and where to return to work after a disaster strikes. They will be under increased stress, especially if the disaster affects their personal lives as well. It's difficult for people to keep their minds on the job if their houses have just been reduced to rubble. Disaster recovery usually involves working long hours beyond the normal working day. So before your employees can concentrate on your business they may have to make arrangements for child or elder care. If the disaster is widespread, you may have to deal with an avalanche of incoming calls from concerned relatives and friends.

If you move your business to an alternative site, you may have to arrange housing for your knowledge workers. For long hours of work you'll need to provide food service for your employees or, at the very least, a directory of sources for obtaining fast food and other necessities. You'll need to make travel arrangements for knowledge workers to the alternative site. You may also have to make special arrangements for disabled workers.

Facilities When you have prioritized business functions and identified minimum equipment needs, locate an acceptable alternative business location. The safest option of all is a *hot site*, which is a separate fully equipped facility to which you can move immediately after the disaster and resume business. Hot sites are popular with financial firms, who spend about $300 million a year to rent hot sites fully equipped with computers and phone lines. The Chubb Contingency Trading Facility, located within walking distance of Wall Street in New York City, is one such hot site. This facility has 10 trading rooms with faxes, copy machines, printers, telexes, backup generators, 1,000 phone lines, a local area network with PCs, uniformed police patrol, and so on.[36] Another alternative is a *cold site*, which does not have computer equipment installed but has backup power generators, a sprinkler system, a security system, and so on.

Your company can install its own hot or cold site, or you can contract with a company specializing in recovery to have one available when you need it. Many companies provide such facilities. The largest three, Comdisco Disaster Recovery Services, IBM Business Recovery Services, and SunGard Recovery Services, provide such facilities. IBM, for example, has 17 hot or cold sites

Business Information This topic was discussed in a previous section but, because it's so important, we'll state the obvious again. The simplest, oldest, and most effective action you can take is to back up information as part of the normal business process. View back up operations as a business process and not an IT process. That means that each knowledge worker is responsible for protecting organizational information. It's not a task that is the sole responsibility of IT specialists.

Computer Equipment A big problem for firms with complex networks is that disaster recovery companies supplying hot sites have difficulty providing client/server facilities, because most networks are unique, multivendor arrays of systems and software. Take NationsBank in Charlotte, North Carolina, for example, which is a conglomerate of 400 mergers and acquisitions.[38] John Sponski, executive vice president of technology services, provides for disaster recovery. With 118 applications running on 77 platforms, including systems from Digital Equipment, Hewlett-Packard, IBM, Stratus, and Tandem, the system is too complex for a recovery service to handle, so John developed an in-house disaster recovery plan. According to John, the cost of the recovery plan

Boatmen's Sails Through Waves of Information

How do you create a disaster recovery plan for the IT system for a bank with 650 branches; 17,000 employees; and 1,800 ATM machines; which together generate 2 million transactions a day? Boatmen's Bank had to answer this question. It chose to move all transaction processing to a technology center in Kansas City equipped with $100 million worth of computers, robots, and optical technology. Technology Center manager Scott Mansker, vice president of Boatmen's Service Co., explained it this way: "We are a manufacturing facility whose product is information." The technology center has 60 employees who staff the center around the clock in staggered 8-hour shifts.

Boatmen's chose the technology center approach to centralize its processing operations. Part of this strategy was to protect IT systems. The technology center is located in the Northland area of Kansas City. Even though this part of the city has never been known to flood, the floors are raised 30 inches above the slab anyway. The security system is state of the art, and the windows are bulletproof. The roof can stand 120-mile-an-hour winds. If a particularly tenacious tornado rips that roof off, there's another one underneath to keep the building dry. The whole technology center was built like that: It has two of everything—power supplies, electrical systems, backup diesel generators, cooling systems. "A lot of companies build two data centers," says Scott. "We built one and made sure it would work."[39] ❖

---

runs into millions of dollars annually, but because a bank's business is contingent upon providing accurate information, the expense is the lesser evil.

CAREER OPPORTUNITY

If you find yourself responsible for formulating a disaster recovery plan, you can get help from many sources. These include

- The Federal Emergency Agency's "Disaster Planning Guide for Business and Industry."
- Publications of the San Francisco Bay Area Earthquake Preparedness Project.
- The Computer Planning and Recovery Planning Institute.
- *The Disaster Recovery Yellow Pages*, published by Systems Audit of Newton, Massachusetts, and costing less than $100, lists everything from equipment sources to water removal services.

For milder types of disasters, like temporary power outages, you can install an uninterruptible power supply (UPS). These battery backup systems will protect your system against fluctuations and short-term power outages. To keep going if your power is gone for more than a short time, you'll need a generator. Maintain an inventory of computer parts on hand. For those parts that are too expensive to stockpile, like network routers, consider pooling a supply with other businesses in the area. You can also make special arrangements with vendors to loan you equipment when you need it.

Communications Infrastructure Loss of communications is one of the biggest problems during a disaster because it is pretty much synonymous with lost revenue. So restoration of communications is a first priority. Have a supply of cellular phones in more than one location. Know which employees have ham radio or CB equipment. Develop alternative telecommunications plans, such as arrangements for employees to communicate on their home computers.

You can never hope to be totally prepared for every emergency that might occur, but with a real commitment from management and detailed planning you can avoid the worst.

Managing Knowledge Workers

Much of your company's information raw material and capital is in databases and data warehouses. However, a considerable amount of valuable information is located

INDUSTRY PERSPECTIVE

Entertainment & Publishing

They Practiced What They Preached

In January 1995 the magazine *Managing Office Technology* ran an article headlined "Disaster Recovery: Are You Ready?" By the end of that very month, Penton, the publisher of the magazine, found that its own disaster recovery plan was sorely tested. It happened on a Saturday afternoon in Cleveland when a water main broke. Forty-pound chunks of asphalt came sailing through office windows followed by a wall of water. It's cold in Cleveland in January, so icicles formed on the windows and the outside of the building, and the carpeted floors became skating rinks. The water in the basement rose to 3 feet and the first 4 floors were covered with 8 inches of water. Water soaked through the floor, then through the ceilings of the floors below, then froze.

Ceiling tiles crumbled and water, ice, and debris came crashing down onto computer equipment, desks and anything else in the way. Drywalls collapsed, file cabinets filled with water, the lower shelves of bookcases were covered in water. The electricity shorted very early in the disaster and information being saved at that time was lost.

The disaster affected 15 of the publisher's 35 publications. Damage was estimated at about $3 million. But Penton was prepared. It had a disaster recovery plan in place, and the company was up and running within hours of the disaster and operating at full power within 2 weeks.

Teams that had been chosen and given their assignments beforehand went to work immediately. A computer technician powered down the main computers in the information-processing center. Temporary office space was secured in an unaffected building across the street. Penton's quality council held marathon meetings to set priorities for the business and to establish procedures for maintaining schedules of affected magazines. A phone bank and message center were set up across the street, staffed by the company's operators and by volunteers. Publishers and department heads contacted employees about the problem and kept them informed. Employees contacted each other to offer support. Corporate Communications issued disaster recovery updates twice daily to inform all employees of progress, help centers, and resources. The company purchased PowerPCs to replace damaged machines and loaned notebooks to employees who wanted to work from home. Because the magazines always backed up their work every night, little information was lost. Diskettes were sent out for cleaning and information restoration.

Because Penton had a disaster recovery plan in place it was able to weather the storm, so to speak, and losses were kept to a minimum. Not that it was easy. The employees worked around the clock to restore operations.[40, 41] ❖

---

in the heads of employees. A good manager knows that human brainpower resides at all levels of the company, not just at the management level. Experienced employees know your business, the industry, your company's competitive strengths and weaknesses, products, customers, and processes. You saw in Chapter 3 how some of the most progressive companies are sharing information among all employees and consulting those in the front lines to determine how to better provide the customer moment of value. Along with different responsibilities and areas of expertise, knowledge workers differ in other ways. For example, the knowledge workers you want working for you may not be located in the city where your business is or they may have been raised in another culture and require help in the transition. All knowledge workers are part of the business organization, which, in turn, is part of the larger organization of society. And, as such, business has a responsibility to act ethically. In discussing the management of knowledge workers we'll examine

- Telecommuting
- Cultural diversity
- Ethics

Responsibilities in the Management of IT Components

	Stability	Change
Control	Provide IT components that work together. Track resources to minimize waste.	New IT components become available constantly; change when it makes good business sense.
Ergonomics	Arrange IT components so that the health of knowledge workers is protected.	People are not built the same, and differences in height and dexterity require adjustment of IT components.
Disaster Recovery	Take steps to minimize the damage of sudden unwelcome change.	Reevaluate disaster plans to accommodate major changes in your IT systems; for example, if you move to a client/server system.

Telecommuting
Home Is Where the Office Is

As you've already seen in Chapters 1, 3, and 6, your knowledge workers don't have to be physically present in your corporate offices to be productive. In fact, you may find that *telecommuting* makes some of your knowledge workers much more productive. There are already about 15 million telecommuters. Table 10.1 shows the proportion of telecommuting employees in selected industries. The Gartner Group expects that number to reach 30 million by the year 2000. Several incentives are contributing to this trend.

- *Legislative* The Clean Air Act (1990) requires that businesses in large cities employing more than 100 people in one location reduce their employees' commute time by 25 percent. Furthermore, in Southern California, each company's impact on air pollution is monitored, and those that exceed the limit are fined up to $25,000. These measures are expected to create about 15 million telecommuting jobs in California alone. The Family and Medical Leave Act mandates unpaid leave for parents of young children. With telecommuting, your employees can work at home so you're not totally without their services, and they will receive a pay check.

- *Productivity* Many companies are finding that a telecommuting program can greatly improve productivity and reduce overhead costs. They can increase productivity by saving knowledge workers the time it takes to commute and work from the office. They can use this time attending to customer service or other business-related tasks. Companies save the cost of office space, heating, air conditioning, electricity, water, and so on.

- *Knowledge workers located in other states* Many situations make telecommuting a good choice for employer and employee. For example, you may want to retain an experienced employee who has relocated. Or you may want to attract knowledge workers who don't want to move to your location. FedEx, for example, has opened several regional data centers so that knowledge workers don't have to move to Tennessee. Three of these data centers are located in Colorado Springs, Dallas, and Orlando.[42]

- *Knowledge workers located in other countries* With telecommuting, you can even employ knowledge workers living in other countries. Northern Telecom Ltd. catalogs its employees' skills on a worldwide basis so that its pool of knowledge workers covers the globe.[43]

TABLE 10.1 Who's Telecommuting?[44, 45]

Industry	Percentage of Employees
Insurance	54%
High technology	44%
Banking/financial	34%
Retail/wholesale	33%
Health care	32%
Public/nonprofit	27%
Manufacturing	26%
Utilities/transportation	22%

Does out of Sight Mean out of Control?

Telecommunications already allows us to connect people all over the world using phone lines. We have phones that belong not to a place but to a person, so one number reaches the person no matter where that owner roams. We have notebook computers that aren't permanently chained to an electrical socket. We have fax machines, e-mail, and groupware so that people can share their ideas and work together while in separate locations. IT allows you to implement a telecommuting program. The question is, can you make it profitable? Telecommuting programs offer many advantages. But managing telecommuting requires skill and careful thought. You must be clear on the *why, what, who, how,* and *where* before you begin (see Figure 10.5).

The *Why* of Telecommuting

Why would you implement a telecommuting program? Well, if it is to be successful it must make business sense. It must increase productivity, reduce costs, retain the right employees, or increase customer contact. It should not be merely a charitable gesture to certain employees. A good example is Dun & Bradstreet. Dun & Bradstreet (D&B) has a successful telecommuting program that was introduced originally to speed up processing cycle time and improve flexibility in meeting customer needs. Now salespeople based in the Dallas office who visit client locations don't have to return to the office to have someone process their orders; they can do it themselves. The cost per worker was reduced to $6,000 from the $30,000 that D&B had been spending on office space, support staff to process orders, and other overhead.[46]

The *What* of Telecommuting

What kinds of jobs or projects are suited to telecommuting? The best kind of jobs for telecommuting are those for which the output is relatively self-contained such as the work product of accountants, insurance claim processors, software developers, or sales representatives. Telecommuting projects should have clearly definable beginning and ending points.

Even relatively autonomous tasks, however, require some group interaction. These tasks can be accomplished by requiring telecommuters to meet in a central site at specified times so that group members may conduct business. This meeting can be a formal meeting on company premises or it can be more casual. For example, the Rizzuti Marketing and Media Group, which consists of six workers who have telecommuted since 1992, meets once a week for breakfast to keep in touch.[47]

Some jobs don't lend themselves to telecommuting. They may require services that are available only at the central office like the mailroom and the corporate library. Some jobs require a constant physical presence, for example, a company administrative assistant may not be a good telecommuting candidate.

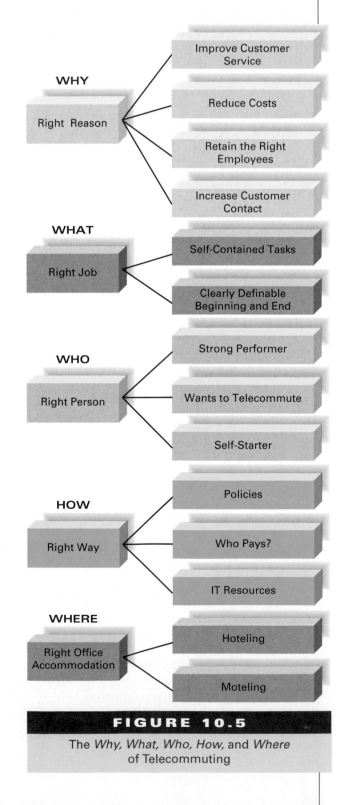

FIGURE 10.5

The *Why, What, Who, How,* and *Where* of Telecommuting

Advantages of Telecommuting

As an Employer

- You benefit from higher employee productivity— between a 5 and 20 percent increase.
- You benefit from reduced absenteeism, on average about 2 days per employee per year.
- You benefit from employee retention, avoiding the costs of hiring and training a new person.
- You benefit from reduced overhead costs, 20 percent on average.
- You benefit by increasing your domestic market, because nonresidents can work for your company.
- You benefit from access to a global labor force, which permits you to hire people from as far away as England or India.
- You benefit from improved employee morale, because employees value the autonomy that

allows them to attend their children's school functions during the day, making up the work time later.

As an Employee

- You can pursue other important activities, such as completing a graduate degree.
- You have greater flexibility to care for children or parents.
- You avoid commuter traffic and bad weather.

As a Citizen

- You reduce pollution. By the year 2000, it is projected that telecommuting will save 1.5 billion gallons of fuel and prevent 3.5 million tons of carbon from polluting the air.[48, 49] ❖

The *Who* of Telecommuting

Who is best suited to telecommuting? Well, certainly not those knowledge workers who agree with Andy Warhol that 80 percent of life is just showing up. A telecommuter must be able to produce results independently. Where the emphasis of management traditionally has been on supervision, in telecommuting the emphasis is on results.

In fact, the key to making telecommuting work is choosing the right employees to participate in the program. Select only employees who are strong performers and who want to be telecommuters. A good telecommuter is someone who is also a self-starter, able to manage time well, and able to balance work and home life. The manager and employee must agree on definitions of good performance and methods of measurement. It's a good idea to provide training for both the employee and the manager to clearly explain the differences between telecommuting and the traditional workplace, and to prepare each to become part of it.

The *How* of Telecommuting

How can you best implement a telecommuting program? Without a sense of trust on the part of the supervisor and a sense of accountability on the part of the employee, telecommuting will not work well. You should establish clear expectation policies. You must decide who will pay

the telecommuter's equipment and overhead costs. You'll also have to provide telecommuters with the IT resources that will enable them to perform their jobs at home.

Who Pays? Telecommuting setup costs vary greatly depending on the type of equipment the telecommuter requires to function effectively. A telecommuter will require, at minimum, a computer and at least one phone line. Two phone lines are preferable, one for voice and one for data. An answering machine, fax machine, and copier may also be necessary. Combination fax, laser printer, copier scanners are now available for less than $1,000.

However, these equipment costs are not the only expenses involved. Employees working at home are using their personal space, heat, light, and air conditioning for the benefit of the company. Telecommuters may need to buy larger homes, or add onto their existing homes to accommodate telecommuting. You might consider giving the telecommuter an expense allowance. While you're evaluating these costs, keep in mind that every person who does not require office space can save you up to 150 square feet, and in many cities, office space rents for $25 per square foot. So you may be saving $3,750 per month per employee in overhead for office space alone—that's $45,000 per employee per year. If just 10 knowledge workers are telecommuters, you could save up to $500,000 annually.

Motivating Knowledge Workers

Motivating knowledge workers means inspiring, directing, and sustaining the kind of behavior that is appropriate for achieving customer moment of value. Knowledge workers tend to be much more effective if they have a clear conceptual understanding of company goals and objectives, how they should be met, and how critical they themselves are to the process. Your knowledge workers not only must understand your vision for the future, but also share in it—they must feel a sense of partnership. Involving knowledge workers in decision making creates a sense of ownership in the success of the company and makes knowledge workers feel as if they're an important part of the organization, thereby encouraging them to give their best.

Giving your knowledge workers latitude in how they perform their jobs is another way to generate a sense of ownership, and it also provides them the opportunity to find more effective ways to operate. Knowledge workers who are allowed to make mistakes without fear of reprisal are likely to be more creative problem solvers. You can't make progress without making mistakes, so allow knowledge workers to fail occasionally. The advent of self-managing workgroups has changed the manager's role from one of supervision to one of coach or mentor. This orientation requires a different skill set. It means encouraging independent thought and risk taking and tolerating a certain amount of failure. ❖

You must also consider liability expense. You don't have the same control over the working conditions of your employees if they're not at the office. What about Worker's Compensation for accidents that occur at home while the employee is working? What about OSHA's health and safety rules? Cigna Insurance, based in Philadelphia, closely monitors the working environment of its telecommuters.[50] Cigna outfits employees with a computer desk, a PC, a well-designed chair, printer, fax machine, and two phone lines. At least twice a year, Cigna inspects the home office to ensure that the employee is in compliance with federal safety regulations and Cigna's own standards.

IT Support: When They Yell "HELP!"

Even though people in business today are increasingly computer literate, they still find themselves in need of help from time to time. Most companies have informal networks of "computer experts" who are willing to help their colleagues, but many companies have formalized the process in the form of a help desk or information center.

Help Desk: First Aid

A **help desk** is a central clearing point for problems. Usually, the help desk staff will answer some questions but refer more complex problems to the appropriate IT experts. The problems that a help desk deals with could range from questions about high-density diskettes to serious difficulties, like an operating system crash. One help desk employee was puzzled by a caller's request for someone to "fix the coffee-cup holder on the computer." The caller was referring to the CD-ROM drive.

Information Centers: The Rescue Team

An **information center** consists of a group of people—IT specialists and people knowledgeable in business practices—who will help you with special information needs. They provide assistance and expertise on accessing information, performing data analysis, and any other information-related requests. Many information centers offer training on software and hardware. The main goal of the information center is to provide immediate assistance to knowledge workers who want to use IT to solve their business problems. Some information centers will actually develop an application for you. They have experts who are skilled in using software packages, such as an expert system or a 4GL. ❖

TEAM WORK

Could You Work a Help Desk?

Some of the questions employees ask a help desk are listed below. Do some research and answer them.

1. I just got a brand new printer. The instructions discuss a "driver." What does that mean?

2. How do I create a shortcut in Windows?

3. What does "General Protection Fault" mean?

4. Why don't I have a toolbar in Microsoft Word?

5. If I delete a file, is it gone forever?

6. How do I search for a file?

7. Why should I use the shutdown feature before I turn off my computer?

8. I'm telecommuting. How do I know what settings my modem should have?

9. If I buy a computer for my home, will I automatically get Internet access? ❖

IT Resources Make sure hardware and software is properly configured before sending it home with employees. This will help you avoid problems and downtime later. Telecommuters need connectivity to the organization's information. Also keep in mind that telecommuters will increase the demand for remote access and they'll increase network access at all hours of the day, night, and weekend.

The *Where* of Telecommuting

Where will you locate telecommuters when they come into the office? Various arrangements are possible. Some may retain their offices, especially if they work only 1 or 2 days a week at home. For employees who spend a large proportion of their work time outside the central office, a virtual office makes sense. In a ***virtual office*** none of the employees has personal work space; rather, they use offices, desks, and computers as needed. In Chapter 3, you learned about virtual organizations, which are located nowhere. Well, the whole organization doesn't have to be virtual. If one group of employees seldom comes into the corporate office, then that segment of your organization is virtual. About 20 percent of IBM North America's 105,000 employees use a virtual office. In Indianapolis, 200 of the 250 workers reserve office space as they need it. They spend the rest of the time at home, with clients, or on the road. Real estate costs have been reduced by more than 65 percent, says John Frank, business leader for IBM's Workforce Mobility Programs.[51] We borrow the lodging industry's language to describe office space for telecommuters.

- ***Hoteling*** is where offices are kept equipped, and knowledge workers reserve space in advance. Often these offices have between four and eight desks.

- ***Moteling*** differs from hoteling in that space is not reserved. Rather it is allocated on a first-come–first-served basis. Essentially, the office becomes a "club" where employees meet on a regular basis, with rooms reserved for certain activities.

CAREER OPPORTUNITY

The business world of today is complex and fast-moving. To remain effective and marketable, you have to keep learning. Learning is not a spectator sport, you must be proactive. It's hard to keep up, but opportunities are available:

- Videotapes are available which are effective for skills training, like learning about software packages.

- You can teach yourself by reading and experimenting with software packages.

- Trade journals are always a good way to learn what's happening in your industry.

- Find out what incentives or financial support your company provides for knowledge workers who want to complete education and training courses.

- Volunteer for on-the-job training programs offered by your company.

Cross-Cultural Diversity
A Mile or Two in Different Shoes

Continuous improvements in telecommunications and transportation and the need to expand markets are spurring more and more companies to become transnational. One in seven equity trades in today's financial markets takes place between parties of different nationalities. In the last 20 years, the proportion of goods and services that the world produced for export has doubled to 20 percent of total output.[52] New alliances are forming as companies coordinate manufacturing, distribution, and marketing strategies on a global scale. The increase in the number of transnational companies is bringing more and more knowledge workers into contact, to a greater or lesser extent, with other nationalities and cultures. You never know when you might have to travel abroad to manage an IT system. Or you might find yourself with knowledge workers from another culture on your staff.

Culture has a profound effect on everything that happens in a society—even IT systems. *Culture* is the collective personality of a nation or society. It encompasses a society's language, traditions, currency, religion, history, music, and acceptable behavior, among other things. Culture is influenced by climate, the society's physical location, its rivers, mountains, history, and anything else that shapes the way people live. For example, because a large number of the first U.S. citizens had fled from oppressive governments, freedom is considered an important right in this country. This concept of freedom extends to information. Most Americans believe that information should be freely available (witness the Freedom of Information Act) and that it is synonymous with power. Other societies don't see it that way. Many societies severely restrict the availability of information and consider information a burden. Under the old Soviet system, for example, there were no phone books in Moscow.

The most significant and powerful factor of expanding a transnational firm's IT system across national boundaries is not hardware- or software-related. It's the effect of *cross-cultural diversity*—the difference in behavior and attitude among people from different cultures—on the parties involved. IT specialists and knowledge workers are often among the first employees to be sent abroad when a company expands. Even companies that

---

Going to College Without Going to College

THE GLOBAL PERSPECTIVE

The largest and most innovative education and training organization in Europe is Britain's Open University which has 218,000 students—141,000 at the undergraduate level and 10,000 at the graduate level. The remaining 67,000 students are not pursuing a specific degree. The university's oldest student thus far was a 93-year-old; its youngest, a 9-year-old prodigy studying mathematics. Many more students audit courses. This huge university lacks a physical campus. It has a small central administration facility, but most faculty and students telecommute—they teach and learn from home.

Students receive course materials by mail or e-mail. Courses are taught (about 700 hours per year) on TV outside prime time. Radio courses (about 150 hours per year) are also available. Students studying science receive home-experiment kits and work through their lab courses at home. Seven thousand tutors and counselors provide help and support to the students through 13 regional centers.

Since the university opened in 1971, about 172,000 undergraduate degrees have been awarded and almost 8,000 master's and Ph.D.-level degrees. Because of the high standards exacted by the Open University, these degrees are respected throughout Europe.

Because of its virtual nature, the Open University is accessible to people in countries outside Britain. All European Union citizens are eligible for admission. But the university also has partnerships with countries outside the European Union including Russia, Hungary, Singapore, and Hong Kong.

Although the Open University in the United Kingdom is the largest in the world, it's not the only one. For example, Israel also has an Open University with an enrollment of 25,000 where the language of instruction is Hebrew. In the United States the idea is becoming popular for graduate degrees.[53] ❖

Vive La Difference

- In Germany, a wedding ring on the left hand means that the wearer is engaged to be married. During the wedding ceremony the ring is transferred to the right hand. So a wedding ring on the right hand means the person is married.

- In Japan, sneezing or blowing your nose in public is considered offensive, whereas slurping your food is considered to be a sign of appreciation.

- In China, it's perfectly acceptable to give someone a photo of him or herself, but if you write the person's name on the photo as identification or in a dedication it is taken to mean that you consider that person to be dead.

- In Russia, and many other countries, commas and decimal points are reversed. For example, the number *12,345.67* would be written as *12.345,67*.

- In predominantly Christian cultures, the Sabbath is Sunday, Israel celebrates the Sabbath on Saturday, and the Moslem countries have their holy day on Friday.

- In England, an ATM is referred to as a "hole in the wall" machine. Germans refer to collecting money from an ATM as "pulling money." ❖

---

send a small representation usually send someone versed in IT. Recognizing the large part that cultural diversity plays in transnational business, Samsung Electronics Co. helps its knowledge workers understand customers in other parts of the world by sending them abroad for a year to learn about other languages and cultures.[54] These knowledge workers are not allowed to contact the local Samsung office and have only one trip home during their time away. Eastman Chemical Co. and Motorola Inc. go one step further by tying advancement to knowledge workers' familiarity with the culture, language, and business practices of countries where the companies do business.[55] Why is it so important to understand cultural diversity?

Cultural differences are like a great river: A big river provides wonderful benefits—water, transportation, power for electricity, and even tourism. However, it can also cause havoc. The way to deal with a powerful river is to understand and respect it. McDonald's recognized the importance of respecting cross-cultural diversity when it recently opened fast-food restaurants in India. Much of India's population is of the Hindu faith, which prohibits the consumption of beef. So McDonald's serves mutton burgers and veggie burgers there instead of its traditional fare.

The Swedish furniture firm of IKEA took a little longer to adapt its merchandise to U.S. preferences.[56] In the beginning IKEA didn't realize how dramatically U.S. home furnishings differ from those in Sweden. Swedish beds are narrower and are not usually sold in matching bedroom sets like American bedroom suites. IKEA's kitchen cupboards were too narrow for the large dinner plates that people here use. The drinking glasses were too small for a nation that thinks a soft drink is not a soft drink until you add ice. In fact, Americans were buying IKEA's flower vases as glasses.

These cross-cultural differences are not limited to eating and sleeping habits. For example, many European democracies have very strict laws concerning name-linked information. Sweden's law is among the most stringent. So, if you find yourself managing an IT system in one of these countries, you may find that you can't send information pertaining to local customers to your corporate headquarters.

Culture Shock
Caution! High Voltage!

Although many of us rejoice in the uniqueness of the peoples in the world and find endless enchantment in exploring our different identities, it's necessary to recognize that the great journey of discovery can be troublesome. If you live and work in another country for any length of time, you're likely to suffer a profound reaction called culture shock. *Culture shock* is the disorientation and confusion that you experience when you're accustomed to one culture and suddenly find yourself in another, where signals, behavior, and beliefs are different. You feel rather like Alice did in Wonderland. Nothing seems to make sense. You experience culture shock when living with extensive change without benefit of familiarity and predictability.

Here's a story to illustrate the point. A young woman, who spoke very little German, went to Germany to work. She had a job in an office where people were as nice to her as they could be without verbal communication. One day, shortly after her arrival during the wine grape harvest

Pick a Country

any sources of information about all the countries in the world are available on the Internet. So choose a country and learn about it.

1. Find a map of your chosen country. One site you could try is http://www.virtualtourist.com.

2. Find general information about the country, such as population, exports, major industries, and so on. The CIA has a Web site with general information at http://www.odci.gov/cia.

3. Listen to or read the news from your chosen country. The World Radio Network (WRN) broadcasts programs by satellite from many countries. WRN also has a Web site where you can listen to news and other programs from across the world. Go to that Web site at http://www.wrn.org, choose a country, and listen to a news broadcast. What was the lead story? Was there any mention of the United States? If so, what was the tone of the report? ❖

season, a colleague brought her a basket of grapes. He walked up to her desk with a big smile and the grapes. She, happy about the welcoming gesture and the prospect of the grapes, said one of the few German words that she knew. She said "Danke" (thanks). The man's smile vanished, he shrugged, turned on his heel, and walked off with the grapes. The young woman was bewildered, and distraught at having caused the disappointment she saw in the man's face. The man was equally confused. What had happened was that the man had understood her to say "No, thanks" instead of "Yes, thanks" which she had meant. Because she had no idea of what had just happened, she didn't know how to rectify the situation.

Did you leave your hometown to go to school? Did you feel sort of lost and lonely? Did the people use different phraseology or have a different accent? Did the weather differ significantly? If the differences you encountered made you feel unsettled, you already know something about culture shock. The difference is one of degree. The farther away you venture, the more intense the culture shock.

If you're sent abroad to manage IT systems, you may encounter unexpected social customs. For example, you may want to promote certain knowledge workers or assign them duties that are contrary to their social norms. You may run into problems just setting up human resources information. For example, if you're in Nigeria, you'd better design your human resources IT system to accommodate up to four wives per male employee.

Managing knowledge workers can be very different too. In the United States it's generally considered an honor for a knowledge worker to be singled out for praise.

You may find that people in other cultures, notably in Asia, are not at all as pleased about that. These are all examples of cultural differences that will affect how you do your job as a manager of IT systems.

What Does Adjustment Feel Like? Culture shock usually has three main phases: The "Isn't that neat" phase, the "Isn't that stupid" phase, and the "It's different but it's fine" phase:

- *"Isn't that neat"* During the early stage of your stay, you find the new environment interesting and amusing.

- *"Isn't that stupid"* The differences become irritating and you feel disoriented and alone. This is the phase in which people tend to become depressed or aggressive.

- *"It's different but it's fine"* You gradually become accustomed to the new environment, make friends, learn what to expect and where to find what you need.

This last phase is where you adjust and come to appreciate your new environment. If you make it to the third phase, you're lucky, because you can then embrace the new without losing the best of the old. Unfortunately some people never make it past the second phase and leave the new location feeling disgruntled, angry, or disdainful.

Being aware of the possible effects of culture shock can help you adjust more quickly to being away from home and help minimize any negative effects on your productivity. Visiting knowledge workers will find it helpful if you understand what they're experiencing.

What Can You Do to Alleviate the Symptoms? In preparation for a relocation, it helps to learn all you can about the new culture—especially the language. Language encompasses much of the identity of a society. You could read the history of your destination, learning about the circumstances that molded the society. You can also find sites on the Internet about the country. If you're going to manage IT systems in another country, be sure to investigate laws pertaining to collecting, storing, and accessing information. If you're transferring information out of the country, you should also investigate laws concerning what can and can't be taken out. In Canada, for example, there are laws prohibiting banking information from being processed outside the country.

Ethics
What's Right?

Consider these recent problems involving unauthorized access or misuse of information:[57, 58]

■ In one year, 440 IRS employees were investigated or disciplined for browsing through the tax

---

INDUSTRY PERSPECTIVE

Transportation

Roadway Services: A Moving Experience

If you want to ship a Ming Dynasty vase, a human heart for transplant, or baby whales, Roadway Services, Inc., can help you. This $4.5 billion company is the world's largest carrier of fragile, valuable, and perishable goods. If an item requires special handling, this company will ship it. In 1992, Roadway Services decided to enter the shipment market in the European Union under the name of Roberts Express Europe (REE). With the formation of the European Union in 1992, Europe joined North America and the Pacific Rim as one of the three major trading blocks in the world.

REE's objective was to meet service commitments every time, regardless of customer location, and to pick up shipments within 90 minutes anywhere in Germany, France, Holland, Belgium, or Luxembourg. Delivery would be guaranteed over any distance. Other shipping companies, like FedEx, centralize operations, but the special characteristics of the EU make a centralized configuration less than feasible. For instance,

■ You must go through customs when moving between countries.

■ German law requires that you have a special permit if you want a non-German truck to pick up goods.

■ France doesn't allow any foreign national trucking company to pick up shipments, under any circumstances.

■ Germany forbids trucks to travel its roads during some weekend hours, and France prohibits truck traffic during weekends in August (the most popular vacation month).

■ Different countries have different holidays when customs offices are closed.

■ The 15 countries of the EU have different currencies and speak 12 different languages.

■ Accounting procedures and rules vary from country to country.

REE chose to centralize planning and control activities but to decentralize physical distribution and some accounting functions. Thus the company needed an IT system that would address local issues but provide centralized control of operations. REE chose a proprietary two-way satellite system for communication. The system collects information on the location of its trucks, storing it in the central database and displaying real-time graphic images of shipment locations on a map of western Europe. REE developed accounting applications for each of the accounting systems within the EU, which are run locally.

To prevent the inevitable errors that occur when people speaking different languages exchange voice and text messages, REE developed applications that accommodate different languages. For drivers, REE developed a set of 25 frequently used messages. The driver identifies his or her native language and selects, by number, the appropriate message. For example, message 12 reads "I am delayed in traffic and will be 15 to 30 minutes late."[59] ❖

records of neighbors, acquaintances, and celebrities, or for creating fraudulent tax refunds.

- State clerks in Maryland's Medicaid office were charged with illegally selling records to HMO representatives for as little as 50 cents each.

- A banker, serving on a state health commission, used his access to medical records to find bank customers who were ill with cancer—and called in their loans.

- Twenty-nine people were charged with cheating New York City out of $20 million in taxes by accessing computer files and wiping out taxes for city landlords in exchange for bribes.

Ethics is the set of standards, policies, and procedures that ensure stability in our society. Constructing workable, nonrestrictive standards and policies for a business is hard enough, but doing that for an entire society is an enormous task. And that's why people have been struggling with the concept of ethics throughout history.

What we do know, however, is that we must have an ethical framework if our society is to function well. Because business is an integral part of society and you're an integral part of both, it's important that you understand and fulfill your role as an ethical knowledge worker. As far back as 44 B.C., Cicero said that ethics are indispensable to anyone who wants to have a good career. That still applies today, and if you're in a management position, it's incumbent on you to foster an ethical working atmosphere.

Ethics is the set of principles or standards that help guide behavior, actions, and choices. It is the effort you make to act reasonably, to take into equal account the interests of each individual who will be affected by your actions, and then to decide on the right course of action. Ethics, like management, is a balancing act. It's the process of reconciling conflicting demands, responsibilities, and goals. Remember that every action, and inaction, has consequences. We label some of those consequences as "right" and others as "wrong." No matter how you view the consequence, you can't deny its existence. For example, if you shoot someone through the heart, that person will be dead. Your act might be viewed by society as murder or as self-defense, but the consequence is that another person is dead. Your act will also be judged by *you*. Unless you act ethically, that can be a heavy burden.

TEAM WORK

What Would You Do?

Analyze the following situation. You have access to the sales and customer information in a flower shop. You discover that the boyfriend of a woman you know is sending roses to three other women on a regular basis. The woman you know is on the flower list, but she believes that she's the only woman in his romantic life. You really think you should tell the woman. Your dilemma is that you have a professional responsibility to keep the company's information private. However, you also believe that you have a responsibility to the woman. Do you tell her?

Are there factors that would change your decision? Each team member should individually consider the additional information below. Then indicate whether any one or more of these factors would change your decision. Then form a consensus with your team. ❖

Additional Facts	Yes	No	Why?
1. The woman is your sister.			
2. The man is your brother.			
3. The woman is about to give the man her life savings as a down payment on a house in the belief that they will soon be married.			
4. The woman is already married.			

Kohlberg's model of ethical development shows three levels of motivation for ethical behavior: First is the **preadolescent stage** in which you keep the rules and do what you think you ought to for fear of punishment and in the hope of rewards. For example, you don't speed on the highway if there is a highway patrol car behind you. Second is the **adolescent stage** in which you do the right thing because of peer pressure and what people will think of you. For example, you wouldn't park in a parking place reserved for the handicapped because your friends would disapprove. Third comes the **adult stage** in which you do the right thing simply because it *is* the right thing and you recognize that if the majority of people in a society don't support reasonable actions, our society will suffer. For example, you stop at a stop light in the middle of the night, even when there's no one around, because you realize that it's important that everyone observe the rules of the road or lives will be endangered.

Ethical dilemmas usually arise, not out of simple situations like traffic decisions, but from a clash among competing goals, responsibilities, and loyalties. Ethical decisions are complex judgments where you're required to balance economic rewards and social responsibility. Your decision process is complicated by the long-term consequences, the many possible alternatives, mixed results, uncertainty about the outcome, and your personal needs and desires.

Let's look at an example. Say your organization is developing a decision support system (DSS) to help formulate treatments for some infectious diseases. Other companies in the industry are working on similar projects. The first system on the market will most likely reap huge profits. You may know that your DSS doesn't yet work properly—it's good, but not yet totally reliable. But you're feeling extreme pressure from your boss to market it immediately. You're worried about the harm that might come to a patient because of this DSS; but, on the other hand, it does work well most of the time. It's not really up to you, is it? You have a family to support and huge student loans to repay. And you like being employed. What do you do?

When entangled in a difficult ethical situation, it might help to answer the questions in Table 10.2. The questions are grouped into four sets of criteria corresponding to the various aspects you might consider when making a difficult ethical decision:

- *Your aversion to punishment* Avoiding unpleasantness is almost always part of the process of evaluating your alternatives. And, depending on the expected level of unpleasantness and its likelihood, it can be a large or small part. However, if this is your only consideration, you're at the lowest level of moral development, according to Kohlberg.

TABLE 10.2 Sets of Criteria for Making Ethical Decisions

Motivation	Viewpoint	Question
Your aversion to punishment	From society	1. Is it legal?
	From your supervisors	2. Is it in line with company policies?
Your image	In your society	3. Would you like your decision to be analyzed on *60 Minutes*?
	Among your colleagues	4. Is it in line with the ethical guidelines of your profession?
	In your social group	5. Would you be proud to report your decision to someone you respect?
Your responsibility	To your society	6. If everyone made this decision, would it be good for all of us?
	To your family and profession	7. To whom do you owe your loyalty, and to what extent?
	To yourself	8. How will the decision make you feel about yourself?
Your capacity to affect others	To cause them hardship	9. If you were one of the others involved, how would you see it?
	To hurt or injure	10. Could your decision hurt or injure others?

Responsibilities in the Management of Knowledge Workers

	Stability	Change
Telecommuting	Provide information access and IT support to telecommuters, but also policies to reduce uncertainty.	Be flexible in dealing with telecommuters who have different needs and face different problems.
Cultural Diversity	Provide a helpful and understanding atmosphere for people already suffering more change than they need.	Being in another country, or having knowledge workers from elsewhere, inherently involves dealing with change.
Ethics	Provide a stable and predictable ethical environment by establishing policies and procedures and setting a good example.	New opportunities and ways of manipulating information require constant vigilance on the part of the IT systems manager.

- *Your image* Most of us care, to a greater or lesser extent, about what other people, at least certain other people, think about us. Your image is important. If people perceive you as honest, hard working, and reliable, you'll receive many more opportunities than you would if the perception were negative. But, once again, your ethical development is incomplete if you consider nothing beyond your image.

- *Your responsibilities* You have responsibilities to many different stakeholders. At the very least, you have responsibilities to your society, your family, your profession, and, very important, yourself. It's often difficult to decide what weights to assign your different responsibilities. The ability to do this well signifies that you're ethically mature.

KNOWLEDGE WORKER'S -LIST

The Nature of Management. *Management of IT systems* means providing stability without stagnation and change without chaos for information, information technology, and knowledge workers.

The Role, Access to, and Protection of Information. Information is both raw material and capital. The management of information involves (1) providing the best means to capture, store, and access the right information, at the right time, in the right form, in the most effective and efficient manner possible; (2) securing your information so that it is safe from loss; and (3) accessing, storing, using, and distributing information responsibly, keeping in mind that information is partnership property.

The Control and Protection of IT Components. *Interoperability* refers to the extent to which IT equipment and software components are compatible with each other. The more interoperability you have in your IT system, the fewer problems you're likely to have. *Cost control* is essential because IT systems components must not be allowed to proliferate without consideration to lifetime costs. *Ergonomics* is the study of how to design and arrange your workplace so that you can achieve maximum productivity and reduce discomfort and adverse health effects. A *disaster recovery plan* is a plan of how you will carry on business if a major catastrophe occurs and knocks out your IT system. The plan should provide for customers, facilities, knowledge workers, business information, computer equipment, and communications infrastructure. A *hot site* is a fully equipped alternative location where you can continue to be productive if you have to leave your office building. A *cold site* is also an alternative location, but it lacks computer equipment.

The Importance of Providing a Work Environment Which Accommodates Diversity and Encourages Ethical Behavior. Without good knowledge workers, the best IT systems are of limited value, so it makes sense to help knowledge workers be productive. Part of this

CAREER OPPORTUNITY

Help is available if you have questions or concerns about what is appropriate behavior for a knowledge worker. The following organizations have formulated codes of ethics regarding the use of computers and the handling of information. Information about these organizations is available on the Internet:

- Computer Professionals for Social Responsibility (CPSR) (http://www.learncd.com/%7Ejgraves/cpsr.htm)
- Association for Computing Machinery (ACM) (http://www.acm.org)
- Association of Information Technology Professionals (AITP)—formerly Data Processing Managers Association (DPMA) (http://nega-duck.cc.vt.edu/DPMA)
- Institute of Electrical and Electronics Engineers (IEEE) (http://www.ieee.org)

- *Your capacity to affect others* Because we all live on the same planet, we affect each other to a lesser or greater extent. As a manager of IT systems, you may have a lot of power to influence the lives of others. This is not a responsibility that you should take lightly. And your ability to positively or adversely affect people far away is growing every day with the shrinking significance of national boundaries. Recognizing your power to affect others, and using it with empathy and compassion, signifies ethical maturity.

People tend to look to those in charge for guidance on what is acceptable within an organization, so you have even more of a responsibility to be ethical if you're in a position of authority. To help your knowledge workers act ethically, you have to set a good example. Of course, the first step is to act ethically yourself. Second, you have to be prepared to take action if you discover unethical behavior. Third, you need to know what your knowledge workers are doing, and you must not reward results that were obtained unethically.

CLOSING CASE STUDY: CASE 1

Don't Fence Me In

Some people who work for Hewlett-Packard (HP) don't go into the company office to work anymore. In an effort to improve sales revenue and sales productivity,

---

involves accommodating diversity whether that means knowledge workers need to work outside the company walls or they're unfamiliar with your cultural environment.

Telecommuting A telecommuting program should be introduced for solid business reasons for self-contained jobs performed by self-motivated knowledge workers. The program should establish clear policies on the division of responsibilities and provide for the right kind of office accommodation. *Hoteling* is where offices are maintained at a central location, and knowledge workers reserve space in advance when they need to come in. *Moteling* is a system where office space is allocated on a first-come–first-served basis.

Cross-cultural diversity is the difference in behavior and attitude among people from different cultures. *Culture* is the collective personality of a nation or society. *Culture shock* is the disorientation and confusion that you experience when you're accustomed to one culture and suddenly find yourself in another. As a manager of IT systems you must be aware that culture shock can seriously affect you or other knowledge workers when you or they have to work away from home.

Ethics Ethics is the set of principles or standards that help guide behavior, actions, and choices. Ethical development has three stages: the *preadolescent stage* in which you do the right thing because of the fear of punishment; the *adolescent stage* in which you do the right thing because of peer pressure; and the *adult stage* in which you do the right thing because it *is* the right thing. As a manager of IT systems, you must foster an ethical working atmosphere by setting an example and formulating policies to guide your knowledge workers in ethical behavior. ❖

Hewlett-Packard Computer System's organization in Palo Alto, California, sent a large proportion of its sales force home. HP didn't fire them—they became telecommuters. HP realized that the hours its salespeople spent commuting to and from work were hours in which the salespeople were not meeting with customers.

HP equipped salespeople with powerful HP notebook computers and software that allowed them to perform from home or other locations the tasks that they previously would have had to perform in the office. Salespeople use their computers to send customer orders to the company or to print sales literature. They can also access the external News Wire Service to obtain the latest information on competitors or ask advice of an industry specialist. Neil Norris, an employee who moved into his home office 2 years ago, says that he was astonished at how much it lessened the stress in his life not to have to commute to downtown Atlanta every day. It's also better for Atlanta's air and traffic control to have fewer cars on the highway.

The results for the company are that its revenue per person has doubled, and people are working more hours. The employees report increased job satisfaction and find that, even though they're spending more hours working, they still have more time for their families than they used to. They have more control over their jobs and feel better about their personal and family relationships.[60] ❖

◄ Questions ►

1. The employees spend more time working yet have more time for their families. How come? Was it just the commute time that was oppressive? How about the journey itself?

2. Examine the HP case using the discussion in the text. How does HP measure up in terms of the *why, what, who, how,* and *where* of telecommuting? Do you have enough information to evaluate each of these dimensions? For areas that lack adequate information, make a judgment as to what would work well.

3. Compare the life of a student to that of an HP telecommuter. What similarities and differences do you find? How much work do you do at the "office," meaning the formal setting of the classroom? How much do you do elsewhere? Is just "showing up" enough? Do you have to be a motivated self-starter to succeed? Are you learning to be a good telecommuter just by being a good student?

4. Does the fact that knowledge workers take computers and information home with them constitute a security worry for managers at HP? Is that information in any more danger than, say, paper files? How about if someone wanted to steal HP's sales records?

5. Which security concern do you think is greater for HP, the loss of the notebook computers or the loss of the information that they contain? Why? Would it make a difference whether a salesperson transmitted orders once a day or once a month?

CLOSING CASE STUDY: CASE 2

Let There Be Light

Nova Scotia's primary electric utility is Nova Scotia Power (NSPI). This company, like other utility, gas, and oil companies, faced new challenges in 1992 with the privatization of the industry in Canada. NSPI reengineered the company to have a customer focus. The focus of the management of IT systems became customer oriented. Because of the lack of competition previous to privatization, the customer's moment of value was not crucial to the survival of the company.

The company's previous centralized system had constrained, rather than served, business needs. Under the old system, when a customer called, a knowledge worker logged the service request into a central mainframe and printed a work order. The central system lacked knowledge about the personnel or equipment available in each region. Work, therefore, was inefficiently scheduled. Also, the company couldn't tell customers when the repair truck would arrive. In a highly competitive environment, this was unsatisfactory.

First, NSPI identified all major business functions and mapped the information flows between them to determine what structure their new IT system should take. The next step was to ensure interoperability and maximize flexibility in the choice of vendors. The mandated interoperability allowed the company to interconnect computers from different vendors and to choose among competing vendors. While choosing hardware and software, NSPI gave careful consideration to future needs, choosing components that could be expanded and upgraded easily.

The system that NSPI developed was a client/server system with commercially available software packages. The new network serves 46 district offices, 4 division offices, 6 thermal plants, several hydroelectric generation stations, and home mobile offices. Now NSPI has increased employee effectiveness in solving customer problems because employees have everything they need at their desks. When a customer calls, the message is logged into the IT system. The IT system then determines the type of vehicle needed, the skills of available staff, the severity of the problem, the completion time requested, and other variables. Because all aspects of the problem will have been considered before an employee goes out to the problem site, NSPI can tell the customer when the truck will arrive and how long the repair job will take.

The benefits of this reengineering effort are many:

- Four hundred nonessential jobs have been eliminated through voluntary retirement and other programs, saving $7.5 million.

- Productivity has increased by 18 percent.

- Each employee now serves 185 customers, compared to 166 before the system was developed.

- NSPI has reduced its truck fleet by 142 vehicles.

- The company is still able to operate without increasing the charge to customers.[61] ❖

◄ Questions ►

1. Why did it become so important for NSPI to revamp its IT systems after privatization? Was there any impetus to do so beforehand?

2. In general, what are the advantages and disadvantages of buying commercial software? Consider price, time from requirements analysis to training, reliability, the fit with the company's business practices, updates, and so on.

3. Since moving from a centralized to a client/server system, what changes in security measures would NSPI have had to make? What information would have to be protected?

4. The case stated that productivity increased by 18 percent, and that each employee serves 19 additional customers. What changes did the reengineering plan implement that contributed to these improvements?

5. Could the employees who handle service requests be telecommuters? Why? Why not? What advantages would the company realize if it were to have telecommuting phone operators?

6. Did using a client/server approach have any effect on the need for disaster recovery? If so, did it increase or decrease that need? Why? Would the consideration of a disaster recovery plan have any effect on the decision to use a client/server business solution?

REAL HOT

Electronic Commerce
Business and You on the Internet

Making Travel Arrangements on the Internet

It's very likely that, in the course of your business dealings, you'll be expected to travel, either within the United States or abroad. If you're interested in getting the most out of your travel dollar, you'll find that you usually get better deals and have fewer problems if you plan carefully. You can use the Internet to check out all aspects of your journey, from mode of travel to the shopping opportunities that are available. The Internet can also give you pointers and direction about aspects of the trip you might not even have thought about.

Some trips are purely business, but you may get a chance to enjoy some personal time during the trip as well. You might want to find nice restaurants, do some sightseeing, or enjoy your hobbies. Here too, the Internet can help.

In this section, we've included a number of Web sites related to making travel arrangements using the Internet. On the Web site that supports this text (http://www.mhhe.com/business/mis/haag, select "Electronic Commerce Projects"), we've provided direct links to all these Web sites as well as many, many more. This is a great starting point for completing this Real HOT section. We would also encourage you to search the Internet for others.

Transportation

If you're not taking your own transportation—your private jet or car—you'll have to find flights, buses, trains, and/or rental cars to suit your needs. Let's look at sites where you can get this kind of information.

Airlines

Some people are happy to travel with whatever airline provides the flight that fits into their schedules. Others insist on certain airlines, or won't travel on particular airlines. No matter how you feel, the Internet can be of benefit in finding a flight. You can even get maps of the airports you'll be using on the Internet. For example, the Quick-AID Airport Information Directories (http://www.quick-aid.com) provides you with all sorts of airport information, from maps to shops, to the airlines that fly in and out. Many airports, like Dallas/Ft. Worth International Airport (http://www.dfwairport.com), have sites on the Internet. These sites can help you with provisions at the airport for disabled people, among other available services.

The Federal Aviation Administration site (http://www.faa.gov) has a comprehensive list of airlines in this country and all over the world. Look at the five airline sites listed in the table on page 449, choose five more (you can use some of the links listed on our text's Web site), and answer the following questions.

A. Can you make a flight reservation online at this site?

B. If you can book flights, does the site ask you to type in your departure and destination cities, or can you choose from a menu?

C. Again, if you can book flights at this site, on a scale of 1 to 10, rate how difficult it is to get to the flight schedule. That is, how many questions do you have to answer, how many clicks does it take, how much do you have to type in?

D. Is there information on when the lowest fares apply? (For example, three-week advance booking, staying over Saturday night, and so forth.)

E. Does the site offer to send you information on special deals via e-mail?

F. Does the site offer information on frequent flier mileage? Can you check your frequent flier account online?

G. Does the site offer you a map of the airports you will be using?

Trains and Buses

If you want to travel by rail or long-distance bus, you can find many helpful sites. Here is a taste of what's available:

- Greyhound's Web site at http://www.greyhound.com has fare and travel time information.
- Monterey Salinas Transit System at http://www.mst.org has information on bus travel in the United States.
- Amtrak at http://www.amtrak.com has a site that lets you look up train travel times and fares and also buy tickets online for train travel in the United States.
- RailEurope at http://www.raileurope.com offers comprehensive coverage of all modes of travel in Europe, including, of course, rail travel.
- Germany's Deutsche Bahn AG site at http://www.bahn.de has ticket ordering information, details on the routing of the trip, and various other useful tidbits.
- The Orient Express site at http://orient-expresstrains.com is a great help if you're interested in traveling by rail in Asia or Australia.

Look at two of these sites and see whether you can book tickets online. Do you need a password to see schedules?

Incidentally, when you're looking up sites outside the United States, remember that the date is often expressed with the day first, then the month, then the year, so that September 10, 1999, would be 10.9.99 or 10-9-99. Also, most of Europe uses 24-hour time, so that 2:15 P.M. would be 14:15.

Rental Cars

When you arrive at your destination, you may need a car. You can often get a better deal if you reserve a car in advance. Some sites like Rental Car Info at http://www.bnm.com have information on multiple companies, and all the large car rental companies have sites on the Internet. Check out three of the car rental Web sites listed in the table on page 449, find three others (don't forget the

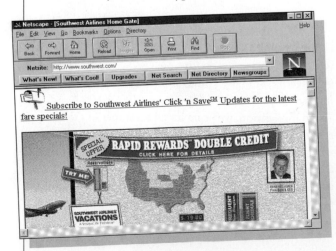

Web site that supports this text has many good links), and answer the following questions.

A. Can you reserve a car at the Web site?

B. Can you search by city?

C. Is there a cancellation penalty? If so, how much?

D. Can you get a list of the car types? Does this company rent sports utility vehicles?

E. Are there special weekend rates?

F. What does the site say about collision insurance purchased from that company in addition to your own insurance?

G. Can you get maps from the site?

H. Are special corporate rates specified on the site?

Road Conditions and Maps

You might want to check road conditions before you set off either in your own car or in a rental. One such site is the Road Conditions site at http://www.theinternet-company.com/truckers/road.htm. Also available are various regional sites such as Oregon's Road Conditions site at http://www.odot.state.or.us/region1/roadcond.htm.

You can even generate maps online at several sites. MapQuest at http://www.mapquest.com is one of the most popular. Its TripQuest section has city-to-city and turn-by-turn directions, and its Map Shortcuts module gives you a list of cities and countries for which you can get maps. Other map sites are listed in the table on page 449, and you can find additional sites on our Web site. Examine three map sites and answer the following questions.

A. Do these sites all give turn-by-turn driving directions?

B. Will they provide a map of an area without start and end points?

C. Do they have zoom-in and zoom-out capabilities?

D. Can you customize the map, perhaps by inserting a landmark or circling an area?

E. Are hotels, restaurants, and so forth marked on the map?

F. If the site offers driving directions, can you specify whether you want the scenic route or the main highways?

G. Are the maps restricted to the United States? If not, what other countries are included?

When you're traveling, the weather is of particular interest to you, both from the point of view of possible travel delays and the kind of clothing to bring along. The Real HOT Electronic Commerce section at the end of Chapter 7 will help you find weather information on the Internet.

Lodging

When you're searching for lodging, consider whether you need accommodations for one night or whether you'll spend enough time in one place to be able to take advantage of special amenities. Also think about whether you'll have to entertain or interview clients, employees, or prospective employees. Perhaps you need to arrange a room for a presentation or for a meeting.

Hotels, especially the larger chains, usually have Web sites. Here you have access to a wealth of information about rates, amenities, and sometimes even information about the hotel's surroundings. The National Hotel Directory at http://www.evmedia.com has lists of a variety of hotels and also trade shows. The Hotel Guide site at http://www.hotelguide.com has information on 60,000 hotels all over the world, and The Trip (http://www.thetrip.com) has hotel reviews and promises discounted prices for certain hotels. The table on page 449 lists Web sites for five hotel chains, and you'll find many more links on our Web site. Choose two of these and two others and answer the following questions

A. Can you search for a particular city?

B. Can you book a room online?

C. Are there properties belonging to this hotel chain outside the United States?

D. Can you see a picture of the room on the Internet?

E. Does the site tell you about special deals or promotions?

F. Is there information about perks you can get by staying there frequently?

G. Do you get a discount for booking online?

One-Stop Travel Sites

Some travel sites on the Internet allow you to book your entire trip from start to finish, offering a combination of airline, hotel, and other helpful information. Two of the most widely used are Microsoft's Expedia at http://expedia.msn.com and Preview at http://www.previewtravel.com. You'll find more sites listed in the table on page 449. Choose five of these and find five more (don't forget to look for good links at the Web site that supports this text) and answer the following questions.

A. How many different booking services are offered from this site (airlines, hotels, rental cars, rail travel, and so on)?

B. If the site offers flight booking, how many flight alternatives does it offer? 3? 10? 20? 30? More than 30?

C. Does the site have information on low-cost specials for airlines, hotels, and rental cars?

D. Is there a traveler's assistance section?

E. Will the site answer your specific questions?

F. Can you search by destination or company for flights and lodging?

Destination Information

You might like to know before you get to your destination what restaurants, museums, shows, shopping, and special attractions are available. Many of the sites previously mentioned have this kind of information. MapQuest (http://www.mapquest.com) is an excellent example of such a site, as are many of the one-stop travel sites. Another great source of city information is from sites specific to the city and local newspapers. At http://www.info-broker.de/infobroker/services/press/northcarolina.html, you'll find a directory of daily newspapers classified by region and state.

No matter what your interest or hobby, the Internet has a site for you. You can find sites dedicated to bird watching, bungee jumping, golf, or anything else that takes your fancy. Many others cater to entertainment events like concerts. You can find destination information sites in the table on page 449 and at the following sites:

■ Excite's travel site (http://city.net) has destination information from Fodor's.

■ The Trip (http://thetrip.com) includes restaurant reviews among its services.

■ Restaurant Row (http://restaurantrow.com) has a list of 100,000 restaurants in 25 countries. You can search by country, city, and cuisine.

■ Open World (http://www.openworld.co.uk /cityguides) has information on 100 of the most popular cities to visit in the world.

More Web site addresses are available at our Web site. Look at two each of the city, newspaper, and special interest sites in the table on page 449. Are the city sites available in multiple languages? Why do you think they are or are not? Are the special interest sites restricted to the United States?

Traveling Abroad

When traveling out of the country, you'll have many additional details to consider in addition to what we've discussed so far. If this is your first trip abroad, be prepared for things to be different. For example, breakfast in Europe often consists of rolls, cheese, and cold cuts of meat washed down with coffee or tea. Don't worry unduly about doing the wrong thing, because people in all countries know that each country has its own customs and idiosyncrasies. You can use the Internet to find out much concerning the country you're about to visit. Many helpful sites are just a click away.

Passports and Visas

Rules of entry differ depending on where you're going and your own nationality. The U.S. State Department (http://travel.state.gov) can help with any questions you have about passports or visas. At this site you can also find travel warnings issued by the U.S. government. Another module has information on embassies and consulates abroad and what they can offer if you need help. Sites originating in the country you're visiting also have entry information as do many of the one-stop travel sites.

Country Information

You can find an enormous volume of information on almost every country in the world on the Internet. Some

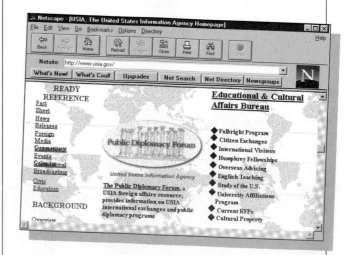

sites, like the World Travel Guide Online (http://www.wtgonline.com), have information on countries all over the world; and some like Africa Online (http://www.africaonline.co.ke), have information on a particular region. You can also find sites designed specifically for business travelers. Other sites can even help you speak the language, while still others offer radio transmissions in English and the native tongue. In the table below, we have provided a variety of sites; if you need more, look at our text's Web site.

Web Sites for Making Travel Arrangements

Airlines	Address	Rental Cars	Address
Southwest	http://www.southwest.com	Hertz	http://www.hertz.com
Singapore Airlines	http://www.singaporeair.com	Avis	http://www.avis.com
American Airlines	http://www.americanair.com	Alamo	http://www.goalamo.com
Delta	http://www.delta-air.com	Dollar	http://www.dollar.com
Aer Lingus	http://www.aerlingus.ie	Rent-a-Wreck	http://www.rent-a-wreck.com

Maps	Address	Hotels	Address
MapsOnUs	http://www.mapsonus.com	Marriott Group	http://www.marriott.com
AutoPilot	http://www.freetrip.com	Embassy Suites	http://www.embassy-suites.com
MapBlast	http://www.mapblast.com	Red Roof Inn	http://www.redroof.com
Excite Maps	http://city.net/maps	Holiday Inn	http://www.holiday-inn.com
DeLorme's CyberRouter	http://route.delorme.com	Hotel Choice	http://www.econolodge.com

One-Stop Travel	Address	Destination Information	Address
Travelocity	http://www.travelocity.com	Kansas City	http://www.kansascity.com
FLIFO	http://www.flifo.com	New York City	http://www.ny.com/nyc
Traveler	http://www.traveler.net	Las Vegas	http://www.pcap.com
Biztravel	http://www.biztravel.com	Specialty Travel	http://www.specialtytravel.com
TravelLinks	http://www.trvltips.com/travellinks.html	Special Interest Travel	http://sitravel.com

Country Information	Address	Government Agencies	Address
Spain and the Spanish	http://gias720.dis.ulpgc.es/spain.html	United States Information Agency	http://www.usia.gov
China Business Directory	http://chinadir.com.hk	U.S. Trade & Development Agency	http://www.tda.gov
Fodor's site	http://www.fodors.com	Trade Data Bank	http://www.stat-usa.gov
Travlang	http://travlang.com	U.S. Department of Commerce	http://www.doc.gov
World Radio Network	http://www.wrn.org	U.S. Agency for International Development	http://www.info.usaid.gov

 Go to the Web site that supports this text: **http://www.mhhe.com/business/mis/haag** and select "Electronic Commerce Projects."

We've included links to over 100 Web sites for making travel arrangements on the Internet.

KEY TERMS AND CONCEPTS

Adolescent Stage
Adult Stage
Carpal Tunnel Syndrome
Cold Site
Computer Virus
Cookie
Cross-Cultural Diversity
Culture
Culture Shock
Disaster Recovery Plan
Ergonomics
Ethics
Firewall
Help Desk
Hot Site

Hoteling
Information as Capital
Information as Raw Material
Information Access
Information Center
Information Security
Internet Loophole
Interoperability
Management of IT Systems
Moteling
Preadolescent Stage
Repetitive Strain Injury (RSI)
Telecommuting
Virtual Office

SHORT-ANSWER QUESTIONS

1. What is the purpose of IT systems management?
2. What are the two roles of business information?
3. What is a computer virus? A firewall? An Internet loophole?
4. Why do employers need to gather information on prospective and current employees?
5. What benefits are provided by the availability of information to consumers and businesses?
6. What does the term ergonomics mean? What is repetitive strain injury?
7. What are the six components of a disaster recovery plan? What is a hot site? What is a cold site?
8. For what reasons should you introduce telecommuting?
9. What is culture? What is culture shock?
10. What are the three levels of ethical development?

DISCUSSION QUESTIONS

1. When selling antiques, you can usually obtain a higher price for those artifacts that have a provenance. A provenance is information detailing the origin and history of the object. For example, the dresses owned by Princess Diana sold for much more than their face value. What kinds of products have value over and above a comparable product because of information? What kind of information makes products valuable? Consider both tangible (resale value) and intangible (sentimental appeal) value.

2. Personal checks that you use to buy merchandise have a standard format. Checks have very few different sizes and almost no variation in format. Consider what would happen if everyone could create his or her own size, shape, and layout of personal check. What would the costs and benefits be to business and the consumer in terms of buying checks, exchanging them for merchandise, and bank check processing?

3. Consider society as a business that takes steps to protect itself from the harm of illegal acts. Discuss the mechanisms and costs that are involved. Examine ways in which our society would be different if no one ever broke a law. Are there ever benefits to our society when people break the law—for example, if they claim that the law itself is unethical or unjust?

4. Many European countries have very strict laws about what you can and can't do with name-linked information. In France, for example, the law stipulates that no information may be saved, electronically or on paper, about a person's religious or political affiliation. Discuss the implications of such laws for an open-information society like the United States. What kinds of information might be appropriate for such laws here, and how would they affect the management of IT systems?

5. Consider movies and TV shows that have dealt with culture shock. Examples are *Moscow on the Hudson, Coming to America,* and *Third Rock from the Sun.* Can you think of any others? Shows on this topic are usually comedies, because cross-cultural diversity can lead to very amusing situations. Think about a show you have seen that dealt with cross-cultural diversity. What kinds of reactions did the parties display? Consider both the visitor and those who are familiar with the culture.

6. Would you like to be a telecommuter? What aspects of telecommuting would appeal to you? What aspects would not? What personality traits would be best for a telecommuter? What home circumstances would help a telecommuter be successful?

7. Can you access all the IT systems at your college or university? What about payroll or grade information about yourself or others? What kind of controls has your college or university implemented to prevent the misuse of information?

8. You know that you can't use a Macintosh to access information stored on a disk formatted on a PC (unless you have a PowerPC or special software). What other instances of the lack of interoperability have you experienced personally or heard of? For example, have you used different versions of PowerPoint or MS Access that won't work on all the PCs to which you have access?

9. Have you experienced computer problems caused by a virus? What did the virus do? Where do you think you got it? How did you fix the problem?

10. If a major disaster like a tornado or flood were to strike your college or university in the middle of the semester, who would be impacted and how? Consider all stakeholders.

11. Say you had a small business and you were considering buying expensive ergonomically designed office furniture such as chairs and desks for your knowledge workers. What would the intangible benefits be to your company of having employees who are comfortable?

CASE STUDY

The Business of the Future— The Cyber Corporation

Today and in the future, technology promises to dramatically change the landscape of business. It will change not only how business is conducted in the marketplace, but also how businesses themselves are established and run. In the age of electronic commerce, the business of the future is the cyber corporation. A *cyber corporation (cybercorp)* is a business established specifically to operate in cyberspace. It has no walls and no formal office space and it completely ignores national boundaries.

The cybercorp of tomorrow must constantly be alert to changes and be able to respond quickly to those changes. Long-range planning will only cover a period of 6 months to 1 year. Beyond that planning will be almost impossible and futile. Other characteristics of a cybercorp follow.

Completely based on electronic commerce A cybercorp exists only in cyberspace. As a customer you won't be able to obtain the products and

IN THE NEWS

Preparing for the Future

It's Your World

services of a cybercorp through mail order or by going to a retail store. Instead you'll obtain products and services through "net order."

Forward-thinking and innovative management Because cybercorps will need to constantly monitor changes and quickly respond, forward-thinking and innovative managers will be a must. Without these types of people, the cybercorp will not survive and will simply become a void in cyberspace.

Virtual Cybercorps will be made up of telecommuting knowledge workers and virtual partnerships. This means a cybercorp will be a virtual organization.

Integrated networks Cyberspace is only possible through integrated IT networks that include internal servers that organize and manage information and external network links that connect a cybercorp to its customers, suppliers, distributors, and partnering organizations.

Outsourcing more than ever before The virtual nature of a cybercorp will mean that it outsources every possible business function, from product design and development to warehousing and delivery to servicing customer accounts.

To some people (pessimists), cybercorps seem like scary and dangerous organizations that can't guarantee job stability. To others (optimists), cybercorps are the most challenging, exciting, and rewarding way of conducting business. No matter what your view of cybercorps, they **are** the business of the future. And your personal success, to a certain extent, will depend on your ability to work in cyberspace in a cybercorp.[1,2] ❖

FEATURES

IN THE INFORMATION AGE, KNOWLEDGE WORKERS UNDERSTAND...

1. The business environment of tomorrow and important factors that will shape it

2. Their role in tomorrow's business as tomorrow's knowledge workers

3. Information technologies that will be important to business tomorrow

Introduction

The business world is indeed changing every day. And it's not just limited to how technology is changing the way business works and how it operates. Throughout this text, we've touched on many technology and non-technology changes that are occurring in business right now. Comparing optimists to pessimists is a good way of viewing these changes. For some people, change can be seen as an impending disaster. To those who relish the unknown and accept the challenge of working in it, change is very exciting and is seen as an opportunity for improvement. Whatever the case, the business world is changing, and we hope you're an optimist who will be able to change with the times.

In this final chapter, we want to look toward the future and speculate about its business environment, knowledge workers, and information technology (see Figure 11.1). Then we want to leave you with some final thoughts about the transparency of technology, how business will be conducted in cyberspace, the fact that knowledge

workers are and will always continue to be the most important resources in business, and that the MIS function is not just for IT specialists. As we look at these issues, we'll pose a series of questions—what we call *frequently asked questions* or *FAQs*. We'll provide our own answers to those questions, but you should also answer them for yourself based on such considerations as your chosen career, the country in which you want to work, whether you plan to further your education, and the industry in which you'd like to work. Remember—the future is your world.

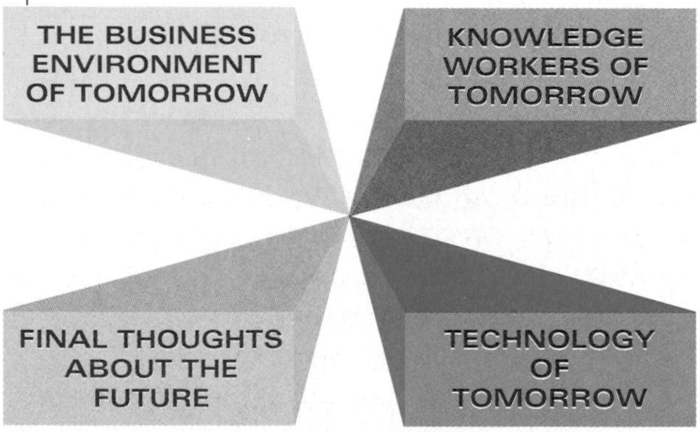

The Business Environment of Tomorrow

The business environment is changing daily. No longer can businesses or people working within those businesses simply settle on a 5-year strategic plan and then assume that changes won't occur. Flexibility is a must in today's fast-paced, changing business environment and will be even more important tomorrow.

FIGURE 11.1

It's the Future

THE BUSINESS ENVIRONMENT OF TOMORROW

KNOWLEDGE WORKERS OF TOMORROW

FINAL THOUGHTS ABOUT THE FUTURE

TECHNOLOGY OF TOMORROW

Security, Privacy, and Ethics

Right now, security, privacy, and ethics issues pervade the business environment. In the future, businesses and knowledge workers will wrestle with the use of technology and information in the best interests of society. The key phrase is ". . . in the best interests of society." Today businesses are exploiting information for competitive advantage; tomorrow they'll increasingly exploit it in the

Frequently Asked Questions

QUESTION In Chapter 1 we discussed six factors currently changing the landscape of business. What new factors will surface tomorrow?

The Obvious	The Not So Obvious
Security, privacy, and ethics	The convergence of business and information technology planning
Information technology as an essential enabler of innovation	Information technology as essential for doing any kind of business
Organizational horsepower strategies that focus on organizational structure	The agile yet fleeting nature of cybercorps

best interests of society (which may mean forgoing a competitive advantage). Your greatest concern as an information-literate knowledge worker will be where to draw the **fine line** between exploiting information to obtain a competitive advantage while, at the same time, acting in a socially and ethically responsible manner.

Information Technology as an Essential Enabler of Innovation

Throughout this text, we've stressed that technology is not a panacea; neither is it innovation by itself. But it is an important **enabler** of business innovation. This will become more important and a focus for all organizations in the future. Technology is and will be a must for innovation.

Organizational Horsepower Strategies That Focus on Organizational Structure

In the next several years, you can expect quality to remain the foundation for generating organizational horsepower (OHP) and business process reengineering to be the primary method for changing the way business occurs. You can also expect businesses to increase their focus on six OHP strategies that will affect the structure of organizations. These include

- **Teams** Groups of people with a shared goal and task interdependence
- **Information partnerships** Agreements between organizations for the sharing of information to strengthen each partner organization

INDUSTRY PERSPECTIVE　　**Health Care**

Your Health Care Supported by a Virtual Health Care Organization

In perhaps no other industry is there a greater need for the virtual organization concept than in health care. You simply cannot go to one place for all your health care needs. If you need glasses or contacts, you go to an optometrist. For routine physicals, you go to your family doctor. If you need x-rays, you may very well have to go to a hospital. And, if a minor emergency occurs, you may end up at an always-open neighborhood clinic. Whatever the case, throughout your lifetime your medical information will be scattered among health care professionals across the country (and perhaps the world). That creates a real problem: How can these health care professionals possibly share all your information?

One solution to aggregating, analyzing, and communicating your health care information among all these professionals is to establish a health information network that creates a virtual organization. In 1996 Andersen Consulting announced such a network, the *Healthcare Information Infrastructure (HII)*. The HII makes available all your information to multiple, independent health care professionals, allowing them to share your information and collaborate across a wide area network—the Internet. For the low cost of connecting to the Internet, health care professionals participating in the HII will be able to access all your health care information—from eye exam results to blood work results and even to routine physical examination results.

At the heart of the HII is your medical information stored in the form of an object. Your medical information object will contain such information as demographics, medical history, allergies, lab results, care plans, and pointers to relatives and primary care physicians. Your object will also contain procedures that allow health care professionals to access your information and provide any new information.

Each participating health care organization in the HII will retain its identity and be completely autonomous. But to you—as a user of various health care services—the system will look like a virtual organization. That is, the HII will become a network of independent organizations linked together by IT to share skills, costs, and market access as they provide you with the best possible health care at the most affordable price.[3] ❖

- **Timeless and locationless operations** Operations without regard to time or location

- **Transnational firms** Production and sales of products and services in countries all over the world in coordinated cooperation

- **Virtual organizations** Networks of independent organizations linked together by IT to exploit market opportunities by sharing skills, costs, and market access

- **Learning organizations** Organizations in which people are continually discovering how to learn together while, at the same time, altering their organization as a result of what they have learned

The Convergence of Business and Information Technology Planning

All too often, people talk about "aligning" business and IT planning. As we discussed in Chapter 8, that unfortunately is wrong—aligning implies two distinct parts. In this case, those two parts are business planning and IT planning. The successful organizations of the future will not align business and IT; instead, they will integrate business and IT planning into a single function that sees technology as a necessary part of doing business. This will require a dramatic change in thinking for most organizations. No longer will organizations be able to view technology as an "add in" or supplement to business

What Will Be Most Important for Business and You in the Future?

In this section, we focus on six new factors that will affect the landscape of business tomorrow. These include:

- Security, privacy, and ethics
- OHP strategies that focus on organizational structure
- IT as essential for doing any kind of business

- IT as an essential enabler of innovation
- The convergence of business and IT planning
- The nature of a cybercorp

Your group's task is threefold. First, order those six factors from most important to least important as far as the overall business environment is concerned. Second, order those six factors from most important to least important as far as which ones offer you (as a knowledge worker) the greatest career opportunity. Finally, develop a list of any additional factors that you think will be important in the future. ❖

Importance to the Overall Business Environment	Importance to You as a Knowledge Worker
1.	1.
2.	2.
3.	3.
4.	4.
5.	5.
6.	6.
New Factors That You Think Will Be Important in the Future	
1.	
2.	
3.	
4.	

Transportation

Technology Is Now Standard for Shipping Products Around the World

Technology is rapidly becoming a standard of doing business. Most organizations need a foundation of technology just to stay in business. That's certainly true in the transportation industry. Let's listen to what some transportation people have to say about using technology every day.

On the Personal Computer

"Of all the technology available to us, I'd say the most important is still the PC, the personal computer."

—Phil Viens, corporate traffic manager for COBE Laboratories

On Electronic Data Interchange

"EDI has to be on everybody's list, even though the technology here is relatively simple."

—Dan Smith, senior associate with Mercer Management

On Scanning and Storage Technologies

"On the other hand, should a consignee, for example, not pay an invoice and claim never to have received a shipment. All you have to do is go to that optical disc and create a copy of the document, complete with date, amount, and signature. It's very convincing."

—Mark Sarago, director of client and product strategy for the Fritz Cos.

On Wireless Technologies

"In the case of railroads, though, they have something like 90 percent to 95 percent of their equipment tagged with radio frequency (RF) tags."

—Jay Farquar, vice president–transportation group for TCSI Corp.

On the Internet

"I see the Internet being used for ordering services, payment services, tracking, and things of that nature. It's just starting to creep in. But there are a few real adventurous companies out there, which makes me believe that within a year or so it will be commonplace."

—Mark Sarago, director of client and product strategy for the Fritz Cos.

Notice that none of these people are really talking about new and exciting technologies, neither are they discussing technology within the context of obtaining and sustaining a competitive advantage. These people see all these technologies—the PC, EDI, scanning and storage technologies, wireless technologies, and the Internet—as standard ways of doing business.[4, 5] ❖

---

planning—they will have to view both business planning and IT planning in a coordinated and integrated fashion.

Information Technology as Essential for Doing Any Kind of Business

That may seem like an obvious statement, but the business world continues to wrestle with this issue. In the future, it will be a matter of fact—you and your organization will need technology just to stay in business.

The Agile Yet Fleeting Nature of Cybercorps

Finally, the business world of tomorrow will be dramatically affected by the newest type of organization—the cyber corporation or cybercorp. Cybercorps promise to forever change the landscape of business in many ways. First, cybercorps will be extremely agile and able to respond to market changes at a moment's notice. This is due in large part to their virtual nature and the fact that they will outsource almost every function. For example, a cybercorp that outsources production will carry less inventory than a traditional product manufacturer, which means the cybercorp will have less obsolete inventory to sell off.

Second, cybercorps will sweep away many of the barriers to entry in most markets. In business, barriers to entry act to prohibit new organizations from entering certain markets. For example, small start-up companies typically suffer from lack of enough capital to effectively advertise and reach a large customer base. That won't be true for cybercorps: By simply setting up Web sites

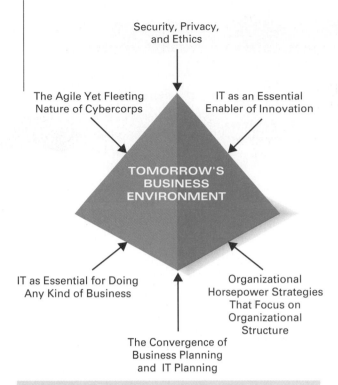

New Factors That Will Affect the Business Landscape of Tomorrow

with product ordering capabilities, cybercorps will be able to reach millions of customers on the Internet on a daily basis.

Finally, the fleeting nature of cybercorps will make it extremely difficult to gather competitive intelligence. Cybercorps can literally appear and disappear in a day. An important aspect of competitive intelligence is knowing who your competition is and what it's doing. With cybercorps continually moving in and out of your market, it may be almost impossible to pinpoint an exact list

of your competitors at any time. Can you imagine doing business when you don't even know who your competition is?

The Knowledge Worker of Tomorrow

No matter how business changes, people—and more specifically, knowledge workers—will always be the key resource. Other resources such as capital, production facilities, information, and technology will also be important. But those resources are meaningless without skilled and intelligent knowledge workers. Let's take a look at the knowledge worker of tomorrow.

Knowledge Workers Will Be Everywhere Doing Everything

Today you can find knowledge workers in all industries performing all types of jobs, and you can certainly expect that to hold true for the future. If anything, knowledge workers will become even more prevalent. Remember, knowledge workers currently outnumber all other types of workers by a four-to-one margin. That margin may very well increase significantly in the future. Why? Because knowledge workers work with and produce information as a product. And information is the basis by which the business world operates. It doesn't matter if your organization is product- or service-oriented, in the retail or manufacturing industry, or perhaps even a cybercorp in cyberspace, information is a key to success. And your ability as a knowledge worker to work with that information is even more important.

Frequently Asked Questions

QUESTION What is the future role of knowledge workers? Where will they be? What will they do? What skills must they possess?

The Obvious	The Not So Obvious
Knowledge workers will be everywhere doing everything.	Knowledge workers will be data miners.
Knowledge workers will possess general skills that include communication, interpersonal, decision-making, and time and project management skills.	Knowledge workers will be systems developers.
	Knowledge workers, for the most part, will be telecommuters.
Knowledge workers will possess IT skills in the areas of personal productivity software and networking.	Knowledge workers will be a "jack of all trades, and master of one."
	Knowledge workers will become just workers.

TEAM WORK

Information Technology for Supporting General Skills

The four general skills that all knowledge workers should possess include communication, interpersonal, decision-making, and time and project management skills. For each of these skills, identify, below, the various IT tools (both hardware and software) that can help you master the skill. ❖

General Knowledge Worker Skills	IT Tool Support
Communication	
Interpersonal	
Decision-making	
Time and project management	

Knowledge Workers Will Possess General Skills That Include Communication, Interpersonal, Decision-Making, and Time and Project Management Skills

The most successful knowledge workers will possess four general skills—communication, interpersonal, decision-making, and time and project management. These skills are vital in any type of business. *Communication skills* relate to your ability to effectively convey your knowledge to other people. This involves making oral presentations, preparing written reports, and the like. *Interpersonal skills* relate to your ability to work with other people. This may involve explaining a warranty to a customer, working in a team environment to solve a

problem, negotiating contract terms with a supplier, or a variety of other people-interactive tasks.

CAREER OPPORTUNITY

Of the four general skills all knowledge workers need to possess, communication may perhaps offer you the greatest career opportunity. Many people have difficulty giving a speech or correctly crafting a well-organized written document. Whenever you can, you should take courses that teach you these skills.

Decision-making skills relate to your ability to recognize a problem or opportunity, generate alternatives to solve the problem or take advantage of the opportunity, evaluate those alternatives, and implement the correct one. Business is all about making decisions, either solving problems or taking advantage of opportunities. Finally, *time and project management skills* relate to your ability to manage your time and the time of others in a team environment. Teams—as an OHP strategy—will receive increased attention in the future. And teams will only be successful if you manage them correctly.

Knowledge Workers Will Possess IT Skills in the Areas of Personal Productivity Software and Networking

If you scan the resumes of most graduating business students today, you'll find several common sections—education, scholarships, recent employment, activities, awards, honors, and so on. You'll also probably find a section entitled "Information Technology Skills" or "Computer Skills." There's a reason for that—all businesses want employees with a basic understanding of certain aspects of IT. Most notably, businesses are looking for students who possess IT skills in the areas of personal productivity software and networking. Your personal productivity software skills should, at a minimum, include the ability to work with word processing, spreadsheet, database, presentation graphics, personal information management, and project management software.

In the area of networking, you should know how to use the Internet and e-mail and perform such functions as setting up a modem connection and distributing e-mail to a group. These types of IT skills are and will be the IT foundation skills that all businesses look for in potential employees.

Knowledge Workers Will Be Data Miners

Tomorrow's knowledge workers will most definitely need to be skilled data miners. Data miners sift through large volumes of information on a daily basis to identify trends, patterns, problems, solutions, and, most important, opportunities that offer a competitive advantage in the marketplace. To be a proficient data miner, you must rely on your other skills as well. For example, good data miners are good decision makers, and good data miners have solid time and project management skills. The best data miners will also know how to define, develop, and work with databases and data warehouses. This means that you'll need to know how to do everything from defining your logical information needs to building a database through normalization to building OLAP queries using multidimensional analysis tools and intelligent agents.

Knowledge Workers Will Be Systems Developers

Knowledge workers will also take on more of a role in systems development. In Chapter 9 we referred to this as *knowledge worker development.* Systems development is among the newest IT skill sets that businesses are beginning

What Skills Do You Need?

In this section, we've identified the four most important general skills that you'll need as a knowledge worker—communication, interpersonal, decision-making, and time and project management. We've also identified the four most important IT skills—personal productivity software, networking, data mining, and systems development. Spend some time looking through job ads in various newspapers from across the country. As you do, focus on ads for the specific career in which you're interested. In the table below, record the general and IT skills that your chosen career requires. ❖

General Skills	IT Skills

to look for in potential employees. You'll definitely increase your chances of landing a job if you know how to use such products as Lotus Notes or PowerBuilder, set up macros in spreadsheet software, and build your own database using a database package.

Knowledge Workers, for the Most Part, Will Be Telecommuters

The knowledge workers of tomorrow will certainly dominate the business world. But they may not necessarily do so in a physical sense. A great number of tomorrow's knowledge workers will probably be telecommuters. As a telecommuter, you may work from home, on the road, or some combination of the two. The real question is, "Do you have the IT skills necessary to be a telecommuter?" That is, do you know how to use such tools as e-mail, videoconferencing software, and groupware? Do you know how to set up a modem connection? Do you know how to transfer word processing and spreadsheet documents through an e-mail system? Do you know how to download files? If you can answer yes to these types of questions, then you're ready to be a telecommuting knowledge worker.

Knowledge Workers Will Be a "Jack of All Trades, and Master of One"

Simply put, knowledge workers will need to be a "jack of all trades, and master of one." That means you need to possess a solid understanding of all areas of business (for example, human resource management, production and logistics, accounting, finance, marketing, and technology) and need to be an expert in one area. That's why your business curriculum requires that you take a variety of business courses in all areas and several concentrated courses in a specific area. The business world today and tomorrow needs generalists in the sense that you must understand every part of how a business works. At the same time, you need a great deal of knowledge about one specific area.

Consider teams in an organization. Which type of team do you think is most effective—a team with several experts who know nothing about each others' areas or a team with several experts who also have a general understanding of each others' areas? Right—the latter is the best type of team. And teams are an important OHP strategy. Successful teams have participants, each of whom is a "jack of all trades, and master of one."

Knowledge Workers Will Become Just Workers

Right now, terms such as the "information age" and "knowledge workers" are hot in the business world. We truly are in a new era of doing business and employees are assuming new information-processing responsibilities. Don't expect that to change in the future. What you can expect is that the business world and its employees will settle into their new environments. When this happens, knowledge workers of tomorrow may not even be called "knowledge" workers. They may take on some glorified distinction, such as wisdom workers, but more than likely we'll probably just refer to them as workers. But no matter what general term is applied, knowledge workers will still work with and produce information as a product. And that's you.

Information Technology of Tomorrow

Perhaps the most difficult predictions to make are in the area of information technology. We've already identified IT as an important factor changing the landscape of business

Frequently Asked Questions

QUESTION   In what ways will the IT systems in Chapter 2 change in the future? Will some be more important than others?

The Obvious	The Not So Obvious
Customer integrated and workgroup support systems will be critical to success.	New systems will emerge that are combinations of others.
New artificial intelligence techniques will surface to support decision-making tasks.	Executive information systems will become everyone's information systems.
Electronic data interchange will be a requirement for doing business.	

today and tomorrow. And technology itself is changing every day. For you to exploit technology as a factor in business, you need to have some perception of what it will look like in the future and how the business world will use it. Some of your perceptions will undoubtedly be wrong (as will many of ours), but it is interesting to try to forecast the future of technology.

Customer Integrated and Workgroup Support Systems Will Be Critical to Success

Because of the explosion of the Internet and electronic commerce, it will become essential for all businesses to provide customer integrated systems (CIS) that allow customers to process their own transactions. Even today you can electronically pay your bills, pay for gas at the pump, and use ATMs to perform your bank transaction processing. These are all examples of CISs, and the future promises even more of them.

A workgroup support system (WSS) is another type of system that will become essential for any business operation. The continued focus on OHP strategies, such as transnational firms, information partnerships, virtual organizations, and teams, will make it absolutely necessary for organizations to focus on WSSs to support the sharing and flow of information among workgroup members who may be geographically dispersed.

New Artificial Intelligence Techniques Will Surface to Support Decision-Making Tasks

As little as 3 years ago, few people had heard of genetic algorithms and even fewer businesses used them. Today that's changing—hundreds of organizations are taking advantage of the unique features of genetic algorithms and their decision support capabilities. The IT industry will continue its research into artificial intelligence (AI) techniques and undoubtedly develop new and better IT-based techniques for supporting the all-important decision-making function.

Electronic Data Interchange Will Be a Requirement for Doing Business

Many large organizations today, including the federal government, refuse to do business with suppliers and distributors if they don't have electronic data interchange

INDUSTRY PERSPECTIVE

Retail

Mass Customization Through Information Technology

Customer moment of value involves guaranteeing perfect delivery of a product or service that meets the customer's expectations in terms of time, location, and form. Of the three, form may very well be the most difficult to provide in the retail industry. For example, if you need a new pair of shoes, form would include size (both length and width). But is your foot really a true 8B, or is

it perhaps somewhere between an 8B and an 8C?

So, because of the variations in form, many retail organizations have turned to technology and a concept called "mass customization" to provide each individual customer with a product tailored to his or her needs. For example, Boston's House of Design uses technology to measure and fit wedding gowns for brides. A bride can even create her own unique wedding gown on a computer and be wearing that special dress in less than 10 days.

And, yes, shoe retailers are following in the same footsteps. For example, in a Custom Foot store

you step on a scanner that measures your foot 14 different ways. Then you choose the style of shoe you want and the color. In less than 3 weeks, you'll be wearing a custom-made pair of shoes that probably costs less than $250.

As a tool for gathering competitive intelligence concerning customers, information technology is great. But once you have that information you should also consider using technology to provide each individual customer with the exact product or service he or she wants. If you can do that, the world will be your oyster.[6,7] ❖

QUESTION How will organizations organize and manage access to information in the future?

The Obvious	The Not So Obvious
Databases will become a standard for supporting online transaction processing.	New technologies will surface for massive information storage.
Data warehouses will be standard for supporting online analytical processing.	Databases and data warehouses will become easier to use and build.

(EDI) capabilities. In the future all organizations, regardless of size, will require EDI capabilities. EDI will become the foundation for all interorganizational communications of information contained in standard business documents.

New Systems Will Emerge That Are Combinations of Others

With respect to the seven types of IT systems, you can expect many to eventually converge into a single system that exhibits a variety of characteristics. You're already seeing that happen to a certain extent. For example, when you use an ATM to withdraw cash or make a deposit, you perform your own transaction processing (CIS), you can obtain a summarized list of your last 10 transactions (MIS), and you participate in the electronic movement of information that would be contained on a standard bank document, such as a deposit slip (EDI). Your opportunity in business is to always critically evaluate the seven types of IT systems and determine how best to combine their features to create a new hybrid system.

Executive Information Systems Will Become Everyone's Information Systems

Right now, executive information systems (EIS) focus on supporting the information needs of strategic management. In the future, that should change in two ways. First, these types of systems will pervade the entire organizational structure and become employee information systems. As an extension of that change, organizations will also begin to give customers the same information-processing capabilities that an EIS provides. When that happens, EISs will become *everyone's information system.* Think of the impact that will have on you as a customer. You'll have the ability to connect to a video store and view your rental history over the past year, including the number of videos you returned late. You'll be able to connect to the electric company and see a graph that compares your electricity usage by month and year. Your ability to perform these functions will definitely enhance your ability to make better personal decisions as a customer.

Databases Will Become a Standard for Supporting Online Transaction Processing

Databases will simply become the standard for organizing and managing access to information to support online transaction processing (OLTP). As far as the relational and object-oriented database models are concerned, you can expect to see both used widely. The relational model will be used extensively in environments that require a logical organization of information according to fields, records, and files. The object-oriented model will be used in environments that require combined information and procedures and the organization of complex data types, such as drawings.

Data Warehouses Will Be Standard for Supporting Online Analytical Processing

Data warehouses primarily support online analytical processing (OLAP), and that will not change in the future. But there will be a growing number of different types of data warehouses. Most notably, organizational data warehouses will support organizationwide OLAP needs, data marts (smaller versions of organizational data warehouses) will support division and department OLAP needs, and personal data warehouses will support your individual OLAP needs.

New Technologies Will Surface for Massive Information Storage

Closely related to databases and data warehouses that organize and manage access to information are technologies

Chefs Are Cooking Up Database Services for Finding Jobs

Databases already are and will continue to be the primary method for organizing and managing access to information within every organization. But there are many other types of databases. One such database is an *external database*—a database maintained by other organizations that you can access to obtain information. Many of these external databases are completely free (especially those that you can find on the Internet) and others charge a small fee for your use.

As a student right now, some external databases are more important than others to you. For example, if you need population statistics for a term paper, you can connect to the U.S. Census Bureau database or other worldwide databases. Most important, if you're looking for a job, you can access and use a variety of employment databases.

If you plan on being a chef or having some other occupation in the food industry, you might want to consider using the employment database provided by the Council on Hotel, Restaurant and Institutional Education and Advantage Systems (CHRIE). CHRIE's database is essentially an electronic job-matching system that contains potential employees and hundreds of

food jobs available all over the world. All you have to do is complete your resume and send it to CHRIE. Once your resume is entered, special job-matching software takes over and produces a list of potential jobs for you. What's really great is that the service is completely free to you as a potential employee.

By the way, if you care nothing about a career as a chef but do enjoy eating good food, there are over 100,000 food and cooking sites on the Internet. Many provide special recipes (for example, mushroom barbecue sauce for ribs), whereas others highlight the menu specialties of over 10,000 restaurants worldwide.[8, 9] ❖

on which database and data warehouse information is stored. These technologies (which we refer to as "cradling technologies") will change dramatically over the next several years by increasing their capacity to store massive amounts of information. This change will have a direct effect on databases and data warehouses. Because of the increased storage capacity, organizations will strive to capture, use, and store even more information. Right now, storage technologies can hold terabytes of information—that's trillions of characters. In the future, that will grow to quadrillions (the next step up from trillions) and possibly to centillions (which is 10^{303}).

Databases and Data Warehouses Will Become Easier to Use and Build

As databases and data warehouses become standard, software providers will strive to create packages that make databases and data warehouses easier to use and build. Right now database packages are probably the most difficult to use of all the personal productivity software tool sets. And we don't even include data warehouse packages in the personal productivity software

tool set. Expect that to change. As we discussed in the section on tomorrow's knowledge workers, it's becoming increasingly more important for you to know how to build and use databases and data warehouses. Your opportunity lies in your ability to understand the concepts, such as normalization and entity-relationship diagramming, behind databases and data warehouses.

Client/Server Will Dominate the Structure of Networks

Client/server will soon become the blueprint by which all organizational networks are built. Client/server's many advantages—which include mirroring organizational workings; transparent distribution of software, information, and processing power; software reuse; and flexibility on the client side—far outweigh any costs associated with its development. For you it will become important to understand (1) how your organization works; (2) the global and local nature of software, information, and processing power; and (3) which client/server implementation model would be best for a given situation.

Frequently Asked Questions

QUESTION   What about networks—how will they change and what will be important?

The Obvious	The Not So Obvious
Client/server will dominate the structure of networks.	Network perfect service will garner more focus than network technologies.
The Internet will become as common as the telephone.	The networked home will form the basis for your personal life.
Intranets will connect organizations to their customers.	The world will be "tele" everything.

The Internet Will Become as Common as the Telephone

The Internet is definitely here to stay. Currently there are over 75 million people using the Internet every day and that number is growing by dramatic leaps and bounds. Undoubtedly the Internet will someday become as common as the telephone.

Intranets Will Connect Organizations to Their Customers

Intranets are nothing more than specialized extensions of the Internet that protect organizations from unauthorized outside access. But intranets also offer something more—they give your organization the ability to set up extranet applications that customers can use to process their own secure transactions over the Internet. The use of extranet applications, which rely on intranets and relatively simple Internet-based technologies, will increase dramatically over the next several years as all organizations strive to electronically communicate with customers.

Network Perfect Service Will Garner More Focus Than Network Technologies

Because network technologies are so rapidly and dynamically changing, many organizations are forced to focus on the technology itself instead of its purpose. That purpose is to provide network perfect service where, how, and when it is wanted. In the coming years, organizations will begin to focus more on network perfect service and less on the technology that provides it. This may seem like a subtle shift in focus, but it's not. The first priority in using technology is to establish the business strategy and then determine how technology can be exploited in executing that strategy.

The Networked Home Will Form the Basis for Your Personal Life

Network technologies will profoundly affect numerous areas of your personal life. One such area is your home. The home of the future will definitely be networked. All appliances, sprinkler systems, lights, televisions, telephones, computers, and anything else you can think of will be interconnected. From any room in your house, you'll be able to control how these devices function and interact. You'll be able to sit at your desk and set the alarm clock in your bedroom. You'll be able to prepare dinner in the kitchen and also control which TV shows your children can watch in the living room.

You'll also see many of the emerging technologies we discussed in Chapter 7 in the networked home of the future. For example, from any television set anywhere in your home, you'll be able to access the Internet. You'll have smart appliances that react to voice commands and determine settings that are consistent with your commands. The networked home of the future is definitely going to be interesting and will probably include more features than you can currently imagine.

The World Will Be "Tele" Everything

Finally, network technologies will bring about many new "tele" applications. Right now, we have telecommunications (moving information electronically) and telecommuting (working somewhere else other than a central location). These are quite common. In the future, we'll also perform such applications as telemedicine and tele-education. *Telemedicine* will allow you to monitor your own physical condition and electronically communicate that information to a physician. You may very well take your own blood pressure and temperature and even perform a simple blood test, all while communicating the results to your doctor. Using virtual reality gloves, you may

AT&T Announces WorldNet to Support Intranets

Interorganizational systems' primary information-processing task is to support communication of information from one location to another or from one person to another. The future holds great promise for IOSs, specifically intranets—a special internal organizational Internet that allows you to communicate information within your organization while preventing unauthorized outside access.

AT&T, one of the world's largest telecommunications service providers, has introduced a product, called WorldNet, to help organizations set up secure intranets. These intranets will support the communication of information to operations throughout the world through the Internet. WorldNet includes software that allows your organization to establish secure internal intranets and worldwide connectivity through the Internet to all of its global operations. Additionally, WorldNet includes firewall software that your organization can customize to create extranet applications. These extranet applications will allow your suppliers and customers access to intranet-stored information.

The future of the business world is definitely electronic commerce. And electronic commerce is only possible through interorganizational systems that allow organizations (and customers) to share information while providing or purchasing products and services. Many people are predicting, and rightfully so, that intranets will form the basis for most electronic commerce activities. If you're interested, you can read more about AT&T's WorldNet at its Web site at http://www.att.com.[10] ❖

then feel the swollen lymph nodes in your neck. Your doctor would use his or her virtual reality gloves to feel the same thing.

In *teleeducation*, you'll live in one location and get a degree from a college or university in another part of the world. Many high schools are even beginning to allow students to stay at home, complete their work, and attend classes through the Internet. "At home" schooling, in which parents teach their own children, will take on a whole new dimension. In this type of high school teleeducation, students will be able to virtually attend classes whenever they want and attend the physical school once a week to take exams.

Automatic Speech Recognition Will Be Everywhere

Let's face it, speech is the most popular, effective, and efficient way of communicating information. It only makes sense then that automatic speech recognition (ASR) will continue to grow in popularity and use. This will occur in the business world and in your personal life. In the business world, expect to create sales contracts, proposal presentations, e-mail messages, and many other documents by simply "speaking" their contents. In your personal life, ASR will indeed be everywhere—from creating

Frequently Asked Questions

QUESTION   What is the future of emerging technologies?

The Obvious	The Not So Obvious
Automatic speech recognition will be everywhere.	Automatic speech understanding will surface.
Multimedia will be standard for presenting information.	Electronic cash will become just "cash."
The wireless revolution will continue.	Virtual reality will be widely used on the Internet and will incorporate taste and smell.
	You may be wirelessly wired.

your term papers and personal letters to turning on the water sprinkler system and starting the coffee.

Multimedia Will Be Standard for Presenting Information

Multimedia is a great way to present information in many forms and allow people to control the order of the presentation. The keys to its popularity are (1) many forms and (2) control. People are simply more apt to use information that comes in many forms (video, sound, text, and so on) and for which they can control the presentation.

The Wireless Revolution Will Continue

The wireless revolution is all about *portability* of technology and your *mobility*. New and better wireless products, such as smart phones that use unguided communications media to transmit information, are hitting retail shelves every day all over the country. This trend has no end in sight as businesses and people strive for wireless connectivity.

Automatic Speech Understanding Will Surface

ASR is about recognizing spoken words, but automatic speech understanding (ASU) will do much more—it will understand what you're saying within the context of a conversation. When speech recognition progresses to the point of speech understanding, you'll be able to walk up to an ATM and ask, "How much money do I have?" or "What's in my checking account?" and receive the requested information. This speech understanding concept focuses on flexibility or ease of use. And as technology becomes easier to use, more people will use it.

INDUSTRY PERSPECTIVE

Entertainment & Publishing

Technology Takes Sporting Events to New Levels of Interactivity

The proliferation of new stadiums has caused upheavals in professional sports. It doesn't matter if the sport is baseball, football, hockey, or basketball, every team wants a new stadium. But these new stadiums are more than just about hardwood floors, astroturf, box seats, or fancy display screens; they are incorporating emerging technologies of all kinds to make your visit more personal and exciting.

Let's look at the technology you may find in the stadium of the future:

- *Stadium credit cards* Many stadiums are beginning to issue stadium credit cards.

With your credit card, you'll be able to purchase tickets and pay for food and sports memorabilia.

- *High-tech food ordering* After you find your seat, don't worry about finding the person yelling "hot dogs" or "peanuts." Instead use a special credit card swiper and keypad located on your armrest to order whatever food you want. That information will be electronically transmitted to the kitchen area, where people will prepare your order and deliver it right to your seat.

- *Personal instant replay screens* Like most new airplanes, some stadiums are giving people their own TV screens. On the screen, you'll be able to watch the game, view instant replays, and even call up the

Internet to check other sports scores at ESPN's Web site. Some players may even wear special cameras that display on your screen what they see while they play the game.

- *Real-time interviews with players* On that same screen, you'll also be able to conduct real-time video interviews with your favorite players. Simply use the keypad to request a personal interview with a player and then view the interview on the screen while you ask questions.

If all this seems a bit far-fetched, think again. The goal of technology, in this case, is to get you off your couch and into the stadium. It's all about entertainment, and entertainment has definitely gone high-tech.[11] ❖

Wireless Technologies Find Sink Holes Before They Surface

Would you believe that soy sauce can be damaging to roads and cause sink holes as large as 100 feet in diameter? It may sound strange, but it's actually quite common in Japan. Soy sauce contains a high sulfur content that gradually eats away at sewer pipes. And if the damaged sewer pipes are underneath roads large sink holes can occur that cost millions of dollars to repair.

The solution is not to stop using soy sauce (which would probably be impossible in Japan) or to fill in the sink holes as they occur, but rather to find the sink holes before they surface and inject cement and other filling solutions to keep the road surfaces even. To do that, Japan has turned to wireless technologies. These wireless technologies emit electromagnetic waves below road surfaces and then interpret the returning waves to determine the exact location of a sink hole and its size. All that's left is to drill a hole in the road surface and inject filling solutions. The whole process can be completed in a matter of just a few hours.

Japan's "road doctor" system based on wireless technologies has a 90 percent success rate and has cut costs by as much as 75 percent. If wireless technologies can find sink holes before they surface, what else can they find—abandoned and fallen mine shafts, old bombs from previous wars, shifts in the earth's surface from volcanic activity? Who really knows? But the business world is certainly taking advantage of wireless technologies; revenues for wireless technologies, such as digital pagers, cellular phones, and satellites are expected to exceed $10 billion before the turn of the century.[12, 13, 14] ❖

THE GLOBAL

PERSPECTIVE

Electronic Cash Will Become Just "Cash"

As different types of products become more prevalent, our view of and references to them tend to change. For example, when color televisions became available, we referred to them as "color TVs." Now that they are more common than black-and-white TVs, we refer to them simply as TVs. The same applies to touch-tone phones. When someone says the word "phone," you don't envision the old rotary-dial telephone; instead you picture a phone with push buttons (or perhaps even a cellular phone without a cord).

In the future, electronic cash (e-cash) may become so prevalent that we simply refer to it as "cash" and refer to folding cash and coins as "hard cash." This may take a while, but many are predicting that it will eventually happen. Who knows, someday retail stores may not even accept folding cash and coins without assessing you an extra fee for using them.

Virtual Reality Will Be Widely Used on the Internet and Will Incorporate Taste and Smell

Virtual reality is one of the newest and hottest technological innovations that promises to forever change how you interact with the presentation of information. In a virtual reality environment, you interact by providing physiological input and receiving physiological output. This creates an exciting and dynamic environment in which you actively and physically participate. In the future, you can expect virtual reality to become very commonplace on the Internet (perhaps through CAVE automatic virtual environments). You can also expect virtual reality researchers to create better and safer ways of incorporating the senses of taste and smell. Imagine putting on your virtual reality gear in the comfort of your own home, connecting to the Internet, and experiencing a Hawaiian Luau, including the scent of the nearby ocean and the taste of roasted vegetables and pig.

You May Be Wirelessly Wired

When most people think of wireless communication, they think of cellular phones, digital pagers, and the like. But what about you as an individual being wirelessly wired? Can you be wired without wires? Many countries are already exploring this by proposing the implantation of a tiny microchip in each of its citizens. The microchip will contain such information as your social security number, your date of birth, your driver's license number, and your medical history. Imagine going to a hospital and having medical personnel use a scanner to obtain a complete profile of your medical history.

This particular proposal has raised heated debates. On one side there are those who see the tremendous advantages. For example, store clerks could determine the real age of people purchasing alcohol. Low earth orbit satellites could instantly locate the position of lost children or fugitives from justice. Doctors could instantly determine which medications might cause you an allergic reaction. The list of advantages is virtually endless.

However, being wirelessly wired also means giving up a great deal of your individual privacy. Those people not in favor of this proposal believe that it will become literally impossible to have any personal privacy at all. And they're right: If you're wearing a microchip that can be electronically located, then any organization with satellite communications capabilities can find you wherever you are. That is indeed a tremendous invasion of your personal privacy if abused. It all boils down to ethics and the social responsibilities of using information in the most appropriate way.

Some Final Thoughts as You Prepare for the Future

The future—what it holds for the business world and for you as a knowledge worker—is certainly an elusive subject. Only 15 short years ago the microcomputer explosion occurred. Today probably almost everyone you know has a PC and many people own more than one. Only a few years ago the Internet was text-based and primarily used by researchers. Today there are over 75 million people using the Internet to communicate with people all over the world and also order products and services. During the middle of the twentieth century the United States was the dominant world economic power. Today global competition has made it vitally important to consider "foreign" competition and to produce and sell products in countries throughout the world. Those types of changes have dramatically altered the business world and your role as a knowledge worker in today's information-based business environment. Tomorrow you can expect changes that are just as dramatic. Unfortunately, you can't accurately predict all those changes; neither can we.

We offer four final notes to you concerning technology, business, knowledge workers, and management information systems as you prepare to take your place in the ever-changing business world. The success of your organization, to a great extent, depends on you as a knowledge worker. And your personal success depends entirely and solely on you. The future is yours.

Technology Will Become Transparent

Information technology is simply a set of tools you use to conduct business. That's true because today's (and tomorrow's) business environment is largely information-based, and IT can help you work with that information. That's also the reason technology is receiving so much attention right now—businesses need to work with information more than ever before, and technology offers a way of doing it efficiently and effectively.

Someday that will probably change. It's not that you won't require technology to work with information or that the business world will no longer rely on information as a key resource; rather, technology will become a normal part of conducting any type of business. When that happens, technology will become *transparent.* Think about electricity: Electricity is necessary for almost every aspect of business. But you don't really think about electricity as being a key business resource (although it really is). You just assume that electricity will always be available and that you will always need it.

Telephones are also a transparent business resource. To do business, you need a telephone to communicate with other people. But you won't find any businesses today that include telephones in their strategic business plan. The assumption is simply that you need a telephone and that telephone communications will always be possible.

That's not true for technology right now—technology is changing every day and the business world is currently wrestling with how best to use it. In the future, technology will indeed become a normal part of doing business. And when it does, technology will become transparent: It will be a standard business resource that everyone assumes will always be needed and will always be available.

Business Will Be Conducted in Cyberspace

Technology—specifically communications technologies such as the Internet—has ushered in a new era of business. That new era involves conducting business in cyberspace. Hundreds of new businesses are opening daily—but they aren't built of brick and mortar and they don't exist on expensive parcels of land in a shopping mall or downtown business district. These new businesses exist in cyberspace, conducting every business operation—from product design to customer service—over the Internet and other forms of communications technology.

Don't underestimate the significance of this trend. Over the next several years, more and more businesses will open and exist only in cyberspace. Existing brick and mortar businesses will increasingly turn to cyberspace.

As this continues to happen it will affect you in a number of ways, including increasing your

- Chances of becoming a telecommuter
- Need to work with people throughout the world
- Need to effectively use IT tools that support electronic commerce
- Mobility to work anywhere anytime
- Need to become an information-literate knowledge worker

The last point is perhaps the most important one for you. In cyberspace, information will continue to be a key resource. Your ability to work with information, make decisions based on available information, and understand the information you work with will define your true success as an information-literate knowledge worker.

Knowledge Workers Will Become the Key to Business

Throughout the history of the business world, people have always been the key resource. That certainly will not change in the future. As a knowledge worker—no matter what your profession or in which industry you work—**you** are the key business resource. As technology becomes more transparent and more business is conducted in cyberspace, your individual success will define the success of your organization. Your ability to work with customers, create new products and services, define the strategic direction of your organization, make decisions, work with information, and perform a host of other activities is really at the heart of any business undertaking.

Management Information Systems Will Not Be for Just Information Technology Specialists

Finally, we would stress that the management information systems (MIS) function in business is not solely the responsibility of IT specialists. Recall from our definition that MIS deals with the planning for, development, management, and use of information technology tools to help people perform all tasks related to information processing and management. As a knowledge worker, you can't delegate the complete MIS function to IT specialists—you need to

INDUSTRY PERSPECTIVE **Manufacturing**

Manufacturers Replace Robots with People

Robotics and other uses of technology in manufacturing assembly lines are big business. Supposedly robots make fewer mistakes, cost less, can work 24 hours a day, and possess a greater production capacity than people. But consider these numbers: In 1991, sales of robotics in Japan peaked at $5.7 billion, and just 3 years later that figure fell to barely $4 billion. Why the turnaround?

Well, a lot of manufacturers are learning that robots do not have a greater production capacity than people and that they cost more than people. Toyota, for example, recently outfitted two different production plants. The first plant was completely automated with robotics at a cost of $333 million. The second plant was outfitted with fewer, simpler robots and hundreds of people working on assembly lines. The second plant has the same production capacity as the first, yet it cost only about $90 million. That's definitely an example of a situation when robots cost more than people and can't produce any more.

Many manufacturers are also finding out that people possess an important trait that you can't build into a robot—flexibility. At NEC's factory in Honjo, Japan, for example, workers can be taught a new assembly list in less than a day. To reprogram robots to perform the same tasks can take as long as 3 months. Robots may be good at performing repetitive tasks thousands of times each day, but they certainly can't adapt to new tasks as quickly as people.

Technology is great—in many instances it **can** perform functions faster and cheaper than people. But technology possesses no intelligence—it can't adapt to change as quickly as people. Technology will never replace people as the most important business resource. Never forget that.[15] ❖

Planning for, Developing, Managing, Using, or Some Combination?

Understanding your knowledge worker role within the management information systems function is a significant career opportunity for you. No matter what career you choose or in which industry you work, you'll definitely be involved in planning for, developing, managing, and using information technology tools—and that's the definition of MIS.

In the table below, we've listed numerous concepts that you've studied in this text. Determine whether part of your job will include planning for, developing, managing, or using these concepts. But before you do, identify your chosen career and in which industry you'd like to work. ❖

Career: _____	Industry: _____			
Concepts	**Planning for**	**Developing**	**Managing**	**Using**
Information Technology Systems (in Chapter 2)				
Transaction processing				
Customer integrated				
Management information				
Workgroup support				
Executive information				
Interorganizational				
Organizational Horsepower Strategies (in Chapter 3)				
Just-in-time				
Teams				
Information partnership				
Timeless and locationless operation				
Transnational firm				
Virtual organization				
Learning organization				
Methods for Organizing Information (in Chapter 4)				
Database				
Data warehouse				
Decision Support and AI Systems (in Chapter 5)				
Decision support				
Group decision support				
Geographic information				
Expert				
Genetic algorithm				
Neural network				
External Electronic Commerce (in Chapter 6)				
Electronic data interchange				
Electronic funds transfer				
Competitive intelligence				
Individualized electronic advertising				
Emerging Technologies (in Chapter 7)				
Automatic speech recognition				
Multimedia				
Virtual reality				
Electronic cash				

participate as well in planning for, developing, managing, and using technology. Information technology is simply a set of tools that **you** use to work with information. To be as successful as possible, you—as a knowledge worker—must also assume responsibility for the MIS function.

Retail Stores in Cyberspace

According to Rudy Puryear, senior partner at Andersen Consulting, half of today's retail companies will no longer exist by the year 2000. Half—that's an astounding number! So what's going to cause the disappearance of 50 percent of the retail stores over the next several years? It's the emergence of metamarts in cyberspace.

A **metamart** is a huge cyberspace-based electronic shopping mall on the Internet. Once you connect to an Internet metamart, you'll be able to simply enter a product type, such as "aerobics shoes for women," then view hundreds of styles, sizes, and name brands. You'll also be able to compare brands and prices much more easily in cyberspace than at traditional stores. For example, you won't have to travel from one department store to another to find the best price on Guess jeans or Polo shirts. Instead the metamart will tell you which cyberspace retail stores are currently having sales and where you can find the best price.

Metamarts will also make it easier for businesses to perform individualized electronic advertising. As you browse an electronic metamart, huge databases will capture information pertaining to you, your product queries, and any products you buy. The retail industry will

KNOWLEDGE WORKER'S ✓-LIST

The Business Environment of Tomorrow and Important Factors That Will Shape It. New factors that will change the landscape of business in the future include

1. *Security, privacy, and ethics* The social implications of using technology and information correctly in the business world.

2. *IT as an essential enabler of innovation* Technology is simply a must for innovation.

3. *Organizational horsepower strategies that focus on organizational structure* Including teams, information partnerships, timeless and locationless operations, transnational firms, virtual organizations, and learning organizations.

4. *The convergence of business planning and IT planning* The melding of the development of the strategic plan of an organization and information technology.

5. *IT as essential for doing any kind of business* You and your organization will need technology just to stay in business.

6. *The agile yet fleeting nature of cybercorps* New cyberspace-based businesses that respond quickly to the market, can overcome barriers to entry, and can come and go without notice.

Their Role in Tomorrow's Business as Tomorrow's Knowledge Workers. Tomorrow's knowledge worker will:

1. Be everywhere and doing everything

2. Possess general skills that include communication, interpersonal, decision-making, and time and project management skills

3. Possess IT skills in the areas of personal productivity software and networking

4. Be a data miner

5. Be a systems developer

6. Be, for the most part, a telecommuter

7. Be a "jack of all trades, and master of one"

8. Become just a worker

Information Technologies That Will Be Important to Business Tomorrow. Information technology is changing the landscape of business, and it's changing daily. To exploit technology in business, you also need to understand how it will change in the future and how the business world will use it.

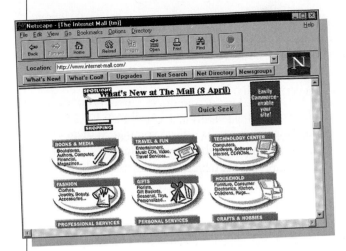

then use that information to send you individualized advertising notices that focus on your exact product desires and purchasing habits.

These Internet metamarts will actually become mega-metamarts where you can find literally any product you want. For example, at the Internet Mall (http://www.internet-mall.com) you can buy books, make travel arrangements, locate a real estate agent, buy clothing and gifts, purchase baseball bats and gloves, and even buy a car from auto dealers all over the country. Metamarts really will become one-stop shopping centers that may put many traditional retail stores out of business.[16] ❖

◄ Questions ►

1. How is the metamart an example of disintermediation through electronic commerce? Do you think this type of disintermediation will have much effect on employment figures around the country? How and why?

The Obvious Predictions	The Not So Obvious Predictions
Information Technology Systems	
Customer integrated and workgroup support systems will be critical to success.	New systems will emerge that are combinations of others.
New artificial intelligence techniques will surface to support decision-making tasks.	Executive information systems will become everyone's information systems.
Electronic data interchange will be a requirement for doing business.	
Organizing and Managing Access to Information	
Databases will become a standard for supporting online transaction processing.	New technologies will surface for massive information storage.
Data warehouses will be standard for supporting online analytical processing.	Databases and data warehouses will become much easier to use and build.
Networks	
Client/server will dominate the structure of networks.	Network perfect service will garner more focus than network technologies.
The Internet will become as common as the telephone.	The networked home will form the basis for your personal life.
Intranets will connect organizations to their customers.	The world will be "tele" everything.
Emerging Technologies	
Automatic speech recognition will be everywhere.	Automatic speech understanding will surface.
Multimedia will be standard for presenting information.	Electronic cash will become just "cash."
The wireless revolution will continue.	Virtual reality will be widely used on the Internet and will incorporate taste and smell.
	You may be wirelessly wired. ❖

2. How is the metamart an example of a cyber corporation (cybercorp), which we discussed in the opening case study? Describe a metamart according to the five characteristics of a cybercorp—completely electronic commerce-based, forward-thinking and innovative management, virtual, integrated networks, and outsourcing more than ever before.

3. In this chapter, we discussed the six organizational horsepower (OHP) strategies that businesses will focus on in the future—teams, information partnerships, timeless and locationless operations, transnational firms, virtual organizations, and learning organizations. Which of these OHP strategies are most important for the success of a metamart? Why do you think this is true? If you had to identify one OHP strategy that was the least important for a metamart, which would it be and why?

4. What do you believe the role of knowledge workers will be in tomorrow's metamarts? What general skills will knowledge workers need for employment at a metamart? What about IT skills? What will be key issues for becoming an information-literate knowledge worker at a metamart?

5. Of the seven IT systems discussed in this chapter and Chapter 2, which will be most important for metamarts? Which will be least important? Be prepared to justify your answers.

6. What will be a metamart's network perfect service in terms of reach, range, and responsiveness? Return to Figure 6.28 in Chapter 6 (p. 264) and describe a metamart's network perfect service according to where it would be on the network perfect service cube.

7. How do you think most people will pay for products they purchase at a metamart? Will they use electronic cash, debit cards, or credit cards? What sort of security issues will be related to purchasing products from a metamart over the Internet?

CLOSING CASE STUDY: CASE 2

You and Your Information

In our final case study, we want to take a look at information pertaining to the most important person in your life—you. Today's business environment is not only information-based, so is all of society. No matter what you do or where you go, your information travels with you and is eventually captured and stored by a number of organizations. In this all-encompassing information environment, let's consider two issues—trust and accuracy. As you'll see, both are very related.

First, answer the questions below, which pertain to your every day life.

1. Do you keep a paper record of all your long-distance phone calls—when you placed them by date and time, to whom, and the length—and then compare that list to your monthly phone bill? □ Y □ N

2. Do you meet with the meter reader to verify the correct reading of your water, gas, or electricity usage? □ Y □ N

3. As you shop, do you keep a record of the prices of your groceries and then compare that record to the register receipt? □ Y □ N

4. Do you frequently ask to see your doctor's medical record on you to ensure that it's correct? □ Y □ N

5. When you receive a tuition bill, do you pull out your calculator, add up the amounts, and verify that the total is correct? □ Y □ N

6. Have you ever purchased a credit report on yourself to make sure your credit information is accurate? □ Y □ N

7. Have you ever called the police department to verify that no outstanding traffic violations have been inadvertently assigned to you? □ Y □ N

8. Do you count your coin change when you receive it from a store clerk? □ Y □ N

9. Do you verify your credit card balance by keeping all your credit card receipts and then matching them to charges on your statement? □ Y □ N

10. Do you keep all your paycheck stubs to verify that the amounts on your W-2 form at the end of the year are correct? □ Y □ N

To how many questions did you answer yes? To how many did you answer no? More than likely, you probably answered no to almost all the questions (if not all of them). What does that have to say about your trust that organizations are maintaining accurate information about you? Well, it basically says that you trust organizations to keep accurate information about you. The real question is, "Is that necessarily the case?"

Now answer the set of questions below, which relate to the level of confidence organizations have in the accuracy of information you give them.

1. When interviewing with potential employers, do they take your word that you have a college degree? □ Y □ N

2. If you deposit several checks into your checking account at once, does the bank trust you to correctly add the amounts? ☐ Y ☐ N

3. When you register for a class that has a prerequisite, does your college or university assume that you have actually taken the prerequisite class? ☐ Y ☐ N

4. When you make a deposit at an ATM and enter the amount, does the bank assume that you entered the correct amount? ☐ Y ☐ N

5. When you're buying a house and negotiating a loan, does the bank assume that the price you're paying for the house is correct and not inflated? ☐ Y ☐ N

6. When insuring your car, does the insurance company assume that you have a good driving record? ☐ Y ☐ N

7. When you apply for a parking permit at your college or university, does it assume that the car belongs to you? ☐ Y ☐ N

8. When you file your taxes, does the IRS assume that you've reported all your income over the past year? ☐ Y ☐ N

The answer to each of those questions is probably no. And what does that say about the extent to which organizations trust you to provide accurate information? In this instance, it may not be strictly a matter of trust. Organizations today can't afford to have *dirty information*—information that's not accurate. Because organizations base so many of their decisions on information, inaccurate information creates a real problem that may equate to inefficient processes and lost revenue.

So, on the one side, you're probably very trusting in your assumptions that organizations are maintaining accurate information about you. On the other side, organizations don't really depend on you to provide accurate information. ❖

◄ Questions ►

1. Should you really trust organizations to maintain accurate information about you? In many instances, is it even worth your time and energy to verify the accuracy of that information?

2. What other examples can you think of in which you simply trust that your information is accurate? What other examples can you think of in which specific organizations don't assume that you're providing accurate information?

3. What sort of impact will cybercorps have on the issues of trust and accuracy? Will it become easier or more difficult for cybercorps to assume that you're providing accurate information? Will you trust cybercorps to maintain your information more accurately than traditional organizations?

4. What are the ethical issues involved in organizations sharing information about you? In some instances it may be okay and in your best interest. But what if the shared information about you is inaccurate? What damage could it cause? What sort of recourse do you have, if any?

5. It's a real dilemma—most people think that credit card offerers charge extremely high interest rates. But how many people do you know who actually go through the process of calculating their average daily balances, applying the interest rates, and then verifying that the interest charged on their accounts is correct? Why do people complain that they are being charged excessive interest rates and then fail to check the accuracy of the interest calculations?

6. What about the future—as more organizations maintain even more information about you, should you become more concerned about accuracy? Why or why not?

Electronic Commerce
Business and You on the Internet

Continuing Your Education Through the Internet

For many of you, this course may mark the end of your endeavors in higher education. Indeed, you may be

preparing right now to enter the business world by sending out resumes and participating in job interviews. If so, we certainly hope you're letting the Internet help (see the Real HOT Electronic Commerce section in Chapter 1, "Using the Internet as a Tool to Find a Job"). For others of you, you may still have another year or two before completing your education. Whatever the case, you need to consider the current landscape of the business world and what it's going to take for you to compete now and in the future.

To be perfectly honest, it's a dog-eat-dog world out there. The competitive landscape of business is more intense than it ever has been. And that competitiveness spills into your personal life. Many of you are in school right now to get an education to better compete in the job market. But many knowledge workers are finding out that an undergraduate degree is simply not enough to compete in the business world.

So, many people are turning once again to higher education to obtain a master's degree, professional certification such as a CPA or CFP (certified financial planner), or perhaps even a Ph.D. in business. You may also be considering the same, either immediately upon graduation or sometime in the near future.

And, just like businesses, graduate schools (and all schools in general) are using the Internet as a way to communicate information to you. Many of these schools are even offering online courses you can complete through the Internet to further your education.

In this section, we've included a number of Web sites related to continuing your education through the Internet. On the Web site that supports this text (http://www.mhhe.com/business/mis/haag, select "Electronic Commerce Projects"), we've provided direct links to all these Web sites as well as many, many more. These are a great starting point for completing this Real HOT section. We would also encourage you to search the Internet for others. One such site is http://www.clas.ufl.edu/CLAS/american-universities.html#U, a great place to find information concerning any school of interest.

MBA Programs

Many of you will undoubtedly choose to continue your education by obtaining an MBA. And you probably should. The market for the best business positions is extremely competitive, with hiring organizations seeking individuals who can speak more than one language, have job experience, and have extended their educational endeavors beyond just getting an undergraduate degree. Indeed, there are over 300,000 people in the United States seeking an MBA right now (that's an all-time high), and you must compete against some of those people in the job market.

Each year, the *U.S. News & World Report* ranks the top business schools in the nation. In the table on page

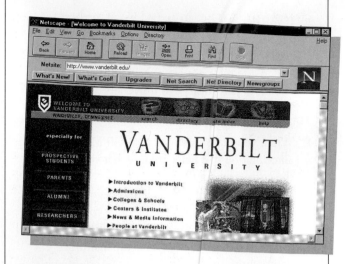

478, we've provided a list of the top five business schools in the nation and where you can find them on the Internet. On the Web site that supports this text, you'll also find a list of the remaining Web sites for the top 50 business schools in the nation.

Choose five different business schools from the list of 50, visit their Web sites, and answer the following questions for each.

A. What business school did you choose?

B. Does that school offer a graduate program in your area of interest?

C. Does the graduate program Web site contain biographical sketches of faculty?

D. Can you order application and admissions information online?

E. Is there a major benefactor for the business school? If so, who is it?

F. Does the site list tuition and fee costs?

G. Does the site contain a list of the graduate courses offered in your area of interest?

As you prepare to enter the workforce and perhaps think about pursuing a master's in business, we would encourage you to return to the Web site that supports this text and visit the list of the top 50 business schools. On a yearly basis, we will update that list to include any new schools among the most elite offering graduate programs in business.

Specialized MBA Programs

In the previous section, you explored a few of the top 50 business schools in the nation. Those schools were ranked irrespective of any specialization, focusing rather on overall academic reputation. *U.S. News & World*

Report also compiles an annual list of the best business schools in 10 specializations: accounting, entrepreneurship, finance, health services administration, management information systems, international business, general business, marketing, nonprofit organizations, and production/operations. And if you're interested in a specialized MBA, you should consider viewing schools in these lists.

In the table on pages 478–479, we've provided a list of 30 of the best business schools in the above areas (3 for each) and where you can find them on the Internet. In that table, we've added any schools that did not appear in the top schools from the previous section. In health services administration, for example, the top-ranked school is Wharton, and we included the University of Minnesota (ranked fifth) and University of California–Irvine (ranked ninth) because they did not appear in the list of the top five. And on the Web site that supports this text, you'll find the complete lists of the top 10 business schools in each area.

Choose at least three schools that offer a specialization in your area of interest and visit their Web sites. Based on what you find, rank those three schools according to your first, second, and third choice. What factors did you consider? Was cost an overriding concern? Before you began your analysis, did you already have a preconceived notion of the best school? Did you change your mind once you visited the schools' sites?

Graduate School Information and Tips

Before you begin your decision-making process concerning which graduate school to attend, you should gather a variety of material. For example, obtaining a directory of universities (both domestic and international) would be helpful. Perhaps even more important,

you should ask yourself several questions. Are you ready for graduate school? Why are you considering going to graduate school? How do you determine which school is best for you based on such issues as price, location, and area of specialization?

Many of these questions are very personal to you. For example, we can't help you determine if you're really ready for graduate school or answer why you're considering going to graduate school. But what we can do is point you toward some valuable resources on the Internet to help you answer some of your questions and find a wealth of information relating to universities. In the table on pages 478–479, we've provided a list of sites on the Internet that either provide school information or help you work through some of your questions. Like most people choosing to continue their education, you'll find these types of sites to be very helpful.

At your leisure, we recommend that you connect to several of these sites and see what they have to offer. Some simply provide a list of universities, whereas others may be particularly useful as you make that all-important decision.

Tele-Education

Throughout this text, you've explored the concept of 24-hour connectivity through information technology. Using IT (part of which is the Internet), organizations today are sending out telecommuting employees, and medical and health facilities are establishing telemedicine practices. And your school may be doing the same—using IT to develop the environment of tele-education.

Tele-education—which goes by a number of terms including e-education, distance learning, distributed learning, and online learning—enables you to get an education without "going" to school. Quite literally, you can enroll in a school on the East Coast and live in Denver, enjoying great winter skiing. Using various forms of IT (videoconferencing, e-mail, chat rooms, and the Internet), you can take courses from schools all over the world. Some of those schools even offer complete degree programs via IT.

And these schools definitely include graduate programs in business. For example, the Massachusetts Institute of Technology and Duke University have graduate programs that combine traditional classroom instruction courses and computer-delivered courses. In 1997, Ohio University (Athens) introduced *MBA without Boundaries,* an MBA program that is completely online except for a required six-week orientation session.

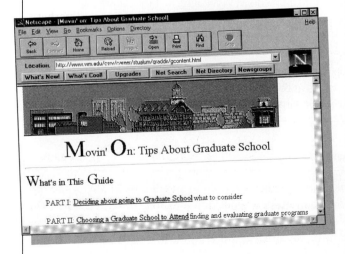

As well, many for-profit organizations offer courses on the Internet that range from preparing for the CPA exam to IT-focused courses such as Windows NT and COBOL programming. In the table below, we've provided a list of sites that have something to do with providing online courses for the Internet. You should definitely connect to the Web site that supports this text

and view the list of other sites related to tele-education. And if you're interested in taking online courses from a specific school, we recommend you connect to its Web site to determine if it offers courses over the Internet.

Connect to at least five of these sites and explore the possibilities of tele-education. As you do, consider the issues that follow on page 480.

Web Sites for Continuing Your Education

University MBA Programs	Address
Harvard University	http://www.hbs.edu
Stanford University	http://www-gsb.stanford.edu
Columbia University	http://www.columbia.edu/cu/business
Massachusetts Institute of Technology (Sloan)	http://web.mit.edu/afs/athena.mit.edu/org/s/sloan/www
University of Pennsylvania (Wharton)	http://www.wharton.upenn.edu

Specialized MBAPrograms

Accounting	Address
1. University of Pennsylvania (Wharton)	http://www.wharton.upenn.edu
2. University of Chicago	http://www.uchicago.edu/uofc/acadunits/GSB.html
3. University of Illinois–Urbana-Champaign	http://130.126.232.20/accountancy

Entrepreneurship	Address
1. Babson College	http://www.babson.edu/mba/el.htm
2. University of Pennsylvania (Wharton)	http://www.wharton.upenn.edu
3. Harvard University	http://www.hbs.edu

Finance	Address
1. University of Pennsylvania (Wharton)	http://www.wharton.upenn.edu
2. University of Chicago	http://www.uchicago.edu/uofc/acadunits/GSB.html
3. Stanford University	http://www-gsb.stanford.edu

Health Services Administration	Address
1. University of Pennsylvania (Wharton)	http://www.wharton.upenn.edu
5. University of Minnesota–Twin Cities (Carlson)	http://www.csom.umn.edu/WWWPages/MHA/program
9. University of California–Irvine	http://www.gsm.uci.edu

Management Information Systems	Address
1. Massachusetts Institute of Technology (Sloan)	http://web.mit.edu/afs/athena.mit.edu/org/s/sloan/www
3. University of Arizona (Eller)	http://www.bpa.arizona.edu/depts/mis/grad_program.html
4. University of Minnesota–Twin Cities (Carlson)	http://www.csom.umn.edu/WWWPages/MHA/program

International Business	Address
1. American Graduate School of International Management (Thunderbird)	http://www.t-bird.edu
2. University of South Carolina	http://www.badm.sc.edu
3. University of Pennsylvania (Wharton)	http://www.wharton.upenn.edu

continued

Web Sites for Continuing Your Education (*continued*)

Specialized MBAPrograms

General Business	Address
1. Northwestern University (Kellogg)	http://www.kellogg.nwu.edu
2. University of Pennsylvania (Wharton)	http://www.wharton.upenn.edu
3. Duke University (Fuqua)	http://www.fuqua.duke.edu

Marketing	Address
1. Northwestern University (Kellogg)	http://www.kellogg.nwu.edu
2. University of Pennsylvania (Wharton)	http://www.wharton.upenn.edu
3. Stanford University	http://www-gsb.stanford.edu

Nonprofit Organizations	Address
1. Yale University	http://www.yale.edu
2. Harvard University	http://www.hbs.edu
7. Case Western Reserve University (Weatherhead)	http://weatherhead.cwru.edu

Production/Operations	Address
1. Massachusetts Institute of Technology (Sloan)	http://web.mit.edu/afs/athena.mit.edu/org/s/sloan/www
2. Carnegie Mellon University	http://www.cmu.cdu
3. Stanford University	http://www-gsb.stanford.edu

Graduate School Information	Address
Helpful questions for going to graduate school	http://www.wm.edu/csrv/career/stualum/graddir/gcontent.html
Another great site for helping you decide if graduate school is right for you	http://www.jobtrak.com/gradschool_docs/gradschool
List of American universities and direct links to them	http://www.clas.ufl.edu/CLAS/american-universities.html
List of universities all over the world	http://www.mit.edu:8001/people/cdemello/univ.html
List of community colleges	http://www.mcli.dist.maricopa.edu/cc

Tele-Education	Address
Real Education is considered to be one the most prominent service providers helping universities and college go online	http://www.realeducation.com
Clearinghouse for over 2,700 courses from 83 providers	http://www.internetuniv.com
One of the most complete collections of online courses (offered by Colorado Community College Online)	http://www.ccconline.com
Free courses on the Internet for learning over 65 languages	http://rivendel.com/%7Eric/resources/coursead.html
Courses in Web page design, Web programming, Internet literacy, IT, and business management	http://www.mhonlinelearning.com/syllabus/coursecatalog.html

Ph.D. Program	Address
Harvard University	http://www.hbs.edu
Princeton University	http://www.princeton.edu/index.shtml
University of Wisconsin–Madison	http://wiscinfo.doit.wisc.edu/bschool
John Hopkins University	http://www.jhu.edu/www/academics/graduate.html
University of Maryland–College Park	http://www.rhsmith.umd.edu/default.asp

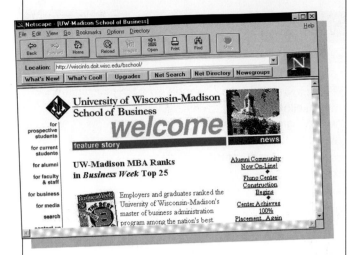

A. Can you just take courses or enroll in a complete degree program?

B. What is the cost of tele-education?

C. What process do you go through to enroll in a tele-education program?

D. How would you feel about staying at home instead of going to class?

E. How do tele-education programs foster interactivity between students and teachers?

F. How much do you think you would learn in a tele-education program compared to a traditional in-class program?

G. For what type of individual is a tele-education program best suited?

Ph.D. Programs

Several years ago, people wanting to gain an advantage in the job market pursued an MBA; and that trend still holds true. But a new trend may be on the horizon—that of developing an even more significant advantage in the job market by obtaining a Ph.D. The thought process is simple. If more people are entering the job market with an MBA, the next logical step is to obtain a Ph.D.

Of course, earning a Ph.D. requires several more years of school beyond an MBA, but a growing number of people are willing to make that investment. In business programs, Ph.D. graduates have two main options: entering the private sector or choosing to stay in academia as a professor. Either option certainly yields tremendous benefits, including significantly higher salaries and great flextime (primarily in academia).

In the table on pages 479, we've provided a list of some of the top institutions in the country offering Ph.D. programs in business and where you can find them on the Internet (you can find a list of others on the Web site that supports this text). Connect to a few of these school sites and explore what it takes to enter a Ph.D. program. Can you see this as a realistic possibility in your lifetime? Can you find a Ph.D. program for your area of interest (e.g., finance, marketing, and so on)? If obtaining a Ph.D. is a new trend for gaining an advantage in the job market, what's next? If you do choose to pursue a Ph.D., how important is it for you also to have some work experience?

As a final note, we would encourage you to keep learning. The business world changes on a daily basis, and you need to change with it. For example, there's always new information technology entering the marketplace everyday. If you don't know how to use it, you've placed yourself behind the eight ball. However you choose to continue your education—through online courses, by obtaining some sort of professional certification, by completing a master's or Ph.D. program, or by simply reading books and learning on your own—never stop learning. Your career depends on it.

 Go to the Web site that supports this text: **http://www.mhhe.com/business/mis/haag** and select "Electronic Commerce Projects."

We've included links to over 100 Web sites for continuing your education through the Internet, including the best business schools in the nation according to *U.S. News & World Report*.

SHORT-ANSWER QUESTIONS

1. What new factors will surface in the future that will further affect the landscape of business?
2. What general skills will knowledge workers need?
3. What IT skills will knowledge workers need?
4. Of the seven IT systems discussed in this chapter and Chapter 2, which will become necessary for just doing business?

5. Why might electronic cash or e-ca become just "cash"?
6. How will the proliferation of cyberspace businesses affect you as a knowledge worker?

DISCUSSION QUESTIONS

1. Many people believe that the business world will eventually "return to the basics" and forgo doing business in cyberspace. What are your feelings on this issue? Is there room in the future for traditional brick and mortar businesses as well as cybercorps?
2. Of the six new factors that will surface in the future that will further affect the landscape of business, which do you believe will receive the greatest attention and why? The least attention and why? What other important factors can you see emerging in the future?
3. Besides communication, interpersonal, decision-making, and time and project management skills, what other skills do you think will be important for

the knowledge workers of tomorrow? Will some skills be more important than others based on different careers or industry settings?

4. Do you think it's possible or even wise for organizations to give their customers executive information system capabilities? Would you, as a customer, use an EIS? If so, for what purposes? What security issues will organizations have to address when providing EIS capabilities to customers?
5. How long do you think it will be before technology becomes transparent in the business world? Do you think it will ever occur? What other things must occur for this to happen?

CASE 1

Assessing the Value of Information

Stapleton Electronics, Inc.

Stapleton Electronics is a world-class manufacturer of components for home stereo systems. Currently, Stapleton has two major manufacturing and distribution centers in the United States—Denver, Colorado, which services the western half of the United States and Roanoke, Virginia, which services the eastern half of the United States (see Figure RH.1). As the director of the distribution center in Denver, you have just received some interesting and somewhat perplexing news from the home office (also located in Denver). Your distribution center currently ships to wholesalers in the following cities in the western United States:

City	State
Los Angeles	California
Portland	Oregon
Seattle	Washington
Little Rock	Arkansas
St. Louis	Missouri
Des Moines	Iowa
Oklahoma City	Oklahoma
Phoenix	Arizona
Butte	Montana

Recently, sales have been booming in all parts of California. Strategic management has decided to open a new manufacturing and distribution facility in Sacramento, California that will service all of California. That means your distribution center will now service all states in the western United States, except California (see Figure RH.2).

Strategic management has also decided that you are using too many carriers for distribution. Carriers are

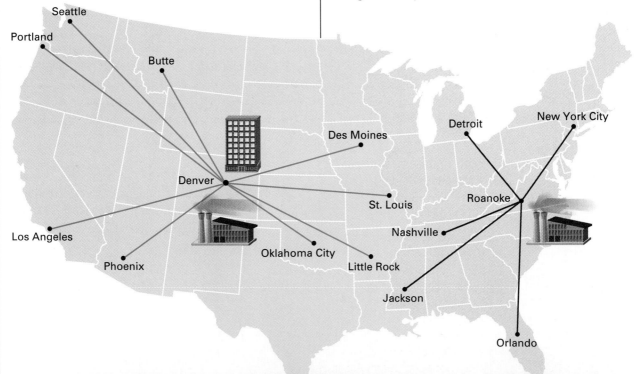

FIGURE RH.1

Stapleton Electronics, Inc.

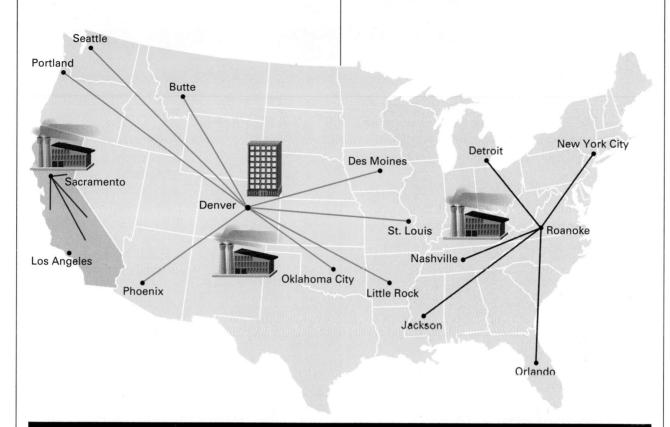

FIGURE RH.2
New Distribution Proposal for Stapleton Electronics

organizations that are subcontracted to carry products from the major distribution centers to the wholesalers. Strategic management has asked you to choose and use only one or two carriers from the current carrier list. Your assistant has provided you with a list of the current carriers and a list of the carrier transactions over the last 27 months. The current list of carriers is as follows:

Carrier Number	Carrier Name
478	Northwest Distribution Lines
623	Rocky Mountain Lines
824	Vans West Distributors
983	Arizona Freighters
767	Lone Star Freighters

All carriers can ship to all destinations except Lone Star Freighters, which cannot ship to Des Moines, Iowa.

The carrier transaction list is in a spreadsheet file containing the fields in the table below. You must analyze the carrier transactions and choose one or two carriers for your new distribution area. Strategic management has asked you to put your analysis in both numeric and graphic forms.

Some Particulars You Should Know

1. All external forces (e.g., the price of gas) will affect all carriers in the same way. So don't worry about external forces—you can't control them anyway.

Column	Name	Description
A	INV. #	An internally generated shipping invoice number.
B	CAR. #	The number of the carrier that made the shipment.
C	DATE	The date the shipment was made.
D	DEST. CITY	The destination city for the shipment.
E	DEST. ST.	The destination state for the shipment.
F	SHIP. WGT.	The total weight of the shipment.
G	TOTAL COST	The total cost of the shipment as charged by the carrier.
H	AGENT	A number that represents the Stapleton employee who arranged for the shipment to be made.

2. Charges for shipments are made according to total shipping weight only, not number of boxes shipped or miles.

3. You may assume that any trends you find in the information will also be present in the coming years. For example, if you find that a given carrier is always the most expensive carrier to a certain destination, you may assume that will hold true in the future.

4. As you consider the information provided to you, think in terms of what information is important and what information is not important. Also don't forget about the time and content dimensions discussed in Chapter 1. Be prepared to justify, by time and content dimension, how you went about your analysis.

5. Upon completing your analysis, please provide concise, yet detailed and thorough, documentation (in narrative, numeric, and graphic forms) that justifies your decision. In this instance, consider the form dimension of information as you prepare your presentation.

6. File: CARRIER (Lotus or Excel file)

CASE 2

Assessing the Value of Information

Affordable Homes Real Estate

In late 1995 a national study announced that Eau Claire, Wisconsin, was the safest place to live. Since then housing development projects have been springing up all around Eau Claire. Six housing development projects are currently dominating the Eau Claire market—Woodland Hills, Granite Mound, Creek Side Huntington, East River Community, Forest Green, and Eau Claire South. These six projects each started with 100 homes, have sold all of them, and are currently developing phase 2.

As one of the three partners and real estate agents of Affordable Homes Real Estate, it is your responsibility to analyze the information concerning the past 600 home sales and choose which development project to focus on for selling homes in phase 2. Because your real estate firm is so small, you and your partners have decided that the firm should focus on selling homes in only one of the development projects.

From the Wisconsin Real Estate Association you have obtained a spreadsheet file that contains information concerning each of the sales for the first 600 homes. It contains the following fields:

Column	Name	Description
A	LOT #	The number assigned to a specific home within each project.
B	PROJECT #	A unique number assigned to each of the six housing development projects (see table below).
C	ASK PRICE	The initial posted asking price for the home.
D	SELL PRICE	The actual price for which the home was sold.
E	LIST DATE	The date the home was listed for sale.
F	SALE DATE	The date on which the final contract closed and the home was sold.
G	SQ. FT.	The total square footage for the home.
H	# BATH.	The number of bathrooms in the home.

The following numbers have been assigned to each of the housing development projects:

Project Number	Project Name
23	Woodland Hills
47	Granite Mound
61	Creek Side Huntington
78	East River Community
92	Forest Green
97	Eau Claire South

It is your responsibility to analyze the sales list and prepare a report that details which housing development project your real estate firm should focus on. Your analysis should be from as many angles as possible.

Some Particulars You Should Know

1. You don't know how many other real estate firms will also be competing for sales in each of the housing development projects.

2. Phase 2 for each housing development project will develop homes similar in style, price, and square footage to their respective first phases.

3. As you consider the information provided to you, think in terms of what information is important and what information is not important. Also, don't forget about the time and content dimensions discussed in Chapter 1. Be prepared to justify, by

time and content, how you went about your analysis.

4. Upon completing your analysis, please provide concise, yet detailed and thorough, documentation (in narrative, numeric, and graphic forms) that justifies your decision. In this instance, consider the form dimension of information as you prepare your presentation.

5. File: REALEST (Lotus or Excel file)

Executive Information System Reporting

B&B Travel Consultants

Benjamin Travis and Brady Austin are coowners of B&B Travel Consultants, a medium-sized travel agency located in Seattle, Washington, that specializes in cruises. Currently, B&B Travel has five different offices in Seattle. At the present time, Ben and Brady are considering various executive information system packages that can show them overall information views of their organization as well as give them the ability to access more detailed information. Ben and Brady have hired you to make recommendations about what reports should be available through the soon-to-be-purchased executive information system.

The table below is a list of the information that will be the foundation for the reports in the proposed executive information system. These five items comprise a record that is created each time a sale is made. To help you develop realistic reports, Ben and Brady have provided you with a spreadsheet file that contains specific sales over the last 6 months.

What Ben and Brady are most interested in is viewing several overall reports and then being able to request more detailed reports. So, as a consultant, your goal is to develop different sets of reports that illustrate the concept of drilling down through information. For example, you should develop a report that shows overall sales by location (each of the five different offices) and then also develop more detailed reports that show sales within each location by agent.

Some Particulars You Should Know

1. Ben and Brady would much rather see information graphically than numerically. So as you develop your reports do so in terms of graphs that illustrate the desired relationships.

2. As you consider the information provided to you, think in terms of overall views first and then detailed views second. This will help you develop a logical series of reports.

3. If you wish, you can explore a variety of software tools to help you create the reports. When complete, prepare your presentation using a presentation graphics package that lets you create a really great presentation of your recommendations.

4. Again your goal is not to create reports that point toward a particular problem or opportunity. Rather you are to design sets of logical series of reports that illustrate the concept of drilling down.

5. File: TRAVEL (Lotus or Excel file)

Building Management Information System Reports from a Database

High-Tech Solutions Inc.

As part of a customer service initiative, High-Tech, a technology solutions provider of networking in the Detroit area for medium-sized businesses, developed a customer call and service center about 2 years ago. The customer call and service center is open 24 hours a day and provides answers to any information requests as well as technical support if any problems arise. The call and service center has been used extensively by High-Tech's 11 customers.

Unfortunately, the customer service software provides management with limited reporting capabilities. So management has no idea of exactly how extensively the

Name	Column	Description
LOCATION #	A	A unique number that identifies which office location recorded the sale.
TRAVEL AGENT #	B	A unique number that identifies which travel consultant recorded the sale.
CRUISE LINE	C	The name of the cruise line for which the package was sold.
TOTAL PACKAGE PRICE	D	The price charged to the customer for the package.
COMMISSION	E	The amount of money B&B made from the sale of the package.

center is used, the nature of the calls, time spent by service representatives, which customers use the center most often and why, and so on.

High-Tech has hired you to propose a series of management information system reports to help alert management to any potential problems or opportunities. Below is a list of the information that will be the foundation for the reports. These eight items comprise a record that is created each time a service representative takes a call. To help you develop realistic reports, High-Tech has provided you with a database that contains specific calls over the last two days.

Name	Description
CALL NUM	A unique number assigned to each call.
CUSTOMER NUM	A unique number assigned to each customer.
SERVICE REP NUM	A unique number assigned to the service representative who handled the call.
CALL LENGTH	Length to complete service call in minutes.
CALL TYPE	Can be informational or a technical problem.
CALL ORIENTATION	Can be operating system, application software, CPU, monitor, or server.
DATE	The date the call was taken.
TIME	The time of day the call was taken.

What High-Tech is most interested in is seeing several MIS reports that are some combination of periodic, exception, and comparative. For example, you should develop a report that shows average call length by customer and also a report that shows average call length by customer according to whether the call was "informational" or a "technical problem" (found in the call type field).

Some Particulars You Should Know

1. High-Tech would like to see information graphically as well as numerically. So as you develop your reports make sure that some of them include graphs.
2. When complete, prepare your presentation of reports using a presentation graphics software package that lets you create a really great presentation of your recommendations.
3. File: HIGHTECH (Access file)

CASE 5

Targeting a Business Process Reengineering Effort

Stewart's MotorSports

Stewart's MotorSports is a bustling motorcycle dealership at the busy corner of Monaco and Alameda in Dallas, Texas. Business has been booming, but lately Jay Stewart, the owner, noticed his income has dropped. Just as alarming has been the increase in customer complaints. Customer satisfaction ratings have dropped as well. Jay hired you as a BPR expert to evaluate his business, target an appropriate business process, and map out a redesign.

Jay's dealership provides many services to its customers. In addition to selling motorcycles, the dealership operates a service department, a parts department, a clothing and accessories store, and even a rider safety training course. After the sale, customer service calls go through Jay's "CustomerFirst" center, which is really three customer service reps answering telephones. Yet, even with this service center, Jay's dealership still has poor customer ratings and that irritates Jay.

One of the reps in the "CustomerFirst" center created a spreadsheet outlining most of the major tasks performed at Jay's dealership—at least to the best of her knowledge. The spreadsheet contains the fields in the table at the top of page 487.

Your job is to perform the following tasks in the following order:

1. Gather information from the spreadsheet about each process. You will use this information to prioritize the processes for redesign using BPR.
2. Select the highest priority process for BPR. Document your reasons for this assessment. Jay will wish to see a written report with your justifications.
3. Based on the information within the spreadsheet, take this highest priority process and map the business process. You may want to use the process map in Chapter 3 as a reference.
4. Take the process map and brainstorm ideas to redesign this process. Consider all information technology and IT systems which you have examined as possibilities for an enabling force. Gather your suggestions and create a presentation for Jay.

Some Particulars You Should Know

1. Don't forget to consider the particular business problems Jay's dealership is having.

Column	Name	Description
A	PROCESS NAME	The name assigned to a specific business process.
B	TASK #	The number assigned to a specific task, based on sequence within a business process.
C	PROCESS CUSTOMER	The name of the customer or person who receives the product of the business process.
D	PROCESS SUPPLIER	The name of the supplier or person who delivers the materials for the business process.
E	TASK COST	A rough estimate of the cost of each task within a process.
F	TASK TIME	Another estimate, this one of the time for each task.

2. When you redesign the business process, keep the concept of perfect service foremost in your discussion. What can be done to advance this concept at Jay's dealership?

3. Consider all possible strategies discussed as possibilities in redesign. Might Jay go locationless or virtual or use teams? And consider all enabling technologies as well. Call around town and see what dealerships (cars and motorcycle) do to make you a welcome customer.

4. File: STEWART (Lotus or Excel file)

CASE 6

Creating a Virtual Organization

McNeal's Machining

Recently, Terry McNeal hired you as a business strategy consultant to help him expand his business in Muncie, Indiana. McNeal's Machining is a small 24-employee machine shop providing machined steel parts to industrial customers. The shop does well; it's just that, lately, Terry has been frustrated with the business's inability to grow. It seems the biggest hurdle is the larger customers that Terry just can't seem to get. All of these customers want more than parts suppliers. They want suppliers who create and take responsibility for whole assemblies. And that's beyond Terry's machining capabilities. He's heard of this virtual organization concept and would like to explore it.

Terry compiled a list of other companies that seem to be in the same situation. Most are small suppliers, some may even be considered competitors. Still, all are potential partners. Terry doesn't need help with deciding which suppliers have complementary products or how to combine assemblies. That part he understands. What he needs help with is deciding what business issues must be considered, what IT is required, and what information must be shared. Terry maintains his supplier list in a spreadsheet that includes the fields shown in the table below.

For your analysis, design three possible virtual organizations. For each design, you must consider the following questions:

- What firm, if any, will be the lead firm?
- How will the partner firms be able to interact using IT and what will be required?
- What part does location play in the partnership?
- What type of information must be shared between each firm and is sharing that information appropriate?

Column	Name	Description
A	SUPPLIER NAME	The name of each possible partner.
B	SUPPLIER PRODUCT OR SERVICE	The individual part or service each possible partner creates.
C	LOCATION	Where is the firm located?
D	A COMPETITOR?	Is this possible partner a competitor?
E	SUPPLIER REPUTATION	Based on an industry survey, on a 1 to 10 scale.
F	CAPABILITIES	What services does this supplier provide in addition to the primary product or service (i.e., part design, subpart assembly)?
G	IT STATUS	Generally, what IT capabilities does this supplier have?
H	COMMENTS	General comments from Terry about each company's suitability.

Create a well-documented proposal detailing each possible organization and a presentation for Terry.

Some Particulars You Should Know

1. File: VIRTUAL (Lotus or Excel file)

Using Relational Technology to Track Technology

REMO Fashions

REMO Fashions is a manufacturer and provider of bicycle accessories located in Phoenix, Arizona. Because of the boom in bicycle sales over the last several years, REMO has been providing its staff with personal computer systems to handle the abundance of paperwork. REMO, however, has little idea of who is using which personal computer systems and what those computer systems are composed of.

Figure RH.3 shows a basic report that REMO's managers would like to see every month concerning who has what technology on their desks. REMO has four different departments—Manufacturing (1011), Advertising (1124), Customer Service (1111), and Distribution (1139). Each of these departments is overseen by a manager. Within each department, each employee has a personal computer system made up of a CPU, a monitor, and one or two printers. Each personal computer system has a unique number that describes it, as does each CPU, monitor, and printer.

REMO decided to implement a relational database model to track technology use in the organization. Originally, REMO decided to let one of its employees handle the construction of the database. However, that employee has not had the time to completely implement the project. REMO has asked you to take over and complete the construction of the database.

**REMO Fashions
Technology Utilization
March 13, 1999**

System:	11379-A		
Price:	$3590	**Department:**	1124—Advertising
Employee:	11439—Samson, Beverly	**Manager:**	Davies, John

CPU:	11367	**Monitor:**	4089
	80586		Packard Bell
	120 MHz		640 × 1028
	16 MB RAM		$540
	$1800		

Printers:	337		338
	Hewlett-Packard		Hewlett-Packard
	LaserJet 4L		LaserJet 5L
	$500		$750

System:	11363-B		
Price:	$2390	**Department:**	1139—Distribution
Employee:	11470—Williams, Bill	**Manager:**	Ko, Julie

CPU:	11368	**Monitor:**	5011
	80486		Packard Bell
	75 MHz		640 × 1028
	8 MB RAM		$540
	$1400		

Printers:	341
	Epson
	Stylus Color II Ink Jet
	$450

FIGURE RH.3

Technology Report for REMO Fashions

The entity classes and primary keys for the database have been identified:

Entity Class	Primary Key
Department	Department Number
Employee	Employee Number
System	System Number
Monitor	Monitor Number
Printer	Printer Number
CPU	CPU Number

The following rules have also been identified:

1. A department can have many employees and must have at least one.
2. An employee must be assigned to one and only one department.
3. An employee is not required to have a system but may have up to two systems.
4. A system can only be assigned to one employee but need not be assigned to any employee.
5. A system must have one and only one CPU and one and only one monitor.
6. A system must have at least one printer and may have two printers.
7. A monitor must be assigned to one and only one system.
8. CPUs and printers need not be assigned to any systems but cannot be assigned to more than one system.

Your job is to be completed in the following phases:

1. Develop and describe the entity-relationship diagram.
2. Use normalization to assure the correctness of the tables.
3. Create the database using a personal DBMS package.
4. Use the DBMS package to create the basic report in Figure RH.3.

Some Particulars You Should Know

1. You may not be able to develop a report that looks exactly like the one in Figure RH.3. However, your report should include the same information.
2. Complete personnel information is tracked by another database. For this application, include only the minimum employee information—number, last name, first name, and department.
3. Information concerning all employees, departments, and systems is not readily available. You should, however, create information for several fictitious systems to include in your database.
4. File: Not applicable

CASE 8

Using a Database to Track English Language Classes

English Is Easy

Building a relational database is sometimes not nearly as easy at it seems. Just ask Troy Kalis, the project development coordinator for *English Is Easy*. *English Is Easy* is a nonprofit organization that offers English language classes in the Chicago area. Troy is in charge of tracking volunteer teachers, students, and class rolls for the English language classes.

Troy spent several months trying to learn how to normalize information in hopes of building a relational database to track the information he needs. What he found was that building a relational database model was not quite as easy as most books said. Figure RH.4 shows the information model he developed. As you can see, Troy tracks volunteer teachers by their occupation and what levels of English they can teach—beginner, intermediate, and advanced. Troy tracks information concerning each class by day and time offered, level, what students are enrolled in each class, and the total enrollment level for each class. Finally, Troy tracks students by name (first and last), level of English literacy, and phone number.

Troy isn't having much luck and he desperately needs your help. You are to start from scratch, develop an initial entity-relationship diagram, normalize the information, and create a database with the information he needs.

Some Particulars You Should Know

1. People—both students and volunteer teachers—can have the same first and last names. So you need to develop a primary key that will uniquely identify each person in his or her respective group.
2. Each class is limited in enrollment to five students.
3. Use whatever DBMS package is available to you to develop the database.
4. File: Not applicable

CASE 9

Building a Decision Support System

Creating an Investment Portfolio

If you plan to have an early retirement you'll need to start an investment plan as soon as possible. The stock market is one possibility for long-term investment. But to decide on your stock portfolio, you'll need a DSS. You

TEACHER

LAST NAME	FIRST NAME	OCCUPATION	LEVEL ABILITY	LEVEL ABILITY	LEVEL ABILITY
Sams	K. C.	Auto worker	Beginner	Intermediate	Advanced
Lowery	Sally	Lawyer	Beginner		
Stevens	Jake	Accountant	Beginner	Intermediate	

CLASS

DAY	TIME	LEVEL	STUD. 1	STUD. 2	STUD. 3	STUD. 4	STUD. 5	TOTAL
Mon.	7 P.M.	Beginner	Ko	Jimenez	Ria			3
Tues.	10 A.M.	Advanced	Jong	Kowalsky				2

STUDENT

LAST NAME	FIRST NAME	LEVEL	PHONE NUMBER
Jimenez	Jose	Beginner	871-9045
Kowalsky	Patrick	Advanced	332-9832
Kuran	Ming-yi	Intermediate	342-4512
Jong	Agus	Advanced	333-5467
Ko	Wong	Beginner	None
Ria	Maria	Beginner	432-4954

FIGURE RH.4

Troy's Attempt at the Relational Model

can use a spreadsheet to do the job. The information you need on 20 stocks is contained in the Word file called STOCKS.DOC. This information consists of

- Two years of weekly price data on 20 different stocks including at least 4 from outside the United States. There is some overlapping of industries in this set of 20.
- Stock market indices from
  - The Dow Jones Industrial Average
  - Standard & Poor
  - NASDAQ Composite
  - The home countries of each of the companies based outside the United States
- Dividends and cash flow per share over the last 10 years (Source: Value Line).

Using this information, build a DSS to perform stock analysis consisting of the following tasks:

1. Examine Diversification Benefits

A. Calculate the average return and standard deviation (σ) of each of the 20 stocks.

B. Form 16 different portfolios: 5 with 2 stocks each; 5 with 5 stocks each; 5 with 10 stocks each; and 1 with all 20.

Answer the following questions using your DSS:

- How does the standard deviation of each portfolio compare to the (average) standard deviation of each stock in the portfolio?

- How does the average return of the portfolio compare to the average return of each stock in the portfolio?

- Do the benefits of diversification seem to increase or diminish as the number of stocks in the portfolio gets larger?

- In the two-stock and five-stock portfolios what happens if you group your stocks toward similar industries?

- In the two-stock and five-stock portfolios what happens if you group your stocks across different countries?

2. Calculate Risk Using ß

Standard deviation measures how risky a stock is. Beta (ß) is also a measure of risk because it measures how sensitive a stock is to the overall market. If ß is greater than 1, then the stock is high risk. A ß less than 1 indicates a low-risk stock. Pick five stocks (making sure to have at least one stock from outside the United States) and calculate ß in both of the following ways:

A. According to the formula:

$$ß = \frac{(\sigma \text{ of individual stock}) (\text{correlation between the stock and the market})}{\sigma \text{ of the market}}$$

B. Using linear regression with the stock return as the dependent variable and the market return as the independent variable. The constant (α) is the "abnormal" or "excess" return, and can be positive or negative.

Answer the following questions using your DSS:

- Do the riskiest stocks, as measured by standard deviation, also appear to be the riskiest when measured by ß?

- Do each of the indices provide the same beta measurements?

- Is the stock from outside the United States different?

3. Calculate the Required Return

The required return is the return you would have to have to invest in stocks. It is the difference between the risk-free rate and your return and is your bonus for taking a risk. For each of the five stocks in **2**, above, calculate the required return using the security market line as follows:

Required return = risk-free rate + ß (ERM – risk-free rate)

where ERM is the expected return on the market.

4. Value Each of the Stocks

A. Estimate the dividend growth rate based on past dividends.

B. Estimate next year's dividend using this year's dividend and the estimated growth rate.

C. Calculate the price of the stock according to the following formula:

Price = estimated dividend/(required return – dividend growth rate)

D. Generate two graphs, one for past dividends and one for estimated dividends for the next 5 years.

Some Particulars You Should Know

1. When calculating any of these values use the weekly returns. That is, use the change in the price each week rather than the prices themselves. This gives you a better basis for calculation because the prices themselves don't usually change very much.
2. Four percent is often used as the risk-free rate and 10 percent as the expected return on the market.
3. File: STOCKS (Word file)

CASE 10

Building an Expert System
What Country Are You Describing?

You've been hired to act as domain expert in the development of an expert system that can identify a country based on certain characteristics such as size, language, population, climate type, and so on. You can find help in the file called COUNTRY.DOC, which contains information taken from the *World Almanac* about multiple countries. Your job is to put that information into a form that a knowledge engineer can use to develop a working expert system. You can represent the country information either in rules structured like those in the box on p. 195 or in a flowchart.

You need to consider the most efficient way of arranging the rules so that the questions the expert system asks will lead to a solution in as short a time as possible. Consider the following guidelines:

- It's more efficient to narrow down the possibilities early in the process. For example, if the first rule that executes asks whether the country has an "R" in its national flag, a "yes" answer will immediately identify the country as Rwanda. That would be good if the circumstances in which the expert system is being used make it very likely that the country you're trying to identify is Rwanda. If not, then this wouldn't be a good first rule.

■ An early rule dealing with whether the country lies completely in the southern hemisphere will split your list of possible countries in two immediately. However, sometimes this "splitting" tactic can lead to duplicate sets of questions. A later rule might ask a question about the language spoken in the country. Because you can only execute a given rule once—you can't double back and ask the same question again—you might have to have two sets of questions about language because some languages, like Spanish, are spoken in both hemispheres.

■ Be certain that you have considered all the possible answers to a question that a rule can ask. For example, the expert system might ask, "Does the country lie fully below the equator?" If we rewrote that rule so that the question states, "Is the country in the southern hemisphere?" we can no longer rely on a yes/no answer because some countries lie on the equator, and are hence in both the northern and southern hemispheres.

■ Some rules will ask questions—like "What's the most widely used language in the country?"—that require more descriptive answers. In this case the expert system must be able to handle any language that the knowledge worker supplies or the expert system will not be able to reach a conclusion.

■ The task you face is to make certain that all the possibilities are accounted for in the most efficient manner possible.

Some Particulars You Should Know

1. Not all countries have the same number of attributes.
2. Your expert system won't be able to identify countries that you haven't explicitly dealt with in your rules, so the expert system must indicate that it can't reach a conclusion.
3. File: COUNTRY (Word file)

CASE 11

Building Value Chains

HealthLife's Customers Define Value

HealthLife Corp. is a small, yet growing, health maintenance organization (HMO). HealthLife began as a small group of doctors offering their services and has evolved into a full-service health organization with doctors all over the Baltimore metropolitan area. Still, with doctors' offices spread across the city, it's hard for Dana Rolleigh, the firm's CEO, to know the level of service customers receive, what customers value, and what they don't. These are important questions for an HMO striving to provide the finest health care services while keeping costs at a minimum.

Dana decided a value chain analysis would be helpful in providing some of this information. So customer surveys were distributed to all the doctors' offices and compiled into a database. The customers were asked to value their experience with various processes in the HMO value chain. Dana customized the value chain process names to best fit their businesses. Specifically, for each value chain process customers were asked whether this area added value to their experience or reduced the value of their experience. The customers then quantified how much each process added or reduced the value of the services they received. Using a total of 100 points for the value chain, each customer distributed those points among HealthLife's processes. The results from all customers were compiled and stored in a database. The survey results table in the database consists of the fields shown in the table at the top of the next page.

So, given the above database, Dana has asked you to gather the raw survey material into two value chains, the value-added chain and the value-reducing chain. You'll create chains that summarize the survey information and size the process areas proportionately as described in Chapter 8. Specifically, your job is to perform the following:

1. Create queries or reports in the provided database to summarize the valued-added amounts and the value-reducing amounts for each process.

2. Draw two value chains using that summary information to size the depicted area for each process. Use the value chains in Chapter 8 as a reference.

3. Compare the value-added and value-reducing process percentages. Do they correlate in any way? If so, why do you think that is? If not, why not?

4. In the table description provided on p. 493, a dashed line is drawn between the purchasing process and the receive and greet customers process. Processes above the line are considered support processes while processes below are considered primary processes. Create a database query to compare how customers value the total of support processes versus primary processes. Do this for both value-added and value-reducing processes. Do the results make sense or are they surprising? Explain why you think either way.

Field Name	Description
SURVEY ID	An ID number uniquely identifying the survey.
VA/VR	A field that identifies whether the current row of information reflects a value-added response or a value-reducing response.
DATE	Survey response date.
MGMT AND ACTG	Customer value of experience, if any, with the HMO management, claims and accounting departments, and the legal department.
HRM	Customer value of the attitude and general personnel environment.
RESEARCH AND DEV	Customer value of the appropriate level of medical research applied to customer treatments. This reflects on the degree to which doctors and other providers stay current in the medical field.
PURCHASING	Customer value placed on the quality of equipment used in providing treatment. This reflects on the HMO's purchasing function.
RECEIVE AND GREET CUSTOMERS	Customer value of patient receiving services and gathering initial information.
PROVIDE MEDICAL SERVICES	Customer value placed on the quality of the medical services provided.
OFFICE LOCATION AND CONVENIENCE	Customer value placed on convenience of office locations and quantity of selection.
SALES AND MARKETING	Customer value placed on the information received when evaluating the service.
CUSTOMER FOLLOWUP	Customer value based on whether calls were returned promptly and subscriptions called in quickly, etc. Covers all after-treatment, nonmedical services.

Note: The Survey ID and VA/VR fields together form the table's primary key.

5. Take the value chains and your other findings and produce a report of suggested changes for Dana. You should base at least part of your suggestions on both what customers value the most (the process with the highest value-added percentage) and what they believe reduces value the most (the process with the highest value-reducing percentage). How do your other findings affect your suggestions?

Some Particulars You Should Know

1. Remember that the total value-added/value-reducing amount for each process must equal 100 percent.
2. The survey values in the database are not percentages although the sum of all responses for a given survey equals 100.
3. File: VALUECHN (Access file)

CASE 12

Evaluating Request for Proposals

ITW Enterprises

In Chapter 9 we followed ITW Enterprises (ITW) as it proceeded through the SDLC to develop its new sys-

tem. Let's suppose that ITW decided to outsource the development of the new system and hired you to evaluate the request for proposal (RFP) returns.

When we discussed the outline of an RFP, we stated that you'd want to include how the RFP returns will be scored. One method of scoring is to list the information and processes you want, assign each a weight, and ask the vendors to check off which their systems support. In Figure RH.5, we include a sample scoring mechanism for ITW's supposed outsourcing concerning information it would like to capture about clients. Notice that each information attribute has been categorized as required, would be nice, or optional. Required information attributes are worth five points, would be nice information attributes are worth three points, and optional information attributes are worth one point.

If a vendor says its system will handle a particular information attribute, we multiply its point value by 1. If a system does not handle a particular information attribute, we multiply its point value by –1. We then sum the scores to determine an overall score.

In a file called RFP.DOC we have provided a portion of the RFP that ITW sent to potential vendors. In that file you'll find a complete list of ITW's information requirements. ITW received three back; these returns are in files called VENDOR1.DOC, VENDOR2.DOC, and VENDOR3.DOC. Your task is to develop a spreadsheet

INFORMATION ATTRIBUTE	INFORMATION ATTRIBUTE CATEGORY			DOES YOUR SYSTEM HANDLE THIS ATTRIBUTE?		SCORE
	REQUIRED (5)	WOULD BE NICE (3)	OPTIONAL (1)	YES (1)	NO (–1)	SCORE
Last Name	X			X		5
First Name	X			X		5
Middle Initial			X	X		1
Pet? (Y/N)	X			X		5
Desire tennis court? (Y/N)	X				X	–5
Desire pool? (Y/N)	X				X	–5
Desire on-site security? (Y/N)	X			X		5
Smoker? (Y/N)			X		X	–1
Age		X		X		3
Number bedrooms	X			X		5
Children? (Y/N)			X		X	–1
Floor (top or bottom)		X			X	–3
Desire covered parking? (Y/N)	X				X	–5
Income level			X	X		1
Desire washer/dryer in apt? (Y/N)		X		X		3
Desire vaulted ceiling? (Y/N)			X		X	–1
Max rent	X			X		5
YOUR TOTAL SCORE FOR THESE INFORMATION ATTRIBUTES:						17

FIGURE RH.5

A Sample Scoring Mechanism

that compares how each vendor scored concerning ITW's information requirements.

Some Particulars You Should Know

1. Each vendor has recommended a system that will work. The only difference is what information is and is not supported by each vendor.
2. In ITW's RFP document, you'll find a complete description of the scoring mechanism. This will help you develop your comparative spreadsheet.
3. When you've completed your analysis, prepare a presentation using a presentation graphics package.

4. File: RFP, VENDOR1, VENDOR2, VENDOR3 (Word files)

CASE 13

Developing Reports Through Prototyping

Revisiting the Video Rental Store

In Chapter 4 we looked at a small database for a video rental store. Your task is to implement that database, load some fictitious information, and then develop several reports. Split your group into two subgroups. The first group will be IT specialists responsible for developing the reports. The second group will be knowledge workers who will define the reports' requirements and review the prototypes.

Your group is to develop reports that would help you perform the following functions:

1. Contact those customers with videos that are at least 1 week overdue.

2. Send a promotional flyer to those customers who have not rented a video in the past 60 days.

3. Determine which videos to take out of rent circulation and place on a sale rack because they are infrequently rented.

4. Determine what categories of videos are rented most often and least often.

5. Determine who the best customers are.

Complete this group project by following the five steps below:

Step 1: Have the knowledge workers supply the IT specialists with the basic requirements of each report.

Step 2: Have the IT specialists develop the reports based on the basic requirements.

Step 3: Have the knowledge workers review the reports and suggest changes.

Step 4: Have the IT specialists update the reports to reflect the requested changes.

Step 5: Repeat steps 3 and 4 until the knowledge workers agree that the reports are exactly what they want.

Some Particulars You Should Know

1. Save each report format under a separate name as you continually enhance the prototype. This will give you the ability to compare the first prototype to the finished product.

2. If you want, you can perform this prototyping process in the form of a JAD workshop so that it becomes RAD.

3. *Knowledge workers* Start with general requirements. As you review the prototypes, become more specific about what you want.

4. *IT specialists* Do not make any assumptions about what the knowledge workers want. Develop the reports according to their exact specifications.

5. When you finish, answer the following questions:

   A. How well did your chosen database package support prototyping?

   B. How many iterations did you go through before finalizing the reports?

   C. How different do the first reports look from the finished reports?

   D. How did you decide which customers are "best"?

   E. Did you find that the two groups had difficulty in communicating?

6. File: Not applicable

CASE 14

Making the Case with Presentation Graphics Software

Information Technology Ethics

Your company is trying to formulate policies and procedures regarding how IT is to be used and protected, and your boss has asked you to make a presentation on the issue of IT-related ethics. Develop the presentation using a presentation package such as Microsoft's PowerPoint.

Sources of Information

■ In the file ETHICS.DOC you'll find information on IT-related crime:

   ◆ Its many forms

   ◆ Estimates of its cost

   ◆ The measures that companies are taking to deal with it

   ◆ Legislation that applies to federal agencies

   ◆ Legislation that applies to the private sector

■ The Association of Computing Machinery's (ACM) Web site has the ACM code of ethics.

Your presentation should also include consideration of the following:

■ Issues affecting the employee-employer relationship such as e-mail, employee monitoring, and the use of company resources for personal purposes. For each topic, present the rights and responsibilities of each of the stakeholders.

■ Consider the collection, use, and access of information on customers. For example, should companies be required to get the permission of customers before collecting or using information about them? Present the advantages and disadvantages from the point of view of both the company and the customer.

■ Consider what the implications are for society and business when software is copied illegally. Consider this problem on both an individual and a national scale. What about very poor countries that will fall further behind the industrial nations if they don't have access to software they can't afford to buy?

Your task is to weave this information into a coherent presentation using graphs and art where appropriate.

Some Particulars You Should Know

1. File: ETHICS (Word file)

APPENDIX A

The Technology Tree

"What technology do I need?" Have you ever asked or heard that question? It's a common question, in both business and personal environments. If someone posed that question to you, how would you answer? Right—you can't answer that question until you know what the person wants to accomplish with information technology (IT). And determining that answer first requires that you ask and answer more questions.

This appendix presents the appropriate questions to ask in order to determine which technology best meets your needs or the needs of your organization. Determining the right technology is like determining the right tools for a home remodeling project. If someone told you about a home remodeling project and wanted to know what tools were needed, you would immediately respond by asking such questions as, "What type of remodeling are you going to do?" "Does your remodeling project involve plumbing?" "Electrical conduit?" "Does your remodeling project involve painting?" and so on.

To find the right technology tools you have to ask questions about people and information. After all, people use IT tools to work with information. So you have to understand what types of information-processing tasks need to be performed before you can determine which IT tools are most appropriate.

Most people in a business environment will tell you that they use information to make decisions. And it's true; the vast majority of today's knowledge workers use information to make some sort of decision. But more specifically, you must learn what their responsibilities are with respect to *managing* and *using* information in an organization. These responsibilities can be categorized as shown at the bottom of this page.

Notice that each of these responsibilities begins with the letter "C" (a neat little mnemonic device)—**C**apturing, **C**reating, **C**onveying, **C**radling, and **C**ommunicating. As you might guess, these five Cs can also be used to categorize IT tools. On the pages to follow, we present the five categories of IT tools according to the 5 Cs of information responsibilities. As we do, we'll pose questions, the answers to which will help you determine what IT tools you need.

The Technology Tree

You can visualize categories of IT tools according to the five Cs of information responsibilities as a tree, with each of the five major branches representing a different technology tool set. When determining the most appropriate technologies, the first question you ask will lead you to one of the five major branches. That question is

What are you trying to do with information— capture, convey, create, cradle, or communicate it?

As you can see from the Technology Tree in Figure A.1 (page 498), that first question will lead you to one of five major types of technology tools (see Figure A.2, page 498)—input technologies (capturing information), output technologies (conveying information), software technologies (creating information), storage technologies (cradling information), or telecommunications technologies (communicating information).

Once you've isolated the appropriate branch of the Technology Tree or set of technology tools, you must ask other questions to finally arrive at the best specific technology tool(s) for a given information management task. Let's look closer at each branch or technology tool set.

Capturing Information
Input Technologies

Input technologies are the tools you use to capture information or commands at the point of origin; they include such tools as a keyboard, mouse, touch screen, and bar code reader. The best input technology for a given situation is one that captures information or commands at the **point of origin.** Consider the following example. As a CEO of a major corporation, you need to send out a letter.

The Five Cs of Information Responsibility

Responsibility	Description
CAPTURING information	Obtaining information at its point of origin
CONVEYING information	Presenting information in its most useful form
CREATING information	Processing information to obtain new information
CRADLING information	Storing information for use at a later time
COMMUNICATING information	Sending information to other people or locations

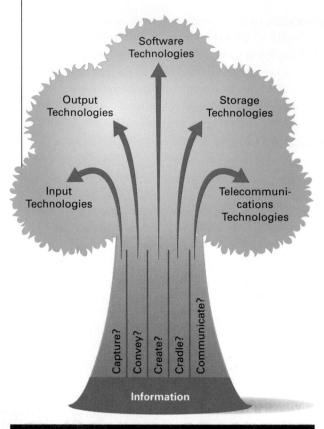

FIGURE A.1
The Technology Tree

You call in your assistant, who writes the letter as you dictate. Your assistant then types the letter and sends it out. Seems straightforward enough but, in reality, the content of the letter was not captured at its point of origin; rather it was captured three times.

Let's review the process. As you dictated the letter, your assistant heard it—that's capture 1. After your assistant heard it, he or she recorded it on paper—that's capture 2. After recording the letter on paper, your assistant typed it—that's capture 3. Now that seemingly straightforward process doesn't make so much sense, does it? Businesses cannot afford to perform the same task three times. Always remember, capturing information or commands at the **point of origin** is the key.

There are many different types of input technologies. Some, like automatic speech recognition systems—which should have been used in the above example—capture information and commands that originate as sounds; others capture information that has already been recorded on paper; still others capture information and commands that originate as physical movement. As you begin to consider which input technologies would be best for a given situation, ask yourself the following question

Am I trying to capture information, commands, or both?

The answer to that question will lead you to one of three categories of input technologies—for capturing information, for capturing commands, or for capturing both (see Figure A.3, page 502).

The second and equally important question to ask in order to determine the best input technology for a given situation is

In what form is the information and/or commands I'm trying to capture?

(continued on page 500)

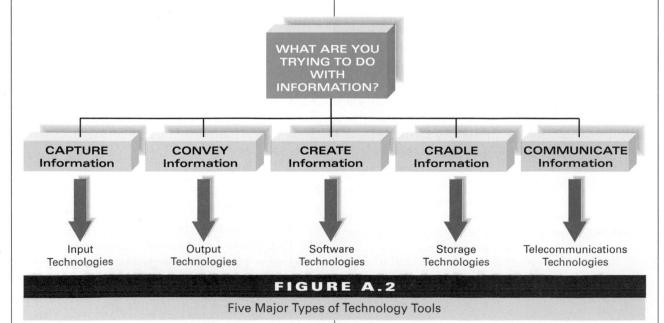

FIGURE A.2
Five Major Types of Technology Tools

PHOTO ESSAY Input Technology Tools

A **keyboard** is today's most popular input technology. It looks similar to a typewriter keyboard, but contains many special keys. Keyboards capture direct input and are effective for both information and command capturing.

A **point-of-sale system (POS system)** captures information and commands at the point of a transaction, typically in a retail environment. POS systems capture direct input and are good for both information and command capturing.

A **sound input** device captures information that originates in audio form. Using sound input devices, you can capture any type of sound (a dog barking, a doorbell ringing, and so on) and record it for later reproduction. Sound input devices capture only information in an audio form.

A **Touch-Tone input** device captures information and commands that originate in audio form from a telephone keypad. Many universities today allow students to register for classes using Touch-Tone–based telephone registration systems. Touch-Tone input devices can capture both information and commands that originate in audio form.

An **automatic speech recognition system (ASR system)** not only captures what you are saying, but also has the ability to distinguish words and sentences. Your speech can then be used as information (for example, the contents of a letter) and commands (for example, save and print the letter). ASR systems capture both information and commands that originate in audio form.

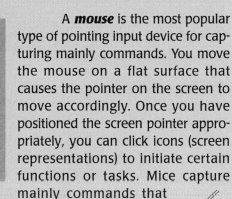

A **mouse** is the most popular type of pointing input device for capturing mainly commands. You move the mouse on a flat surface that causes the pointer on the screen to move accordingly. Once you have positioned the screen pointer appropriately, you can click icons (screen representations) to initiate certain functions or tasks. Mice capture mainly commands that originate in a screen representation form.

A **trackball** is an upside-down, stationary mouse in which you move the ball instead of the device. Trackballs are popular for use on portable systems when there is limited room for moving a mouse. Trackballs capture mainly commands that originate in a screen representation form.

A **pen mouse** looks like a fountain pen and performs similarly to mice and trackballs. A pen mouse has a ball at the tip that causes the pointer on the screen to move as you move the pen mouse across a flat surface. Pen mice capture mainly commands that originate in a screen representation form.

A **pointing stick** is a small rubberlike device that causes the pointer to move on the screen as you apply directional pressure. Pointing sticks are used almost exclusively on portable systems and most often appear in the middle of the keyboard. Pointing sticks mainly capture commands that originate in a screen representation form.

A **touch screen** is a special screen that lets you use your finger to literally point at and touch a particular

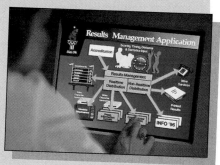

function you want to perform. Touch screens are popular for use in make-your-own greeting card systems and information centers. Although you can enter information using a touch screen, most touch screens capture mainly commands that originate in a screen representation form (icons).

A *light pen* is a special light-producing input device used in conjunction with a light-sensitive (photoelectric) screen or pad. With a light pen, you point to the screen where you want more information to appear or where a function is located that you want to perform. Air traffic controllers use light pens to point at aircraft on a screen to make more information appear, including the aircraft type and altitude. Light pens capture mainly commands that originate in a screen representation form.

A *bar code reader* captures information in a predetermined format that exists as a series of vertical bars whose width and distance apart determine a number. Bar code readers are a popular device in retail environments for capturing universal product code (UPC) information. Bar code readers mainly capture

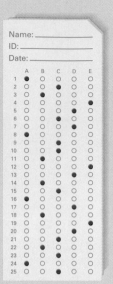

information that must exist in a predetermined format on paper.

An *optical mark recognition (OMR)* input device detects the presence or absence of a mark in a predetermined place. Most collegiate aptitude examinations are graded using OMR devices, and many professors grade true/false and multiple-choice exams using OMR devices. Optical mark recognition devices mainly capture information that must exist in a predetermined format on paper.

A *magnetic-ink character recognition (MICR)* input device reads a set of preprinted electronic symbols, usually numbers and characters. The banking industry originally used MICR devices to process the billions of checks each month written by consumers and businesses. Magnetic-ink character recognition devices capture information that exists in a predetermined format on paper.

An *optical character recognition (OCR)* input device can capture information that exists in both predetermined and non-predetermined formats. For information that exists in a predetermined format, optical character recognition devices (called *formatted OCR devices*) read a set of symbols (usually just characters and numbers) whose format

The answer to that question will lead you to one of six categories of input technologies—audio, direct, screen representation, formatted text and images, unformatted text and images, or motion.

By answering these two questions, you can determine which input technologies are best according to what you're trying to capture (information, commands, or both) and in what form the information and/or commands originate. Now you've reviewed the left-hand technology tree branch (Figure A.1 on page 498) and understand input technologies according to what you are trying to capture and the form of the information or

commands. For a good review of specific input technology tools, take a look at the photo essay "Input Technology Tools" on pages 499–501.

Conveying Information
Output Technologies

Output technologies are the tools you use to see, hear, or otherwise accept the results of your information-processing requests. The best output technology for a given situation is one that presents information **in its**

has been standardized by the American National Standards Institute (ANSI). Formatted OCR devices are often used in retail environments for scanning price tags. Formatted optical character recognition devices capture information that must exist in a predetermined format on paper.

Some types of optical character recognition input devices can capture information that exists on paper but not in a predetermined format (such as handwriting and text generated by a printer). These types of OCR devices are called **unformatted OCR devices**. Unformatted OCR devices capture information and then put it into an editable format so that you can change the information. **Pen-based computers** are special computers that use a writing stylus (with which you write on the screen) and unformatted OCR for writing on the screen. Unformatted OCR devices mainly capture information that already exists on paper but not in a predetermined format.

An **image scanning** input device captures information (usually pictures, diagrams, and graphs) that is not in a predetermined format. Image scanning devices differ from unformatted OCR input devices in that they usually just capture the information for inclusion in a document and do not give you the ability to make changes to the captured information. Image scanning devices capture information that does not exist in a predetermined format on paper.

A **glove** input device captures the movement of your hand and fingers, including dexterity and strength of movement. Glove input devices are used in computer-based puppetry, computer-based sign language systems, and most often in virtual reality systems. Glove input devices capture information and commands that originate as motion.

A **headset** input device captures the movement of your head, side to side and up and down. As with gloves, headsets are mainly used in virtual reality systems. Headsets capture information and commands that originate as motion.

A **walker** input device captures the movement of your legs and feet, including speed of travel and directional movement. A walker looks similar to an exercise treadmill. As with headsets and gloves, walkers are mainly used in virtual reality systems. Walkers capture information and commands that originate as motion. ❖

most useful form. Output form, then, should be your first question:

What form do I need to convey information?

The answer to that question will lead you to one of three categories of output technologies—audio, on-screen, and printed (see Figure A.4, page 502).

Although the most appropriate form of presentation is the key to determining the correct output technology, you can't stop there. You must also determine the quality of information produced by an output technology. This issue of quality relates most directly to on-screen output technologies (called screens or monitors) and printed output technologies (printers and plotters). For an overview of output technologies, including the issue of quality for on-screen and printed output technologies, review the photo essay "Output Technology Tools" on pages 503–504.

Now you've reviewed the second technology tree branch and understand output technologies according to the form of the information conveyed and according to the quality of information produced by on-screen and printed output technologies.

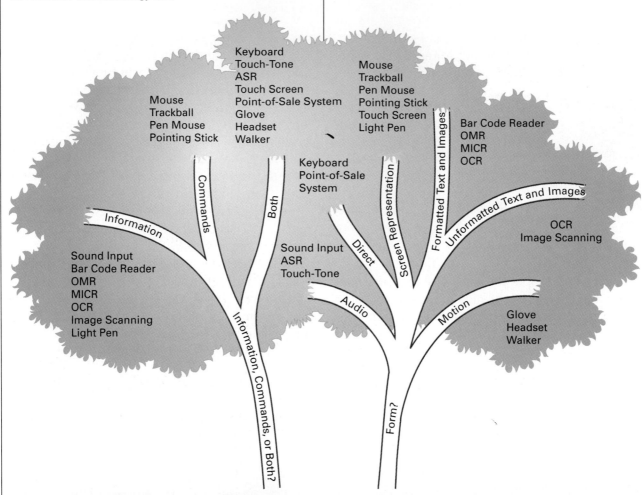

FIGURE A.3

The Input Branch of the Technology Tree

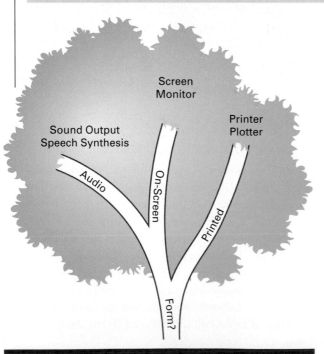

FIGURE A.4

The Output Branch of the Technology Tree

Creating Information

Software Technologies

Software technologies are the tools you use to process information to obtain new information. That is, software is the set of instructions that performs a particular information-processing task for you. As you can probably guess, you have to know which information-processing task you're trying to perform before you can determine the best software technology.

The first and most important question to ask to determine the best software technology for a given situation is

> ***Are the information-processing tasks specific to me and my business functions or to technology management?***

The answer to that question will lead you to one of the two major categories of software technologies—application software and operating system software. We often refer to these software technology categories as *layers* of

(continued on page 505)

PHOTO ESSAY: Output Technology Tools

A *sound output* device reproduces previously recorded and stored sounds. Sound output devices are the output equivalent to sound input devices. Sound output devices simply convey pre-recorded information in audio form.

A *speech synthesis* output device creates speech output from text. Speech synthesis output devices are the flipside of automatic speech recognition input devices. Speech synthesis devices convey information in audio form.

A *plotter* is a special type of printer that draws output on paper. That is, a plotter uses a writing instrument attached to a moveable arm that moves over the paper and positions the writing instrument appropriately. Many plotters let you use different colors to create output. Make-your-own greeting card systems most often use a plotter as the output device for creating the card. Plotters convey information in printed form.

Q uality of on-screen output technologies is affected by the graphics adapter card, color, resolution, size, and the flicker question.

A *graphics adapter card* connects the monitor to the rest of the hardware. The quality of the graphics adapter card determines, to a large extent, the number of pixels that will be displayed on the screen and the number of colors used.

A pixel is a screen element that can be turned on or off and made different shades of colors.

Monitors that use only one color are called *monochrome monitors*. Other monitors can produce up to 17 million different colors. *Resolution* is determined by the number of pixels on a screen. A *pixel* is the smallest display element on a screen that can be turned on or off and made different shades of colors. For example, a monitor whose resolution is 1,024 × 768 has 1,024 rows and 768 columns of pixels (over 750,000 total pixels). Thus the more pixels the higher the resolution.

Size definitely affects presentation quality. Most people are moving toward using 16-inch and 17-inch monitors as opposed to the standard 12-inch monitors.

Some monitors make two passes to produce information on the screen—these are called **interlaced monitors**. Monitors that make only one pass to produce information are called **noninterlaced monitors**. Interlaced monitors seem to flicker and can be hard on your eyes and can adversely affect presentation quality.

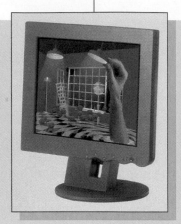

On-screen technologies for portable systems are called **flat panel displays**. Because of the technology used to convey information on flat panel displays, their quality is less than that of a standard monitor with the same resolution, color capability, and graphics adapter card. You can also now find flat panel displays for desktop systems (see photo at left).

Quality of print technologies is affected by impact versus nonimpact, use of preformed character sets, color, dot matrix versus letter quality, graphics, and special printing needs.

Printers that strike the page with some sort of mechanism are called **impact printers**, whereas printers that do not strike the page are called **nonimpact printers**. Nonimpact printers are quieter, cleaner, and typically provide better-quality output than impact printers. Nonimpact printers are also the choice for most color printing needs.

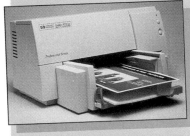

Many printers are equipped with preformed character sets. If they are, they have a difficult time creating graphics, but provide high-quality output of the preformed character sets.

Color affects the presentation quality of print technologies. Some printers work with no color (called **monochrome printers**), whereas others support up to 16 colors.

Dot matrix printers use a matrix of pins to form characters and then strike those pins through a printer ribbon onto a page. Dot matrix printer quality is near but not letter quality. **Letter quality printers**, on the other hand, use other technologies to create images on a page. For example, preformed character set printers are letter quality printers, **ink jet printers** spray ink onto a page to create letter quality output, and **laser printers** use a special laser technology and inklike toner to create letter quality output.

"A picture is worth a thousand words." That's especially true for print technologies. Laser and ink jet printers provide the best graphics, followed by dot matrix printers. Most preformed character printers produce little or no graphics because they have to use already-formed characters (dashes, periods, and the like) to create a "pseudo" graphic image.

Some printers work with one size of paper and lack extended functional capabilities. Other printers allow you to use different sizes of paper and such special output forms as gum labels and envelopes. ❖

Dot matrix printer

High-resolution laser printer

software between you and the processing engine (the internal memory and CPU, which we'll discuss later), as shown in Figure A.5. Let's focus on the operating system software layer before we ask more questions pertaining to application software.

The ***operating system software*** is designed to handle tasks specific to technology management and coordinates the interaction of all the IT components. So operating system software is the layer of software closest to the processing engine. Operating system software also contains utility software, which handles specific technology management tasks such as virus protection and disk backup.

Application software is the software designed to help you solve problems specific to business operations or perform specific business tasks. Application software then is the layer of software closest to you. To determine the most appropriate application software, ask this question

What specific information-processing tasks am I trying to perform?

The answer to that question will lead you to one of seven categories of application software—general business function, industry-specific, tasks specific to your business, education, personal productivity, group work, or specialized applications (see Figure A.6 on page 506). Let's quickly review these seven different categories of application software, and then we'll ask more questions to further define specific software technologies within them.

- *General business function* General business function software helps automate tasks that most businesses perform periodically, such as payroll, project management, accounts receivable, and inventory control.

- *Industry-specific* Industry-specific software automates tasks that businesses in a particular industry perform. For example, a number of

businesses offer software that automates tasks in the health care industry, such as patient admission and billing, radiology, nursing administration, and so on.

- *Tasks specific to your business* Software in this category automates tasks that are specific to a particular business. Unlike general business function and industry-specific software, which can be purchased from a variety of software vendors, this software must be custom-developed to incorporate the exact information-processing tasks you need to perform. In this text, we've devoted all of Chapter 9 to the development of this category of software.

- *Education* Simply put, education software helps you learn about topics or areas of interest.

- *Personal productivity* Personal productivity software is designed to help you do things that you could probably otherwise do manually. Personal productivity software includes such tools as word processing, spreadsheet, presentation graphics, personal information management, and database management systems.

- *Group work* Group work software (also called "groupware") supports the collaborative efforts of workgroups by facilitating communication, information sharing, and group decision support efforts. Throughout this text and especially in Chapter 2, you'll find extensive discussions of group work software.

- *Specialized applications* Specialized application software includes software technologies that do not fit easily into one of the other categories. Examples of specialized application software are virtual reality, video capturing and editing, and multimedia.

You should keep in mind that these categories of application software are not mutually exclusive. For example, Holiday Inn Inc. chose to write its own multimedia

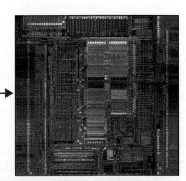

APPLICATION SOFTWARE

Solve Problems Specific to Business Operations or Perform Specific Business Tasks

OPERATING SYSTEM SOFTWARE

Tasks Specific to Technology Management

FIGURE A.5

Viewing Software Technologies as Layers

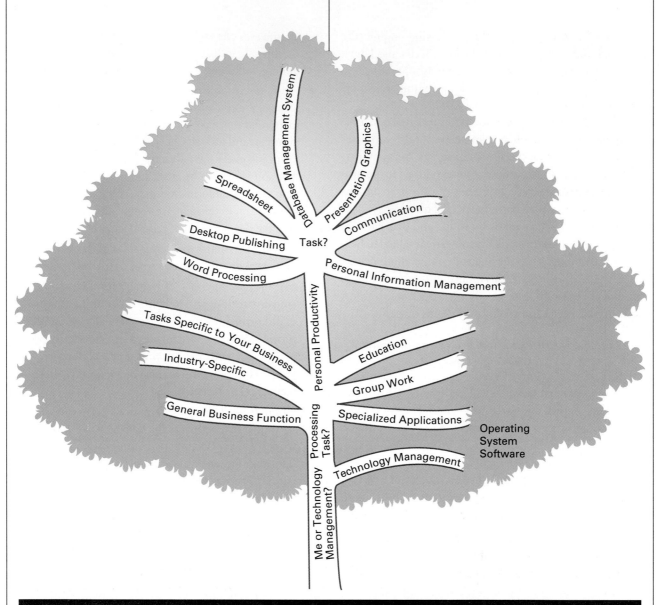

Spreadsheet

Database Management System

Presentation Graphics

Desktop Publishing

Task?

Communication

Word Processing

Personal Information Management

Tasks Specific to Your Business

Personal Productivity

Industry-Specific

Education

Group Work

General Business Function

Specialized Applications

Operating System Software

Me or Technology Management?

Processing Task?

Technology Management

FIGURE A.6

The Software Branch of the Technology Tree

software to teach its hotel managers how to deal with certain personnel issues. That software, then, is an example of specialized application software (multimedia) incorporating education (teaching) and tasks specific to that organization (developed for Holiday Inn only).

Let's now take a closer look at personal productivity software and ask another question. For personal productivity software, that question is

What tasks am I trying to perform that I could probably otherwise do manually?

The answer to that question will lead you to one of seven categories of personal productivity software—word processing, desktop publishing, spreadsheet, database

management system, presentation graphics, communication, or personal information management. You're probably already familiar with many personal productivity software tools. For a good review of some of these, take a look at the photo essay "Personal Productivity Software" on pages 507–511.

Now you've reviewed the third technology tree branch and understand software technologies according to business-specific tasks versus technology management and application software according to what information-processing tasks you are trying to perform. Don't forget, we cover many of the categories of application software and certain aspects of operating system software throughout this text.

PHOTO ESSAY Personal Productivity Software

Word Processing Software

Word processing software is designed to help you work with documents that consist primarily of text. Most word processing software, however, does support your work with pictures and freehand drawings.

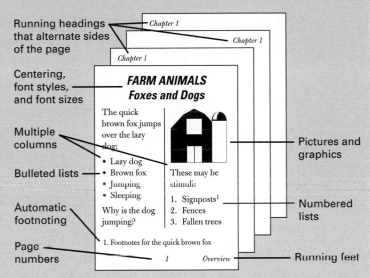

Running headings that alternate sides of the page

Centering, font styles, and font sizes

Multiple columns

Bulleted lists

Automatic footnoting

Page numbers

Pictures and graphics

Numbered lists

Running feet

Chapter 1

Chapter 1

Chapter 1

FARM ANIMALS
Foxes and Dogs

The quick brown fox jumps over the lazy dog:

- Lazy dog
- Brown fox
- Jumping
- Sleeping

Why is the dog jumping?

These may be stimuli

1. Signposts[1]
2. Fences
3. Fallen trees

1. Footnotes for the quick brown fox

1   Overview

Desktop Publishing Software

Desktop publishing software extends word processing software to give you the ability to create documents that cannot be created easily with word processing software. In fact, in many instances word processing software may not contain many of the functions you want to perform. As you can see at right, desktop publishing software can vary color shades within boxes, easily manipulate the orientation of text, overlay text onto artwork, create sidebar note areas, and produce high-quality reproductions of photos.

Today, the distinction between word processing software and desktop publishing software is narrowing. However, desktop publishing software still offers many capabilities that word processing software does not. These capabilities will help you create really great-looking documents, such as menus, advertising flyers, and books.

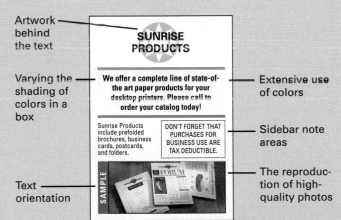

Artwork behind the text

Varying the shading of colors in a box

Text orientation

Extensive use of colors

Sidebar note areas

The reproduction of high-quality photos

SUNRISE PRODUCTS

We offer a complete line of state-of-the art paper products for your desktop printers. Please call to order your catalog today!

Sunrise Products include prefolded brochures, business cards, postcards, and folders.

DON'T FORGET THAT PURCHASES FOR BUSINESS USE ARE TAX DEDUCTIBLE.

FORUM

SAMPLE

Gene's Pizza
APPETIZERS

Garlic Bread	$2.25
Caesar Salad	$2.25
Cold Antipasto	$5.75
House Salad	$3.25
W/Cheese	$3.75

Body Balance for Performance

Spreadsheet Software

Spreadsheet software helps you work primarily with numeric information. Using spreadsheet software, you enter information in a cell (the intersection of a row and column). Then you can use the cell address to specify, with formulas and functions, how other cells mathematically relate to that cell.

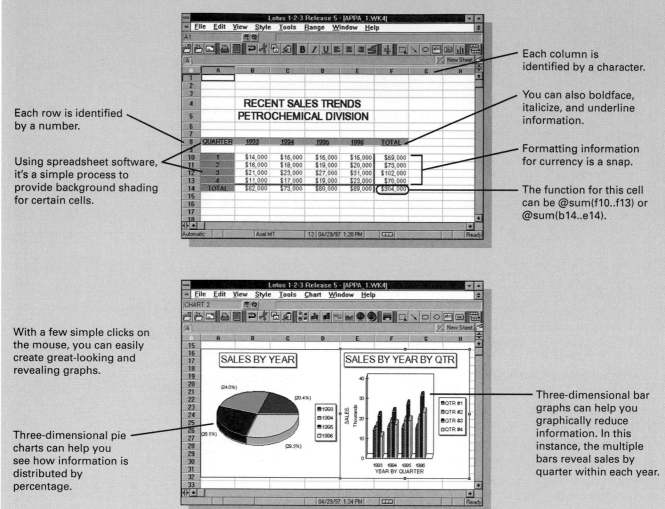

Each row is identified by a number.

Using spreadsheet software, it's a simple process to provide background shading for certain cells.

Each column is identified by a character.

You can also boldface, italicize, and underline information.

Formatting information for currency is a snap.

The function for this cell can be @sum(f10..f13) or @sum(b14..e14).

With a few simple clicks on the mouse, you can easily create great-looking and revealing graphs.

Three-dimensional pie charts can help you see how information is distributed by percentage.

Three-dimensional bar graphs can help you graphically reduce information. In this instance, the multiple bars reveal sales by quarter within each year.

Cradling Information

Storage Technologies

Storage technologies are the tools you use to more permanently store information for use at a later time. Although we use the term "permanent" for storage technologies, most storage technologies give you the ability to change your information or erase it altogether. When considering the use of storage technologies, you should ask two questions to determine which storage technology is best for your needs. The first question is

Will I need to update my information later?

The answer to that question will lead you to one of three types of storage technologies: (1) those that provide easy updating capabilities, (2) those that provide updating capabilities that are sometimes difficult and slow, and (3) those that do not allow you to update your stored information (see Figure A.7, page 512).

Database Management System Software

D*atabase management system (DBMS) software* is designed to help you manage information in multiple files that have related information. Suppose, for example, that you owned a video rental store. You would maintain such files as a *Video* file that contains information about each video in your store, a *Customer* file that contains specific information about each of your customers, and a *Video Rental* file that contains details concerning who has rented which videos. All of these files obviously contain related pieces of information.

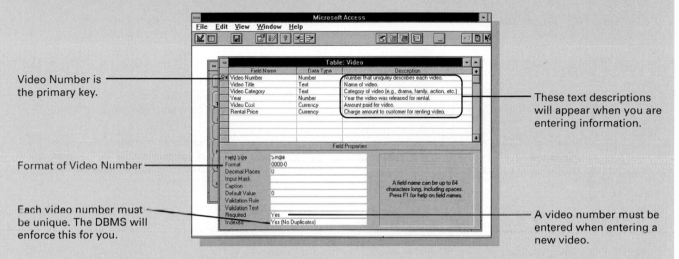

Video Number is the primary key.

These text descriptions will appear when you are entering information.

Format of Video Number

Each video number must be unique. The DBMS will enforce this for you.

A video number must be entered when entering a new video.

When you first create a database, you define what the files look like by establishing a data dictionary (shown above). The ***data dictionary*** contains a description of each of the fields in a given file.

Notice that a DBMS file looks similar to a spreadsheet, except that columns in a DBMS file have logical names as opposed to column characters.

Because Video Number is the primary key, all video numbers are unique.

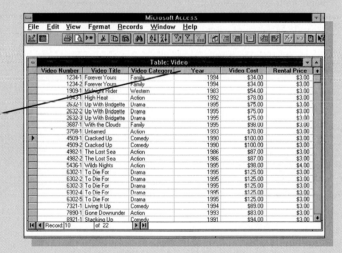

These categories of storage technologies can also be used if you ask an alternative form of the above question. That is, "How often will I need to update my information?" If the answer is never, you might want to consider storage technologies that do not give you the ability to update your information. If changes are going to occur only rarely, you may want to consider those storage technologies that provide updating capabilities that are sometimes difficult and slow. And if you need to update your information frequently, you should definitely consider only those storage technologies that provide easy updating capabilities.

The second question you should ask is

How much information do I need to store?

The answer to that question will lead you to one of two categories of storage technologies—limited and massive (see Figure A.7 on page 512).

(continued on page 512)

Because DBMS software allows you to maintain logical relationships among your files, it can also help you easily create reports that contain information from several files, such as the report below that details how many videos each of your customers has rented from each video category.

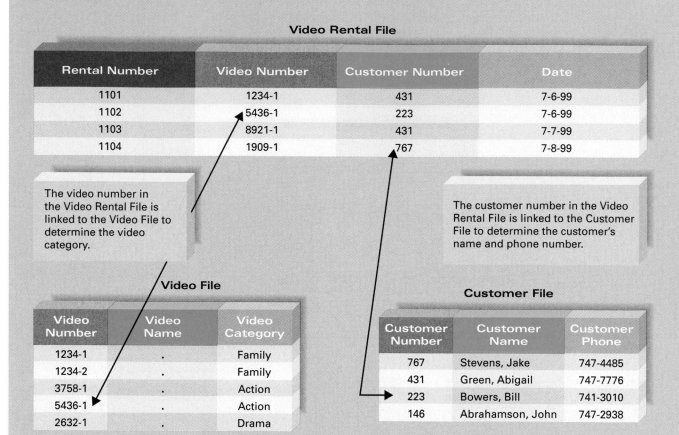

Video Rental File

Rental Number	Video Number	Customer Number	Date
1101	1234-1	431	7-6-99
1102	5436-1	223	7-6-99
1103	8921-1	431	7-7-99
1104	1909-1	767	7-8-99

The video number in the Video Rental File is linked to the Video File to determine the video category.

The customer number in the Video Rental File is linked to the Customer File to determine the customer's name and phone number.

Video File

Video Number	Video Name	Video Category
1234-1	.	Family
1234-2	.	Family
3758-1	.	Action
5436-1	.	Action
2632-1	.	Drama

Customer File

Customer Number	Customer Name	Customer Phone
767	Stevens, Jake	747-4485
431	Green, Abigail	747-7776
223	Bowers, Bill	741-3010
146	Abrahamson, John	747-2938

Video Rental Report by Category for Each Customer

Customer Name	Customer Phone	Category	Total Rentals in Each Category
Abrahamson, John	747-2938	Family	3
Bowers, Bill	741-3101	Comedy	1
		Action	1
Green, Abigail	747-7776	Action	4
		Drama	2
		Family	1
		Comedy	3
Stevens, Jake	747-4485	Western	6
		Comedy	7

Presentation Graphics Software

Presentation graphics software is designed to help you create really exciting presentations of information. After creating your presentation, many presentation software graphics packages will help you build a set of notes to which you can refer and which you can distribute to your group while presenting the information. Many presentation graphics software packages can even generate 35-mm slides and project your presentation during a meeting.

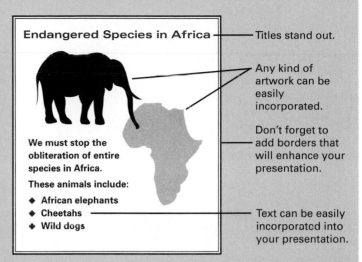

Titles stand out.

Any kind of artwork can be easily incorporated.

Don't forget to add borders that will enhance your presentation.

Text can be easily incorporated into your presentation.

Personal Information Management Software

Personal information management software is designed to help you manage information relating to contacts, schedules, to-do lists, and finances. ❖

Add, delete, or edit names and addresses in your electronic address book.

Electronic address book.

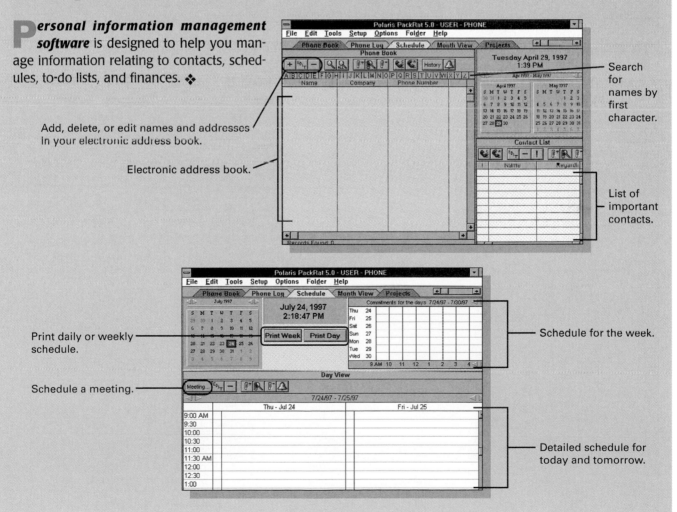

Search for names by first character.

List of important contacts.

Print daily or weekly schedule.

Schedule a meeting.

Schedule for the week.

Detailed schedule for today and tomorrow.

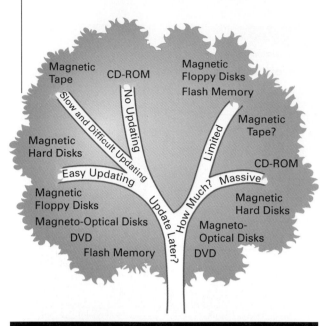

FIGURE A.7

The Storage Branch of the Technology Tree

Now you've reviewed the fourth technology tree branch and understand storage technologies according to necessity of updating and amount of storage requirements. For a good review of specific storage technologies, take a look at the photo essay "Storage Technologies" on pages 513–515.

Communicating Information

Telecommunications Technologies

Telecommunications technologies are the tools you use to send information to and receive it from another person or location. Telecommunications technologies represent the fastest growing and most widely varied of all the technology tools. Telecommunications technologies are often associated with the term network. A *network* is

(continued on page 514)

Let's Add a Little Perspective

Most industry analysts predict that by the year 1998 a typical magneto-optical disk (which is slightly smaller than a CD-ROM disk) will be able to hold 10 gigabytes of information. Ten gigabytes is equivalent to 10 billion characters. For the sake of argument, let's say you have 10 magneto-optical disks that are completely full of text information (for a total of 100 billion characters). Below is an interesting comparison of various storage technologies. ❖

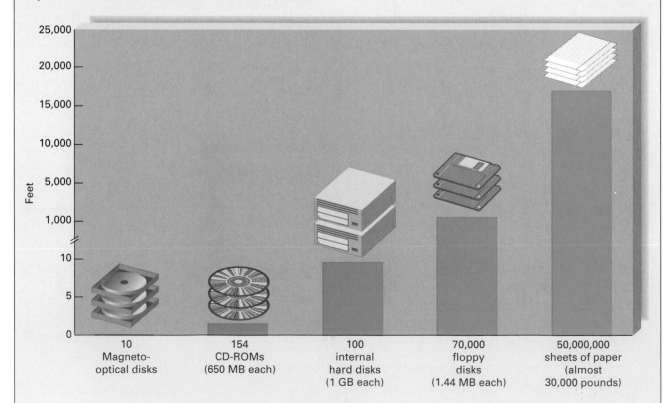

PHOTO
ESSAY
Storage Technologies

Magnetic Tape Storage Technologies

Magnetic tape storage technologies store information on and retrieve it from a tape using a sequential method of access. That is, in order to read information halfway through the tape, the first half of the tape must be passed over (using something similar to fast-forward with a cassette tape). Magnetic tapes are primarily used for backing up information and software that exist on another storage technology.

For small computer systems, such as your personal computer, magnetic tapes are about one-half the size of a standard VCR tape. On larger systems, a magnetic tape looks like a large reel-to-reel tape.

The amount of storage on a tape is referred

Magnetic tape for large systems

Columns run up and down the tape. A single character can be stored in each column.

A single bit is stored in the intersection of a track and column.

Tracks run the length of the tape.

An on bit (1) is represented by a magnetized position.

An off bit (0) is represented by a nonmagnetized position.

to as tape density. **Tape density** is measured in **bytes per inch** or **BPI**. So a tape with a density of 9,600 BPI can hold 9,600 bytes or characters per inch.

Disk Storage Technologies

Disk storage technologies separate the storage medium (called the "disk") into tracks, with each track divided into several sectors. Disk storage technologies use a direct method of access, which means you can move directly to the information you need without passing over the previous information. Disk storage technologies comprise the majority of the storage technologies used today and include magnetic floppy disks, magnetic hard disks, optical disks, and magneto-optical disks.

Magnetic hard disk storage technologies store information on multiple disks called platters. Magnetic hard disks come in a variety of forms, including internal hard disks, external hard disks, hard disk cartridges, and hard cards.

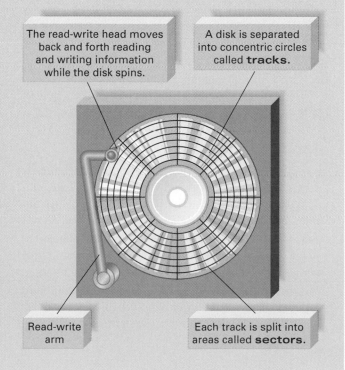

The read-write head moves back and forth reading and writing information while the disk spins.

A disk is separated into concentric circles called **tracks**.

Read-write arm

Each track is split into areas called **sectors**.

Hard disk pack for large systems

An ***internal hard disk*** rests inside the cabinet of your computer. From the front you can't even tell an internal hard disk is present.

An ***external hard disk*** sits outside the cabinet of your computer.

Hard disk cartridges are storage technologies in which the multiple disks or platters can be easily removed from the disk drive and replaced with another cartridge of disks or platters. Hard disk cartridges for large computer systems are called ***hard disk packs***.

Hard cards are storage technologies that exist on a board that can be inserted into an expansion slot on your computer.

Optical Disk Storage Technologies

Optical disk storage technologies use a laser beam to read and write information to an optical disk. Because of the precision of laser technology, optical disks can hold more information than a magnetic disk. When the laser creates information on an optical disk, it burns ***pits*** into the disk surface to represent an off bit (bit 0). The areas between the pits are called ***lands*** and represent an on bit (bit 1).

When the laser reads information from an optical disk, the laser penetrates the bottom layer of protective plastic and emits a light source against the layer of reflective aluminum. If the light strikes a pit, the light is scattered and isn't reflected back. If the light strikes a land, it is reflected and interpreted as an on bit.

The most common type of optical disk is ***CD-ROM***. And, because the laser must physically alter the surface of the disk (by creating pits), information cannot be changed once written to the disk. That's why CD-ROMs are ROM, or read-only memory.

OPTICAL DISK WITH INFORMATION

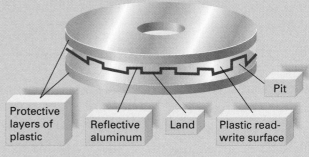

Protective layers of plastic · Reflective aluminum · Land · Plastic read-write surface · Pit

Like magnetic disks, optical disks are separated into concentric circles called "tracks."

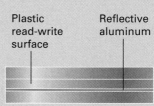

Plastic read-write surface · Reflective aluminum

If you cut a blank CD in half, you will find the plastic read-write surface between two layers of protective plastic.

a connection of two or more IT components (typically computers) that gives people the ability to share software, share information, share peripheral devices, communicate with each other, and share processing power. Examples of a network include two computers connected to the same printer or the literally millions of computers connected all over the world that make up the Internet. We've devoted all of Chapter 6 to these very important topics of telecommunications and networks, so we'll discuss them only briefly here (also refer to Figure A.8 on page 516).

As you begin to consider which telecommunications technologies would be best for a given situation, ask yourself the following question

How tightly do I need to control processing on a network?

The answer to that question will lead you to one of three categories of networks—centralized, distributed, or hybrid (see Figure A.9 on page 516).

Centralized networks have one main CPU that handles all communication within the network and performs

Magneto-Optical Disk Storage Technologies

Magneto-optical disk storage technologies use a laser for reading and writing information and a form of magnetization to give you the ability to alter the stored information. The disks used in magneto-optical disk storage technologies are often called **erasable optical disks**.

An erasable optical disk has a crystalline alloy that contains crystal-like objects and can be heated, which allows the crystal-like objects to move. To write information, the laser heats the alloy, and the crystals are adjusted to represent information through a form of magnetization. To read information, a laser source is emitted against the crystals. A given alignment of crystals can (1) block the light so that it is not reflected against the layer of reflective aluminum or (2) allow the light to pass through the crystals and reflect against the layer of reflective aluminum and back to the laser.

Most people would place **digital video disks (DVD)** in the category of magneto-optical technologies. Technically, that may be correct sometimes and incorrect in others. First generation DVD technologies, for example, are still read-only (ROM) but have an initial capacity of 4.6GB with a possible upgrade to 17GB. As well, first generation DVDs can read CD-ROM. Newer generations of DVD (DVD-RAM and DVD+RW) truly are erasable optical disks. These generations possess rewritable capabilities, but often are not compatible with existing CD-ROM technologies.

Whatever the case, CD-ROM is on its way out, and DVD is its successor. If you're interested in learning about DVD technologies, connect to the Web site that supports this text and select "Emerging Technologies." ❖

Laser

To write information, the laser first heats the alloy, which allows the crystals to move.

Plastic
Crystalline alloy
Aluminum
Plastic

Next a magnetic writing device adjusts the alignment of the crystals.

For reading, the alignment of the crystals determines how the laser light will be reflected off the aluminum.

all information-processing requests. With a centralized network, you can easily control what functions can be performed. Because of this, centralized networks provide you with a great amount of control. **Distributed networks** (which are often called "decentralized" networks) are a collection of connected CPUs. In a distributed network, each person has a CPU and, therefore, can perform whatever processing is necessary for his or her job. For that reason, distributed networks provide you with the least amount of control.

Finally, **hybrid networks** are basically a combination of a centralized and a distributed network. With a hybrid network, you can employ one main CPU to handle functions that need to be tightly controlled and, at the same time, distribute many CPUs to people who need to do independent processing.

Another important question to ask concerning the most appropriate use of telecommunications technologies is

What is the geographic distance that I'm trying to cover?

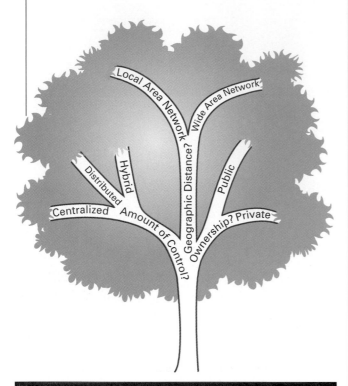

FIGURE A.8
The Communications Branch of the Technology Tree

The answer to that question will lead you to one of two types of networks—local area networks and wide area networks (see Figure A.10). A *local area network (LAN)* covers a limited geographic distance, such as an office, office building, or a group of buildings within close proximity to each other. A *wide area network (WAN)* covers large geographic distances, such as a state, a country, or even the entire world.

A third question to ask concerning the most appropriate use of telecommunications technologies is

Who should have ownership of the telecommunications technologies?

The answer to that question will lead you to one of two types of networks—public networks and private networks. *Public networks* are networks on which your organization competes for time and use with other people and organizations. The public telephone system is an example of a public network. A *private network* is a network that your organization either owns or exclusively leases the right to use. In the instance of a private network, your organization may actually own the telecommunications technologies or have exclusive lease rights.

Again, we've devoted all of Chapter 6 to telecommunications technologies, so we have only touched on them

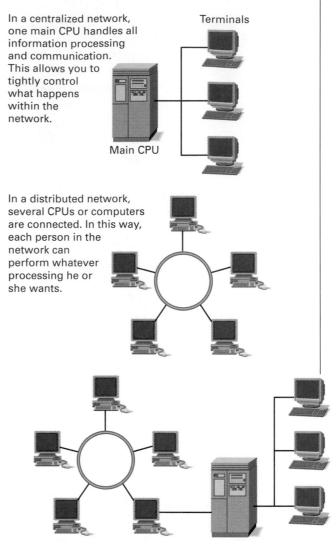

In a centralized network, one main CPU handles all information processing and communication. This allows you to tightly control what happens within the network.

In a distributed network, several CPUs or computers are connected. In this way, each person in the network can perform whatever processing he or she wants.

A hybrid network is a combination of a centralized and a distributed network. In this way, you can tightly control who does what within the centralized network portion and, at the same time, give complete processing freedom to those people in the distributed network portion.

FIGURE A.9
Telecommunications Technology According to Control

here. What you have just read about telecommunications technologies represents only the tip of the iceberg about this most fascinating and exciting aspect of IT.

The Foundation of the Technology Tree

The Processing Engine

The five Cs—capturing, conveying, creating, cradling, and communicating—provide a powerful way to view the various categories of information technologies. Just

A local area network (LAN) covers a limited geographic area such as the building above.

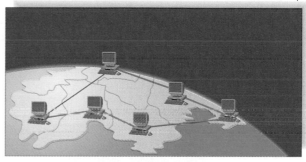

A wide area network (WAN) can cover a large geographic area such as the several countries above.

FIGURE A.10

Telecommunications Technology According to Distance

by asking the right questions, you can determine the best technology or technologies for your needs. However, noticeably absent from our categorizations is the very heart of IT—the processing engine.

The processing engine really forms the foundation of the Technology Tree (see Figure A.11, page 518). The processing engine contains two components—the internal memory and the central processing unit. The internal memory is the common connection among all the hardware in an IT system, and the central processing unit is the part of the hardware that actually executes the software instructions and coordinates the interaction of all the other hardware devices. Let's quickly review these two critical components.

The Central Processing Unit

The *central processing unit (CPU)* is the hardware in an IT system that interprets and executes the software instructions and coordinates how all the other hardware devices work together. The CPU has two components—the control unit and the arithmetic/logic unit (see Figure A.12, page 518). The *control unit* interprets software instructions and literally tells the other hardware devices what to do, based on the software instructions. As you might guess, the *arithmetic/logic unit (A/L unit)* performs all arithmetic operations (for example, addition and subtraction) and all logic operations (such as sorting and comparing numbers).

The Internal Memory

The *internal memory* is a temporary storage that holds three things:

1. Information you are working with
2. The application software you are using
3. The operating system software

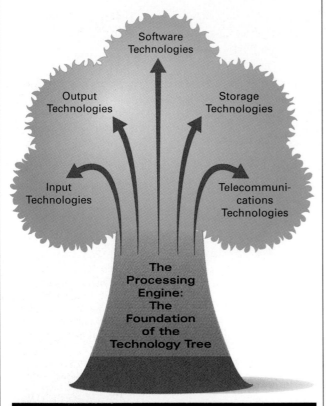

FIGURE A.11

The Foundation of the Technology Tree

The internal memory takes on the role of a notepad that the CPU uses to temporarily store information and instructions.

The internal memory has two distinct sections—random access memory and read-only memory (see Figure A.13). *Random access memory (RAM)* is what most people equate with the internal memory. RAM is the part of the internal memory that holds the three things listed on page 517. *Read-only memory (ROM)* is the part of the internal memory that comes with permanent, built-in instructions. These instructions perform such tasks as getting your system going when you first turn it on and handling input and output (for example, receiving input from a keyboard and sending output to a monitor).

Putting It All Together

It's actually quite simple to view the different tool sets of information technology individually. The real challenge is in combining them to create a complete and beneficial system that achieves the intended goal. That's what this text is about—helping you determine the right technology tools for a given situation, then showing you how to put them together and make them work to achieve an advantage. In Figure A.14, you can see how the five

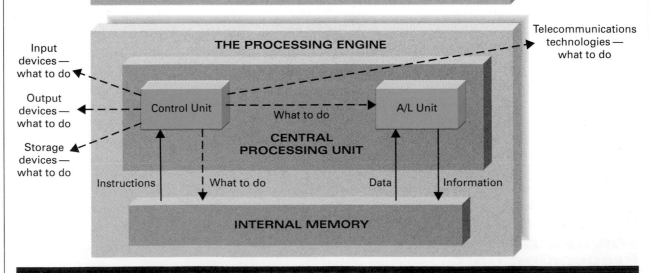

FIGURE A.12

The Components of the Central Processing Unit

INTERNAL MEMORY

Random Access Memory (RAM)

Read-Only Memory (ROM)

Random access memory (RAM) is volatile. That means you can change its contents, but it also loses its contents when the computer is turned off.

Read-only memory (ROM) cannot be changed. It comes with built-in instructions that help your system get going and handles basic input/output tasks.

FIGURE A.13
The Internal Memory

technology tool sets and the processing engine work together. Now it's up to you to decide which tools to use and when.

In general, if you're starting from scratch to create a new system, we suggest you climb through the Technology Tree in the following fashion:

❶ Go to the software technologies branch. Choose the application software technologies tree branch and determine exactly which application software you need.

❷ Go to the input technologies tree branch. Choose the type of input technologies that will capture information and commands at their points of

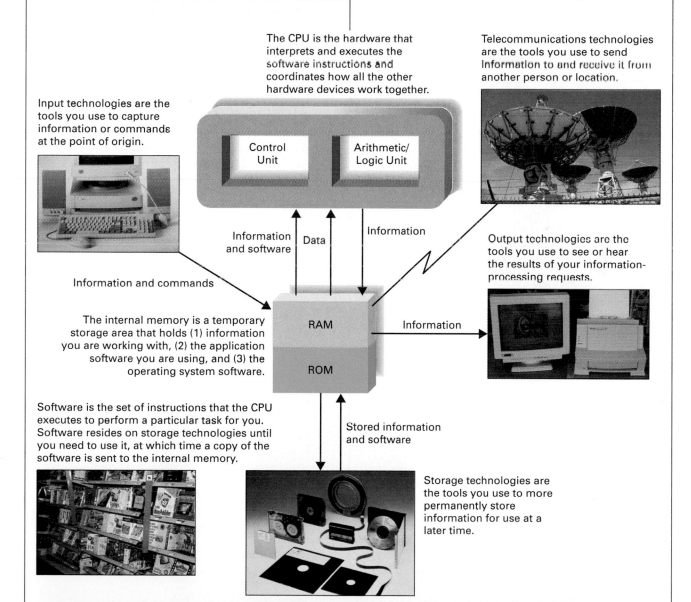

The CPU is the hardware that interprets and executes the software instructions and coordinates how all the other hardware devices work together.

Telecommunications technologies are the tools you use to send information to and receive it from another person or location.

Input technologies are the tools you use to capture information or commands at the point of origin.

Control Unit

Arithmetic/Logic Unit

Information and software

Data

Information

Output technologies are the tools you use to see or hear the results of your information-processing requests.

Information and commands

The internal memory is a temporary storage area that holds (1) information you are working with, (2) the application software you are using, and (3) the operating system software.

RAM

ROM

Information

Software is the set of instructions that the CPU executes to perform a particular task for you. Software resides on storage technologies until you need to use it, at which time a copy of the software is sent to the internal memory.

Stored information and software

Storage technologies are the tools you use to more permanently store information for use at a later time.

FIGURE A.14
The Complete Technology Tool Set

origin and those technologies most suited for capturing information, commands, or both. Verify that the application software you chose will support your desired input technologies.

❸ Go to the output technologies tree branch. Choose the type of output technologies that will convey information in its most useful form and those technologies that have the required level of quality.

❹ Go to the telecommunications technology tree branch. Then choose the most appropriate telecommunications technologies according to geographic distance, control, and ownership. Don't forget, we have devoted all of Chapter 6 to telecommunications technology; that chapter will help you answer many questions.

❺ Go back to the software technologies tree branch. This time choose the operating system software technologies tree branch, and select the best operating system that will support the application software, input, output, and telecommunications technologies you have chosen.

❻ Go to the storage technologies tree branch. Choose the most appropriate storage technologies according to your needs for updating your information and how much information (and software) you have to store.

❼ Finally, climb down the tree and take a look at the trunk. Now you'll want to find a CPU and identify the amount of internal memory that will provide you with the necessary power and speed to support all the other technologies you have chosen.

Climbing a real tree requires some physical dexterity and strength. Likewise, climbing the Technology Tree requires intellectual dexterity and strength. Your ability to move quickly through the Technology Tree will depend on your ability to ask and answer the right questions.

From an organizational perspective, we would bring up one important note here. All organizations work with limited resources—people, money, expertise, and so on. The greatest limitation in choosing the absolute best technology is always **money.** All organizations would like to choose the very best technology to meet their current and future needs. Most often, however, that's simply not possible because organizations have limited money resources. If you purchase a personal system for yourself, you'll find the same to be true.

APPENDIX B

The Internet

Perhaps the most visible and explosive information technology tool is the Internet. No matter where you look or what you read, someone always seems to be referring to the Internet. On television commercials, you'll find Internet addresses displayed (such as http://www.ibm.com for an IBM commercial or http://www.toyota.com for a Toyota commercial). In almost every magazine, you'll find some sort of article about the Internet. Most major business publications, such as *Fortune, Forbes,* and *Business Week,* devote entire issues each year to the Internet and how to use it for electronic commerce.

You'll also hear people use hundreds of different terms when talking about the Internet, such as Web, World Wide Web, browser, client, server, search engine, chat room, and so on. Unfortunately, these hundreds of different terms are sometimes why certain people hesitate to learn about the Internet. After all, don't hundreds of terms imply that the Internet is very complicated and difficult to learn? How useful or much fun can the Internet be if you first have to memorize a couple of hundred different definitions?

Once exposed to the Internet though, people find that the Internet is, in fact, a most enjoyable, simple, and easy-to-use computer-based tool. If you've never cruised or surfed the Internet, the next few pages explain how to do just that. And after reading the next four pages and participating in one of the two Internet scavenger hunts on pages 526–528, you'll **really** be a skilled Internet cruiser (or surfer if you prefer the ocean to the highway). It's true—the Internet really is easy to learn, and in a matter of a few short hours you may find yourself not wanting to leave cyberspace.

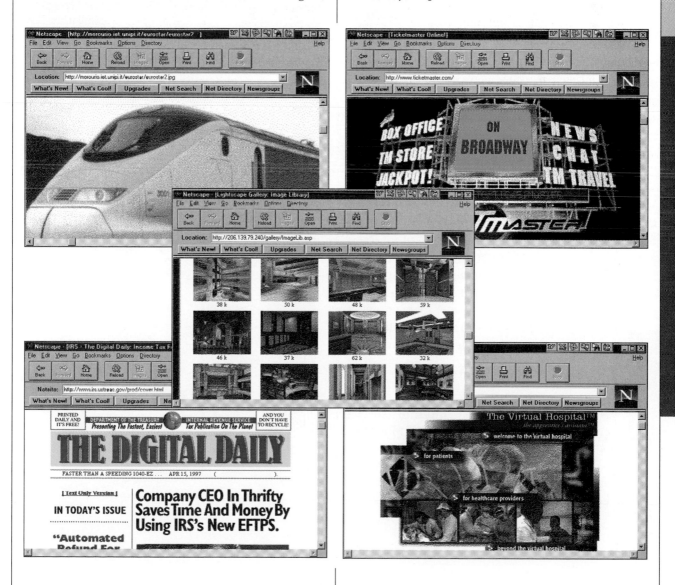

A Tour of the Internet

The **Internet** is basically a network of networked computers all over the world. Schools, businesses, government agencies, and many others have all connected their internal computer networks to the Internet, making it truly a large *network* of *networked computers*. Today people use the terms Internet and Web interchangeably. Technically, that's not correct. But, in reality, who cares?

There are two types of computers on the Internet—servers and clients. **Servers** are computers that provide information and services to Internet cruisers. For example, if you connect to Disney's Web site at http://www.disney.com you're essentially using the Internet to connect to a large computer that has a Web name of *disney* and is supported by Disney. If your school has a Web site on the Internet, that Web site is really on a server computer that your school supports. And, if your school lets you build a Web page (many do today), your Web page is contained on your school's server computer. Incidentally, the terms "Web page" and "Web site" are used interchangeably. Technically, they're different; in reality, who cares.

As an Internet cruiser, you connect to the Internet through an **Internet service provider**—an organization that supports many people who want to access and use the Internet. There are a variety of types of Internet service providers (abbreviated as ISPs). For example, your school is probably an ISP because it gives students access to the Internet. In your town or region, you may know of local Internet service providers. For example, in the Denver area, one of the biggest local Internet service providers is Rocky Mountain Internet. Finally, there are a number of Internet service providers that have a worldwide presence, such as America Online, Compuserve, Prodigy, and Microsoft Network (MSN).

When cruising the Internet, your computer is called a client. A **client** is simply a computer that accesses and uses the information and services provided by a server.

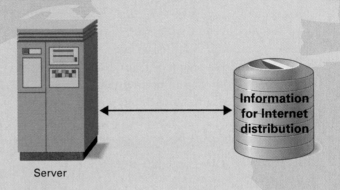

Server

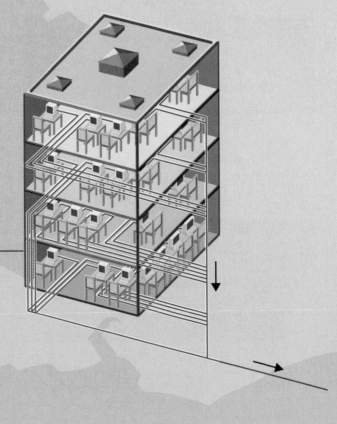

Information for Internet distribution

In short, the **World Wide Web, WWW,** or **Web** (whichever you choose to call it) is the Internet in a linked multimedia form. Before the Web, the Internet was all text-based; you saw no icons, you couldn't use a mouse, and video was an impossibility. In pre-Web days, you had to know where to go on the Internet to find what you needed; cruising, surfing, and searching were not terms associated with the Internet. Now, because of the Web, the Internet supports information in a variety of forms (sound, video, graphics, text, and so on). That information can also be linked to other places that may have similar information.

Just like the regular postal service system, every place (page or site) on the Internet has an address. If you know the address, you simply type it in and you're instantly there. If you don't know the address, you use a variety of powerful search engines (discussed on the next page) to find where you want to go.

Most addresses start with http://www, which stands for hypertext transfer protocol (http) and World Wide Web (www). The remaining portion of the address is unique to each location. Somewhere in that part you'll find an organizational identifier, which is usually one of the following:

COM or CO—commercial organization

EDU—educational institution

GOV—government agency

MIL—military agency

NET—network support center

ORG—other organization (mostly nonprofit)

For example, the Web site below at left is for Disney, so you'll find "com" somewhere in the title. And in the Web site below for the British newspaper *The Telegraph,* you'll find "co" as the organizational identifier.

What comes before and after the organizational identifier gets a little more complicated (and less relevant). If something appears after the organizational identifier (usually starting with a "/"), it's probably a subdirectory path that enables you to get to the right portion of the server computer. What comes before the organizational identifier is really the logical name for the server. For Disney it's "disney"; for *The Telegraph,* it's "telegraph."

You may also find something between the organizational identifier and the path name. If you do, it's the country identifier. For example, *The Telegraph* comes from Britain, so its country identifier ("uk" for United Kingdom) appears after its organizational identifier.

Almost all Web addresses start with http://www.

The Telegraph is a commercial organization located in England. So, its address includes "co" (commercial organization) and "uk" (which is the country identifier).

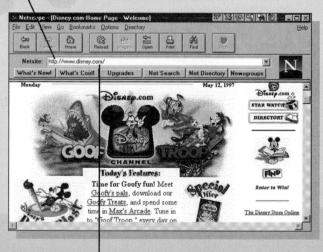

Disney is a commercial organization so its address has "com" as the organizational identifier.

Once you've connected to a Web site, feel free to click on icons, buttons, or terms to see more information.

As we discussed before, the Internet is an information resource in which information on one Web site may be linked to other Web sites that have similar information. So it's a relatively simple process to search for all Web sites that contain similar information. To do so you use a search engine. A **search engine** is a software tool that allows you to search for Internet information by using key words or terms. And there are a variety of search engines from which you can choose. On this page we describe two.

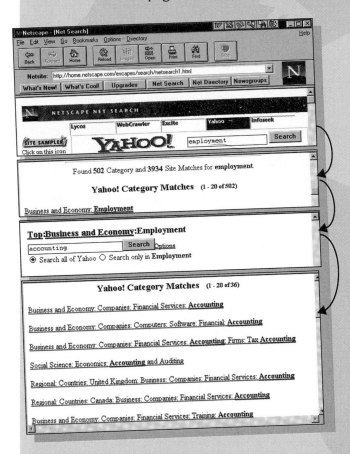

Yahoo (shown above) is the most popular and widely used search engine on the Internet. In fact, the creators of Yahoo also publish the *Internet Yellow Pages,* which lists thousands of sites by topic. To start Yahoo, we clicked on the *Net Search* button and then chose Yahoo from a list of available search engines. Then we decided to look up employment information so we used that as the key word; Yahoo responded by telling us that it found 502 categories of employment and 3,934 Web sites that contained employment information.

We then chose to look at the first category called "Business and Economy: Employment." Yahoo then asked for another key word and we typed in "accounting." Yahoo responded by telling us that it found 36 different matches. As you can see in the final screen, we could then choose from different types of accounting jobs–perhaps accounting in the financial services or computer software industries or tax accounting. Whatever the case, we would continue this dialog with Yahoo until our search became refined enough so that Yahoo could actually present us with a listing of job opportunities in accounting.

Another popular search engine is WebCrawler (shown below). To use WebCrawler, we once again clicked on the *Net Search* button and this time chose WebCrawler from the list of available search engines. For this search, we decided to look up information relating to jazz music on the Internet so we used "jazz music" for the key word. WebCrawler responded by telling us that it found an amazing 128,663 Web sites that contained jazz music information. Notice also that WebCrawler immediately displayed a listing of all the Web sites. To choose a particular Web site (such as Stein's Haus of Jazz Music), all we would have to do is point and click on it–WebCrawler would immediately take us to that Web site.

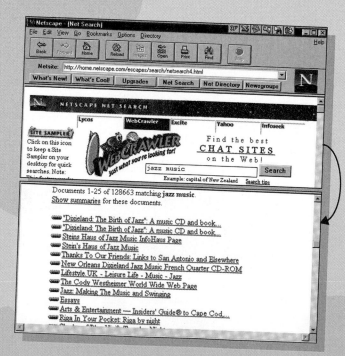

To move around the Internet, cruise to new cyber destinations, and surf some of the hottest and wildest sites, you need a piece of communications software called a ***browser.*** The two most popular browsers today are Netscape Communicator and Internet Explorer (shown below). Using either of these two, you can access search engines (such as Yahoo and WebCrawler), print Web pages, save the locations of your favorite and most often visited sites, and perform a vast array of other functions. What's really great is that learning how to use browser software is simple. In fact, the best way to learn is simply to sit down and take off into cyberspace using whatever browser you have. ❖

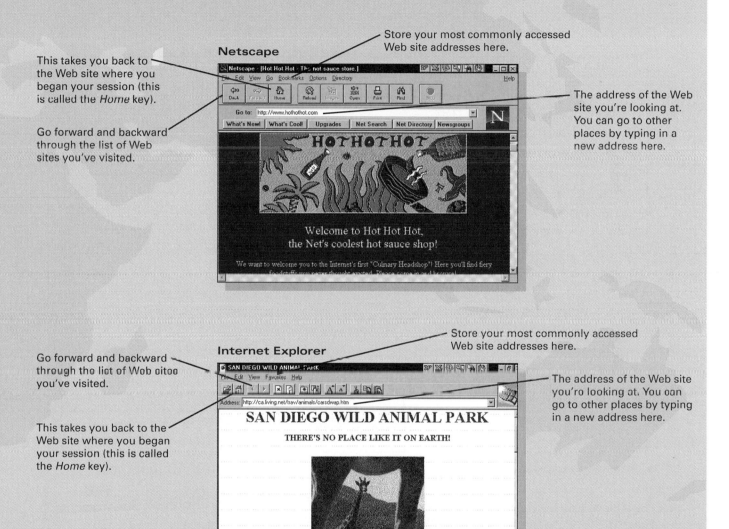

Netscape

Store your most commonly accessed Web site addresses here.

This takes you back to the Web site where you began your session (this is called the *Home* key).

Go forward and backward through the list of Web sites you've visited.

The address of the Web site you're looking at. You can go to other places by typing in a new address here.

Internet Explorer

Store your most commonly accessed Web site addresses here.

Go forward and backward through the list of Web sites you've visited.

This takes you back to the Web site where you began your session (this is called the *Home* key).

The address of the Web site you're looking at. You can go to other places by typing in a new address here.

Scavenger Hunts

For each of the scavenger hunt exercises you find on these pages, find a Web site that provides the appropriate information. When you find the Web site, record its address in the space provided by each exercise. You cannot use encyclopedia Web sites such as the one for *Encyclopedia Britannica.*

Scavenger Hunt 1

1. The weight of the moon.
    http://_____

2. Tomorrow's weather forecast for Puget Sound.
    http://_____

3. The state flower of New Hampshire.
    http://_____

4. The first person to reach the South Pole.
    http://_____

5. The state that borders Alabama to the north.
    http://_____

6. The Seven Dwarfs.
    http://_____

7. The value at which the stock market closed on the most recent trading day.
    http://_____

8. Last year's winner of the Oscar for best director.
    http://_____

9. The average temperature of the sun.
    http://_____

10. The current population of the United States.
    http://_____

11. The real name of The Mad Monk.
    http://_____

12. The conversion process between Fahrenheit and centigrade.
    http://_____

13. What the abbreviation cwt. stands for.
    http://_____

14. The IQ level which is considered to be the beginning of genius.
    http://_____

15. What the Statue of Liberty wears on her feet.
    http://_____

16. Who won the Indy 500 car race last year.
    http://_____

17. The average weight of a cairn terrier dog.
    http://_____

18. The oldest college in the United States.
    http://_____

19. The biggest airport in Spain.
    http://_____

20. The country with the largest sheep population.
http://_____

21. The film that made Rudolph Valentino a star.
http://_____

22. The red-haired, freckle-faced boy on the cover of *Mad* magazine.
http://_____

23. The fear associated with triskaidekaphobia.
http://_____

24. Your congressperson's name, address, and phone number.
http://_____

25. The UN ambassador from the United States.
http://_____

26. The color of a car license plate from Texas.
http://_____

27. The year the *Mona Lisa* was painted.
http://_____

28. Who Lee Harvey Oswald allegedly killed in addition to John F. Kennedy.
http://_____

29. The Great Lake that Pennsylvania borders.
http://_____

30. The last five Pulitzer prize winners.
http://_____

Scavenger Hunt 2

1. The moons surrounding the planet Jupiter.
http://_____

2. The current temperature in Mexico City, Mexico.
http://_____

3. Donald Duck's nephews.
http://_____

4. The state bird of Alaska.
http://_____

5. The four presidential likenesses carved in Mount Rushmore.
http://_____

6. The largest living relative of the hog.
http://_____

7. The unemployment level of your state.
http://_____

8. The price the postal service charges for delivering a 2-pound package overnight.
http://_____

9. The currency used in Thailand.
http://_____

10. The seven wonders of the ancient world.
http://_____

11. Robert Zimmerman's stage name.
http://_____

12. Today's prime interest rate.
http://_____

13. The month you were born in if your birthstone is amethyst.
http://_____

14. The number of witches burned at the stake in Salem, Massachusetts.
http://_____

15. The transitional periods of the zodiac.
http://_____

16. A translation lexicon between English and Klingon.
http://_____

17. The country to which the Isthmus of Corinth is connected.
http://_____

18. The line that divided the north and south in the U.S. Civil War.
http://_____

19. The most commonly spoken language in Belgium.
http://_____

20. The country whose anthem begins "From peaceful Ypiranga's banks."
http://_____

21. The 1936 Miss Hungary who had her title taken away because she was under age.
http://_____

22. A list of *Billboard*'s top five songs.
http://_____

23. Why the Marquis de Sade served 27 years in prison.
http://_____

24. The location of the International Court of Justice.
http://_____

25. The U.S. military newspaper.
http://_____

26. The three colors of ink used to print a U.S. dollar bill.
http://_____

27. The D-Day invasion password.
http://_____

28. The number of points in the maple leaf on the Canadian flag.
http://_____

29. The capital of South Dakota.
http://_____

30. The exchange rate between the U.S. dollar and the Japanese yen.
http://_____

APPENDIX C

Object-Oriented Technologies

Object-oriented—it's one of the hottest topics in information technology right now, and it's destined to occupy the spotlight for many years to come. Every computer person and IT specialist is scrambling to learn how to write software in object-oriented programming languages, create databases using object-oriented database management systems, and design new systems using object-oriented analysis and design. Every software provider—such as Netscape, Microsoft, Borland, Corel,

and IBM—is in the midst of changing its personal productivity software so that it's *object-oriented*. Below, you can review the object-oriented representation for the video rental store we discussed in Chapter 4.

But what is object-oriented? Why are object-oriented concepts and techniques becoming so popular? Why is knowing something about object-oriented concepts and techniques important to you as a knowledge worker? These are all great questions, and we hope to answer them here. We certainly don't claim that you'll be an object-oriented expert just by reading the next few pages, but you will have a good understanding of the whole object-oriented environment and why everyone seems to be moving toward objects.

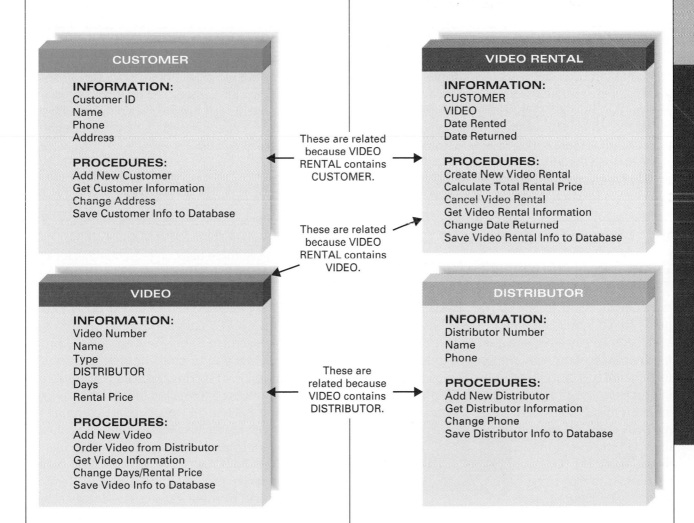

What Does It Mean to Be Object-Oriented?

An **object** is simply a software module that contains information, which describes something (for example, a person, place, or thing), along with a list of procedures that can act on the information. So an **object-oriented (O-O) approach** is any approach—perhaps a programming language or a DBMS—that combines information and procedures into a single object. For example, the STUDENT object at your school contains information about you as well as the procedures to work with your information. Some of these procedures include the ability to change your address, assign you a major, and specify a graduation date.

Combining information and procedures is quite different from other approaches. Most often, information is stored separately from procedures. In other approaches it's possible to have the information but not be able to do anything with it (because you may not have the procedures). Likewise, you could have the procedures (in the form of software) but not be able to do anything with them because you don't have any information to work with.

A Home Stereo System

For a good analogy think of a home stereo system as an object-oriented system with each of the components being an object. The objects in a typical home stereo include an amplifier, a CD player, a cassette deck, an equalizer, and a set of speakers. Each of these objects works with one specific group of information and has procedures for working with just that information. The information for the CD player, for example, is the CD itself. The methods in the CD player include how to read the music from the CD, in what order to play songs according to how you programmed it, and so on. But what the CD player can't do is actually output the music for you to hear.

Why? Because that's not the responsibility of the CD player. So, when you want to hear music on a CD, the CD player must read the music from the CD and pass it to the amplifier. In that object, you can manipulate the volume. In fact, manipulating the volume of the music is a primary method of the amplifier object. From there the music is passed to the speakers with associated volume information.

Thus each component in a home stereo system really is an object. As an object, each component works with only certain information and performs certain functions. If one component needs another function performed, it must send a message to another object (or component) that can perform that function.

One other thing you should notice about objects is that a complete system needs only one object of each kind. Consider the speakers. You don't need one set of speakers for the CD player, one set for the amplifier, and one set for the cassette player. Instead, each of those components can use the speaker object by simply sending to it the music to be played (through the amplifier object).

A Resort Rental Agency

As a business example, let's consider the use of O-O concepts for a resort rental agency. In Figure C.1, you can see three object representations for a resort rental agency that rents vacation properties to renters on a weekly basis—RENTER, RENT CONTRACT, and VACATION PROPERTY. Let's take a closer look at the RENT CONTRACT object. This object contains information concerning a rent contract and the procedures that allow you to perform such functions as creating a new rent contract, calculating total rent, and saving contract information to a database. Notice also that the RENT CONTRACT object contains the RENTER object. So, for example, if you were completing a new rent contract and the renter stated that his or her address had changed, you could easily change the address while using the RENT CONTRACT object. Objects as a part of another object makes logical business sense. For our resort rental agency from a technical point of view, we're saying that the RENT CONTRACT object contains both the RENTER and VACATION PROPERTY objects. In business terms, this means that our resort rental agency rents a vacation property to a renter by creating a rent contract.

To see how this works, let's examine the procedures list more closely for RENTER and RENT CONTRACT. In Figure C.2, we've detailed what some of those procedures involve. When you begin creating a new rent contract (using the RENT CONTRACT object), the first step in that procedure involves calling the *Get Renter Info* procedure in the RENTER object. You are then prompted to enter the renter's name, after which the *Get Renter Info* procedure attempts to find a match in the database. When a match is found, *Get Renter Info* sends the renter's information back to *Create New Rent Contract* in the RENT CONTRACT object. You then see the renter's information on the screen and are asked if the information is correct. If it's not, the next step is to call the *Change Address* procedure in the RENTER object which would prompt you for the new address and then store the renter's new information (by calling the *Save Renter Info to Database* procedure). ❖

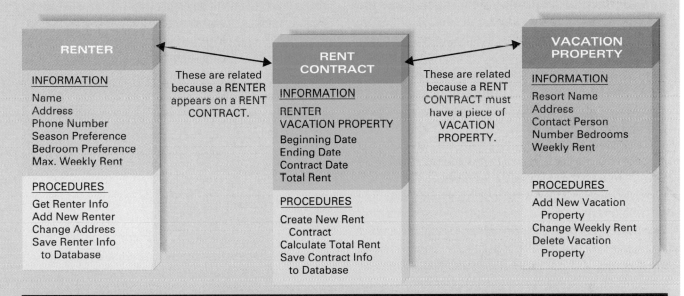

RENTER

INFORMATION

Name
Address
Phone Number
Season Preference
Bedroom Preference
Max. Weekly Rent

PROCEDURES

Get Renter Info
Add New Renter
Change Address
Save Renter Info
  to Database

These are related because a RENTER appears on a RENT CONTRACT.

RENT CONTRACT

INFORMATION

RENTER
VACATION PROPERTY
Beginning Date
Ending Date
Contract Date
Total Rent

PROCEDURES

Create New Rent
  Contract
Calculate Total Rent
Save Contract Info
  to Database

These are related because a RENT CONTRACT must have a piece of VACATION PROPERTY.

VACATION PROPERTY

INFORMATION

Resort Name
Address
Contact Person
Number Bedrooms
Weekly Rent

PROCEDURES

Add New Vacation
  Property
Change Weekly Rent
Delete Vacation
  Property

FIGURE C.1

An Object Representation of a Resort Rental Agency

RENTER OBJECT PROCEDURES

GET RENTER INFO
1. Accept renter name from user
2. Retrieve renter info from database
3. If no match found
    3.1 Display "Invalid renter name"
    3.2 Go to 1
4. Return renter info

CHANGE ADDRESS
1. Accept new address from user
2. Call **Save Renter Info to Database**

SAVE RENTER INFO TO DATABASE
1. Write renter info to database

RENT CONTRACT OBJECT PROCEDURES

CREATE NEW RENT CONTRACT
1. Call **Get Renter Info** in *RENTER* object and return information
2. Display information and ask user if address is correct
3. If answer is no
    3.1 Call **Change Address** in *RENTER* object **. . .**
9. Call **Calculate Total Rent**
10. Ask user if total rent is okay
11. If answer is yes
    11.1 Call **Save Contract Info to Database**

CALCULATE TOTAL RENT
1. Number weeks = (ending date – beginning date) /7
2. Total rent = number weeks * weekly rent

SAVE CONTRACT INFO TO DATABASE
1. Write contract info to database

FIGURE C.2

Object Interaction Through Procedures

Why Are Object-Oriented Concepts and Techniques Becoming So Popular?

O-O Concepts Closely Model How You View the World

In business you actually view a given business process as a combination of information and the procedures that you need to act on that information. In a payroll environment for example, you view employees (which would be an object) as information—name, salary, number of dependents, and so on—and procedures that act on that information. Some of these procedures include adding a new employee, changing an employee's salary, calculating gross pay, and making the necessary deductions to calculate net pay. So, O-O concepts basically provide the same technical view as your logical business view.

O-O concepts make good business sense, and they also make sense in your personal life. Have you ever purchased a product that requires "some assembly" such as a mountain bike or gas grill? Upon opening the box and spreading out the contents you immediately reach for the instruction booklet (which is an example of an object-oriented approach). In the instructions you'll find a detailed set of steps concerning assembly along with a description of the various parts. You won't find the set of instructions separate from the description of the parts—they are combined because it makes the most sense to do so.

Reuse Leads to Productivity

From our rental resort agency example, you can easily see another reason why people are beginning to use an object-oriented approach—*reuse*. In an O-O environment, you simply define a procedure once and then allow any other object to use it as necessary. This reuse principle has significantly reduced the time it takes to develop software because procedures are only defined once and then literally reused time and time again. A good analogy here is that of our amplifier in a home stereo. You just need one amplifier; all other components—the CD player, cassette deck, and equalizer—share in the use of the amplifier.

According to a survey of the 30 largest insurance companies in the United States, more than two-thirds include objects in their IT strategy. Why? Because a significant percentage of IT budgets in the insurance industry goes toward maintaining and modifying existing systems. For insurance companies, object technologies promise to reduce the time it takes to modify and maintain existing systems through code reuse. This is true not only for the insurance industry, but also for most other industries.

O-O Databases Support Complex and Unique Data Types

Besides combining information and procedures into a single object, O-O databases (discussed in Chapter 4) also work better with complex data types than other database models. Complex data types include diagrams, schematic drawings, video, sound, and text documents. The relational database model, although it may allow you to store and view such data types, does not include good mechanisms for allowing you to manipulate and change information within those data types. For example, you can include a CAD drawing of a part as a field in a relational database table, but it's literally impossible to work with any specific information in the drawing (such as cuts, specific components, and the ordering of assembly) without having that information also stored in other fields of the same table. O-O databases don't restrict information storage to two-dimensional tables, which gives you greater flexibility in storing and defining procedures that work with complex data types. In fact, most of today's multimedia applications rely on the use of objects and object-oriented databases.

Most other database models also restrict you to working with specific data types—alphabetic, numeric, decimal, currency, date, and so on. In an O-O database environment, however, you can create and work with data types that may be unique to a certain business process. In our earlier example of the resort rental agency, the VACATION PROPERTY object includes information concerning address. With an O-O database, you could easily define that this field includes not only a street address but also a unit number. You could then define a procedure that requires the entry of both. This is an example of a unique data type that requires not only a street address, but also a unit number.

O-O Concepts Support Reengineering Efforts

Many businesses today are seeking to reengineer business processes (we discuss business process reengineering in Chapter 3). Many of the "traditional" IT systems that support business processes separate information from procedures. Often, this separation is not closely aligned with how many people view the supported business processes. The Commercial Airline Group at Boeing, for example, has decided to use object technologies to reengineer its business processes—including manufacturing, procurement, finance, and sales. When complete, the new object-based system will be used by more than 55,000 Boeing employees.

O-O Technologies Are Becoming More Prevalent

One of the most significant drawbacks to the use of O-O concepts in recent years has been the lack of O-O technologies that are specifically designed to work with objects. Traditional third-generation programming languages such as COBOL and FORTRAN and database query languages such as SQL are designed to treat information and procedures separately.

Today, however, a growing number of fourth- and fifth-generation languages, natural languages, and DBMS packages directly support the use of objects. Some of these new programming languages include C++, Smalltalk, OOCOBOL, Eiffel, Objective-C, CLOS, Actor, Object Pascal, and Java. Of all these, you can expect Java to have the most widespread use. As far as DBMS packages that support objects are concerned, Table C.1 contains a list of some of the more popular ones.

O-O Concepts Are Well-Suited to Client/Server

In Chapter 6, we explore client/server as the emerging blueprint for organizational networks, and most organizations are choosing to develop client/server networks through object-oriented technologies. Formally defined, a **client/server network** is a network that contains one or more host computers (called "servers") that provide some type of service to the other computers (called "clients") in the network. Spreading objects across a client/server network makes logical sense: client workstations contain objects with local procedures for working with local information, and servers contain objects with global procedures for working with global information. To see how objects work in a client/server environment, let's look at the example of a client/server model 3 implementation found in Chapter 6. If you want, you can refer to pages 226–229 in Chapter 6 where we completely detail this example.

In a model 3 client/server implementation model, the server handles the entire data management function, the client handles the entire presentation function,

TABLE C.1 Object-Oriented Database Management Systems Packages			
DBMS Package	**Vendor**	**DBMS Package**	**Vendor**
Gemstone/S	Gemstone Systems	Objectivity/DB 5.0	Objectivity Inc.
Matisse 3.0	ADB Inc.	ObjectStore PSE	Object Design Inc.
Ontos*Integrator	Ontos Inc.	Poet 5.0	Poet Software
Versant ODBMS 5.0	Versant	Jeevan 2.0	W3Apps
O$_2$ Systems	Ardent Software	Vision	Insyte

and both share in processing the logic or business rules. So the server object contains procedures for retrieving and storing information (data management) and for processing some of the logic or business rules. Likewise, the client object contains procedures for some of the logic or business rules and for presenting information (the presentation function). To demonstrate the model 3 implementation, we assume that you are the manager of the manufacturing division in an organization and need to give pay raises to each of your employees. For assigning pay raises, you also have to follow several rules—some for just your division and some for all organizational employees.

In an object-oriented environment, your client workstation contains an object for assigning pay raises to manufacturing division employees according to manufacturing division rules and formatting and presenting information to you. The server contains an object for assigning pay raises according to organizational rules and for retrieving information from and saving information to the database. In Figure C.3, you can see how this actually works.

First, your MANUFACTURING DIVISION EMPLOYEE object (which we'll call the client object) asks you for an employee and sends a message to the ORGANIZATIONAL EMPLOYEE object (which we'll call the server object) to retrieve that employee's information from the database and return it. Your client object then executes the rules for determining pay raises for manufacturing employees, displays that information to you, and sends the proposed pay raise to the server object. The server object then executes the organizational rules for assigning pay raises and returns the modified pay raise to your client object. Your client object then displays that information to you and allows you to submit the finalized pay raise for processing to the server object. Finally, the server object updates the Employee database to reflect the employee's pay raise.

And while you're assigning pay raises to manufacturing division employees, other managers could be doing the same for their employees. In this instance, you and the other managers essentially share the server object—another excellent example of reuse. ❖

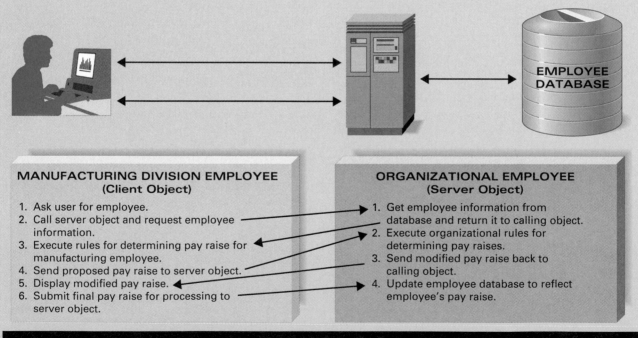

MANUFACTURING DIVISION EMPLOYEE
(Client Object)

1. Ask user for employee.
2. Call server object and request employee information.
3. Execute rules for determining pay raise for manufacturing employee.
4. Send proposed pay raise to server object.
5. Display modified pay raise.
6. Submit final pay raise for processing to server object.

ORGANIZATIONAL EMPLOYEE
(Server Object)

1. Get employee information from database and return it to calling object.
2. Execute organizational rules for determining pay raises.
3. Send modified pay raise back to calling object.
4. Update employee database to reflect employee's pay raise.

FIGURE C.3

Object-Oriented Technologies and Client/Server—The Perfect Match

So Why Are Object-Oriented Concepts and Techniques Important to You?

As we close our discussion of O-O concepts and techniques, let's address the most important question of all; that is, "Why is knowing something about O-O concepts and techniques important to you as a knowledge worker?" After all, we've already stated that the use of objects is really transparent to you. For example, when you access a Web page with animated movement, you actually get an object that contains information (a description of the animated figures, their color, shape, and so on) and procedures that act on that information (how the figures are supposed to move, their speed, and so on). But if this is transparent to you, why is it important that you understand it?

Well, recall from Chapter 1 that an important part of knowledge worker computing includes developing some systems for yourself or a group. That's why you learned how to build your own database in Chapter 4. The simple fact of the matter is that you will—in all probability—develop some of your own systems. And as you do, you'll probably do so using object-oriented technologies, specifically what we call applications development tools.

Applications development tools (which also go by the names *enterprise resource planning tools* and *enterprise software tools*) are software packages that help you develop systems based primarily on object-oriented technologies. Using these tools which include easy-to-use graphic user interfaces you'll define business processes in terms of objects—a combination of information and the procedures that act on that information. Then you'll define how the objects are related—messages and information that are passed between the objects, which objects contain other objects, and so on. And, as you do this, you'll be taking advantage of the many benefits of object-oriented technologies (reuse for example).

There are a number of powerful and popular applications development tools in use today. These tools (and their providers) include:

- OneWorld (JD Edwards)
- R/3 (SAP)
- Designer/Developer (Oracle)
- BAAN IV (Baan)
- PeopleTools (PeopleSoft)
- LANSA (Aspect Development)
- Lawson Insight (Lawson)
- Magic Enterprise (Magic Software)

Unfortunately, it's impossible to show you how these tools work by simply talking about them in a book. So, we've included a description of each and links to their provider on the Web site for this book at http://www.mhhe.com/business/mis/haag (select "Systems Development" and then "Applications Development Tools"). You should definitely check it out.

NOTES

Chapter 1

1. DeJong, Jennifer, "Turbocharging Customer Service," *Inc. Technology*, June 13, 1995, pp. 35–39.

2. De Koszmovsky, Kristina, "The Culture Wars," *Men's Health*, November 1996, pp. 140–141.

3. Zuckerman, Mortimer, "America's Silent Revolution," *U.S. News & World Report*, July 18, 1994, p. 90.

4. Kelly, Kevin, "Case Digs Out from Way Under," *Business Week*, August 14, 1995, pp. 62–63.

5. Lubove, Seth, "The Berserk-ley Boys," *Forbes*, August 14, 1995, pp. 42–43.

6. Thayer, Taylor, "Marketing: The Next Generation," *Sales & Marketing Management*, February 1995, pp. 43–44.

7. Robins, Gary, "Data Warehousing: Retailers on the Cutting Edge," *STORES*, September 1995, pp. 19, 24–28.

8. Stewart, Thomas, "Getting Real About Brainpower," *Fortune*, November 27, 1995, pp. 201–203.

9. Zelner, Wendy, "Back to 'Coffee, Tea, or Milk?'" *Business Week*, July 3, 1995, pp. 52–54.

10. Naughton, Keith, "Ford Opens the Throttle," *Business Week*, September 18, 1995, pp. 66–68.

11. Kerwin, Kathleen, "Let's Make a Deal," *Business Week*, September 25, 1995, pp. 54–55.

12. Zeiger, Dinah, "On-line Service Tracks Flights with FAA Data," *The Denver Post*, December 5, 1996, pp. 1–2C.

13. Arnst, Catherine, "The Networked Corporation," *Business Week*, June 26, 1995, pp. 86–89.

14. Stahl, Stephanie, "Make Documents, Not War," *InformationWeek*, May 20, 1996, pp. 46–47.

15. *The World Almanac*, Funk & Wagnalls Corporation, NJ, 1994.

16. *Fortune*: August 1975; August 11, 1980; August 19, 1985; July 30, 1995; and August 7, 1995.

17. "The Fortune Global 500," *Fortune*, August 7, 1995, pp. 123–197.

18. McWilliams, Gary, "Small Fry Go Online," *Business Week*, November 20, 1995, pp. 158–164.

19. "Business Is Blooming, Thanks," *Business Week*, November 20, 1995, p. 164.

20. Beresford, Lynn, "Young Millionaires," *Entrepreneur*, November 1995, pp. 112–120.

21. Keohan, Martin, "The Virtual Office: Impact and Implementation," *Business Week*, September 11, 1995, pp. 95–98.

22. Mailloux, Jacqueline, "New Menu at PepsiCo," *Computerworld*, November 1996, p. 86.

23. Langhoff, June, "Telecommute America," *Fortune*, October 30, 1995, pp. 229–235.

24. Langhoff, June, "Telecommute America," *Fortune*, October 30, 1995, pp. 229–235.

25. Baig, Edward, "Welcome to the Officeless Office," *Business Week*, June 26, 1995, pp. 104–106.

26. Currid, Cheryl, "Managing Today's Corporations Using Mobile Technology," *Fortune*, May 29, 1995, pp. 157–172.

27. Moukheiber, Zina, "Open-A Little," *Forbes*, December 16, 1996, pp. 43–44.

28. Verity, John, "A Trillion-Byte Weapon," *Business Week*, July 31, 1995, pp. 80–81.

29. Arnst, Catherine, "MCI Is Swarming Over the Horizon," *Business Week*, February 19, 1996, pp. 68–69.

30. Novack, Janet, "The Data Edge," *Forbes*, September 11, 1995, pp. 148–152.

31. "Buried Treasure in Credit Cards," *Business Week*, October 28, 1996, p. 136.

32. Partially adapted from O'Brien, James, *Management Information Systems: A Managerial End User Perspective*, Irwin, Homewood, IL, 1990.

33. Mandel, Michael, "A World Wide Web for *Tout Le Monde*," *Business Week*, April 1, 1996, p. 36.

34. Forest, Stephanie, "J. C. Penney's Fashion Statement," *Business Week*, October 14, 1996, pp. 66–67.

35. "Who's Reading Your Medical Records?" *Consumer Reports*, October 1994, pp. 628–632.

36. McMenamin, Brigid, "It Can't Happen Here," *Forbes*, May 20, 1996, pp. 252, 254.

37. Kallman, Ernest, and John Grillo, *Ethical Decision Making and Information Technology*, McGraw-Hill, San Francisco, 1993.

38. Peyser, Marc, and Steve Rhodes, "When E-Mail Is Ooops Mail," *Newsweek*, October 16, 1995, p. 82.

39. Stewart, Thomas, "What Information Costs," *Fortune*, July 10, 1995, pp. 119–121.

40. Royal, Weld, "Do Databases Really Work?" *Sales & Marketing Management*, September 1995, pp. 66–74.

41. Morais, Richard, "Buying a Piece of Vacationland," *Forbes*, December 2, 1996, pp. 62, 64.

42. Novack, Janet, "The Data Miners," *Forbes*, February 12, 1996, pp. 96–97.

Chapter 2

1. Weber, Joseph, "Just Get It to the Stores on Time," *Business Week*, March 6, 1995, pp. 66–67.

2. Darling, Charles, and William Semich, "Extreme Integration," *Datamation*, November 1996, pp. 48–58.

3. Baxter, Andrew, "Smart Response to a Changing Market," *Financial Times*, March 1, 1995, p. 13.

4. Sprout, Alison, "The Internet inside Your Company," *Fortune*, November 27, 1995, pp. 161–168.

5. Ibid.

6. Kight, Betty, "The Smart Way to Build a Data Warehouse," *Datamation*, October 1996, pp. 91–94.

7. Haag, Stephen and Peter Keen, *Information Technology: Tomorrow's Advantage Today*, McGraw-Hill, New York, 1996.

8. de Llosa, Patty, and Henry Goldblatt, "What Information Costs," *Fortune*, July 10, 1995, pp. 119–121.

9. Lunce, Steve, "An Examination of the Managerial Issues Involved in the Contingency Planning for Information Systems," The University of Texas at Arlington, 1994.

10. Dwyer, Paula, "Modernize This Old-Boy Club? Rubbish!" *Business Week*, January 22, 1996, p. 39.

11. Young, Jeffrey, "Can Computers Really Boost Sales?" *Forbes ASAP*, August 28, 1995, pp. 84–98.

12. Wagner, Mitch, "That's the Ticket," *Computerworld*, May 6, 1996, pp. 77, 81.

13. "Hechinger's Client/Server Strategy: Mission Critical Applications from Kenan Technologies First," *Chain Store Age Executive with Shopping Center Age*, September 1995, pp. 20–21.

14. Zweig, Phillip, "Beyond Bean-Counting," *Business Week*, October 28, 1996, pp. 130–132.

15. Keating, Stephen, "Telemedicine: A Reality Checkup," *The Denver Post*, December 8, 1996, pp. 1, 18I.

16. Braly, Damon, "Groupware and Your Health," *Health Management Technology*, September 1995, pp. 20–22.

17. Hammer, Michael, and James Champy, *Reengineering the Corporation*, HarperCollins, New York, 1993, pp. 36–39.

18. Jacobs, April, "Info-boom Fattens Paper Glut," *Computerworld*, July 15, 1996, pp. 120–121.

19. Hensdill, Cherie, "Yield Management: An Holistic Approach," *HOTELS*, January 1996, p. 58.

20. Rao, Srikumar, "The Hot Zone," *Forbes*, November 18, 1996, pp. 252–255.

21. Begley, Sharon, "Software au Naturel," *Newsweek*, May 8, 1995, pp. 70–71.

22. "How General Motors Used an Expert System to Speed New Products to Market," *I/S Analyzer Case Studies*, March 1995, pp. 9–12.

23. "New Executive Info System Keeps Calgary Competitive," *Chain Store Age*, March 1996, p. 40.

24. Raymar, Bruce, "All Roads Lead to IT," *Computerworld—The Global 100*, May 1, 1995.

25. Haag and Keen, op. cit.

26. "World Insurance Network Pursues E-Commerce," *Insurance & Technology*, 1996, pp. 10–12.

27. Moukheiber, Zina, "He Who Laughs Last," *Forbes*, January 1, 1996, pp. 42–43.

28. Prokesch, Steven, "Making Global Connections at Caterpillar," *Harvard Business Review*, March–April 1996, pp. 88–89.

29. "Powerful Reservations, Marketing and Sales Create Occupancy Premiums," *HOTELS*, October 1995, pp. 51–53.

30. Morais, Richard, "Buying a Piece of Vacationland," *Forbes*, December 2, 1996, pp. 62,64.

31. Fryer, Bronwyn, "Allied Signal Technical Services," *Computerworld Client/Server Journal*, August 1996, pp. 8–9.

Chapter 3

1. Schafer, Sarah, "How Information Technology Is Leveling the Playing Field," *Inc. Technology*, November 14, 1996, p. 94.

2. Martin, Justin, "Are You as Good as You Think You Are?" *Fortune*, September 30, 1996, pp. 142–144.

3. Stevens, Tim, "More Panes, More Gains," *Industry Week*, December 18, 1995, pp. 59–63.

4. Plotkin, Hal, "Dining à la Data," *Inc. Technology*, November 14, 1996, pp. 85–86.

5. Nash, Kim, "Overnight Services Duke It Out Online," *Computerworld*, April 22, 1996, pp. 1, 64.

6. Stewart, Thomas, "3M Fights Back," *Fortune*, February 5, 1996, pp. 94–99.

7. Fisher, Anne, "Corporate Reputations," *Fortune,* March 4, 1996, pp. 96–97.

8. Hisey, Pete, "Quality Essential to Building Image," *Discount Store News,* May 6, 1996, p. 107.

9. Fierman, Jaclyn, "Americans Can't Get No Satisfaction," *Fortune,* December 11, 1995, p. 186.

10. Sherman, Stratford, "You Can Have It All," *Fortune,* March 4, 1996, p. 193.

11. Brown, Stuart, "Detroit to Suppliers: Quality or Else," *Fortune,* September 30, 1996, pp. 134C–134S.

12. Jenish, D'Arcy, "Cleaning Up," *Maclean's,* December 12, 1994, p. 46.

13. "Oiling the Wheels of Customer Satisfaction," *Nation's Business,* April 1996, p. 12.

14. McGraw, Dan, "Staying Loose in a Tense Tech Market," *U.S. News & World Report,* July 8, 1996, p. 46.

15. Conners, Mary, "Baxter's Big Makeover in Logistics," *Fortune,* July 8, 1996, pp. 106C–106N.

16. Garner, Rochelle, "Flight Crew," *Computerworld,* Februrary 5, 1995, pp. 66–67.

17. Stodghill II, Ron, "One Company, Two Cultures," *Business Week,* January 22, 1996, p. 68.

18. Nelson, Frank, "New Client/Server Systems Create Competitive Edge," *Best's Review,* April 1996, pp. 92–94.

19. Ouellette, Tim, "Database Decorum," *Computerworld,* August 12, 1996, p. 45.

20. Borsham, Tim, "Companies Learn to Share Secrets," *Business Review Weekly,* December 5, 1994, pp. 80–81.

21. Kling, Julia, "Sharing IS Secrets," *Computerworld,* September 23, 1996, pp. 1, 131.

22. Owen, Jean, "JM Mold: Small but Agile," *Manufacturing Engineering,* June 1996, pp. 69–74.

23. Carlton, Jim, "Think Big," *The Wall Street Journal,* June 17, 1996, p. R27.

24. Zachary, G. Pascal, "Hard Labor," *The Wall Street Journal,* June 17, 1996, p. R26.

25. Ibid.

26. Leib, Jeffery, "Customer Service Pays for TeleTech," *The Denver Post,* December 8, 1996, pp. I-1, I-18.

27. Moore, Mark, "Telecommuting Olympiad," *PC Week,* July 15, 1996, p. 105.

28. Berger, Melanie, "Making the Virtual Office a Reality," *Sales & Marketing Management,* June 1996, p. S18.

29. Ibid.

30. Taylor, Alex III, "The Man Who Put Honda Back on Track," *Fortune,* September 9, 1996, pp. 92–100.

31. Goff, Leslie, "Silicon Alley," *Computerworld,* April 22, 1996, pp. 81–83.

32. Kmitch, Janet, et al., "International Comparisons of Manufacturing Compensation," *Monthly Labor Review,* October 1995, p. 3.

33. Shia, Pei-yuan, "Citibanking the World," *Bank Management,* July/August 1995, pp. 30–37.

34. Reinhardt, Andy, and Seanna Browder, "Booming Boeing," *Business Week,* September 30, 1996, pp. 118–125.

35. Roberts, Bill, "Long-Distance Relationships," *Inc.,* May 1996, pp. 64–68.

36. Ibid.

37. Hoffman, Thomas, "Prescription for Savings," *Computerworld,* July 1, 1996, p. 57.

38. Harreld, J. Bruce, "Creating a Flexible Company," *Across the Board,* October 1995, p. 56.

39. Reuteman, Rob, "Boston Chicken's Beck Blames Self for Laying an Egg," *The Rocky Mountain News,* June 8, 1997.

40. Bylinski, Gene, "To Create Products, Go into a CAVE," *Fortune,* February 5, 1996, pp. 80A–80H.

41. Kling, Julia, "Decision-Support Software Cuts Loan Processing Time," *Computerworld,* February 19, 1996, pp. 63–64.

42. Verespej, Michael, "Reengineering Isn't Going Away," *Industry Week,* February 20, 1996, p. 42.

43. Spiro, Leah, "Global Gamble," *Business Week,* February 12, 1996, pp. 63–72.

44. Levine, Ron, "Wireless LANs Extend Reach on Tough Factory Floor," *Communications News,* June 1996, p. 38.

45. Smart, Tim, "Jack Welch's Encore," *Business Week,* October 28, 1996, pp. 154–160.

46. Stewart, Thomas, "3M Fights Back," *Fortune,* February 5, 1996, pp. 94–99.

Chapter 4

1. Zulman, Shelley, "Dressing Up Data," *Oracle Magazine,* January–February 1995, pp. 46–49.

2. "The Chain Store Age 100," *Chain Store Age,* August 1996, p. 3A.

3. "Swamped with Data, H-E-B Turns to Red Brick to Make Sense of It All," *Chain Store Age Executive with Shopping Center Age,* September 1995, pp. 6–7B.

4. Hoffman, Thomas, and Kim Nash, "Data Mining Unearths Customers," *Computerworld,* July 10, 1995, pp. 1, 28.

5. Diltea, Steve, "Managing Sales with Software," *Nation's Business,* March 1996, pp. 29–31.

6. Hutheesing, Nikhil, "Speaking with One Voice," *Forbes,* September 23, 1996, pp. 214–215.

7. Cash, James, "Gaining Customer Loyalty," *InformationWeek,* April 10, 1995, p. 88.

8. "Sybase Lands $3 Million Deal," *Computerworld,* July 21, 1996, p. 70.

9. Hamilton, Joan, "Medicine's New Weapon: Data," *Business Week,* March 27, 1995, pp. 184–188.

10. Wendy Knight & Associates, "Think You Know Your Health Plan? Think Again," *Newsweek,* September 16, 1996, special advertising section.

11. Anthes, Gary, "Car Dealer Takes the Personal out of PCs," *Computerworld,* August 14, 1995, p. 48.

12. Byrnes, Nanette, "On the Cutting Edge," *Business Week,* October 28, 1996, pp. 134–136.

13. Bruno, Lee, "Database Relating Key Information to Hospitals," *The Business Journal,* October 9, 1995, pp. 36–37.

14. Bessen, Jim, "Riding the Marketing Information Wave," *Harvard Business Review,* September–October 1993, pp. 150–160.

15. Chandler, Susan, "Data Is Power. Just Ask Fingerhut," *Business Week,* June 3, 1996, p. 69.

16. Hoffman, Thomas, "Good-bye, Legacy Skills," *Computerworld,* January 22, 1996, pp. 73, 76.

17. Royal, Weld, and David Sheldon, "Do Databases Really Work?" *Sales & Marketing Management,* April 1996, pp. 66–74.

18. Rudnitsky, Howard, "Another Agricultural Revolution," *Forbes,* May 20, 1996, pp. 159–161.

19. Kling, Julia, "OLAP Gains Fans among Data-Hungry Firms," *Computerworld,* January 8, 1996, pp. 43, 48.

20. Hutheesing, Nikhil, "Surfing with Sega," *Forbes,* November 4, 1996, pp. 350–351.

21. Watterson, Karen, "A Data Miner's Tools," *BYTE,* October 1995, pp. 91–96.

22. DeJesus, Edmund, "Dimensions of Data," *BYTE,* April 1995, pp. 139–148.

23. Cafasso, Rosemary, "OLAP: Who Needs It?" *Computerworld,* February 2, 1995, p. 12.

24. Radding, Alan, "Blue Cross Climbs Mountain of Data with OLAP," *InfoWorld,* January 30, 1995, p. 64.

25. Nash, Kim, "MasterCard Extends Its Limit," *Computerworld,* July 31, 1995, p. 6.

26. Babcock, Charles, "Slice, Dice, & Deliver," *Computerworld,* November 13, 1995, pp. 129–132.

27. Karon, Paul, "Subaru Aims to Take the Guesswork out of Consumer Trends," *InfoWorld,* January 22, 1996, p. 63.

28. Phillips, Ben, "Ice Service's Data Warehouse Goes with the Flow," *PC Week,* January 22, 1996, pp. 45–46.

29. Fryer, Bronwyn, "Fast Data Relief," *InformationWeek,* December 2, 1996, pp. 133–137.

30. Sager, Ira, "IBM's Tollbooth for the I-Way," *Business Week,* May 13, 1996, pp. 114–115.

31. Fryer, Bronwyn, "Zeneca Takes Its Medicine," *InformationWeek,* March 18, 1996, pp. 74–76.

32. LaPlante, Alice, "Big Things Come in Smaller Packages," *Computerworld,* June 24, 1996, pp. DW/6–7.

Chapter 5

1. "When Intelligence Rules, the Manager's Job Changes," *Management Review,* July 1994, pp. 33–35.

2. Gambon, Jill, "A Database That 'Ads' Up," *InformationWeek,* August 7, 1995, pp. 68–69.

3. Maynard, Roberta, "Leading the Way to Effective Marketing," *Nation's Business,* October 1996, pp. 10–11.

4. Hobeika, A. G., et al., "A Decision Support System for Developing Evacuation Plans Around Nuclear Power Plant Stations," *Interfaces,* September–October 1994, pp. 22–35.

5. Freemantle, Michael, "Ten Years After Chernobyl Consequences Are Still Emerging," *Chemical & Engineering News,* April 29, 1996, pp. 18–28.

6. Simon, Herbert, *The New Science of Management Decisions,* rev. ed., Prentice-Hall, Englewood Cliffs, NJ, 1977.

7. Maslakowski, Carla, "Cut Adverse Drug Reactions with Clinical Decision Support," *Health Management Technology,* August 1996, pp. 28–30.

8. Brown, Gerald G., et al., "Scheduling Coast Guard District Cutters," *Interfaces,* March–April 1996, pp. 59–72.

9. Rakshit, Ananda, et al., "System Operations Advisor: A Real-Time Decision Support System for

Managing Airline Operations at United Airlines," *Interfaces,* March–April 1996, pp. 50–58.

10. "Turning Data into Useful Information," *Progressive Grocer,* July 1994, p. 14.

11. Hayes, Frank, "Hormel Makes Client/Server Move," *Computerworld,* August 26, 1996, p. 28.

12. Hoffman, Thomas, and Mitch Wagner, "Visions of Holiday $ugarplums," *Computerworld,* December 4, 1995, pp. 1, 147.

13. Scheier, Robert L., "Timing Is Everything," *Computerworld,* August 5, 1996, pp. 62–63.

14. DiDio, Laura, "Pizzeria Eats Up Client/Server Pie," *Computerworld,* March 4, 1996, pp. 69–70.

15. Townsend, Anthony M., Michael E. Whitman, and Anthony R. Hendrickson, "Computer Support System Adds Power to Group Processes," *HR Magazine,* September 1995, pp. 87–90.

16. Jackson, Neal, et al., "Support Group Decisions via Computer Systems," *Quality Progress,* May 1995, pp. 75–78.

17. Connors, Daniel P., and David D. Yao, "Methods for Job Configuration in Semiconductor Manufacturing," *IEEE Transactions on Semiconductor Manufacturing,* August 1996, pp. 401–410.

18. Nunamaker, J.F., Jr., et al., "Electronic Meeting Systems to Support Group Work: Theory and Practice at Arizona," Working paper, College of Business, University of Arizona, March 1990.

19. Bers, Joanna Smith, "Accelerating the Decision Process," *Bank Systems and Technology,* August 1996, p. 22.

20. Aiken, Milam, Mahesh Vanjami, and James Krosp, "Group Decision Support Systems," *Review of Business,* Spring 1995, pp. 38–42.

21. Fabris, Peter, "Felon Television," *CIO,* September 1, 1990, pp. 24–26.

22. Gillooly, Caryn, "Bright Light," *InformationWeek,* November 20, 1995, p. 56.

23. Wagner, Mitch, "Mapping Software Heads in New Direction," *Computerworld,* July 15, 1996, p. 67.

24. Patterson, David, "Mapping Out Your Future," *Nursing Homes,* October 1995, pp. 34–35.

25. Bird, Jane, "Computers versus Crime," *Management Today,* April 1996, pp. 66–68.

26. Swenson, John, "GIS Software Goes Corporate," *InformationWeek,* June 3, 1996, p. 103.

27. Woodbury, Carol, "GIS Software," *Journal of Property Management,* September–October 1996, pp. 60–62.

28. Duenas, Mark, "Ada County Rewrites the Book with GIS," *American City & County,* February 1995, p. 84.

29. Dunkin, Amy, "The Quants May Have Your Numbers," *Business Week,* September 25, 1995, pp. 146–147.

30. Clerking, Daniel, Peter J. Fox, and Frederick E. Petty, "A Decision Support System for Hospital Bed Alignment," *Hospital and Health Services Administration,* Fall 1995, pp. 386–400.

31. Port, Otis, "Computers that Think Are Almost Here," *Business Week,* July 17, 1995, pp. 68–71.

32. Cossack, S., "Expert System Offers Relief for Child Abuse," *Computerworld,* July 29, 1991, p. 37.

33. Stuart, Ann, "A Dose of Accuracy," *CIO,* May 15, 1996, pp. 22–24.

34. Baum, David, "U.N. Automates Payroll with AI System," *Datamation,* November 1996, pp. 129–131.

35. "FAA Expert System Aims Sky High," *Computerworld,* March 7, 1994, pp. 73, 75.

36. Anthes, Gary H., "$1B Award to Fix Air Traffic Systems," *Computerworld,* September 23, 1996, p. 8.

37. Malhorta, Manish, et al., "Artificial Neural Systems in Commercial Lending," *Bankers Magazine,* November–December 1994, pp. 40–44.

38. Mandelman, Auker, "The Computer's Bullish!" *Barron's,* December 14, 1992, pp. 16–17.

39. Punch, Linda, "Battling Credit Card Fraud," *Bank Management,* March 1993, pp. 18–22.

40. "Cigna, IBM Tech Tool Targets Health Care Fraud," *National Underwriter Property & Casualty-Risk & Benefits,* October 1994, p. 5.

41. Glatzer, Hal, "Neural Networks Take On Real-World Problems," *Computerworld,* April 18, 1994, pp. 133–135.

42. Perry, William, "What Is Neural Network Software?" *Journal of Systems Management,* September 1994, pp. 12–15.

43. Port, Otis, "Diagnoses That Cast a Wider Net," *Business Week,* May 22, 1995, p. 130.

44. Baxt, William G., and Joyce Skora, "Prospective Validation of Artificial Neural Network Trained to Identify Acute Myocardial Infarction," *The Lancet,* January 6, 1997, pp. 12–15.

45. Perry, loc. cit.

46. McCartney, Laton, "Technology for a Better Bottom Line," *InformationWeek,* February 26, 1996, p. 40.

47. Port, loc. cit.

48. Rao, Srikumar S., "The Hot Zone," *Forbes,* November 18, 1996, pp. 252–254.

49. Michaels, Jenna, "Looking for Every Opportunity," *Wall Street & Technology,* December 1992, pp. 25, 28.

50. Hoffman, Thomas, "Swamp Thing," *Computerworld,* August 7, 1995, pp. 83–84.

51. Warren, P., "Police to Pinpoint 'Problem' Kids with Neural Technology," *Computing,* October 19, 1995, p. 16.

52. Begley, S., "Software au Naturel," *Newsweek,* May 8, 1995, pp. 70–71.

53. "Qual-Med to Introduce Fourth Generation Medical Management," *Health Care Strategic Management,* April, 1996, p. 15.

54. "White-Collar Computers," *Economist,* August 1, 1992, pp. 57–58.

55. Knightly, John, "Intelligent Systems," *Mortgage Banking,* May 1996, pp. 30–38.

56. McDermott, Kevin, "Ducking Foreign Legal Troubles," *D&B Reports,* March–April 1994, p. 42.

57. Armstrong, Bob, and Jeff Patterson, "The Fast Lane to Success with NAFTA," *CA Magazine,* October 1994, pp. 49–51.

58. Berry, Jonathan, "A Potent New Tool for Selling: Database Marketing," *Business Week,* September 5, 1994, pp. 56–62.

59. Bird, Jane, "Logical Guides to Marketing," *Management Today,* February 1995, pp. 60–63.

60. McCartney, loc. cit.

61. Hample, Scott, "R U Ready for A I?" *American Demographics,* May 1996, pp. 60–62.

62. Naik, Gautam, "In Sunlight and Cells, Science Seeks Answers to High-Tech Puzzles," *The Wall Street Journal,* January 16, 1996, pp. A1, A8.

63. Johnstone, Bob, "Research and Innovations: Remaking Markets," *Far Eastern Economic Review,* March 25, 1993, p. 50.

64. Heichler, Elizabeth, "Expert System Keeps UK TV Ads in Line," *Computerworld,* December 20, 1993, p. 30.

65. Goldberg, David E., "Genetic and Evolutionary Algorithms Come of Age," *Communications of the ACM,* March 1994, pp. 113–119.

66. Girishankar, Saroja, "Nabisco Net Brings Sweet Success," *Communicationsweek,* May 22, 1995, p. 63.

67. Wilder, Clinton, "Important Information—Fast," *InformationWeek,* November 14, 1995, pp. 77–82.

68. Wilder, Clinton, "Intelligent Agents Add Spark to Electronic Commerce," *InformationWeek,* July 24, 1995, p. 89.

69. Judge, Paul, "Why Firefly Has Mad Ave. Buzzing: The Internet Startup Takes Word of Mouth to New Level," *Business Week: Industrial/Technology Edition,* October 7, 1996, p. 101.

70. McGee, Marianne K., "Rapid-Fire Home Loans," *InformationWeek,* November 7, 1994, pp. 38–40.

71. "Electronic Assistant Keeps Pilot 'In the Loop,'" *Aviation Week and Space Technology,* May 13, 1996, pp. 47–48.

72. Fitzgerald, Michael, "Waste Not," *Computerworld,* June 7, 1993, p. 89.

73. Gray, Robert, "Putting the Show on the Road," *Marketing,* June 20, 1996, pp. 27–29.

74. Price, Susan, "Identifying Potentially Profitable Credit Card Customers with Artificial Intelligence," *Bank Systems and Technology,* May 1996, p. 17.

75. Sankaran, Jayaram K., and Rahul R. Ubgade, "Routing Tankers for Dairy Milk Pickup," *Interfaces,* September–October 1994, pp. 59–66.

76. "Software in India; Bangalore Bytes," *Economist,* March 23, 1996, p. 67.

77. Tsui, Eric, "Global Outlook: Australia," *Best's Review,* April 1996, p. 16.

Chapter 6

1. Mullich, Joe, "Setting It Straight," *PC Week,* August 12, 1996, p. 40.

2. "The Network 25," *Computerworld/NetworkWorld,* September 9, 1996, pp. 48–55.

3. O'Leary, Chris, "Buehler Foods Makes Its Move to Open Systems," *Supermarket Foods,* November 13, 1995, pp. 15–16.

4. Strachman, Daniel, "Investment in Client-Server Technology Serving Fannie Mae Well," *American Banker,* July 5, 1994, pp. 6A–7A.

5. Schatz, Willie, "Hourly Loan Approvals for $1,000 Less," *Computerworld Client/Server Journal,* June 1995, pp. 22–23.

6. Wilde, Candee, "No Pulp Here," *Computerworld Client/Server Journal,* June 1995, p. 20.

7. Dicarlo, Lisa, "Toy Supplier Plays to Win at Client/Server Game," *PC Week,* February 6, 1995, pp. 125, 127.

8. Wilson, Linda, "A Beautiful Relationship," *Computerworld Client/Server Journal,* June 1995, p. 23.

9. "How to Revitalize Host Systems for Client/Server Computing Today and Tomorrow," *Datamation,* April 1, 1995, pp. S1–S24.

10. Hoffman, Thomas and Rosemary Cafasso, "The Last Laugh," *Computerworld,* March 18, 1996, pp. 74–75.

11. Alexander, Steve, "An IT Elixir for the Health Care Crisis?" *Computerworld Client/Server Journal,* June 1995, pp. 42–43.

12. Blodgett, Mindy, "A Wireless LAN Landslide," *Computerworld,* April 1, 1996, p. 59.

13. Comaford, Christine, "The Great Unseen Cost of Client/Server," *PC Week,* July 11, 1994, p. 18.

14. Gerber, Cheryl, "Lean 'n' Mean in Texas," *Computerworld Client/Server Journal,* June 1995, p. 44.

15. Schalon, Lisa, "Sales Automation Systems Increase Sales, Productivity," *Best's Review—Life-Health Insurance Edition,* January 1996, pp. 100–102.

16. Manchester, Philip, "Opportunities for Innovators," *The Financial Times,* March 6, 1996, p. FTS8.

17. "Global Alliances Spawn New International Virtual Private Networks," *Data Communications,* September 1995, pp. 47–48.

18. Dudman, Jane, "Privates on Parade," *Computer Weekly,* May 23, 1996, pp. 36–37.

19. Jackson, Tim, "Peapod's Vision," *The Financial Times,* December 4, 1995, p. 15.

20. Cleland, Kim, "Web Grocery Biz Gets a New Player," *Advertising Age,* April 26, 1996, p. 38.

21. Kalakota, Ravi, and Andrew Whinston, *Frontiers of Electronic Commerce,* Addison-Wesley, Cambridge, MA, 1996.

22. Hayes, Frank, "Toronto Stock Exchange: Going, Going, Gone," *Computerworld,* July 22, 1996, pp. 1, 16.

23. "Wilkerson, Robert, "Intranet Experiment Pays Off in the Lab," *PC Week,* April 1, 1996, p. N9.

24. Callaway, Erin, "Setting the Standard," *PC Week,* July 15, 1996, p. 47.

25. Korseniowski, Paul, "Breaking Fertile Intranet Ground," *PC Week,* April 1, 1996, pp. N5–N15.

26. Cortese, Amy, "Updates? Just a Mouse Click Away," *Business Week,* February 26, 1996, p. 84.

27. Paul, Lauren, "The Outside Intranet," *PC Week,* July 8, 1996, p. 48.

28. Gibbs, Mark, "Seeking All the Hits," *Computerworld/NetworkWorld,* September 9, 1996, pp. 32–33.

29. Morant, Adrian, "Keeping Your Company's Information Up-to-Date," *Management Accounting,* June 1996, p. 40.

30. Mayor, Tracy, "The Easy Fit," *PC Week,* July 22, 1996, p. 44.

31. Langhoff, June, "Telecommute America," *Fortune,* October 30, 1995, pp. 229–235.

32. "Federated Puts Faith in At-Home Telecommuting," *Chain Store Age Executive with Shopping Center Age,* January 1996, p. 100.

33. Richards, Bill, "Inside Story: Intranets Foundation for Early Electronic Commerce," *The Wall Street Journal Reports: Technology,* June 17, 1996, p. R23.

34. Bob, Steve, "Telecommuting: Concepts and Resources," *Business Credit,* January 1996, pp. 36–39.

35. Hildreth, Suzanne, "Trimming Telecommuting's Price Tag," *Computerworld,* April 8, 1996, p. 100.

36. Goff, Leslie, "Home@Sweet.Home," *Computerworld,* February 12, 1996, pp. 68–69.

37. Boroughs, Don, "Paperless Profits," *U.S. News & World Report,* July 17, 1995, pp. 40–42.

38. Banham, Russ, "The Hidden Risks of Telecommuting," *Risk Management,* July 1996, pp. 58–62.

39. Cooper, Richard, "Telecommuting: The Good, the Bad and the Particulars," *Supervision,* February 1996, pp. 10–13.

40. Gareiss, Robin, "The Pepsi Challenge," *Data Communications,* May 21, 1996, pp. 54–61.

41. Nash, Kim, "Learn Your Lessons Well," *Computerworld,* July 15, 1996, p. 65.

42. Adapted from Keen, Peter, and J. Michael Cummins, *Networks in Action,* Wadsworth, Belmont, CA, 1994.

43. "Federal Express Eyes Internet Software," *The Denver Post,* October 10, 1996, p. 2C.

44. Rice, Valerie, "Health Group Gets Intranet Treatment," *PC Week,* May 6, 1996, p. 51.

45. Fisher, Susan, "Snug Fit or Mishmash," *PC Week,* March 11, 1996, pp. E1, E9.

Chapter 7

1. Guttman, Monika, "Hollywood Falls in Love with Technology," *U.S. News & World Report,* February 16, 1996, pp. 73–74.

2. Kim, Albert, "Hollywired," *Entertainment Weekly,* October 13, 1995, pp. 21–22, 26, 30, 32.

3. Daly, Steve, "Don't Believe Your Eyes," *Entertainment,* July 16, 1995, p. 279.

4. Coy, Peter, "3-D Computing," *Business Week,* September 4, 1995, pp. 70–77.

5. Mannes, George, "Machines That Listen," *Popular Mechanics,* July 1995, pp. 46–49.

6. Syedain, Hashi, "Technology Finds a New Voice," *Marketing,* November 17, 1994, p. XIV.

7. Remich, Norman, "Speech Market Growing 35% Annually," *Appliance Manufacturer,* July 1993, pp. 57–58.

8. Nutheesing, Nikhil, "The Mother of Development," *Forbes,* January 22, 1996, pp. 88–89.

9. Dennis, Verl, "How Interactive Instruction Saves Time," *Journal of Instructional Delivery Systems,* Winter 1994, pp. 25–28.

10. O'Leary, Chris, "Nature's Fresh Is Sowing Technology," *Supermarket News,* January 22, 1996, p. 18.

11. Melcher, Richard, "Not Just Ink-Stained Wretches," *Business Week,* March 28, 1994, pp. 56–59.

12. Melcher, Richard, "The Press of New Business," *Business Week,* January 15, 1996, pp. 64–65.

13. Wilson, Craig, "Where the Work Is in the Computer Era," *USA Today,* March 29, 1995, p. 1D.

14. Dataquest, 1995.

15. McConnaughey, Janet, "Virtual Reality Used to Treat Autism," *The Denver Post,* October 20, 1996, p. 39A.

16. Adams, Nina, "Lessons from the Virtual World," *Training,* June 1995, pp. 45–47.

17. Flynn, Laurie, "VR and Virtual Spaces Find a Niche in Real Medicine," *The New York Times,* June 5, 1995, p. C3.

18. Gross, Neil, "Seasick in Cyberspace," *Business Week,* July 10, 1995, pp. 110, 113.

19. Schwartz, Bruce, "A Video Game Accessory That Works by Mind Control," *USA Today,* June 16, 1995, p. D1.

20. Queenan, Joe, "Getting (Virtually) Real," *Chief Executive,* November 1995, p. 70.

21. Maney, Kevin, "High-Tech Rooms with 3-D View," *USA Today,* May 11, 1995, pp. 1B–2B.

22. Callaway, Erin, "Setting the Standard," *PC Week,* July 15, 1996, p. 47.

23. Zeiger, Dinah, "A Digital Wallet in Your Computer," *The Denver Post,* September 9, 1996, pp. 7G, 12G.

24. Bloom, Jennifer, "Web Pioneers Unite to Seek Open Standard for Payments," *American Banker,* April 18, 1996, pp. 1, 17.

25. Bloom, Jennifer, "Atlanta Group Aims to Create a Local Internet-Only Bank," *American Banker,* February 29, 1996, p. 14.

26. Templin, Neal, "Cash Crunch," *The Wall Street Journal,* June 17, 1996, p. R22.

27. Caldicott, Karen, "Sholom Rosen: Citibank V.P.: Emerging Technologies," *Forbes ASAP,* August 26, 1996, p. 71.

28. Dalton, Laura, "Virtual Pet Store on Information Superhighway," *Pet Product News,* April 1995, p. 10.

29. Tanaka, Jennifer, "Calling All Cows," *Newsweek,* April 17, 1995, p. 13.

30. Blodgett, Mindy, "A Wireless LAN Landslide," *Computerworld,* April 1, 1996, p. 59.

31. Larsen, Amy, "Wireless LANs: Worth a Second Look," *Data Communications,* November 1995, pp. 95–100.

32. Moeller, Michael, "Fortune 500 Ramps Up Wireless Net Projects; Early Adopters Take Calculated Risk," *PC Week,* March 27, 1995, pp. 1–2.

33. Moeller, Michael, "Government Goes Wireless in Indiana," *PC Week,* July 3, 1995, pp. 23–24.

34. Bozman, Jean, "Practicality of Wireless Applications Grows," *Computerworld,* January 16, 1995, pp. 53, 58.

35. Hapgood, Fred, "High-Tech Harvest," *Inc. Technology,* September 12, 1995, pp. 52–56.

36. Lutton, Christine, "Cyberfarm," *Forbes,* July 15, 1996, pp. 86–87.

37. Levine, Ron, "Wireless LANs Extend Reach on Tough Factory Floor," *Communications News,* June 1996, pp. 38–39.

38. Blodgett, loc. cit.

39. Murphy, Elena, "Telecom Growth Leaps," *Purchasing,* April 25, 1996, pp. 86–87.

40. Zeiger, Dinah, "Smart Card Technology to Get Boost," *The Denver Post,* October 10, 1996, p. 2C.

41. McCarthy, Joseph, "Wireless Wonders: Using Satellites and Cellular Links, Wireless Networks Are Becoming Popular. But Watch Those Costs," *Financial World,* January 2, 1996, pp. 80–81.

42. "Vacuum Cleaner Features a Smart Analog Controller," *Appliance Manufacturer,* February 1995, pp. 91–93.

43. Dryden, Patrick, "Flash That Decoder Ring," *Computerworld*, March 3, 1995, p. 14.

44. Rao, Srikumar, "Good Morning, Hal," *Financial World*, October 10, 1995, pp. 92–93.

45. "First Fuzzy Logic for Cooktop Controller," *Appliance Manufacturer*, February 1996, pp. 86–87.

46. Robins, Gary, "Hybrid Modeling for Site Selection," *STORES*, January 1995, pp. 88–90.

47. Bongiorno, Lori, "The Pepsi Regeneration," *Business Week*, March 11, 1996, pp. 70–73.

48. Nairn, Geoff, "Washer Features Fuzzy Logic, Virtual Sensors," *Design News*, September 25, 1995, p. 50.

49. Rogers, Dale, "A Case for Fuzzy Thinking: The Fuzzy Logic Algorithm Will Make the Logistics Professional's Job Go a Lot Smoother in the Near Future," *Transportation & Logistics*, March 1996, pp. 108–110.

50. Baker, Andrea, "Intelligent Dishwasher Outsmarts Dirt," *Design News*, April 4, 1995, pp. 69–72.

51. Cookson, Clive, "The Rise of the Robot Nose," *Word Press Review*, September 1995, p. 36.

52. Wilke, Michael, "Nix to Tix at Some Airlines," *Advertising Age*, August 14, 1995, pp. 8, 10.

53. Lavitt, Michael, "Airlines Offer PC-Based Ticketing to Top Fliers," *Aviation Week and Space Technology*, October 3, 1995, p. 36.

54. "Delta Tests Ticketless Travel on Shuttle Flights with AT&T Smart Card Technology," *Delta News*, 1995.

55. Parker-Pope, Tara, "Shoppers Get Chance to Scan Store Products," *The Denver Post*, July 16, 1995, p. 5H.

56. Robins, Gary, "Customer Scanning," *STORES*, May 1994, pp. 63–64.

Chapter 8

1. Bartholomew, Doug, "California Chaos," *InformationWeek*, May 6, 1996, pp. 48–56.

2. *Merriam-Webster's Collegiate Dictionary*, Merriam-Webster, Inc., Springfield, MA, 1994, p. 28.

3. Keen, Peter G. W., "Information Technology and the Management Difference: A Fusion Map," *IBM Systems Journal*, Vol. 32, no. 1, 1993, pp. 17–39.

4. Keen, Peter G. W., "Do You Need an IT Strategy?" in *Competing in the Information Age: Strategic Alignment in Practice*, Jerry N. Luftman, ed. Oxford University Press, New York, 1996, p. 157.

5. Stahl, Stephanie, "Information Is Part of the Package," *InformationWeek*, September 9, 1996, p. 208.

6. Porter, Michael E., *Competitive Strategy: Techniques for Analyzing Industries and Competitors*, The Free Press, New York, 1980.

7. Kahaner, Larry, *Competitive Intelligence*, Simon and Schuster, New York, 1996.

8. Kling, Julia, "Schwab Dials Up Stock Quote System," *Computerworld*, October 14, 1996, p. 88.

9. Kahaner, loc. cit.

10. Porter, Michael, and Victor Milar, "How Information Gives You Competitive Advantage," *Harvard Business Review*, July–August 1985, pp. 64–76.

11. Wagner, Mitch, "Travel Service to Target Needs of Businesses," *Computerworld*, August 12, 1996, pp. 63–65.

12. Edwards, Owen, "Bow Tech: ASAP Case Study," *Forbes ASAP*, June 3, 1996, pp. 54–58.

13. Richter, M. J., "Managing for Tomorrow by Going Wireless Today," *Fortune*, November 11, 1996, advertising supplement.

14. Allen, Brandt R., and Andrew C. Boynton, "Information Architecture: In Search of Efficient Flexibility," *MIS Quarterly*, December 1991, pp. 435–445.

15. Rockart, John F., "Chief Executives Define Their Own Data Needs," *Harvard Business Review*, March–April 1979, pp. 81–93.

16. Hoffman, Thomas, "Will Customers Go Ballistic?" *Computerworld*, May 6, 1996, p. 98.

17. Morrison, Ian, *The Second Curve*, Ballantine Books, New York, 1996.

18. Gill, Philip J., "IT Helps Integrate the Food Chain," *InformationWeek*, September 9, 1996, p. 138.

19. DePompa, Barbara, "Sharing the Cost of Recovery," *InformationWeek*, September 9, 1996, p. 146.

20. Adapted from Laudon, Kenneth C., and Jane P. Laudon, *Management Information Systems: Organization and Technology*, Prentice-Hall, Englewood Cliffs, NJ, 1996.

21. Caldwell, Bruce, "We Are the Business," *InformationWeek*, October 28, 1996, pp. 36–38.

22. DePompa, Barbara, "Disaster Strikes! Are You Ready?" *InformationWeek*, May 15, 1996, p. 48.

23. Preston, Kathryn, "Disaster Recovery Planning," *Industrial Distribution*, December 1994, p. 65.

24. Smith, Laura, "Spend a Penny, Save a Bundle," *PC Week*, May 29, 1995, p. E8.

25. Hoffman, Thomas, "Publisher Does Disaster Planning by the Book," *Computerworld*, May 20, 1996, p. 74.

26. Cohodas, Marilyn C., "Just Walk Away," *PC Week*, May 29, 1995, p. E8.

27. DePompa, op. cit., p. 51.

28. Adapted from Fried, Louis, *Managing Information Technology in Turbulent Times*, Wiley-QED, New York, 1995.

29. Moad, Jeff, "All Around the World," *PC Week*, May 13, 1996, pp. E1–E6.

30. Caldwell, op. cit., pp. 36–37.

31. Melymuka, Kathleen, "The Vision Thing," *Computerworld*, December 12, 1994, pp. 84–86.

32. Fortune 500, *Fortune*, April 29, 1996, p. F46.

33. Hoffman, Thomas, "VW Rides Information Highway South of Border," *Computerworld*, November 18, 1996, p. 84.

34. Mahoney, William F., and Charles K. Wessendorf, "How to Get Investors Online," *Financial Executive*, January–February 1996, pp. 41–43.

Chapter 9

1. *The Wall Street Journal*, August 24, 1995, advertising supplement.

2. Simpson, David, "Win95 vs. NT Workstation: You Make the Call!" *Datamation*, December 1996, pp. 110–113.

3. Caldwell, Bruce, "Wal-Mart Ups the Pace," *InformationWeek*, December 9, 1996, pp. 37–49.

4. Garner, Rochelle, "Why JAD Goes Bad," *Computerworld*, April 25, 1994, pp. 87–88.

5. Lane, Randall, "FAA, Inc." *Forbes*, August 26, 1996, p. 48.

6. Bartholomew, Doug, "Objects Take Off," *InformationWeek*, February 26, 1996, pp. 14–15.

7. Fryer, Bronwyn, "When Users Take Notes," *Computerworld*, August 8, 1994, p. 82.

8. Mortlock, Thomas, "Rapid Application Delivery," *http://www.singnent.com/sg —customers/maxinfo/ti.html*, 1996.

9. Haag, Stephen, and Peter Keen, *Information Technology: Tomorrow's Advantage Today*, McGraw-Hill, New York, 1996.

10. Scheier, Robert, "Highest Bidder," *PC Week*, July 31, 1995, pp. E1–E2.

11. Verity, John, "Let's Order Out for Technology," *Business Week*, May 13, 1996, p. 47.

12. Anderson, Howard, "Innovators in Outsourcing," *Forbes*, October 23, 1995, pp. 1–15 (special advertising supplement).

13. McHugh, Josh, "Bowling Ball, Marbles, and Garden Hose," *Forbes*, October 21, 1996, pp. 84–92.

14. Hoffman, Thomas, and Julia Kling, "Utility Unplugs Object Project," *Computerworld*, February 26, 1996, pp. 1, 125.

15. Caldwell, Bruce, "The New Outsourcing Partnership," *InformationWeek*, June 24, 1996, pp. 50–64.

16. Verity, loc. cit.

17. Caldwell, "The New Outsourcing Partnership," loc. cit.

18. Byrne, John, "Has Outsourcing Gone Too Far?" *Business Week*, April 1, 1996, pp. 26–28.

19. Girard, Kim, "MasterCard Upgrade Gives Network a Charge," *Computerworld*, May 6, 1996, p. 86.

20. Tolworthy, Leslie (managing editor), "Arranger 1.1," *Information Matters*, Texas Instruments Publication, 1996, pp. 8–10.

21. Hoffman, Thomas, "BellSouth Breathes New Life into Old Billing System," *Computerworld*, March 4, 1996, p. 70.

22. Frank, Maurice, "The Evolution of Client/Server CASE: New CASE Tools Simplify Management, Technology, Information," *DBMS*, January 1996, pp. 91–93.

23. Knowles, Anne, "Peace Talks," *PC Week*, December 11, 1995, pp. 21–22.

24. Dixon Murray, Teresa, "Projecting Success: Bell & Howell Cut a Crucial Process from Two Months to Two Days: That's Got to Be Good for Business," *Small Business News–Akron*, November 1995, p. 7.

25. "FDM Aids Spinal Implant Design for Danek Medical Group," *http://www.stratasys.sb2.html*, 1996.

26. Tolworthy, Leslie (managing editor), "Global Efficiency: AT&T Streamlines Information Delivery Using Composer," *Information Matters*, Texas Instruments Publication, 1996, pp. 5–7.

27. Halper, Mark, "Power Ploy," *Forbes ASAP*, February 26, 1996, pp. 32–36.

Chapter 10

1. Bounds, Greg, Lyle York, Mel Adams, and Gipsie Ranney, *Beyond Total Quality Management: Toward the Emerging Paradigm*, McGraw-Hill, New York, 1994.

2. Gambon, Jill, "Sales Sleuths Find Solutions," *InformationWeek,* July 22, 1996, pp. 51–52.

3. Caldwell, Bruce, "We Are the Business," *InformationWeek,* October 28, 1996, pp. 36–50.

4. Ibid.

5. Bartholomew, Doug, "Hyatt's Spirit Gets Boost," *InformationWeek,* August 5, 1996, p. 90.

6. English, Larry P., "Help for Data-Quality Problems," *InformationWeek,* October 7, 1996, pp. 53–62.

7. "Tighter Control of Medical Records Urged," *Computerworld,* March 10, 1997, p. 8.

8. Turetsky, Ken, "Hospital REhabilitates from Its Paper Overdose: Optical Character Recognition, Artificial Intelligence Are the Right Prescription for St. Alphonsus," *Infoworld,* July 3, 1995, p. 49.

9. Adams, Dawn L., "Another Platform Heard From," *Training & Development,* May 1996, pp. 79–80.

10. Wilder, Clinton, "Location, Location, Location," *InformationWeek,* March 25, 1996, pp. 73–75.

11. Eastwood, Alison, "End-Users: The Enemy Within?" *Computing Canada,* January 4, 1996, p. 41.

12. Sharp, Kevin R., "When Disaster Strikes," *Computerworld,* September 5, 1994, pp. 97–99.

13. Needle, David, "Betting the Store on Technology," *InformationWeek,* September 9, 1996, pp. 192–197.

14. Black, George, "Get Your Data Back!" *Datamation,* December 15, 1995, pp. 54–57.

15. Karaim, Reed, "The Invasion of Privacy," *Civilization,* October–November 1996, pp. 70–77.

16. Ibid.

17. Greengard, Samuel, "Privacy: Entitlement or Illusion?" *Personnel Journal,* May 1996, pp, 74–82.

18. Morris-Lee, James, "It's Everyone's Business Now!" *Direct Marketing,* April 1996, pp. 40–43.

19. Spinello, Richard A., "The End of Privacy: Companies That Collect Information for a Specific Purpose Can Resell or Reuse It for Other Purposes with Impunity," *America,* January 4, 1997, pp. 9–13.

20. Posch, Robert J., "The 25-Year Privacy Debate Has an Institutional Memory." *Direct Marketing,* April 1996, pp. 54–56.

21. Morris-Lee, loc. cit.

22. Rule, James, and Lawrence Hunter, "Privacy Wrongs: Corporations Have More Right to Your Data Than You Do," *Washington Monthly,* November 1996, pp. 17–20.

23. Foley, John, "Data Dilemma," *InformationWeek,* June 10, 1996, pp. 14–16.

24. Ibid.

25. Morris-Lee, loc. cit.

26. Rule and Hunter, loc. cit.

27. Morris-Lee, loc. cit.

28. van Kirk, Doug, "Poor Asset Management Is Breaking the Bank," *Infoworld,* January 23, 1995, pp. 69–71.

29. "How to Save 13% of Your IS Budget," *Datamation,* August 1996, p. 13.

30. Caldwell, Bruce, "No Management Medals," *InformationWeek,* August 19, 1996, p. 80.

31. "Ergonomic Posturing," *CIO,* March 15, 1996, p. 22.

32. Dessoff, Alan L., "What's Wrong with Your Computer Workstation?" *Safety & Health,* October 1995, pp. 60–63.

33. Johnson, Stuart J., "Chevron Takes Control," *InformationWeek,* November 4, 1996, pp. 97–102.

34. Ichikawa, Atsushi, "Coping with Urban Disasters," *OECD Observer,* December 1996, pp. 15–16.

35. Dietrich, Robert S., "Tunnel Vision," *Computerworld,* March 6, 1995, pp. 77–78.

36. Kahan, Stuart, "Hot Sites: The Solution When Business Interruption Is Fatal," *The Practical Accountant,* July 1994, pp. 58–63.

37. "Disaster Recovery: Are You Ready?" *Managing Office Technology,* January 1995, pp. 26–32.

38. DePompa, Barbara, "Averting a Complete Disaster," *InformationWeek,* July 15, 1996, pp. 40–50.

39. Sichkinger, Ted, "A Bank's Brain," *Kansas City Star,* September 24, 1996, pp. D1, D15.

40. "Disaster Recovery: Our *Real* Story," *Managing Office Technology,* June 1995, pp. 24–25.

41. Buehler, Steve, "The Sky Is Falling," *PC Magazine,* October 22, 1996, p. 30.

42. McGee, Marianne K., "Stretched to the Limit," *InformationWeek,* December 2, 1996, p. 36–48.

43. Hildebrand, Carol, "Shopping Around," *CIO,* August 1996, p. 22.

44. Jones, David C., "Insurance Industry in Telecommuting Vanguard," *National Underwriter: Property & Casualty/Risk & Benefits Management,* June 26, 1995, p. 5.

45. Davis, Eileen, "Have Modem, Won't Travel," *Management Review,* April 1995, p. 7.

46. Ogilvie, Heather, "This Old Office," *Journal of Business Strategy,* September–October 1994, pp. 27–30.

47. "Rizzuti's Virtual Adventure," *Sales & Marketing Management,* November 1995, p. 14.

48. Smith, Bob, "Welcome to the Virtual Office," *HRFocus,* November 1994, p. 16.

49. Greengard, Samuel, "Workers Go Virtual," *Personnel Journal,* September 1994, p. 71.

50. Howard, Lisa, "Telecommuting Gaining Converts among Insurers," *National Underwriter: Property & Casualty/ Risk & Benefits Management,* May 13, 1996, pp. 3, 40.

51. Kim, Irene, and Ken Fouhy, "Telecommuters: They're Not Just at Home," *Chemical Engineering,* October 1995, p. 37.

52. Qureshi, Zia, "Globalization: New Opportunities, Tough Challenges," *Finance & Development,* March 1996, pp. 30–33.

53. Web, www.openu.ac.uk/OU/Intro/What Is.html.

54. Dragoon, Alice, "CIO 100-World Leaders-Samsung Electronics: Not Accidental Tourists," *CIO,* August 1996, p. 62.

55. Dragoon, Alice, "When in Rome . . . ," *CIO,* August 1996, p. 28.

56. "Furnishing the World," *The Economist: Management Briefs, 1994–1996,* pp. 6–7.

57. Karaim, Reed, "The Invasion of Privacy," *Civilization,* October–November 1996, pp. 70–77.

58. "New York Uncovers Huge Tax Fraud Scheme," *Associated Press* report, *Morning Sun,* November 22, 1996, p. 10.

59. Shore, Barry, "Using Information Technology to Coordinate Transnational Service Operations: A Case Study in the European Union," *Journal of Global Information Systems,* Spring 1996, pp. 5–14.

60. O'Connell, Sandra, "HP's Sales Team Gets Boost in Revenue and Morale," *HRMagazine,* March 1996, p. 56.

61. Covey, Kathy, and Wally Leonard, "Computing Increases Competitiveness," *Transmission & Distribution World,* March 1996, pp. 68–69.

Chapter 11

1. Betts, Mitch, "Turn Your Company into a Cybercorp. It's Wired. It's Virtual. It's Agile," *Computerworld,* October 9, 1995, p. 41.

2. Wells, Jennifer, "Virtual Revenge," *MaClean's,* May 27, 1996, pp. 36–37.

3. Drapin, Lois, "Andersen Creates Disease Management Network," *Health Management Technology,* January 1996, pp. 22, 24.

4. Lamb, J. J., "Whiz-Bang!" *World Trade,* June 1995, pp. 58–68.

5. Hayashi, Alden, "Six Hot Technologies for the 21st Century," *Datamation,* August 1996, pp. 68–73.

6. Hildebrand, Carol, "If the Gown Fits . . ." *CIO,* June 1, 1996, p. 16.

7. "A Shoe That Really Fits," *Forbes,* June 3, 1996, pp. 126–127.

8. Velgos, Monica, "Gigs from Gigabytes," *Food Careers,* February 1996, p. 89.

9. Dogar, Rana, and Damon Darlin, "Recipes That Grandma Never Used," *Forbes,* October 21, 1996, pp. 190–200.

10. Rooney, Paula, "AT&T Has Plans to Extend WorldNet for Intranet Use," *PC Week,* July 22, 1996, p. 40.

11. McGraw, Dan, "Playing the Stadium Game," *U.S. News & World Report,* June 3, 1996, pp. 46–51.

12. Takita, Hiroaki, "Success Below the Surface: Geo Search Inspects Roads and Clears Mines," *Tokyo Business,* May 1995, pp. 14–16.

13. Blodgett, Mindy, "A Wireless LAN Landslide," *Computerworld,* April 1, 1996, p. 59.

14. Murphy, Elena, "Telecom Growth Leaps," *Purchasing,* April 25, 1996, pp. 86–87.

15. Thornton, Emily, "Japan Lays Off Its Robots," *World Press Review,* July 1996, pp. 31–32.

16. Bleecker, Samuel, "The Emerging Meta-Mart," *The Futurist,* May–June 1995, pp. 17–19.

GLOSSARY

A

Ad hoc decision also called a **nonrecurring decision**; a decision that you make infrequently (perhaps only once) and you may even have different criteria for determining the best solution each time.

Adolescent stage the second stage of ethical development.

Adult stage the third and final stage of ethical development.

Analytical processing creating information to support your decision-making tasks.

Application development facility a wealth of building blocks that you can use to create applications quickly, so teams can literally "get to work."

Application generation subsystem facilities to help you develop transaction-intensive applications in a database environment.

Application software software designed to help you solve problems specific to business operations or perform specific business tasks.

Arithmetic/logic unit (A/L unit) the part of the central processing unit that performs all arithmetic operations and all logic operations.

Artificial intelligence (AI) the science of making machines imitate human thinking and behavior.

Asynchronous transfer mode (ATM) a transmission method for sending information that divides a long transmission into smaller units (called "packets").

Atomic primary key a primary key that uses only one field to create a unique description.

Automated clearinghouse (ACH) an intermediary organization that handles the electronic movement of money between two banks.

Automatic speech recognition (ASR) not only captures spoken words, but also distinguishes word groupings to form sentences.

B

Bandwidth the range of frequencies available on a communications medium. Bandwidth determines the capacity of the communications medium.

Bridge an internetworking unit that connects two networks of the same kind.

Broadcast radio an unguided communications medium similar to microwaves and satellites, except that the receiving locations needn't be in line of sight or have a dish shaped antenna to receive information transmissions.

Bus topology a network topology in which all computers are connected to a single communications medium over which all communications travel.

Business process a sequence of activities that takes raw materials from a supplier and serves an outcome to a customer.

Business process reengineering (BPR) the reinventing of processes within a business.

Business systems planning (BSP) identifies information requirements by documenting the relationships between business processes and information classes.

C

Cable modem a special communications processor that connects your television to a cable TV service provider, giving you access to the Internet through your TV.

Cable-ready computer a computer that you can connect directly to a cable TV outlet to receive programming you can watch on your monitor.

Capital investment analysis calculating a quantitative measure of IT systems value.

Carpal tunnel syndrome a type of repetitive strain injury in which the wrist becomes inflamed and swells when the median nerve is pinched where it passes through the bones of the wrist.

Cave automatic virtual environment (CAVE) a special 3-D, virtual reality room that can display images of other people located in other CAVEs all over the world.

Central processing unit (CPU) the hardware in an IT system that interprets and executes the software instructions and coordinates how all the other hardware devices work together.

Centralized database a database that maintains all database information in one location.

Character the smallest logical unit of information for a knowledge worker.

Chief information officer (CIO) the strategic level IT manager who directs all IT systems and personnel while communicating directly with the highest levels of the organization.

Choice the third step in the decision-making process where you decide on a plan to address the problem or opportunity.

Client/server network a network that contains one or more host computers (called "servers") that provide some type of service to the other computers (called "clients") in the network.

Cluster controller a communications processor that manages a group of devices that share a single high-speed communications medium connected to another location.

Coaxial cable a guided communications medium with one or more central wires surrounded by thick insulation.

Cold site an alternative site where a company sets up its IT system in case of a disaster. A cold site does not have computer equipment installed but has backup power generators, a sprinkler system, a security system, and so on.

Communications media the paths, or physical channels, in a network over which information travels from one place to another.

Communications processor a hardware device that unites the various communications media and computers and routes communications throughout a network.

Communications service provider an organization—such as AT&T or Sprint—that provides communications services to individuals and other organizations.

Comparative report a report that shows two or more sets of similar information in an attempt to illustrate a relationship.

Competition a characteristic of today's business environment. Competition is greater today than ever before for a number of reasons, not the least of which is the use of information technology.

Competitive advantage providing the best perceived perfect service at the customer's moment of value.

Competitive forces model a tool to formulate strategy by examining the environment in which your organization competes.

Competitive intelligence information about the internal workings of your organization as well as the external market surrounding your organization.

Competitive scanning continuous competitive intelligence.

Composite primary key a primary key that uses more than one field to create a unique description.

Computer-aided software engineering (CASE) tool software that automates some or all steps in the systems development life cycle.

Contingency planning the process of examining the possibilities of losing an IT system and formulating procedures to minimize the damage.

Continuous automatic speech recognition an automatic speech recognition system that can process continuous streams of words—that is, normal speech patterns.

Control chart a graphic means of identifying causes to problems that are controllable.

Control unit the part of the central processing unit that interprets software instructions and literally tells the other hardware devices what to do, based on the software instructions.

Cookie a little chunk of information about you, which a Web site stores on your hard disk when you visit that site.

Cost-benefit analysis the process of evaluating IT systems for development by comparing systems costs with systems benefits.

Critical success factor (CSF) a factor critical to organizational success.

Cross-cultural diversity the difference in behavior and attitude between people from different cultures.

Crossover part of a genetic algorithm where portions of good outcomes are combined in the hope of creating an even better outcome.

Culture the collective personality of a nation or society, encompassing language, traditions, currency, religion, history, music, and acceptable behavior, among other things.

Culture shock the disorientation and confusion that you experience when you're accustomed to one culture and suddenly find yourself in another, where signals, behavior, and beliefs are different.

Customer integrated system (CIS) a system which is an extension of a transaction processing system that places technology in the hands of an organization's customers and allows them to process their own transactions.

Customer moment of value providing service when the customer wants it (time), where the customer wants it (location), how the customer wants it (form), and in a manner guaranteed to the customer (perfect delivery).

Cybersickness eyestrain, simulator sickness, and flashbacks that many people experience who participate in virtual reality environments.

D

Data any raw facts or observations that describe a particular phenomenon.

Data administration the function in an organization that plans for, oversees the development of, and monitors the information resource.

Data administration subsystem helps you manage the overall database environment by providing facilities for backup and recovery, security management, query optimization, reorganization, concurrency control, and change management.

Data definition subsystem helps you create and maintain the data dictionary and define the structure of the files in a database.

Data dictionary contains the logical structure of information in a database.

Data management the component of a decision support system (DSS) that performs the function of storing and maintaining the information that you want your DSS to use.

Data manipulation subsystem helps you add, change, and delete information in a database and mine it for valuable information.

Data mart a subset of a data warehouse, in which a highly summarized or focused portion of the data warehouse is kept.

Data mining tool a software tool you use to query information in a data warehouse.

Data warehouse a logical collection of information—gathered from many different operational databases—that supports business analysis activities and decision-making tasks.

Database a collection of information that you organize and access according to the logical structure of that information.

Database administration the function in an organization that is responsible for the more technical and operational aspects of managing the information contained in operational databases.

Database management system (DBMS) the software you use to specify the logical organization for a database and access it.

Database management system engine (DBMS engine) accepts logical requests from the various other DBMS subsystems, converts them to their physical equivalent, and actually accesses the database and data dictionary as they exist on a storage device.

Decentralized computing the concept of splitting the computing power of an organization and locating it in functional business areas.

Decision support system (DSS) a highly flexible and interactive IT system that is designed to support decision making when the problem is not structured.

Decision support system generator (DSS generator) software that enables you to develop a DSS for a specific task. Spreadsheet programs are an example.

Design the second step of the decision-making process. It's where you consider possible ways of solving the problem, filling the need, or taking advantage of the opportunity.

Dimensions of information include time (the when aspect of information), content (the what aspect of information), and form (the how aspect of information).

By viewing information according to these definitions, you can determine its value.

Disaster recovery cost curve a depiction of the organization's disaster recovery costs based on how quickly you wish to recover.

Disaster recovery plan a comprehensive plan to anticipate and recover from a major catastrophe.

Discrete automatic speech recognition an automatic speech recognition system which requires that you pause between each spoken word.

Disintermediation the elimination of organizations in the chain of providing goods and services.

Distributed database a database in which information is distributed to various locations.

Domain expert the person who provides the domain expertise in the form of problem-solving strategies.

E

Electronic cash (e-cash; digital cash) an electronic representation of cash.

Electronic commerce a modern methodology that addresses the use of information technology as an essential enabler of business. Electronic commerce supports both internal and external business functions.

Electronic data interchange (EDI) the direct computer-to-computer transfer of transaction information contained in standard business documents, such as invoices and purchase orders.

Electronic funds transfer (EFT) the electronic passing of funds (money) among businesses and banks and their customers.

Electronic meeting software lets a team have a "virtual" meeting through information technology.

Electronic meeting support the component of groupware that helps you schedule meetings and carry out those meetings.

Electronic messaging the software component of groupware that helps team members communicate.

Electronic publishing the publication of items such as books, magazines, newspapers, and advertising flyers in an electronic format rather than in the print-on-paper format associated with traditional publishing processes.

Emerging technology a technology that falls into one of the two following categories: (1) it is so new that most businesses haven't exploited it or (2) it is fairly well-established, but businesses haven't fully exploited it.

Entity class a concept—typically people, places, or things—about which you wish to store information and that you can identify with a unique key.

Entity-relationship (E-R) diagram a graphic method of representing entity classes and their relationships.

Ergonomics the study of how to design and arrange your workplace so that you can achieve maximum productivity, reducing discomfort and adverse health effects.

Ethernet a communications standard for connecting components in a local area network by making use of a shared communications medium.

Ethics sets of principles or standards that help guide behavior, actions, and choices.

Exception report a report that shows only a subset of available information based on some selection criteria.

Executive information system (EIS) a highly interactive management information system combined with decision support systems and artificial intelligence for helping managers identify and address problems and opportunities.

Expert system an artificial intelligence system that applies reasoning capabilities to reach a conclusion.

Expert system shell a software package designed to facilitate the development of an expert system.

Explanation module the part of an expert system where the "why" information, supplied by the domain expert, is stored to be accessed by knowledge workers who want to know why the expert system asked a question or reached a conclusion.

External database a database that exists outside the organization.

External electronic commerce addresses the use of information technology to support how a business interacts with the marketplace.

External information information that describes the environment surrounding the organization.

Extranet a special application that allows other organizations and people access to information published on an intranet.

F

Feasibility review the reviewing of a proposed system to determine if it is feasible from a cost, technical, and time point of view.

Feature analysis the first step in automatic speech recognition; it captures your words as you speak into a microphone, eliminates any background noise, and actually converts the digital signals of your speech into phonemes.

Fiber distributed data interface (FDDI) a communications standard for connecting high-speed local area networks or links among geographically dispersed LANs.

Field a logical grouping of characters.

File a logical grouping of records.

Firewall the special security software that protects an intranet against outside access.

Fishbone diagram a line diagram that begins with a problem (the effect) and branches out into problem causes.

Flaming the distribution of an online communication that offends someone because of the use of obscene, derogatory, or inappropriate language.

Foreign key a primary key of one file that also appears in another file.

Front-end processor a communications processor which is a special computer that handles the communications function for a host computer or server in a network.

Fuzzy logic a method of working with "fuzzy" information; that is, information that is incomplete, ambiguous, or imprecise.

G

Gateway an internetworking unit that connects networks that are completely dissimilar with respect to how they work and communicate internally.

Genetic algorithm an artificial intelligence system that mimics the evolutionary, survival-of-the-fittest process to generate increasingly better solutions to a problem.

Geographic information system (GIS) a decision support system designed specifically to work with spatial information.

Global configuration a configuration in which all international operations depend on headquarters for resources and direction.

Global positioning system (GPS) a collection of 24 earth-orbiting satellites that continuously transmit radio signals you can use to determine where you are.

Globalization a characteristic of today's business environment. It simply states that business today is global business; customers, suppliers, distributors, retailers, and competitors exist all over the world for any type of business.

Glove an input device in virtual reality that captures and records the shape and movement of your hand and fingers and the strength of your hand and finger movements.

Group decision support system (GDSS) a type of decision support system that facilitates the formulation of and solution to problems by a team.

Group document database a powerful storage facility for organizing and managing all documents related to specific teams.

Group scheduling software provides facilities for maintaining the day-to-day electronic calendars of team members and evaluating those calendars to schedule optimal meeting times.

Groupware the popular term for the software component that supports the collaborative efforts of a team.

Guided communications media communications media that transmit information over a closed path (such as a wire).

H

Headset a combined input and output device in virtual reality that (1) captures and records the movements of your head and (2) displays various views of an environment on a screen that covers your entire field of vision.

Help desk a central clearing point for problems that knowledge workers encounter when using IT systems. Usually, the help desk staff will answer some questions but refer more complex problems to the appropriate IT experts.

Histogram a graphic representation of frequency distributions, or counts of how often different things occur.

Hot site a separate, fully equipped facility with IT to which knowledge workers can move immediately after a disaster and resume business.

Hoteling offices which are kept equipped at a central location for telecommuters. When they need it, knowledge workers reserve space in advance.

Hybrid model a model that combines two or more artificial intelligence techniques to help you solve complex problems more effectively than you could with the help of any one AI technique.

I

Implementation the final step in the decision-making process where you put your plan into action.

Individualized electronic advertising the use of technology to determine who gets what advertisements and electronically send those advertisements to only those people.

Inference engine the processing component of an expert system. It reasons through your problem facts and the domain expertise in the knowledge base to reach a conclusion.

Information data that has a particular meaning within a specific context.

Information access to do their jobs, knowledge workers need to be able to get the right information, at the right time, and in the right form.

Information age how today's business environment is characterized. It is a time when businesses depend on their information and when knowledge is power.

Information architecture describes what information your organization needs and which people within your organization need that information.

Information center a group of IT specialists and people knowledgeable in business practices who help knowledge workers with special information needs.

Information-literate knowledge worker a knowledge worker who can define what information is needed, knows how and where to obtain that information, understands the meaning of the information once received, and can act appropriately, based on the information, to help the organization achieve the greatest advantage. In all instances, an information-literate knowledge worker always uses information according to ethical and legal constructs.

Information partnership an agreement between organizations for the sharing of information to strengthen each partner organization.

Information security the protection of information from loss or damage because of errors, accidents, or malicious actions.

Information technology (IT) any computer-based tool that people use to work with information and support the information and information-processing needs of an organization.

Information technology fusion (IT fusion) this occurs when the information technology within your organization is indistinguishable from the business processes and the people who exploit the information technology.

Information technology systems plan (IT systems plan) the documented results of IT systems planning.

Information technology systems planning (IT systems planning) the process that uses the goals, strategies, objectives, processes, and information requirements of your organization as a foundation for identifying and selecting which IT systems to develop and deciding when to develop them.

Information technology systems risk the possibility that a system will not achieve the predicted benefits.

Information unavailability cost curve a depiction of the cost to the organization of the unavailability of information.

Infrared an unguided communications medium that uses a red light (below the visibility of the human eye) to transmit information.

Input technologies the tools you use to capture information or commands at the point of origin.

Instance an occurrence of an entity class that can be uniquely described.

Intangible benefit a systems benefit that cannot be monetarily quantified.

Integrated CASE tool a CASE tool which supports the entire systems development life cycle, from planning through support.

Integrated services digital network (ISDN) both the plan and the international communications standard for the transition of the world's public telephone system from analog to digital for the purpose of transmitting all formats of information (voice, video, text, and so on) simultaneously over twisted-pair telephone lines.

Integrity constraint a rule that helps assure the quality of information.

Intelligence the first step in the decision-making process where you find or recognize a problem, need, or opportunity (also called the diagnostic phase of decision making).

Intelligent agent an artificial intelligence system which can move around your computer or network performing repetitive tasks independently, adapting itself to your preferences.

Intelligent home appliance an appliance that contains an embedded IT system that controls numerous functions and is capable of making some decisions.

Internal electronic commerce addresses the use of information technology to support internal processes, functions, and operations.

Internal information information that describes specific operational aspects of the organization.

Internal memory a temporary storage area that holds three things: (1) information you are working with, (2) the application software you are using, and (3) the operating system software.

International virtual private network (international VPN) a virtual private network that combines the capabilities of telephone service providers around the world.

Internet a network of networked computers all over the world.

Internet loophole a point of entry to your internal IT system from your Internet site.

Internet PC a computer that supports only Internet access.

Internet service provider an organization that supports many people who want to access and use the Internet.

Internet telephone the technology tools required to carry on a phone conversation over the Internet.

Internet virtual private network (Internet VPN) a network that provides your organization with a way of establishing a *virtual* Internet network that consists of only you, your customers, and suppliers.

Internetworking unit a special hardware device that connects two or more networks.

Interoperability also known as standardization, refers to the extent to which IT equipment and software components are compatible.

Interorganizational system (IOS) a system that automates the flow of information between organizations to support the planning, design, development, production, and delivery of products and services.

Intersection relation a relation you create to eliminate a repeating group.

Intranet an internal organizational Internet that is guarded against outside access by special security software.

J

Joint application development (JAD) a workshop that unites management, IT specialists, and knowledge workers to define and specify the logical requirements and technical alternatives for a proposed system.

Joint application development (JAD) facilitator although he or she has no decision-making power, this person runs the JAD workshop, keeps the participants moving forward through the agenda, and resolves conflicts between participants.

Just-in-time (JIT) an approach that produces or delivers a product or service *when* the customer wants it.

K

Knowledge acquisition the component of the expert system that the knowledge engineer uses to enter the rules.

Knowledge base the part of the expert system that stores the rules.

Knowledge-based system also called an **expert system**, is an artificial intelligence system that applies reasoning capabilities to reach a conclusion.

Knowledge engineer the person who formulates the domain expertise into an expert system.

Knowledge worker a person who works with and produces information as a product.

Knowledge worker computing places technology, technology power, software, information, and technology knowledge in the hands of those who need it—knowledge workers.

Knowledge worker database a database designed and maintained by a knowledge worker to support his or her personal information needs.

Knowledge worker development the development and support of IT systems by knowledge workers with little or no help from IT specialists.

L

Language processing the third step of automatic speech recognition; it attempts to make sense of what you're saying by comparing the possible word phonemes (generated in step 2) with a language model database.

Learning organization an organization whose people are continually discovering how to learn together while, at the same time, altering their organization as a result of what they learn.

Levels of information literacy different levels or stages that describe your understanding of information. These levels include professional (only understanding information at its face value), expert, and innovator (understanding what information truly means).

Local area network (LAN) a network that covers a limited geographic distance, such as an office, office building, or a group of buildings within close proximity.

Locationless operation operating without regard to location.

Logical view focuses on how you as a knowledge worker need to arrange and access information to meet your particular business needs.

Lower CASE tool a CASE tool which supports the back-end steps of the systems development life cycle, including design, implementation, and support.

M

Management information system (MIS) a system that provides periodic and predetermined reports that summarize information within a database.

Management information systems (MIS) deals with the planning for, development, management, and use of information technology tools to help people perform all tasks related to information processing and management.

Management information systems (MIS) challenge a challenge that all businesses must strive to meet. That challenge deals with how to coordinate the use of a business's three most important resources — information, information technology, and people— while providing products and services at the customer's moment of value.

Manufacturing resource planning (MRP II) systems that tie material requirements from MRP systems into other organizational systems to integrate financial, human resource, and marketing needs into the scheduling.

Materials requirements planning (MRP) systems that take the production schedule and determine which raw materials and components are required and when.

Microwave an unguided communications medium that uses a high-frequency band of radio broadcast transmission and dish-shaped antennae for sending and receiving information.

Model management the part of the decision support system that consists of both the DSS models and DSS model management system.

Modem a device that converts the digital signals of your computer into an analog form that can be transmitted over a telephone line and then converts the analog signal back to digital signals at the other end of the transmission.

Moteling offices are kept equipped for telecommuters at a central location and, when they need it, knowledge workers are allocated space on a first-come–first-served basis.

Multidimensional analysis (MDA) tool a slice-and-dice technique that allows you to view multidimensional information from different perspectives.

Multimedia the simultaneous presentation of information through many forms of media that you can control.

Multimedia authoring software software specifically designed to help you create a multimedia application.

Multinational configuration a configuration in which international operations operate independently, reporting only financial information to headquarters.

Multiplexer a communications processor that aggregates several communications media and allows them to share a single communications medium that operates at a much higher capacity.

Mutation part of a genetic algorithm; it's the process of randomly trying combinations and evaluating the success (or failure) of the outcome.

N

Network (computer network) a connection of two or more IT components (typically computers) that gives people the ability to share software, share information, share peripheral devices, communicate with each other, and share processing power.

Network operating system (NOS) the system software that determines how a network functions.

Network perfect delivery the extent to which your organization can meet the where, how, and when characteristics of the network, and the extent to which your organization can guarantee those characteristics.

Network perfect service the delivery of networking capabilities where, how, and when they are wanted.

Network range the information and transactions that must travel across your network.

Network reach the people, organizations, and business processes that your network should include.

Network responsiveness the level of service—speed, reliability, and security—your network must provide.

Network topology the physical arrangement of computers in a network.

Neural network an artificial intelligence system which is capable of learning because it's patterned after the human brain.

Nonrecurring decision also called an **ad hoc decision**, is a decision that you make very infrequently (perhaps only once) and you may even have different criteria for determining the best solution each time.

Nonstructured decision decisions for which there may be several "right" answers, and there is no precise way to get a right answer.

Normalization a process of assuring that a relational database structure can be implemented as a series of two-dimensional tables.

O

Object a software module containing information that describes an entity class along with a list of procedures that can act on the information describing the entity class.

Object-oriented approach any approach —perhaps a programming language or a DBMS—that combines information and procedures into a single object.

Object-oriented database (O-O database or OODB) a database model that brings together, stores, and allows you to work with both information and procedures that act on the information.

Object-oriented database management system (O-O DBMS or OODBMS) the DBMS software that allows you to develop and work with an object-oriented database.

Objective information information that quantifiably describes something that is known.

Online analytical processing (OLAP) the manipulation of information to support decision making.

Online database a database that exists outside an organization.

Online transaction processing (OLTP) involves gathering input information, processing that information, and updating existing information to reflect the gathered and processed information.

Operating system software software designed to handle tasks specific to technology management and coordinate the interaction of all the IT components.

Operational database a database that supports online transaction processing.

Operational management the level of management that manages and directs the day-to-day operations and the implementation of goals and strategies.

Optical fiber a communications medium that uses a very thin glass or plastic fiber through which pulses of light travel. Optical fiber is the fastest and most reliable guided communications medium.

Organizational force meeting as many customer expectations as possible.

Organizational horsepower (OHP) a measure of an organization's ability to exert force in the market with speed.

Organizational speed meeting customers' expectations quickly.

Output technologies the tools you use to see, hear, or otherwise accept the results of your information-processing requests.

Outsourcing the delegation of specific work to a third party for a specified length of time, at a specific cost, and at a specified level of service.

P

Paperless office an office in which materials are maintained in electronic instead of paper form.

Parallel conversion moving from the old system to the new system by using both the old and new systems until you're sure that the new system performs correctly.

Pareto chart a sorted chart of frequencies of various problem causes.

Partitioned database a database that maintains certain files of information in different locations—usually where that information is most often used.

Pattern classification the second step of automatic speech recognition; it attempts to recognize your spoken phonemes by locating a matching phoneme sequence among the words stored in an acoustic model database.

Peer-to-peer network a network that provides two abilities: (1) the ability to communicate with other people and (2) the ability to share peripheral devices.

Perfect delivery understanding a customer's moment of value in terms of time, location, and form and taking the necessary steps to assure that those characteristics can be met.

Periodic report a report that is produced at a predetermined time interval—daily, weekly, monthly, yearly, and so on.

Permanent team a team designed to support permanent processes and not intended to be disbanded.

Physical view deals with how information is physically arranged, stored, and accessed on some type of secondary storage device.

Piecemeal conversion moving from the old system to the new system by converting to only a portion of the new system until you're sure that it works correctly and then converting to the remaining portions of the new system.

Pilot conversion moving from the old system to the new system by having only a small group of people use the new system until you know that it works correctly and then converting the remaining people.

Plunge conversion moving from the old system to the new system by discarding the old system completely and immediately using the new system.

Preadolescent stage the first stage of ethical development.

Primary intelligence competitive intelligence gathered directly from the primary source.

Primary key a field in a database file that uniquely describes each record.

Private network a network that your organization either owns or exclusively leases the right to use the communications media to connect network components.

Project plan includes a list of people who will participate on the project team, a preliminary budget, and a time frame for completing each major step or task.

Project repository a database that contains information pertaining to all the systems development projects that your organization has undertaken using a CASE tool.

Project team a team designed to accomplish specific one-time goals which is disbanded once the project is complete.

Proof-of-concept prototype a prototype you use to prove the technical feasibility of a proposed system.

Prototype a model of a proposed product, service, or system.

Prototyping the process of building a model that demonstrates the features of a proposed product, service, or system.

Public network a network on which your organization competes for time and use with other people and organizations.

Q

Quality meeting customer expectations.

Query-by-example (QBE) tool helps you graphically design the answer to a question.

Query-and-reporting tool found in a data warehouse environment. These tools are similar to query-by-example tools, structured query language, and report generators in a typical database environment.

R

Random access memory (RAM) the internal memory that holds your information and the operating system and application software you're working with.

Rapid application development (RAD) a systems development method that combines prototyping and joint application development to increase the effectiveness of the systems development process.

Read-only memory (ROM) the part of the internal memory that comes with permanent, built-in instructions.

Record a logical grouping of fields.

Recurring decision a decision that you have to make repeatedly, and often periodically, either weekly, monthly, quarterly, or yearly.

Relation a two-dimensional table in the relational database model.

Relational database model a database model that uses a series of two-dimensional tables or files to store information.

Repetitive strain injury (RSI) also referred to as cumulative trauma disorder (CTD), is characterized by headache, neckache, eyestrain, wrist pain, fatigue, and stress caused by repetitive actions.

Replicated database a database that maintains multiple copies of information in different locations.

Report generator helps you quickly define formats of reports and what information you want to see in a report.

Request for proposal (RFP) a formal document that outlines your logical requirements of a proposed system and invites outsourcing organizations (which we'll refer to as "vendors") to submit bids for its development.

Reverse engineering the analysis of existing software and the creation of design specifications from it.

Ring topology a network topology in which all computers are connected to a single communications medium (similar to a bus), and that communications medium is connected at both ends to form a closed loop.

Robot a mechanical device equipped with simulated human senses and capable of taking action on its own.

Router an internetworking unit that connects networks that are somewhat dissimilar with respect to certain communications aspects, such as how computers are addressed and the size of messages sent.

Rule-based expert system the type of expert system that expresses the problem-solving process as rules.

S

Satellite an unguided communications medium which is an amplifier, or repeater, that receives information from one location on earth, repeats the information, and sends it to one or more receiving locations on earth.

Scatter diagram a plot of paired data on a two-axis graph.

Search engine a software tool that allows you to search for Internet information by using key words or terms.

Secondary intelligence competitive intelligence gathered indirectly from a source other than the primary source.

Selection part of a genetic algorithm which gives preference to better outcomes.

Selfsourcing the development and support of IT systems by knowledge workers with little or no help from IT specialists.

Selling prototype a prototype you use to convince people of the worth of a proposed system.

Shared information locating an organization's information in a single location so all people throughout the organization can have access to whatever information they need.

Smart card a small plastic card (about the size of a credit card) that contains a memory chip on which a sum of money can be recorded and updated.

Smart phone a cellular phone that also acts as a transmittal and reception station for digital page messages, e-mail messages, and faxes and also has Internet access capabilities.

Software technologies the tools you use to process information to obtain new information.

Speaker-dependent automatic speech recognition an automatic speech recognition system that lets you "train" it to recognize your voice.

Speaker-independent automatic speech recognition an automatic speech recognition system that can be used by anyone, but often contains a limited vocabulary that cannot be expanded.

Star topology a network topology that contains a central computer from which all other computers radiate.

Statistical process control (SPC) a method of gathering and analyzing product or service measurements to identify and solve quality problems.

Storage technologies the tools you use to more permanently store information for use at a later time.

Storyboard a visual representation of multimedia objects.

Strategic management the level of management that provides an organization with overall direction and guidance.

Structured decision a decision where processing a certain kind of information in a specified way will always provide the right answer.

Structured query language (SQL) a standardized fourth-generation query language found in most database environments.

Subjective information information that attempts to describe something that is currently unknown.

Summarized report a report that aggregates information in some way.

T

Tactical management the level of management that develops the goals and strategies outlined by strategic management.

Tangible benefit a systems benefit that can be monetarily quantified.

Team a group of people with a shared common goal and task interdependence.

Telecommunications the electronic movement of information from one location to another.

Telecommunications technologies the tools you use to send information to and receive it from another person or location.

Telecommuter someone who works for an organization either at home or at a satellite work location at least part of the time while connected to the main office through some form of communications technology.

Telecommuting the use of communications technology to work in a place other than a central location.

Three-dimensional (3-D) a technology presentation of information that gives you the illusion that the object you're viewing is actually in the room with you.

Timeless operation operating without regard to time.

Token ring a communications standard for connecting components in a local area network, which makes use of a single shared communications medium and an electronic token that is passed around and used in turn by each component.

Total quality management (TQM) meeting customer expectations through continuous improvement and organizationwide quality ownership.

Traditional systems development life cycle (traditional SDLC) a structured step-by-step approach to developing systems that creates a separation of duties among IT specialists and knowledge workers.

Transaction processing the processing of transactions that occur within an organization.

Transaction processing system (TPS) a system that processes transactions that occur within the organization.

Transborder data flow information crossing borders.

Transmission control protocol/Internet protocol (TCP/IP) the communications standard by which the Internet works.

Transnational configuration the configuration of a transnational firm.

Transnational firm a firm that produces and sells products and services in countries all over the world in coordinated cooperation.

Twisted-pair cable two insulated copper wires twisted in a spiral. Twisted-pair cable is a guided communications medium and the most popular form of all communications media.

U

Unguided communications media communications media that transmit information through the air—in much the same way as radio stations broadcast their programming.

Upper CASE tool a CASE tool that supports the front-end steps of the systems development life cycle, including planning, scoping, analysis, and design.

User interface management the part of the decision support system that allows the user, or knowledge worker, to communicate with the DSS.

V

Value-added network (VAN) a semipublic network that provides additional services beyond the simple communication of information from one place to another.

Value chain a tool that views the organization as a chain—or series—of processes each of which adds value to the product or service for the customer.

Videoconferencing software allows a team to have a "face-to-face" meeting when members are geographically dispersed.

View allows you see the content of a database file, make whatever changes you want, perform simple sorting, and query to find the location of specific information.

Virtual office an office where none of the employees has personal workspace; rather, they use offices, desks, and computers as needed.

Virtual organization a network of independent organizations linked together by IT to exploit market opportunities by sharing skills, costs, and market access.

Virtual private network (VPN) a public network that guarantees availability to your organization, but does not provide you with a dedicated line or with communications media.

Virtual reality a three-dimensional computer simulation in which you actively and physically participate.

Virtual workplace a technology-enabled workplace. No walls. No boundaries. Work anytime, anyplace, linked to other people and information you need, wherever they are.

Virus a program which someone develops with malicious intent to harm an IT system. A computer virus can cause damage when it finds its way into a set of instructions like an .EXE file or an MS-Word macro.

W

Walker an input device in virtual reality that captures and records the movement of your feet as you walk or turn in different directions.

Whiteboard software lets team members meet and interactively edit and share documents.

Wide area network (WAN) a network that covers large geographic distances, such as a state, a country, or even the entire world.

Wireless local area network (wireless LAN) a network that covers a limited distance in which all components or computers are connected without physical cables.

Work flow automation software software designed to support the flow of business documents in a specific work process or procedure.

Workgroup support system (WSS) a system that is designed specifically to improve the performance of teams by supporting the sharing and flow of information.

World Wide Web (WWW) the Internet in a linked multimedia form.

X

X.12 the communications standard for transmitting common-formatted information during electronic data interchange.